BIORHYTHM SPORTS FORE- CASTING

Bernard Gittelson

ARCO PUBLISHING COMPANY INC.
219 Park Avenue South, New York, N.Y. 10003

To
PROFESSOR VANDORLO BIDOSH

Published by Arco Publishing Company, Inc.
219 Park Avenue South, New York, N.Y. 10003

Library of Congress Cataloging in Publication Data

Gittelson, Bernard.
  Biorhythm sports forecasting.

  Bibliography p. 71
  1. Sports—Physiological aspects.   2.   Biological
rhythms.   I.   Title.

GV706.G57   796'.01   77-2583
ISBN: 0-668-04145-5 (Cloth Edition)

Contents

Introduction

The author recently appeared with Fran Tarkenton on an NBC-TV coast-to-coast hook-up. Utilizing biorhythms to forecast the results of the Greater Greensboro Golf Classic, Gittelson was able to project Al Geiberger as the winner—and the prediction came true. No magic was involved; no crystal ball necessary. What *was* involved was a careful analysis of biorhythms and the sporting profile of Geiberger—and the knowledge that that particular golfer performs well during intellectual and emotional highs.

The purpose of this book is to provide the reader with information about the history of biorhythm, to discuss how it works, and to explore the pros and cons of this fascinating science. A main objective will be to relate biorhythm to sports in such a way as to enable us to forecast and understand the reasons for the peaks and the valleys of performance and all the areas in between.

Biorhythm is in its early stages of development. It works in approximately 80 per cent of the cases it is applied to. As such, it is in good company. Aspirin does not work for everybody. Not everyone is born with ten toes and ten fingers. Some people are allergic to penicillin. Yet, in the area of application of biorhythm to accidents, 60 to 80 per cent of accidents occur on 20 per cent of the days of our lives. This is a significant starting area for the student of behavior.

To use this book effectively, it should be considered a means to the end of viewing an individual's performance potential on any given day. Thus, track the profile of your favorite athlete. Ask the questions: Is this performance in line with the biorhythmic profile? Is the performance relative to the accomplishments of the competition? What trends and patterns exist for the athlete that should be filed for future reference?

In doing this, you will become a student of behavior. Patterns, norms, percentages will be your focus, not a crystal ball.

Biorhythms may be one of the missing links that explains behavior. Much more study is needed in the whole area of biocycles. I urge you to write to me. The more information I obtain, the more insights into human behavior that can be provided, the faster and the deeper can the exploration of biorhythms grow.

BERNARD GITTELSON
Summit, New Jersey
June, 1977

5

Sports Forecasting with Biorhythm

Tom Seaver of the New York Mets pitches against the lowly Montreal Expos. He lasts but a few innings. His fast ball has no zip. His control is poor. His curve ball does not break. A few weeks later against the same Expos, Tom Seaver is Tom Terrific. He goes the distance yielding but three hits. He strikes out a dozen batters. His curve ball dips and darts. His fast ball has "something on it." His control is perfect, and he wins the game easily.

Walt Frazier of the New York Knickerbockers throws up shots from all angles, and the basketball finds its way into the hoop. On defense, he seems to cover his opponent like a tent. In the next game he plays, Clyde's shots hit the rim and bounce out. His passes go over the outstretched arms of teammates. He has many defensive lapses.

Terry Metcalf of the St. Louis Cardinals in a game against the Dallas Cowboys is a veritable scoring machine. He runs back kick-offs, giving his team excellent scoring opportunities. He squiggles through the line of scrimmage past the straining arms and legs of the opposition. He breaks away for two long touchdown runs. In the next game against the same Dallas team a few weeks later, Metcalf is horrible. He fumbles the ball, bumps into blockers, slips, can't execute, is unable to do anything right.

Franco Harris of the Pittsburgh Steelers huffs and puffs his way through a contest against the then weak Houston Oilers on December 10, 1972. He fails to gain 100 yards for the first time in seven weeks. Just 13 days later, Harris makes a mind-boggling, finger-tip snatch of the football giving Pittsburgh a dramatic win over Oakland in the play-offs. His effort is billed "the catch of the century."

These "on" and "off" days are what the language and the legends of sports are filled with. Sports writers talk of *hot hands, cold nights, streak shooters, momentum, being up for a contest, being down, grooving, slumps, rising to the occasion.* Yet, beyond the romance and mystique of some alleged romantic force that seizes athletes, there is apparently another and more logical explanation. For, all things considered, professional athletes are honed to a fine competitive edge. They are carefully conditioned physically to perform at the top of their game each time out. They have the emotional inducements of pride and prestige. They have the financial incentives of large paydays. Why then are they, like most people in the world, "on" some days and "off" on other days? How different would things be if athletes and mere mortals like us could predict the "up" times and the "down" days? THE ANSWER TO THESE QUESTIONS MAY BE FOUND IN BIORHYTHM.

Life Rhythms—An Overview

Our world has hundreds of cycles—

rhythms that regularly repeat themselves. The earth rotating around the sun initiates the annual cycle of the seasons and is reflected in the blossoming time, growth rate, and other aspects of all green plants. Every 12½ hours, tides ebb and flow. Most women experience a menstrual cycle every 28 days. The moon reappears every 25 hours. Grasshopper plagues come 9.2 years apart. Rhythms, cycles continually affect life on earth.

The gestation period for human birth is exactly nine lunar months or 266 plus 14 days. Parenthetically, a study of the birth dates of over a quarter-million children born in New York municipal hospitals revealed that the birthrate—and, it logically follows, the conception rate—was highest during the three days around full moon.

There is a definite regularity of changes in man—from body make-up to mental and mood performances—that affects more than 100 functions and structural elements. The skin renews itself especially between midnight and four A.M. A metabolic ability peak for the liver is reached just before or after rising each day. And early morning is peak activity time for the male sex hormone. Perhaps the best known of all cycles is that associated with the earth's rotation on its axis that influences light and darkness—the *circadian cycle.*

Scientists, thinkers, and physicians have always been concerned with cycles, with rhythms, as clues to the nature of man's life on earth. As long ago as 2400 years, in the time of the Greek physician Hippocrates, there was an awareness and a respect for the rhythms of life. Hippocrates urged his colleagues and his students to observe the "good" and the "bad" days among the healthy and the ill and to consider them in the treatment of patients.

Studies aimed at identifying and understanding cycles have been conducted in widely different fields. The rhythmic cy-

cles that characterize business activity were first studied by Dr. Hyde Clarke, an Englishman, in 1883. Eight years before Clarke, Samuel Bennet of the United States was the first to note the rhythmic cycles in prices. The American naturalist, Ernest Thompson Seton, spotlighted the rhythmic variations in the populations of animals.

Biological Rhythms

The end of the nineteenth century and the beginning of the twentieth century saw a breakthrough in the question of why man's disposition differs from day to day. These studies concerned themselves with *biorhythms,* a compound of two Greek words, *bios* and *rhythmos,* which mean *life* and a *periodic beat.*

As early as 1890, a University of Vienna psychology professor, Dr. Hermann Swoboda, sought to determine if man's feelings and actions were influenced by rhythmic fluctuations. Swoboda had noted a periodicity in heart attacks, in the outbreak of fevers, and in the recurrence of dreams, creative impulses, and creative ideas. He began to delve into discovering whether some pattern or cycle existed and whether these rhythms could be pre-calculated.

Operating independently of Swoboda, Dr. Wilhelm Fliess, President of the German Academy of Medicine and a medical researcher, grappled with the question of biological rhythms in his patients. Fliess, a friend and physician to Sigmund Freud, was intrigued by the fact that some children he treated who were exposed to contagious diseases remained immune for days, only to eventually give in on a periodic day.

Both Swoboda and Fliess involved themselves in massive documentation of periods of anxiety in their patients, outbreak of disease, tissue swelling, fevers, and heart attacks.

Swoboda's studies led him to the conclusion that all of these physical phenomena appeared to recur rhythmically. He even found a certain "rhythmical turning point" in asthma attacks. Swoboda's main premise was perhaps best indicated in a paper he delivered to the University of Vienna in 1900:

> Life is subject to consistent changes. This understanding does not refer to changes in our destiny or to changes that take place in the course of life. Even if someone lived a life entirely free of outside forces, of anything that could alter his mental and physical state, still his life would *not* be identical from day to day. The best of physical health does not prevent us from feeling ill sometimes, or less happy than usual.

In 1904, Swoboda published the results of his research in a book titled *The Periodicity in Man's Life.* Identified were a 23-day physical cycle and a 28-day emotional cycle—BIORHYTHMS—that Swoboda viewed as influencing the rhythmical fluctuations that govern the ups and downs in human life.

It is one of the intriguing aspects of science that Fliess, operating 300 miles away from Swoboda in Berlin, came to the same conclusions. Fliess recorded his theory on the existence of a 23-day and a 28-day biorhythm in his 564-page volume *The Course of Life.*

Fliess concluded that the 23–day physical rhythm originated in the muscle cells or fibers. He believed that its fluctuations affected physical strength, endurance, energy, physical confidence, and resistance. Fliess maintained that each individual inherits both male and female characteristics, that everyone has elements of bisexuality in his make–up. The German physician attributed the physical cycle to mas-

culine origins and ascribed the 28-day emotional rhythm to feminine origins.

A third biorhythm, the one involving intelligence, was determined in the 1920's by Alfred Teltscher, an Austrian doctor of engineering who taught at the University of Innsbruck. As a teacher, he was curious about the good and the bad days his students had, the ebb-and-flow of intellectual awareness and performance. Teltscher collected massive amounts of data regarding student birthdates and examination performance. He sifted through this information searching for a pattern. The results of his study led to his postulation of an intellectual cycle of 33 days. He concluded that there were periods when a student could easily understand and grasp new subjects and periods when thinking ability and perception were dimmed. Teltscher's intellectual cycle was a biorhythm that, he reasoned, affected intelligence, memory, mental alertness, logic, reasoning power, reaction, and ambition.

In 1929, two Americans, Drs. Rexford B. Hersey and Michael J. Bennett, of the University of Pennsylvania, came up with research findings that supported Teltscher's theory. They noted, in extensive studies of behavior patterns of workers in the shops of the Pennsylvania Railroad, rhythmic swings in mood in 33- to 36-day cycles apparently unrelated to external events.

Evolved Biorhythm Theory

Today, more and more people in all walks of life are becoming interested in the theory of biorhythm. There is nothing supernatural about the theory and over the years the work of Swoboda, Fliess and Teltscher has been synthesized, clarified and, as we shall see, applied to many aspects of human behavior.

George S. Thommen, a major force in the explication of biorhythm theory, and a man with over fifty years of research and experimentation in the field, stated in his authoritative book, *Is This Your Day?*:

> The problem has been one of convincing man . . . who has held that *man might be born and conceived under nature's laws . . . but there was no reason why he had to live under them!*

What follows is a brief overview of the three biorhythm cycles that begin at the moment of birth in the positive phase and continue regularly in their ebb and flow until death.

The 23-Day Physical Rhythm

This rhythm encompasses physical strength, endurance, energy, resistance to disease, and confidence. During the first half of the cycle, the first 11½ days, an analogy may be drawn to a battery that is giving off energy. All systems are plus. Better coordination, greater resistance to disease, and generally better physical condition highlight this first half of the cycle. It is a good time for athletics or for any activity that demands physical stamina. The individual is able to work hard for longer periods of time.

During the 11½ days of the second half of this physical cycle, an analogy may be drawn to the battery that needs to be recharged. One is aware in most cases of reduced vitality. Athletes, for example, can more easily fall into slumps at this time. Most of the time they simply do not function as efficiently as they did in the first half, the positive days of the cycle. Individuals in reasonably good condition should expect no problems during their negative days, but there will simply be a reduction in physical potential. It helps to view the recharging half of the physical cycle as a period which is passive as contrasted to the first half of the cycle which is very active.

Concern and caution during the physical cycle's negative phase should in most cases not be operative factors for the individual. If one is in fairly good condition there will generally be no problems. Only during the critical cycle days—the time when there is a change in the rhythm from positive to negative or vice versa—is extra caution called for. This would serve to offset a physical rhythm that is unstable and unpredictable.

The 28-Day Emotional Cycle

Sometimes termed the "sensitivity" cycle, the emotional biorhythm governs sensibility, nerves, feelings, intuition, cheerfulness, moodiness and creative ability.

The first 14 days, the plus days, are times when the individual is predisposed to cheerfulness and optimism. Such things as creative endeavor, love, cooperation, feelings, and all coordination connected with the nervous system are favorably influenced. It is a time of getting along better with ourselves and with others.

The second 14 days constitute a recuperative phase. It is a time for recharging, and again the analogy to a battery might be made. Excitability and irritability prevail. These days are not especially suited to cooperation and teamwork. Industrial and transportation accidents are more likely to take place in this emotional negative phase.

The emotional rhythm is very powerful. Many times it can have a significant influence on the physical and mental components of an individual. In "mind" sports such as golf or running, a person in a sub-par stage physically may still manage to be "up" if he is operating at an emotional high in his cycle.

The critical days of the emotional cycle are times to be on guard. They can leave us open to self-inflicted harm, violent arguments, or a moodiness that might seem totally irrational to others. Emotional rhythms and emotionally critical days are easier to keep track of than physical or intellectual, for we are all in most cases better able to evaluate our feelings and moods than our body or mind.

The 33-Day Intellectual Rhythm

This rhythm affects intelligence, memory, mental alertness, logic, reasoning power, reaction, and ambition. It is divided into a positive phase of 16½ days and a negative phase of equal duration.

In the positive phase, individuals have more open minds, more retentive memories, quicker comprehension and adaptation. It is the best time to absorb new subjects. It is a good time for studying, for creative thinking. These plus 16½ days may be viewed as prime time for artists, thinkers, and writers.

The second half of the intellectual cycle is characterized by reduced thinking capacity and by difficulty in concentrating. Most individuals find it a difficult time to learn new things. Most of us find it tempting to function with a closed mind during this period in order for the brain cells to be recharged. These "minus" days are perhaps most efficiently utilized if they are spent in rehearsal or in practice of things already learned.

Critical Days

The day your cycle changes from plus to minus or from minus to plus is considered critical. You are neither "up" nor "down." What is actually taking place is a switch-over, a state of limbo. The phenomenon of the critical day can perhaps best be perceived through the analogy biorhythm theorists draw to the electric light bulb.

When a light bulb blows out, it generally does so with a flash the instant the switch is turned on. Electricians would explain that this happens because the current entering a cold filament causes it to snap if it has become physically weakened.

Human critical days are similar to the light bulb switch-point day. A person should be more careful on these days and not tax the system which seems to be in a state of flux, possessing a high degree of instability. Critical days in and of themselves are not dangerous, for unless external events place a person in a potentially dangerous situation, critical days will generally go their way without being noticed.

A single critical day—a day when one of the cycles crosses the baseline—takes place about six times a month. A double critical day—a day when two cycles cross the baseline—takes place about six times a year. A triple critical day is experienced about once a year—when all three cycles pass through zero within 24 hours. Each cycle has two critical days. One of these critical days is at the start of the cycle and the other takes place at the midpoint of the cycle. Critical days represent less than 20 per cent of an individual's lifetime.

On a physically critical day, there is less resistance to disease. Strength, speed and coordination are at low points, Emotionally critical days make the individual open to self-inflicted harm, to violent argument, to behaving in a disagreeable manner. There is a down spiral for analysis and decision-making when the intellectually critical days take place. This is also a time when accidents occur due to negligence, or a time for "human error."

An emotionally critical day can be easily calculated by an individual. Since the emotional rhythm moves from positive to negative (or vice versa) every two weeks and begins on the day of birth, the first emotionally critical day takes place two weeks after the date of birth. And then for the rest of a person's life, this emotionally critical day will occur at this two-week interval. Thus, a person born on a Friday can be aware of the fact that every other Friday will be critical. In effect, all that is needed is the knowledge of the day of the week you were born to ascertain your emotionally critical days.

Recently, there has been a great deal of speculation and interest in the concept of the "mini-critical day." According to the prevailing theory, the mini-critical period occurs when sine curves reach their apexes and valleys and, suddenly, change spins and directions. This reversal places the individual in an unstable condition similar to that of a critical period. Although this new concept sounds feasible, much more research is necessary before anyone can speak of a mini-critical with certainty.

The Sporting Life

In virtually every sport, in all aspects of athletic endeavor, the valleys and peaks of performers stand out clearly. The money, the glamor, the romance, the competitiveness of athletics has made what happens in the fantasy world of sports of interest to most of us in the real world.

A great deal of interest also exists concerning the interrelationship of sports and biorhythms. One of the main areas of study and developing concern is why some performers on any given day or days are more inspired, less inspired, more effective, less effective. This concern has gone beyond the mystique of such terms as momentum, hot hands, slumps, etc., and has sought to explain the cycles, the rhythms of performance.

Another area of study has centered on forecasting and projecting trends, patterns, results. Jimmy (the Greek) Snyder and others report that they employ biorhythms in their computation of odds and in their ultimate decision about the outcome of sporting events.

For the student of biorhythms, for the student of athletic competition, for the fans, the coaches, the professors, owners, managers, for all of us, there is a need to know and much to study, ponder, contemplate in the interrelationship between sports and biorhythms. Some of the research and the examples that already exist are reviewed on the following pages.

Auto Racing

Sports forecasting on the basis of biorhythmic calculations always has to take into consideration the unexpected and unforseen factors that may affect and alter predictions. This is especially true in the sport of auto racing. It is not only the driver who ultimately affects the outcome of a race. Weather and track conditions, the mechanical condition of vehicles, the crowd—all of these are intangible factors that can have a major impact on a racing result. All of these were in evidence in the 1975 Indianapolis 500 Automobile race.

An *Argosy* magazine article written by John Brooks based on the examination of the biorhythms of the leading drivers came up with some interesting predictions. Brooks determined that two drivers seemed to have the best biorhythmic opportunity for good performances: Bobby Unser and Gordon Johncock. Unser was at peaks in his physical and intellectual cycles. Johncock had an even better bio-cycle readout. He was operating under a triple high. For the rest of the competition, the outlook was less favorable from a biorhythm point of view. Among this group was A. J. Foyt. He had low physical rhythms even though he was emotionally high with the presumed capability for making the fine split-second judgments so necessary for auto racing.

Rain shortened the race to only 174 laps instead of 200. Technical problems, engine mishaps, and accidents further reduced the field. Foyt, handicapped biorhythmically, led the field for 47 laps. Johncock had led the field for the first seven laps, but he dropped to second behind Foyt and then was forced to retire from the competition because of engine trouble.

Towards the end of the race, Unser found himself in a battle with Johnny Rutherford for first place. Unser drove a careful and shrewd race and finished first, as his biorhythms indicated he would. Rutherford, whose physical and intellectual rhythms were negative, with only his emotional rhythms positive, was second. Foyt finished the race in third place.

Thus, the biorhythmic forecasts of Brooks in *Argosy* may have been entirely accurate for the individual drivers, but they were modified by the uncontrollable factors that figure so prominently in any prediction of motor sports results.

A sad example of bio-cycles and auto racing concerns Jean Behra. The French racing car driving champion from 1947-52, Behra died in an accident in Berlin on August 1, 1959. It was a triple low period for him, an especially poor situation for anyone in the dangerous sport of auto racing. Especially poignant was the absolute high he had been under in the days before the accident, and the long series of dramatic successes he had racked up.

In October, 1976, Richard Petty won the $140,000 American 500 Grand National Stock Car Race at Rockingham, North Carolina. A report in *The New York Times* indicated that Petty "used yellow caution laps to maximum advantage." How much did the winning of the race, the using of the yellow laps effectively, have to do with the fact that Petty's bio-cycle for the race revealed that he was physically and intellectually high?

There are several other interesting linkages between biorhythms and racing performances: Al Unser won the Indianapolis 500 on May 30, 1970. His bio-cycle readout was just perfect for that spectacular performance: triple high!

On June 3, 1973, Jackie Stewart triumphed in the Monaco Grand Prix in a record 1 hour and 57 minutes and 44.3 seconds. Emotionally, Stewart was at his highest point in his cycle and, he was also operating under an intellectual plus. The biorhythms for Stewart underscore the theory that for racing car drivers emotion and intellect are of even greater significance than the physical rhythm. On that June day, Stewart was physically low, yet he was able to use judgment and daring, timing and insight, to wrap up his record-setting Grand Prix triumph.

Baseball

Not much research has been conducted concerning baseball and biorhythms. The nature of the game, its cooperative team sport elements make analysis a bit difficult. Yet, there are some interesting cases to survey in this popular sport.

An ambitious study was conducted by computer scientist Bob Hambley. He calculated the charts of pitchers in eleven no-hit games—four by Sandy Koufax in 1962, 1963, 1964 and 1965; a Jack Kralick performance in 1962; Juan Marichal's gem in 1963; a Bob Lemon no-hitter in 1948; and no-hitters by Don Larsen in 1956 and Cy Young in 1897. The back-to-back no-hitters tossed by Johnny Vander Meer in 1938 completed the list.

The findings revealed that nine of the eleven no-hitters coincided with a critical day in the biorhythms of the pitchers, and that most of these critical days were in the physical rhythm.

George Thommen has suggested that the pitchers may have been so "charged up that they disregarded all caution." Others studying Hambley's results are puzzled by the ability of the pitchers to have so much overall command of the ball when they should have been physically unstable according to their bio-cycles.

A quartet of former New York Yankee greats provides further interesting examples of possible bio-cycle influence. On December 11, 1951, Joe DiMaggio announced that he was retiring from baseball. For many it appeared to be a decision difficult to understand. On that December day, DiMaggio was high physically and emotionally, but critical intellectually. On a critical day an individual is usually in an unstable condition and prone to hasty judgment or action. Could such have been the case with the great "Joe D"?

Mickey Mantle, DiMaggio's successor in center field, was involved in an episode that apparently had biorhythmic connotations. On May 18, 1962, Mantle slashed a hard drive into the outfield for a base hit. Running toward first base, he suddenly collapsed. A check of the Yankee center fielder's bio-cycles for that May day shows he was high physically and mentally, and emotionally critical; a combination of high accident affinity existed—too much strength in relation to coordination and nerve reaction.

Yankee immortal Babe Ruth's 1927 feat of 60 home runs provides an interesting retrospective biorhythm analysis. All but 13 of those home runs were slugged on days when Ruth was at or near a physical peak. In short, relying on biorhythm charts alone, somebody who knew nothing about Ruth's condition during the different days of the 1927 season would have been 79 per cent accurate in forecasting the "Bambino's" home run heroics.

Lou Gehrig, Ruth's teammate for many of those Yankee glory years, blasted four home runs in four consecutive trips to the plate on June 3, 1932. Gehrig almost notched a fifth straight homer except for an exceptional catch by Al Simmons. Gehrig's bio-cycle readout for that June 3: emotionally low on June 3, intellectually critical the day before, June 2. Analysis of the emotional low shows that for Gehrig it was part of the biorhythmic pattern under which he operated best. A cool, patient batter, on June 3, he waited calmly for the right pitch.

Gehrig's biorhythms—a significant factor during his famed career—were to have a fateful influence on him on June 2, 1941. On that date, with his physical cycle at its lowest point, Gehrig died of amyotrophic lateral sclerosis.

Bob Gibson—17 World Series Strikeouts

"It was the greatest pitching performance I've ever seen." That was the statement made by Detroit manager Mayo Smith after Bob Gibson on October 2, 1968, had struck out a record 17 Tigers, allowed but five hits, and powered his St. Louis team to a 4-0 victory.

The record of 15 strikeouts for a pitcher in a World Series had been set by Sandy Koufax in 1963. Gibson had to go to the ninth inning of this first game of the 1968 series to break the record and set a new one.

Going into the ninth inning he fanned Al Kaline for the third time and the scoreboard lights flashed number 15. Three flailing swings by Norm Cash gave Gibson number 16. Now it was Willie Horton versus Bob Gibson. Horton looked at a called strike three, and Gibson had his record-setting 17th strikeout.

From a biorhythm point of view Gibson had a lot going for him. He operated under a triple high that autumn day in 1968 and registered very high emotionally and very high intellectually—classic form for a classic performance.

Years later, Ted Simmons reminisced about Gibson: "He never let up. He challenged the hitters and he challenged himself." And Gibson on Gibson: "There have been plenty of people playing in this game with talent. But the basic thing is desire and determination . . . people are going to remember what they want to remember about you anyway . . . but the thing that pleases me is what I accomplished, and that's good enough for me."

The 1975 World Series

The Red Sox of Boston and the Reds of Cincinnati met in a seesaw battle for the 1975 World Championship that was filled with biorhythmic overtones. Game three saw Cincy's Joe Morgan single in the winning run in the 10th inning to give the Reds a 6-5 win. The little second baseman was at his highest point in his physical cycle and was high emotionally.

Home run hitters in the third game had a lot going for them in their bio-cycles. Johnny Bench had a triple high and was at his highest point intellectually when he picked the right pitch to slug for a two-run homer. The game was tied in the ninth inning by Boston's Dwight Evans with a two-run home run. Evans was at his highest point physically, and was emotionally and intellectually high. Thus, much of the action and the drama of the third game of the 1975 world series came from individuals who were primed by their bio-cycles.

On October 15, the two teams met in game four. Boston won 5–4. Evans was still operating under a triple high. He was a key figure in the Boston triumph, tripling in two runs and later scoring from third to account for three of the five Red Sox scores.

Suffering through a double critical and a

minus emotionally in his cycle, Cincinnati's Fred Norman was hit hard. The pitching log for Norman: four runs given up in 3-1/3 innings.

Don Gullett put on a one-man show to pace Cincinnati's 6-2 fifth-game victory on October 16. Striking out seven, walking one, and stroking a base hit for himself, Gullett yielded but five opposition hits. His bio-cycle: triple high, with the intellectual cycle registering at its highest point.

October 21 was another tough game, and when all the efforts of the day had been tallied the final score was Boston 7 and Cincinnati 6. Individual biorhythmic highlights included: Boston's Carl Yastrzemski—three hits, operating under very high physical and intellectual cycles; Pat Darcy, the losing pitcher for the Reds, operating under lows emotionally and intellectually and responsible for giving up the game-winning homer to Boston's Carlton Fisk in the bottom of the 12th inning; Boston's Rick Wise, relief pitcher in the 12th inning credited with the win—intellectually very high and physically plus in his cycle.

The final game of the World Series took place on October 22. Pete Rose and Tony Perez, both functioning under triple highs, were largely responsible for the Reds 4-3 win. Perez smashed a two-run homer, and Rose had two hits including the game-tying RBI.

Jim Burton—Boston relief pitcher—should have stayed in bed. Emotionally he was critical, physically he was very low, intellectually his rhythm was low. Burton pitched 2/3 of an inning, walking two and yielding the game-winning hit to Cincinnati's Joe Morgan.

The 1976 Season

During the 1976 baseball season, there

were many interesting sidelights on the interrelationship of the national pastime and biorhythms.

The personalities of two pitchers—one a rookie and one a veteran—revealed some pathways worth future study.

Detroit's Mark (the Bird) Fidrych excited all of Michigan and in fact all of baseball with his winning ways and collegiate-type enthusiasm. Fidrych would run to take his position on the pitching mound and run off it back to the dugout after he concluded pitching an inning. He would shout encouragement to his infielders. And in a nationally televised game, the young hurler became the first player to come back onto the field to accept the applause of the crowd after he had notched an impressive victory.

On September 3, "the Bird" was not flying. He had one of his worst outings of the season against a Milwaukee Brewer team that was going nowhere in the American League standings. On that date, Fidrych lasted but 3-2/3 innings as the Brewers lashed him for 9 runs and sent him to an early shower. The final score of the game was Milwaukee 11 and Detroit 2. The scoring for Fidrych as regards his biorhythms: physically he was positive, but emotionally he was at his lowest point. For an athlete like Fidrych, whose strength as a pitcher comes in large part from his enthusiasm, an emotional low is not the most opportune of circumstances.

On the other hand, Mike Torrez, veteran pitcher on the Oakland A's, performed splendidly with generally poor emotional rhythms going for him. This is understandable when one considers that in forecasting performances by veteran class pitchers, little stock generally need be placed in emotional rhythms. Veteran pitchers have been "through the mill," and confidence is one aspect of their play not lacking, and therefore not significantly influencing performance.

Mike Torrez clearly demonstrated this. In five September starts, his record was as follows:

	P	E	I*
September 3: 3-0 win, yielded two hits	−	−	+
September 7: 4-0 win, yielded four hits	−	−	+
September 11: 1-0 win	+	−	C
September 15: 5-2 win	+	C	−
September 28: 1-0 win, yielded two hits	−	+	C

*Physical (P), Emotional (E), Intellectual (I).

This masterful pitching record compiled by Torrez was accomplished when his emotional rhythms in three of the victories were minus, and on another occasion were in the critical phase. This record buttresses the belief that for "class" pitchers the emotional cycle is generally of least validity in forecasting performance.

On the other hand, Torrez was high intellectually in two of the starts, and at the zero critical point in two other victories. Did heightened powers of concentration come into play enabling Torrez to compensate for apparently poor physical and emotional rhythms? A final item of note is the September 15th performance of Torrez. On that date, he was down intellectually and yielded runs for the first time in his amazing five-game winning streak. How much did his physical high and emotional critical compensate for the intellectual low in the poorest performance of the five wins?

In late September of 1976, the Oakland Athletics were struggling desperately to cut the lead of the Kansas City Royals. Larry Gura, physically high, and at his highest point emotionally and intellectually, was given the ball on September 29 and told to hold back the A's. Gura responded with a nifty four-hit shutout enabling Kansas City to win 4-0 and move on to the Ameri-

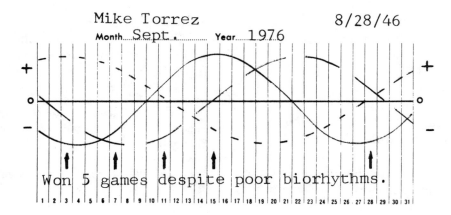

Mike Torrez   8/28/46
Month Sept.   Year 1976

Won 5 games despite poor biorhythms.

can League championship playoffs against the New York Yankees.

Gura, low in all cycles, was racked for 12 hits in the opening game, and the former Yankee pitcher was put down by his former manager, Billy Martin: "He pitched very well." In the fourth game on October 13, with the incentives of getting back at Martin, at his old teammates, and with keeping Kansas City in the playoffs, Gura again took the mound. His bio-cycle readout showed: physically low, intellectually low. Whatever boost he needed from his emotional cycle was not forthcoming, for Gura was at the lowest point in his emotional cycle. The lefthander lasted two innings, yielding six hits and two runs.

The interrelationship of biorhythms and top pitching performances is further underscored by the efforts of the New York Mets' Tom Seaver and Dennis Leonard of Kansas City. In a crucial game in Kansas City's drive for the American League West pennant, Leonard snapped his team's losing streak, trimming Texas 7-0, and yielding only six hits. The Kansas City hurler was physically at the highest point in his cycle as well as emotionally and intellectually plus.

The heavy hitting Pirates managed just five hits off Tom Seaver on September 13.

Tom Terrific shut out the Bucs and fanned a dozen batters. Seaver was high in all three cycles that September day.

The American League 1976 Championship

The temperature was in the 50s, but a jammed house kept warm by screaming itself hoarse. This cool Thursday night October 14, the New York Yankees and the Kansas City Royals slugged it out in the final game of the American League championship series at Yankee Stadium.

Pitching on his 28th birthday, Ed Figueroa of the Yankees, intellectually and physically low, but at his highest point in his emotional rhythm, struggled on the mound. When the laboring hurler finally left the game after yielding a single in the top of the eighth inning, he had surrendered seven hits and three runs. But the Yankees led, 6-3. Had the constant chant by the thousands and thousands of home town rooters—"Eddie, Eddie, Eddie"—coupled with his emotional biorhythmic peak kept him and the Yanks in the game for those seven innings?

In the eighth inning, a dramatic biorhythmic confrontation took place. Grant Jackson came in for New York to relieve Figueroa. Perhaps the Yankees' premier

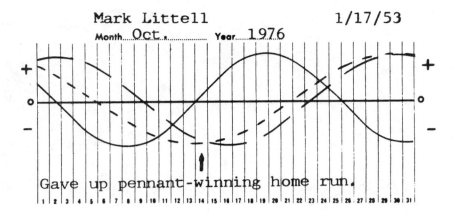

Mark Littell   1/17/53
Month Oct.   Year 1976

Gave up pennant-winning home run.

pitcher during the waning weeks of the 1976 season, Jackson's bio-cycle was: physically low, intellectually close to his lowest point. He was emotionally high, but this is generally not considered a significant factor for veteran pitchers like Jackson.

With two men on base, Kansas City's George Brett, the American League's batting champion, faced Jackson. The 23-year-old Brett showed low physical rhythm, was within 24 hours of an emotional critical, but intellectually he was high. Brett blasted a three-run homer tying the score, 6–6. Jackson said, "I *let* a fast ball *slip*." Brett, not known for his home run hitting, said: "I was *going* for a home run. The fence was 310 feet. I *knew* I could hit the ball 310 feet."

Thus, the Brett-Jackson confrontation was a clash between one athlete's intellectual high and another's intellectual low. One admitted he was governed by his intellect and consciously went for a home run. The other admitted that a mental lapse was an operating factor in the surrendering of the home-run pitch.

The contest remained tied, 6–6, until the bottom of the ninth inning. Then another and more dramatic pitcher-batter confrontation with interesting biorhythmic side-

lights ensued.

Mark Littell, a power-pitcher, had choked off the Yankees in the 8th inning. Littell had pitched 104 innings during the regular season and allowed but one home run. Biorhythmically, however, this cold October night was not the best time for him. His cycle revealed that he was physically critical, emotionally low, and intellectually at his lowest point.

Chris Chambliss came to bat for the Yankees, and Littell surrendered only his second home run of the year. Chambliss blasted the ball into the right field stands to give the Yankees their first pennant in a dozen years.

"I challenged him. I didn't want to walk him," said Littell. "I'm not gonna feel sorry for myself. I gave him my best pitch."

How good Littell's best pitch was will be discussed for decades by sports fans. How much his biorhythms influenced the outcome of the American League championship is another matter that will be pondered for a long time.

The 1976 World Series

GAME # 1: *Cincinnati Reds 5, New York Yankees 1*

Their front line pitching depleted from

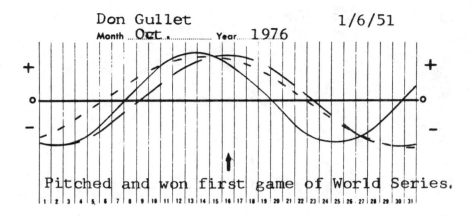

the dogfight series with the Kansas City Royals, Yankee manager Billy Martin selected 26-year-old Doyle Alexander to open the World Series against the Cincinnati Reds. Don Gullet was the starter for the Reds.

The bio-cycles for Alexander and Gullet were a study in contrasts. Alexander was at the lowest point in his physical rhythm, emotionally minus. The only thing he had going for him was an intellectual plus. A triple high characterized Gullet's rhythms and emotionally, he was at his highest point, significant for a young pitcher.

The "Big Red Machine" racked Alexander for five runs and nine hits in seven innings. Gullet, enjoying his triple high, was in command all the way. The Yankees only managed five hits and one run off the Cincinnati ace who left the game in the eighth inning with a pain in his ankle.

The hitting stars for Cincinnati were Joe Morgan and Tony Perez. Morgan, operating under a triple high, and at his highest point physically, got the Reds off to an early lead with a first inning home run. He also made three outstanding fielding plays. Perez notched two singles, a double, and drove in a run. The Cincinnati first baseman on that chilly October day showed intellectual and emotional highs in his

rhythms. As a veteran ballplayer, he undoubtedly was able to compensate for a low in his physical cycle.

GAME # 2: *Cincinnati Reds 4, New York Yankees 3*

The three million dollar man, Catfish Hunter, started and finished this contest for the New York Yankees. Biorhythmically, Hunter was intellectually low, physically coming off his lowest point—not the best of conditions for one facing the "Big Red Machine." Only emotionally did Hunter have something in his favor: He was a day away from his highest point.

For the first four innings, Yankee outfielders were transformed into track stars. Hunter was hit hard. He was laboring. He was constantly behind the batters. Yet, though the Reds had the 30-year-old right-hander on the ropes, they couldn't knock him out. Bio-cycle and Cincinnati notwithstanding, he settled down and held the Reds in check.

As the game moved into the bottom of the ninth inning, the line score was identical for both teams: three runs, nine hits, no errors. Then with two outs and Cincinnati's Ken Griffey on second base as a result of an error, Tony Perez came to bat. Perez singled sharply to left field giving the Reds a 4–3 win. Hunter, almost echoing his physical and intellectual position, said: "I wanted the pitch back the minute I threw it."

Other biorhythm sidelights of the first Sunday night game in the history of the World Series included: Elliot Maddox of New York (triple low) striking out twice and grounding into a rally-killing double play; and Joe Morgan of Cincinnati (plus physically and plus intellectually) rapping two hits, one a triple, and producing five brilliant fielding plays.

GAME # 3: *Cincinnati 6, New York 2*

The World Series shifted to Yankee Stadium for the third game on October 19. The big show that night in the cold of New York City was Cincy's Dan Driessen. Operating under an emotional high and an intellectual high, Driessen almost single-handedly demolished the Yankees. In the third inning, he singled. In the fourth inning, he homered. In the sixth inning, he doubled. He stole a base, and wound up with one RBI and two runs scored.

The 13-hit Cincinnati barrage came against veteran Yankee pitchers Dock Ellis and Grant Jackson. The 31-year-old Ellis, within 24 hours of a physically critical day and intellectually negative, was removed in the fourth inning. He had been shelled for seven hits and four runs. His successor, Jackson, lasted 3-2/3 innings and departed after giving up four hits and two runs.

GAME # 4: *Cincinnati Reds 7, New York Yankees 2*

"This World Series was boredom compared to last year," said Cincinnati's Pete Rose as the Reds swept the Yanks in four games to string together back-to-back world championships. It was the first time a National League team won consecutive championships in 54 years. Throughout the series, biorhythms spotlighted and underscored individual performances and decisions. This was greatly in evidence in the fourth and final game.

The bio-cycles of the relief pitchers used by both teams were especially interesting. Hugh McEnaney succeeded Gary Nolan on the mound for the Reds and pitched the last 2-1/3 innings. The young hurler had not had a good season pitching for Cincinnati, but in this relief appearance, he was flawless. He gave up no hits, no runs, and completely throttled any Yankee hopes of victory. McEnaney's bio-cycle: double critical—physically and emotionally, but intellectually within a day of his highest point. It's obvious that his thinking ability was sharp and given the moment of clinching the championship of the world for his team, he was able to turn the double critical to his advantage.

An opposite bio-cycle readout existed for Dick Tidrow, Yankee reliever; an opposite pitching performance also resulted. Tidrow was low in all three rhythms and had just passed out of an emotional and a physical critical. In the ninth inning Tidrow took the mound in relief of Ed Figueroa. Johnny Bench smashed a three-run home run off him. The Reds scored their fourth, fifth, and sixth runs. Then Tidrow gave up back-to-back doubles to Geronimo and Concepcion for the Reds' seventh run. The game was out of reach and Tidrow was removed.

In the midst of the ninth inning debacle for the Yankees, another New Yorker was also removed—their manager, Billy Martin. Within 24 hours of a physically critical day and within 24 hours of an intellectually critical day, and emotionally minus, Martin charged out of the Yankee dugout to do battle with the umpires. Handicapped by his bio-cycles, Martin's temper tantrum apparently made him say and do things he should not have said or done. He was tossed out of the game by the men in blue.

The starting pitchers in this final game performed creditably and their biorhythms, in effect, forecast this behavior. Cincinnati's Gary Nolan was physically and intellectually high. In the 6-2/3 innings he pitched, he held the Yankees to two runs. Yankee starter Ed Figueroa labored into the ninth supported by an intellectual high. When he was removed from the game in favor of Tidrow, he had yielded three runs and six hits.

The 1976 World Series belongs now to the record books. Sports fans, however, and biorhythm analysts, will probably be reviewing and evaluating its implications for a long, long time.

Baseball Forecasting Combined with Handicapping

All over America, numerous individuals and organizations have harnessed biorhythms to their sports forecasting operations. "Jimmy the Greek" Snyder has gone on record as stating that he uses biorhythms as one of the methods to help him select winners in National Football League contests.

One man who has been highly successful in forecasting baseball results is professional handicapper Kenneth S. Cammisa. "Biorhythms used in conjunction with my baseball handicapping methods," Cammisa states, "have increased my 64 per cent win factor to a fantastic 87 per cent."

Cammisa's theory is based on individual player case histories with the prime focus on pitchers. "The key factor," he states, "is the pitcher and the support factor is the bio charts of the key players of the rest of the team." Cammisa looks only for special games where there is a "class" pitcher and the support is high and the opposition pitcher and the team is low. "Otherwise," he observes, "I will pass."

In the June 1, 1975, to June 1, 1976, period, Cammisa selected 132 games for play. "Out of the 132 games selected," he notes, "there were 115 winners for an amazing percentage of 87.12. Even more outstanding was the fact that the opposition in all those 132 games averaged only 1.92 (earned runs) per game. The biorhythm-approved teams averaged 5.08 runs per game," Cammisa maintains. "Because of the large sampling, I feel my results are very significant."

Cammisa is emphatic about the following: "Unless you have developed a highly sophisticated method of evaluating the skills and incentives involved in athletic competition, biorhythms cannot be utilized to their fullest extent." In other words, Cammisa sees biorhythms as a supplement and acknowledges a host of other factors that must also be involved in any kind of forecasting. He also argues that one must fully understand biorhythms and sports to be able to forecast intelligently.

Cycles and Pitchers

THE PHYSICAL CYCLE: Cammisa maintains that there is a direct relationship between the physical rhythm and the age of the pitcher. "The older the pitcher," he notes, "the more importance I attach to his physical cycle, which I feel governs his endurance level."

With older quality pitchers, such as Jim Palmer or Tom Seaver, the physical cycle in the view of Cammisa has much significant value. Whereas Cammisa believes that for a young pitcher like Frank Tannana, of the California Angels, "the physical cycle has very little value."

THE INTELLECTUAL CYCLE: This cycle is cited by Cammisa as the one having the greatest value in forecasting. "When you are dealing with strictly class pitchers," he acknowledges, "it has a direct

PRIME EXAMPLES OF SELECTIONS MADE DURING THE 1976 BASEBALL SEASON
(Only "class" or "quality" pitchers used)

Birth Date	Bio Symbol	Pitcher	Opponent	Date of Game	Hits Allowed	Runs Allowed	Win Lose	Comments
7-3-53	ENT	Frank Tanana	Kansas City	7-7-76	9 innings 4 hits	1 run	Win	A young, class pitcher
12-22-44	SFF	Steve Carlton	St. Louis	8.8.76	8 innings 2 hits	1 run	Win	Older pitcher. Physical at peak high.
7-28-49	SEB	Vida Blue	Mil.	8-10-76	9 innings 5 hits	1 run	Win	Peak high intellectually.
11-23-40	X3A	Lou Tiant	Cal.	8-12-76	10 innings 6 hits	1 run	Win	Older pitcher. Peak high Physically.
5.25-50	U1F	John Montefusco	Philly	8-13-76	9 innings 6 hits	0 runs	Win	Young pitcher. Intellectually near peak.
4-2-45	DXH	Don Sutton	Cubs	8-15-76	9 innings 6 hits	2 runs	Win	Near peak intellectually.
9-4-50	GQJ	Doyle Alexander	Texas	8-17-76	9 innings 5 hits	1 run	Win	Near peak intellectually.
5-8-51	XKY	Dennis Leonard	Texas	9-4-76	9 innings 6 hits	0 runs	Win	Peak physically. Near peak intellectually.
6-23-49	F18	Dave Goltz	Texas	9-9-76	9 innings 3 hits	0 runs	Win	Peak intellect.
11-17-44	F2D	Tom Seaver	Pitts.	9-13-76	9 innings 5 hits	0 runs	Win	Near peak Intellect.
10-15-45	QXF	Jim Palmer	Yanks	9-22-76	9 innings 4 hits	0 runs	Win	Older pitcher, Physical peak.

effect on the concentration capabilities of each pitcher. And concentration is of prime concern when evaluating 'class' or quality pitchers."

THE EMOTIONAL CYCLE: Cammisa places the least value on the emotional cycle for forecasting purposes. "The only influence it may have is on the confidence of the pitchers," he argues. "But when you are dealing with and evaluating 'class' pitchers, confidence is one factor they definitely do not lack!"

Basketball

Though a team game with numerous substitutions, the sport of basketball is many times controlled by the efforts of one individual. Scoring points, playing super defense, tallying assists, or sweeping the boards for rebounds, the basketball player throughout history has "risen to the occasion." From the biorhythm perspective, many of these moments could have been predicted.

On November 24, 1960, Wilt Chamberlain, then a member of the Philadelphia 76'ers, hauled in a record 55 rebounds against the Boston Celtics. Charged up via a plus in his emotional cycle, the main contributing factor to Chamberlain's historic performance appeared to be the peak point he was under in his physical rhythm.

Chamberlain's forte, at seven-foot-plus, was rebounding. Basketball Hall of Famer Bob Cousy's forte was play-making. On February 27, 1959, very high physically and exceptionally high intellectually, Cousy notched a record 28 assists. Competing for the Boston Celtics against the old Minneapolis Laker franchise, Cousy's uncanny passing accounted for 56 of his team's points. It was heads-up basketball, courtesy of Cousy's biorhythms.

NBA—1976

A survey of some individual performances of the 1976 National Basketball Association season reveals some more dramatic examples of the interrelationship of biorhythms and basketball.

Artis Gilmore, the gigantic center of the Chicago Bulls, exemplifies the personal ups and the downs that apparently correlate so well with bio-cycle study. On October 26, Gilmore's Chicago team nipped the Milwaukee Bucks 90-88. A Gilmore shot in the final minute of the game was the Chicago margin of victory. It is worth noting that Gilmore was physically plus that evening.

Just four days later, Gilmore's physical cycle was critical. The Bulls also suffered through a critical time as they were routed by the Milwaukee Bucks 102-74. The Chicago center was of no value to his team. In a complete reversal of form from his efforts against Milwaukee four days before, Gilmore had a miserable night. He could manage but six points and six rebounds.

Boston's John Havlicek, Houston's Rudy Tomjanovich, Washington's Elvin Hayes, Portland's Maurice Lucas, San Antonio's George Gervin, and Golden State's Charles Dudley recorded impressive performances on dates where all of them operated under physical rhythms at their highest points.

Boston defeated Indiana on October 21 and Hondo Havlicek scored eight of his game-high 32 points in overtime. Hayes popped in a jump shot with 33 seconds remaining to lift the Bullets to a 98-97 win over the Detroit Pistons on October 23. Rudy T. had 38 points in Houston's 129-126 win over Phoenix on October 23.

Hauling in 15 rebounds and pacing all scoring with 24 points, Lucas powered Portland to a 131–97 win over Detroit on October 30. San Antonio's Gervin notched a game-high 37 in his team's October 30

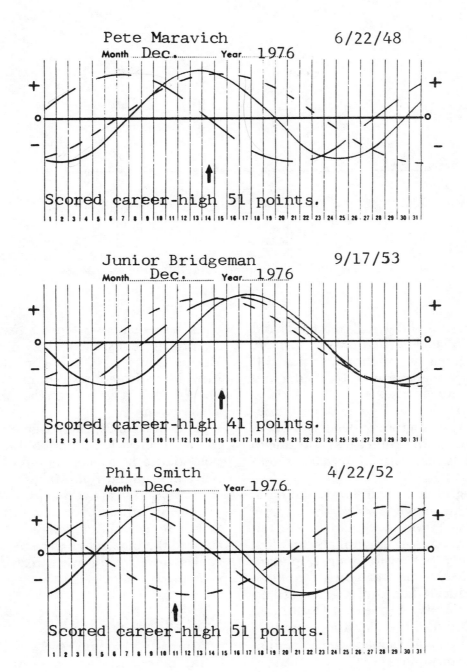

Pete Maravich　6/22/48
Month Dec.　Year 1976
Scored career-high 51 points.

Junior Bridgeman　9/17/53
Month Dec.　Year 1976
Scored career-high 41 points.

Phil Smith　4/22/52
Month Dec.　Year 1976
Scored career-high 51 points.

loss to Boston, 126–117.

Dudley, though negative in his two other cycles, was aided by being physically at his highest point in the Golden State 112-92 triumph over Portland on October 28. Doing almost everything but sell tickets, Dudley scored 19 points, notched 12 assists and managed four steals.

Other Basketball-Biorhythm Links

The last week of October 1976 will long be remembered by Larry Kenon of San Antonio. Operating under a triple high, on October 27, Kenon led the Spurs to a 115-106 win over Phoenix. He spurred the Spurs with an NBA season high to that

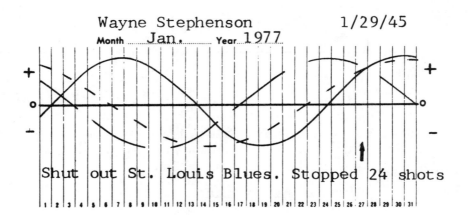

Wayne Stephenson   1/29/45
Month   Jan.   Year 1977

Shut out St. Louis Blues. Stopped 24 shots

point of 41, pulled down 12 rebounds and racked up 5 steals. Then on October 30, operating under an emotional critical, all Kenon could manage was 14 points and numerous defensive lapses.

On October 30, the Houston Rockets defeated the Washington Bullets, 105–92. A large reason for the Bullet loss was due to the ineffectiveness of Elvin Hayes and Dave Bing.

Operating under a triple low, and emotionally at his lowest point, the usually high–scoring Hayes was held to just ten points. Bing was low emotionally and low intellectually, but even more important biorhythmically—he was going through a physical critical. The Bullet guard scored only eight points—his season low to that point. With 2/5 of their starting team biorhythmically handicapped, the Washington loss to Houston was easily justifiable.

Bill Walton was born November 5, 1952. On November 5, 1976, the giant red–headed center collected 26 points and 16 rebounds to lead Portland to a 146–104 win over Philadelphia. His birthday was made happy by his biorhythms, which showed physical and emotional highs operative.

A good little man can beat a big man any day of the week—especially if the little man has a physical edge in his biorhythms.

This was demonstrated on November 6, 1976. The Houston Rockets defeated the Boston Celtics, 117-111, and little Calvin Murphy defeated six-foot-nine-inch Sidney Wicks in a fist fight in the third quarter of the game.

Both players registered emotional lows in their cycles. Thus, both of them had the potential to be especially out of sorts that November night. But, Murphy was physically plus in his rhythm while Wicks was physically minus. A barrage of lefts and rights to the head floored Wicks and amazed the fans who had come out to see a basketball game but were treated to an impromptu boxing match.

Dave Cowens Quits His Job

Stunned Celtic fans reacted with dismay to the news that Dave Cowens was quitting his job on the Boston NBA team. While the announcement seemed out of the blue to the average basketball follower, friends indicated the 6'–8½" center had suffered through blue periods before in which he would seriously question the value of spending his years as a professional athlete. They felt he was liable to just "wake up one morning and quit."

He did just that during an emotionally

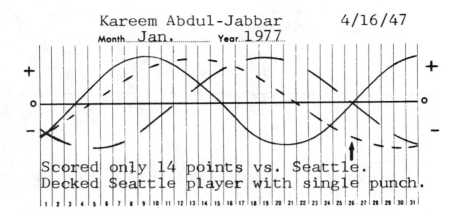

Kareem Abdul-Jabbar 4/16/47
Month Jan. Year 1977

Scored only 14 points vs. Seattle.
Decked Seattle player with single punch.

low day, quite possibly another one of the "blue periods" friends had noticed. While Cowens' job called for peak physical performance on the basketball court and consistently cool intellectual judgment, it seems that it was the emotional side of the amiable red-headed athlete that drew him to the Celtics. He has claimed that he doesn't play for the money or the glory, but simply because he likes to play basketball. The nature of the sport and the life–style of a professional athlete appealed to him—till that November day in 1976, when harkening to a different emotional message, during a low point in his bio-cycle, Dave Cowens left the Boston Celtics. How much of the emotional side of the former Celtic star was speaking when he claimed: "I don't feel like a superstar. I just feel like a normal person who has quit his job. . . . Some people won't understand what I'm doing, but I don't live for other people." Cowens has since rejoined the Celtics.

The Pearl and the Pistol

Earl ("the Pearl") Monroe and the New York Knickerbockers came up against the New Orleans Jazz and "Pistol" Pete Maravich on Saturday night, October 30, 1976, before 14,342 fans at Madison Square Garden.

The Monroe-Maravich confrontation was a biorhythm shootout and a classic confrontation between two of the slickest scorers in the National Basketball Association.

The bio-cycles for the two were nearly identical: Maravich was low intellectually and emotionally, but within 24 hours of his highest point physically. Monroe was at his highest point physically and also down intellectually and emotionally. The veteran stars did not need a hype from their intellectual or emotional rhythms as the results of the night revealed. Their skills all came from the timing, the driving, the spinning of their physical ability.

Maravich was a one-man scoring machine. Driving at will, he popped in 20-foot jump shots, notched ten assists and wound up with 39 points.

Monroe was Mr. Magic. Whirling, spinning, faking, he tallied 36 points and six key assists.

Both players performed at fever pitch physically and at sub-par emotionally. They indicated the emotional lows and the attendant irascibility from these lows via post-game comments. Maravich said, "It was the closest thing to a Central Park mugging I can get. They tried to do everything but kill me." He pointed to a big

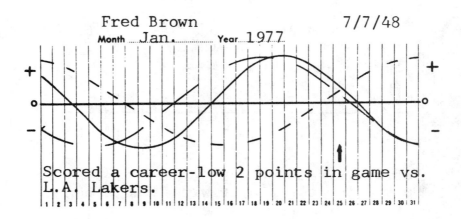

Fred Brown   7/7/48

Month Jan.   Year 1977

Scored a career-low 2 points in game vs. L.A. Lakers.

gash on his left hand. "I think Monroe pulled a switchblade on me."

Monroe was also not in the most even-tempered of moods. The officials charged him with a technical foul that cost him $75 for losing his "cool" in a highly emotional protest.

Continuing on his physical high, Pete Maravich scored an impressive 43 points three nights later, leading the New Orleans Jazz to a 115–97 triumph over the Boston Celtics. With a 48-45 halftime lead, the Jazz profited from the physically plus Maravich who in the second half of the game managed 26 points and thereby a big assist in widening the margin of victory.

The NBA All-Star Game

On Sunday, February 13, the National Basketball Association held its annual all-star game in Milwaukee, Wisconsin. The game was exciting from start to finish as the world's most outstanding players demonstrated their individual skills. The lead changed hands up until the last 38 seconds when Phoenix' Paul Westphal scored to give the West squad a three-point lead. The East was able to come within one point with 16 seconds remaining but a key steal by Westphal squelched any chance of

an East comeback. The final score was West 125, East 124.

From a biorhythmic point of view, this game confirmed that basketball players score best while high physically. The other two cycles don't seem to have an effect on scoring, though they do seem to affect the passing and rebounding aspects of the game. A study of the 24 participants of the all-star game reveals that 12 were high physically on the day of the game. Furthermore, those 12 players accounted for 67 per cent of the total points scored during the game. It would seem significant that 50 per cent of the players scored 67 per cent of the points.

Individually, the results were equally profound. Paul Westphal, the West's dominant player, was very high physically. The same held true for Julius Erving, the game's MVP, and for Bob McAdoo, the game's leading scorer. Rick Barry of the West team opened the game with four consecutive baskets. He, too, was very high physically. The disappointing showings were turned in by George McGinnis, who scored a mere four points; George Gervin, who couldn't score a single point; and Pete Maravich, who lost the ball with 16 seconds remaining in the game. Each player was low physically. Despite these statistics

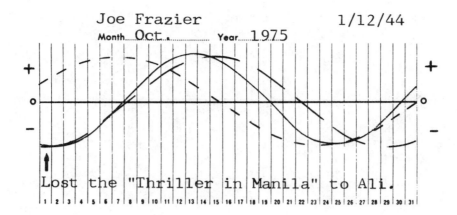

Joe Frazier   1/12/44

Month....Oct.............. Year....1975

Lost the "Thriller in Manila" to Ali.

no definitive connection between scoring potential and the physical cycle is being made at this time. More research is necessary.

Boxing

Some of the most spectacular examples of the role of biorhythm in athletic competition come from the world of boxing. Just two athletes, glove to glove, in a small ring, pitted against each other very clearly spotlight the individual's biorhythms.

A classically poignant case is the tragedy of Benny ("the Kid") Paret. On March 24, 1962, Paret's biorhythmic position revealed that he was triple critical. He entered the ring against Emile Griffith. Paret was carried out of the ring after being battered into a state of unconsciousness by Griffith. Ten days later, on his very next critical day, never having regained consciousness, Paret died.

A significant role was played by biorhythm in a series of boxing matches between Floyd Patterson and Ingemar Johansson in 1960.

In their first bout, Johansson showed emotional and intellectual highs and was concluding a recuperative period in his physical cycle. Patterson's only positive operating factor was a high in his emotional rhythm. Johansson won the match to the surprise of many of the sporting public.

Their second match saw Patterson the victor. Johansson was outmatched in the ring and in the bio-cycles. Patterson's cycles were high both physically and emotionally while the Swedish boxer was low in these rhythms.

A third match was scheduled. Johansson did his best to avoid the rigorous training routine that boxers must maintain to keep in peak form. He entered the ring against Patterson with the advantage of a triple high. Patterson defeated him in the fifth round even though Floyd was under the influence of a triple low. It is worth noting that even a triple high cannot guarantee victory for a poorly-conditioned, poorly-trained fighter. It is also worth noting that in any attempt to predict or to forecast the influence of biorhythms on sporting events, other factors such as training and discipline and will must be taken into account.

A major factor influencing a number of Muhammad Ali's fights has been biorhythm. On March 31, 1973, Ken Norton shattered Ali's jaw, his pride, and his professional standing. Ali's bio-cycle for that

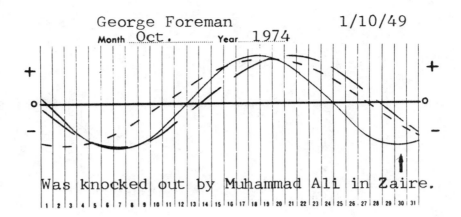

George Foreman   1/10/49
Month Oct.   Year 1974

Was knocked out by Muhammad Ali in Zaire.

1 2 3 4 5 6 7 8 9 10 11 12 13 14 15 16 17 18 19 20 21 22 23 24 25 26 27 28 29 30 31

date records a near critical for both his physical and emotional rhythms.

Back on February 25, 1964, when Ali was known to the world as Cassius Clay, he defeated Sonny Liston for the heavyweight championship of the world. Liston biorhythmically had nothing going for him, and many observers recall that he also had nothing going for him in the fight. Physically he was critical and he showed negative readings in the two other cycles.

The doctors at ringside reported that Clay "had the fear of death." His physical cycle was critical, and he was intellectually low in his rhythms. Emotionally, Clay was very high and was perhaps more so after notching his seventh-round kayo.

Ali met George Foreman for the title on October 30, 1974. Both men were negative in all three cycles. Ali scored an eighth-round knockout. Was the result of the fight dictated by the fact that Foreman was at the lowest point in his physical cycle while Ali was just plain low? Observers recall that both boxers displayed a great deal of physical fatigue, but that Foreman tired faster.

In a bout that resulted in Joe Frazier winding up with an enforced hospital stay for several weeks, Ali lost the title on a decision. Biorhythmically, Ali was outclassed by Frazier, who was physically very high while Ali was very low. Emotionally Frazier was also very high; Ali was just plus. Only intellectually did Ali have the edge. The rhythms of the fighters were reflected in the rhythm of the match. Frazier, stubborn, determined, and the stronger of the two, bulled his way to victory and also to the hospital stay. Ali lost the match but avoided serious damage to his body.

The two men met again on October 1, 1975, in the battle that has been called "the Thriller in Manila." It was a close bout that saw Ali seemingly get stronger after the twelfth round and finally kayo Frazier in the fourteenth.

The changed momentum of the match is reflected in their physical rhythms for that day: Ali was physically very high while Frazier operated at his lowest point.

On May 25, 1976, Ali defended his title against a little-known but game fighter by the name of Richard Dunn. No one really took this fight too seriously until the bell sounded and the fight began. Ali, who was coming off his worst fight and a near loss to Jimmy Young, needed a fast and easy victory to quiet his disappointed fans. Dunn seemed oblivious to this fact and came out swinging wild and high, hoping for a miracle blow to land. Biorhythmically, however, this was not to be a miraculous night for Richard Dunn. While Ali was critical physically, he was high emotionally and very high intellectually. Dunn, at the same time, was low in all three cycles. The results were predictable. Ali survived a shaky few rounds and then charged back with a fury to knock his opponent out.

The long-awaited rematch between Muhammad Ali and Ken Norton took place on September 28, 1976, at Yankee Stadium in New York. Neither fighter performed up to expectations, but then, again, neither fighter was high biorhythmically. The fight lasted the full fifteen rounds with no knockdowns and few spirited exchanges. Ultimately, Ali prevailed, but this fight will long be remembered for his lackluster showing.

Joe Louis and Biorhythm

As in the case of Jesse Owens, there are athletes who defy any biorhythmic stereotyping. Such an athlete was Joe Louis. In some of his key major championship fights, the Brown Bomber prevailed while generally under the influence of poor biorhythm cycles.

On June 22, 1937, Louis confronted Braddock for the heavyweight championship of the world. Braddock went down and was counted out in the eighth round as Louis took the title. Intellectually, Louis was very low and, even more significantly, he was operating under a double critical in his cycles. Anyone attempting to forecast the result of that June 22, 1937, bout on the basis of Joe's negative biorhythms would have had some difficulty. Yet, the opposite would have been the case had they realized the Joe Louis bio-cycle performance pattern: He prevailed under poor cycles.

In perhaps the only real "grudge" fight of his career—against Max Schmeling on

June 22, 1938—Louis again went against traditional biorhythm forecasting. Physically and intellectually low, and emotionally critical, he battered and bruised the German fighter to notch a first-round knockout. How much the Nazi propaganda swipes at America—and the denigration of Louis because of his color—had to do with Joe's frenzied fighting is a matter of record. How much the emotional critical of Louis had to do with the results of the match is a matter for the student of biorhythm forecasting to contemplate.

In two championship matches against Jersey Joe Walcott, Louis again prevailed despite poor biorhythm cycles. Critical physically, critical intellectually, and emotionally low on December 5, 1947, Louis squeaked by Walcott for a fifteen-round decision.

On June 25, 1948, in a re-match with Walcott, the Brown Bomber managed an eleventh-round kayo. However, in this fight as in so many others, Louis persevered despite negative rhythms: He was low physically and intellectually. It was the only time in the four championship matches under discussion that Louis registered a plus in any cycle. Emotionally he was high in his rhythms.

Thus, the bio-cycle readouts on Joe Louis in his two fights against Walcott, his destruction of Schmeling, and his victory over Braddock should alert the student of biorhythm forecasting to an important point: *Pattern, track record,* and *trend* are important and significant elements of any sports forecasting through biorhythms.

A postscript to the career of Joe Louis and biorhythms came on September 27, 1950. The Brown Bomber, a shadow of his former self, attempted to make a ring comeback against Ezzard Charles. The old champ survived for fifteen rounds only to lose the fight by a decision. The battle was

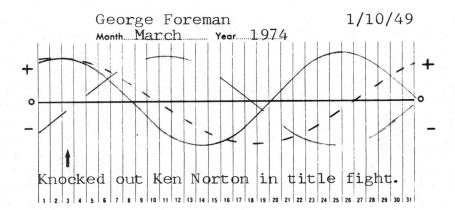

George Foreman   1/10/49
Month....March........ Year....1974

Knocked out Ken Norton in title fight.

| 1 | 2 | 3 | 4 | 5 | 6 | 7 | 8 | 9 | 10 | 11 | 12 | 13 | 14 | 15 | 16 | 17 | 18 | 19 | 20 | 21 | 22 | 23 | 24 | 25 | 26 | 27 | 28 | 29 | 30 | 31 |

a biorhythmic confrontation as well as one of youth and age, the future and the past.

Charles was physically and intellectually high and at his highest point emotionally for the contest. Louis was just the opposite. Emotionally critical, he was minus in the two other rhythms. In the past, it would have been a biorhythm pattern that he could have coped with. This late in his career, over the hill, the combination of poor rhythms and failing skills was too much.

A year before, an edge in his biorhythms had enabled Charles to eke by Walcott in a close fight for the heavyweight championship. On June 22, 1949, Charles faced Walcott; the bio-cycles for both were

Charles—physcially (critical)
            emotionally (lowest point)
            intellectually (positive)

Walcott—physically (critical)
            emotionally (very low)
            intellectually (very low)

The only edge Charles had was in the intellectual cycle and in this close fight it was enough to give him the victory.

Rocky Marciano was a very physical fighter and also a man with a lot of pride who was greatly influenced by his emotions in the ring. These facts about Marciano were graphically intertwined with his biorhythms in two of his matches.

On September 23, 1952, Marciano kayoed Walcott in the thirteenth round to win the heavyweight title. Physically and intellectually both boxers were down—Walcott, in fact, was at his lowest point. Emotionally, they were both positive. It was a very close match. How much of an edge did Marciano have as a result of his emotional plus is perhaps seen by his thirteenth round kayo.

In the last hurrah, the final fight of his career, Marciano faced Archie Moore. Physically high, intellectually low, Marciano was at near peak emotionally in his rhythms. Moore was at his lowest point physically and emotionally and was intellectually plus. Marciano knocked out Moore in the ninth round and retired gracefully. How much did his emotional plus versus Moore's emotional minus influence Rocky's triumphant exit from boxing?

Anyone scanning the following bio-cycles would have perhaps been willing to speculate on the outcome of a fight between the two individuals these cycles represented:

	P
Fighter "A"	highest point
Fighter "B"	negative

E	I
critical	highest point
negative	plus

The above was the biorhythm contrast between George Foreman (Fighter "A") and Ken Norton (Fighter "B") on March 3, 1974. Foreman demolished Norton in a match that was no contest, scoring a second-round knockout.

Chess and Cricket

From such widely dissimilar sports as chess and cricket come examples of the interesting and significant influence of bioryhthms on performance.

Chess

When Bobby Fischer contested Boris Spassky in Reykjavic, Iceland, in 1972, for the world championship, he had a favorable bio-cycle reading most of the time of the competition. On the two days that were critical in Fischer's cycle, by coincidence no matches were scheduled.

Fischer won the world championship and got all the attendant publicity. How different would the result of the matches have been had Fischer been required to perform on critical days or on days when his bio-cycle was not in the favorable position?

Cricket

Glen Turner, the remarkable New Zealand cricketeer, star of the New England cricket team, was competing in the last days of May, 1973, at Northampton, and was not out at the close of the first day's play. He still needed 23 runs to reach 1,000 runs in May, a feat accomplished by only five others in history.

Although tired, fretful and nervous after the previous day's play, a physical high in his cycle on the last day of the month gave him the reserve energy he needed to complete the 1,000 runs.

Cycling

In cycling, a sport that demands much of the individual in terms of physical ability, intellectual acuteness, and emotional awareness, biorhythms have been an accepted and indeed integral component of the regimen of many of Europe's greatest stars.

Hugo Koblet, Ferdi Kubler, Gino Bartali, Fritz Schar, etc., have all declared that their top performances took place on the days of their strongest rhythm positions. By contrast, they have explained that despite all the exertion of will possible on their days of physical low positions, their strength simply did not last.

"I consider," Ferdi Kubler wrote, "biorhythmically regulated training valuable for every athlete." And Fritz Schar, Swiss Champion in 1953 and Swiss Long Distance Champion in 1953, observed: "I have been training with great success according to biorhythms since 1945. Thanks to the training schedule, I have not had to overcome any long crises for many years in spite of continuous races at home and abroad."

A study of the effects of bio-cycles on the performances of cyclist Hugo Koblet, born March 21, 1925, is very revealing:

On June 17, 1948, Koblet was the victor in the difficult Tour-de-Suisse stretch that led from Altdorf over the Gotthard Pass in Switzerland down to Lugano in Italy. On that date, Koblet's rhythms registered an absolute high.

Again, in 1951, Koblet won a difficult competition in the Gioro d' Italia, a contest that saw him faced with the rigors and ob-

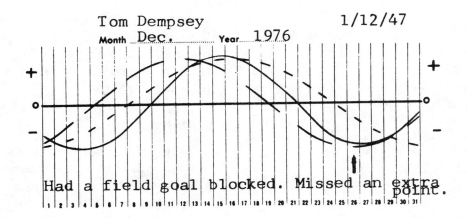

stacles of difficult mountain passes. In this competition, Koblet again was operating under an absolute high in his rhythms.

In the Tour-de-France, Koblet again racked up impressive victories as follows:

July 15, 1951—Brive-Agen stretch
July 18, 1951—Tarbes-Aspin stretch
July 20, 1951—Carcassone-Montpellier stretch
July 27, 1951—Aix les Bains-Geneva stretch

In all of these, Koblet's bio-cycle indicated positive positions. There were no critical situations.

On the other side of the coin, there were competitions in which Koblet did not do as well: in point of fact, he did quite poorly. A prime example is how he fared in the 1954 Tour-de-France.

On July 18, he suffered a fall during the Bordeaux-Bayonne stretch. A day later there was another fall, a worse one, in the Bayonne-Pau. Finally, on July 21, Koblet was so discouraged that he abandoned the race. All three of these happenings took place while Koblet was in an absolute low in all three cycles.

Foreshadowing the triple debacle, the two falls and the withdrawal from competition, he had an impressive victory on July

7th in the Oerlikon-Zurich race. Apparently, the triple high of that date had a great deal to do with the triumph.

Football

The sport of football is a complicated game of inches and seconds. Offensive teams and defensive teams and special teams and substitutes trot off and on the field, further complicating the sport. Nevertheless, some highly interesting studies and some remarkable individual bio-cycles exist that are worth examining as regards forecasting and evaluating the inter-relationship of the game and biorhythms.

Missouri Southern State College Study

Harold R. Willis joined forces with his students to engage in a predictive study of his college's football team. During spring practice, Willis constructed a program to evaluate the performances of 24 backfield and end candidates for the Missouri Southern State football team. The ratings were on a ten-point scale in each of six special categories: effort, mistakes, attitude, execution of tasks, endurance, self-control. An overall rating was then arrived at.

For a 27-day period, each candidate was given a daily rating. Curves were then

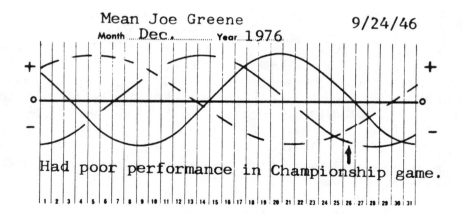

Mean Joe Greene   9/24/46

Month Dec.   Year 1976.

Had poor performance in Championship game.

plotted of each of the player's performances and superimposed over the biorhythm chart for the period. Willis noted a close correlation between both curves.

Willis applied biorhythmic predictions to the final spring practice games. He reported that there was a 60 per cent accuracy rate. Given a ten-point overall performance scale, that statistic is 50 per cent more accurate than random predictions might have been.

So delighted was Willis by the results of the spring training biorhythmic applications, he extended his study into the regular season. It developed that of 13 injuries to the team during the season, 13 took place on critical days. It also developed that there was a 77 per cent accuracy rate for the forecasts of player performances utilizing biorhythms. Most significant of all, for the first time in its history the football team of Missouri Southern State won all its games and the divisional title. Undoubtedly, something other than superior football talent made the championship possible. For with much the same roster of players the following season, MSSC lost more than half of its games.

Wallerstein and Roberts

Researchers Michael R. Wallerstein and Nancy Lee Roberts conducted a study to relate football teams and their bio-curves to performance. The thrust of their focus was on "total" offensive and/or defensive team biorhythms.

In the University of Southern California-UCLA game of November 18, 1972, the bio-curves for USC's offensive and defensive teams were at a high point for the season. Conversely, UCLA was at the zero point offensively and down in the physical rhythm defensively. As Wallerstein and Roberts concluded and then predicted, USC won the football game.

In a National Football League game held on December 17, 1973, the Washington Redskins were operating under physical and emotional lows defensively. The Washington team was upset by the underdog New England Patriots. The following week in a playoff game, Washington trimmed Green Bay 16-3. The Packers were able to manage only a field goal in their trimming by Washington, whose defensive unit bio-curve was on the upswing.

Joe Namath's Ego, Tom Dempsey's Toe

Two of the more dramatic performances in NFL history took place when athletes had only one of their rhythms in the positive phase. Yet, for Joe Namath and for

Tom Dempsey, it was enough to put their names in the record book.

On January 12, 1969, Namath took the field against the Baltimore Colts in the Super Bowl. Broadway Joe had promised the world that his New York Jets would upset the favored Colts. And though his physical and intellectual cycles were negative, Joe's emotional rhythm was at its highest point. The final score of the Super Bowl was Namath's Jets 16, Colts 7.

Dempsey made his mark in 1970 with a record 63-yard field goal enabling New Orleans to nip Detroit 19-17. Physically, he was very high in his rhythms although emotionally and intellectually he was very low. Apparently no one has to tell Dempsey that for long kicks the important cycle is the physical cycle.

Bart Starr's Dive

On December 31, 1967, the bio-cycle log for Green Bay Quarterback Bart Starr showed: Emotionally—highest point; intellectually—high. With 13 seconds left in the National Football League championship game against Dallas, Starr and his Packers trailed 17–14. Charged by his emotional high and being at peak form intellectually, Starr made his move. He picked his spot and powered over in a one-yard dive to give Green Bay a 21–17 come-from-behind victory.

O.J. Simpson

One of the things O.J. Simpson is noted for as a football player is his consistency. The Buffalo back, a calm and collected athlete no matter what the circumstances, has always managed to harness his talents and maximize his efforts. In doing these things Simpson has shunned the erratic ups and downs that characterize so many other athletes. Yet, in three back-to-back contests in 1976, O.J. was anything but consistent.

On September 19, he carried the ball 16 times for only 38 yards as Houston trimmed his Buffalo team, 13–3. The following week Buffalo eked by Tampa, 14–9, and O.J. had his worst day as a professional athlete. He carried the ball 20 times, compiling only 39 yards. In the September 19 contest, Simpson was physically low. When he had the worst game of his pro career, he was physically critical. Even O.J. Simpson could not overcome the handicap of his biorhythms.

Then, one week after the worst day of his pro career, O.J. had a complete reversal of form. His emotional rhythm was high. His physical rhythm was exceptionally high. And his statistics for that October 3 clearly revealed the condition of his biocycle.

Performing like a one man gang, O.J. carried the football 24 times for a total of 130 yards rushing. Twelve of Buffalo's points came on the individual effort of Simpson as the charged up runner cracked over for two touchdowns.

On Sunday, November 8, 1976, O.J. Simpson took the field for Buffalo on a day when his bio-cycle revealed he was minus in all three rhythms. For the first time in an eight-year career, O.J. was ejected from a football game after he came up swinging at Mel Lunsford, a 250-pound defensive end for the New England Patriots.

The incident took place six minutes into the first period of the game played at Foxboro, Massachusetts. Simpson had gained but eight yards in six carries when he unloaded his frustrations on Lunsford who had stopped his forward momentum for no gain.

The usually calm, cool, collected and gentlemanly Simpson engaged in behavior that shocked many of the fans and even the officials. It was a classic example of an athlete, handicapped by a triple down in his cycle, lashing out to attempt to do something about it.

While Simpson had a historic first that Sunday, November 8, so did Joe Theismann in leading the Washington Redskins to a 24–21 triumph over the San Francisco 49ers. Theismann had his best day ever as a professional athlete. He passed for 302 yards, threw touchdown passes of 18, 33, and 3 yards. His most spectacular moment came when he ran for a first down on a fake field goal play. The faked field goal gave the Redskins better field position for an actual field goal attempt that gave Washington its three-point victory margin. Emotionally and physically, the Washington quarterback was very high in his rhythms.

If football is a game of inches, it is also a game of seconds. And in two 1976 National Football League contests, with only seconds remaining, dramatic happenings took place.

Los Angeles and Minnesota, two of the League's premier teams, were locked in a brawl on September 19. Neither team would give an inch. With less than a minute remaining and the score tied 10–10, the Vikings were apparently driving for victory. Then Fran Tarkenton uncorked a pass that was intercepted, stopping the Minnesota drive. The final score was Minnesota 10 and Los Angeles 10. Tarkenton's errant throw shocked the fans and some of his teammates. His physical rhythm was low, and he was emotionally negative. Intellectually, he was positive but going down. How much, one wonders, did his bio-cycle have to do with the pass the veteran quarterback probably wished he hadn't released?

The other incident took place in a game between Oakland and Pittsburgh. For years and years, George Blanda had been the old reliable place kicker for the Oakland Raiders. Finally, pushing 50 years of

age, Blanda was forced into retirement and Fred Steinfort replaced him. With 18 seconds to play on September 12, the rookie kicker's field goal gave Oakland a 31–28 triumph over Pittsburgh. Steinfort was emotionally and intellectually high when his toe deftly propelled the ball 21 yards in the air and through the goal posts.

Biorhythmic Highlights of the 1976 NFL Season

In National Football League action on October 24, 1976, numerous examples of biorhythmic influence were in evidence, particularly among quarterbacks.

Detroit's Greg Landry and Jim Zorn, of the Seattle Seahawks, were a study in biocycle and quarterback performances. Landry notched 18 completions in 27 attempts for 233 yards and three touchdowns—and he didn't even play in the fourth quarter. His bio-cycle—triple high. Zorn was physically and intellectually low and emotionally critical. On the football field, he threw a record six interceptions, one of which was returned 70 yards by Detroit's Levi Johnson for a score. The final score of the game was Lions 41, Seahawks 14.

In two very close games, intellectually high quarterbacks were the margin of difference. The Oakland Raiders eked by Green Bay, 18–14, behind quarterback Kenny Stabler, and Cleveland edged San Diego, 21–17, behind quarterback Brian Sipe. Calling a very smart game that correlated well with his intellectual rhythm at its highest point, Stabler's arm accounted for all three Oakland touchdowns. Sipe completed 23 of 28 passes for two touchdowns and 246 yards. Though emotionally low, a physical and especially an intellectual high linked up well in Sipe's performance.

At Orchard Park, New York, only the super play of O.J. Simpson gave Buffalo Bill fans anything to be happy about. Otherwise October 24, 1976, was disastrous as the Bills suffered a double loss. They were beaten by New England 26–22, and quarterback Joe Ferguson was lost for the season.

Emotionally at the lowest point in his rhythm and also physically low, Ferguson was tackled and injured while on a nine-yard run in the second quarter. It was later reported that he sustained fractures in the lower back.

Simpson, who was the only bright spot in the day for Buffalo, rushed for 110 yards on 25 carries and scored two touchdowns to become the second leading rusher in NFL history with 8,609 yards. O.J.'s bio-cycle for the day: Physically at his highest point; intellectually at his highest point; and it didn't hurt that he was also plus emotionally.

Baltimore's Roger Carr put on a one-man show as the Colts mangled the hapless New York Jets, 20–0. The swift wide receiver accounted for two Baltimore touchdowns as he caught five passes good for 210 yards. Carr's dramatics came as he was operating under a triple high in his bio-rhythms.

Thus, on October 24, 1976, anyone reading the bio-cycles of Carr, Simpson, Stabler, Sipe, Zorn, Ferguson, and Landry would have been able to come up with fairly sophisticated forecasting of their football performances.

James (Shack) Harris and Terry Bradshaw: Invalids Return

Both James (Shack) Harris of the Los Angeles Rams and Terry Bradshaw of the Pittsburgh Steelers will remember Sunday, October 31, 1976—Halloween Day. Harris and Bradshaw both returned to action for their teams after being out of the lineup due to injuries.

Out of action since October 11, due to a shoulder injury, Harris showed up to lead the Rams to a 45–6 rout of the Seattle Seahawks. In the first half, Harris threw two touchdown passes, powering the Rams to a 31–3 lead. When he left the game to rest midway through the final quarter, Harris had accumulated 208 yards, hitting 14 of 25 passes and notching two more scoring passes of 15 and 20 yards. The bio-cycle readout for the L.A. quarterback: high physically and intellectually.

Bradshaw came in for the Steelers late in the first half after having missed two games because of a neck injury. Physically Bradshaw was at the highest point in his rhythms. He was also very high emotionally. Abetted by his biorhythms, Bradshaw turned it on in a seven-minute span in the final quarter. He orchestrated three Pittsburgh touchdowns to give the Steelers a 23–0 triumph over the San Diego Chargers.

Tarkenton Sets Record

At Chicago on October 31, Tarkenton's Vikings suffered their first defeat in eight games, losing 14–13 to the Bears. But for Tarkenton, it was a memorable day. Spurred by an emotional high, buoyed by a critical in the physical rhythm—a pattern many athletes seem to respond to well— Tarkenton surpassed Johnny Unitas' passing record of 40,239 career yards.

The Viking quarterback hit on 24 of 46 pass attemps for 272 yards giving him a career total of 40,421 yards. And he ran two yards himself to score the only Minnesota T.D., capping an 80-yard drive.

Bartkowski's Injury

October 10, 1976, is a day that Steve Bartkowski will long remember. Physically, his bio-cycle revealed that he was very low. Emotionally he was minus in his rhythms. And intellectually, there was not any help—he was minus in this area as well.

The underdog New Orleans team crushed Bartkowski's Atlanta squad, 30–0. However, more significant than the Atlanta defeat was the crippling injury to their quarterback, Bartkowski, the man with the triple low, was hurt badly enough that October 10 that his injury put him out of action for the entire season.

Jones and Stabler: Negative Cycles Equal Negative Days

Star quarterbacks Bert Jones and Kenny Stabler took the field on November 14. Events later showed that it was not an auspicious day for these two men to engage in the grueling competition of professional football.

Jones, Baltimore's pride and joy and the leading quarterback in the NFL, had his worst day of the season.Twice he was intercepted, and he completed only 10 of 25 passes for 139 yards.

Stabler, the southpaw star of the Oakland Raiders, managed four errant throws that went for interceptions. His timing was off and his play selection left much to be desired.

A check of the respective bio-cycles revealed:

	P	E	I
Jones	Critical	–	–
Stabler	–	–	–

With their rhythms in these negative positions, the disastrous performances of Stabler and Jones were not surprising.

On the other hand, New England Patriots quarterback Steve Grogan, boosted by highs in his physical and emotional rhythms and responding well to an intellectual critical, had a grand day November 14. He scored two touchdowns on individual runs and completed 12 of 17 passes.

Splendid bio-cycle meshing took place as the St. Louis Cardinals eked by the Los Angeles Rams, 30–28 on November 14, 1976. Quarterback Jim Hart and wide receiver Ike Harris—both intellectually very near their highest points—linked up to account for much of the Cardinal scoring.

Hart completed 20 of 33 passes and notched 324 yards. Harris was on the receiving end of eight of the Hart passes and recorded 130 yards. It is worth noting that Hart's main passing target—Mel Gray—was out of the game due to a face injury. Harris and Hart managed very well. One can only ponder the dramatic effects of their intellectual rhythms on their tremendous performances.

The Ups and Downs of Jim Bakken

On successive Sundays in November, St. Louis Cardinal place kicker Jim Bakken illustrated the startling effects of biorhythms on performance.

On November 7, the usually highly accurate Bakken missed three of four field goal attempts as the Cardinals barely squeaked by the Philadelphia Eagles. The veteran field goal kicker performed with a triple low in his biorhythms.

One week later, St. Louis opposed the favored Los Angeles Rams. The game saw the lead change hands several times. The Cardinals were able to stay in the game due to Bakken's field goal kicking. With three seconds left to play, St. Louis trailed by one point, 28–27. Bakken's fourth field goal of the day gave St. Louis a 30–28 come-from-behind triumph. Biorhythmically, Bakken was physically at his highest point, a necessary asset for a field goal kicker.

The Too-Soon Spike

A judgment error and a crushing physical injury in two November 1976 National Football League games also were apparently attributable to player bio-cycles. Minnesota's Sammy White caught a 52-yard pass from Fran Tarkenton. White raised the ball to spike it, believing he was in the goal area. He was tackled at the three yard line and fumbled the ball away. A check of White's bio-cycle showed that physically he was low and, more significantly as far as the premature spiking, intellectually he was very low.

Houston defensive end Elvin Bethea showed up for combat against the Cincinnati Bengals on November 14, with his bio-cycle registering a triple low. It was not a day for this man to be on a football field. Bethea sustained a severe neck injury battling for a thrown ball and was rushed out of the Cincinnati ball park to the hospital for treatment.

Joe Namath Returns

Sidelined for several weeks, Joe Namath returned to action for the New York Jets on November 15. He said he hadn't lost any confidence during the time on the sideline. "This wasn't a game to prove anything." But with his bio-cycle at triple high, Namath proved a lot. The Jets, with Broadway Joe leading them on four scoring drives, dumped Tampa, 34–0.

"I know exactly what to do day in and day out as a football player," he said. "So I know exactly where I stand. Over the years I've had criticism, but I get over it better now. I don't want to feel bad, and I don't allow myself to feel bad."

With a triple high in his rhythms, Namath was emotionally, mentally, and physically able to respond to the challenge of a return to action and to the barbs of some fans, as evidenced by his performance against Tampa.

Down Cycles Prove Down Time for Quarterbacks

Five National Football League quarterbacks shared the boos of the fans and the aches of injuries on November 21, 1976. All five quarterbacks shared virtually the same bio-cycles—negative.

New York Jet fans jeered "Broadway Joe" Namath as the New England Patriots topped their team, 38–24. Namath, experiencing a triple negative in his rhythms, threw five interceptions—and had two of them run back for touchdowns.

Jim Plunkett of the San Francisco 49ers also experienced a triple negative in his bio-cycles. Plunkett had a miserable time. He completed just 4 of 16 passes and was intercepted three times. This poor play caused him to be removed from the game.

A physically and intellectually low Roger Staubach, Dallas quarterback, threw three interceptions that led to a 17–10 upset Dallas defeat. It was significant from the point of view of what biorhythms can do to the performance of the steadiest athlete. Staubach had been intercepted but four times during the preceding ten games. How significant was the Dallas quarterback's physical and emotional low this November 21? The question answers itself.

Quarterbacks Craig Morton of the Giants and Steve Ramsey of Denver took the field on November 21 with lows in their physical and emotional cycles. Most of the players on both teams were around and on their feet at the end of the game, but Ramsey and Morton both suffered injuries and had to leave the playing field. They shared injuries, and they shared the same minus readings in two of their rhythms.

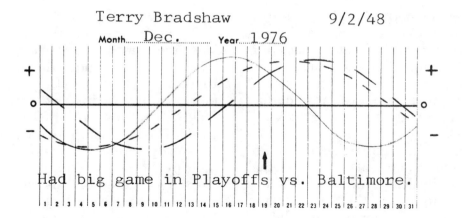

Terry Bradshaw   9/2/48

Month.....Dec.......Year....1976

+   +

o   o

−   −

Had big game in Playoffs vs. Baltimore.

National Football League Playoffs

The "second season" of the NFL began the weekend of December 18-19, 1976. When the weekend was over, Oakland, Los Angeles, Minnesota and Pittsburgh looked forward to the league championship games. And the teams they defeated could look ahead to the 1977 National Football League season. Biorhythms figured prominently in the results of the four games played.

The Minnesota Vikings crushed the Washington Redskins, 35–20 behind quarterback Fran Tarkenton and the power running of Chuck Foreman and Brent McClanahan. Tarkenton, intellectually positive in his rhythms and critical emotionally, completed 12 of 21 passes for 170 yards. As with many other athletes—Tarkenton turned an emotional critical to his advantage. "We were at an emotional peak," he said. "We can do anything under those conditions as a team."

Foreman and McClanahan rushed for over a hundred yards each. Foreman was operating under a triple high in his rhythms, and his bull-like plunges underscored the fact that he was at the highest point in his physical cycle. McClanahan's bio-cycle readout: He was within 24 hours of his highest emotional point, in a plus

situation intellectually, and within 24 hours of a physical critical. As with Tarkenton, McClanahan was able to turn a critical day in a cycle to an advantage.

The Pittsburgh Steelers completely outplayed the Baltimore Colts on Sunday, December 19 piling up a 40–14 triumph. The differences in the two teams were highlighted by contrasting biorhythms of two premier running backs:

		P	E	I
Pittsburgh	Franco Harris	+	+	critical
Baltimore	Lydell Mitchell	−	within 24 hours of critical	critical

Harris carried the ball 18 times and wound up with 132 yards rushing. He also tallied 24 yards on three receptions. Mitchell was held to but 55 yards rushing on 16 carries and notched 42 yards receiving on five catches. Thus, both the biorhythms and the performances of Harris and Mitchell were a study in contrasts. The key area of difference was in the physical cycle—so crucial to a power runner's performance.

The biorhythm standout in the Pittsburgh-Baltimore contest, however, was Steeler quarterback, Terry Bradshaw. Positive in both the physical and emotional cycles and very high in the intellectual cycle—a significant area for a quarterback—

Bradshaw completed 14 of 18 passes for 264 yards. He also threw three touchdown passes. Absent from six Steeler games during the season due to injuries, Bradshaw's peak biorhythms boosted him to a performance that removed any doubts about his ability to lead the Pittsburgh team.

Quarterback Ken Stabler, operating under highs in his emotional and intellectual cycles and a physical critical, was the key man as Oakland nipped the New England Patriots, 24–21. With ten seconds left to play in the game, Stabler snaked over for a T.D. in a one-yard rollout, providing the margin of victory.

It was a courageous, audacious, and brilliant move by Stabler. How significant were the southpaw quarterback's favorable rhythms in determining the outcome of the seesaw game is another of the myriad biorhythm sport situations worth pondering.

In the final play-off game of the long weekend, there was more material to mull over concerning sports forecasting and biorhythm. In the Dallas-Los Angeles game, scrutiny of a couple of performances underscored the fact that the pattern of a player's performance and the condition of the opposition must always be taken into account.

Both L.A. quarterback Pat Haden and Ram receiver Harold Jackson had little going for them biorhythmically. Both men operated under triple lows in their cycles. Haden was so hampered by his rhythms and the after-effects of surgery the previous week, that he was able to complete only 10 of 21 pass attempts, managed no touchdown tosses and was intercepted three times. "I know I'm going to be a lot better next week," Haden said. Jackson, also sub-par biorhythmically, nevertheless was able to snare six passes for 116 yards.

Somehow, Los Angeles was able to parlay the efforts of Haden and Jackson into a 14–12 cliff-hanger win.

On the other side of the field, the Dallas side, their great quarterback Roger Staubach also was "under the weather" biorhythmically. Physically at his lowest point, minus in his two other rhythms, Staubach hit only 15 of 37 passes for 150 yards. The leadership so often provided by the steady Staubach was not on the field in their play-off encounter with Los Angeles. Anyone checking out his bio-cycle would have been able to see that Sunday, December 19 would not be a good day for Roger Staubach on a football field.

National Football League Championship Games

Clever quarterbacking by Minnesota's Fran Tarkenton and Oakland's Ken Stabler brought their two teams into Super Bowl competition. Behind Tarkenton, Minnesota trimmed Los Angeles 24–13. Stabler's direction enabled the Raiders to trounce the Pittsburgh Steelers, 24–7.

Sunday, December 26, 1976, was a frigid day in Minnesota and a pleasant day in Oakland, California. But it seemed that Tarkenton and Stabler were influenced more by their biorhythms than the temperature.

The veteran Viking quarterback was high in both his emotional and intellectual rhythms and was seasoned enough to adjust to a physical low. He hit on 12 of 27 passes for 143 yards. When he was in danger, he simply threw the ball away rather than allow an interception by the Rams. The highlight of Tarkenton's action on the football field was a well-placed pass that allowed Chuck Foreman to break away for a 62-yard run that set up a touchdown.

Stabler operated under a triple high in his rhythms. Passing for one touchdown, he managed to complete ten of 16 passes for 88 yards. Like Tarkenton, it was the quality of his play selection and the sureness of his passing and hand offs that powered his team to victory.

The most interesting biorhythmic sidelight of the day was the performance of Minnesota defender Bobby Bryant. His bio-cycle readout was:

physically—low
emotionally—within 24 hours of a
   critical day
intellectually—positive

For Bryant and for the Vikings, it was the ideal combination of rhythm positions for a defender in a critical game. As with so many other athletes experiencing a critical or on the verge of experiencing a critical day, Bryant took chances and performed at a new defensive peak. He was also aided by his positive intellectual rhythms.

In the opening minutes of the game, Minnesota grabbed a psychological edge and an edge on the scoreboard as Bryant picked up a blocked Los Angeles field goal attempt and raced 90 yards for a touchdown. "It was something," Bryant said. "I glanced over my shoulder when I fielded the ball, and I knew nothing would stop me unless I stumbled or they put a jet in there. I just took off, but I was getting a little tight at the end."

With about three minutes left in the game, Bryant again was Minnesota's good luck charm. He intercepted L.A. quarterback Haden's pass on the Viking eight-yard line. "I saw the ball thrown," Bryant smiled, "and I was able to get to it."

Thus, Tarkenton, Stabler, Bryant—just three of the dozens and dozens of men that played that Sunday, December 26—influenced the outcome of NFL championship games. The biorhythms of the three men apparently had a lot to do with the scores.

Super Bowl XI

The Minnesota Vikings continued their habit of losing their final game of the season as they were blown out of Super Bowl XI by a score of 32–14. The Oakland Raiders were methodical in their destruction of the older Minnesota team, running virtually at will and stymieing the Viking offense throughout most of the game. For researchers of biorhythm, the Super Bowl takes on an added significance, for it places men before a huge audience and dangles a world championship before them. With so much at stake, players from both teams supposedly give their maximum effort to win. When one team completely dominates the game, as did the Oakland Raiders, one may look to biorhythm for answers.

Excluding all other factors and strictly on the basis of individual biorhythms, the Oakland Raiders had to win Super Bowl XI. While both quarterbacks were low in all three cycles, Minnesota's Fran Tarkenton was extremely low emotionally and intellectually. The normally exceptional Tarkenton completed less than 50 per cent of his passes and threw two key interceptions.

Minnesota actually had an early opportunity to be competitive when they blocked a Ray Guy punt and recovered the ball inside the Oakland 5-yard line. By the way, the punt was the first ever blocked on Ray Guy. (His biorhythms showed that he was low physically and emotionally.) Minnesota's running back, Brent McClanahan, had the chance to score from the 3-yard line but was hit and fumbled away the ball. This error is considered a key play in the game, for the Vikings never challenged again. Biorhythmically, McClanahan was low physically, critical emotionally and low intellectually.

Oakland set a Super Bowl record by

Super Bowl XI Biorhythm Chart

January 9, 1977

Final Score: Raiders 32–Vikings 14

Below are the names of the Minnesota Vikings and Oakland Raiders players. Beneath each name is a code which represents the player's date of birth. Each letter of the code represents a position on the biorhythm cycle. A + means high or strong, – means low or weak, and c means critical or unstable. The first letter and sign stands for the position on the physical cycle, the second letter and sign stands for the position on the emotional cycle, and the third letter and sign stands for the position on the intellectual cycle.

OAKLAND RAIDERS

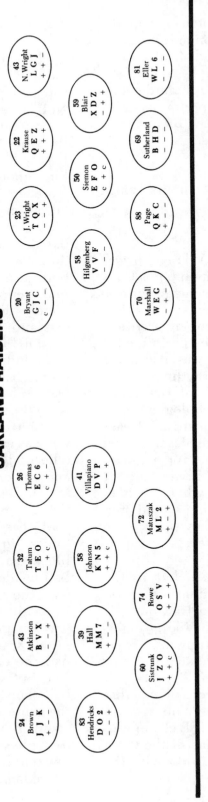

MINNESOTA VIKINGS

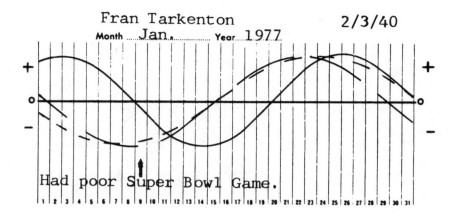

rushing for 266 yards on the ground. Clarence Davis alone ran for 137 yards. Pete Banaszak ran for two touchdowns. Were the Raiders that good or were the Viking defenders that bad? The answer, according to biorhythm, is a little of both. Davis and Banaszak were at their highest and second from highest points respectively on the physical cycle. By contrast, every member of the vaunted Minnesota defensive front four was either critical or low in at least two of the three cycles. Jeff Siemon, the Minnesota middle linebacker and the man who is responsible for calling the defensive signals, was critical intellectually. Wally Hilgenberg, Minnesota's most experienced linebacker, was very low in all three cycles. In light of these facts, it is not surprising that Oakland was able to move the ball against the Vikings.

The Oakland defense, like the offense, was highly successful on Super Bowl Sunday. Minnesota's star running back, Chuck Foreman, was held to just 44 yards on the ground while Fran Tarkenton was pressured into inaccurate throws all day. Unlike the Minnesota front four, the Raider defensive linemen were all very high physically. Willie Hall, the Oakland linebacker, not only recovered McClanahan's fumble but also intercepted a pass at a key juncture in the game. Not surprisingly, he was at his highest point physically.

While it would be irresponsible to assert that Oakland won due to favorable biorhythms, we cannot overlook the preceding facts. On Sunday, January 9, the Oakland players had what it took to win while the Minnesota players didn't. Minnesota coach Bud Grant may have said it best when he offered this analysis after the debacle: "We just played them on the wrong day. Next time we'll play them on Wednesday."

Golf

The sport of golf is a very intriguing area to observe the effects of biorhythms on performance and forecasting. It is an area where judgment, personality, physical condition and concentration are especially relevant.

One of the classic examples of biorhythms and golf took place in July of 1962. Despite the heat, the bustling crowds, and a sore back, Arnold Palmer won the British Open handily at Troon, Scotland, July 9–13. He finished with a 276, four strokes ahead of his nearest rival.

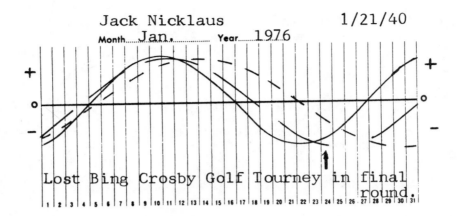

Jack Nicklaus   1/21/40
Month....Jan.....   Year....1976

Lost Bing Crosby Golf Tourney in final round.

Palmer's bio-cycle reveals that he was operating under a triple high, and his shot selection, his uncanny skills in judging distances, and his pleasant manner to the large crowd indicated just how positive he was feeling.

Just two weeks later, Palmer's three rhythms had dropped off from their peak to a triple low. He was a very different person; he was a much different golfer. Performing in the Professional Golfer Association matches, he showed irritability to the crowd and vastly diminished golfing skills. Palmer finished the match tied for seventeenth place, ten strokes behind Gary Player.

Record-setting scores by golfers Tom Weiskopf, Jack Nicklaus and Lee Trevino all correlate very well with the bio-cycles of these three famous golfers.

Trevino notched a record 275 to win the 1968 U.S. Open June 13–16. For those days, Trevino's bio-cycle was: Physically very high, emotionally very high. Apparently the two high cycles compensated for an intellectual low.

At the U.S. Open the year before, 1967, Nicklaus also recorded a record 275 for 72 holes. The dates of the competition were June 15–18. Nicklaus was under the influence of a triple high in his rhythms and was especially high in his physical and intellectual cycles.

Tom Weiskopf took the field on July 11–14, 1973, in the British Open. He operated under a high in all three cycles, and as the days of the match moved on he was moving progressively higher in both the physical and emotional cycles. Weiskopf set a record with a 72-hole total of 276 to the cheers of the crowd. There wasn't much more he could have possibly wanted out of golf during those July days in 1973.

The record shows that, for all three golfers, their days of triumph, their days of nearly perfect biorhythms, were days marked by intelligent shot selection and with moments when everything seemed to be going just right. Even the crowds, which have been known to ruffle more than a few golfers, were not viewed as disturbances.

In 1970–1971, four top golf tournaments were won by four different golfers whose biorhythms interrelated significantly with the outcome of the matches.

At his highest point both physically and emotionally, Billy Casper staged a brilliant performance in taking the Masters Golf Tourney Championship on April 13, 1970. Tony Jacklin was the winner of the U.S. Open on June 21, 1970. Jacklin's bio-cycle: Physically and intellectually, he was at his highest point.

The following year, again on June 21, and again with biorhythm aid, Lee Trevino triumphed in the U.S. Open Golf Championship. Trevino was operating under a physical high. Perhaps even more significant, though, was the heads-up golf he displayed, the intelligent shot selection that underscored the fact that biorhythmically he was at his highest point intellectually. And on July 25, 1971, Arnold Palmer, with an emotional and intellectual high in his favor, won the Westchester Classic, one of the richest golf tourneys.

More recently, the case of Jack Nicklaus and Ben Crenshaw underscored the interrelationship between golf and biorhythms. At the Bing Crosby Pebble Beach National Golf Tournament on January 24, 1976, Nicklaus led the field going into the fourth and final round. Suddenly, his game fell apart. He recorded two triple, one double, and five single bogeys, and dropped from the lead to finish the match in 22nd place. An analysis of the Nicklaus biorhythm graph reveals that intellectually, physically and emotionally he was low or critical during all four days of the match.

Thus, even the man touted as the greatest golfer of all time could not fight back against the handicap of low or critical biocurves. And instead of holding the lead and winning the top prize money of $37,000, Nicklaus had a $2,200 payday.

The golfer who won the match was Ben Crenshaw, who was also emotionally and physically low or critical during the tournament, but at an intellectual peak during the last three days, which brought on a period of sharp adjustment.

A few weeks later, after picking up the Hawaiian Open's $46,000 first prize, Crenshaw noted: "I just knew that I could win the golf tournament. I finally believed in myself. I can't explain it." Perhaps his biocycles can. When he won the Hawaiian Open, Crenshaw's physical and emotional rhythms had reached a high point. And, apparently, his recent victory in the Bing Crosby match helped boost his emotional cycle, which was at a low point.

Close friends Mac McLendon and Hubert Green had virtually similar bio-cycle charts going into the final round of the $215,000 Southern Open Golf Tournament at Columbus, Georgia:

	P	E	I
McLendon	−2	+2	+2
Green	−3	+1	+3

The closeness of their cycles underscored the closeness of their golfing performances as McLendon narrowly edged Green in the final on October 24, 1976, to win his first individual title.

"I've seen these other guys out here that win," McLendon said, "they seem to just let it happen. That's what I'm gonna try to do." How much the thin biorhythmic edge the 32-year-old golfer from Birmingham, Alabama, had over Green allowed him to "let it happen" is highly interesting to contemplate.

A consistent biorhythmic profile leading to consistent winning ways is demonstrated by the bio-cycle analysis of Al Geiberger in two tournaments in 1975 and 1976. Geiberger performs very well when he is under the influence of emotional and intellectual highs. I told a national NBC television audience that Geiberger would win the 1976 Greater Greensboro Open Golf Tournament despite the stiff competition of Lee Trevino and others.

Geiberger was very low physically, yet very high emotionally and intellectually positive and moving up. He won the 1976 tournament despite the challenge of Trevino, who dogged him through each round of the tightly contested tournament.

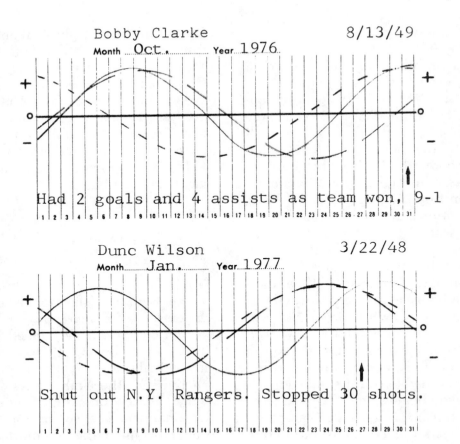

Bobby Clarke   8/13/49
Month Oct.   Year 1976

Had 2 goals and 4 assists as team won, 9–1

Dunc Wilson   3/22/48
Month Jan.   Year 1977

Shut out N.Y. Rangers. Stopped 30 shots.

August 21–24, 1975, Geiberger won the Tournament Players Championship with the same biorhythm pattern. From a physical perspective, he had nothing going for him in his rhythm—it registered low. But emotionally and intellectually, he was positive. It was the bio-cycle profile that he functioned best under, and no doubt this was the chief reason for his championship play.

Ice Hockey

Split-second timing and quick thinking, physical agility and endurance, emotional stability and the will to win—all of these traits and more characterize the top hockey players.

There are numerous instances where biorhythms have influenced performance and could have been significant in the forecasting of individual achievement.

On October 31, 1976, Philadelphia's Bobby Clarke must have looked to Minnesota as if he had on the meanest of all Halloween costumes. Clarke, at the highest point in his physical and intellectual cycles and plus emotionally, banged in two goals and was credited with four assists as the Flyers destroyed the North Stars, 9–1.

A triple high in his rhythms on October 13 enabled Gregg Sheppard of the Boston Bruins to score in each period for the second time in his career and pace the 5–1 victory over the Rangers at New York's Madison Square Garden. Sheppard thus capped a string that saw him notch five

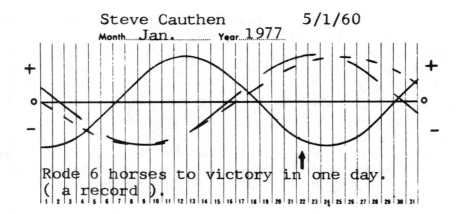

Steve Cauthen   5/1/60
Month Jan.   Year 1977

Rode 6 horses to victory in one day. (a record).

goals in four games. "I'm usually a slow starter," Sheppard said, expressing amazement at how well he had been performing. Had he checked his biorhythms, he might have been aware of part of the reason for his fine stick work.

Dramatic examples of favorable biorhythms boosting hockey performances took place during the month of November 1976 in National Hockey League action.

On November 21, the Pittsburgh Penguins trimmed the Chicago Black Hawks, 5–0. Pittsburgh goalie Dunc Wilson stopped 25 shots including a rare penalty shot. Physically Wilson was at his highest point in his cycle and intellectually he was very positive.

That same night Montreal's Steve Shutt paced his team's 9–5 shoot-out triumph over Toronto. Shutt's three-goal hat trick gave him 23 goals in 23 games. The Shutt bio-cycle: Physically and emotionally high.

On November 19, Detroit's Dan Maloney's hat trick paced the 5–2 Red Wings' victory over Cleveland. As with so many other athletes, Maloney turned an intellectual critical to his advantage. He was also helped by plus readings in his two other cycles.

In another game played that night, New York Islander Clark Gillies scored the first

hat trick in his professional career to pace his team's 6–2 victory over Vancouver. Gilles functioned under a triple high, and he was at his highest point in his physical cycle.

On November 20, Gil Perreault of Buffalo showed the following bio-cycle: highest physical point, emotionally plus, intellectually critical. With 32 seconds left in the game he slapped in the puck to give Buffalo a 4–3 win over the L.A. Kings.

Jockeys and Horse Racing

The sport of horse racing is a blend of rider and mount, a partnership of man and horse. And many times the difference between an "also ran" and a winner is the way the jockey rides his race. Thus, the bio-cycle of a jockey is a significant element in forecasting and comprehending why some long shots win going away and why some favorites fade in the stretch.

When Bill Shoemaker, veteran jockey, showed up at California's Santa Anita track on November 6, 1976, his bio-cycle showed that physically he was very positive; emotionally, he was minus; and intellectually, he was critical. The significant rhythm for a veteran jockey like Shoemaker is the physical rhythm, since emotion is not a factor of any consequence for a rider who has been tested over and over again in championship races. And before Shoemaker even mounted his horse, he had decided what type of race to run. Thus, a great deal depended on his physical rhythm—his reflexes, agility, steadiness—to steer and guide his mount the way he wanted to.

Riding King Pellinore, Shoemaker stalked Honest Pleasure through the first mile of the mile-and-an-eighth feature race, the $350,000 Champions. Then the jockey turned his horse loose in the stretch. King Pellinore opened a daylight lead in mid-stretch and held on to win by a nose. It was a $240,000 payday.

Three thousand miles away on that same Saturday, November 6, 1976, at Aqueduct Race Track in New York City, another jockey was experiencing an intellectually critical day, showed an emotional minus, and was within 24 hours of a critical physical. His day's activities seemed to mesh well with the biorhythms he was experiencing.

Jacinto Vasquez collected the place money in the first three races. He was riding well, but not well enough to win. Then things changed in the big race of the day—the $54,000 Queens County Handicap.

Vasquez had been told to use his own judgment in the handling of "It's Freezing," a frisky, 4-year-old colt. How clouded the judgment and also the physical ability of Vasquez were might have been revealed by the fact that, despite the jockey's efforts, the horse rushed out, burning up ground and itself. "Trainer Basile had also told Vasquez not to rush," *The New York Times* reported.

Luckily for Vasquez, "It's Freezing" still had a little left and was able to hug the rail in a stretch run that saw the field fan out in what appeared to be a five-across cavalry charge. Vasquez and "It's Freezing" wound up just a head in front of Dis-

tant Land at the finish of the mile-and-three-sixteenths event.

Thus, though Vasquez was intellectually critical and physically not up to par, the combination of a slow field and a spirited horse combined to offset his biorhythmic handicaps. But the events of the day at Aqueduct served to indicate just how difficult forecasting is on the basis of biorhythms, especially as regards horse racing.

Skating

It is a truism that in the sport of skating, an extra dose of energy or daring at a critical time is a major factor for success. On February 13, 1976, nineteen-year-old Dorothy Hamill won the Gold Medal in the Women's Figure Skating Championship Olympic competition. The lovely skater was experiencing a physically critical day, and her bio-cycle showed that she was one day past emotional critical.

A similar situation took place as Sheila Young took the Gold Medal in the Olympic Women's 500 Meter Skating Championship. Ms. Young's biorhythms revealed that she was physically critical and emotionally high on February 6, 1976, the day of her gold medal triumph.

For both Hamill and Young, as with so many other athletes, the ability to go all out physically, to reach for a bit more in a situation of stress and pressure appears interwoven with their experiencing a physically critical day.

It is ironic and hardly a coincidence that the biorhythm patterns of both of these Olympic Champion skaters are similar to those of no-hit pitchers. As was previously mentioned, nine of eleven no-hitters studied occurred on days when the pitcher was experiencing a critical period; particularly a physical critical period. During an outstanding performance, the athlete reached back inside and pushed himself beyond the bounds of his own expectations. During a physical critical, both a no-hit pitcher and a championship skater ignore caution and procedure and let their instincts lead them. Therefore, it is not surprising to find that both extraordinary performances and unexpected failures occur at such times.

Soccer

The champion soccer team of Switzerland, the Basel Soccer Team, can trace its superior performance to intelligent application of biorhythmic principles. Coach Helmut Benthaus became very interested in the possibilities of biorhythms as an aid in athletic competition. He started by making forecasts of a player's performance based on his particular rhythms for a given day. Coming up with impressive results, Benthaus soon found himself using biorhythmic calculations on a regular basis in planning lineups and in handling his players.

Yet, Benthaus maintains, an athlete's biorhythms are only part of his performing story. A first-class player will do better than a second-class player even if biorhythmically the prediction would indicate otherwise. Benthaus also affirms an important aspect of soccer competition is teamwork which should not be broken up because of particular biorhythmic readings.

What Benthaus does is make careful and intelligent use of individual biorhythmic profiles. He will schedule hard physical training when a player is physically high. Fearing vulnerability to injury or overexertion during an athlete's physical low cycle, Benthaus limits extensive training. During competition, the keen-eyed coach uses bio-

rhythmic information to develop plays where stronger parts of his team are more exposed, weaker parts protected. However, Benthaus keeps his calculations secret, not wanting his players to know their predictions and thus become overly fearful or overly confident. Thus far, his efforts have met with great success.

Swimming

A study conducted at the University of Utah is an interesting sidelight on sports forecasting with biorhythms. It also adds significant scientific weight to the importance of further research into the influence of rhythms upon human behavior. It made some interesting observations about swimming and biorhythms.

John Lewis Martin's 1973 University of Utah dissertation, "Relationship of Selected Biological Rhythms to Performance of Competitive Swimmers," concluded that there is solid evidence of "frequent similarities between individual performance and physical biological rhythms." The study also made the point that there is close correlation between performance and emotional rhythms.

For his investigation, Martin recorded the performance times of 31 college and university competition swimmers. These recordings spanned a two-year period. Martin then correlated the results on a biorhythm grid for each individual swimmer.

His work involved swimming coaches at West Liberty State College (West Liberty, West Virginia), State University of New York (Buffalo, New York), and Winona State College (Winona, Minnesota). Meet results, observations about swimmers, and birth dates were supplied by the coaches.

Martin's findings revealed that 23 of the 31 subjects surveyed "depicted a definite relationship between biological rhythms and performance." He also discovered that when the physical and emotional curves were in conjuction, "a close relationship between performance and biological clock occurred."

Martin further noted that the emotional and intellectual cycles working in similar patterns were not significant or substantial indicators of athletic performance. The same point was made as regards the dovetailing of the physical and intellectual curves.

In sum, Martin's major premise was that swimmers gave their best efforts operating under emotional and physical highs in their bio-cycles.

Mark Spitz

Martin's conclusions seem especially applicable to the heroics of Mark Spitz. In the 1972 Olympics, Spitz operated under a physical and emotional high during ten days in late August and early September. He went on to become the first person to win seven gold medals during one session of the Olympic Games. Earlier, in Mexico City, the performance of Spitz had been disappointing.

Apparently, Spitz owes much to his high physical and emotional rhythms for the seven gold medals and the resultant fame and riches that came as a result of those ten days of superlative swimming in the Summer Olympics.

Tennis

In the finals at Wimbledon on July 5, 1975, Arthur Ashe defeated Jimmy Connors. The match was not only a battle between two great tennis players, but also a biorhythmic confrontation:

	P	E	I
Ashe	−	+	+
Connors	−	−	−

September 3, 1976, was an emotionally critical day for Ilie Nastase. At the United States Tennis Open at Forest Hills, New York, the excitable Rumanian outdid himself. He screamed at fans and at officials, engaged in obscene gestures and was finally cited for "extraordinary and unsportsmanlike conduct." A perusal of his biorhythm chart would have enabled one to forecast that September 3, 1976, would not be an "on" day even for the tempestuous tennis ace.

Just a little before Thanksgiving Day, 1976, Jimmy Connors engaged in a competition that he had a lot to be thankful for—and a large part of it was due to a slim biorhythm edge.

On November 21, Connors competed against Roscoe Tanner in the $125,000 International Tennis Tourney. The bio-cycle readouts for the two tennis stars were:

	P	E	I
Connors	−3	−2	+2
Tanner	−4	+1	−5

A careful scrutiny of the biorhythms of the two athletes indicates the slight biorhythmic edge Connors had in the physical rhythm and in the intellectual rhythm. Intellectually, there was actually a big difference, in that Connors was up and Tanner was down.

Beset by an injured ankle, back trouble, and a down feeling, Connors was advised by his physician not to play the match. Jimmy compromised and agreed to play three sets.

The contest was close, but with the edge in his rhythms and the abbreviated contest providing some support, Connors squeaked by to victory: 3–6, 7–6, 6–4.

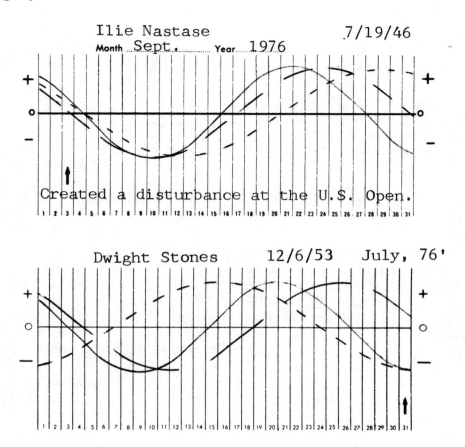

Ilie Nastase   7/19/46
Month ...Sept.......... Year ...1976

Created a disturbance at the U.S. Open.

1 2 3 4 5 6 7 8 9 10 11 12 13 14 15 16 17 18 19 20 21 22 23 24 25 26 27 28 29 30 31

Dwight Stones   12/6/53   July, 76'

1 2 3 4 5 6 7 8 9 10 11 12 13 14 15 16 17 18 19 20 21 22 23 24 25 26 27 28 29 30 31

The triumph of Connors is an excellent example of the sophistication needed to forecast the results of athletic competition. A key factor that must always be considered is the biorhythm of one performer versus the biorhythm of another. In this case, a slight edge possessed by Connors over Tanner was all that was needed.

Track and Field

A couple of classic examples of track and field accomplishments meshing with the influence of biorhythms exist.

In the now legendary performance of Jesse Owens in the 1939 Berlin Olympics, the amazing qualities of Owens and the operation of intangibles are fascinating to contemplate.

On August 3, Owens shattered the world record in the quarter finals and the finals in the 100-meter dash. His time was disallowed because of what was claimed to be "a favoring wind." Owens was physically critical on that date.

On August 4, Owens set an Olympic broad jump record. He also shattered all the records for the trials of the 200-meter dash. On that date, he was physically and emotionally low.

On August 5, Owens was the victor in the 200-meter dash.

On August 8, Owens was a member of the winning 400-meter relay team. On that date he was intellectually critical and his other two rhythms were low.

Thus, there is inconsistency in the inter-relationship of the biorhythms to performance, and in the attempts that anyone would have made to forecast what the accomplishments of Owens might have been. No one could search the great athlete's heart, fathom his feelings about America, the Olympics, and what place he wanted for himself in history. The intangibles must always be taken into consideration in any attempt to "read" biorhythms and athletes.

More predictable apparently would have been the behavior of track star Jim Ryun. On June 23, 1967, he set the record for the mile, and then on July 8, he did the 1500 meters in 3 minutes, 33.1 seconds. At that time in Ryun's life of track and field records, his bio-cycle reveals that he was critical in all three areas around the times he accomplished his feats.

The case of John Uelses illustrates the dramatic ups and downs in an athlete's fortunes and abilities due to biorhythmic fluctuation. On February 3, 1962, at Madison Square Garden, Uelses pole vaulted 16 feet and one-quarter inch to notch a new world record. However, at Louisville, two weeks later, he was unable to clear 14 feet. The Madison Square Garden record-setting feat took place with Uelses operating under a physical and emotional high. At Louisville, the bio-cycle graph for Uelses showed him low emotionally and physically.

1976 Olympic Track and Field

On July 31 in the 1976 Olympics, highly regarded Dwight Stones, favored to do very well in the high jump event, performed well below his and everyone else's expectations. The slender athlete's biorhythm for that Olympic Saturday: Physically and intellectually almost at his lowest point and emotionally within 24 hours of a critical day. It was not a day for a record-breaking performance.

Frank Shorter, who had been there before and won, was part of the mass in the grueling Marathon competition. Favored to win the event, Shorter finished second. His physical stamina—so imperative in the Marathon—was probably negatively influenced by his physical low. Shorter was also within 24 hours of an emotionally critical day. All he had going for him biorhythmically was an intellectual high. But for the Marathon runner, the competition does not significantly involve thinking. In fact, too much thinking about the pain and strain of the run has been the undoing of many an athlete.

The Future of Biorhythm

The impact of biorhythm is beginning to be felt in many areas, from medicine to safety studies to aviation to athletic performances to examinations of the variety of human behavior. Yet, like other speculative sciences, biorhythm it still in its infancy, still in need of extensive research to provide answers to often baffling questions.

Still to be discovered is why biorhythms exist and what is their physical basis? How do they interact and integrate with all the other cycles of life? Why do individuals vary in their susceptibility to biorhythmic cycles, some being so strongly influenced by them, some seemingly very insignificantly influenced? How are the three rhythms influenced, weakened, strengthened, altered by environment or different stages of life or circumstance? How can mankind best be taught to adapt to and use biorhythmic cycles? How can biorhythms best be used in the service of humanity?

These questions are enormous in scope and will require extensive thought, research, and application if the full potential of this field is to be realized. The hope here, however, is to begin this enormous undertaking through pointing the way, setting a direction for the future of biorhythms and perhaps in the process suggest some answers to the questions posed.

Probably the simplest way each individual can test biorhythm theory is through application to his or her own self. Maintaining a "blind diary" of emotional, physical and mental fluctuations in one's daily life and then comparing it with one's fluctuations in the biorhythmic cycles can determine how strongly biorhythms influence a given individual. The rare persons who are "arhythmic" will probably find no correlation between their diaries and biorhythm readouts. For the great majority, though, biorhythms will work and can provide a tool that can guide one toward success and away from disaster throughout life.

Why do biorhythms exist? Why do they work? Why are we subject to so many cycles, circadian and otherwise? Such speculations have puzzled philosophers since time began. Some hold that the phase of the moon one is born under increases an individual's accident prone-ness at each reappearance of that phase. Lunar influence on menstrual cycles and on emotional mood tend to support this theory. The lunar cycle corresponds to the biorhythmic emotional cycle, both being 28 days long. Perhaps, therefore, there is a lunar influence in the emotional cycle. Could the same gravitational forces which pulls the tides affect the sensitivities of human beings? Could there be other gravitational forces which exert a "pull" on our physical and intellectual rhythms? Could geomagnetism be a regulator of circadian cycles, as many students of biological rhythms have suggested? If so, perhaps the earth's magnetism plays a role in biorhythms.

Then again, biorhythms may stem from internal forces rather than external ones, or perhaps a combination of the two. We may respond to both external clocks, such as the predictable stages of the moon, and to internal clocks, such as the one mentioned over a decade ago in the *New York State Journal of Medicine.* Drs. Robert O. Becker, Charles H. Bachman and Howard Friedman described in an article, "The Direct Current Control System: A Link Between Environment and Organism," results of an experiment they conducted in which they measured the charging capacity of the brain to transport electrical current.

> Since the cranial direct current potential appeared to be particularly important . . . in the state of consciousness and level of irritability in the human being, the possibility that it was the controlling mechanism for biologically cyclic behavior was considered. In a very preliminary study, the transcranial d.c. potential of two normal subjects and two schizophrenic subjects was determined daily for a period of two months. A definite cycle pattern was evident in all four subjects, with a periodicity of approximately twenty-eight days and with all four following similar cycles.

According to this research, therefore, electrical potential is a factor in an individual's moods and varies regularly over a 28-day period. Might it not therefore be the central mechanism of the emotional biorhythm?

On the other hand, an examination of the process of cell reproduction leads to speculation on the possibility of a radically different source of biorhythmic patterns. Cells reproduce and regulate their metabolisms through the syntheses of DNA (dioxyribonucleic acid) and RNA (ribonucle-

ic acid). Dr. A. Ehret, in a recent paper, reported the discovery of small bodies called chronons which are situated in the complex DNA molecule. Ehret's thought was that chronons regulate the speed with which RNA is synthesised. Therefore, he speculated, they might also regulate a number of physiological and circadian rhythms. If this is so, is it not possible that different chronon configurations could interact to influence the 23-day physical rhythm and perhaps the other two rhythms as well?

Turning to an entirely different aspect of biorhythmic speculation, let us consider the variety of human response to the three biorhythms: emotional, physical and intellectual. Why are some individuals more sensitive to biorhythms than others? What distinguishes the sensitive subject from the individual who is not sensitive? Can it be that some people can better handle themselves in varying situations and thus mask the effects of their biorhythmic curves? Or do the strengths of the sine-waves which represent the curves vary in different individuals and in the same individuals at different times? In dealing with these questions, three broad areas of research are indicated: the regularity of biorhythms; the interaction of biorhythms with heredity; and the characteristics of situations (environments) which demonstrate biorhythmic effects.

Early work in biorhythm indicated that bio-cycles are absolutely regular and do not vary an iota from the moment of birth until the moment of death. Today, however, even those who still subscribe to this traditionalist's formula accept the concept that environment and physical condition can produce some irregularity in biorhythms. Less conservative researchers are more flexible in their outlook. They maintain that biorhythms, like other natural rhythms, are not absolutely precise. Nor, they would add, are they so irregular as to render useless biorhythmic charting and prediction. As Douglas Neil indicated: "Our (biorhythm) studies are showing that there's definitely something there. . . . Biorhythms may be similar to circadian rhythms. But there are probably individual differences, just as there are in menstrual cycles." When one considers the vulnerability of individuals on days preceding and following critical days, as revealed in accident research, this contention has much validity.

In considering the role of heredity and biorhythms, it is generally accepted that since biorhythmic timing begins at the moment of birth, heredity plays no role unless the time of birth is inherited. What is interesting and worthy of study is how inherited traits combine with the ever-changing biorhythmic profiles and thereby affect an individual's actions and performance. Since research in the area is so inconclusive and limited to date—for example, tracing an inherited ability through genetic combination—there is no way thus far of solving the problem of the interaction of biorhythm and heredity.

Far more evidence can be mustered in an examination of the role of biorhythm and environment. After all, it is environment which brings to light a particular biorhythmic response: There must be the automobile accident in order to determine the individual's reaction to that particular situation. A student must take a test if his results are to be analyzed in terms of his or her biorhythms on that date. An athlete must be involved in some form of competition or performance if his actions are to be measured against his individual cycles. On an average, unchallenging day, there will be nothing to measure biorhythms against; they will be masked beneath ordinary performance. Therefore, the problem to be studied is how challenging the environ-

ment must be to bring biorhythms into full play, or, to put it another way: What is the challenge threshold, the point below which biorhythms will be masked and above which they will be apparent? Being able to recognize such a threshold in various human activities would bring the potential of biorhythm into full play. We would then be able to know when biorhythms must be given full attention and when they can be safely ignored. We would then be able to go much further than merely following such general prescriptions as avoiding hard exercise during physically negative or critical days, taking extra precautions on critical days, guarding against moodiness and irritability on emotionally low days, leaving important intellectual decisions to days when we are intellectually high.

The various biorhythmic combinations in concert with the enormous variety of life's situations make this a problem with extensive ramifications. In addition, there is the question of how administrators can handle biorhythmic information they have on their workers. Is it sufficient to warn a worker when a critical day is coming on? Should jobs be altered to meet biorhythmic exigencies? Or should workers be left unaware of biorhythms, thereby avoiding the dangers of self-fulfilling prophecies, and simply be subtly manipulated so as to best avoid possible biorhythmic consequences? Such questions will be answered as the applied discipline—the study of biorhythm in industry—develops and grows. Similarly, applied medical biorhythm must be developed if biorhythms are to be effectively used in the fields of health and medicine.

Interpreting biorhythmic curves is another problem worthy of much research and study. While the nature and consequences of critical days are well known and while triple highs and lows also can be interpreted with much accuracy, mixed rhythm days remain less clear and require guideposts for adequate interpretation. Wallerstein and Roberts, known for their successful bio-curves for football teams, pointed out the significance of the direction of a particular rhythm, indicating that this direction could be as important—and perhaps more important—than whether a rhythm was above or below the zero line. Opposing rhythms have also been given much thought by contemporary researchers. It has been maintained that days of "opposed crossing" can be much like critical days, involving rhythmic instability or confusion. If a rising physical rhythm crosses an emotional rhythm that is declining, an individual may experience conflict and confusion. Certainly these hypotheses warrant more attention and research.

What is needed, it seems clear, is a more systematic approach to the study of biorhythm. It must be remembered that biorhythm, like psychoanalysis, can never be an exact and accurately predicted science. Individual differences and the influence of environment preclude exactness such as that found in the physical sciences. Presently, there is not a general, widely accepted classification or typology of rhythmic positions and combinations. Too much depends on the particular analyst or specialist who is using biorhythm. It is necessary that the terms of biorhythm be defined and clarified so that the field can be defended against charges that it is modified to meet whatever predictions are required.

Methodology is another aspect of biorhythm that must be clarified and studied. So far, most biorhythmic analysis has been limited to critical days. While results of such analysis have been most impressive, we cannot forget that it is limited to a small portion of the entire biorhythmic theory—only 20 per cent of the days of an individual's life are critical. In order for the theory

to gain broader acceptance and be put into more widespread use, the remaining 80 per cent must be correlated with biorhythms. It must be determined how up days, down days and in-between days correspond to bio-curves. "Blind diaries" are a good method, but limited in scope since they can only be used case by case and only with a fully cooperating subject. What is needed is a standard procedure for biorhythm analysis which all researchers can use, involving techniques which are clear, widely accepted, and could be utilized in testing the theory as a whole. Unless such a procedure is devised, biorhythm cannot progress from the stage of being a collection of empirical studies, few of which deal with the theory as a whole. A step in this direction, is the approach devised by Neil, which called for developing an objective performance scale, rating individual behavior on that scale over long periods of time and comparing the results with bio-curves. While this method had the advantage of testing biorhythm theory at all points, not just the worst ones, it represented a small sample and was very complicated. So a systematic and all-encompassing procedure for analysis of biorhythms still remains an outstanding need of this fledgling field of study.

This, then, is a broad summary of the research requirements of biorhythms: a study of the roots of biorhythm, an analysis of the regularity of the three rhythms, a determination of the roles of heredity and environment on a particular individual's biorhythm, the development of systems of applied biorhythm, the establishment of a systematic approach to interpretation, and agreement on a standard procedure for analysis. As the theory develops and is put to greater and greater use in the service of humanity, undoubtedly many of these fields will be broadened, many of the problems will be studied and many of the questions answered.

We can expect to see within the next decade biorhythm being put to use in a myriad of different ways. There are virtually limitless opportunities for application of biorhythm in industry. Reducing accidents and injuries, improving worker performance and morale, increasing productivity and boosting management–worker relationships are only some of these.

There is also great potential for the use of biorhythm in the area of government. In foreign relations and diplomacy, it would be most useful to know the biorhythmic profiles of our own and foreign diplomats, especially during times of negotiation and discussion. Military commanders and top level officials could, when necessity does not dictate otherwise, wait for high rhythmic days in the intellectual and emotional cycles to make important decisions. Tasks could be assigned to military groups, as in business and industry, according to biorhythmic profiles of a particular group.

In the field of medicine, the implications of biorhythm is very great. The scheduling of surgery, the care of heart attack victims, the anticipation of behavior patterns of mental patients, the use of biorhythms for surgeons themselves in scheduling difficult operations—all are areas with tremendous potential for the good of mankind.

Application of biorhythm to athletic performance presents another area of limitless opportunity in terms of training, avoidance of injury, prediction of performance, team lineups, etc.

Engineering, education, training for the handicapped, aviation safety—these are just a few more areas where biorhythmic analysis can play a significant role.

Biorhythm, even now in its infancy, is a science in the service of humanity. Ultimately, every individual can be the recipient of the rewards of biorhythmic knowledge. For it is through realizing our own biorhythmic curves and learning how to interpret our own profiles that we can take its messages to heart and thereby find a life-long guide to business and financial success, to good personal relationships, to better health, to a long and full life.

Working Out Biorhythm Charts

All that is needed to work out an individual's biorhythm for a particular day is a code letter or number for each of his physical, emotional and intellectual rhythms. (Many athletes' codes are provided in this text.) To determine your own code or that of someone you know, simply consult the birth charts (pages 122-202) and trace your day, month and year of birth.

Biorhythm charts are provided on a monthly basis from 1977 to 1979. With the code in hand, it is simple to trace one's biorhythms on any date. The midpoint of any chart refers to the zero or critical day of a particular cycle—physical, emotional or mental. Above the critical line, the positive or high days can be traced, climbing to the apex or highest day and then descending until once again, the critical day is reached. Likewise, beneath the critical line are the negative or low days, which descend to their lowest point and then climb once again to the critical line where the cycle is repeated.

Precise Interpretations of the Physical, Emotional, Intellectual Cycles of Biorhythms

C = Critical
+ = High or Strong
− = Low or Weak

P E I

C C C On this day, all three of the rhythms pass through a zero, and each one begins a new phase. It is a time to stay calm and take things easy. Extreme caution in involvement and judgment is required. This is an accident-prone day.

C C + Both the Physical and Emotional rhythms on this day are under stress and strain. All deliberations should be made with extra care. Your Intellectual high favors clear thinking. This is an accident-prone day.

C C − At this time, as a result of both your Emotional and Physical rhythms being in the "critical" position, you are exposed to a sluggish disposition. This condition, coupled with a low in the Intellectual cycle, should encourage you to take special care to avoid trouble. This is an accident-prone day.

P E I

C + C In this phase, the "critical" day in your Intellectual rhythm serves to intensify your "critical" disposition Physically. It is a time for you to allow your favorable Emotional disposition to guide you. This is an accident-prone day.

C + + This is a time of tremendous instability and a spent quality for you physically. Compensation can be obtained from your high Emotional and Intellectual condition. This is an accident-prone day.

C + − Though you may feel spent Physically, your Emotions are in plus. This should provide some assistance to the Physically "critical" condition you are in. Awareness is required for you to take steps to adjust to and to overcome your Intellectual low. This is an accident-prone day.

C − C You are characterized by a Physical condition that is dead beat, on a crossover. It is possible that you feel down and low Emotionally. This day could be very trying and exceptionally enervating, especially since you are also at zero point in your Intellectual rhythm. This is an accident-prone day.

P E I

C − + The only fortunate thing about your condition this day is the Intellectual plus you will be operating under. You probably will feel wiped-out Physically because of the "critical" status of this cycle. Emotionally, there will be depression. This is an accident-prone day.

C − − Lows in both your Emotional and Intellectual rhythms will further intensify the tired-out feeling that characterizes this day—a "critical" day for you Physically. This is an accident-prone day.

+ C C This is a day for you to think before you act. In general, the Physical plus indicates that you will have ample energy and endurance, but you may feel depressed Emotionally and Intellectually with both these rhythms at zero. This is an accident-prone day.

+ C + At this time, a state of well being will influence your actions and your thinking, since your Physical and Intellectual rhythms are at plus. However, guard your Emotions—you may feel weary and lethargic. This is an accident-prone day.

P E I

+ C — Though operating under a Physical plus, it is counterbalanced and offset this day by a "critical" day in your Emotions. It is necessary to think twice to avoid problems and pitfalls. Your Intellectual rhythm is coasting. This is an accident-prone day.

+ + C It is a potent, positive, primed day for you Physically and Emotionally. However, with your Intellectual rhythm in "critical," it is highly imperative that you carefully monitor your thinking. This is an accident-prone day.

+ + + Triple plus—today is your day! This is an outstanding period, with all three rhythms in high. Take full advantage of this time and seize the moment. It is a day when you can go all out.

+ + — Good cheer and brimming vitality are yours on this excellent day. You should be feeling very good. The only caution might be that, because of the low in your Intellectual rhythm, you should weigh all decisions with the utmost care.

P E I

+ — C It is a good time for you to concentrate on Physical activity, especially tasks that do not require much concentration. You may feel down Emotionally, and you should take into consideration the "critical" condition of your Intellectual rhythm. This is an accident-prone day.

+ — + The only inopportune aspect of an otherwise fine phase is the minus Emotional rhythm. You should try not to let the "blue" feeling that can possibly derive from your Emotional rhythm affect you. Concentrate as much as possible on Physical activity. It is a good time for thinking, for decision-making, for study—you are in top form Intellectually.

+ — — From a Physical point of view, all things should be possible. You can go all out. However, you must guard your Emotions. Since your Intellectual rhythm is negative, carefully ponder and review all decisions.

P E I

P E I

– C C   On this type of day, all kinds of things can happen to an unwary person. Extra caution is dictated, almost obligatory. Intellectual and Emotional "critical" signifies handicaps in and of themselves. Coupled with a Physical low, all activities must be undertaken with extreme preparedness. This is an accident-prone day.

– C +   The best approach to behavior on a day such as this—a Physical low and an Emotional "critical," both creating conditions making you feel weary and blue—is for you to utilize your Intellectual high and allow it to dominate your action. This is an accident-prone day.

– C –   This is a day for you to just take it as easy as possible. Avoid hasty decisions and attempt to obtain as much rest as is possible. You will find your system sapped by physical fatigue from the Physical low. You will also feel uninspired as a result of your Emotional rhythm being at a cross point. It is not a day to be feared as much as it is a day to be guided by caution. This is an accident-prone day.

– + C   You can concentrate on making this a good day as a result of the positive Emotional rhythm that should characterize your system. Physically you are below par, out of sorts, and intellectually you are at the zero point, but your Emotional cycle can help you through this day if you let it. This is an accident-prone day. *human error*

– + +   You will have a tired feeling that evolves from your Physical low. It can easily be offset if you take advantage of your high Emotional and excellent Intellectual condition. Avoid physical activities, but enjoy other life pursuits.

– + –   A low-pitched day for you Physically and Intellectually. The best thing to do is concentrate on your capacity for creative work and take advantage of your plus Emotional rhythm.

– – C   In this condition, recharging your system is prescribed. You will find it to be a slow day, you are down Physically and Emotionally. Vitality and vigor are lacking. Be conscious of the effects of

P E I

the zero position in your Intellectual rhythm and guard against it. This is an accident-prone day.

– – + A good book, cheerful company, a movie or any type of pleasant diversion might help you make it through this type of day more easily. You will find that your feet are dragging and that you feel down in the dumps. However, your positive in

P E I

the Intellectual rhythm will enable you to think clearly. Take it easy and take advantage of your mind's capacity to enjoy the stimulation of diversion.

– – – This time is an interlude of calm—Physical, Emotional, Intellectual. Strive to shake off the anxieties of the triple low. Relax with the thought that better days are not far away.

Epilogue

As we go to press, once again the newspapers are replete with headlines that are partially explained by the theory of Biorhythm. Frank Sinatra's mother died, with the rest of the occupants, in the crash of an airplane flying from Palm Springs to Las Vegas. Early reports were that the cause of the accident was human error. The pilot was intellectually critical, which may have slowed him in making the fast decisions necessary that fateful night. Readers of my recent book, *Biorhythm: A Personal Science*, read of scores of airplane crashes where the pilot or co-pilot was flying on critical days. A person has six or seven critical days a month. A commercial pilot only has to fly seventeen days a month. Why take chances?

Freddie Prinze, the young TV star, committed suicide on a low day emotionally, within 24 hours of a physical critical; a weak and helpless, frustrating day for a person in a depression.

Evel Knievel practice jumped over a tank of sharks, broke several bones and was hospitalized. Mr. Knievel was emotionally critical and intellectually low. Two years ago *Argosy* Magazine carried a story wherein I stated that if I were Evel Knievel I would postpone the Snake River Canyon jump. That event also ended in a hospital. On that day, Mr. Knievel was physically critical.

Sixteen-year-old jockey Steve Cauthen, an apprentice, won six races in one day, and it was not surprising to note that he was on an intellectual and emotional high. He was at his best for a jockey.

While I was lecturing in Australia recently, the newspapers carried the story that David Graham, the golfer, won the Wentworth and Surrey Golf Tournament in England by upsetting Hale Irwin on the last day of the tournament. In analyzing

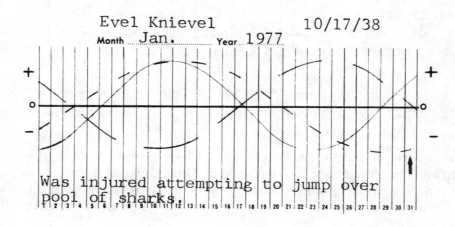

Evel Knievel   10/17/38
Month Jan.   Year 1977

Was injured attempting to jump over pool of sharks.

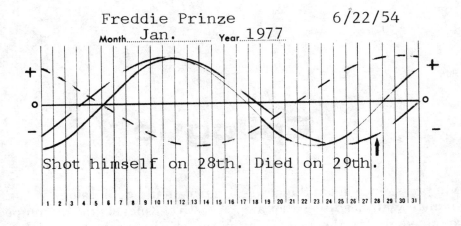

Freddie Prinze   6/22/54

Month Jan.   Year 1977

Shot himself on 28th. Died on 29th.

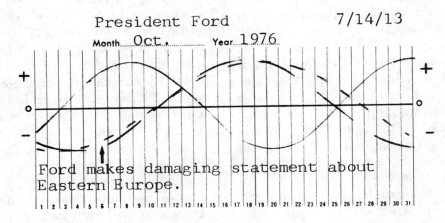

President Ford   7/14/13

Month Oct.   Year 1976

Ford makes damaging statement about
Eastern Europe.

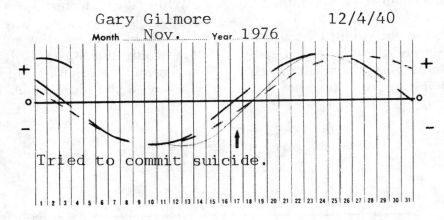

Gary Gilmore   12/4/40

Month Nov.   Year 1976

Tried to commit suicide.

the biorhythm charts of both men, it was no surprise to me that on October 10, 1976, Graham was emotionally and intellectually high and Irwin was emotionally critical and in between a critical intellectual and critical physical day.

This book and a pencil makes you a researcher. You can prove to yourself whether Biorhythm works for you or others. But remember, Biorhythm is only one of the factors you should be concerned with. Age, condition, environment, pressure, experience, the condition of the opponent—all are true factors. Biorhythm is just one more . . . maybe it's the X factor.

Biorhythm Products

Many Biorhythm products are now being marketed. Some are accurate while others are confusing or misleading.

Biorhythm Computers, Inc., at 298 Fifth Avenue, New York City, 10003, was started by George Thommen and is now directed by Bernard Gittelson. This company is the worldwide center for Biorhythm research and information. They produce a Cyclograf Kit which allows the individual to chart his own biorhythms. The Dialgraf is perfect for those who want the ease of a calculator at a fraction of the price. *The Biorhythm Newsletter* is a monthly publication that keeps the reader informed of all new and late-breaking developments in the Biorhythm field. Twelve- and six-month computerized charts are also available which supply the owner with day-by-day interpretations.

The Kosmos I Biorhythm Calculator is the most advanced device ever created for instant, electronic computation of biorhythms. In addition to its ability to calculate and present an individual's biorhythms at the touch of a few buttons, it also contains a dual memory bank which allows for compatibility studies. On critical or minicritical days, the Kosmos I lets you know this information by way of red or amber indicating lights. The producers are Kosmos International of Atlanta, Georgia.

The Bio-Rhythm Computer works like a digital clock and can be electronically set to show one's daily rhythms. It is accurate, convenient, and an attractive addition to any desk. It is produced by Bio-Rhythm Equipment Corp. of Cincinnati, Ohio.

The Bio-Rhythmi-Calendar is a 12-month calendar with red, blue and green dots placed next to each day indicating the individual's position on each cycle. It is easy to read and the instructions are adequate. It is marketed by Ms. Caroline Helmuth of New York City.

The products mentioned here have been tested and found to be accurate. Unfortunately, the same does not hold true for all Biorhythm products. The Biorhythm machines found in supermarkets and bus terminals are totally inaccurate. Several plastic Biorhythm products come with incorrect instructions and have been found to come apart too easily.

Bibliography

Anderson, Russell K. "Biorhythm—Man's Timing Mechanism," *American Society of Safety Engineers Journal,* February 1973, pp. 17–21.

Aschoff, Jurgen (ed.). *Circadian Clocks.* Amsterdam: North-Holland Publishing Company, 1965.

Astrand, Per-Olf and Kaare Rodahl. *Textbook of Work Physiology.* New York: McGraw-Hill Book Company, 1970.

Ault, Michael, and Kinkade, Kenna. *Biorhythm Analysis of Single Car Fatalities.* Joplin, Mo.: Missouri Southern State College, 1973.

Barnes, Jack. "Everybody's Got Biorhythm," *Sunday Magazine,* May 20, 1973, pp. 2–7.

Bennett, M. *Living Clocks in The Animal World.* Springfield, Illinois: Thomas, 1974.

Best, John W. *Research in Education,* Englewood Cliffs, New Jersey: Prentice-Hall, Inc., 1970.

Bierhuizen, J.F. (Chairman) *Circadian Rhythmicity.* Proceedings of the International Symposium on Circadian Rhythmicity, Wageningen: Center for Agricultural Publishing and Documentation, 1972.

Bochow, Reinhold, *Der Unfall im landwirtschaftlichen Betrieb.* Wissenschaftliche Zeitschrift der Humbolt University, no. 6, 1954/1955.

Brown, Frank A., J. Woodland Hastings, and John D. Palmer. *The Biological Clock, Two Views.* New York, London: Academic Press, 1970.

Brown, Frank. *Rhythms, Biological,* Encyclopedia, 1968.

Bunning, Erwin. *The Physiological Clock.* New York: Springer-Verlag New York, Inc., 1967.

Case, Jan. *Predictive Powers in Bio-Rhythm Analysis in the Performance of Football Players.* Joplin, Mo.: Missouri Southern State College, 1972.

Coates, Lloyd D., et al. *A Study of Bio-Rhythm Cycles, Astrological Forecasts, and Personal Evaluations.* Joplin, Mo.: Missouri Southern State College, 1972.

Cohen, Daniel. *Biorhythms in Your Life.* New York: Fawcett Publications, Inc., 1976.

Cloudsley-Thompson, J.L. *Rhythmic Acitivity in Animal Physiology and Behavior.* New York and London: Academic Press, 1961.

Coloquhoun, W.P. (ed.). *Biological Rhythms and Human Performance.* London and New York: Academic Press, 1971.

Conroy, R.T.W.L. and J.N. Mills, *Human Circadian Rhythms.* London: J. and A. Churchill, 1970.

Crammer, L. "Periodic Psychoses," *British Medical Journal,* 1:545-549, 1959.

Dale, Arbie. *Biorhythm.* New York: Pocket Books, 1976.

DeVries, Herbert A. *Physiology and Exercise for Physical Education and Athletics.* Dubuque, Iowa: Wm. C. Brown Publishers, 1974.

Dewey, Edward R. *Cycles, The Mysterious Forces That Trigger Events.* New York: Hawthorn Books, 1971.

Donaldson, V.H. and R.R. Evans. "A Biochemical Abnormality in Hereditary Angioneurotic Edema. Absence of Serum Inhibitor of C'1 Esterase," *American Journal of Medicine,* 35:37–42, 1963.

Edholm, O.G., and A.L. Bącharach (eds.). *The Physiology of Human Performance.* London and New York: Academic Press, 1965.

Ferguson, George A., *Statistical Analysis in Psychology and Education.* New York: McGraw-Hill Book Co., 1971.

Fliess, Wilhelm. *Der Ablauf Des Lebens.* Leipzig-Vienna: Franz Deuticke, 1906.

Fliess, Wilhelm. *Von Leben und vom Tod.* Jena: Diederichs, 1909.

Fliess, Wilhelm. *Das Jahr im Lebendigen.* Jena: Diederichs, 1918.

Fliess, Wilhelm. *Zur Periodenlehre.* Leipzig: Ebenda, 1925.

Fraisse, Paul. *The Psychology of Time.* New York, Evanston, and London: Harper and Row, Publishers, 1963.

Frueh, Hans. *Von der Periodenlehre zur Biorhythmenlehre.* Zurich-Leipzig: Wegweiser, 1939–1942.

Frueh, Hans. *Rhythmenpraxis.* Zurich: Frueh, 1943.

Frueh, Hans. *Kraft, Gesundheit und Leistung.* Basserdorf: Frueh, 1946.

Frueh, Hans. *Deine Leistungskurve.* Basserdorf-Zurich: Frueh, 1953.

Frueh, Hans. *Triumph der Lebensrhythmen.* Buedingen-Gettenbach: Lebensweiser, 1953.

Gittelson, Bernard. *Biorhythm: A Personal Science.* New York: Arco Publishing Co., Inc., 1975.

Goodwin, B.C. *Temporal Organization in Cells.* London and New York: Academic Press, 1967.

Gross, Hugo Max. *Biorhythms.* Motivation Development Centre, 1975.

Halberg, Franz. "Some Physiological and Clinical Aspects of Twenty-Four Hour Periodicity," *Lancet,* 20–30, January 1953.

Halberg, Franz. "Chronobiology," *Annual Review of Physiology,* 31:675–725, 1969.

Halberg, F., et al., "Authorhythmometry—Procedures for Physiologic Self-Measurements and Their Analysis," *Physiology Teacher,* 1:1–11, 1972.

Halberg, F., et al., "Toward a Chronotherapy of Neoplasia: Tolerance of Treatment Depends on Host Rhythms," *Experientia,* 29:909–934, 1973.

Hersey, R.B. *Workers' Emotions in Shop and Home.* Philadelphia: University of Pennsylvania Press, 1932.

Johnson, Dale, *A Relationship of Selected Biological Rhythms to Football Injuries.* Unpublished doctoral dissertation, University of Utah, 1974.

Karlins, Marvin, and Lewis M. Andrew. *Biofeedback.* Philadelphia and New York: J.B. Lippencott Company, 1972.

Klein, Marcia. *Biorhythm in the Prediction of Heart Attacks Suffered by American Business Men.* Joplin, Mo.: Missouri State Southern College, 1973.

Kleitman, W. *Sleep and Wakefulness.* Chicago: University of Chicago Press, 1939.

Krause-Poray, B.J. *I Wish I Had Known.* Brisbane, Australia: Biorhythm Research and Information Centre, 1974.

Kuhn, Robert I., *Control Your Destiny with Biorhythms.* Fla: *Fiesta,* Fiesta de Florida Publishing Inc., Boca Raton, January 1975.

Leeks, Richard C. *The Influence of Biorhythms in Traffic Accidents.* Unpublished Masters Theses, Arizona State University, May 1976.

Linton, Marigold and Philip S. Gallo, Jr. *The Practical Statistician: Simplified Handbook of Statistics.* Monterey, Calif.: Brooks/Cole Publishing Company, 1975.

Luce, Gay Gaer. *Biological Rhythms in Human and Animal Physiology.* New York: Dover Publications, Inc., 1971.

Luce, Gay Gaer. *Biological Rhythms in Psychiatry and Medicine.* Published by the National Institute on Mental Health, 5454 Wisconsin Avenue, Chevy Chase, Maryland, 1970.

Luce, Gay Gaer. *Bodytime Physiological Rhythms and Social Stress.* New York: Pantheon Books, Division of Random House, 1971.

Mallardi, Vincent. *Biorhythms & Your Behavior.* Media America, Inc., 1976.

Martin, John L. *Relationship of Selected Biological Rhythms to Performance of Competitive Swimmers.* Unpublished doctoral dissertation, University of Utah, 1973.

Mayersbach, H. von (ed.) *The Cellular Aspects of Biorhythms, Symposium on Rhythmic Research.* New York: Springer-Verlag New York Inc., 1967.

Menaker, Michael (ed.). *Biochronometry.* Washington, D.C.: National Academy of Science, 1971.

Mills, J.N. *Biological Aspects of Circadium Rhythms.* London and New York: Plenum Press, 1973.

Moore, Ruth. *The Coil of Life.* New York: Alfred A. Knopf, 1969.

Morehouse, Laurence E. *Laboratory Manual for Physiology of Exercise.* St. Louis: The C.V. Mosby Company, 1972.

Morley, A. "Periodic Diseases, Physiological Rhythms and Feedback Control—A Hypothesis," *Australias Annual of Medicine,* 19:244–249, 1970.

Neil, Douglas E. *Biorhythms and Industrial Safety.* Monterey, California: Naval Postgraduate School (unpublished).

Neil, Douglas E., Louis J. Giannotti, and Thomas A. Wyatt. *Statistical Analysis of the Theory of Biorhythms.* Monterey, California: Naval Postgraduate School (unpublished).

O'Neil, Barbara and Phillips, Richard. *Biorhythms, How To Live With Your Life Cycles.* Pasadena, Calif.: Ward Ritchie Press, 1975.

Palmer, John D. *An Introduction to Biological Rhythms.* New York: Academic Press, 1976.

Pavlidis, Theodosios. *Biological Oscillations: Their Mathematical Analysis.* New York and London: Academic Press, 1965.

Pengelley, Eric T. (ed.) *Circannual Clocks: Annual Biological Rhythms.* New York: Academic Press, 1976.

Reimann, Hobart A. "Periodic Arthralgia in Twenty-Three Members of Five Generations of a Family," *Journal of American Medical Association,* 146:713–716, 1951.

Reimann, Hobart A. "Hereditary Periodic Edema. Interrelation of Familial Periodic Disorders," *American Journal of Medical Science,* 243:727–739, 1962.

Reimann, Hobart A. *Periodic Diseases.* Philadelphia: F.A. Davis Co., 1963.

Reimann, H.A., E.D. Coppola, and G.R. Villegas. "Serum Component Defects in Periodic Diseases, *Annual of International Medicine,* 73:737–740, 1970.

Reimann, Hobart A. "Haemocytic Periodicity and Periodic Disorders. Periodic Neutropenia, Thrombocytopenia, Lymphocytoses, and Anaemia. *Postgraduate Medical Journal,* 47:504–510, 1971.

Reimann, Hobart A. "Periodic Synoviosis (intermittent hydrarthrosis) With Observations and Studies on a Patient." *Postgraduate Medical Journal,* 50:33–39, 1974.

Reimann, Hobart A. "Colchicine For Periodic Peritonitis," *Journal of American Medical Association,* 231:64–66, 1975.

Reimann, Hobart A. "Clinical Insight on the Nature of Periodic Diseases," *Modern Medicine,* April 1975.

Reinberg, Alain, and Jean Ghata. *Biological Rhythms.* New York: Walker and Company, 1964.

Richter, Paul Curt. *Biological Clocks in Medicine and Psychiatry.* Springfield, Illinois: Charles C. Thomas Publisher, 1965.

Roethlisbrger, F.J. and W.J. Dickson. *Management and the Worker.* Cambridge: Harvard University Press, 1946.

Rogers, Charles W., R. Leo Sprinkle and Fred H. Lindberg. "Biorhythms: Three Tests of the Predictive Validity of the 'Critical Day' Hypotheses," *International Journal of Chronobiology,* Vol. 2, pp. 247–252, 1974.

Sacher, D. *The Influence of Biorhythmic Criticality on Aircraft Mishaps.* Unpublished Masters Thesis, Naval Postgraduate School, Monterey, California, 1974.

Saline, Carol. "Blame It on Your Biorhythms," *Boston Magazine,* June, 1974, pp. 7–14.

Sanhein, Jacob M. *Biorhythm Analysis as Applicable to Safety.* Prepared by Quality Assurance Department, Weapons Support Center, Crane, Indiana, 1975.

Scheving, L. et al. "Circadian Rhythm in Arabinosyl Cytosine Tolerance by Mice," *Cancer Research,* 36:1133–1137, 1976.

Schlieper, Hans. *Der Rhythmus des Lebendigen.* Jean: Diedrichs, 1909.

Schlieper, Hans. *Das Jahr im Raum.* Jena: Diedrichs (undated).

Schwing, H. *Ueber Biorhythmen und Deren Technische Anwendung.* Paper presented at the Swiss Federal Institute of Technology, Zurich.

Senzaburo, Oka. *The Purpose of Driver's Self Control.* Hikone, Japan: Ohmi Railway Co., 1969.

Siegel, S. *Nonparametric Statistics.* New York: McGraw-Hill, 1956.

Smith, Robert E. *The Complete Book of Biorhythm Life Cycles.* New York: Aardvark Publishers, Inc., 1976.

Sollberger, A. *Biological Rhythm Research.* Amsterdam, London, and New York: Elsevier Publishing Company, 1965.

Steindler, E.M. "Nature's Built-In Clocks," *Today's Health,* November 1965, pp. 49–53.

Still, Henry. *Of Time, Tides, and Inner Clocks.* Harrisburg, Pa.: Stackpole Books, 1972.

Strughold, Hubertus. *Your Body Clock.* New York: Charles Scribner's Sons, Publishers, 1971.

Swain, A.D., J.W. Altman, and L.W. Rook Jr. *Human Error Qualification.* Albuquerque, N.M.: Sandia Corp. 1963.

Swoboda, H. *Das Siebenjahr.* Vienna-Leipzig: Orion-Verlag, 1917.

Swoboda, Hermann. *Die Perioden des menschlichen Lebens in ihrer psychologischen und biologischen Bedeutung.* Leipzig-Vienna: Deuticke, 1904.

Swoboda, Hermann. *Studien zur Grundlegung der Psychologie.* Liepzig-Vienna: Deuticke, 1905.

Swoboda, Hermann. *Die Kritischen Tage des Menschen.* Leipzig-Vienna: Deuticke, 1909.

Swoboda, Hermann. *Die Bedeutung des Siebenjahr Rhythmus fur die menschliche Vererbung.* Florence, Italy: Industria Tipografica Fiorentina, 1954.

Thommen, George. *Is This Your Day?* New York: Crown Publishers, Inc., 1973, 1964.

Tope, Otto. *Biorhythmische Einflüsse und ihre Auswirkung in Fuhrparkbetrieben* Hanover, Germany: Staedtehygiene, 1956.

Wallerstein, Michael, and Nancy Lee Roberts. "All Together on the Bio-curve," *Human Behavior,* April 1973, 2, 8–15.

Ward, Ritchie R. *The Living Clocks.* New York: Alfred A. Knopf, 1971.

Wernli, Hans J. *Biorhythm,* New York: Cornerstone Library, 1976.

Willis, H.R. *Biorhythm and its Relationship to Human Error.* Paper presented at the 16th Annual Meeting Human Factors Society, October 1972.

Willis, Harold R. *Biorhythm—Phantom of Human Error.* Dallas, Texas: Ling-Temco-Vought Corp., 1969.

Willis, Harold R. *The Effect of Biorhythm Cycles—Implications for Industry.* Miami Beach, Fla.: Proceedings of the American Industrial Hygiene Conference, 1974.

How to Chart Biorhythm Curves

Look up the date of birth. Following it you will find three symbols, such as "J, V, Y." The first symbol refers to the Physical rhythm, the second to the Emotional, and the third to the Intellectual. Then turn to the Biorhythm Charts (pages 203-238), where you will find each month of the years 1977 to 1979 duplicated three times—once for each biorhythm—and numbered to correspond to the days of that month. Do not be confused by the swarms of symbols that appear within the columns; simply refer to the first symbol you found under the birth date, locate the same symbol in the monthly table for the physical rhythm, and draw a line passing through the physical symbol. The result will be an accurate sine wave chart of the physical rhythm. Repeat the process for the monthly emotional and intellectual rhythm charts—drawing a line through the second and third symbols respectively—and you will have a complete biorhythm chart in three parts.

...JANUARY..	..FEBRUARY..	...MARCH...	...APRIL...	....MAY....	...JUNE....
P--E--I	P--E--I	P--E--I	P--E--I	P--E--I	P--E--I
1) S..J..D	1) C..M..B	1) J..N..6	1) R..Q..4	1) A..S..1	1) J..V..Y
2) T..K..E	2) D..N..C	2) K..O..7	2) S..R..5	2) B..T..2	2) K..W..Z
3) U..L..F	3) E..O..D	3) L..P..8	3) T..S..6	3) C..U..3	3) L..X..1
4) V..M..G	4) F..P..E	4) M..Q..A	4) U..T..7	4) D..V..4	4) M..Y..2
5) W..N..H	5) G..Q..F	5) N..R..B	5) V..U..8	5) E..W..5	5) N..Z..3
6) X..O..J	6) H..R..G	6) O..S..C	6) W..V..A	6) F..X..6	6) O..1..4
7) A..P..K	7) J..S..H	7) P..T..D	7) X..W..B	7) G..Y..7	7) P..2..5
8) B..Q..L	8) K..T..J	8) Q..U..E	8) A..X..C	8) H..Z..8	8) Q..3..6
9) C..R..M	9) L..U..K	9) R..V..F	9) B..Y..D	9) J..1..A	9) R..A..7
10) D..S..N	10) M..V..L	10) S..W..G	10) C..Z..E	10) K..2..B	10) S..B..8
11) E..T..O	11) N..W..M	11) T..X..H	11) D..1..F	11) L..3..C	11) T..C..A
12) F..U..P	12) O..X..N	12) U..Y..J	12) E..2..G	12) M..A..D	12) U..D..B
13) G..V..Q	13) P..Y..O	13) V..Z..K	13) F..3..H	13) N..B..E	13) V..E..C
14) H..W..R	14) Q..Z..P	14) W..1..L	14) G..A..J	14) O..C..F	14) W..F..D
15) J..X..S	15) R..1..Q	15) X..2..M	15) H..B..K	15) P..D..G	15) X..G..E
16) K..Y..T	16) S..2..R	16) A..3..N	16) J..C..L	16) Q..E..H	16) A..H..F
17) L..Z..U	17) T..3..S	17) B..A..O	17) K..D..M	17) R..F..J	17) B..J..G
18) M..1..V	18) U..A..T	18) C..B..P	18) L..E..N	18) S..G..K	18) C..K..H
19) N..2..W	19) V..B..U	19) D..C..Q	19) M..F..O	19) T..H..L	19) D..L..J
20) O..3..X	20) W..C..V	20) E..D..R	20) N..G..P	20) U..J..M	20) E..M..K
21) P..A..Y	21) X..D..W	21) F..E..S	21) O..H..Q	21) V..K..N	21) F..N..L
22) Q..B..Z	22) A..E..X	22) G..F..T	22) P..J..R	22) W..L..O	22) G..O..M
23) R..C..1	23) B..F..Y	23) H..G..U	23) Q..K..S	23) X..M..P	23) H..P..N
24) S..D..2	24) C..G..Z	24) J..H..V	24) R..L..T	24) A..N..Q	24) J..Q..O
25) T..E..3	25) D..H..1	25) K..J..W	25) S..M..U	25) B..O..R	25) K..R..P
26) U..F..4	26) E..J..2	26) L..K..X	26) T..N..V	26) C..P..S	26) L..S..Q
27) V..G..5	27) F..K..3	27) M..L..Y	27) U..O..W	27) D..Q..T	27) M..T..R
28) W..H..6	28) G..L..4	28) N..M..Z	28) V..P..X	28) E..R..U	28) N..U..S
29) X..J..7	29) H..M..5	29) O..N..1	29) W..Q..Y	29) F..S..V	29) O..V..T
30) A..K..8		30) P..O..2	30) X..R..Z	30) G..T..W	30) P..W..U
31) B..L..A		31) Q..P..3		31) H..U..X	

....JULY....	...AUGUST...	..SEPTEMBER.	..OCTOBER...	.NOVEMBER..	.DECEMBER..
P--E--I	P--E--I	P--E--I	P--E--I	P--E--I	P--E--I
1) Q..X..V	1) A..1..T	1) J..A..R	1) Q..C..O	1) A..F..M	1) H..H..J
2) R..Y..W	2) B..2..U	2) K..B..S	2) R..D..P	2) B..G..N	2) J..J..K
3) S..Z..X	3) C..3..V	3) L..C..T	3) S..E..Q	3) C..H..O	3) K..K..L
4) T..1..Y	4) D..A..W	4) M..D..U	4) T..F..R	4) D..J..P	4) L..L..M
5) U..2..Z	5) E..B..X	5) N..E..V	5) U..G..S	5) E..K..Q	5) M..M..N
6) V..3..1	6) F..C..Y	6) O..F..W	6) V..H..T	6) F..L..R	6) N..N..O
7) W..A..2	7) G..D..Z	7) P..G..X	7) W..J..U	7) G..M..S	7) O..O..P
8) X..B..3	8) H..E..1	8) Q..H..Y	8) X..K..V	8) H..N..T	8) P..P..Q
9) A..C..4	9) J..F..2	9) R..J..Z	9) A..L..W	9) J..O..U	9) Q..Q..R
10) B..D..5	10) K..G..3	10) S..K..1	10) B..M..X	10) K..P..V	10) R..R..S
11) C..E..6	11) L..H..4	11) T..L..2	11) C..N..Y	11) L..Q..W	11) S..S..T
12) D..F..7	12) M..J..5	12) U..M..3	12) D..O..Z	12) M..R..X	12) T..T..U
13) E..G..8	13) N..K..6	13) V..N..4	13) E..P..1	13) N..S..Y	13) U..U..V
14) F..H..A	14) O..L..7	14) W..O..5	14) F..Q..2	14) O..T..Z	14) V..V..W
15) G..J..B	15) P..M..8	15) X..P..6	15) G..R..3	15) P..U..1	15) W..W..X
16) H..K..C	16) Q..N..A	16) A..Q..7	16) H..S..4	16) Q..V..2	16) X..X..Y
17) J..L..D	17) R..O..B	17) B..R..8	17) J..T..5	17) R..W..3	17) A..Y..Z
18) K..M..E	18) S..P..C	18) C..S..A	18) K..U..6	18) S..X..4	18) B..Z..1
19) L..N..F	19) T..Q..D	19) D..T..B	19) L..V..7	19) T..Y..5	19) C..1..2
20) M..O..G	20) U..R..E	20) E..U..C	20) M..W..8	20) U..Z..6	20) D..2..3
21) N..P..H	21) V..S..F	21) F..V..D	21) N..X..A	21) V..1..7	21) E..3..4
22) O..Q..J	22) W..T..G	22) G..W..E	22) O..Y..B	22) W..2..8	22) F..A..5
23) P..R..K	23) X..U..H	23) H..X..F	23) P..Z..C	23) X..3..A	23) G..B..6
24) Q..S..L	24) A..V..J	24) J..Y..G	24) Q..1..D	24) A..A..B	24) H..C..7
25) R..T..M	25) B..W..K	25) K..Z..H	25) R..2..E	25) B..B..C	25) J..D..8
26) S..U..N	26) C..X..L	26) L..1..J	26) S..3..F	26) C..C..D	26) K..E..A
27) T..V..O	27) D..Y..M	27) M..2..K	27) T..A..G	27) D..D..E	27) L..F..B
28) U..W..P	28) E..Z..N	28) N..3..L	28) U..B..H	28) E..E..F	28) M..G..C
29) V..X..Q	29) F..1..O	29) O..A..M	29) V..C..J	29) F..F..G	29) N..H..D
30) W..Y..R	30) G..2..P	30) P..B..N	30) W..D..K	30) G..G..H	30) O..J..E
31) X..Z..S	31) H..3..Q		31) X..E..L		31) P..K..F

CODES: P-PHYSICAL BIORHYTHM CURVE,E-EMOTIONAL BIORHYTHM CURVE,I-INTELLECTUAL BIORHYTHM CURVE

PHYSICAL

1	2	3	4	5	6	7	8	9	10	11	12	13	14	15	16	17	18	19	20	21	22	23	24	25	26	27	28	29	30	31	±
SU	M	TU	W	TH	F	SA	SU	M	TU	W	TH	F	SA	SU	M	TU	W	TH	F	SA	SU	M	TU	W	TH	F	SA	SU	M	TU	
AX	BA	CB	DC	ED	FE	GF	HG	JH	KJ	LK	ML	NM	ON	PO	QP	RQ	SR	TS	UT	VU	WV	XW	AX	BA	CB	DC	ED	FE	GF	HG	
BW	CX	DA	EB	FC	GD	HE	JF	KG	LH	MJ	NK	OL	PM	QN	RO	SP	TQ	UR	VS	WT	XU	AV	BW	CX	DA	EB	FC	GD	HE	JF	
CV	DW	EX	FA	GB	HC	JD	KE	LF	MG	NH	OJ	PK	QL	RM	SN	TO	UP	VQ	WR	XS	AT	BU	CV	DW	EX	FA	GB	HC	JD	KE	
DU	EV	FW	GX	HA	JB	KC	LD	ME	NF	OG	PH	QJ	RK	SL	TM	UN	VO	WP	XQ	AR	BS	CT	DU	EV	FW	GX	HA	JB	KC	LD	+
ET	FU	GV	HW	JX	KA	LB	MC	ND	OE	PF	QG	RH	SJ	TK	UL	VM	WN	XO	AP	BQ	CR	DS	ET	FU	GV	HW	JX	KA	LB	MC	
FS	GT	HU	JV	KW	LX	MA	NB	OC	PD	QE	RF	SG	TH	UJ	VK	WL	XM	AN	BO	CP	DQ	ER	FS	GT	HU	JV	KW	LX	MA	NB	0
GR	HS	JT	KU	LV	MW	NX	OA	PB	QC	RD	SE	TF	UG	VH	WJ	XK	AL	BM	CN	DO	EP	FQ	GR	HS	JT	KU	LV	MW	NX	OA	
HQ	JR	KS	LT	MU	NV	OW	PX	QA	RB	SC	TD	UE	VF	WG	XH	AJ	BK	CL	DM	EN	FO	GP	HQ	JR	KS	LT	MU	NV	OW	PX	−
JP	KQ	LR	MS	NT	OU	PV	QW	RX	SA	TB	UC	VD	WE	XF	AG	BH	CJ	DK	EL	FM	GN	HO	JP	KQ	LR	MS	NT	OU	PV	QW	
KO	LP	MQ	NR	OS	PT	QU	RV	SW	TX	UA	VB	WC	XD	AE	BF	CG	DH	EJ	FK	GL	HM	JN	KO	LP	MQ	NR	OS	PT	QU	RV	
LN	MO	NP	OQ	PR	QS	RT	SU	TV	UW	VX	WA	XB	AC	BD	CE	DF	EG	FH	GJ	HK	JL	KM	LN	MO	NP	OQ	PR	QS	RT	SU	
M	N	O	P	Q	R	S	T	U	V	W	X	A	B	C	D	E	F	G	H	J	K	L	M	N	O	P	Q	R	S	T	

EMOTIONAL

1	2	3	4	5	6	7	8	9	10	11	12	13	14	15	16	17	18	19	20	21	22	23	24	25	26	27	28	29	30	31	±
SU	M	TU	W	TH	F	SA	SU	M	TU	W	TH	F	SA	SU	M	TU	W	TH	F	SA	SU	M	TU	W	TH	F	SA	SU	M	TU	
W	X	Y	Z	1	2	3	A	B	C	D	E	F	G	H	J	K	L	M	N	O	P	Q	R	S	T	U	V	W	X	Y	
XV	YW	ZX	1Y	2Z	31	A2	B3	CA	DB	EC	FD	GE	HF	JG	KH	LJ	MK	NL	OM	PN	QO	RP	SQ	TR	US	VT	WU	XV	YW	ZX	
YU	ZV	1W	2X	3Y	AZ	B1	C2	D3	EA	FB	GC	HD	JE	KF	LG	MH	NJ	OK	PL	QM	RN	SO	TP	UQ	VR	WS	XT	YU	ZV	1W	
ZT	1U	2V	3W	AX	BY	CZ	D1	E2	F3	GA	HB	JC	KD	LE	MF	NG	OH	PJ	QK	RL	SM	TN	UO	VP	WQ	XR	YS	ZT	1U	2V	
1S	2T	3U	AV	BW	CX	DY	EZ	F1	G2	H3	JA	KB	LC	MD	NE	OF	PG	QH	RJ	SK	TL	UM	VN	WO	XP	YQ	ZR	1S	2T	3U	+
2R	3S	AT	BU	CV	DW	EX	FY	GZ	H1	J2	K3	LA	MB	NC	OD	PE	QF	RG	SH	TJ	UK	VL	WM	XN	YO	ZP	1Q	2R	3S	AT	
3Q	AR	BS	CT	DU	EV	FW	GX	HY	JZ	K1	L2	M3	NA	OB	PC	QD	RE	SF	TG	UH	VJ	WK	XL	YM	ZN	1O	2P	3Q	AR	BS	
AP	BQ	CR	DS	ET	FU	GV	HW	JX	KY	LZ	M1	N2	O3	PA	QB	RC	SD	TE	UF	VG	WH	XJ	YK	ZL	1M	2N	3O	AP	BQ	CR	0
BO	CP	DQ	ER	FS	GT	HU	JV	KW	LX	MY	NZ	O1	P2	Q3	RA	SB	TC	UD	VE	WF	XG	YH	ZJ	1K	2L	3M	AN	BO	CP	DQ	
CN	DO	EP	FQ	GR	HS	JT	KU	LV	MW	NX	OY	PZ	Q1	R2	S3	TA	UB	VC	WD	XE	YF	ZG	1H	2J	3K	AL	BM	CN	DO	EP	−
DM	EN	FO	GP	HQ	JR	KS	LT	MU	NV	OW	PX	QY	RZ	S1	T2	U3	VA	WB	XC	YD	ZE	1F	2G	3H	AJ	BK	CL	DM	EN	FO	
EL	FM	GN	HO	JP	KQ	LR	MS	NT	OU	PV	QW	RX	SY	TZ	U1	V2	W3	XA	YB	ZC	1D	2E	3F	AG	BH	CJ	DK	EL	FM	GN	
FK	GL	HM	JN	KO	LP	MQ	NR	OS	PT	QU	RV	SW	TX	UY	VZ	W1	X2	Y3	ZA	1B	2C	3D	AE	BF	CG	DH	EJ	FK	GL	HM	
GJ	HK	JL	KM	LN	MO	NP	OQ	PR	QS	RT	SU	TV	UW	VX	WY	XZ	Y1	Z2	13	2A	3B	AC	BD	CE	DF	EG	FH	GJ	HK	JL	
H	J	K	L	M	N	O	P	Q	R	S	T	U	V	W	X	Y	Z	1	2	3	A	B	C	D	E	F	G	H	J	K	

INTELLECTUAL

1	2	3	4	5	6	7	8	9	10	11	12	13	14	15	16	17	18	19	20	21	22	23	24	25	26	27	28	29	30	31	±
SU	M	TU	W	TH	F	SA	SU	M	TU	W	TH	F	SA	SU	M	TU	W	TH	F	SA	SU	M	TU	W	TH	F	SA	SU	M	TU	
Q	R	S	T	U	V	W	X	Y	Z	1	2	3	4	5	6	7	8	A	B	C	D	E	F	G	H	J	K	L	M	N	
RP	SQ	TR	US	VT	WU	XV	YW	ZX	1Y	2Z	31	42	53	64	75	86	A7	B8	CA	DB	EC	FD	GE	HF	JG	KH	LJ	MK	NL	OM	
SO	TP	UQ	VR	WS	XT	YU	ZV	1W	2X	3Y	4Z	51	62	73	84	A5	B6	C7	D8	EA	FB	GC	HD	JE	KF	LG	MH	NJ	OK	PL	
TN	UO	VP	WQ	XR	YS	ZT	1U	2V	3W	4X	5Y	6Z	71	82	A3	B4	C5	D6	E7	F8	GA	HB	JC	KD	LE	MF	NG	OH	PJ	QK	
UM	VN	WO	XP	YQ	ZR	1S	2T	3U	4V	5W	6X	7Y	8Z	A1	B2	C3	D4	E5	F6	G7	H8	JA	KB	LC	MD	NE	OF	PG	QH	RJ	
VL	WM	XN	YO	ZP	1Q	2R	3S	4T	5U	6V	7W	8X	AY	BZ	C1	D2	E3	F4	G5	H6	J7	K8	LA	MB	NC	OD	PE	QF	RG	SH	+
WK	XL	YM	ZN	1O	2P	3Q	4R	5S	6T	7U	8V	AW	BX	CY	DZ	E1	F2	G3	H4	J5	K6	L7	M8	NA	OB	PC	QD	RE	SF	TG	
XJ	YK	ZL	1M	2N	3O	4P	5Q	6R	7S	8T	AU	BV	CW	DX	EY	FZ	G1	H2	J3	K4	L5	M6	N7	O8	PA	QB	RC	SD	TE	UF	
YH	ZJ	1K	2L	3M	4N	5O	6P	7Q	8R	AS	BT	CU	DV	EW	FX	GY	HZ	J1	K2	L3	M4	N5	O6	P7	Q8	RA	SB	TC	UD	VE	0
ZG	1H	2J	3K	4L	5M	6N	7O	8P	AQ	BR	CS	DT	EU	FV	GW	HX	JY	KZ	L1	M2	N3	O4	P5	Q6	R7	S8	TA	UB	VC	WD	
1F	2G	3H	4J	5K	6L	7M	8N	AO	BP	CQ	DR	ES	FT	GU	HV	JW	KX	LY	MZ	N1	O2	P3	Q4	R5	S6	T7	U8	VA	WB	XC	
2E	3F	4G	5H	6J	7K	8L	AM	BN	CO	DP	EQ	FR	GS	HT	JU	KV	LW	MX	NY	OZ	P1	Q2	R3	S4	T5	U6	V7	W8	XA	YB	−
3D	4E	5F	6G	7H	8J	AK	BL	CM	DN	EO	FP	GQ	HR	JS	KT	LU	MV	NW	OX	PY	QZ	R1	S2	T3	U4	V5	W6	X7	Y8	ZA	
4C	5D	6E	7F	8G	AH	BJ	CK	DL	EM	FN	GO	HP	JQ	KR	LS	MT	NU	OV	PW	QX	RY	SZ	T1	U2	V3	W4	X5	Y6	Z7	18	
5B	6C	7D	8E	AF	BG	CH	DJ	EK	FL	GM	HN	JO	KP	LQ	MR	NS	OT	PU	QV	RW	SX	TY	UZ	V1	W2	X3	Y4	Z5	16	27	
6A	7B	8C	AD	BE	CF	DG	EH	FJ	GK	HL	JM	KN	LO	MP	NQ	OR	PS	QT	RU	SV	TW	UX	VY	WZ	X1	Y2	Z3	14	25	36	
78	8A	AB	BC	CD	DE	EF	FG	GH	HJ	JK	KL	LM	MN	NO	OP	PQ	QR	RS	ST	TU	UV	VW	WX	XY	YZ	Z1	12	23	34	45	

Baseball

NAME	DATE OF BIRTH	CODE			NAME	DATE OF BIRTH	CODE		
Aaron, Henry (Hank) OF	Feb 5, 1934	A	J	1	Boone, Robert C	Nov 19, 1947	W	D	M
Abbott, William P	Feb 16, 1951	L	N	J	Borbon, Pedro P	Dec 2, 1946	P	Q	X
Acosta, Cecilio P	Nov 22, 1946	E	F	N	Borgmann, Glenn C	May 25, 1950	U	1	F
Adams, Robert OF	Jul 22, 1948	P	1	2	Bosman, Richard P	Feb 17, 1944	H	E	2
Alomar, Santos (Sandy) 2ND	Oct 19, 1943	B	Y	E	Bostock, Lyman OF	Nov 22, 1950	R	L	W
Albury, Victor P	May 12, 1947	P	J	T	Boswell, Ken 2ND	Feb 23, 1946	J	O	E
Alcala, Santo P	Dec 23, 1952	U	R	Z	Bourque, Patrick 1ST	Mar 23, 1947	L	P	B
Alexander, Doyle P	Sep 4, 1950	G	Q	J	Bowa, Lawrence SS	Dec 6, 1945	W	T	Z
Alexander Jr., Matthew IF	Jan 30, 1947	E	T	Q	Bradford, Charles (Buddy) OF	Jul 25, 1944	F	Y	V
Allen, Lloyd P	May 8, 1950	C	J	W	Bradley, Thomas P	Mar 16, 1947	D	H	3
Allen, Richard (Dick) 1ST	Mar 8, 1942	K	W	J	Braun, Stephen OF	May 8, 1949	F	H	U
Alou, Jesus OF	Mar 24, 1943	X	L	2	Breeden, Harold 1ST	Jun 28, 1944	B	Z	2
Alvarado, Luis Cesar IF	Jan 15, 1949	H	G	F	Brett, George 3RD	May 15, 1953	B	U	C
Alvarez, Jesus Orlando OF	Feb 28, 1952	U	1	X	Brett, Kenneth P	Sep 18, 1948	D	3	T
Anderson, Michael OF	Jun 22, 1951	W	2	C	Brewer, James P	Nov 17, 1937	B	S	V
Andujar, Joaquin P	Dec 21, 1952	S	P	X	Briggs, John OF	Mar 10, 1944	G	2	Q
Apodaca, Robert P	Jan 31, 1950	V	Y	Y	Briles, Nelson P	Aug 5, 1943	T	E	4
Armbrister, Edison (Ed) OF	Jul 4, 1948	U	H	J	Brinkman, Edwin SS	Dec 8, 1941	M	Q	S
Arnold, Christopher OF	Nov 6, 1947	J	T	7	Broberg, Peter P	Mar 2, 1950	E	1	V
Auerbach, Fredrick (Rick) SS	Feb 15, 1950	N	L	F	Brock, Louis OF	Jun 18, 1939	E	H	E
Ayala, Benigno (Benny) OF	Feb 7, 1951	B	D	8	Brohamer Jr., John 2ND	Feb 26, 1950	A	W	R
					Brown, Jackie P	May 31, 1943	W	X	1
Bahnson, Stanley P	Dec 15, 1944	L	2	7	Brown, Ollie OF	Feb 11, 1944	B	2	V
Bailey, Robert 3RD	Oct 13, 1942	W	R	5	Brown, William (Gates) OF	May 2, 1939	D	R	Y
Baker, Johnnie (Dusty) 2ND	Jun 15, 1949	V	S	Z	Bryant, Ronald P	Nov 12, 1947	P	Z	E
Baldwin, Ricky P	Jun 1, 1953	T	J	U	Brye, Stephen OF	Feb 4, 1949	E	2	1
Bando, Salvatore (Sal) 3RD	Feb 13, 1944	D	A	X	Buckner, William OF	Dec 14, 1949	T	D	J
Bannister, Alan OF	Sep 3, 1951	C	Q	K	Bumbry, Alonza OF	Apr 21, 1947	R	Q	6
Barr, James P	Feb 10, 1948	N	C	4	Burgmeier, Thomas P	Aug 2, 1943	Q	B	1
Baylor, Donald OF	Jun 28, 1949	L	C	E	Burleson, Richard (Rick) SS	Apr 29, 1951	O	A	P
Beckert, Glenn 2ND	Oct 12, 1940	D	O	Z	Burroughs, Jeffrey OF	Mar 7, 1951	G	D	3
Beene, Fred P	Nov 24, 1942	S	C	F	Busby, Steven P	Sep 29, 1949	M	M	7
Belanger, Mark SS	Jun 8, 1944	E	E	G	Buskey, Thomas P	Feb 20, 1947	C	M	D
Bell, David (Buddy) 3RD	Aug 27, 1951	T	J	C	Butler, William P	Mar 12, 1947	X	D	Y
Bench, Johnny C	Dec 7, 1947	R	W	5					
Beniquez, Juan OF	May 13, 1950	H	O	2	Cabell Jr., Enos IF	Oct 8, 1949	V	V	H
Berry, Allen (Ken) OF	May 10, 1941	G	3	D	Caldwell, Ralph P	Jan 22, 1949	P	O	N
Bevacqua, Kurt IF	Jan 23, 1947	V	M	J	Campaneris, Dagoberto (Bert) SS	Mar 9, 1942	L	X	K
Bibby, James P	Oct 29, 1944	K	H	S	Campbell, David IF	Jan 14, 1942	C	Z	W
Bittner, Lawrence OF	Jul 27, 1945	E	2	Z	Campbell, William P	Aug 9, 1948	K	Q	M
Billingham, John (Jack) P	Feb 21, 1943	P	H	4	Capra, Lee (Buzz) P	Oct 1, 1947	T	L	4
Billings, Richard C	Dec 4, 1942	E	N	Q	Carbo, Bernie OF	Aug 5, 1947	H	K	E
Bird, James P	Mar 5, 1950	H	A	Y	Cardenal, Jose OF	Oct 7, 1943	N	M	1
Blair, Dennis P	Jun 5, 1954	U	O	1	Cardenas, Leonardo (Leo) SS	Dec 17, 1938	F	V	U
Blair, Paul OF	Feb 1, 1944	P	R	L	Carew, Rodney 2ND	Oct 1, 1945	B	J	Z
Blanks, Larvell IF	Jan 28, 1950	S	V	V	Carlton, Steven P	Dec 22, 1944	S	F	F
Blomberg, Ronald OF	Aug 23, 1948	A	B	1	Carrithers, Donald P	Sep 15, 1949	V	1	S
Blue Jr., Vida P	Jul 28, 1949	S	E	B	Carroll, Clay P	May 2, 1941	W	U	4
Blyleven, Rikalbert (Burt) P	April 6, 1951	O	F	Z	Carroll, Thomas P	Nov 5, 1952	S	Z	K
Bochte, Bruce 1ST	Nov 12, 1950	G	A	M	Carter, Gary C	Apr 8, 1954	H	M	A
Boisclair, Bruce OF	Dec 9, 1952	F	C	L	Carty, Ricardo (Rico) OF	Sep 1, 1939	L	2	O
Bonds, Bobby Lee OF	Mar 15, 1946	F	F	Z	Casanova, Paulino (Paul) C	Dec 31, 1941	M	L	H
Bonham, William P	Oct 1, 1948	R	N	7					

NAME	DATE OF BIRTH	CODE			NAME	DATE OF BIRTH	CODE		
Cash Jr., David **2ND**	Jun 11, 1948	U	N	T	Egan, Thomas **C**	Jun 9, 1946	X	H	M
Cater, Danny **1ST**	Feb 25, 1940	D	H	1	Ellis Jr., Dock **P**	Mar 11, 1945	E	A	T
Cadeno, Cesar **OF**	Feb 25, 1951	U	W	S	Ellis, John **C**	Aug 21, 1948	W	3	Y
Cey, Ronald **3RD**	Feb 15, 1948	S	H	A	Etchebarren, Andrew **C**	Jun 20, 1943	T	P	Q
Chalk, David Lee **SS**	Aug 30, 1950	B	L	D	Evans, Darrell **3RD**	May 26, 1947	F	X	8
Chambliss, Carroll **1ST**	Dec 26, 1948	L	P	T	Evans, Dwight **OF**	Nov 3, 1951	S	V	E
Champion Jr., Buford Billy **P**	Sep 18, 1947	F	1	Q	Fairey, James **OF**	Sep 22, 1944	T	2	O
Chaney, Darrel **SS**	Mar 9, 1948	S	C	Y	Fairly, Ronald **OF**	Jul 12, 1938	J	C	2
Christenson, Larry **P**	Nov 10, 1953	U	C	R	Fanzone, Carmen **IF**	Aug 30, 1941	D	3	R
Cleveland, Reginald **P**	May 23, 1948	A	W	8	Ferguson, Joseph **C**	Sep 19, 1946	K	1	P
Clines, Eugene **OF**	Oct 6, 1946	D	P	7	Fidrych, Mark **P**	Aug 14, 1954	V	3	5
Clyde, David **P**	Apr 22, 1955	T	2	R	Figueroa, Edwardo **P**	Oct 14, 1948	G	1	M
Coggins, Richard **OF**	Dec 7, 1950	J	1	D	Fingers, Roland **P**	Aug 25, 1946	H	A	X
Colbert Jr., Nathan (Nate) **OF**	Apr 9, 1946	H	C	R	Fisk, Carlton **C**	Dec 26, 1947	N	A	Q
Colborn, James **P**	May 22, 1946	E	S	2	Fitzmorris, Alan **P**	Mar 21, 1946	M	M	6
Coleman, Joseph **P**	Feb 3, 1947	J	X	U	Floyd, Robert **IF**	Oct 20, 1943	C	Z	F
Coluccio Jr., Robert **OF**	Oct 2, 1951	J	R	F	Flynn Jr., Robert **SS**	Apr 18, 1951	C	S	D
Concepcion, David **SS**	Jun 17, 1948	C	T	Z	Foli, Timothy **SS**	Dec 8, 1950	K	2	E
Conigliaro, Anthony **OF**	Jan 7, 1945	L	W	W	Folkers, Richard **P**	Oct 17, 1946	P	1	K
Cooper, Cecil **1ST**	Dec 20, 1949	B	K	P	Foote, Barry **C**	Feb 16, 1952	H	O	L
Corbin, Alton **P**	Feb 12, 1949	N	G	A	Ford Sr., Darnell **OF**	May 19, 1952	J	X	E
Correll Jr., Victor **C**	Feb 5, 1946	O	Y	U	Forsch, Kenneth **P**	Sep 8, 1946	W	P	D
Cosgrove, Michael **P**	Feb 17, 1951	M	O	K	Forsch, Robert **P**	Jan 13, 1950	C	F	F
Cowens Jr., Alfred (Al) **OF**	Oct 25, 1951	J	M	4	Forster, Terry **P**	Jan 14, 1952	V	J	L
Cox, James **2ND**	May 28, 1950	X	A	J	Fosse, Raymond **C**	Apr 4, 1947	X	2	0
Cox, Larry **C**	Sep 11, 1947	W	T	J	Foster, Alan **P**	Dec 8, 1946	V	W	4
Crawford, Willie **OF**	Sep 7, 1946	V	O	C	Foster, George **OF**	Dec 1, 1948	J	S	2
Crosby, Edward **IF**	May 26, 1949	A	1	E	Foster, Leonard **SS**	Feb 2, 1951	U	2	3
Crowley, Terrence **IF**	Feb 16, 1947	W	H	8	Foucalt, Steven **P**	Oct 3, 1949	Q	Q	C
Cruz, Cirilo (Tommy) **OF**	Apr 2, 1953	E	E	1	Frailing, Kenneth **P**	Jan 19, 1948	O	J	G
Cruz, Hector **OF**	Apr 2, 1953	E	E	1	Fregosi, James **SS**	Apr 4, 1942	O	V	C
Cruz, Jose **OF**	Aug 8, 1941	L	N	H	Freisleban, David **P**	Oct 31, 1951	P	S	B
Cuellar, Miguel (Mike) **P**	May 8, 1937	Q	V	1	Frias, Jesus **SS**	Jul 14, 1948	G	S	T
Culver Jr., George **P**	Jul 8, 1943	O	E	A	Fryman, Woodrow **P**	Apr 12, 1940	E	2	G
Curtis, John **P**	Mar 9, 1948	S	C	Y	Fuentes, Rigoberto (Tito) **2ND**	Jan 4, 1944	K	R	Q
D'Acquisto, John **P**	Dec 24, 1951	X	Q	X	Fuller, James **OF**	Nov 28, 1950	X	R	3
Dal Canton, John **P**	Jun 15, 1942	R	J	J	Gallagher, Robert **OF**	Jul 7, 1948	X	L	M
Darcy, Patrick **P**	May 12, 1950	G	N	1	Gamble, Oscar **OF**	Dec 20, 1949	B	K	P
Darwin, Arthur **OF**	Feb 16, 1943	K	C	Y	Garber, Henry **P**	Nov 13, 1947	Q	1	F
Davis, Herman (Tommy) **OF**	Mar 21, 1939	H	C	P	Garcia, Pedro **2ND**	Apr 17, 1950	E	Q	A
Davis, William **OF**	Apr 15, 1940	H	B	K	Garland, Marcus **P**	Oct 26, 1950	N	M	3
Decinces, Douglas **3RD**	Aug 29, 1950	A	K	C	Garman, Michael **P**	Sep 16, 1949	W	2	T
Decker Jr., George (Joe) **P**	Jun 16, 1947	D	Q	V	Garner, Philip **2ND**	Apr 30, 1949	V	3	M
Demery, Lawrence **P**	Jun 4, 1953	W	M	X	Garr, Ralph **OF**	Dec 12, 1945	E	Z	6
Dempsey, John Rick **C**	Sep 13, 1949	T	Y	Q	Garrett Jr., Henry **OF**	Jan 13, 1943	M	P	N
Denny, John **P**	Nov 8, 1952	V	3	N	Garrett, Ronald **3RD**	Dec 3, 1947	N	S	1
Dent, Russell (Bucky) **SS**	Nov 25, 1951	R	P	2	Garvey, Steven **1ST**	Dec 22, 1948	G	L	P
Didier, Robert **C**	Feb 16, 1949	R	L	E	Gaston, Clarence **OF**	Mar 17, 1944	O	F	X
Dierker, Lawrence **P**	Sep 22, 1946	N	A	S	Gentry, Gary **P**	Oct 6, 1946	D	P	7
Dobson, Charles (Chuck) **P**	Jan 10, 1944	Q	X	W	Geronimo, Cesar **OF**	Mar 11, 1948	U	E	1
Dobson Jr., Patrick **P**	Feb 12, 1942	J	1	S	Gibson, Robert **P**	Nov 9, 1935	W	G	H
Doherty, John **1ST**	Aug 22, 1951	O	D	6	Giusti Jr., David **P**	Nov 27, 1939	F	B	B
Downing, Alphonso (Al) **P**	Jun 28, 1941	K	V	U	Gogolewski, William **P**	Oct 26, 1947	V	H	V
Downing, Brian **C**	Oct 9, 1950	T	X	L	Goltz, David **P**	Jun 23, 1949	F	1	8
Doyle, Robert (Denny) **2ND**	Jan 17, 1944	X	B	4	Gomez, Luis **SS**	Aug 19, 1951	L	A	3
Drago, Richard **P**	Jun 25, 1945	T	X	1	Goodman Jr., James **3RD**	Jan 25, 1948	U	P	N
Driessen, Daniel **1ST**	Jul 29, 1951	N	H	G	Gossage, Richard **P**	Jul 5, 1951	M	M	Q
Duffy, Frank **SS**	Oct 14, 1946	M	X	G	Grabarkewitz, Billy **IF**	Jan 18, 1946	T	F	B
Duncan, David **C**	Sep 26, 1945	U	D	U	Granger, Wayne **P**	Mar 15, 1944	M	D	V
Dunning, Steven **P**	May 15, 1949	N	P	2	Greif, William **P**	Apr 25, 1950	N	Y	J
Dwyer, James **OF**	Jan 3, 1950	Q	Y	4	Grich, Robert **2ND**	Jan 15, 1949	H	G	F
Dyer, Don (Duffy) **C**	Aug 15, 1945	A	S	L	Grieve, Thomas **OF**	Mar 4, 1948	N	1	T
Easterly, James **P**	Feb 17, 1953	G	R	P	Griffey, George Kenneth **OF**	Apr 10, 1950	V	J	2
Eastwick III, Rawlins **P**	Oct 24, 1950	L	K	1	Griffin Jr., Douglas **2ND**	Jun 4, 1947	P	D	J
Eckersley, Dennis **P**	Oct 3, 1954	B	W	O	Griffin, Thomas **P**	Feb 22, 1948	B	P	H

79

NAME	DATE OF BIRTH	CODE			NAME	DATE OF BIRTH	CODE		
Grimsley II, Ross **P**	Jan 7, 1950	U	3	8	Jackson, Grant **P**	Sep 28, 1942	G	B	P
Gross, Gregory **OF**	Aug 1, 1952	O	N	N	Jackson, Reginald **OF**	May 18, 1946	A	O	X
Grote, Gerald (Jerry) **C**	Oct 6, 1942	P	K	X	Jefferson Jr., Jesse **P**	Mar 3, 1950	F	2	W
Grubb Jr., John **OF**	Aug 4, 1948	E	L	G	Jenkins, Ferguson **P**	Dec 13, 1943	L	X	2
Guerrero, Mario (Mike) **SS**	Sep 28, 1950	H	M	8	John, Thomas **P**	May 22, 1943	N	O	U
Gullett, Donald **P**	Jan 6, 1951	Q	3	A	Johnson, Alexander **OF**	Dec 7, 1942	H	Q	T
Gura, Lawrence **P**	Nov 26, 1947	F	L	T	Johnson, Clair (Bart) **P**	Jan 3, 1950	Q	Y	4
Hahn, Donald **OF**	Nov 16, 1948	R	C	M	Johnson Jr., Clifford **OF**	Jul 22, 1947	R	Y	Y
Hall, Tom **P**	Nov 23, 1947	C	H	Q	Johnson, David **2ND**	Jan 30, 1943	Q	O	G
Hairston, Jerry **OF**	Feb 16, 1952	H	O	L	Johnson, Deron **1ST**	Jul 17, 1938	O	H	7
Hale, John **OF**	Aug 5, 1953	P	S	T	Johnson, Jerry **P**	Dec 3, 1943	A	N	R
Halicki, Edward **P**	Oct 4, 1950	O	S	F	Johnson, Robert **P**	Apr 25, 1943	J	P	1
Hamilton, David **P**	Dec 13, 1947	X	3	C	Johnson, Thomas **P**	Apr 2, 1951	K	B	V
Hands, Jr., William **P**	May 6, 1940	F	X	6	Johnson, Timothy **SS**	Jul 22, 1949	M	2	4
Haney, Wallace (Larry) **C**	Nov 19, 1942	N	1	A	Johnstone Jr., John (Jay) **OF**	Nov 20, 1945	F	C	J
Hansen, Robert **1ST**	May 26, 1948	D	Z	C	Jones, Cleon **OF**	Aug 4, 1942	V	C	1
Hardy, Howard **P**	Jan 10, 1948	E	3	6	Jones, Randell **P**	Jan 12, 1950	B	E	E
Hargan, Steven **P**	Sep 8, 1942	K	K	3	Jorgensen, Michael **OF**	Aug 16, 1948	R	X	T
Hargrove, Dudley (Michael) **1ST**	Oct 26, 1949	Q	L	1	Joshua, Von **OF**	May 1, 1948	B	3	L
Harmon, Terry **SS**	Apr 12, 1944	R	D	Q	Kaat, James **P**	Nov 7, 1938	M	J	N
Harper, Tommy **OF**	Oct 14, 1940	F	Q	2	Kelly, Harold **OF**	Jul 30, 1944	L	A	1
Harrah, Colbert (Toby) **SS**	Oct 26, 1948	T	K	Y	Kendall, Fred **C**	Jan 31, 1949	A	X	W
Harrelson, Derrell (Bud) **SS**	Jun 6, 1944	C	C	E	Kennedy, Junior Raymond **IF**	Aug 9, 1950	D	S	Q
Harris, Victor **2ND**	Mar 27, 1950	G	X	N	Kessinger, Donald **SS**	Jul 17, 1942	C	N	H
Harrison, Roric **P**	Sep 20, 1946	L	2	Q	Kingman, David **OF**	Dec 21, 1948	F	K	O
Hassler, Andrew **P**	Oct 18, 1951	B	E	W	Kirby Jr., Clayton **P**	Jun 25, 1948	L	2	8
Haely, Francis **C**	Sep 6, 1946	U	N	B	Kirkpatrick, Edgar **OF**	Oct 8, 1944	M	P	5
Hebner, Richard **3RD**	Nov 26, 1947	F	L	T	Kison, Bruce **P**	Feb 18, 1950	Q	O	J
Hedlund, Michael **P**	Aug 11, 1946	R	P	J	Kline, Steven **P**	Oct 6, 1947	A	Q	A
Hegan, James **1ST**	Jul 21, 1942	G	R	M	Knowles, Darold **P**	Dec 9, 1941	N	R	T
Heidemann, Jack **SS**	Jul 11, 1949	A	Q	S	Knox, John **2ND**	Jul 26, 1948	T	B	6
Heintzelman, Thomas **IF**	Nov 3, 1946	J	P	2	Kobel, Kevin **P**	Oct 2, 1953	D	U	L
Heise, Robert **IF**	May 12, 1947	P	J	T	Koosman, Jerry **P**	Dec 23, 1942	A	D	B
Helms, Tommy **2ND**	May 5, 1941	B	X	7	Kosco, Andrew **OF**	Oct 5, 1941	R	H	U
Henderson, Kenneth **OF**	Jun 15, 1946	F	O	S	Kranepool, Edward **1ST**	Nov 8, 1944	U	S	3
Hendrick Jr., George **OF**	Oct 18, 1949	H	C	S	Krausse Jr., Lewis **P**	Apr 25, 1943	J	P	1
Hendricks, Elrod (Ellie) **C**	Dec 22, 1940	F	A	5	Kubiak, Theodore **IF**	May 12, 1942	F	C	H
Hernandez, Enzo **SS**	Feb 12, 1949	N	G	A	Kucek, John **P**	Jun 8, 1953	C	Q	2
Hernandez, Ramon **P**	Aug 31, 1940	H	3	Q	Kusick, Craig **1ST**	Sep 30, 1948	Q	M	6
Herrmann, Edward **C**	Aug 27, 1946	K	C	Z	LaCock Jr., Ralph (Pete) **OF**	Jan 17, 1952	A	M	O
Hilgendorf, Thomas **P**	Mar 10, 1942	M	Y	L	Lacy, Leondaus (Lee) **2ND**	Apr 10, 1949	A	M	Z
Hiller, John **P**	Apr 8, 1943	P	1	J	LaGrow, Lerrin **P**	Jul 8, 1948	A	M	N
Hilton, John **IF**	Sep 15, 1950	S	2	U	Lahoud, Jr., Joseph **OF**	Apr 14, 1947	K	J	Y
Hiser, Gene **OF**	Dec 11, 1948	T	3	D	Lamont, Gene **C**	Dec 25, 1946	P	L	N
Hisle, Larry **OF**	May 5, 1947	H	B	M	Lange, Richard **P**	Sep 1, 1948	K	L	B
Hodges, Ronald **C**	Jun 22, 1949	E	Z	7	LaRoche, David **P**	May 14, 1948	P	N	Y
Hoerner, Joseph **P**	Nov 12, 1936	X	M	O	Lavelle, Gary **P**	Jan 3, 1949	T	X	2
Holdsworth, Frederick **P**	May 29, 1952	T	E	P	Lee, Leron **OF**	Mar 4, 1948	N	1	T
Holt, James **OF**	May 27, 1944	Q	V	3	Lee III, William **P**	Dec 28, 1946	S	O	Q
Holtzman, Kenneth **P**	Nov 3, 1945	M	O	Z	LeFlore, Ronald **OF**	Jun 16, 1952	O	X	8
Hood, Donald **P**	Oct 16, 1949	F	A	Q	Leon, Eduardo (Eddie) **IF**	Aug 11, 1946	R	P	J
Hooton, Burt **P**	Feb 7, 1950	E	C	6	Leon, Maximino **P**	Feb 4, 1950	B	3	3
Horton, Willie **OF**	Oct 18, 1942	D	W	B	Leonard, Dennis **P**	May 8, 1951	X	K	Y
Hosley, Timothy **C**	May 10, 1947	N	G	R	Lersch, Barry **P**	Sep 7, 1944	D	M	7
Hough, Charles **P**	Jan 5, 1948	X	X	1	Linblad, Paul **P**	Aug 9, 1941	F	G	4
House, Thomas **P**	Apr 29, 1947	B	Y	F	Lintz, Larry **SS**	Oct 10, 1949	X	X	K
Howard, Wilbur **OF**	Jan 8, 1949	A	3	7	Linzy, Frank **P**	Sep 15, 1940	X	P	6
Howe Jr., Arthur **3RD**	Dec 15, 1946	E	A	C	Lis, Joseph **1ST**	Aug 15, 1946	V	T	N
Hrabosky, Alan **P**	Jul 21, 1949	L	1	3	Llenas, Winston **IF**	Sep 23, 1943	W	1	M
Hughes, James **P**	Jul 2, 1951	J	J	N	Locker, Robert **P**	Mar 15, 1938	E	Y	G
Humphrey, Terryal **C**	Aug 4, 1949	B	M	J	Locklear, Gene **OF**	Jul 19, 1949	J	Y	1
Hundley, Cecil **C**	Jun 1, 1942	C	X	3	Lockwood Jr., Claude (Skip) **P**	Aug 17, 1946	X	V	P
Hunt, Ronald **IF**	Feb 23, 1941	X	H	2	Lolich, Michael (Mickey) **P**	Sep 12, 1940	U	M	3
Hunter, James (Catfish) **P**	Apr 8, 1946	G	B	Q	Lonborg, James **P**	Apr 16, 1942	C	E	P
Hutton, Thomas **1ST**	Apr 20, 1946	T	O	U	Lopes, David **2ND**	May 3, 1946	J	2	H
Ivie, Michael **1ST**	Aug 8, 1952	V	U	U	Lovitto Jr., Joseph **OF**	Jan 6, 1951	Q	3	A

NAME	DATE OF BIRTH	CODE			NAME	DATE OF BIRTH	CODE		
Lowenstein, John **IF**	Jan 27, 1947	B	Q	N	Moran, Carl **P**	Sep 26, 1950	F	K	6
Lum, Michael **OF**	Oct 27, 1945	E	G	S	Moret, Rogelio (Roger) **P**	Sep 16, 1949	W	2	T
Luzinski, Gregory **OF**	Nov 22, 1950	R	L	W	Morgan, Joe **2ND**	Sep 19, 1943	S	W	H
Lyle, Albert (Sparky) **P**	Jul 22, 1944	C	V	S	Morlan, John **P**	Nov 22, 1947	B	G	P
Lynn, Fredric **OF**	Feb 3, 1952	S	A	6	Morris, John **P**	Aug 23, 1941	U	V	K
Maddox, Elliott **OF**	Dec 21, 1948	F	K	O	Morton, Carl **P**	Jan 18, 1944	A	C	5
Maddox, Garry **OF**	Sep 1, 1949	G	M	D	Moses, Gerald **C**	Aug 9, 1946	P	N	G
Madlock Jr., Bill **3RD**	Jan 2, 1951	M	Y	5	Mota, Manuel **OF**	Feb 18, 1938	C	2	P
Mangual, Angel **OF**	Mar 19, 1947	G	L	6	Munson, Thurman **C**	Jun 7, 1947	S	G	M
Mangual, Jose **OF**	May 23, 1952	N	2	J	Murcer, Bobby **OF**	May 20, 1946	C	Q	Z
Marshall, Michael **P**	Jan 15, 1943	A	2	Z	Murphy, Thomas **P**	Dec 30, 1945	X	P	Q
Martinez, Felix **P**	May 31, 1950	C	D	M	Murray, Dale **P**	Feb 2, 1950	X	1	1
Martinez, John (Buck) **C**	Nov 7, 1948	H	W	C	Murrell, Ivan **OF**	Apr 24, 1945	C	R	5
Martinez, Teodoro (Teddy) **IF**	Dec 10, 1947	U	Z	8	Muser, Anthony **1ST**	Aug 1, 1947	D	F	A
Mason, James **SS**	Aug 14, 1950	J	X	V	Nelson, David **2ND**	Jun 20, 1944	R	R	T
Matlack, Jonathan **P**	Jan 19, 1950	J	M	M	Nelson, Roger **P**	Jun 7, 1944	D	D	F
Mattews, Gary **OF**	Jul 5, 1950	P	L	O	Nettles, Graig **3RD**	Aug 20, 1944	J	W	O
May, Carlos **OF**	May 17, 1948	S	Q	2	Nettles Jr., Morris **OF**	Jan 26, 1952	K	V	X
May, David **OF**	Dec 23, 1943	V	E	D	Niekro, Joseph **P**	Nov 7, 1944	T	R	2
May, Lee **1ST**	Mar 23, 1943	W	K	1	Niekro, Philip **P**	Apr 1, 1939	T	O	1
May, Milton **C**	Aug 1, 1950	T	K	H	Nolan, Gary **P**	May 27, 1948	E	1	D
May Jr., Rudolph **P**	Jul 18, 1944	W	R	O	Norman, Fredie **P**	Aug 20, 1942	O	T	J
Mayberry, John **1ST**	Feb 18, 1950	Q	O	J	North, William **OF**	May 15, 1948	Q	2	Q
McAnally, Ernest **P**	Aug 15, 1946	V	T	N	Northrup, James **OF**	Nov 24, 1939	C	2	7
McBride, Arnold Ray **OF**	Feb 3, 1949	D	1	Z	Oates, Johnny **C**	Jan 21, 1946	W	J	E
McCarver, James **C**	Oct 16, 1941	E	T	6	Odom, Johnny (Blue Moon) **P**	May 29, 1945	P	Y	7
McCovey, Willie **1ST**	Jan 10, 1938	K	Q	J	Office, Rowland **OF**	Oct 25, 1952	G	O	7
McCraw, Tommy **OF**	Nov 21, 1940	V	1	7	Oglivie, Benjamin **OF**	Feb 11, 1949	M	F	8
McDaniel, Lyndall **P**	Dec 13, 1935	K	N	J	Oliva, Antonio (Tony) **OF**	Jul 20, 1940	M	O	G
McEnaney, William **P**	Feb 14, 1952	F	M	J	Oliver, Jr., Albert **OF**	Oct 14, 1946	M	X	G
McGlothen, Lynn **P**	Mar 27, 1950	G	X	N	Oliver, Robert **OF**	Feb 8, 1943	B	X	Q
McGraw Jr., Frank (Tug) **P**	Aug 30, 1944	T	D	Y	Ontiveros, Steven **IF**	Oct 26, 1951	K	N	5
McIntosh, Joseph **P**	Aug 4, 1951	T	O	N	Orta, Jorge **2ND**	Nov 26, 1950	V	P	1
McMullen, Kenneth **3RD**	Jun 1, 1942	C	X	3	Osteen, Claude **P**	Aug 9, 1939	L	D	Y
McNally, David **P**	Oct 31, 1942	R	G	P	Otis, Amos **OF**	Apr 26, 1947	W	V	C
McRae, Harold **OF**	Jul 10, 1946	H	L	K	Paciorek, Thomas **OF**	Nov 2, 1946	H	O	1
Medich, George **P**	Dec 9, 1948	R	1	B	Pagan, David **P**	Sep 15, 1949	V	1	S
Melendez, Luis **OF**	Aug 11, 1949	J	T	Q	Palmer, James **P**	Oct 15, 1945	Q	X	F
Melton, William **3RD**	Jul 7, 1945	H	G	E	Parker, David **OF**	Jun 9, 1951	J	O	X
Mendoza, Mario **SS**	Dec 26, 1950	E	R	X	Parker, Harry **P**	Sep 14, 1947	B	W	M
Meoli Jr., Rudolph **IF**	May 1, 1951	Q	C	R	Patek, Freddie **SS**	Oct 9, 1944	N	Q	6
Merritt, James **P**	Dec 9, 1943	G	T	X	Pattin, Martin **P**	Apr 6, 1943	N	Y	G
Messersmith, John (Andy) **P**	Aug 6, 1945	P	J	B	Pena, Orlando **P**	Nov 17, 1934	K	O	O
Metzger, Roger **SS**	Oct 10, 1947	E	U	E	Perez, Atanasio (Tony) **1ST**	May 14, 1942	H	E	K
Millan, Felix **2ND**	Aug 21, 1943	M	V	M	Perry, Gaylord **P**	Sep 15, 1938	E	M	1
Miller, Charles **IF**	Mar 3, 1947	O	X	P	Perry Jr., James **P**	Oct 30, 1936	K	2	A
Miller, Norman **OF**	Feb 5, 1946	O	Y	U	Peterson, Fred (Fritz) **P**	Feb 8, 1942	E	W	O
Miller, Richard **OF**	Apr 19, 1948	N	Q	7	Petrocelli, Americo (Rico) **3RD**	Jun 27, 1943	C	W	X
Miller, Robert **P**	Feb 18, 1939	X	3	R	Phillips, Michael **SS**	Aug 19, 1950	O	3	1
Milner, John **1st**	Dec 28, 1949	K	S	X	Pizarro, Juan **P**	Feb 7, 1937	S	P	B
Mingori, Stephen **P**	Feb 29, 1944	U	R	F	Plummer, William **C**	Mar 21, 1947	J	N	8
Mitchell, Robert **OF**	Oct 22, 1943	E	2	H	Pole, Richard **P**	Oct 13, 1950	X	2	P
Mitterwald, George **C**	Jun 7, 1945	A	E	H	Popovich, Paul **SS**	Aug 18, 1940	S	P	C
Moffitt, Randall **P**	Oct 13, 1948	F	Z	L	Porter, Darrell **C**	Jan 17, 1952	A	M	O
Monday Jr., Robert (Rick) **OF**	Nov 20, 1945	F	C	J	Powell, John **1ST**	Aug 17, 1941	O	P	D
Money, Donald **3RD**	Jun 7, 1947	S	G	M	Rader, David **C**	Dec 26, 1948	L	P	T
Montague Jr., John **P**	Sep 12, 1947	X	U	K	Rader, Douglas **3RD**	Jul 30, 1944	L	A	I
Montanez, Guillermo (Willie) **1ST**	Apr 1, 1948	S	1	O	Ramirez, Orlando **SS**	Dec 18, 1951	R	K	R
					Randle, Leonard **SS**	Feb 12, 1949	N	G	A
Montefusco Jr., John **P**	May 25, 1950	U	1	F	Randolph, William **2ND**	Jul 6, 1954	E	R	Y
Montgomery, Robert **C**	Apr 16, 1944	V	H	U	Rau, Douglas **P**	Dec 15, 1948	X	D	H
Moore, Balor Lilbon **P**	Jan 25, 1951	M	T	U	Ray, James **P**	Dec 1, 1944	U	N	S
Moore Jr., Charles **C**	Jun 21, 1953	Q	A	G	Reed, Ronald **P**	Nov 2, 1942	T	J	R
Moose Jr., Robert **P**	Oct 9, 1947	D	T	D	Reitz, Kenneth **3RD**	Jun 23, 1951	X	3	D
Morales, Jose **C**	Dec 30, 1945	X	P	Q	Renko, Jr., Steven **P**	Dec 10, 1944	F	W	2
Morales, Julio **OF**	Feb 18, 1949	T	N	G	Rettenmund, Mervin **OF**	Jun 6, 1943	E	A	B

NAME	DATE OF BIRTH	CODE			NAME	DATE OF BIRTH	CODE		
Reuschel, Ricky **P**	May 16, 1949	O	Q	3	Spittorff, Paul **P**	Oct 8, 1946	F	R	A
Reuss, Jerry **P**	Jun 19, 1949	B	W	4	Sprague, Edward **P**	Sep 16, 1945	K	W	K
Reynolds, Robert **P**	Jan 21, 1947	T	K	G	Stanhouse, Donald **P**	Feb 12, 1951	G	J	E
Rhoden, Richard (Rick) **P**	May 16, 1953	C	V	D	Stanley, Frederick **SS**	Aug 13, 1947	Q	S	N
Rice, James **OF**	Mar 8, 1953	C	H	A	Stanley, Mitchell **OF**	Jul 20, 1942	F	Q	L
Richard, James **P**	Mar 7, 1950	K	C	1	Stanton, Leroy **OF**	Apr 10, 1946	J	D	S
Rivers, John (Mickey) **OF**	Oct 31, 1948	A	P	4	Stargell, Wilver (Willie) **OF**	Mar 6, 1941	L	T	E
Roberts, David Arthur **P**	Sep 11, 1944	H	Q	C	Staub, Daniel (Rusty) **OF**	Apr 1, 1944	F	V	E
Roberts, David Wayne **IF**	Feb 17, 1951	M	O	K	Stearns, John **C**	Aug 21, 1951	N	C	5
Roberts, Leon **OF**	Jan 22, 1951	J	Q	R	Stennett, Renaldo **2ND**	Apr 5, 1951	N	E	Y
Robertson, Robert **1ST**	Oct 2, 1946	X	L	3	Stinson III, Gorrell **C**	Oct 11, 1945	M	T	B
Robinson, Jr., Brooks **3RD**	May 18, 1937	C	C	C	Stone Jr., George **P**	Jul 9, 1946	G	K	J
Robinson, Craig **SS**	Aug 21, 1948	W	3	Y	Stone, Steven **P**	Jul 14, 1947	J	Q	Q
Robinson, Jr., William **OF**	Jun 26, 1943	B	V	W	Strom, Brent **P**	Oct 14, 1948	G	1	M
Rodriguez, Aurelio **3RD**	Dec 28, 1947	P	P	S	Sudakis, William **1F**	Mar 27, 1946	S	S	D
Rodriguez, Eduardo **P**	Mar 6, 1952	D	E	5	Sundberg, James **C**	May 18, 1951	K	U	A
Rodriguez, Eliseo **C**	May 24, 1946	G	U	4	Sutherland, Gary **1F**	Sep 27, 1944	A	D	T
Rogers, Stephen **P**	Oct 26, 1949	Q	L	1	Sutton, Donald **P**	Apr 2, 1945	D	X	H
Rojas, Octavio (Cookie) **2ND**	Mar 6, 1939	Q	Q	8	Swan, Craig **P**	Nov 30, 1950	B	T	5
Romo, Vicente **P**	May 21, 1943	M	N	T	Swisher, Steven **C**	Aug 9, 1951	A	T	S
Roof, Philip **C**	Mar 5, 1941	K	S	D	Tanana, Frank **P**	Jul 3, 1953	E	N	T
Rooker, James **P**	Sep 23, 1941	E	Y	H	Tate, Randall **P**	Oct 23, 1952	E	M	5
Rose, Peter **3RD**	Apr 14, 1942	A	C	N	Taveras, Franklin **SS**	Dec 24, 1950	C	P	V
Rosello, David **SS**	Jun 26, 1950	F	B	E	Taylor, Antonio (Tony) **1F**	Dec 19, 1935	Q	T	P
Ross, Gary **P**	Sep. 16, 1947	D	Y	O	Tenace, Gene **C**	Oct 10, 1946	H	T	C
Royster, Jeron (Jerry) **IF**	Oct 18, 1952	X	G	Z	Terrell, Jerry **IF**	Jul 13, 1946	L	O	N
Rudi, Joseph **OF**	Sep 7, 1946	V	O	C	Thomas, Derrel **IF**	Jan 14, 1951	A	H	J
Rudolph, Kenneth **C**	Dec 29, 1946	T	P	R	Thomasson, Gary **1ST**	Jul 29, 1951	N	H	G
Ruhle, Vernon **P**	Jan 25, 1951	M	T	U	Thompson, Danny **SS**	Feb 1, 1948	D	W	U
Russell, William **SS**	Oct 21, 1948	O	E	T	Thornton, Andre **1ST**	Aug 13, 1949	L	V	S
Ruthven, Richard **P**	Mar 27, 1952	D	Y	P	Tiant, Luis **P**	Nov 23, 1940	X	3	V
Ryan Jr., Lynn **P**	Jan 31, 1947	F	U	R	Tidrow, Richard **P**	May 14, 1947	R	L	A
Sadecki, Raymond **P**	Dec 26, 1940	K	E	A	Tolan, Robert **OF**	Nov 19, 1945	E	B	H
Sanders, Jr., Kenneth **P**	Jul 8, 1941	U	C	5	Torre, Joseph **3RD**	Jul 18, 1940	K	M	E
Sanders, Reginald (Reggie) **1st**	Sep 9, 1949	P	U	M	Torres, Jr., Rusty **OF**	Sep 30, 1948	Q	M	6
Sands, Charles **C**	Dec 17, 1947	D	D	G	Torrez, Michael **P**	Aug 28, 1946	L	D	1
Sanguillen, Manuel **C**	Mar 21, 1944	S	K	2	Tovar, Cesar **2B**	Jul 3, 1940	S	Z	X
Scarce, Guerrant (Mac) **P**	Apr 8, 1949	W	F	X	Trillo, Manny **2ND**	Dec 25, 1950	D	Q	W
Scherman, Jr., Frederick **P**	Jul 25, 1944	F	Y	V	Twitchell, Wayne **P**	Mar 10, 1948	T	D	Z
Schmidt, Michael **3RD**	Sep 27, 1949	K	K	5	Tyson, Michael **2ND**	Jan 13, 1950	C	F	F
Schneck, David **OF**	Jun 18, 1949	A	V	3	Unser, Delbert **OF**	Dec 9, 1944	E	V	1
Schueler, Ronald **P**	Apr 14, 1948	H	L	2	Upshaw Jr., Cecil **P**	Oct 22, 1942	H	1	F
Scott Jr., George **1ST**	Mar 23, 1944	U	M	4	Valentine, Robert **1F**	May 13, 1950	H	O	2
Seaver, George (Tom) **P**	Nov. 17, 1944	F	2	D	Velez, Otto **OF**	Nov 29, 1950	A	S	4
Segui, Diego **P**	Aug 17, 1938	W	L	5	Washington, Claudell **OF**	Aug 31, 1954	P	R	O
Sells, David **P**	Sep 18, 1946	J	Z	O	Watson, Robert **1ST**	Apr 10, 1946	J	D	S
Sharon, Richard **OF**	Apr 15, 1950	C	O	7	Watt, Eddie **P**	Apr 4, 1942	O	V	C
Sharp, William **OF**	Jan 18, 1950	H	L	L	White Jr., Frank **2ND**	Sep 4, 1950	G	Q	J
Shellenback, James **P**	Nov 18, 1943	J	1	B	White, Roy **OF**	Dec 27, 1943	B	J	H
Siebert, Wilfred (Sonny) **P**	Jan 14, 1937	R	T	L	Wilcox, Milton **P**	Apr 20, 1950	H	T	D
Simmons, Ted **C**	Aug 9, 1949	G	R	O	Williams, Billy **OF**	Jun 15, 1938	E	D	8
Simpson, Wayne **P**	Dec 2, 1948	K	T	3	Williams, Charles **P**	Oct 11, 1947	F	V	F
Singer, William **P**	Apr 24, 1944	F	Q	3	Williams Jr., Earl **C**	Jul 14, 1948	G	S	T
Singleton, Kenneth **OF**	Jun 10, 1947	V	K	P	Winfield, David **OF**	Oct 3, 1951	K	S	G
Sizemore, Ted **2ND**	Apr 15, 1945	R	H	V	Wise, Rick **P**	Sep 13, 1945	G	T	G
Slaton, James **P**	Jun 19, 1950	W	X	6	Wohlford, James **OF**	Feb 28, 1951	X	Z	V
Slayback, William **P**	Feb 21, 1948	A	O	G	Wood Jr., Wilbur **P**	Oct 22, 1941	L	Z	D
Smith, Carl (Reggie) **OF**	Apr 2, 1945	D	X	H	Woodson, Richard **P**	Mar 30, 1945	A	U	E
Soderholm, Eric **SS**	Sep 24, 1948	K	F	Z	Wright, Clyde **P**	Feb 20, 1943	O	G	3
Solaita, Tolia **1ST**	Jan 15, 1947	N	D	A	Wynn, James **OF**	Mar 12, 1942	O	1	N
Sosa, Elias **P**	Jun 10, 1950	N	O	W	Yastrzemski, Carl **OF**	Aug 22, 1939	A	R	D
Speier, Chris **SS**	Jun 28, 1950	H	D	G	Yeager, Stephen **C**	Nov 24, 1948	B	L	U
Spencer, James **1ST**	Jul 30, 1947	B	D	7	Yount, Robin **SS**	Sep 16, 1955	E	F	7
Spikes, Leslie Charles **OF**	Jan 23, 1951	K	R	S	Zachary, Patrick **P**	Apr 24, 1952	G	1	N
Spillner, Daniel **P**	Nov 27, 1951	T	R	4	Zisk, Richard **OF**	Feb 6, 1949	G	A	3
Spinks, Scipio **P**	Jul 12, 1947	G	O	O					

Basketball

NAME	DATE OF BIRTH	CODE			NAME	DATE OF BIRTH	CODE		
Abdul-Aziz, Zaid	Apr 7, 1946	F	A	P	Davis, Mel	Nov 9, 1950	D	1	J
Abdul-Jabbar, Kareem	Apr 16, 1947	M	L	1	Davis, Mickey	Jun 16, 1950	T	U	3
Adams, Don	Nov 27, 1947	G	M	U	Denton, Randy	Feb 18, 1949	T	N	G
Adelman, Rick	Jun 16, 1946	G	P	T	Dickey, Derrek	Mar 20, 1951	U	R	H
Allen, Lucius	Sep 26, 1947	O	F	Y	Digregorio, Ernie	Jan 15, 1951	B	J	K
Archibald, Nate	Apr 18, 1948	M	P	6	Drew, John	Sep 30, 1954	W	T	L
Ard, Jim	Sep 19, 1948	E	A	U	Driscoll, Terry	Aug 28, 1947	H	E	3
Averitt, William	Jul 22, 1952	D	C	C	Dudley, Charles	Mar 5, 1950	H	A	Y
Awtrey, Dennis	Feb 22, 1948	B	P	H	Eakins, Jim	May 24, 1946	G	U	4
Bantom, Mike	Dec 3, 1951	B	X	B	Eberhard, Al	May 10, 1952	X	O	4
Barnes, Marvin	Jul 27, 1952	J	H	H	Ellis, Leroy	Mar 10, 1940	S	W	G
Barnett, Jim	Jul 7, 1944	L	F	C	Elmore, Len	Mar 28, 1952	C	2	T
Barry, Rick	Mar 28, 1944	B	R	A	Erickson, Keith	Apr 19, 1944	A	L	X
Beard, Butch	May 4, 1947	G	A	L	Erving, Julius	Feb 22, 1950	U	S	N
Bing, Dave	Nov 24, 1943	P	D	H	Ford, Chris	Jan 11, 1949	D	C	B
Block, John	Apr 16, 1944	V	H	U	Foster, Fred	Mar 18, 1946	J	J	3
Boerwinkle, Tom	Aug 23, 1945	J	I	T	Fox, Jim	Apr 7, 1943	O	Z	H
Boone, Ron	Sep 6, 1946	U	N	B	Frazier, Walt	Mar 29, 1945	X	T	D
Bracey, Steve	Aug 1, 1950	T	K	H	Garrett, Rowland	Jul 16, 1950	C	W	Z
Brewer, Jim	Dec 3, 1951	B	X	B	Gervin, George	Apr 27, 1952	K	A	Q
Bridges, Bill	Apr 4, 1939	W	R	4	Gianelli, John	Jun 10, 1950	N	O	W
Brisker, John	Jun 15, 1947	C	P	U	Gibbs, Dick	Dec 20, 1948	E	J	N
Bristow, Allan	Aug 23, 1951	P	E	7	Gilliam, Herm	May 5, 1946	L	A	K
Brokaw, Gary	Jan 11, 1954	N	J	N	Goukas, Matt	Feb 25, 1944	Q	N	B
Brown, Fred	Jul 7, 1948	X	L	M	Goodrich, Gail	Apr 23, 1943	G	N	Y
Brown, John	Dec 14, 1951	N	F	N	Gray, Leonard	Dec 19, 1951	S	L	S
Brown, Roger	May 22, 1942	Q	N	S	Green, Lamar	Mar 22, 1947	K	O	A
Burleson, Tom	Feb 24, 1952	Q	W	T	Haskins, Clem	Aug 11, 1944	X	N	E
Calhoun, Corky	Nov 1, 1950	T	S	A	Havlicek, John	Apr 8, 1940	A	X	C
Calvin, Mack	Jul 27, 1948	U	C	7	Hawes, Steve	May 26, 1950	V	2	G
Carr, Austin	Mar 10, 1948	T	D	Z	Hawkins, Connie	Jul 17, 1942	C	N	H
Carter, Fred	Feb 14, 1945	C	D	2	Hawthorne, Nate	Jan 15, 1950	E	H	H
Catchings, Harvey	Sep 2, 1951	B	P	J	Hayes, Elvin	Nov 17, 1945	C	3	F
Chaney, Don	Mar 22, 1946	N	N	7	Haywood, Spencer	Apr 22, 1949	N	U	D
Charles, Ken	Jul 10, 1951	R	R	V	Heard, Garfield	May 3, 1948	D	B	N
Chenier, Phil	Oct 30, 1950	R	Q	7	Henderson, Tom	Jan 26, 1952	K	V	X
Chones, Jim	Nov 30, 1949	E	S	3	Hewitt, Bill	Aug 8, 1944	U	K	B
Clark, Archie	Jul 15, 1941	D	K	D	Hudson, Lou	Jul 11, 1944	P	K	G
Cleamons, Jim	Sep 13, 1949	T	Y	Q	Hummer, John	May 4, 1948	E	C	O
Clemens, Barry	May 1, 1942	S	U	5	Jackson, Phil	Sep 17, 1945	L	X	L
Coleman, E. C.	Sep 25, 1950	E	J	5	James, Aaron	Oct 5, 1952	K	W	M
Collins, Doug	Jul 28, 1951	M	G	F	Johnson, Charles	Mar 31, 1949	O	1	P
Counts, Mel	Oct 16, 1941	E	T	6	Johnson, George	Dec 18, 1948	C	G	L
Cowens, Dave	Oct 25, 1948	S	J	X	Johnson, Ollie	May 11, 1949	J	L	X
Dampier, Louie	Nov 20, 1944	J	B	G	Johnson, Wallace	Aug 31, 1952	V	P	K
Dandridge, Bob	Nov 15, 1947	S	3	H	Jones, Dwight	Feb 27, 1952	T	Z	W
Dark, Jessie	Sep 2, 1951	B	P	J	Jones, James	Jan 1, 1945	E	Q	Q
Davis, Dwight	Oct 28, 1949	S	N	3	Kauffman, Bob	Jul 13, 1946	L	O	N
Davis, Jim	Dec 18, 1941	W	1	3	Kozelko, Tom	Jul 1, 1951	H	H	M

83

NAME	DATE OF BIRTH	CODE			NAME	DATE OF BIRTH	CODE		
Kuberski, Steve	Nov 6, 1947	J	T	7	Saunders, Fred	Jun 13, 1951	N	S	2
Kunnert, Kevin	Nov 11, 1951	C	A	N	Schlueter, Dale	Nov 12, 1945	V	X	A
Lacey, Sam	Mar 28, 1948	O	W	K	Scott, Charlie	Dec 15, 1948	X	D	H
Lanier, Bob	Sep 10, 1948	T	U	L	Silas, Paul	Jul 12, 1943	S	J	E
Lantz, Stu	Jul 13, 1946	L	O	N	Skinner, Talvin	Sep 10, 1952	H	Z	U
Lee, Clyde	Mar 14, 1944	L	C	U	Sloan, Jerry	Mar 28, 1942	G	O	4
Love, Bob	Dec 8, 1942	J	R	U	Smith, Bobby	Feb 26, 1946	M	R	H
Love, Stan	Apr 9, 1949	X	G	Y	Smith, Don	Oct 10, 1951	R	Z	O
Maravich, Pete	Jun 22, 1948	H	Y	5	Smith, Elmore	May 9, 1949	G	J	V
Marin, Jack	Oct 12, 1944	Q	T	A	Smith, Greg	Jan 28, 1947	C	R	O
Martin, LaRue	Mar 30, 1950	K	1	Q	Smith, Phil	Apr 22, 1952	E	Y	L
May, Don	Jan 3, 1946	D	T	U	Smith, Randy	Dec 12, 1948	U	A	E
McAdoo, Bob	Sep 25, 1951	B	K	7	Snyder, Dick	Feb 1, 1944	P	R	L
McGlocklin, Jon	Jun 10, 1943	J	E	F	Sojourner, Mike	Oct 16, 1953	S	F	Z
McIntosh, Kennedy	Jan 21, 1949	O	N	M	Stacom, Kevin	Sep 4, 1951	D	R	L
McMillian, Jim	Mar 11, 1948	U	E	1	Stallworth, Bud	Jan 18, 1950	H	L	L
McNeill, Larry	Jan 31, 1951	S	Z	1	Stallworth, Dave	Dec 20, 1941	A	3	5
Meely, Cliff	Jul 10, 1947	E	M	M	Steele, Larry	May 5, 1949	C	E	R
Melchionni, Gary	Jan 19, 1951	F	N	O	Thompson, George	Nov 29, 1947	J	O	W
Meminger, Dean	May 13, 1948	O	M	X	Thurmond, Nate	Jul 25, 1941	O	U	O
Mengelt, John	Oct 16, 1949	F	A	Q	Tomjanovich, Rudy	Nov 24, 1948	B	L	U
Mix, Steve	Dec 30, 1947	R	R	U	Trapp, George	Jul 11, 1948	D	P	Q
Money, Eric	Feb 6, 1955	N	H	H	Unseld, Wes	Mar 14, 1946	E	E	Y
Monroe, Earl	Nov 21, 1944	K	C	H	Van Arsdale, Dick	Feb 22, 1943	Q	J	5
Moore, Otto	Aug 27, 1946	K	C	Z	Van Arsdale, Tom	Feb 22, 1943	Q	J	5
Mullins, Jeff	Mar 18, 1942	U	D	T	Van Lier, Norm	Apr 1, 1947	U	Y	L
Murphy, Calvin	May 9, 1948	K	H	T	Walk, Neal	Jul 29, 1948	W	E	A
Neal, Lloyd	Dec 10, 1950	M	A	G	Walker, Jimmy	Apr 8, 1944	N	3	M
Nelson, Don	May 15, 1940	P	D	G	Walton, Bill	Nov 5, 1952	S	Z	K
Nelson, Louie	May 28, 1951	U	B	L	Warner, Cornell	Aug 12, 1948	N	T	P
Newlin, Mike	Jan 2, 1949	S	W	1	Washington, Jim	Jul 1, 1943	G	1	2
Norwood, Willie	Aug 8, 1947	L	N	H	Washington, Kermit	Sep 17, 1951	R	B	Y
Patterson, Steve	Jun 24, 1948	K	1	7	Watts, Don	Jul 21, 1951	E	3	7
Perry, Curtis	Sep 13, 1948	W	X	O	Weatherspoon, Nick	Jul 20, 1950	G	1	4
Petrie, Geoff	Apr 17, 1948	L	O	5	Wedman, Scott	Jul 29, 1952	L	K	K
Porter, Howard	Aug 31, 1948	J	K	A	Weiss, Bob	May 7, 1942	A	1	C
Porter, Kevin	Apr 17, 1950	E	Q	A	Wesley, Walt	Apr 25, 1945	D	S	6
Price, Jim	Nov 27, 1949	B	P	Z	Westphal, Paul	Nov 30, 1950	B	T	5
Ratleff, Ed	Mar 29, 1950	J	Z	P	White, Jo Jo	Nov 16, 1946	W	3	G
Ray, Clifford	Jan 21, 1949	O	N	M	Wicks, Sidney	Sep 19, 1949	B	B	W
Restani, Kevin	Dec 23, 1951	W	P	W	Wilkes, Jamaal	May 2, 1953	M	G	X
Riley, Pat	Mar 20, 1945	O	K	3	Williams, Earl	Mar 24, 1951	A	V	M
Riley, Ron	Nov 11, 1950	F	3	L	Williams, Nate	May 2, 1950	U	C	Q
Riordan, Mike	Jul 9, 1945	K	J	G	Williams, Ron	Sep 24, 1944	V	A	Q
Roberson, Rick	Jul 7, 1947	B	J	J	Wilson, Bobby	Jan 15, 1951	B	J	K
Rowe, Curtis	Jul 2, 1949	P	G	J	Winfield, Lee	Feb 4, 1947	K	Y	V
Russell, Cazzie	Jun 7, 1944	D	D	F	Wingo, Hawthorne	Sep 9, 1948	S	T	K
Russell, Campy	Jan 12, 1952	T	G	J	Winters, Brian	Mar 1, 1952	W	3	Z

Cricket

NAME	DATE OF BIRTH	CODE			NAME	DATE OF BIRTH	CODE		
Abberley, Neal	Apr 22, 1944	D	O	1	Cowdrey, Colin	Dec 24, 1932	G	V	O
Abrahams, John	Jul 21, 1952	C	B	B	Cowley, Nigel	Mar 1, 1953	T	A	2
Acfield, David	Jul 24, 1947	T	1	1	Cumbes, James	May 4, 1944	Q	1	E
Amiss, Dennis	Apr 7, 1943	O	Z	H	Davey, Jack	Sep 4, 1944	A	J	4
Armstrong, Gregory	May 11, 1950	F	M	Z	Davis, Roger	Jan 15, 1946	Q	C	7
Arnold, Geoffrey	Sep 3, 1944	X	H	3	Davison, Brian	Dec 21, 1946	L	G	J
Asif Iqbal, Razvi	Jun 6, 1943	E	A	B	Denness, Michael	Dec 1, 1940	H	H	J
Aworth, Christopher	Feb 19, 1953	J	T	R	Denning, Peter	Dec 16, 1949	V	F	L
Bairstow, David	Sep 1, 1951	A	O	H	Dixon, John	Mar 3, 1954	S	D	6
Baker, Raymond	Apr 9, 1954	J	N	B	D'Oliveira, Basil	Oct 4, 1931	U	W	4
Balderstone, Christopher	Nov 16, 1940	Q	V	2	Dudleston, Barry	Jul 16, 1945	R	Q	O
Barclay, John	Jan 22, 1954	A	U	Y	Dudley-Jones, Robert	May 26, 1952	Q	B	M
Barlow, Graham	Mar 26, 1950	F	W	M	Dunstan, Malcolm	Oct 14, 1950	A	3	Q
Bedi, Bishan	Sep 25, 1946	Q	D	V	Dye, John	Jul 24, 1942	K	U	P
Birch, John	Jan 18, 1955	G	3	H	Ealham, Alan	Aug 30, 1944	T	D	Y
Birkenshaw, Jack	Nov 13, 1940	N	S	Y	East, Raymond	Jun 20, 1947	H	U	Z
Bolus, Brian	Jan 31, 1934	T	D	V	Edmeades, Brian	Sep 17, 1941	W	S	B
Booth, Peter	Nov 2, 1952	P	W	G	Edmonds, Phil	Mar 8, 1951	H	E	4
Bore, Michael	Jun 2, 1947	N	B	G	Edrich, John	Jun 21, 1937	O	J	D
Botham, Ian	Nov 24, 1955	E	T	B	Ellis, Geoffrey	May 24, 1950	T	Z	E
Bourne, William	Nov 15, 1952	E	G	U	Elms, Richard	Apr 5, 1949	T	C	U
Boyce, Keith	Oct 11, 1943	R	Q	5	Emburey, John	Aug 20, 1952	K	D	7
Boycott, Geoffrey	Oct 21, 1940	N	X	A	Engineer, Farokh	Feb 25, 1938	K	F	W
Brain, Brian	Sept 13, 1940	V	N	4	Faber, Mark	Aug 15, 1950	K	Y	W
Brassington, Andrew	Aug 9, 1954	Q	X	Z	Featherstone, Norman	Aug 20, 1949	S	3	Z
Breakwell, Dennis	Jul 2, 1948	S	F	G	Field, Maxwell	Mar 23, 1950	C	T	J
Brearley, Michael	Apr 28, 1942	P	R	2	Fletcher, Keith	May 20, 1944	J	O	V
Briers, Nigel	Jan 15, 1955	O	O	T	Foat, James	Nov 21, 1952	L	N	1
Brown, Anthony	Jun 24, 1936	U	L	E	Francis, Arthur	Nov 29, 1953	Q	W	C
Brown, David	Jan 30, 1942	T	N	E	Gardom, Keith	Dec 31, 1952	E	Z	8
Burgess, Graham	May 5, 1943	T	Z	C	Gifford, Norman	Mar 30, 1940	P	O	2
Buss, Antony	Sep 1, 1939	L	2	O	Gilliat, Richard	May 20, 1944	J	O	V
Butcher, Alan	Jan 7, 1954	J	E	J	Gomes, Larry	Jul 13, 1953	P	X	4
Butcher, Roland	Oct 14, 1953	Q	D	X	Gooch, Graham	Jul 23, 1953	B	E	F
Carrick, Fergus	Jul 16, 1952	V	Z	5	Good, Antony	Nov 10, 1952	X	B	P
Cartwright, Harold	May 12, 1951	D	O	3	Goodwin, Keith	Jun 21, 1938	L	K	F
Cartwright, Thomas	Jul 22, 1935	D	J	5	Graham, Norman	May 8, 1943	W	3	F
Cass, Rodney	Apr 23, 1940	Q	K	S	Graham, Brown	Jul 11, 1951	S	S	W
Cheatle, Giles	Jul 31, 1953	K	N	O	Graveny, David	Jan 2, 1953	G	2	B
Clapp, Robert	Dec 12, 1948	U	A	E	Graves, Peter	May 19, 1946	B	P	Y
Clinton, Grahame	May 5, 1953	P	K	1	Greenidge, Geoffrey	May 29, 1948	D	Z	C
Close, Brian	Feb 24, 1931	E	Y	E	Greenidge, Gordon	May 1, 1951	Q	C	R
Cook, Geoffrey	Oct 9, 1951	Q	Y	N	Greig, Anthony	Oct 6, 1946	D	P	7
Cook, John	Jun 5, 1946	T	D	H	Griffiths, James	Jun 13, 1949	T	Q	X
Cooke, Robert	Sep 30, 1943	F	E	T	Groome, Jeremy	Apr 7, 1955	D	M	B
Cope, Geoffrey	Feb 23, 1947	F	P	G	Hacker, Peter	Jul 16, 1952	V	Z	5
Cordle, Anthony	Sep 21, 1940	F	V	D	Hampshire, John	Feb 10, 1941	K	X	O
Cottam, Robert	Oct 16, 1944	U	X	E	Hardie, Brian	Jan 14, 1950	D	G	G
Coverdale, Stephen	Nov 20, 1954	D	O	4	Harris, Michael	May 25, 1944	O	T	1

NAME	DATE OF BIRTH	CODE			NAME	DATE OF BIRTH	CODE		
Harrison, Stuart	Sep 21, 1951	V	F	3	McKenzie, Graham	Jun 24, 1941	F	R	Q
Harvey-Walker, Ashley	Jul 21, 1944	B	U	R	McVicker, Norman	Nov 4, 1940	D	J	P
Hassan, Basharat	Mar 24, 1944	V	N	5	Mansell, Alan	May 19, 1951	L	V	B
Hayes, Frank	Dec 6, 1946	T	U	2	Marshall, Roger	Feb 28, 1952	U	1	X
Headley, Ronald	Jun 29, 1939	Q	T	Q	Mendis, Gehan	Apr 24, 1955	V	A	T
Hemmings, Edward	Feb 20, 1949	V	P	J	Miller, Geoffrey	Sep 8, 1952	F	X	S
Hemsley, Edward	Sep 1, 1943	X	D	X	Morley, Jeremy	Oct 20, 1950	G	F	W
Hendrick, Michael	Oct 22, 1948	P	F	U	Morris, Alan	Aug 23, 1953	K	H	D
Herman, Robert	Nov 30, 1946	N	O	V	Moseley, Hallam	May 28, 1948	F	2	E
Higgs, Kenneth	Jan 14, 1937	R	T	L	Mottram, Thomas	Sep 7, 1945	A	N	A
Hignell, Alastair	Sep 4, 1955	Q	W	U	Murray, Deryck	May 20, 1943	L	M	S
Hill, Alan	Jun 29, 1950	J	E	H	Murray, John	Apr 1, 1935	G	J	R
Hill, Leonard	Apr 14, 1942	A	C	N	Murtagh, Andrew	May 6, 1949	D	F	S
Hill, Michael	Jul 1, 1951	H	H	M	Mushtaq, Mohammad	Nov 22, 1943	N	B	F
Hills, Richard	Jan 8, 1951	S	B	C	Nanan, Nirmal	Aug 19, 1951	L	A	3
Hobbs, Robin	May 8, 1942	B	2	D	Nash, Malcolm	May 9, 1945	S	D	M
Hodgson, Alan	Oct 27, 1951	L	O	6	Nicholls, David	Dec 8, 1943	F	S	W
Holder, Vanburn	Oct 8, 1945	J	Q	7	Nicholson, Anthony	Jun 25, 1938	P	O	K
Hopkins, John	Jun 16, 1953	L	Y	B	Norman, Michael	Jan 19, 1933	K	T	G
Howarth, Geoffrey	Mar 29, 1951	F	1	R	Old, Christopher	Dec 22, 1948	G	L	P
Hughes, David	May 13, 1947	Q	K	U	Oldham, Stephen	Jul 26, 1948	T	B	6
Humpage, Geoffrey	Apr 24, 1954	A	3	R	Ormrod, Alan	Dec 22, 1942	X	C	A
Humphries, David	Aug 6, 1953	Q	T	U	Owen-Thomas, Dudley	Sep 20, 1948	F	B	V
Illingworth, Raymond	Jun 8, 1932	P	S	N	Page, Julian	May 1, 1954	H	G	Y
Imrankhan, Niazi	Nov 25, 1952	P	R	5	Page, Michael	Jun 17, 1941	W	K	J
Inchmore, John	Feb 22, 1949	X	R	L	Parker, John	Feb 21, 1951	Q	S	O
Intikhab, Alam Khan	Dec 28, 1941	J	H	E	Parks, James	Oct 21, 1931	O	L	N
Jackman, Robin	Aug 13, 1945	W	Q	J	Parsons, Austin	Jan 9, 1949	B	A	8
Jameson, John	Jun 30, 1941	M	X	W	Perryman, Stephen	Oct 22, 1955	S	O	B
Jesty, Trevor	Jun 2, 1948	L	D	K	Phillipson, Paul	Feb 10, 1952	B	H	E
Johnson, Colin	Sep 5, 1947	Q	N	C	Pilling, Harry	Feb 23, 1943	R	K	6
Johnson, Graham	Nov 8, 1946	O	U	7	Pocock, Patrick	Sep 24, 1946	P	C	U
Johnson, Ivan	Jun 27, 1953	W	G	N	Pont, Keith	Jan 16, 1953	V	N	Q
Johnson, Peter	Nov 12, 1949	K	3	K	Price, John	Jul 22, 1937	W	M	B
Jones, Alan	Nov 4, 1938	J	F	K	Pridgeon, Paul	Feb 22, 1954	J	X	W
Jones, Allan	Dec 9, 1947	T	Y	7	Procter, Michael	Sep 15, 1946	F	W	L
Jones, Alan	Jun 1, 1957	H	O	4	Radley, Clive	May 13, 1944	B	G	O
Jones, Eifion	Jun 25, 1942	D	T	T	Randall, Derek	Feb 24, 1951	T	V	R
Julien, Bernard	Mar 13, 1950	Q	J	7	Ratcliffe, Robert	Nov 29, 1951	V	T	6
Kallicharran, Alvin	Mar 21, 1949	D	Q	E	Reidy, Bernard	Sep 18, 1953	N	F	5
Kanhai, Rohan	Dec 26, 1935	X	1	W	Rice, Clive	Jul 23, 1949	N	3	5
Kennedy, Andrew	Nov 4, 1949	B	U	B	Richards, Barry	Jul 21, 1945	W	V	T
Khan, Majid Jahangir	Sep 28, 1946	T	G	Y	Richards, Gwyn	Nov 29, 1951	V	T	6
Kitchen, Mervyn	Aug 1, 1940	A	1	T	Richards, Vivian	Mar 7, 1952	E	F	6
Knew, George	Mar 5, 1954	U	F	8	Roberts, Andy	Jan 29, 1951	Q	X	Y
Knight, Roger	Sep 6, 1946	U	N	B	Robinson, Rocker	Aug 17, 1946	X	V	P
Knott, Alan	Apr 9, 1946	H	C	R	Roebuck, Peter	Mar 6, 1956	Q	K	F
Lamb, Timothy	Mar 24, 1953	T	Y	R	Romaines, Paul	Dec 25, 1955	N	W	8
Larkins, Wayne	Nov 22, 1953	J	P	4	Roope, Graham	Jul 12, 1946	K	N	M
Latchman, Harry	Jul 26, 1943	J	X	T	Rose, Brian	Jun 4, 1950	G	H	Q
Leadbeater, Barrie	Aug 14, 1943	E	O	E	Ross, Nigel	Apr 5, 1953	H	H	4
Lee, Peter	Aug 27, 1945	N	B	X	Rouse, Mick	Jan 20, 1949	N	M	L
Lever, John	Feb 24, 1949	B	T	N	Rowe, Charles	Nov 27, 1951	T	R	4
Lever, Peter	Sep 17, 1940	B	R	8	Russell, Philip	May 9, 1944	V	C	K
Lewington, Peter	Jan 30, 1950	U	X	X	Sadiq, Mohammad	May 3, 1945	M	1	F
Lewis, Richard	Aug 6, 1947	J	L	F	Sainsbury, Peter	Jun 13, 1934	O	Z	W
Llewellyn, Michael	Nov 27, 1953	O	U	A	Sarfraz, Nawaz	Dec 1, 1948	J	S	2
Lloyd, Barry	Sep 6, 1953	A	W	6	Schepens, Martin	Aug 12, 1955	Q	2	5
Lloyd, Clive	Aug 31, 1944	U	E	Z	Selvey, Michael	Apr 25, 1948	T	W	E
Lloyd, David	Mar 18, 1947	F	K	5	Senghera, Ravinder	Jan 25, 1947	X	O	L
Long, Arnold	Dec 18, 1940	B	Z	1	Shackleton, Julian	Jan 29, 1952	N	Y	1
Luckhurst, Brian	Feb 5, 1939	K	P	D	Sharp, George	Mar 12, 1950	P	H	6
Lumb, Richard	Feb 27, 1950	B	X	S	Sharpe, Philip	Dec 27, 1936	W	A	1
Lyon, John	May 17, 1951	J	T	8	Shepherd, David	Dec 27, 1940	L	F	B
McEwan, Kenneth	Jul 16, 1952	V	Z	5	Shepherd, John	Nov 9, 1943	X	R	1

NAME	DATE OF BIRTH	CODE			NAME	DATE OF BIRTH	CODE		
Shuttleworth, Kenneth	Nov 13, 1944	B	X	8	Taylor, Robert	Jul 17, 1941	F	M	F
Sidebottom, Arnold	Apr 1, 1954	A	E	2	Taylor, William	Jan 24, 1947	W	N	K
Simmons, Jack	Mar 28, 1941	K	N	2	Thomas, Richard	Jun 18, 1944	P	P	R
Skinner, Lonsdale	Sep 7, 1950	K	T	M	Titmus, Frederick	Nov 24, 1932	X	T	R
Slocombe, Philip	Sep 6, 1954	V	X	U	Todd, Paul	Mar 12, 1953	G	M	E
Smedley, Michael	Oct 28, 1941	R	C	K	Tolchard, Jeffrey	Mar 17, 1944	O	F	X
Smith, David	Jan 9, 1956	E	J	P	Tolchard, Roger	Jun 15, 1946	F	O	S
Smith, Kenneth David	Jul 9, 1956	C	X	7	Townsley, Andrew	Jun 24, 1952	W	C	H
Smith, Michael	Jan 4, 1942	Q	P	M	Trim, Geoffrey	Apr 6, 1956	A	N	D
Smith, Neil	Apr 1, 1949	P	2	Q	Tunnicliffe, Trevor	Mar 4, 1950	G	3	X
Snow, John	Oct 13, 1941	B	Q	3	Turner, David	Feb 5, 1949	F	3	2
Solanky, John	Jun 30, 1942	J	Y	Y	Turner, Glenn	May 26, 1947	F	X	8
Southern, John	Sep 2, 1952	X	R	M	Turner, Stuart	Jul 18, 1943	A	P	L
Spencer, Terry	Aug 18, 1931	T	C	P	Underwood, Derek	Jun 8, 1945	B	F	J
Spencer, John	Oct 6, 1949	T	T	F	Venkataraghavan	Apr 21, 1946	U	P	4
Squires, Peter	Aug 4, 1951	T	O	N	Vernon, Martin	Jul 4, 1951	L	L	P
Stead, Barry	Jun 21, 1939	H	L	H	Verrinder, Alan	Jul 28, 1955	A	M	P
Steele, David	Sep 29, 1941	L	B	O	Virgin, Roy	Aug 26, 1939	E	V	H
Steele, John	Jul 23, 1946	V	Y	X	Wadey, Alan	Sep 12, 1950	P	Y	R
Stephenson, Robert	Nov 19, 1942	N	1	A	Waller, Christopher	Oct 3, 1948	T	P	A
Stevenson, Graham	Dec 16, 1955	D	N	Y	Ward, Alan	Aug 10, 1947	N	P	K
Stevenson, Keith	Oct 6, 1950	Q	U	H	White, Robert	Oct 6, 1936	J	C	K
Still, Stuart	Dec 14, 1957	U	O	2	Whitehouse, John	Apr 8, 1949	W	F	X
Stovold, Andrew	Mar 19, 1953	O	T	M	Whiteside, Christopher	Aug 12, 1953	W	Z	1
Sullivan, John	Feb 5, 1945	R	X	S	Wilcock, Gordon	Feb 26, 1950	A	W	R
Swarbrook, Fred	Dec 17, 1950	T	H	O	Wilkins, Alan	Aug 22, 1953	J	G	C
Tavare, Christopher	Oct 27, 1954	C	S	E	Wilkinson, Philip	Aug 23, 1951	P	E	7
Taylor, Derek	Nov 12, 1942	F	T	2	Willey, Peter	Dec 6, 1949	L	Y	A
Taylor, Michael	Nov 12, 1942	F	T	2	Williams, Lawrence	Nov 20, 1946	C	D	8
					Williams, Richard	Aug 10, 1957	J	3	8
					Willis, Robert	May 30, 1949	E	B	J
					Wood, Barry	Dec 26, 1942	D	G	E
					Woolmer, Robert	May 14, 1948	P	N	Y

Football

NAME	DATE OF BIRTH	CODE			NAME	DATE OF BIRTH	CODE		
Adamle, Michael **RB**	Oct 10, 1949	X	X	K	Burrow, Kenneth **WR**	Mar 29, 1948	P	X	L
Adams, Anthony **QB**	Mar 19, 1950	W	P	E	Bussey, Dexter **RB**	May 11, 1952	A	P	5
Adams, Robert **TE**	Aug 15, 1946	V	T	N	Butler, William (Skip) **PK**	Oct 21, 1947	Q	C	Q
Adkins, Margene **WR**	Apr 30, 1947	C	Z	G	Cain, James **WR**	Jul 22, 1951	F	A	8
Alston Jr., Mack **TE**	Apr 27, 1947	X	W	D	Calhoun, Donald **RB**	Apr 29, 1952	M	C	S
Amundson, George **RB**	Mar 31, 1951	H	3	T	Cappelletti, John **RB**	Aug 9, 1952	W	V	V
Anderson, Kenneth **QB**	Feb 15, 1949	Q	K	D	Carlson, Dean **QB**	Aug 1, 1950	T	K	H
Anderson, Robert **RB**	Oct 11, 1947	F	V	F	Carmichael, Harold **WR**	Sep 22, 1949	E	E	Z
Andrews, John **TE**	Nov 2, 1948	C	R	6	Carr, Roger **WR**	Jul 1, 1952	F	K	P
Armstrong, Otis **RB**	Nov 15, 1950	K	D	P	Casper, David **TE**	Sep 26, 1951	C	L	8
Ashton Jr., Josh **RB**	Aug 24, 1949	W	D	4	Caster, Richard **WR**	Oct 16, 1948	J	3	O
Bailey, George **RB**	Feb 2, 1949	C	Z	Y	Chandler, Robert **WR**	Apr 24, 1949	P	W	F
Baker, Vernon **RB**	Feb 16, 1945	E	F	4	Chesson III, Wesley **WR**	Jan 15, 1949	H	G	F
Baker, Melvin **WR**	Aug 12, 1950	G	V	T	Chester, Raymond **TE**	Jun 28, 1948	O	B	C
Bakken, James **K**	Nov 2, 1940	B	G	N	Childs, Henry **TE**	Apr 16, 1951	A	Q	B
Banaszak, Peter **RB**	May 21, 1944	K	P	W	Cipa, Larry **QB**	Oct 5, 1951	M	U	J
Bankston, Warren **TE**	Jul 22, 1947	R	Y	Y	Clark, Charles (Boobie) **RB**	Nov 8, 1950	C	Z	H
Barkum, Jerome **WR**	Jul 18, 1950	E	Y	2	Clark, Wayne **QB**	May 30, 1947	K	2	D
Barnes, Allen **WR**	Jul 4, 1949	R	J	L	Clements Jr., Vincent **RB**	Jan 4, 1949	U	Y	3
Bartkowski, Steven **QB**	Nov 12, 1952	B	D	R	Cockroft, Donald **K-P**	Feb 6, 1945	S	Y	T
Beasley, John **TE**	Apr 6, 1945	H	2	M	Coleman, Ronnie **RB**	Jul 9, 1951	Q	Q	U
Beasley, Terry **WR**	Feb 5, 1950	C	A	4	Collier, Michael **RB**	Sep 21, 1953	Q	J	8
Beirne, James **WR**	Oct 15, 1946	N	Y	H	Concannon Jr., John **QB**	Feb 25, 1943	T	M	8
Bell, Edward **WR**	Sep 13, 1947	A	V	L	Coslet, Bruce **TE**	Aug 5, 1946	L	J	C
Berra, Timothy **WR**	Sep 23, 1951	X	H	5	Cousins, Gary **RB**	Jan 21, 1949	O	N	P
Berry, Robert **QB**	Mar 10, 1942	M	Y	L	Cox, Frederick **K**	Dec 11, 1938	X	P	O
Bertelsen, James **RB**	Feb 26, 1950	A	W	R	Craig, Steve **TE**	Mar 13, 1951	N	K	A
Biletnikoff, Frederick **WR**	Feb 23, 1943	R	K	6	Crosby, Steven **RB**	Jul 3, 1950	N	J	M
Bjorklund, John **RB**	Jun 5, 1950	H	J	R	Crosswhite, Leon **RB**	Apr 28, 1951	N	3	O
Blanda, George **QB-K**	Sep 17, 1927	O	3	C	Csonka, Lawrence **RB**	Dec 25, 1946	P	L	N
Bleier, Robert **RB**	Mar 5, 1946	T	Y	P	Cunningham, Julian **RB**	Sep 14, 1945	H	U	W
Bonner, Glen **RB**	May 5, 1952	S	J	Y	Cunningham Jr., Samuel **RB**	Aug 15, 1950	K	Y	W
Boryla, Michael **QB**	Mar 6, 1951	F	C	2	Curran, Patrick **TE**	Sep 21, 1945	P	2	P
Bradshaw Jr., Morris **WR**	Nov 19, 1952	J	L	Y	Curtis, Isaac **WR**	Oct 20, 1950	G	F	W
Bradshaw, Terry **QB**	Sep 2, 1948	L	M	C	Danelo, Joseph **K**	Sep 2, 1953	U	S	O
Branch, Clifford **WR**	Aug 1, 1948	B	H	D	Davis, Charles **RB**	Jan 6, 1952	N	A	C
Braxton, James **RB**	May 23, 1949	V	X	B	Davis, Clarence **RB**	Jun 28, 1949	L	C	E
Briscoe, Marlin **WR**	Sep 10, 1945	D	Q	D	Davis III, Harrison **WR**	Feb 20, 1952	M	S	P
Brister, Willie **TE**	Jan 28, 1952	M	X	Z	Davis, Steven **RB**	Nov 10, 1948	L	Z	F
Brockington, John **RB**	Sep 7, 1948	Q	R	H	Dawkins III, Joe **RB**	Jan 27, 1948	W	R	P
Brown, Kenneth **RB**	Nov 8, 1945	R	T	5	Dawson, Leonard **QB**	Jun 20, 1935	S	E	6
Brown, Larry **TE**	Jun 16, 1949	W	T	1	Demory, John **QB**	Dec 1, 1950	C	U	6
Brown, Larry **RB**	Sep 19, 1947	G	2	R	Dempsey, Thomas **K**	Jan 12, 1947	K	A	6
Brunet, Robert **RB**	Jul 29, 1946	D	B	4	Dennison, Douglas **RB**	Dec 18, 1951	R	K	R
Brunson, Larry **WR**	Aug 11, 1949	J	T	Q	Denson, Moses **RB**	Jul 6, 1944	K	E	B
Bryant, Bobby **DB**	Jan 24, 1944	G	J	C	Dickey, Lynn **QB**	Oct 19, 1949	J	D	T
Bryant, Cullen **RB**	May 20, 1951	M	W	C	Dodd, Alvin **WR**	Aug 21, 1945	G	Y	R
Bulaich, Norman **RB**	Dec 25, 1946	P	L	N	Dolbin, John Tice **WR**	Oct 12, 1948	E	Y	K
Burrough, Kenneth **WR**	Jul 14, 1948	G	S	T	Domres, Martin **QB**	Apr 17, 1947	N	M	2

NAME	DATE OF BIRTH	CODE	NAME	DATE OF BIRTH	CODE
Doughty, Glenn **WR**	Jan 30, 1951	R Y Z	Hill, Talmadge **WR**	Apr 15, 1947	L K Z
Douglass, Robert **QB**	Jun 22, 1947	K W 2	Holland, John **WR**	Feb 28, 1952	U 1 X
Dressler, Douglas **RB**	Mar 19, 1948	E N A	Howard, Ronald **TE**	Mar 3, 1951	C 3 Y
Dunbar, Jubilee **WR**	May 17, 1949	P R 4	Hubbard, Marvin **RB**	May 7, 1946	N C M
DuPree, Billy Joe **TE**	Mar 7, 1950	K C 1	Huff, Gary **QB**	Apr 27, 1951	M 2 N
Edwards, Cleophus (Cid) **RB**	Sep 10, 1943	J N 7	Hufnagel, John **QB**	Sept 13, 1951	N 1 U
Elliott, Lenvil **RB**	Sep 2, 1951	B P J	Humm, David **QB**	Apr 2, 1952	H D Y
Evans, Jack **RB**	Jan 10, 1948	E 3 6	Hunt, George **K**	Aug 3, 1949	A L H
Farmer, George **WR**	Apr 19, 1948	N Q 7	Hunter, Scott **QB**	Nov 19, 1947	W D M
Ferguson Jr., Joe **QB**	Apr 23, 1950	L W G	Jackson, Clarence (Jazz) **RB**	Mar 5, 1952	C D 4
Fleming, Marvin **TE**	Jan 2, 1942	O N K	Jackson, Harold **WR**	Jan 6, 1946	G W X
Foreman, Walter (Chuck) **RB**	Oct 26, 1950	N M 3	Jackson, Randy **RB**	Nov 13, 1948	O 3 J
Fouts, Daniel **QB**	Jun 10, 1951	K P Y	Jackson, Wilbur **RB**	Nov 19, 1951	L J V
Francis, Wallace **WR**	Nov 7, 1951	W Z J	James, Ron (Po) **RB**	Mar 19, 1949	B O C
Freitas, Jesse **QB**	Sep 19, 1951	T D 1	Jankowski, Bruce **WR**	Aug 12, 1949	K U R
Fritsch, Toni **K**	Jul 10, 1945	L K H	Jarvis, Leon (Ray) **WR**	Feb 2, 1949	C Z Y
Fritts, Stan **RB**	Dec 18, 1952	P M U	Jaworski, Ronald **QB**	Mar 23, 1951	X U L
Fugett Jr., Jean **TE**	Dec 16, 1951	P H P	Jaynes, David **QB**	Dec 12, 1952	J F O
Fuqua, John **RB**	Sep 12, 1946	C T H	Jessie, Ron **WR**	Feb 4, 1948	G Z X
Gabriel Jr., Roman **QB**	Aug 5, 1940	E B X	Johnson Jr., Albert **RB**	Jun 17, 1950	U V 4
Gant, Reuben **TE**	Apr 12, 1952	S O A	Johnson, Andrew **RB**	Oct 18, 1952	X G Z
Garrett, Carl **RB**	Aug 31, 1947	L H 6	Johnson, Charles **QB**	Nov 22, 1938	D Y 3
Garrison, Gary **WR**	Jan 21, 1944	D F 8	Johnson, Essex **RB**	Oct 15, 1946	N Y H
Geredine, Thomas **WR**	Jun 17, 1950	U V 4	Johnson, Kermit **RB**	Feb 22, 1952	O U R
Gerela, Roy **K**	Apr 2, 1948	T 2 P	Johnson, Randolph **QB**	Jun 17, 1944	O O Q
Gillette, Walker **WR**	Mar 16, 1947	D H 3	Johnson, Ronald **RB**	Oct 17, 1947	M 2 M
Gilliam, Joe **QB**	Dec 29, 1950	H U 1	Johnson, Samuel **RB**	Sep 22, 1952	U J 7
Gilliam, John **WR**	Aug 7, 1945	Q K C	Johnson, William **WR**	Jan 21, 1952	E Q S
Ginn, Hubert **RB**	Jan 4, 1947	B V X	Joiner Jr., Charles **WR**	Oct 14, 1947	J Y J
Glass, Charles **TE**	June 25, 1947	N Z 5	Jones, Bertram **QB**	Sep 7, 1951	G U O
Goodman Jr., Leslie **RB**	Sep 1, 1950	D N F	Jones, Jimmy **RB**	Jun 15, 1950	S T 2
Gossett, Bruce **K**	Nov 9, 1941	F P W	Jones, Lawrance **WR**	Mar 4, 1951	D A Z
Graff, Neil **QB**	Jan 12, 1950	B E E	Jones, Steve **RB**	Mar 6, 1951	F C 2
Grandberry, Kenneth **RB**	Jan 25, 1952	J U W	Keithley, Gary **QB**	Jan 11, 1951	V E F
Grant, Frank **WR**	Feb 15, 1950	N L F	Kendrick, Vincent **RB**	Mar 18, 1952	Q R J
Gray,Melvin **WR**	Sep 28, 1948	O K 4	Keyworth, Jonathan **RB**	Dec 15, 1950	R F M
Green Jr., Woodrow **RB**	July 20, 1952	B A A	Kiick, James **RB**	Aug 9, 1946	P N G
Gresham, Robert **RB**	Jul 9, 1948	B N O	Kilmer Jr., William **QB**	Sep 5, 1939	P C S
Griese, Robert **QB**	Feb 3, 1945	P V Q	Kingsriter, Douglas **TE**	Jan 29, 1950	T W W
Grim, Robert **WR**	May 8, 1945	R C L	King, Horace **RB**	Mar 5, 1953	X E 6
Grogan, Steven **QB**	Jul 24, 1953	C F G	Kinney, Jeff **RB**	Nov 1, 1949	W R 7
Grossman, Randy **TE**	Sep 20, 1953	P H 7	Klein, Robert **TE**	Jul 27, 1947	W A 4
Haden, Patrick **QB**	Jan 23, 1953	E U X	Knight, David **WR**	Feb 1, 1951	T 1 2
Hadl, John **QB**	Feb 15, 1940	R 1 Q	Kotar, Doug **RB**	Jun 11, 1951	L Q Z
Hammond, Gary **WR**	July 31, 1949	V H E	Kwalick, Thaddeus (Ted) **TE**	Apr 15, 1947	L K Z
Hampton, David **RB**	May 7, 1947	K D O	Lamonica, Daryle **QB**	Jul 17, 1941	F M F
Hanratty, Terrence **QB**	Jan 19, 1948	O J G	Landry, Gregory **QB**	Dec 18, 1946	H D F
Hardeman, Donald Ray **RB**	Aug 13, 1952	C Z Z	Lane, MacArthur **RB**	Mar 16, 1942	S B R
Harraway Jr., Charles **RB**	Sep 21, 1944	S 1 N	Lash, Jim **WR**	Nov 12, 1951	D B O
Harrell, Willard **RB**	Sep 16, 1952	O C 1	Lawrence, Larry **QB**	Apr 11, 1949	B J 1
Harris, Franco **RB**	Mar 7, 1950	K C 1	Leahy, Patrick **K**	Mar 19, 1951	T Q G
Harris, Ike **WR**	Nov 27, 1952	R T 7	Leaks, Roosevelt **RB**	Jan 31, 1953	N 3 6
Harris, James L. **QB**	July 20, 1947	P W W	Lefear, Billy **WR**	Feb 12, 1950	K H C
Harrison, James H. **RB**	Sep 10, 1948	T U L	Leigh, Charles **RB**	Oct 29, 1945	G J U
Hart, Harold **RB**	Jul 13, 1952	S W 2	LeVias, Jerry **WR**	Sep 5, 1946	T M A
Hart, James **QB**	Apr 29, 1944	L V 8	Lewis, Frank **WR**	Jul 4, 1947	W F F
Hawkins, Benjamin **WR**	Mar 22, 1944	T L 3	Leypoldt, John **K**	Mar 31, 1946	W W H
Hayes, Robert **WR**	Dec 20, 1942	V A 7	Livingston, Michael **QB**	Nov 14, 1945	X Z C
Hayes, Wendell **RB**	Aug 5, 1940	E B X	Longley Jr., Clinton **QB**	Jul 28, 1952	K J J
Hermann, Donald **WR**	Jun 5, 1947	Q E K	Lynch, Francis **RB**	Dec 13, 1945	F 1 7
Herrera, Efren **K**	Jul 30, 1951	O J H	Malone, Arthur **RB**	Mar 20, 1948	F O B
Herron, Mack **RB**	Jul 24, 1948	R 3 4	Malone, Ben **RB**	Feb 3, 1952	S A 6
Highsmith, Donald **RB**	Mar 12, 1948	V F 2	Mandich, Jim **TE**	Jul 30, 1948	X F B
Hill, Calvin **RB**	Jan 2, 1947	X T V	Mann, Errol **K**	Jun 27, 1941	J U T
Hill, J.D. **WR**	Oct 30, 1948	X O 3	Manning III, Archie **QB**	May 19, 1949	R T 6

89

NAME	DATE OF BIRTH	CODE	NAME	DATE OF BIRTH	CODE
Marangi, Gary **QB**	Jul 29, 1952	L K K	Ray Jr., Edward **RB**	Apr 5, 1947	A 3 P
Marcol, Czeslaw **K**	Oct 24, 1949	O J Y	Reamon, Thomas **RB**	Mar 12, 1952	K L C
Marinaro, Ed **RB**	Mar 31, 1950	L 2 R	Reaves, John **QB**	Mar 2, 1950	E 1 V
Masters, William **TE**	Mar 15, 1944	M D V	Reed, Alvin **TE**	Aug 1, 1944	N C 3
Matthews, William **RB**	Nov 15, 1951	G E R	Reed, Joseph **QB**	Jan 8, 1948	C 1 4
Maxson, Alvin **RB**	Nov 12, 1951	D B O	Reed, Oscar **RB**	Mar 24, 1944	V N 5
McCauley Jr., Donald **RB**	May 12, 1949	K M Y	Rentzel, Lance **WR**	Oct 14, 1943	U T 8
McClanahan, Brent **RB**	Sep 21, 1952	T H 6	Rhodes, Raymond **WR**	Oct 20, 1950	G F W
McCullough, Earl **WR**	Jan 10, 1946	L 1 2	Richards, Golden **WR**	Dec 31, 1950	K W 3
McCullum, Samuel **WR**	Nov 30, 1952	U W B	Riggins, John **RB**	Aug 4, 1949	B M J
McCutcheon, Lawrence **RB**	Jun 2, 1950	E F O	Robinson, Paul **RB**	Dec 19, 1944	P C C
McDaniel, Johnny **WR**	Sep 23, 1951	X H 5	Rodgers Jr., Willie **RB**	Feb 8, 1949	J C 5
McGee, Sylvester (Molly) **RB**	Aug 26, 1952	Q K E	Rucker, Reginald **WR**	Sep 21, 1947	J A T
McGee, Willie **WR**	May 14, 1950	J P 3	Sanders, Charles **TE**	Aug 25, 1946	H A X
McGeorge, Richard **TE**	Sep 14, 1948	X Y P	Scarber, Sam **RB**	Jun 24, 1949	G 2 A
McKinnis Jr., Hugh **RB**	Jun 9, 1948	S L R	Schreiber, Lawrence **RB**	Aug 11, 1947	O Q L
McMakin, John **TE**	Sep 24, 1950	D H 4	Scott, Freddie **WR**	Aug 5, 1952	S R R
McNeill, Rodney **RB**	Mar 26, 1951	C X O	Scott, James **WR**	Mar 28, 1952	C 2 T
McQuay, Leon **RB**	Mar 19, 1950	W P E	Scott, Robert (Bo) **RB**	Mar 30, 1943	F R 8
McQuilken, Kim **QB**	Feb 26, 1951	V X T	Scott, Robert Benson **QB**	Apr 2, 1949	Q 3 R
Metcalf, Terrance **RB**	Sep 24, 1951	A J 6	Scribner, Robert **RB**	Apr 9, 1951	R J 3
Mike-Mayer, Nicholas **K**	Mar 1, 1950	D Z U	Seal, Paul **TE**	Feb 27, 1952	T Z W
Milan, Don **QB**	Jan 12, 1949	E D C	Seymour, Paul **TE**	Feb 6, 1950	D B 5
Miller Jr., Cleophus **RB**	Sep 5, 1951	E S M	Shaw, Dennis **QB**	Mar 3, 1947	O X P
Mitchell, James **TE**	Oct 19, 1947	O A O	Siani, Michael **WR**	May 27, 1950	W 3 H
Mitchell, Lydell **RB**	May 30, 1949	E B J	Simmons, Jerry **WR**	Nov 14, 1942	H V 4
Montgomery, James **WR**	Jul 10, 1949	X P R	Simpson, O.J. **RB**	Jul 9, 1947	D L L
Moore, Nathaniel **WR**	Sep 19, 1951	T D 1	Sipe, Brian **QB**	Aug 8, 1949	F Q N
Moore, Robert **TE**	Feb 12, 1949	N G A	Smith, Barrett **WR**	Jan 15, 1951	B J K
Morin, Milton **TE**	Oct 15, 1942	A T 7	Smith, Barton **RB**	Mar 23, 1952	V W O
Morrall, Earl **QB**	May 17, 1934	K 1 3	Smith, Charles **WR**	Jul 26, 1950	N D H
Morris, Eugene (Mercury) **RB**	Jan 5, 1947	C W Y	Smith, Charles Henry **RB**	Jan 18, 1946	T F B
Moseley, Mark **K**	Mar 12, 1948	V F 2	Smith, Gerald **TE**	Jul 19, 1944	X S P
Munson, William **QB**	Aug 11, 1941	H J 6	Smith, Jackie **TE**	Feb 23, 1940	B F Y
Myers, Phil (Chip) **WR**	Jul 9, 1945	K J G	Smith, John **K**	Dec 30, 1949	M U Z
Namath, Joseph **QB**	May 31, 1943	W X 4	Smith, Larry **RB**	Sep 2, 1947	N K 8
Nelson, Ralph **RB**	Jan 23, 1954	B V Z	Snead, Norman **QB**	Jul 31, 1939	B X P
Newhouse, Robert **RB**	Jan 9, 1950	W B B	Snow, Jack **WR**	Jan 25, 1943	L J B
Newland, Robert **WR**	Oct 27, 1948	U L Z	Solomon, Freddie **WR**	Jan 11, 1953	Q H L
Nottingham, Don **RB**	Jun 28, 1949	L C E	Spurrier Jr., Stephen **QB**	Apr 20, 1945	W N L
Odom, Steve **WR**	Sep 5, 1952	C U P	Stabler, Ken **QB**	Dec 25, 1945	S K L
Odoms, Riley **TE**	Mar 1, 1950	D Z U	Staggers Jr., Jonathan **WR**	Dec 14, 1948	W C G
Osborn, David **RB**	Mar 18, 1943	R E V	Stallworth, Johnny **WR**	Jul 15, 1952	U Y 4
Otis, James **RB**	Apr 29, 1948	X 1 J	Staubach, Roger **QB**	Feb 5, 1942	B T L
Owen, Willis **QB**	Sep 1, 1952	W Q L	Stenerud, Jan **K**	Nov 26, 1942	U E H
Owens, Steve **RB**	Dec 9, 1947	T Y 7	Stevens, Jr., Howard **RB**	Feb 9, 1950	G E 8
Parker, Joseph **WR**	Apr 23, 1952	F Z M	Stewart, Wayne **TE**	Aug 18, 1947	V X S
Parks, William **WR**	Jan 1, 1948	T T W	Stingley, Darryl **WR**	Sep 18, 1951	S C Z
Partee, Dennis **K**	Sep 1, 1946	P H 5	Strachan, Michael **RB**	May 24, 1953	L A M
Pastorini Jr., Dante **QB**	May 26, 1949	A 1 E	Strock, Donald **QB**	Nov 27, 1950	W Q 2
Payne Jr., Kenneth **WR**	Oct 6, 1950	Q U H	Stroud Jr., Morris **TE**	May 17, 1946	X N W
Payton, Walter **RB**	Jul 25, 1954	A H K	Sullivan, Patrick **QB**	Jan 18, 1950	H L L
Pearson, Barry **WR**	Feb 2, 1950	X 1 1	Sullivan, Thomas **RB**	Mar 5, 1950	H A Y
Pearson, Drew **WR**	Jan 12, 1951	W F G	Summerell, Carl **QB**	Dec 6, 1951	E 1 E
Pearson, Preston **RB**	Jan 17, 1945	V D 7	Swann, Lynn **WR**	Mar 7, 1952	E F 6
Phillips, Jess **RB**	Feb 28, 1947	L U M	Tagge, Jerry **QB**	Apr 12, 1950	X L 4
Phipps, Michael **QB**	Nov 19, 1947	W D M	Tarkenton, Francis **QB**	Feb 3, 1940	E O D
Pinder, Cyril **RB**	Nov 13, 1946	T Z D	Tarver, John **RB**	Jan 1, 1949	R V Z
Pitts, Frank **WR**	Nov 12, 1943	C U 4	Taylor, Altie **RB**	Sep 29, 1947	R J 2
Plunkett Jr., James **QB**	Dec 5, 1947	P U 3	Taylor, Charles **WR**	Sep 28, 1941	K A N
Podolak, Edward **RB**	Sep 1, 1947	M J 7	Taylor Jr., Otis **WR**	Aug 11, 1942	E K 8
Pruitt, Gregory **RB**	Aug 18, 1951	K 3 2	Thaxton, James **TE**	Jan 11, 1949	D C B
Ramsey, Stephen **QB**	Apr 22, 1948	Q T B	Theismann, Joseph **QB**	Sep 9, 1949	P U M
Rashad, Ahmad **WR**	Nov 19, 1949	R G R	Thomas, Duane **RB**	Jun 21, 1947	J V 1
Rather, David (Bo) **WR**	Oct 7, 1950	R V J	Thomas, Earl **WR**	Oct 4, 1948	U Q B

NAME	DATE OF BIRTH	CODE			NAME	DATE OF BIRTH	CODE		
Thomas, Malcolm (Mike) **RB**	Jul 17, 1953	T	2	8	Washington, Gene **WR**	Jan 14, 1947	M	C	8
Thomas, Robert **RB**	Aug 23, 1948	A	B	1	Washington, Victor **RB**	Mar 23, 1946	O	O	8
Thompson, Thomas **RB**	Sep 22, 1951	W	G	4	Watkins, Lawrence **RB**	Oct 5, 1946	C	O	6
Trumpy Jr., Robert **TE**	Mar 6, 1945	X	Y	O	White, Daniel **QB-P**	Feb 9, 1952	A	G	D
Tucker Sr., Robert **TE**	Jun 8, 1945	B	F	J	Williams, Delvin **RB**	Apr 17, 1951	B	R	C
Turner, James **K**	Mar 28, 1941	K	N	2	Williams, Edward **RB**	Jun 19, 1950	W	X	6
Twilley Jr., Howard **WR**	Dec 25, 1943	X	G	F	Williams, Perry **RB**	Dec 11, 1946	A	Z	7
Upchurch, Rickie **WR**	May 20, 1952	K	Y	F	Willis III, Frederick **RB**	Dec 9, 1947	T	Y	7
Van Eeghen, Mark **RB**	Apr 19, 1952	B	V	H	Windsor, Robert **TE**	Dec 19, 1942	U	3	6
Van Heusen, William **WR**	Aug 27, 1946	K	C	Z	Woods, Ray **RB**	Feb 17, 1951	M	O	K
Vataha, Randel **WR**	Dec 4, 1948	M	V	5	Wright, Elmo **WR**	Jul 3, 1949	Q	H	K
Voight, Stuart **TE**	Aug 12, 1948	N	T	P	Yepremian, Garo **K**	Jun 2, 1944	W	2	A
Wade, Charles **WR**	Feb 23, 1950	V	T	O	Young, Charles Edward **TE**	Feb 5, 1951	X	B	6
Wages, Harmon **RB**	May 18, 1946	A	O	X	Young, Charles Lee **RB**	Oct 13, 1952	S	B	U
Walton, Larry **WR**	Feb 8, 1947	O	3	Z	Young, Rickey **RB**	Dec 7, 1953	A	B	L
Warfield, Paul **WR**	Nov 28, 1942	W	G	K	Zimmerman, Don **WR**	Nov 22, 1949	U	K	U

Golf

NAME	DATE OF BIRTH	CODE			NAME	DATE OF BIRTH	CODE		
Aaron, Tommy	Feb 22, 1937	K	B	R	Douglass, Dale	Mar 5, 1936	A	M	1
Abrameit, Roy	Oct 20, 1944	A	2	J	Dowen, Gary	Jan 4, 1950	R	Z	5
Adams, Sam	May 9, 1946	P	E	O	Eastwood, Bob	Feb 9, 1946	S	3	Y
Albus, Jim	Jun 18, 1940	C	K	H	Edwards, Danny	Jun 14, 1951	O	T	3
Allin, Brian	Oct 13, 1944	R	U	B	Eichelberger, Dave	Sep 3, 1943	B	F	Z
Alsup, Terry	Feb 8, 1947	O	3	Z	Elder, Lee	Jul 14, 1934	W	3	U
Altgelt, Stanton	Nov 5, 1948	F	U	A	Elliott, Dan	May 8, 1945	R	C	L
Archer, George	Oct 1, 1939	S	A	L	Erickson, Bob	Jan 23, 1933	O	X	L
Armstrong, Wally	Jun 19, 1945	N	R	U	Erskine, Randy	Jul 8, 1948	A	M	N
Baird, Butch	Jul 20, 1936	X	J	6	Evans, Tom	Sep 2, 1948	L	M	C
Barber, Jerry	Apr 25, 1916	P	K	7	Ewing, Jack	May 21, 1944	K	P	W
Barber, Miller	Mar 31, 1931	R	C	G	Feather, Randy	Oct 11, 1948	D	X	J
Bayer, George	Sep 17, 1925	U	1	7	Ferrier, James	Feb 24, 1915	C	D	B
Bean, Andy	Mar 13, 1953	H	N	F	Fezler, Forrest	Sep 23, 1949	F	F	1
Beard, Frank	May 1, 1939	C	Q	X	Finger, Sherman	Feb 2, 1944	Q	S	M
Benson, Bobby	Jul 15, 1940	G	J	B	Finsterwald, Dow	Sep 6, 1929	V	U	5
Bies, Don	Dec 10, 1937	B	N	L	Fitzsimmons, Patrick	Dec 15, 1950	R	F	M
Blancas, Homero	Mar 7, 1938	U	Q	7	Fleckman, Marty	Apr 23, 1944	E	P	2
Bolt, Tommy	Mar 31, 1918	G	P	L	Fleisher, Bruce	Oct 16, 1948	J	3	O
Boros, Julius	Mar 3, 1920	U	S	V	Floyd, Ray	Sep 4, 1942	F	F	Y
Brewer, Gay	Mar 19, 1932	C	V	6	Ford, Doug	Aug 6, 1922	J	H	Q
Brown, Pete	Feb 2, 1935	S	G	Z	Funseth, Rod	Apr 3, 1933	P	J	P
Burns, George	Jul 29, 1949	T	F	C	Furgol, Ed	Mar 22, 1917	A	E	8
Butler, Duke	Oct 13, 1948	F	Z	L	Galbraith, Alexander	Aug 14, 1945	X	R	K
Cadle, George	May 9, 1948	K	H	T	Garrett, Bill	Sep 6, 1940	O	F	W
Caldwell, Rex	May 5, 1950	X	F	T	Geiberger, Al	Sep 1, 1937	R	Z	K
Canipe, David E.	Aug 31, 1953	S	Q	M	Gilbert, Gibby	Jan 14, 1941	F	Y	U
Casper, Billy	Jun 24, 1931	K	D	1	Gilder, Bob	Dec 31, 1950	K	W	3
Cerda, Antonio	Apr 24, 1948	S	V	D	Glenz, David	Dec 15, 1948	X	D	H
Cerrudo, Ron	Feb 4, 1945	Q	W	R	Goalby, Bob	Mar 14, 1929	F	M	T
Charles, Bob	Mar 14, 1936	K	V	B	Goin, Ted Alan	Jan 9, 1950	W	B	B
Clayton, Ernie	Sep 2, 1941	G	C	U	Graham, David	May 23, 1946	F	T	3
Colbert, Jim	Mar 9, 1941	O	W	H	Graham, Lou	Jan 7, 1938	G	N	F
Cole, Bobby	May 11, 1948	M	K	V	Green, Al	Aug 26, 1939	E	V	H
Conner, Frank	Jan 11, 1946	M	2	3	Green, Hubert	Dec 28, 1946	S	O	Q
Coody, Charles	Jul 13, 1937	N	C	1	Greene, Bert	Feb 11, 1944	B	2	V
Crampton, Bruce	Sep 28, 1935	C	V	7	Groh, Gary	Oct 11, 1944	P	S	8
Crawford, Richard	Jun 28, 1939	P	S	P	Haas, Freddie	Jan 3, 1916	R	J	S
Crenshaw, Ben	Jan 11, 1952	S	F	H	Hamilton, Garnard	Aug 26, 1949	A	F	6
Cullins, Guy	Jul 25, 1949	P	B	7	Harris, John	Jun 13, 1952	L	U	5
Curl, Rod	Jan 9, 1943	S	V	T	Harris Jr., Labron	Sep 27, 1941	J	3	M
Dent, Jim	May 11, 1942	E	B	G	Hayes, Dale	Jan 7, 1952	O	B	D
Devlin, Bruce	Oct 10, 1937	K	H	Q	Hayes, Mark	Jul 12, 1949	B	R	T
Dickinson, Gardner	Sep 27, 1927	A	K	N	Heard, Jerry	May 1, 1947	D	1	H
Dickson, Bob	Jan 25, 1944	H	K	D	Hebert, Lionel	Jan 20, 1928	A	N	4
Diehl, Terry	Nov 9, 1949	G	Z	G	Heck, Marlon	Aug 28, 1939	G	X	K
Dill, Terrance	May 13, 1939	P	3	B	Henry, Bunky	Feb 8, 1944	W	Y	S
Dills, Joey	Nov 22, 1951	O	M	Y	Hill, Dave	May 20, 1937	E	E	E
Dougherty, Ed	Nov 4, 1947	G	R	5	Hill, Mike	Jan 27, 1939	A	F	3

NAME	DATE OF BIRTH	CODE			NAME	DATE OF BIRTH	CODE		
Hinkle, Lon	Jul 17, 1949	G	W	Y	Morley, Michael	Jun 17, 1946	H	Q	U
Hinson, Larry	Aug 5, 1944	R	G	7	Murphy, Bob	Feb 14, 1943	H	A	W
Hiskey, Babe	Nov 21, 1938	C	X	2	Nelson, Larry	Sep 10, 1947	V	S	H
Humphries, Earl	Sep 29, 1950	J	N	A	Nevil, Dwight	Aug 25, 1944	O	2	T
Inman, Joe	Nov 29, 1947	J	O	W	Newquiat, Dave	Aug 27, 1950	W	H	A
Irwin, Hale	Jun 3, 1945	U	A	D	Nichols, Bobby	Apr 14, 1936	S	Y	8
Iverson, Don	Oct 28, 1945	F	H	T	Nicklaus, Jack	Jan 21, 1940	P	A	Y
Jacklin, Tony	Jul 7, 1944	L	F	C	Nieporte, Tom	Oct 21, 1928	X	H	Z
Jacobs, John	Mar 18, 1945	M	H	1	Nixon, Mike	Sep 16, 1946	G	X	M
Jacobs, Tommy	Feb 13, 1935	F	S	C	North, Andy	Mar 9, 1950	M	E	3
Jaeckel, Barry	Feb 14, 1949	P	J	C	O'Neill, Dan	Mar 21, 1951	V	S	J
Jamieson, Jim	Apr 21, 1943	E	L	W	Oosterhuis, Peter	May 3, 1948	D	B	N
January, Don	Nov 20, 1929	D	L	F	Pace, Roy	Jun 27, 1941	J	U	T
Jenkins, Tom	Dec 14, 1947	A	A	D	Palmer, Arnold	Sep 10, 1929	B	Y	A
Johnson, George	Dec 8, 1938	U	M	L	Parker, Roger	Mar 10, 1947	V	B	W
Johnson, Howie	Sep 8, 1925	L	R	X	Pate, Jerry	Sep 16, 1953	L	D	3
Johnston, Bill	Jan 2, 1925	P	U	E	Payne, Bob	Nov 29, 1943	U	J	N
Johnston, Ralph	Nov 18, 1941	P	Y	6	Pearce, Eddie	Mar 16, 1952	F	U	B
Jones, Grier	May 6, 1946	M	B	L	Peete, Calvin	Jul 18, 1943	A	P	L
Karl, Richie	Sep 28, 1944	B	E	U	Pfeil, Mark	Jul 18, 1951	B	Z	4
Kelley, Spike	Oct 8, 1947	C	S	C	Pilcher, Johnny	Nov 2, 1952	P	W	G
Kite, Tom	Dec 9, 1949	O	2	D	Player, Gary	Nov 1, 1936	M	A	C
Knight, Dwaine	Oct 14, 1947	J	Y	J	Pooley, Don	Aug 27, 1951	T	J	C
Knudson, George	Jun 28, 1937	V	Q	L	Porter, Joe	Jun 5, 1945	W	C	F
Koch, Gary	Nov 21, 1952	L	N	1	Pott, Johnny	Nov 6, 1935	T	D	E
Leach, Ray	Jun 12, 1950	P	Q	Y	Purtzer, Tom	Dec 5, 1951	D	Z	3
Lee, Stan	Sep 1, 1952	W	Q	L	Rachels, Sammy	Sep 23, 1950	C	G	3
Leslie, Perry	Dec 31, 1942	J	M	K	Rawley, Zeno	Jul 4, 1946	B	E	D
Lietzke, Bruce	Jul 18, 1951	B	Z	4	Reasor, Mike	Dec 4, 1941	H	M	O
Lind, David	Jun 3, 1949	J	F	N	Refram, Dean	Nov 11, 1936	W	L	N
Lister, John	Mar 9, 1947	U	A	V	Rhyan, Dick	Nov 28, 1935	S	1	2
Littler, Gene	Jul 21, 1930	R	B	S	Risch, Bob	Aug 4, 1947	G	J	D
Lott, Lyn	Apr 9, 1950	U	H	1	Robertson, Ken	Dec 27, 1946	R	N	P
Lotz, Dick	Oct 15, 1942	A	T	7	Rodgers, Phil	Apr 3, 1938	A	P	1
Lundstrom, David	Jun 7, 1947	S	G	M	Rodriguez, Juan	Oct 23, 1935	E	S	Y
Lunn, Bob	Apr 24, 1945	C	R	5	Rogers, Bill	Sep 10, 1951	K	X	R
Mahaffey, John	May 9, 1948	K	H	T	Rosburg, Bob	Oct 21, 1926	E	E	B
Mallon, Bill	Feb 2, 1952	R	3	5	Rudolph, Mason	May 23, 1934	Q	D	A
Maltbie, Roger	Jun 30, 1951	G	G	L	Sabo, Ed	Mar 1, 1949	G	Y	S
Mancour, Larry	Jan 1, 1935	J	C	1	Sanders, Doug	Jun 24, 1933	E	G	6
Mancuso, Chipper	Dec 17, 1946	G	C	E	Sanudo, César	Oct 26, 1943	J	C	M
Marr, Dave	Dec 27, 1933	G	Z	T	Schlee, John	Jun 2, 1939	M	U	W
Marti, Fred	Nov 15, 1940	P	U	I	Schroeder, John	Nov 12, 1945	V	X	A
Marvel, Mike	Apr 21, 1945	X	O	2	Shaw, Bob	Dec 24, 1944	U	H	H
Massengale, Don	Apr 23, 1937	A	F	L	Shaw, Tom	Dec 13, 1942	O	W	Z
Massengale, Rik	Feb 6, 1947	M	1	X	Shillington, Brian	Jan 9, 1947	G	1	3
Masserio, James	Oct 13, 1948	F	Z	L	Sifford, Charles	Jun 3, 1923	L	A	U
McCord, Gary	May 23, 1948	A	W	8	Sifford, Curtis	May 6, 1942	X	Z	B
McCullough, Mike	Mar 21, 1945	P	L	4	Sikes, Dan	Dec 7, 1930	S	A	Z
McDonald, Pat	Apr 23, 1950	L	W	G	Sikes, R. H.	Mar 6, 1940	O	S	C
McGee, Jerry	Jul 21, 1943	D	S	O	Simons, Jim	May 15, 1950	K	Q	4
McGinnis, Tommy	Nov 27, 1947	G	M	U	Smith, Bob E.	Dec 2, 1942	C	L	O
McLendon, B. R.	Aug 10, 1945	T	N	F	Smith, Dave	Mar 29, 1946	U	U	F
McNickle, Artie	Sep 29, 1945	X	G	X	Smith, David	Jan 14, 1950	D	G	G
Melnick, John	Nov 26, 1951	S	Q	3	Snead, J.C.	Oct 14, 1941	C	R	4
Melnyk, Steve	Feb 26, 1947	J	S	K	Snead, Sam	May 27, 1912	M	J	W
Menne, Bob	Feb 19, 1942	Q	E	Z	Sneed, Ed	Aug 6, 1944	S	H	8
Metz, Craig	Mar 14, 1942	Q	3	P	Spray, Steve	Dec 16, 1940	X	X	Y
Miller, Allen	Aug 10, 1948	L	R	N	Stanton, Bob	Jan 20, 1946	V	H	D
Miller, Johnny	Apr 29, 1947	B	Y	F	Starks, Nate	Jun 20, 1940	E	M	K
Mitchell, Bobby	Feb 23, 1943	R	K	4	Stevens, Johnny	Aug 17, 1942	L	Q	F
Molina, Florentino	Dec 30, 1938	T	F	8	Still, Ken	Feb 12, 1935	E	R	B
Moody, Orville	Dec 9, 1933	M	G	A	Stockton, Dave	Nov 2, 1941	W	H	P
Moran, Paul	Jun 5, 1938	S	W	X	Stroble, Bobby	Dec 4, 1944	X	Q	V
Morgan, Gil	Sep 25, 1946	Q	D	V	Tabar, Greg	May 9, 1949	G	J	V

NAME	DATE OF BIRTH	CODE			NAME	DATE OF BIRTH	CODE		
Tallach, Ed	Jan 9, 1946	K	Z	1	Walzel, Bob	Sep 26, 1949	J	J	4
Tapie, Alan	Mar 24, 1949	G	T	H	Watson, Tom	Sep 4, 1949	K	P	G
Taylor, Steven	Aug 22, 1949	U	B	2	Weaver, De Witt	Sep 14, 1939	A	M	2
Tewell, Doug	Aug 27, 1949	B	G	7	Weiskopf, Tom	Nov 9, 1942	C	Q	Y
Thompson, Barney	Nov 6, 1948	G	V	B	White, Carlton	Feb 26, 1949	D	V	P
Thompson, Leonard	Jan 1, 1947	W	S	U	Wiechers, Jim	Aug 7, 1944	T	J	A
Thompson, Rocky	Oct 14, 1943	U	T	8	Williams, Evan	Feb 28, 1948	H	V	O
Thorpe, Jim	Feb 1, 1949	B	Y	X	Wintz, Gary	Oct 13, 1948	F	Z	L
Toepel, John	May 16, 1944	E	K	R	Wynn, Bob	Jan 27, 1940	V	G	5
Trevino, Lee	Dec 1, 1939	K	F	F	Wynn, Mike	Oct 22, 1944	C	A	L
Twitty, Howard	Jan 15, 1949	H	G	F	Yancey, Bert	Aug 6, 1938	L	3	T
Unger, Bob	Jul 14, 1943	U	L	G	Zarley, Kermit	Sep 29, 1941	L	B	O
Venturi, Ken	May 15, 1931	Q	U	T	Zender, Bob	Jun 22, 1943	V	R	S
Veriato, Steve	May 6, 1946	M	B	L	Ziegler, Larry	Aug 12, 1939	O	G	2
Wadkins, Bobby	Jul 26, 1951	K	E	D	Ziobro, Billy	Sep 11, 1948	U	V	M
Wadkins, Lanny	Dec 5, 1949	K	X	8	Zoeller, Fuzzy	Nov 11, 1951	C	A	N
Walkingstick, Guy	Apr 27, 1949	S	Z	J					
Wall Jr., Art	Nov 25, 1923	B	H	5					

_____
_____
_____
_____
_____
_____

Horse Racing

NAME	DATE OF BIRTH	CODE			NAME	DATE OF BIRTH	CODE		
Adams, Larry	Jun 13, 1936	J	3	2	Maple, Eddie	Nov 8, 1948	J	X	D
Arcaro, Eddie	Feb 19, 1916	S	3	7	Pincay Jr., Laffit	Dec 29, 1946	T	P	R
Baeza, Braulio	Mar 26, 1942	E	M	2	Rotz, John L.	Dec 16, 1934	Q	P	K
Baltazar, Chuck	May 22, 1947	B	T	4	Shoemaker, Willie	Aug 19, 1931	U	D	Q
Belmonte, Eddie	Feb 5, 1943	W	U	N	Turcotte, Ron	Jul 22, 1951	F	A	8
Blum, Walter	Sep 28, 1934	F	U	5	Ussery, Bob	Sep 3, 1935	A	Y	G
Cauthen, Steve	May 1, 1960	P	P	E	Valenzuela, Maguel	Dec 25, 1934	B	Y	T
Cordero, Angel	May 8, 1942	B	2	D	Vasquez, Jacinto	Jan 4, 1944	K	R	Q
Dancer, Stanley	Jul 25, 1927	F	B	P	Velasquez, Jorge	Dec 28, 1948	N	R	V
Fires, Earlie	Mar 19, 1947	G	L	6	Ycaza, Manuel	Feb 1, 1938	J	K	6
Hartack, Bill	Dec 9, 1932	P	F	7					
Haughton, William	Nov 2, 1923	B	N	G					

Ice Hockey

NAME	DATE OF BIRTH	CODE			NAME	DATE OF BIRTH	CODE		
Ahern, Fred	Feb 12, 1952	D	K	G	Cowick, Bruce	Aug 18, 1951	K	3	2
Alexander, Claire	Jun 16, 1945	K	O	R	Crashley, Barton	Jun 15, 1946	F	O	S
Anderson, Earl	Feb 24, 1951	T	V	R	Crisp, Terrance	May 28, 1943	T	U	1
Anderson, Murray	Aug 28, 1949	C	H	8	Croteau, Gary	Jun 20, 1946	L	T	X
Anderson, Ronald	Jan 21, 1950	L	O	O	Dailey, Robert	May 3, 1953	N	H	Y
Apps Jr., Sylvanus	Aug 1, 1947	D	F	A	DeMarco Jr., Albert (Ab)	Feb 27, 1949	E	W	Q
Arnason, Charles (Chuck)	Jul 15, 1951	W	W	1	Dionne, Marcel	Aug 3, 1951	S	N	M
Atkinson, Steven	Oct 16, 1948	J	3	O	Doak, Gary	Feb 25, 1946	L	Q	G
Awrey, Donald	Jul 18, 1943	A	P	L	Dornhoefer, Gerhardt (Gary)	Feb 2, 1943	T	R	K
Backstrom, Ralph	Sep 18, 1937	L	O	2	Drouin, Jude	Oct 28, 1948	V	M	1
Bailey, Garnet (Ace)	Jun 13, 1948	W	P	V	Dube, Normand	Sep 12, 1951	M	Z	T
Barber, William	Jul 11, 1952	Q	U	Z	Dudley, Richard (Rick)	Jan 31, 1949	A	X	W
Barrett, Frederick	Jan 26, 1950	Q	T	T	Dunlop, Blake	Apr 4, 1953	G	G	3
Bennett, Curt	Mar 27, 1948	N	V	J	Dunn, David	Aug 19, 1948	V	1	W
Berenson, Gordon (Red)	Dec 8, 1939	R	N	N	Dupere, Denis	Jun 6, 1948	P	H	O
Bergeron, Michel	Nov 11, 1954	S	E	U	Dupont, Andre	Jul 27, 1949	R	D	A
Bergman, Gary	Oct 7, 1938	D	F	P	Durbano, Steven	Dec 12, 1951	L	D	L
Berry, Robert	Nov 29, 1943	U	J	N	Ecclestone, Timothy	Sep 24, 1947	M	D	W
Beverley, Nicholas	Apr 21, 1947	R	Q	6	Edestrand, Darryl	Nov 6, 1945	P	R	3
Bialowas, Dwight	Sep 8, 1952	F	X	S	Egers, John	Jan 28, 1949	V	U	T
Bladon, Tom	Dec 29, 1952	C	X	6	Esposito, Philip	Feb 20, 1942	R	F	1
Boddy, Gregg	Mar 19, 1949	B	O	C	Fairbairn, William	Jan 7, 1947	E	Y	1
Boldirev, Ivan	Aug 15, 1949	N	X	U	Ferguson, George	Aug 22, 1952	M	F	A
Bordeleau, Jean-Pierre	Jun 13, 1949	T	Q	X	Flesch, John	Jul 15, 1953	R	Z	6
Bordeleau, Paulin	Jan 29, 1953	L	1	4	Flett, William	Jul 21, 1943	D	S	O
Boucha, Henry	Jun 1, 1951	A	F	P	Forbes, David	Nov 16, 1948	R	C	M
Bouchard, Pierre	Feb 20, 1948	X	N	F	Frig, Leonard	Oct 30, 1950	R	Q	7
Boudrias, Andre	Sep 19, 1943	S	W	H	Gagnon, Germain	Dec 9, 1942	K	S	V
Bourne, Robert	Jun 21, 1954	N	B	J	Gainey, Robert	Dec 13, 1953	G	H	R
Brooks, Gordon	Sep 11, 1950	O	X	Q	Gardner, David	Aug 23, 1952	N	G	B
Brown, Arnie	Jan 28, 1942	R	L	C	Gare, Danny	May 14, 1954	V	U	D
Brown, Larry	Apr 14, 1947	K	J	Y	Gassoff, Robert	Apr 17, 1953	U	U	H
Bucyk, John	May 12, 1935	B	W	Z	Gibbs, Barry	Sep 28, 1948	O	K	4
Burns, Robert (Robin)	Aug 27, 1946	K	C	Z	Gilbert, Edward	Mar 12, 1952	K	L	C
Byers, Michael	Sep 11, 1946	B	S	G	Gilbert, Rod	Jul 1, 1941	N	Y	X
Cameron, Craig	Jul 19, 1945	U	T	R	Gilbertson, Stanley	Oct 29, 1944	K	H	S
Campbell, Colin	Jan 28, 1953	K	Z	3	Gilles, Clark	Apr 7, 1954	G	L	8
Carleton, Kenneth	Aug 4, 1946	K	H	B	Giroux, Larry	Aug 28, 1951	U	K	D
Carr, Eugene	Sep 17, 1951	R	B	Y	Glennie, Brian	Aug 29, 1946	M	E	2
Carriere, Larry	Jan 3, 1952	K	1	8	Goldsworthy, William	Aug 24, 1944	N	1	S
Cashman, Wayne	Jun 24, 1945	B	Y	W	Goodenough, Larry	Jan 19, 1953	A	Q	T
Charron, Guy	Jan 24, 1949	R	Q	P	Goring, Robert (Butch)	Oct 22, 1949	M	G	W
Christie, Michael	Dec 20, 1949	B	K	P	Gould, John	Jan 15, 1949	H	G	F
Clarke, Robert (Bobby)	Aug 13, 1949	L	V	S	Grant, Daniel	Feb 21, 1946	G	M	C
Clement, Bill	Dec 20, 1950	W	L	R	Gratton, Normand	Dec 22, 1950	A	N	U
Collins, William	Jul 13, 1943	T	K	F	Graves, Hilliard	Oct 18, 1950	E	D	U
Comeau, Reynald	Oct 25, 1948	S	J	X	Greschner, Ronald	Dec 22, 1954	N	S	3
Corrigan, Michael	Jan 11, 1946	M	2	3	Grisdale, John	Aug 23, 1948	A	B	1
Cournoyer, Yvan	Nov 22, 1943	N	B	F	Gryp, Robert	May 6, 1950	A	G	U

NAME	DATE OF BIRTH	CODE		
Gueremont, Jocelyn	Mar 1, 1951	A	1	W
Hadfield, Victor	Oct 4, 1940	T	F	R
Hajt, William	Nov 18, 1951	K	H	U
Hampton, Rick	Jun 14, 1956	A	1	G
Harper, Terrence	Jan 27, 1940	V	G	5
Harris, Ronald	Jun 30, 1942	J	Y	Y
Harris, William	Jan 29, 1952	N	Y	1
Hart, Gerald	Jan 1, 1948	T	T	W
Harvey, Buster	Feb 4, 1950	B	3	3
Henderson, Paul	Jan 28, 1943	O	M	E
Henning, Lorne	Feb 23, 1952	P	V	S
Hess, Robert	May 19, 1955	X	1	L
Hextall, Bryan	May 23, 1941	U	N	R
Hextall, Dennis	Apr 17, 1943	A	G	S
Hicke, Ernest	Nov 7, 1947	K	U	8
Hicks, Douglas	May 29, 1955	K	H	V
Hodge, Kenneth	Jun 25, 1944	W	W	Y
Hogaboam, William	Sep 5, 1949	L	Q	H
Howatt, Gary	Sep 26, 1952	A	N	C
Howe, Gordon	Mar 31, 1928	C	3	A
Hrechkosy, David	Nov 1, 1951	Q	T	C
Hrycuik, James	Oct 7, 1949	U	U	G
Hudson, David	Dec 28, 1949	K	S	X
Hughes, Brenton	Jun 17, 1943	Q	M	N
Hull, Dennis	Nov 19, 1944	H	A	F
Hull, Robert	Jan 3, 1939	X	K	D
Huston, Ronald	Apr 8, 1945	K	A	O
Irvine, Ted	Dec 8, 1944	D	U	Z
Jarrett, Douglas	Apr 22, 1944	D	O	1
Jarry, Pierre	Mar 30, 1949	N	Z	O
Jarvis, Doug	Mar 24, 1955	N	1	V
Johnston, Joey	Mar 3, 1949	J	1	U
Johnston, Larry	Jul 20, 1943	C	R	N
Joly, Greg	May 30, 1954	O	H	U
Kannegiesser, Sheldon	Aug 15, 1947	S	U	P
Kearns, Dennis	Sep 27, 1945	V	E	V
Kehoe, Rick	Jul 15, 1951	W	W	1
Kelly, Bob	Jun 6, 1946	U	E	J
Kelly, Robert	Nov 25, 1950	U	O	Z
Kindrachuk, Orest	Sep 14, 1950	R	1	T
King, Wayne	Sep 4, 1951	D	R	L
Komadoski, Neil	Nov 5, 1951	M	U	J
Korab, Gerald	Sep 15, 1948	A	Z	Q
Korney, Michael	Sep 15, 1953	K	C	2
Koroll, Clifford	Oct 1, 1946	W	K	2
Kozak, Don	Feb 2, 1952	R	3	5
Kryskow, David	Dec 25, 1951	A	R	Y
L'Abbe, Maurice (Moe)	Sep 4, 1947	P	M	B
Labre, Yvon	Nov 29, 1949	D	R	2
LaFleur, Guy	Sep 20, 1951	U	E	2
Laframboise, Peter	Jan 18, 1950	H	L	L
Lalonde, Robert	Mar 27, 1951	D	Y	P
Lalonde, Ronald	Oct 30, 1952	M	T	D
Lambert, Yvon	May 20, 1950	P	V	A
Lapointe, Guy	Mar 18, 1948	D	M	8
Larose, Claude	Mar 2, 1942	D	Q	C
Larouche, Pierre	Nov 16, 1955	U	L	2
Lavender, Brian	Apr 20, 1947	Q	P	5
Leach, Reginald	Apr 23, 1950	L	W	G
Lefley, Charles	Jan 20, 1950	K	N	N
Leiter, Robert	Mar 22, 1941	D	G	V
Lemaire, Jacques	Sep 7, 1945	A	N	A
Lemieux, Jean	May 31, 1952	V	G	R
Lemieux, Richard	Apr 19, 1951	D	T	E
Lesuk, William	Nov 1, 1946	G	N	Z
Lever, Donald	Nov 14, 1952	D	F	T
Lewis, David	Jul 3, 1953	E	N	T
Libett, Nick	Dec 9, 1945	B	W	3
Lochead, Bill	Oct 13, 1954	M	D	Y
Lonsberry, Ross	Feb 7, 1947	N	2	H
Lorentz, James	May 1, 1947	D	1	H
Luce, Donald	Oct 2, 1948	S	O	8
Lynch, Jack	May 28, 1952	S	D	O
Lysiak, Thomas	Apr 27, 1953	G	B	S
Mac Adam, Alan	Mar 6, 1952	D	E	5
MacDonald, Lowell	Aug 30, 1941	D	3	R
MacLeich, Richard	Jan 3, 1950	Q	Y	4
MacMillan, William	Mar 7, 1943	F	W	K
Magnuson, Keith	Apr 27, 1947	X	W	D
Mahovlich, Frank	Jan 10, 1938	K	Q	J
Mahovlich, Peter	Oct 10, 1946	H	T	C
Maloney, Daniel	Sep 24, 1950	D	H	4
Maloney, David	Jul 31, 1956	B	R	V
Manery, Randy	Jan 10, 1949	C	B	A
Marcotte, Donald	Apr 15, 1947	L	K	Z
Marks, John	Mar 28, 1948	O	W	K
Marotte, Gilles	Jun 7, 1945	A	E	H
Marshall, Bert	Nov 22, 1943	N	B	F
Marson, Mike	Jul 24, 1955	U	H	L
Martin, Pit	Dec 9, 1943	G	T	X
Martin, Richard (Rick)	Jul 26, 1951	K	E	D
Martineau, Donald	Apr 25, 1952	H	2	O
McCreary, Keith	Jun 19, 1940	D	L	J
McDonald, Lanny	Feb 16, 1953	F	Q	O
McElmury, James	Oct 3, 1949	Q	Q	C
McKechnie, Walter	Jun 19, 1947	G	T	Y
McKenny, James	Dec 1, 1946	O	P	P
McKenzie, John	Dec 12, 1937	D	P	N
McManama, Robert	Oct 7, 1951	O	W	L
McNab, Peter	May 8, 1952	V	M	2
Meehan, Gerald	Sep 3, 1946	R	K	7
Merrick, Wayne	Apr 23, 1952	F	Z	M
Middleton, Rick	Dec 4, 1953	V	2	H
Mikita, Stanley	May 20, 1940	U	J	M
Mikkelson, William	May 21, 1948	W	U	6
Mohns, Douglas	Dec 13, 1933	Q	L	E
Monahan, Garry	Oct 20, 1946	S	A	N
Morrison, Lewis	Feb 11, 1948	B	D	5
Mott, Morris	May 25, 1946	H	V	5
Mulvey, Grant	Sep 17, 1956	D	J	C
Murdoch, Robert	May 17, 1947	U	O	Y
Murphy, Michael	Sep 12, 1950	P	Y	R
Murray, Robert	Jul 16, 1948	J	U	V
Nanne, Louis	Jun 2, 1941	G	X	2
Neely, Robert	Nov 9, 1953	T	B	Q
Neilson, James	Nov 28, 1940	E	E	F
Nevin, Robert	Mar 18, 1938	H	2	K
Nicholson, Paul	Feb 16, 1954	C	R	Q
Nolet, Simon	Nov 23, 1941	U	A	C
Nowak, Henry	Nov 24, 1950	T	N	Y
Nystrom, Bob	Oct 10, 1952	P	2	R
O'Brien, Dennis	Jun 10, 1949	Q	N	U
Oddleifson, Christopher	Sep 7, 1950	K	T	M
O'Flaherty, Gerard	Aug 31, 1950	C	M	E
Ogilvie, Brian	Jan 30, 1952	O	Z	2
O'Reilly, Terry	Jun 7, 1951	G	M	V
Orr, Bobby	Mar 20, 1948	F	O	B
Pappin, James	Sep 10, 1939	U	H	X
Paradise, Robert	Apr 22, 1944	D	O	1
Patey, Larry	Feb 17, 1953	G	R	P

NAME	DATE OF BIRTH	CODE		
Patrick, Craig	May 20, 1946	C	Q	Z
Perreault, Gilbert	Nov 13, 1950	H	B	N
Pesut, George	Jun 17, 1953	M	Z	C
Plager, Barclay	Mar 26, 1941	H	L	Z
Plante, Pierre	May 14, 1951	F	Q	5
Polis, Gregory	Aug 8, 1950	C	R	P
Potvin, Denis	Oct 29, 1953	H	T	E
Potvin, Jean	Mar 25, 1949	H	U	J
Powis, Lynn	Apr 19, 1949	K	R	A
Pratt, Tracy	Mar 8, 1943	G	X	L
Price, Noel	Dec 9, 1935	F	J	E
Pronvost, Jean	Dec 18, 1945	L	C	D
Quinn, Pat	Jan 29, 1943	P	N	F
Ramsey, Craig	Mar 17, 1951	R	O	E
Ratelle, Jean	Oct 3, 1940	S	E	Q
Redmond, Mickey	Dec 27, 1947	O	O	R
Redmond, Dick	Aug 14, 1949	M	W	T
Reid, Allan	Jun 24, 1946	P	X	2
Richard, Jacques	Oct 7, 1952	M	Y	O
Robert, Rene	Dec 31, 1948	Q	U	Y
Roberto, Phillip	Jan 1, 1949	R	V	Z
Roberts, Douglas	Oct 28, 1942	O	D	M
Roberts, James	Apr 9, 1940	B	Y	D
Robinson, Larry	Jun 2, 1951	B	G	Q
Robitaille, Michael	Feb 12, 1948	P	E	6
Rochefort, Leon	May 4, 1939	F	T	1
Romanchych, Larry	Sep 7, 1949	N	S	K
Rombough, Douglas	Jul 8, 1950	S	O	R
Rota, Darcy	Feb 16, 1953	F	Q	O
Rota, Randy	Aug 16, 1950	L	Z	X
Rupp, Duane	Mar 29, 1938	T	K	V
Russell, Philip	Jul 1, 1952	F	K	P
Sabourin, Gary	Dec 4, 1943	B	O	S
Sacharuk, Lawrence	Sep 16, 1952	O	C	1
St. Laurent, Andre	Feb 16, 1953	F	Q	O
St. Marseille, Francis	Dec 14, 1939	X	T	T
Saleski, Donald	Nov 10, 1949	H	1	H
Salming, Borje	Apr 17, 1951	B	R	C
Sanderson, Derek	Jun 16, 1946	G	P	T
Sather, Glen	Sep 2, 1943	A	E	Y
Savard, Andre	Feb 9, 1953	W	J	G
Savard, Serge	Jan 22, 1946	X	K	F
Schmautz, Robert	Mar 28, 1945	W	S	C
Schock, Ronald	Dec 19, 1943	R	A	8
Schoenfeld, James	Sept 4, 1952	B	T	O
Schultz, David	Oct 14, 1949	D	2	O
Seiling, Rod	Nov 14, 1944	C	Y	A
Sheppard, Gregory	Apr 23, 1949	O	V	E
Shutt, Stephen	Jul 1, 1952	F	K	P
Simmer, Charles	Mar 20, 1954	M	V	P
Sims, Allan	Apr 18, 1953	V	V	J
Sittler, Darryl	Sep 18, 1950	V	B	X
Smith, Dallas	Oct 10, 1941	W	N	Z
Spencer, Brian	Sep 3, 1949	J	O	F
Stackhouse, Ronald	Aug 26, 1949	A	F	G
Stanfield, Frederic	May 4, 1944	Q	1	E
Stapleton, Patrick	Jul 4, 1940	T	1	Y
Stemkowski, Peter	Aug 25, 1943	Q	Z	Q
Stewart, John	May 16, 1950	L	R	5

NAME	DATE OF BIRTH	CODE		
Stewart, Robert	Nov 10, 1950	E	2	K
Stoughton, Blaine	Mar 13, 1953	H	N	F
Talafous, Dean	Aug 25, 1953	M	K	F
Tallon, Dale	Oct 19, 1950	F	E	V
Tardif, Marc	Jun 12, 1949	S	P	W
Thompson, Errol	May 28, 1950	X	A	J
Thornson, Floyd	Jun 14, 1949	U	R	Y
Tkaczuk, Walter	Sep 29, 1947	R	J	2
Tremblay, Mario	Sep 2, 1956	M	W	V
Turnbull, Ian	Dec 22, 1953	Q	R	1
Unger, Garry	Dec 7, 1947	R	W	5
Vadnais, Carol	Sep 25, 1945	T	C	T
Vail, Eric	Sep 16, 1953	L	D	3

Goaltenders

NAME	DATE OF BIRTH	CODE		
Adams, John	Jul 27, 1946	B	3	2
Belanger, Yves	Sep 30, 1952	E	R	G
Belhumeur, Michel	Sep 2, 1949	H	N	E
Bouchard, Daniel	Dec 12, 1950	O	C	J
Brooks, Ross	Oct 17, 1937	R	P	X
Cheevers, Gerry	Dec 2, 1940	J	J	K
Crozier, Roger	Mar 16, 1942	S	B	R
Davidson, John	Feb 27, 1953	R	2	Z
Dryden, Ken	Aug 7, 1947	K	M	G
Edwards, Gary	Oct 5, 1947	X	P	8
Esposito, Tony	Apr 23, 1943	G	N	Y
Farr, Norman (Rocky)	Apr 7, 1947	C	B	R
Favell, Douglas	Apr 5, 1945	G	1	L
Gilbert, Gilles	Mar 31, 1949	O	1	P
Grant, Douglas	Jul 27, 1948	U	C	7
Herron, Denis	Jun 18, 1952	Q	Z	B
Inness, Gary	May 28, 1949	C	3	G
Johnson, Robert	Nov 12, 1948	N	2	H
Johnston, Eddie	Nov 24, 1935	O	W	X
Larocque, Michel	Apr 6, 1952	M	H	3
Lockett, Ken	Aug 30, 1947	K	G	5
LoPresti, Peter	May 23, 1954	G	A	N
Low, Ronald	Jun 21, 1950	A	Z	8
Maniago, Cesare	Jan 13, 1939	K	U	O
McDuffe, Peter	Feb 16, 1948	T	J	B
McKenzie, William	Mar 12, 1949	S	G	4
McRae, Gordon	Apr 12, 1948	F	J	Z
Meloche, Gilles	Jul 12, 1950	W	S	V
Myre, Phil	Nov 1, 1948	B	Q	5
Parent, Bernie	Apr 3, 1945	E	Y	J
Plasse, Michel	Jun 1, 1948	K	C	J
Resch, Glenn	Apr 17, 1948	L	O	5
Rivard, Fern	Jan 17, 1946	S	E	A
Rutherford, Jim	Feb 17, 1949	S	M	F
Smith, Gary	Feb 4, 1944	S	U	O
Stephenson, Wayne	Jan 29, 1945	K	Q	L
Thomas, Robert	Sep 9, 1947	U	R	G
Vachon, Rogatien	Sep 8, 1945	B	O	B
Villemure, Gilles	May 30, 1940	G	T	W
Wilson, Duncan	Mar 22, 1948	H	Q	D

Tennis

NAME	DATE OF BIRTH	CODE			NAME	DATE OF BIRTH	CODE		
Alexander, John (Austral.)	Jul 4, 1951	L	L	P	Cornejo, Patricio (Chile)	Jun 6, 1944	C	C	E
Amaya, Victor (USA)	Jul 2, 1954	A	N	U	Court, Margaret (Austral.)	Jul 16, 1942	B	M	G
Amritraj, Anand (India)	Mar 20, 1952	S	T	L	Cox, Mark (Gr. Brit.)	Jul 5, 1943	L	B	6
Amritraj, Vijay (India)	Dec 14, 1953	H	J	S	Cramer, Patrick (S. Africa)	Mar 21, 1947	J	N	8
Anderson, Malcolm (Mal) (Austral.)	Mar 3, 1935	A	H	V	Crealy, Dick (Austral.)	Sep 18, 1944	P	X	K
Andrews, John (USA)	May 2, 1952	P	F	V	Cuypers, Brigitte (S. Africa)	Dec 3, 1955	O	3	L
Anliot, Helena (Sweden)	Sep 26, 1956	N	S	M	Darmon, Rosie (France)	Mar 23, 1939	K	E	R
Anthony, Julie (USA)	Jan 13, 1948	H	C	A	Davidson, Owen (Austral.)	Oct 4, 1943	K	J	X
Appel, Elly (Netherlands)	Jul 27, 1952	J	H	H	Dell, Dick (USA)	Dec 29, 1947	Q	Q	T
Ashe, Arthur (USA)	Jul 10, 1943	Q	G	C	Dent, Philip (Austral.)	Feb 14, 1950	M	K	E
Austin, W. Jeffrey (USA)	Jul 5, 1951	M	M	Q	Dibbs, Eddie (USA)	Feb 3, 1951	V	3	4
Ball, Sydney (Austral.)	Jan 24, 1950	O	R	R	Dibley, Colin (Austral.)	Sep 19, 1944	Q	Y	L
Baranyi, Szabolcs (Hungary)	Jan 31, 1944	O	Q	K	Dimond, Jenny (Austral.)	Nov 13, 1955	R	H	Y
Barazzutti, Corrado (Italy)	Feb 19, 1953	J	T	R	Dominguez, Patrice (France)	Jan 12, 1950	B	E	E
Barker, Sue (Gr. Brit.)	Apr 19, 1956	O	1	R	Dowdeswell, Colin (Rhodesia)	May 12, 1955	Q	T	D
Barthes, Pierre (France)	Sep 13, 1941	S	O	6	Dowdeswell, Roger (Rhodesia)	Feb 16, 1944	G	D	1
Bassi, Lucia (Italy)	Dec 12, 1936	G	O	L	Downs, Barbara (USA)	Mar 4, 1954	T	E	7
Battrick, Gerald (Gr. Brit.)	May 27, 1947	G	Y	A	Drysdale, Cliff (S. Africa)	May 26, 1941	X	Q	U
Beaven, Lindsey (Gr. Brit.)	Jan 1, 1950	O	W	2	DuPont, Laura (USA)	May 4, 1949	B	D	Q
Bengtson, Ove (Sweden)	Apr 5, 1945	G	1	L	DuPre, Patrick (USA)	Sep 16, 1954	H	E	5
Bentzer, Ingrid (Sweden)	Dec 6, 1943	D	Q	U	Durr, Francoise (France)	Dec 25, 1942	C	F	D
Bertolucci, Paulo (Italy)	Aug 3, 1951	S	N	M	Ebbinghaus, Katja (W. Germany)	Jan 6, 1948	A	Y	2
Bertram, Byron (S. Africa)	Oct 29, 1952	L	S	C	Edlefsen, Tom (USA)	Dec 12, 1941	Q	U	W
Blachford, Lindsay (Gr. Brit.)	Apr 6, 1953	J	J	5	Edmondson, Mark (Austral.)	Jun 28, 1954	U	J	Q
Bonicelli, Fiorella (Peru)	Dec 21, 1951	U	N	U	Elschenbroich, Harald (W. Germany)	Jun 19, 1941	A	M	L
Borg, Bjorn (Sweden)	Jun 6, 1956	Q	S	7	el Shafei, Ismail (UAR)	Nov 15, 1947	S	3	H
Borowiak, Jeff (USA)	Sep 25, 1949	H	H	3	Emerson, Roy (Austral.)	Nov 3, 1936	O	C	E
Bostrom, Patricia (USA)	Nov 25, 1950	U	O	Z	Estep, Mike (USA)	Jul 19, 1949	J	Y	1
Brasher, Shirley (Gr. Brit.)	Jun 13, 1934	O	Z	W	Evert, Chris (USA)	Dec 21, 1954	M	R	2
Brown, William L. (USA)	Jan 14, 1945	S	A	4	Evert, Jeanne (USA)	Oct 5, 1957	T	3	X
Browning, Francoise (France)	Dec 25, 1942	C	F	D	Ewert, Ernie (Austral.)	Jun 5, 1954	U	O	1
Burton, Veronica (Gr. Brit.)	Jan 27, 1952	L	W	Y	Fairlie, Brian (New Zealand)	Jun 13, 1948	W	P	V
Carmichael, Bob (Austral.)	Jul 4, 1940	T	1	Y	Farrell, Mark (Gr. Brit.)	May 6, 1953	Q	L	2
Casals, Rosemary (USA)	Sep 19, 1948	E	A	U	Fassbender, Jurgen (W. Germany)	May 21, 1948	W	U	6
Case, Ross (Austral.)	Nov 1, 1951	Q	T	C	Fawcett, Anthony (Rhodesia)	Jun 29, 1951	F	F	K
Caujolle, Jean-Francois (France)	Mar 31, 1953	C	C	Y	Fayter, Jackie (Gr. Brit.)	Jun 10, 1951	K	P	Y
Chanfreau, Jean Baptiste (France)	Jan 17, 1947	P	F	C	Feaver, John (Gr. Brit.)	Feb 16, 1952	H	O	L
Chanfreau, Gail (France)	Apr 3, 1945	E	Y	J	Fernandez, Isabel (Colombia)	Sep 18, 1950	V	B	X
Lesley, Charles (Gr. Brit.)	Jul 15, 1952	U	Y	4	Fibak, Wojciech-Jan (Poland)	Aug 30, 1952	U	O	J
Clifton, John (Gr. Brit.)	Feb 19, 1946	E	K	A	Fillol, Jaime (Chile)	Jun 3, 1946	R	B	F
Coe, Annette (Gr. Brit.)	Mar 4, 1954	T	E	7	Fleming, Peter (USA)	Jan 21, 1955	U	U	Z
Coles, Glynis (Gr. Brit.)	Feb 20, 1954	G	V	U	Fletcher, Ian (Austral.)	Dec 1, 1948	J	S	2
Collins, Michael (Gr. Brit.)	May 19, 1952	J	X	E	Franulovic, Zeljko (Yugoslavia)	Jun 13, 1947	A	N	S
Conner, Judith (New Zealand)	Nov 18, 1953	E	L	Z	Freer, Billy (S. Africa)	Mar 9, 1951	J	F	5
Connors, Jimmy (USA)	Sep 2, 1952	X	R	M	Fretz, Tory Ann (USA)	Aug 8, 1942	B	G	5
Cooper, Jill (Gr. Brit.)	Apr 14, 1949	E	M	4	Froehling III, Frank (USA)	May 19, 1942	N	K	P
Cooper, John (Austral.)	Nov 4, 1946	K	Q	3	Fromholtz, Dianne Lee (Austral.)	Aug 10, 1956	M	2	6

99

NAME	DATE OF BIRTH	CODE	NAME	DATE OF BIRTH	CODE
Fuchs, Natalie (**France**)	Sep 3, 1952	A S N	Koch, Thomaz (**Brazil**)	May 11, 1945	U F O
Ganz, Donna (**USA**)	Nov 9, 1954	Q C S	Kodes, Jan (**Czech.**)	Mar 1, 1946	P U L
Ganzabal, Julian (**Argentina**)	Aug 25, 1946	H A X	Korotkov, Vladimir (**USSR**)	Apr 23, 1948	R U C
Gardiner, Alvin (**Austral.**)	Feb 11, 1951	F H D	Krantzcke, Karen (**Austral.**)	Feb 1, 1947	G V S
Gerken, Paul (**USA**)	Mar 15, 1950	S L A	Kronk, Paul (**Austral.**)	Sep 22, 1954	O L C
Gerulaitis, Vitas (**USA**)	Jul 26, 1954	B J X	Krulevitz, Steve (**USA**)	May 30, 1951	W D N
Giltinan, Bob (**Austral.**)	Jul 4, 1949	R J L	Kuhnke, Christian (**W. Germany**)	Apr 13, 1939	H 1 E
Giorgi, Monica (**Italy**)	Jan 3, 1946	D T U	Kuki, Jun (**Japan**)	Dec 28, 1945	V N O
Gisbert, Juan (**Spain**)	May 4, 1942	V X 8	Kukal, Jan (**Czech.**)	Sep 13, 1942	P P 8
Giscafre, Raquel (**Argentina**)	May 15, 1949	N P 2	Kuykendall, Kathy (**USA**)	Nov 23, 1956	B U D
Gohn, Judith (**Rumania**)	May 10, 1945	T E N	Lall, Premjit (**India**)	Oct 20, 1940	M W 8
Goolagong, Evonne (**Austral.**)	Jul 31, 1951	P K J	Lara, Marcelo (**Mexico**)	Oct 5, 1947	X P 8
Gorman, Tom (**USA**)	Jan 19, 1946	U G C	Laver, Rod (**Austral.**)	Aug 9, 1938	O C W
Gottfried, Brian (**USA**)	Jan 27, 1952	L W Y	Leonard, Tom (**USA**)	Jul 15, 1948	H T U
Gourlay, Helen (**Austral.**)	Dec 23, 1946	N J L	Lewis, Richard (**Gr. Brit.**)	Dec 6, 1954	U B M
Goven, Georges (**France**)	Apr 27, 1948	V Y G	Lloyd, David (**Gr. Brit.**)	Jan 3, 1948	V V Y
Graebner, Clark (**USA**)	Nov 4, 1943	S M V	Lloyd, John (**Gr. Brit.**)	Aug 27, 1954	L N K
Gregg, Pat (**Austral.**)	May 13, 1953	X S A	Lloyd, William (Bill) (**Austral.**)	May 7, 1949	E G D
Guerrant, Romana (**USA**)	Nov 28, 1948	F P Y	Louie, Marcelyn (Marcie) (**USA**)	Oct 9, 1953	L 2 S
Gulyas, Istvan (**Hungary**)	Oct 14, 1931	G D F	Loyo-Mayo, Joaquin (**Mexico**)	Aug 16, 1945	B T M
Gunter, Nancy (**USA**)	Aug 23, 1942	R W M	Lutz, Bob (**USA**)	Aug 29, 1947	J F 4
Gurdal, Michele (**Belgium**)	Nov 30, 1952	U W B	McKinley, Bob (**USA**)	Aug 5, 1950	C J W
Guzman, Francisco (Pancho) (**Ecuador**)	May 24, 1946	G U 4	McManus, Jim (**USA**)	Sep 16, 1940	A Q 7
			McMillan, Frew (**S. Africa**)	May 20, 1942	O L Q
Hancock, Keith (**Austral.**)	Feb 3, 1953	Q C A	McNamee, Paul (**Austral.**)	Nov 12, 1954	T F V
Harris, Kerry (**Austral.**)	Sep 19, 1949	B B W	Mandarino, Jose Edison (**Brazil**)	Mar 26, 1941	H L Z
Hawcroft, Barbara (**Austral.**)	Oct 13, 1950	X 2 P	Mappin, Sue (**Gr. Brit.**)	Nov 7, 1947	K U 8
Heldman, Julie (**USA**)	Dec 8, 1945	A V 2	Martin, Billy (**USA**)	Dec 25, 1956	L Y C
Hemmes, Fred (**Netherlands**)	Jun 14, 1950	R S 1	Martinez, Cecilia (**USA**)	May 24, 1947	D V 6
Hewitt, Bob (**S. Africa**)	Jan 12, 1940	F U P	Masters, Geoff (**Austral.**)	May 19, 1950	O U 8
Higueras, Jose (**Spain**)	Mar 1, 1953	T A 2	Masthoff, Helga (**W. Germany**)	Nov 11, 1941	H R Y
Hirai, Ken (**Japan**)	Mar 19, 1950	W P E	Maud, Robert (**S. Africa**)	Aug 12, 1946	S Q K
Hoesl, Helga (**W. Germany**)	Feb 2, 1940	D N C	May, Kathy (**USA**)	Jun 18, 1956	E B L
Hogan, Patti (**USA**)	Dec 21, 1949	C L Q	Mayer Jr., Sandy (**USA**)	Apr 5, 1952	L G 2
Holecek, Milan (**Czech.**)	Oct 23, 1943	F 3 J	Meer, Saeed (**Pakistan**)	Nov 25, 1947	E K S
Holmes, Norman (**USA**)	Oct 5, 1949	S S E	Meiler, Karl (**W. Germany**)	Apr 30, 1949	V 3 M
Hombergen, Patrick (**Belgium**)	Sep 8, 1946	W P D	Melville, Kerry (**Austral.**)	Aug 7, 1947	K M G
Hordijk, Jan (**Netherlands**)	Feb 5, 1950	C A 4	Metreveli, Alexander (**USSR**)	Nov 2, 1944	O M W
Hrebec, Jiri (**Czech.**)	Sep 19, 1950	W C Y	Meyer, Carrie (**USA**)	Aug 22, 1955	C J G
Hudson-Beck, Salli (**Rhodesia**)	Oct 30, 1953	J U F	Michel, Margaret (Peggy) (**USA**)	Feb 2, 1949	C Z Y
Hume, Joyce (**Gr. Brit.**)	Jul 22, 1944	C V S	Mignot, Bernard (**Belgium**)	Mar 12, 1948	V F 2
Hunt, Lesley (**Austral.**)	May 29, 1950	A B K	Molesworth, Corinne (**Gr. Brit.**)	Jun 18, 1949	A V 3
Hunt, Robyn Rhona (**New Zealand**)	Dec 3, 1950	E W 8	Molina, Ivan (**Columbia**)	Jun 16, 1946	G P T
Iqbal, Munawar (**Pakistan**)	Feb 27, 1948	G U N	Moore, Penny (**Gr. Brit.**)	Jul 7, 1951	O O S
Jauffret, Francois (**France**)	Feb 9, 1942	F X P	Moore, Ray (**S. Africa**)	Aug 24, 1946	G 3 W
Jausovec, Mima (**Yugoslavia**)	Jul 20, 1956	O F K	Moreno, Jose (**Spain**)	Aug 30, 1953	R P L
Janes, Christine (**Gr. Brit.**)	Jan 16, 1941	H 1 W	Morgan, Mandy (**Austral.**)	Jul 4, 1953	F O U
Johansson, Kjell (**Sweden**)	Feb 12, 1951	G J E	Morozova, Olga (**USSR**)	Feb 22, 1949	X R L
Johansson, Lief (**Sweden**)	Jun 3, 1952	A K U	Mottram, Christopher (**Gr. Brit.**)	Apr 25, 1955	W B U
Joubert, Dean (**S. Africa**)	Jun 10, 1953	E S 4	Mottram, Linda (**Gr. Brit.**)	May 17, 1957	Q 2 O
Jovanovic, Boro (**Yugoslavia**)	Oct 21, 1939	P V 6	Mukerjea, Jaidip (**India**)	Apr 21, 1942	H K U
Kachel, Christopher (**Austral.**)	Jun 19, 1955	H A J	Mulligan, Martin (**Italy**)	Oct 18, 1940	K U 6
Kakulia, Teimuraz (**USSR**)	Apr 26, 1947	W V C	Munoz, Antonio (**Spain**)	Mar 1, 1951	A 1 W
Kaligis, Lany (**Indonesia**)	Apr 22, 1949	N U D	Nagelsen, Betsy (**USA**)	Oct 23, 1956	R R F
Kalogeropoulos, Nicky (**Greece**)	Feb 18, 1945	G H 6	Nastase, Ilie (**Rumania**)	Jul 19, 1946	R U T
Kamiwazumi, Jun (**Japan**)	Oct 1, 1947	T L 4	Nasuelli, Maria (**Italy**)	Jul 19, 1947	O V V
Kanderal, Peter (**Austral.**)	Jan 16, 1948	L F D	Navratilova, Martina (**Czech.**)	Oct 18, 1956	M M A
Kary, Hans (**Austria**)	Feb 23, 1949	A S M	Neely, Armistead C. (**USA**)	Mar 19, 1947	G L 6
Keldie, Ray (**Austral.**)	Jan 17, 1946	S E A	Newberry, Janet (**USA**)	Aug 6, 1953	Q T U
Kindler, Marianne (**Switzerland**)	Jul 16, 1948	J U V	Newcombe, John (**Austral.**)	May 23, 1944	M R Y
King, Billie Jean (**USA**)	Nov 22, 1943	N B F	N'Godrella, Wanaro (**France**)	Oct 19, 1949	J D T
Kirk, Brenda (**S. Africa**)	Jan 11, 1951	V E F	Nowicki, Tadeusz, (**Poland**)	Jul 7, 1946	E H G
Kiyomura, Ann (**USA**)	Aug 22, 1955	C J G	Okker, Tom (**Netherlands**)	Feb 22, 1944	N K 7
Kloss, Ilana (**S. Africa**)	Mar 26, 1956	N B 1	O'Neill, Chris (**Austral.**)	Mar 19, 1956	F X T
			Orantes, Manuel (**Spain**)	Feb 6, 1949	G A 3

NAME	DATE OF BIRTH	CODE
Orth, Heide (**W. Germany**)	Aug 10, 1942	D J 7
Overton, Wendy (**USA**)	Mar 31, 1947	T X K
Ovici, Toma (**Rumania**)	May 31, 1949	F C K
Pachta, Sonja (**Austria**)	Apr 25, 1941	P N W
Paish, John (**Gr. Brit.**)	Mar 25, 1948	L T G
Paish, Wendy (**Austral.**)	May 17, 1950	M S 6
Pala, Frantisek (**Czech.**)	Mar 28, 1944	B R A
Palmeova-West, Alena (**Czech.**)	Jan 7, 1945	L W W
Panatta, Adriane (**Italy**)	Jul 9, 1950	T P S
Parun, Onny (**New Zealand**)	Apr 15, 1947	L K Z
Pasarell, Charles (**USA**)	Feb 12, 1944	C 3 W
Pattison, Andrew (**Rhodesia**)	Jan 30, 1949	X W V
Peisachov, Paulina (**Israel**)	Apr 20, 1950	H T D
Pericoli, Lea (**Italy**)	Mar 22, 1935	U 2 G
Phillips-Moore, Barry (**Austral.**)	Jun 9, 1938	W 1 2
Pigeon, Kristy (**USA**)	Aug 15, 1950	K Y W
Pilic, Nikki (**Yugoslavia**)	Aug 27, 1939	F W J
Pinner, Ulli (**W. Germany**)	Feb 17, 1954	D S R
Pinterova, Marie (**Czech.**)	Aug 16, 1946	W U O
Pinto Bravo, Jaime (**Chile**)	Oct 9, 1939	C J T
Plotz, Hans-Joachim (**W. Germany**)	Feb 26, 1944	R O C
Pohmann, Hans-Jurgen (**W. Germany**)	May 23, 1947	C U 5
Ponce, Gina (**Mexico**)	Sep 28, 1955	R S L
Pretorius, Patricia (**S. Africa**)	Feb 12, 1946	V C 2
Procter, Maryna (**Rhodesia**)	Sep 9, 1944	F O A
Proisy, Patrick (**France**)	Sep 10, 1949	Q V N
Pryde, Marilyn (**New Zealand**)	May 15, 1952	E T A
Rahim, Haroon (**Pakistan**)	Nov 12, 1949	K 3 K
Ralston, Dennis (**USA**)	Jul 27, 1942	N X S
Ramirez, Raul (**Mexico**)	Jun 20, 1953	P 3 F
Redondo, Marita (**USA**)	Feb 19, 1956	X W X
Richey, Cliff (**USA**)	Dec 31, 1946	V R T
Riessen, Martin (**USA**)	Dec 4, 1941	H M O
Robinson, Martin (**Gr. Brit.**)	Oct 19, 1955	P L 7
Roche, Tony (**Austral.**)	May 17, 1945	C M U
Rodriguez, Patricio (**Chile**)	Dec 20, 1938	J Y X
Rosewall, Ken (**Austral.**)	Nov 2, 1934	S 2 7
Rossouw, Laura (**S. Africa**)	Jul 15, 1946	N Q P
Roubin, Odile de (**France**)	Sep 28. 1948	O K 4
Rowley, Laurie (**USA**)	Jun 14, 1955	C Y D
Ruffels, Ray (**Austral.**)	Mar 23, 1946	O O 8
Ruzici, Virginia (**Rumania**)	Jan 31, 1955	G B B
Saila, Pekka (**Finland**)	Dec 20, 1941	A 3 5
Sakai, Toshiro (**Japan**)	Nov 23, 1947	C H Q
Sandbert, Christina (**Sweden**)	Jan 11, 1948	F A 7
Sawamatsu, Kazuko (**Japan**)	Jan 5, 1951	P 2 8
Schaar, Marijke (**Netherlands**)	Nov 12, 1944	A W 7
Schallau, Ramona Anne (**USA**)	Nov 28, 1948	F P Y
Seegers, Reyno (**S. Africa**)	Feb 29, 1952	V 2 Y
Seewagen, George (**USA**)	Jun 13, 1946	D M Q
Shaw, Kris (**USA**)	Jul 25, 1952	G F F
Simionescu, Mariana (**Rumania**)	Nov 27, 1956	F Y H
Simpson, Jeffrey (**New Zealand**)	Oct 29, 1950	Q P 6
Simpson, Russell (**New Zealand**)	Feb 22, 1954	J X W
Singh, Jasjit (Jay) (**India**)	Feb 4, 1948	G Z X
Siviter, Philip (**Gr. Brit.**)	Mar 16, 1953	L Q J
Slaughter, Wendy (**Gr. Brit.**)	Nov 5, 1951	U X G
Smith, Jonathan (**Gr. Brit.**)	Jan 29, 1955	E 3 8
Smith, Stan (**USA**)	Dec 14, 1946	D 3 B
Solomon, Harold (**USA**)	Sep 17, 1952	P D 2
Stap, Susan (**USA**)	Jun 3, 1954	S M Y
Stewart, Sherwood (**USA**)	Jun 6, 1946	U E J
Stilwell, Graham (**Gr. Brit.**)	Nov 15, 1945	A 1 D
Stockton, Dick (**USA**)	Feb 18, 1951	N P L
Stone, Allan (**Austral.**)	Oct 14, 1935	T J P
Stove, Betty (**Netherlands**)	Jun 24, 1945	S W Z
Strandberg, Margaretta (**Sweden**)	Mar 20, 1951	U R H
Sugiarto–Liem, Lita (**Indonesia**)	Feb 27, 1946	N S J
Szabo, Eva (**Hungary**)	Oct 30, 1945	H K V
Szoke, Peter (**Hungary**)	Aug 8, 1947	L N H
Tanner, Roscoe (**USA**)	Oct 15, 1951	W B T
Taroczy, Balazs (**Hungary**)	May 9, 1954	Q P 7
Taylor, Roger (**Gr. Brit.**)	Oct 14, 1941	C R 4
Teeguarden, Pam (**USA**)	Apr 17, 1951	B R C
Tenney, Laurie (**USA**)	Nov 4, 1955	H 2 P
Thung, Rolf (**Netherlands**)	Jul 27, 1951	L F E
Tiriac, Ion (**Rumania**)	May 9, 1939	L Y 6
Tomanova, Renata (**Czech.**)	Dec 9, 1954	X E P
Tuero, Linda (**USA**)	Oct 21, 1950	H G X
Turnbull, Wendy (**Austral.**)	Nov 26, 1952	Q S 6
Ulrich, Torben (**Denmark**)	Oct 4, 1928	F T X
Van Dillen, Erik (**USA**)	Feb 21, 1951	Q S O
Vilas, Guillermo (**Argentina**)	Aug 17, 1952	G A 4
Vopickova, Vlasta (**Czech.**)	Mar 26, 1944	X P 7
Wade, Virginia (**Gr. Brit.**)	Jul 10, 1945	L K H
Walhof, Trudy (**Netherlands**)	Jan 15, 1944	V 3 2
Walsh, Sharon (**USA**)	Feb 24, 1952	Q W T
Warbach, Brigitta (**Finland**)	Jan 14, 1948	J D B
Warboys, Stephen (**Gr. Brit.**)	Oct 25, 1953	D P A
Warwick, Kim (**Austral.**)	Apr 8, 1952	O K 5
Wells, Christopher (**Gr. Brit.**)	Sep 24, 1955	N O G
Whitlinger, John (**USA**)	Feb 4, 1954	O E D
Wikstedt, Mimmi (**Sweden**)	Apr 3, 1954	C G 4
Wooldridge, Winnie (**Gr. Brit.**)	Jan 18, 1947	Q G D
Young, Janet (**Austral.**)	Oct 22, 1951	F J 1
Yuill, John (**S. Africa**)	Dec 12, 1948	U A E
Zednik, Vladimir (**Czech.**)	Feb 1, 1947	G V S
Ziegenfuss, Valerie (**USA**)	Jun 29, 1949	M D F
Zugarelli, Antoni (**Italy**)	Jan 17, 1950	G K K
Zwaan, Tina (**Netherlands**)	Jun 17, 1947	E R W

World Champion Drivers

NAME	DATE OF BIRTH	CODE			NAME	DATE OF BIRTH	CODE		
Arfons, Arthur Eugene	Feb 3, 1926	V	Z	F	Hawthorn, John Michael	Apr 10, 1929	K	L	N
Ascari, Alberto	Jul 13, 1918	T	G	Q	Hill, Phil	Apr 20, 1927	B	S	S
Brabham, Jack	Apr 2, 1926	K	2	6	Rindt, Jochen	Aug 18, 1942	M	R	G
Clark, Jim	Mar 14, 1936	K	V	B	Surtees, John	Feb 11, 1934	G	P	7
Fangio, Juan-Manuel	Jun 24, 1911	T	G	O	Stewart, Jackie	Jun 11, 1939	V	A	6
Farina, Dr. Giuseppe (Nino)	Oct 30, 1906	X	R	7					

_____

_____

_____

_____

_____

World Class Drivers

NAME	DATE OF BIRTH	CODE			NAME	DATE OF BIRTH	CODE		
Amon, Chris	Jul 20, 1943	C	R	N	Merzario, Arturo	Mar 11, 1943	K	1	O
Andretti, Mario	Feb 28, 1940	G	L	4	Pace, Carlos	Oct 6, 1944	K	N	3
Belso, Tom	Aug 27, 1943	S	2	S	Pearson, David	Dec 22, 1934	W	V	Q
Beltoise, Jean-Pierre	Apr 6, 1937	G	R	2	Pescarolo, Henri	Sep 25, 1942	D	2	M
Brambilla, Vittorio	Nov 11, 1937	T	M	P	Peterson, Ronnie	Feb 14, 1944	E	B	Y
Depailler, Patrick	Aug 9, 1944	V	L	C	Pryce, Tom	Jun 11, 1949	R	O	V
Donohue, Mark	Mar 18, 1937	L	1	H	Regazzoni, Gianclaudio	Sep 5, 1939	P	C	S
Fittipaldi, Emerson	Dec 12, 1946	B	1	8	Reutemann, Carlos	Apr 12, 1942	W	A	L
Fittipaldi, Wilson	Dec 24, 1943	W	F	E	Rutherford, Johnny	Feb 12, 1938	U	V	J
Foyt, A. J.	Jan 16, 1935	A	S	H	Scheckter, Jody	Jan 29, 1950	T	W	W
Ganley, Howden	Dec 24, 1941	E	D	A	Schenken, Tim	Sep 26, 1943	B	A	P
Hailwood, Mike	Apr 4, 1940	U	T	7	Stommelen, Rolf	Jul 11, 1943	R	H	D
Hill, Graham	Feb 15, 1929	B	N	Z	Stuck, Hans Joachim	Jan 1, 1951	L	X	4
Hunt, James	Aug 29, 1947	J	F	4	Unser, Al	May 29, 1939	H	Q	S
Ickx, Jacky	Jan 1, 1945	E	Q	Q	Unser, Bobby	Feb 20, 1934	Q	Y	H
Jarier, Jean-Pierre	Jul 10, 1946	H	L	K	Watson, John	May 4, 1946	K	3	J
Laffite, Jacques	Nov 21, 1943	M	A	E	Wilds, Mike	Jan 7, 1946	H	X	Y
Lauda, Niki	Feb 22, 1949	X	R	L	Yarborough, Cale	Mar 27, 1939	Q	J	V
Mass, Jochen	Sep 30, 1946	V	J	1					

Future World Class Drivers

NAME	DATE OF BIRTH	CODE			NAME	DATE OF BIRTH	CODE		
Ashley, Ian	Oct 26, 1947	V	H	V	Larrousse, Gerard	May 23, 1940	X	M	P
Barnett, Chris	Feb 26, 1956	G	A	5	Leclere, Michel	Mar 18, 1947	F	K	5
Brise, Tony	Mar 28, 1952	C	2	T	Lunger, Brett	Nov 14, 1945	X	Z	C
Coulon, Jacques	Jan 15, 1942	D	1	X	Magee, Damien	Nov 17, 1945	C	3	F
Crawford, Jim	Feb 13, 1948	Q	F	7	McRae, Graham	Mar 5, 1940	N	R	B
Dean, Tony	Jul 23, 1932	O	G	Z	Morgan, Dave	Aug 7, 1944	T	J	A
Edwards, Guy	Dec 30, 1942	H	L	J	Morgan, Richard	Aug 17, 1953	D	B	6
Evans, Bob	Jun 11, 1947	W	L	Q	Nicholson, John	Oct 6, 1941	S	J	V
Forbes-Robinson, Elliott	Oct 31, 1943	O	H	R	Pilette, Teddy	Jul 26, 1942	M	W	R
Gethin, Peter	Feb 21, 1940	X	D	W	Purley, David	Jan 26, 1945	G	N	H
Graham, Stuart	Jan 9, 1942	V	U	R	Schuppan, Vern	Mar 19, 1943	S	F	W
Henton, Brian	Sep 19, 1946	K	1	P	Scott, Richard	Nov 8, 1946	O	U	7
Hezemans, Toine	Apr 14, 1943	V	D	P	South, Stephen	Feb 19, 1952	L	R	O
Holland, Keith	Dec 6, 1935	C	F	B	Tambay, Patrick	Jun 25, 1949	H	3	B
Hobbs, David	Jun 8, 1939	S	1	3	Taylor, Ian	Jan 28, 1947	C	R	O
Jabouille, Jean Pierre	Oct 1, 1942	K	E	S	Walker, Dave	Jun 10, 1941	P	C	B
Jones, Alan	Nov 2, 1946	H	O	1	Walkinshaw, Tom	Aug 14, 1946	U	S	M
Klausler, Tom	Jul 14, 1945	P	O	M	Wentz, Ted	Nov 7, 1946	N	T	6
Kuwashima, Masami	Sep 14, 1950	R	1	T	Wunderink, Roelof	Dec 12, 1948	U	A	E

_____

_____

_____

_____

_____

The European Champions

NAME	DATE OF BIRTH	CODE			NAME	DATE OF BIRTH	CODE		
Borzov, Valery	Oct 20, 1949	K	E	U	Kuschmann, Manfred	Jul 25, 1950	M	C	A
Bruzsenyak, Ilona	Sep 14, 1950	R	1	T	Malinowski, Bronislaw	Jun 4, 1951	D	J	S
Briesenick, Hartmut	Mar 17, 1949	X	M	A	Melnik, Faina	Jul 9, 1945	K	J	G
Chizhova, Nadyezhda	Sep 29, 1945	X	G	X	Mennea, Pietro	Jun 28, 1952	C	G	M
Drut, Guy	Dec 6, 1950	H	Z	C	Pascoe, Alan	Oct 11, 1947	F	V	F
Foster, Brendan	Jan 12, 1948	G	B	8	Podluzhny, Valeriy	Aug 22, 1952	M	F	A
Fuchs, Ruth	Dec 14, 1946	D	3	B	Siitonen, Hannu	Mar 18, 1949	A	N	B
Golubnichiy, Vladimir	Jun 2, 1936	V	R	Q	Skowronek, Ryszard	May 1, 1949	W	A	N
Hoffmeister, Gunhild	Jul 6, 1944	K	E	B	Spiridonov, Aleksey	Nov 20, 1951	M	K	W
Hohne, Christoph	Feb 12, 1941	M	Z	Q	Susanj, Luciano	Nov 10, 1948	L	Z	F
Holmen, Nina	Sep 29, 1951	F	O	C	Szewinska, Irena	May 24, 1946	G	U	4
Honz, Karl	Jan 28, 1951	P	W	X	Thompson, Ian	Oct 16, 1949	F	A	Q
Justus, Klaus-Peter	Jul 1, 1951	H	H	M	Tomova, Lilyana	Aug 9, 1946	P	N	G
Kishkun, Vladimir	Nov 5, 1951	U	X	G	Torring, Jesper	Sep 27, 1947	P	G	Z
					Witschas, Rosemarie	Apr 4, 1952	K	F	1

World Celebrities and Notables

NAME	DATE OF BIRTH	CODE			NAME	DATE OF BIRTH	CODE		
Abbott, George (**producer**)	Jun 25, 1887	S	G	3	Anderson, Dame Judith (**actress**)	Feb 10, 1898	O	1	R
Abel, Sid (**hockey**)	Feb 22, 1918	Q	F	G	Anderson, Dick (**football**)	Feb 10, 1946	T	A	Z
Abel, Walter (**actor**)	Jun 6, 1898	P	B	A	Anderson, Donny (**football**)	Apr 3, 1949	R	A	S
Abernathy, Ralph					Anderson, Eddie. *See* Rochester.				
(**civil rights leader**)	Mar 11, 1926	L	E	J	Anderson, Jack (**journalist**)	Oct 19, 1922	O	1	Y
Abrams, Creighton	Sep 15, 1914	B	K	E	Anderson, Lynn				
Abzug, Bella (**politician**)	Jul 24, 1920	B	V	7	(**country music artist**)	Sep 26, 1947	O	F	Y
Acuff, Roy (**musician**)	Sep 15, 1903	J	Y	N	Anderson, Marian (**contralto**)	Feb 17, 1902	J	J	7
Adams, Don (**actor**)	Apr 19, 1927	A	R	R	Anderson, Robert (**playwright**)	Apr 28, 1917	P	O	D
Adams, Edie (**actress**)	Apr 16, 1929	Q	R	T	Anderson, Sparky (**baseball**)	Feb 22, 1934	S	1	K
Adams, Joey (**comedian**)	Jan 6, 1911	L	F	K	Andersson, Bibi (**actress**)	Nov 11, 1935	A	J	K
Adamson, Joy (**naturalist**)	Jan 20, 1910	E	T	W	Andreadis, Christina Onassis				
Addams, Charles (**cartoonist**)	Jan 7, 1912	J	H	N	(**heiress**)	Dec 11, 1950	N	B	H
Adderly, Herbert A. (**football**)	Jun 8, 1939	S	1	3	Andress, Ursula (**actress**)	Mar 19, 1938	J	3	L
Adler, Larry (**musician**)	Feb 10, 1914	P	R	T	Andrews, Dana (**actor**)	Jan 1, 1909	M	2	A
Adler, Richard (**songwriter**)	Aug 3, 1921	J	D	L	Andrews, Julie (**actress, singer**)	Oct 1, 1935	F	Y	B
Agnew, Spiro (**ex-Vice Pres.**)	Nov 9, 1918	X	O	C	Angeles, Victoria de los (**soprano**)	Nov 1, 1924	W	O	J
Aherne, Brian (**actor**)	May 2, 1902	O	2	G	Anka, Paul (**singer**)	Jul 30, 1941	T	Z	T
Ailey, Alvin (**choreographer**)	Jan 5, 1931	A	B	V	Ann-Margret (**actress**)	Apr 28, 1941	S	Q	Z
Aimee, Anouk (**actress**)	Apr 24, 1934	K	C	E	Anouilh, Jean (**playwright**)	Jun 23, 1910	V	E	L
Albanese, Licia (**soprano**)	Jul 22, 1913	T	K	O	Antonioni, Michelangelo				
Albee, Edward (**playwright**)	Mar 12, 1928	G	J	P	(**director**)	Sep 29, 1912	W	W	P
Alberghetti, Anna Maria (**singer**)	May 15, 1936	C	2	6	Arden, Eve (**actress**)	Apr 30, 1912	H	K	3
Albert, Carl (**politician**)	May 10, 1908	F	P	4	Arendt, Hannah (**historian**)	Oct 14, 1906	G	A	Q
Albert, Eddie (**actor**)	Apr 22, 1908	L	Z	L	Arkin, Alan (**actor-director**)	Mar 26, 1934	D	B	J
Albright, Lola (**actress**)	Jul 20, 1925	G	X	F	Arlen, Harold (**composer**)	Feb 15, 1905	W	L	D
Alda, Alan (**actor**)	Jan 28, 1936	K	C	W	Arlen, Richard (**actor**)	Sep 1, 1900	D	G	1
Alda, Robert (**actor**)	Feb 26, 1914	H	E	B	Armstrong, Neil A. (**astronaut**)	Aug 5, 1930	J	R	8
Aldrin Jr., Edwin E. (**astronaut**)	Jan 20, 1930	T	Q	A	Armstrong-Jones, Anthony	Mar 7, 1930	T	F	O
Algren, Nelson (**novelist**)	Mar 28, 1909	F	A	V	Arnaz, Desi (**actor, producer**)	Mar 2, 1917	D	N	N
Ali, Muhammad (**boxing**)	Jan 18, 1942	G	A	1	Arness, James (**TV actor**)	May 26, 1923	C	V	M
Alioto, Joseph L.					Arnold, Eddy (**singer**)	May 15, 1918	F	D	X
(**Mayor: San Fran.**)	Feb 12, 1916	L	V	Z	Arrau, Claudio (**pianist**)	Feb 6, 1904	P	3	Z
Allen, Mel (**sportscaster**)	Feb 14, 1913	W	U	V	Arthur, Bea (**actress**)	May 13, 1926	E	M	F
Allen, Steve (**TV entertainer**)	Dec 26, 1921	Q	J	Y	Arthur, Jean (**actress**)	Oct 17, 1908	E	G	Y
Allen, Woody (**comedian**)	Dec 1, 1935	V	A	5	Asimov, Isaac (**author**)	Jan 2, 1920	E	N	1
Allison, Bobby (**hockey**)	Dec 3, 1937	S	F	D	Askew, Reubin (**Gov. of Florida**)	Sep 11, 1928	F	Y	8
Allyson, June (**actress**)	Oct 7, 1923	W	P	O	Asner, Edward (**actor**)	Nov 15, 1929	W	F	A
Alpert, Herb (**band leader**)	Mar 31, 1935	F	H	Q	Astaire, Fred (**dancer, actor**)	May 10, 1899	H	D	J
Alsop Jr., Joseph W.	Oct 11, 1910	Q	C	W	Astor, Mary (**actress**)	May 3, 1906	D	E	R
Alston, Walter (**baseball**)	Dec 1, 1911	S	2	J	Atkins, Chet (**guitarist**)	Jun 20, 1924	C	U	G
Altman, Robert (**director**)	Feb 20, 1925	S	N	V	Atkinson, Brooks (**drama critic**)	Nov 28, 1894	R	D	B
Alworth, Lance (**football**)	Aug 3, 1940	C	3	V	Attenborough, Richard (**actor**)	Aug 29, 1923	F	D	H
Ambler, Eric (**suspense writer**)	Jun 28, 1909	F	J	O	Aumont, Jean-Pierre (**actor**)	Jan 5, 1913	E	H	O
Ameche, Don (**actor**)	May 31, 1908	D	H	R	Autry, Gene (**singer, actor**)	Sep 29, 1907	M	P	C
Amis, Kingsley (**novelist**)	Apr 16, 1922	M	H	C	Avalon, Frankie (**singer**)	Sep 18, 1940	C	S	A
Amory, Cleveland (**writer**)	Sep 2, 1917	D	A	7	Axelrod, Albert (**fencing**)	Feb 21, 1921	G	J	N
Amos (**radio comedian**)	May 5, 1899	C	2	D	Axelrod, George (**playwright**)	Jun 9, 1922	U	F	Y
Amsterdam, Morey (**actor**)	Dec 14, 1914	X	Q	4	Ayres, Lew (**actor**)	Dec 28, 1908	H	X	5
Anders, William A. (**astronaut**)	Oct 17, 1933	E	K	O	Aznavour, Charles (**singer, actor**)	May 22, 1924	U	T	L

NAME	DATE OF BIRTH	CODE		NAME	DATE OF BIRTH	CODE	
Babashoff, Shirley (swimming)	Jan 31, 1957	B E G		Bergen, Edgar (ventriloquist)	Feb 16, 1903	E J 8
Bacall, Lauren (actress)	Sep 16, 1924	W Y 4		Bergen, Polly (actress, singer)	Jul 14, 1930	K X L
Bacharach, Burt (composer)	May 12, 1929	T P M		Bergerac, Jacques (actor)	May 26, 1927	P 1 V
Backus, Jim (actor)	Feb 25, 1913	K C 7		Bergman, Ingmar (director)	Jul 14, 1918	U H R
Baez, Joan (singer)	Jan 9, 1941	A T P		Bergman, Ingrid (actress)	Aug 29, 1917	X Z 3
Bagnold, Enid (novelist)	Oct 27, 1889	W W Z		Berle, Milton (comedian)	Jul 12, 1908	X W 1
Bailey, F. Lee (lawyer)	Jun 10, 1933	O V R		Berlin, Irving (composer)	May 11, 1888	R U T
Bailey, Pearl (singer)	Mar 29, 1918	E N J		Berman, Shelley (comedian)	Feb 3, 1926	V Z F
Baird, Bill (puppeteer)	Aug 15, 1904	W X S		Berning, Susie Maxwell (golf)	Jul 22, 1941	L R L
Baker, Carroll (actress)	May 28, 1935	S K H		Bernstein, Carl (author)	Feb 14, 1944	E B Y
Baker, Howard (U.S. Senator)	Nov 15, 1925	K A Z		Bernstein, Leonard (conductor)	Aug 25, 1918	Q W 1
Baker, Kenny (singer, actor)	Sep 30, 1912	X X Q		Berra, Yogi (baseball)	May 12, 1925	G K C
Baker, Russell (columnist)	Aug 14, 1925	J U 6		Betjeman, Sir John (Poet Laureate)	Aug 28, 1906	F K B
Balanchine, George (choreographer)	Jan 9, 1904	K 3 5		Bikel, Theodore (actor)	May 2, 1924	X 2 Y
Baldwin, Faith (writer)	Oct 1, 1893	H A H		Bing, Sir Rudolf (opera manager)	Jan 9, 1902	Q 1 1
Baldwin, James (novelist)	Aug 2, 1924	X G R		Bishop, Jim (author)	Nov 21, 1907	T M X
Ball, Catherine (swimming)	Sep 30, 1951	G P D		Bishop, Joey (comedian)	Feb 3, 1919	R Q X
Ball, George (diplomat)	Dec 21, 1909	V R Z		Bisset, Jacqueline (actress)	Sep 13, 1944	K S E
Ball, Lucille (comedienne)	Aug 6, 1911	Q W Y		Bixby, Bill (actor)	Jan 22, 1934	K X M
Ballard, Kaye (actress)	Nov 20, 1926	M G 7		Black, Shirley Temple (actress, ambassador)	Apr 23, 1928	C X Y
Balmain, Pierre (fashion designer)	May 18, 1914	U B R		Blackman, Honor, (actress)	Aug 22, 1929	F E P
Balsam, Martin (actor)	Nov 4, 1919	P K 8		Blackmun, Harry (judge)	Nov 12, 1908	H E R
Bancroft, Anne (actress)	Sep 17, 1931	C E M		Blaine, Vivian (actress, singer)	Nov 21, 1924	T F 4
Banks, Ernie (baseball)	Jan 31, 1931	D 3 O		Blair, Janet (actress)	Apr 23, 1921	W O H
Bannister, Roger (runner)	Mar 24, 1929	Q W 4		Blake, Eubie (pianist)	Feb 7, 1883	F D N
Barber, Red (sports announcer)	Feb 17, 1908	P Q M		Blanda, George (football)	Sep 17, 1927	O 3 C
Barber, Samuel (composer)	Mar 9, 1910	G L D		Blass, Bill (designer)	Jun 22, 1922	K T D
Barenbom, Daniel (pianist)	Nov 15, 1942	J W 5		Bliss, Ray C.	Dec 16, 1907	V J P
Barry, Gene (actor)	Jun 4, 1922	P A T		Blondell, Joan (actress)	Aug 30, 1912	P U S
Barth, John (novelist)	May 27, 1930	H C 4		Bloom, Claire (actress)	Feb 15, 1931	T P 4
Bartholomew, Freddie (actor)	Mar 28, 1924	L U W		Bloomgarden, Kermit (producer)	Dec 15, 1904	F E H
Basehart, Richard (actor)	Aug 31, 1919	T A A		Blyth, Ann (actress)	Aug 16, 1928	C 1 G
Basie, Count (band leader)	Aug 21, 1904	E A Y		Bogarde, Dirk (actor)	Mar 28, 1921	T Q P
Bates, Alan (actor)	Feb 17, 1934	N V E		Bogdanovich, Peter (producer)	Jul 30, 1939	A W O
Baudouin (King)	Sep 7, 1930	T W 8		Bok, Derek	Mar 22, 1930	L V 4
Baugh, Sammy (football)	Mar 17, 1914	D Y V		Bolger, Ray (dancer, actor)	Jan 10, 1904	L A 6
Baxter, Anne (actress)	May 7, 1923	G B 1		Bond, Julian (legislator)	Jan 14, 1940	H W R
Bayh, Birch (U.S. Senator)	Jan 22, 1928	C P 6		Bono, Sonny (singer)	Feb 16, 1940	S 2 R
Bayi, Filbert (runner)	Jun 23, 1953	S C J		Boone, Pat (singer)	Jun 1, 1934	B N K
Baylor, Elgin (basketball)	Sep 16, 1934	R H S		Boone, Richard (actor)	Jun 18, 1917	U J W
Beame, Abraham (mayor)	Mar 20, 1906	F R F		Booth, Shirley (actress)	Aug 30, 1909	X Q L
Beamon, Bob (long jumper)	Aug 2, 1946	H F 8		Boozer, Emerson (football, sportscaster)	Jul 4, 1943	K A 5
Bean, Alan (astronaut)	Mar 15, 1932	W R 2		Borge, Victor (pianist)	Jan 3, 1909	O A C
Bean, Orson (actor)	Jul 22, 1928	A A P		Borgnine, Ernest (actor)	Jan 24, 1917	N D J
Beaton, Cecil (photographer)	Jan 14, 1904	P E B		Borman, Frank (astronaut)	Mar 14, 1928	J L R
Beatty, Warren (actor, producer)	Mar 30, 1937	X K U		Bosley, Tom (actor)	Oct 1, 1927	E O R
Beckett, Samuel (playwright)	Apr 13, 1906	G N 5		Boston, Ralph (long jumper)	May 9, 1939	L Y 6
Beery Jr., Noah (actor)	Aug 10, 1916	G E G		Boulez, Pierre (conductor)	Mar 26, 1925	F T W
Belafonte, Harry (singer)	Mar 1, 1927	V Y A		Bouton, Jim (baseball, sportscaster)	Mar 8, 1939	S S B
Beliveau, Jean (hockey)	Aug 31, 1931	J Q 3		Bowles, Chester (diplomat)	Apr 5, 1901	N 2 L
Bellamy, Ralph (actor)	Jun 17, 1904	J U Z		Bowman, Lee (actor)	Dec 28, 1914	O B K
Belli, Melvin	Jul 29, 1907	T J G		Boyd, Stephen (actor)	Jul 4, 1928	F L 5
Bellow, Saul (novelist)	Jul 10, 1915	A 3 F		Boyer, Charles (actor)	Aug 28, 1899	C B U
Belmondo, Jean-Paul (actor)	Apr 9, 1933	V P V		Bracken, Eddie (actor)	Feb 7, 1920	S V 4
Beman, Deane (golf)	Apr 22, 1938	U F M		Bradbury, Ray Douglas (writer)	Aug 22, 1920	H W 3
Benjamin, Richard (actor)	May 22, 1938	D H J		Bradley, Omar N. (5-Star Gen.)	Feb 12, 1893	G W H
Bennett, Joan (actress)	Feb 27, 1910	U A 2		Bradley, Thomas (Mayor: L.A.)	Dec 29, 1917	G G S
Bennett, Robert Russell (composer)	Jun 15, 1894	M F A		Brailowsky, Alexander (pianist)	Feb 16, 1896	B A S
Bennett, Tony (singer)	Aug 3, 1926	S K W		Brando, Marlon (actor)	Apr 3, 1924	R 1 3
Bentsen, Lloyd (U.S. Senator)	Feb 11, 1921	U Z C		Brandt, Willy (Chancellor)	Dec 18, 1913	G T 6
Berg, Patty (golf)	Feb 13, 1918	G Z 6		Braun, Wernher von (scientist)	Mar 23, 1912	Q 3 X
Bergen, Candice (actress)	May 9, 1946	P E O				

NAME	DATE OF BIRTH	CODE		NAME	DATE OF BIRTH	CODE	
Brazzi, Rossano (actor)	Sep 18, 1916	X Q N		Calisher, Hortense (novelist)	Dec 20, 1911	O S 3	
Brel, Jacques (singer)	Apr 8, 1929	H J L		Callas, Maria (soprano)	Dec 4, 1923	L R F	
Brennan, William J. (judge)	Apr 25, 1906	T Z J		Calloway, Cab (band leader)	Dec 25, 1907	G S Y	
Brent, George (actor)	Mar 15, 1904	G K 5		Calvet, Corinne (actress)	Apr 30, 1926	P 2 1	
Breslin, Jimmy (journalist)	Oct 17, 1930	N F G		Cameron, Rod (actor)	Dec 7, 1912	W G S	
Brewer, Teresa (singer)	May 7, 1931	H M L		Campanella, Roy (baseball)	Nov 19, 1921	B 3 U	
Brewster, Kingman (Pres. of Yale)	Jun 17, 1919	N K Z		Campbell, Glen (singer)	Apr 22, 1938	U F M	
Brezhnev, Leonid I. (Secretary)	Dec 16, 1906	A H N		Caniff, Milton (cartoonist)	Feb 28, 1907	F 1 V	
Bridges, Beau (actor)	Dec 9, 1941	N R T		Cannon, Dyan (actress)	Jan 4, 1937	G J A	
Bridges, Lloyd (actor)	Jan 15, 1913	P S Y		Canova, Judy (actress)	Nov 20, 1916	R X K	
Brinkley, David (newscaster)	Jul 10, 1920	L G S		Cantinflas (comedian)	Aug 12, 1911	W 3 5	
Britt, May (actress)	Mar 22, 1936	S A K		Caponi, Donna Maria (golf)	Jan 29, 1945	K Q L	
Britten, Benjamin (composer)	Nov 22, 1913	D V E		Capote, Truman (novelist)	Sep 30, 1924	N K K	
Brook, Peter (director)	Mar 21, 1925	A O R		Capp, Al (cartoonist)	Sep 28, 1909	F R G	
Brooke, Edward (U.S. Senator)	Oct 26, 1919	F A Y		Cappelletti, Gino (football)	Mar 26, 1934	D B J	
Brooks, Geraldine (actress)	Oct 29, 1925	Q M H		Capra, Frank (producer)	May 18, 1897	W K N	
Brooks, Gwendolyn (poet)	Jun 7, 1917	J 1 L		Cardin, Pierre (fashion designer)	Jul 7, 1922	B F T	
Brown, Doris (runner)	Sep 17, 1942	T T D		Carey, Macdonald (actor)	Mar 15, 1913	E V R	
Brown Jr., Edmund G. (governor)	Apr 7, 1938	E T 5		Carlisle, Kitty (singer, actress)	Sep 3, 1915	K 2 3	
Brown, Helen Gurley (author)	Feb 18, 1922	A G M		Carlos, John (sprinter)	Jun 5, 1945	W C F	
Brown, James (singer)	May 3, 1934	T M O		Carlson, Richard (actor)	April 29, 1912	G J 2	
Brown, Jimmy (football)	Feb 17, 1936	G X J		Carmichael, Hoagy (song writer)	Nov 22, 1899	U D G	
Brown, Pamela (actress)	Jul 8, 1918	O B L		Carner, Joanne Gunderson (golf)	Mar 4, 1939	O O 6	
Brubeck, Dave (musician)	Dec 6, 1920	W Q B		Carney, Art (actor)	Nov 4, 1918	S J 6	
Brynner, Yul (actor)	Jul 11, 1920	M H T		Carnovsky, Morris (actor)	Sep 5, 1897	R H Y	
Buchanan, Patrick (columnist)	Nov 2, 1938	G D H		Caron, Leslie (actress)	Jul 1, 1931	R L 8	
Buccholz, Horst (actor)	Dec 4, 1933	G B 4		Carpenter, Malcolm Scott (astronaut)	May 1, 1925	T 2 Z	
Buchwald, Art (columnist)	Oct 20, 1925	G C 7		Carr, Catherine (swimming)	May 27, 1954	L E R	
Buckley, James (U.S. Senator)	Mar 9, 1923	R 2 8		Carr, Vikki (singer)	Jul 19, 1942	E P K	
Buckey Jr., William F. (journalist)	Nov 24, 1925	T K A		Carradine, David (actor)	Dec 8, 1936	C K G	
Bujold, Genevieve (actress)	Jul 1, 1942	K Z Z		Carradine, John (actor)	Feb 5, 1906	J B 4	
Bumbry, Grace (singer)	Jan 4, 1937	G J A		Carroll, Diahann (actress)	Jul 17, 1935	W D Z	
Bundy, McGeorge (Pres., Ford Found.)	Mar 30, 1919	C P M		Carroll, Madeleine (actress)	Feb 26, 1909	W 2 Y	
Bundy, William Putnam (editor)	Sep 24, 1917	C X V		Carroll, Pat (comedienne)	May 5, 1927	R E 8	
Bunuel, Luis (director)	Feb 22, 1900	U M 8		Carson, Johnny (TV entertainer)	Oct 23, 1925	K F B	
Burger, Warren (judge)	Sep 17, 1907	X C Y		Carter, Jimmy (President of U.S.)	Oct 1, 1924	O L L	
Burke, Adm. Arleigh A. (Naval Chief)	Oct 19, 1901	C 3 K		Case, Clifford (U.S. Senator)	Apr 16, 1904	Q O 4	
Burnett, Carol (comedienne)	Apr 26, 1936	G H M		Cash, Johnny (singer)	Feb 26, 1932	D 2 J	
Burns, Arthur, F.	Apr 27, 1904	D Z G		Cass, Peggy (comedienne)	May 21, 1926	N U O	
Burns, George (comedian)	Jan 20, 1896	V B Y		Cassavetes, John (actor)	Dec 9, 1929	X B Z	
Burr, Raymond (actor)	May 21, 1917	P J 2		Cassidy, David (singer)	Mar 12, 1950	P H 6	
Burrows, Abe (playwright)	Dec 18, 1910	P P Y		Cassini, Oleg (designer)	Apr 11, 1913	J U L	
Burstyn, Ellen (actress)	Dec 7, 1932	N D 5		Castellano, Richard (actor)	Sep 2, 1934	C W D	
Burton, Michael (swimming)	Jul 3, 1947	V E E		Castro Rux, Fidel (Premier)	Aug 13, 1927	B V A	
Burton, Richard (actor)	Nov 10, 1925	E Y U		Catton, Bruce (historian)	Oct 9, 1899	W Q 4	
Bush, George (politician)	Jun 12, 1924	S M 7		Cavett, Dick (TV entertainer)	Nov 19, 1936	G T V	
Butkus, Dick (football)	Dec 9, 1942	K S V		Celler, Emmanuel (politician)	May 6, 1888	M P O	
Buttons, Red (actor)	Feb 5, 1919	T S Z		Cernan, Eugene Andrew (astronaut)	Mar 14, 1934	P S 5	
Butz, Earl (politician)	Jul 3, 1909	L O T		Chagall, Marc (painter)	Jul 7, 1887	G T G	
Buzzi, Ruth (comedienne)	Jul 24, 1936	D N B		Chamberlain, Richard (actor)	Mar 31, 1935	F H Q	
Byrd, Robert (U.S. Senator)	Jan 15, 1918	A Y B		Chamberlain, Wilt (basketball)	Aug 21, 1936	J N 5	
Cadmus, Paul (painter, etcher)	Dec 17, 1904	H G K		Champion, Gower (choreographer)	Jun 22, 1921	N S B	
Caesar, Sid (comedian)	Sep 8, 1922	T N Q		Champion, Marge (actress)	Sep 2, 1923	K H M	
Cagney, James (actor)	Jul 17, 1900	D R N		Chancellor, John (TV commentator)	Jul 14, 1927	S T D	
Cahn, Sammy (song writer)	Jun 18, 1913	H D N		Channing, Carol (actress)	Jan 31, 1923	C S 4	
Caine, Michael (actor)	Mar 14, 1933	S R 3		Chaplin, Charles (actor)	Apr 16, 1889	M Y 4	
Caldwell, Erskine (novelist)	Dec 17, 1903	K E G					
Caldwell, Taylor (novelist)	Sep 7, 1900	K N 7					
Caldwell, Zoe (actress)	Sep 14, 1933	S E O					

NAME	DATE OF BIRTH	CODE	NAME	DATE OF BIRTH	CODE
Chaplin, Sydney (actor)	Mar 31, 1926	H Z 4	Cooper, Leroy Gordon, Jr. (astronaut)	Mar 6, 1927	C A F
Chapot, Frank (equestrian)	Feb 24, 1934	U 3 M	Copland, Aaron (composer)	Nov 14, 1900	J Z A
Charisse, Cyd (dancer)	Mar 8, 1923	Q 1 7	Corelli, Franco (tenor)	Apr 8, 1943	P 1 J
Charles, Ray (singer)	Sep 23, 1932	G N V	Cosby, Bill (actor)	Jul 12, 1937	M B Z
Chase, Ilka (author, actress)	Apr 8, 1905	E G X	Cosell, Howard (sportscaster)	Mar 25, 1929	R X 5
Chavez, Carlos (composer)	Jun 13, 1899	T K K	Courreges, Andre (fashion designer)	Mar 9, 1923	R 2 8
Chavez, Cesar (labor leader)	Mar 31, 1927	E 1 6	Court, Margaret Smith (tennis)	Jul 16, 1942	B M G
Chayefsky, Paddy (playwright)	Jan 29, 1923	A Q 2	Courtenay, Tom (actor)	Feb 25, 1937	N E U
Cheney, Richard (politician)	Jan 30, 1941	W M C	Cousins, Norman (publisher)	Jun 24, 1912	R J R
Cher (singer)	May 20, 1946	C Q Z	Cousteau, Jacques Ives (explorer)	Jun 11, 1910	J V 7
Chirico, Giorgio de (painter)	Jul 10, 1888	H Y N	Cousy, Bob (basketball)	Aug 9, 1928	T T 8
Chisholm, Shirley (congresswoman)	Nov 30, 1924	E P E	Cowles, Gardner (newspaper publ.)	Jan 31, 1903	M V R
Christian, Linda (actress)	Nov 13, 1924	L 1 V	Cox, Archibald (professor of law)	May 17, 1912	B 2 M
Christie, Julie (actress)	Apr 14, 1941	D B L	Cozzens, James Gould (novelist)	Aug 19, 1903	E Z T
Church, Frank (U.S. Senator)	Jul 25, 1924	P 2 J	Crabbe, Buster (actor)	Feb 7, 1908	E F B
Churchill, Sarah (actress)	Oct 7, 1914	A D 2	Crain, Jeanne (actress)	May 25, 1925	U X Q
Cilento, Diane (actress)	Oct 5, 1933	Q 1 B	Cranston, Alan (U.S. Senator)	Jun 19, 1914	F F Q
Clair, Rene (director)	Nov 11, 1898	M U 2	Crawford, Broderick (actor)	Dec 9, 1911	C G R
Claire, Ina (actress)	Nov 15, 1895	A U Y	Crawford, Cheryl (producer)	Sep 24, 1902	V D U
Clark, Dane (actor)	Feb 18, 1915	U 1 4	Crawford, Joan (actress)	Mar 23, 1908	D X 6
Clark, Dick (TV personality)	Nov 30, 1929	O V Q	Crenna, Richard (actor)	Nov 30, 1927	T S L
Clark, Petula (singer)	Nov 15, 1934	H M M	Crichton, Michael (novelist)	Oct 23, 1942	J 2 G
Clark, Ramsey (politician)	Dec 18, 1927	O H 4	Cronin, A.J. (novelist)	Jul 19, 1896	S P G
Clay, Cassius. See Ali.			Cronin, Joe (baseball)	Oct 12, 1906	E 2 O
Clay, Lucius D. (banker)	Apr 23, 1897	U N V	Cronkite, Walter (newscaster)	Nov 4, 1916	A G 2
Clemens, S.L. See Twain, Mark			Cronyn, Hume (actor)	Jul 18, 1911	U C E
Cliburn, Van (pianist)	Jul 12, 1934	U 1 S	Crosby, Bing (singer)	May 2, 1904	J B M
Clifford, Clark M. (Sec. of Defense)	Dec 25, 1906	K R W	Crosby, Bob (musician)	Aug 23, 1913	E O N
Clooney, Rosemary (singer)	May 23, 1928	K Z V	Cugat, Xavier (band leader)	Jan 1, 1900	O Q O
Clurman, Harold (producer)	Sep 18, 1901	S Z M	Cukor, George (director)	Jul 7, 1899	U F A
Cobb, Lee J. (actor)	Dec 9, 1911	C G R	Cullen, Bill (radio & TV entertainer)	Feb 18, 1920	F D G
Coburn, James (actor)	Aug 31, 1928	S N W	Culp, Robert (actor)	Aug 16, 1931	R A N
Cochran Barbara Ann (skiing)	Jan 4, 1951	O 1 7	Cummings, Robert (actor)	Jun 9, 1910	G T 5
Cochran, Marilyn (skiing)	Feb 7, 1950	E C 6	Cunningham, R. Walter (astronaut)	Mar 16, 1932	X S 3
Cochran, Robert (skiing)	Dec 11, 1951	K C K	Curtin, Phyllis (soprano)	Dec 3, 1927	W V O
Coco, James (actor)	Mar 21, 1929	N T 1	Curtis, Tony (actor)	Jun 3, 1925	F D Z
Colbert, Claudette (actress)	Sep 13, 1905	B Z Q	Curzon, Clifford (pianist)	May 18, 1907	Q V A
Colby, William (politician)	Jan 4, 1920	G P 3	Dahl, Arlene (actress)	Aug 11, 1928	V V B
Collingwood, Charles (TV commentator)	Jun 4, 1917	F X H	Dailey, Dan (actor)	Dec 14, 1917	P U C
Collins, Dorothy (singer)	Nov. 18, 1926	K E 5	Dali, Salvador (painter)	May 11, 1904	S L V
Collins, Judy (singer)	May 1, 1939	C Q X	Daly, James (actor)	Oct 23, 1918	F Z T
Collins, Michael (astronaut)	Oct 31, 1930	D U V	Daly, John (news analyst)	Feb 20, 1914	B 2 4
Comden, Betty (writer)	May 3, 1919	O V N	d'Amboise, Jacques (dancer)	Jul 28, 1934	N O A
Commager, Henry Steele (historian)	Oct 25, 1902	F G S	Damone, Vic (singer)	Jun 12, 1928	G R H
Como, Perry (singer)	May 18, 1913	X A P	Danilova, Alexandra (ballerina)	Jan 20, 1904	V L H
Conant, James B. (educator)	Mar 26, 1893	C H R	Darcel, Denise (actress)	Sep 8, 1925	L R X
Connally, John B. (politician)	Feb 28, 1917	B L L	Darren, James (actor)	Jun 8, 1936	D X W
Connelly, Marc (playwright)	Dec 13, 1890	U O H	Darrieux, Danielle (actress)	May 1, 1917	S R G
Connery, Sean (actor)	Aug 25, 1930	F J U	daSilva, Howard (actor)	May 4, 1909	U K Z
Connors, Chuck (actor)	Apr 10, 1921	J A 3	Dassin, Jules (director)	Dec 18, 1911	M Q 1
Connors, Mike (actor)	Aug 15, 1925	K V 7	Dauphin, Claude (actor)	Aug 19, 1903	E Z T
Conrad Jr., Charles (astronaut)	Jun 2, 1930	O J B	Davenport, Willie (hurdler)	Jun 8, 1943	G C D
Conrad, William (actor)	Sep 27, 1920	V B 6	Davis, Angela	Jan 26, 1944	J L E
Considine, Bob (columnist)	Nov 4, 1906	E W D	Davis, Bette (actress)	Apr 5, 1908	R H 2
Constantine II (ex-King)	Jun 2, 1940	K W Z	Davis, Miles (trumpeter)	May 25, 1926	R Y S
Coogan, Jackie (actor)	Oct 26, 1914	U X N	Davis, Ossie (actor)	Dec 18, 1917	T Y G
Cooke, Alistair (TV narrator)	Nov 20, 1908	Q N Z	Davis Jr., Sammy (actor)	Dec 8, 1925	K Y P
Cooke, Terence (churchman)	Mar 1, 1921	P R V			
Cooper, Alice (rock musician)	Feb 4, 1948	G Z X			
Cooper, Jackie (actor)	Sep 15, 1922	C U X			
Cooper, John Sherman	Aug 23, 1901	P 2 T			

NAME	DATE OF BIRTH	CODE			NAME	DATE OF BIRTH	CODE		
Day, Dennis (singer)	May 21, 1917	P	J	2	Dunne, Irene (actress)	Dec 20, 1904	L	K	N
Day, Doris (singer)	Apr 3, 1924	R	1	3	Durante, Jimmy (comedian)	Feb 10, 1893	E	U	F
Day, Laraine (actress)	Oct 13, 1920	O	S	O	Durbin, Deanna (actress)	Dec 4, 1922	O	Q	D
Dayan, Moshe (Minister of Israel)	May 20, 1915	T	E	V	Durocher, Leo (baseball)	Jul 27, 1906	U	F	C
Dean, Jimmy (singer)	Aug 10, 1928	U	U	A	Durrell, Lawrence (novelist)	Feb 27, 1912	O	C	6
De Bakey, Michael E. (surgeon)	Sep 7, 1908	L	X	R	Duvalier, Jean-Claude	Jul 3, 1951	K	K	O
de Beauvoir, Simone (novelist)	Jan 9, 1908	W	E	F	Dylan, Bob (singer)	May 24, 1941	V	O	S
DeBusschere, Dave (basketball)	Oct 16, 1940	H	S	4	Eagleton, Thomas (U.S. Senator)	Sep 4, 1929	T	S	3
DeCarlo, Yvonne (actress)	Sep 1, 1924	G	J	O	Eastland, James O. (U.S. Senator)	Nov 28, 1904	M	Q	Y
Dee, Ruby (actress)	Oct 27, 1924	R	J	D	Ebsen, Buddy (actor)	Apr 2, 1908	O	E	Y
DeFore, Don (actor)	Aug 25, 1917	T	V	Y	Eckstine, Billy (singer)	Jul 8, 1914	B	Z	B
DeHavilland, Olivia (actress)	Jul 1, 1916	N	V	8	Eden, Sir Anthony (Prime Minister)	Jun 12, 1897	A	G	E
DeKooning, Willem (painter)	Apr 24, 1904	A	W	D	Edwards, Vincent (actor)	Jul 7, 1928	J	O	8
de La Renta, Oscar (designer)	Jul 22, 1932	N	F	Y	Egan, Richard (actor)	Jul 29, 1923	V	A	K
De Laurentiis, Dino (producer)	Aug 8, 1919	T	F	L	Eggar, Samantha (actress)	May 3, 1939	E	S	Z
Delon, Alain (actor)	Nov 8, 1935	V	F	G	Eglevsky, Andre (choreographer)	Dec 21, 1917	W	2	K
Del Rio, Dolores (actress)	Aug 3, 1905	G	M	H	Ehrlichman, John	Mar 20, 1925	X	N	Q
Demarest, William (actor)	Feb 27, 1892	A	G	U	Eisele, Donn F. (astronaut)	Jun 23, 1930	M	B	X
Dempsey, Jack (boxing)	Jun 24, 1895	S	Q	M	Eisenhower, Mamie Doud	Nov 14, 1896	V	V	1
Deneuve, Catherine (actress)	Oct 22, 1943	E	2	H	Eisenhower, Milton S. (educator)	Sep 15, 1899	V	U	E
Dennis, Sandy (actress)	Apr 27, 1937	E	K	P	Ekberg, Anita (actress)	Sep 29, 1931	P	R	Y
Denver, John (singer)	Dec 31, 1943	F	N	M	Eldridge, Florence (actress)	Sep 5, 1901	E	M	7
Desmond, Johnny (composer)	Nov 14, 1921	U	X	P	Elgart, Larry (band leader)	Mar 20, 1922	H	J	J
De Valera, Eamon (Pres. of Ireland)	Oct 14, 1882	E	3	4	Elliott, Michael (skiing)	Apr 3, 1942	N	U	B
Devine, Andy (actor)	Oct 7, 1905	C	V	G	Ellis, Jimmy (equestrian)	Feb 24, 1940	C	G	Z
De Vries, Peter (novelist)	Feb 27, 1910	U	A	2	Erhard, Ludwig (ex-Chancellor)	Feb 4, 1897	L	T	J
Dickey, James (poet)	Feb 2, 1923	E	U	6	Erickson, Leif (actor)	Oct 27, 1911	F	U	G
Dickenson, Angie (actress)	Sep 30, 1931	Q	S	Z	Erikson, Erik H. (psychoanalyst)	Jun 15, 1902	M	P	S
Diefenbaker, John G. (Prime Minister)	Sep 18, 1895	M	S	7	Ervin, Frank (harness racing)	Aug 12, 1904	T	U	P
Dietrich, Marlene (actress)	Dec 27, 1904	S	R	U	Evans, Dale (actress)	Oct 31, 1912	H	1	O
Dietz, James W. (rowing)	Jan 12, 1949	E	D	C	Evans, Dame Edith (actress)	Feb 8, 1888	Q	L	Z
Diller, Phyllis (comedienne)	Jul 17, 1917	C	K	S	Evans, Lee (runner)	Feb 25, 1947	H	R	J
Dillman, Bradford (actor)	Apr 14, 1930	L	Q	T	Evans, Maurice (actor)	Jun 3, 1901	C	B	D
DiMaggio, Joe (baseball)	Nov 25, 1914	D	Z	K	Evers, Charles (leader)	Sep 14, 1923	W	U	Y
Doctrow, E. L. (novelist)	Jan 6, 1931	B	C	W	Ewell, Tom (actor)	Apr 29, 1909	P	E	U
Dole, Robert (U.S. Senator)	Jul 22, 1923	O	W	C	Fabian (singer)	Feb 6, 1943	X	V	O
Dolin, Anton (dancer)	Jul 27, 1904	C	D	7	Fabray, Nanette (actress)	Oct 27, 1922	W	F	7
Dominguin, Luis Miguel (bullfighter)	Dec 9, 1926	H	1	S	Fadiman, Clifton (critic)	May 15, 1904	W	P	Z
Domino, Fats (musician)	Feb 26, 1928	P	W	8	Fairbanks Jr., Douglas (actor)	Dec 9, 1909	J	E	N
Donahue, Troy (actor)	Jan 27, 1938	D	E	1	Faith, Percy (musician)	Apr 7, 1908	T	K	4
Doolittle, James H. (general)	Dec 14, 1896	E	X	X	Falk, Peter (actor)	Sep 16, 1927	N	2	B
Dorati, Antal (conductor)	Apr 9, 1906	C	J	1	Farentino, James (actor)	Feb 24, 1938	J	E	V
Douglas, Helen Gahagan	Nov 25, 1900	U	H	M	Farmer, James (civil rights leader)	Jan 12, 1930	P	X	C
Douglas, Kirk (actor)	Dec 9, 1916	N	O	4	Farrell, Eileen (soprano)	Feb 13, 1920	A	2	B
Douglas, Melvyn (actor)	Apr 5, 1901	N	2	L	Farrell, James T. (novelist)	Feb 27, 1904	N	V	N
Douglas, William (former judge)	Oct 16, 1898	J	W	A	Farrow, Mia (actress)	Feb 9, 1946	S	3	Y
Dowling, Eddie (actor)	Dec 9, 1894	E	P	N	Fast, Howard (novelist)	Nov 11, 1914	N	L	4
Downs, Hugh (TV entertainer)	Feb 14, 1921	X	B	F	Faye, Alice (actress)	May 5, 1915	D	S	F
Drake, Alfred (singer)	Oct 7, 1914	A	D	2	Feiffer, Jules (cartoonist)	Jan 26, 1929	E	V	E
Drury, Allen (novelist)	Sep 2, 1918	A	B	A	Feldon, Barbara (actress)	Mar 12, 1941	R	Z	L
Drysdale, Don (baseball)	Jul 23, 1936	C	M	A	Feliciano, Jose (singer)	Sep 10, 1945	D	Q	D
Dubcek, Alexander (Pres. of Czech.)	Nov 27, 1921	K	H	3	Fellini, Federico (director)	Jan 20, 1920	X	C	L
Dubinsky, David (labor leader)	Feb 22, 1892	T	B	P	Ferrell, Barbara (sprinter)	Jul 28, 1947	X	B	5
Duchin, Peter (pianist)	Jul 28, 1937	E	S	H	Ferrer, Jose (actor)	Jan 8, 1912	K	J	O
Duke, Patty (actress)	Dec 14, 1946	D	3	B	Ferrer, Mel (actor)	Aug 25, 1917	T	V	Y
Dullea, Keir (actor)	May 30, 1936	S	O	N	Fiedler, Arthur (conductor)	Dec 17, 1894	N	X	V
Du Maurier, Daphne (novelist)	May 13, 1907	L	Q	4					
Dunaway, Faye (actress)	Jan 14, 1941	F	Y	U					

NAME	DATE OF BIRTH	CODE			NAME	DATE OF BIRTH	CODE		
Fields, Gracie (comedienne)	Jan 9, 1898	E	W	S	Gardner, Ava (actress)	Dec 24, 1922	L	H	Y
Finch, Peter (actor)	Sep 28, 1916	K	1	X	Gardner, John (politician)	Oct 8, 1912	H	C	Y
Finch, Robert (politician)	Oct 9, 1925	T	U	V	Gargan, William (actor)	Jul 17, 1905	N	X	Y
Finley, Charles O. (sportsman)	Feb 22, 1918	Q	F	G	Garland, Judy (actress)	Jun 10, 1922	V	G	Z
Finney, Albert (actor)	May 9, 1936	U	V	Z	Garner, Erroll (jazz pianist)	May 15, 1921	V	H	5
Firkusny, Rudolf (pianist)	Feb 11, 1912	V	P	P	Garner, James (actor)	Apr 7, 1928	K	G	H
Fischer, Bobby (chess)	Mar 9, 1943	H	Y	M	Garner, Peggy Ann (actress)	Feb 3, 1932	D	D	T
Fischer-Dieskau, Dietrich (baritone)	May 28, 1925	X	1	T	Garroway, Dave (TV host)	Jul 13, 1913	K	A	E
Fisher, Eddie (singer)	Aug 10, 1928	U	U	A	Gassman, Vittorio (actor)	Sep 1, 1922	M	F	J
Fittipaldi, Emerson (auto racer)	Dec 12, 1946	B	1	8	Gavin, James	Mar 22, 1907	E	U	K
Fitzgerald, Ella (singer)	Apr 25, 1918	J	M	C	Gavin, John (actor)	Apr 8, 1935	O	Q	Y
Fitzgerald, Geraldine (actress)	Nov 24, 1914	C	Y	J	Gaynor, Janet (actress)	Oct 6, 1906	W	V	H
Flack, Roberta (singer)	Feb 10, 1940	M	V	L	Gaynor, Mitzi (actress)	Sep 4, 1931	N	U	7
Fleming, Peggy Gale (ice skating)	Jul 27, 1948	U	C	7	Gazzara, Ben (actor)	Aug 28, 1930	J	M	X
Fleming, Rhonda (actress)	Aug 10, 1923	K	N	W	Geddes, Barbara Bel (actress)	Oct 31, 1922	C	K	C
Foch, Nina (actress)	Apr 20, 1924	L	P	M	Gehringer, Charlie (baseball)	May 11, 1903	U	J	S
Fonda, Henry (actor)	May 16, 1905	U	R	3	Genevieve (entertainer)	Apr 17, 1930	O	T	W
Fonda, Jane (actress)	Dec 21, 1937	N	Y	W	Genn, Leo (actor)	Aug 9, 1905	N	S	O
Fonda, Peter (actor)	Feb 23, 1939	E	E	W	Geoffrion, Bernie (hockey)	Feb 14, 1931	S	O	3
Fong, Hiram (U.S. Senator)	Oct 1, 1907	O	R	E	Gernreich, Rudi (designer)	Aug 8, 1922	L	K	S
Fontaine, Joan (actress)	Nov 22, 1917	Q	1	O	Gershwin, Ira (lyricist)	Dec 6, 1896	U	P	P
Fonteyn, Dame Margot (ballerina)	May 18, 1919	F	H	3	Getz, Stan (saxophonist)	Feb 2, 1927	R	Z	G
Ford, Elizabeth (Mrs. Gerald)	Apr 8, 1918	P	X	T	Gielgud, Sir John (actor)	Apr 14, 1904	O	M	2
Ford, Gerald R. (ex-President)	Jul 14, 1913	L	B	F	Gifford, Frank (sportscaster)	Aug 16, 1930	U	3	L
Ford, Glenn (actor)	May 1, 1916	V	Q	E	Giles, Warren (baseball)	May 28, 1896	M	T	V
Ford II, Henry (auto maker)	Sep 4, 1917	F	C	A	Gillespie, Dizzy (trumpeter)	Oct 21, 1917	G	W	P
Ford, Tennessee Ernie (singer)	Feb 13, 1919	D	1	8	Gilmore, Artis (basketball)	Sep 21, 1949	D	D	Y
Ford, Whitey (baseball)	Oct 28, 1928	G	P	O	Gingold, Hermione (actress)	Dec 9, 1897	U	T	U
Foreman, George (boxing)	Jan 10, 1949	C	B	A	Ginsberg, Allen (poet)	Jun 3, 1926	C	E	2
Forsythe, John (actor)	Jan 29, 1918	P	K	Q	Giovanni, Nikki (poet)	Jun 7, 1943	F	B	C
Fosbury, Richard (high jumper)	Mar 6, 1947	R	1	S	Gish, Lillian (actress)	Oct 14, 1896	N	S	3
Fosse, Bob (choreographer)	Jun 23, 1927	U	1	Q	Givency, Hubert (designer)	Feb 21, 1927	N	Q	1
Foxx, Redd (actor)	Dec 9, 1922	T	V	J	Gleason, Jackie (actor)	Feb 26, 1916	B	G	F
Foy, Eddie, Jr. (dancer)	Feb 4, 1905	L	3	1	Glenn Jr., John Hershel (astronaut)	Jul 18, 1921	Q	Q	3
Francescatti, Zino (violinist)	Aug 9, 1905	N	S	O	Godard, Jean Luc (director)	Dec 3, 1930	O	Z	V
Franciosa, Anthony (actor)	Oct 25, 1928	D	M	L	Goddard, Paulette (actress)	Jun 3, 1911	V	O	1
Francis, Connie (singer)	Dec 12, 1938	A	Q	P	Godfrey, Arthur (entertainer)	Aug 31, 1903	R	J	6
Franciscus, James (actor)	Jan 31, 1924	X	T	6	Goldberg, Arthur J. (politician)	Aug 8, 1908	D	V	U
Franklin, Aretha (singer)	Mar 25, 1942	D	L	1	Golden, Harry (author)	May 6, 1902	S	C	L
Frazier, Joe (boxing)	Jan 12, 1944	S	Z	Y	Goldwater, Barry M. (U.S. Senator)	Jan 1, 1909	M	2	A
Frieden, Betty (feminist)	Feb 4, 1921	N	U	4	Gonzalez, Pancho (tennis)	May 9, 1928	T	L	G
Friedman, Milton (economist)	Jul 31, 1912	H	S	V	Goodman, Benny (clarinetist)	May 30, 1909	X	H	S
Fromm, Erich (psychoanalyst)	Mar 23, 1900	C	N	4	Gordon, Richard Francis (astronaut)	Oct 5, 1929	D	V	1
Frost, David (TV entertainer)	Apr 7, 1939	B	U	7	Gordon, Ruth (actress)	Oct 30, 1896	F	F	L
Fry, Christopher (playwright)	Dec 18, 1907	X	L	R	Gore, Albert A. (ex-Senator)	Dec 26, 1907	H	T	Z
Fulbright, J. William (politician)	Apr 9, 1905	F	H	Y	Goren, Charles H. (bridge expert)	Mar 4, 1901	D	X	M
Fuller, Buckminster (educator)	Jul 12, 1895	N	F	5	Gorme, Eddie (singer)	Aug 16, 1931	R	A	N
Funston, George Keith	Oct 12, 1910	R	D	X	Gould, Elliott (actor)	Aug 29, 1938	L	X	J
Furness, Betty (actress)	Jan 3, 1916	R	J	S	Gould, Glenn (pianist)	Sep 25, 1932	J	P	X
Gabin, Jean (actor)	May 17, 1904	A	R	2	Gould, Morton (composer)	Dec 10, 1913	W	L	X
Gable, Dan (wrestling)	Oct 25, 1945	C	E	Q	Goulet, Robert (singer)	Nov 26, 1933	W	W	V
Gabor, Zsa Zsa (actress)	Feb 6, 1923	J	Y	B	Graham, Billy (evangelist)	Nov 7, 1918	V	M	A
Galbraith, John Kenneth (economist)	Oct 15, 1908	C	E	W	Graham, Katherine Meyer (publisher)	Jun 16, 1917	S	G	U
Gallagher, Michael (skiing)	Oct 3, 1941	P	F	S	Graham, Otto Everett (football)	Dec 6, 1921	T	R	D
Gallico, Paul (novelist)	Jul 26, 1897	W	X	Q	Grahame, Gloria (actress)	Nov 28, 1929	M	T	O
Gallup, George H. (poll taker)	Nov 18, 1901	K	B	G	Grange, Red (football)	Jun 13, 1904	E	Q	V
Gandhi, Indira (ex-Prime Minister)	Nov 19, 1917	N	X	L	Granger, Farley (actor)	Jul 1, 1925	L	D	U
Garbo, Greta (actress)	Sep 18, 1905	G	B	V	Granger, Stewart (actor)	May 6, 1913	L	R	C
					Grant, Cary (actor)	Jan 18, 1904	T	J	F

111

NAME	DATE OF BIRTH	CODE			NAME	DATE OF BIRTH	CODE		
Grass, Gunter (novelist)	Oct 16, 1927	U	A	7	Hasso, Signe (actress)	Aug 15, 1915	O	H	J
Grasso, Ella (Governor)	May 10, 1919	V	3	U	Hatfield, Mark O. (U.S. Senator)	Jul 12, 1922	G	L	Y
Gravel, Mike (U.S. Senator)	May 13, 1930	R	R	P	Haver, June (actress)	Jun 10, 1926	K	M	A
Graves, Peter (actor)	Mar 18, 1926	S	M	Q	Hawn, Goldie (actress)	Nov 21, 1945	G	D	K
Graves, Robert (poet)	Jul 26, 1895	D	U	L	Hayakawa, S. I. (U.S. Senator)	Jul 18, 1905	O	Y	Z
Gray, Barry (radio interviewer)	Jul 2, 1916	O	W	A	Hayden, Melissa (ballerina)	Apr 25, 1928	E	Z	1
Gray, Dolores (singer)	Jun 7, 1930	T	O	G	Hayes, Helen (actress)	Oct 10, 1900	U	S	7
Grayson, Kathryn (singer)	Feb 9, 1923	M	2	E	Hayes, Isaac (composer)	Aug 20, 1942	O	T	J
Greco, Buddy (singer)	Aug 14, 1926	F	V	8	Hayworth, Rita (actress)	Oct 17, 1918	X	T	N
Greco, Jose (dancer)	Dec 23, 1918	V	B	O	Head, Edith (designer)	Oct 28, 1907	S	Q	7
Green, Adolph (actor)	Dec 2, 1915	H	E	T	Hearst Jr., William Randolph (publisher)	Jan 27, 1908	R	X	Y
Green, Paul (playwright)	Mar 17, 1894	O	3	K	Heath, Edward (ex-Prime Minister)	Jul 9, 1916	V	A	H
Greene, Charles E. (sprinter)	Mar 21, 1945	P	L	4	Heatherton, Joey (actress)	Sep 14, 1944	L	T	F
Greene, Graham (novelist)	Oct 2, 1904	A	P	8	Heckart, Eileen (actress)	Mar 29, 1919	B	O	L
Greene, Lorne (actor)	Feb 12, 1915	O	U	X	Hefner, Hugh (publisher)	Apr 9, 1926	R	F	E
Greenspan, Alan (economist)	Mar 6, 1926	F	3	D	Heifetz, Jascha (violonist)	Feb 2, 1901	U	V	P
Greenwood, Joan (actress)	Mar 4, 1921	S	U	Y	Heller, Joseph (novelist)	May 1, 1923	A	Y	U
Greer, Germaine (feminist)	Jan 29, 1939	C	H	5	Heller, Walter (economist)	Aug 27, 1915	C	U	V
Grey, Joel (actor)	Apr 11, 1932	C	Q	V	Hellman, Lillian (playwright)	Jun 20, 1905	J	Y	5
Griffin, Merv (TV entertainer)	Jul 6, 1925	Q	J	Z	Helms, Richard (politician)	Mar 30, 1913	U	H	7
Griffin, Robert (U.S. Senator)	Nov 6, 1923	F	R	L	Henderson, Florence (actress)	Feb 14, 1934	K	S	B
Griffith, Andy (actor)	Jun 1, 1926	A	C	Z	Henderson, Skitch (conductor)	Jan 27, 1918	N	H	O
Grimes, Tammy (actress)	Jan 30, 1934	S	C	U	Henreid, Paul (actor)	Jan 10, 1908	X	F	G
Grizzard, George (actor)	Apr 1, 1928	D	A	B	Hepburn, Audrey (actress)	May 4, 1929	L	G	D
Gromyko, Andrei A. (diplomat)	Jul 5, 1909	N	Q	V	Hepburn, Katherine (actress)	Nov 8, 1909	A	B	P
Grove, Lefty (baseball)	Mar 6, 1900	J	Y	M	Herblock (political cartoonist)	Oct 13, 1909	V	D	W
Groza, Lou (football)	Jan 25, 1924	R	N	Z	Herman, Woody (band leader)	May 16, 1913	V	2	N
Guardino, Harry (actor)	Dec 23, 1925	B	L	5	Heston, Charlton (actor)	Oct 4, 1924	R	O	O
Guinness, Sir Alec (actor)	Apr 2, 1914	U	M	D	Heyerdahl, Thor (explorer)	Oct 6, 1914	X	C	1
Gurney, Edward (politician)	Jan 12, 1914	J	Q	X	Hickcox, Charles (swimming)	Feb 6, 1947	M	1	X
Guthrie, Arlo (singer)	Jul 10, 1947	E	M	M	Hickel, Walter (politician)	Aug 18, 1919	F	Q	V
Hackett, Bobby (trumpeter)	Jan 31, 1915	B	H	L	Hildegarde (singer)	Feb 1, 1906	E	1	Z
Hackett, Buddy (actor)	Aug 31, 1924	F	H	N	Hillary, Sir Edmund (climber)	Jul 20, 1919	X	P	Z
Hackman, Gene (actor)	Jan 30, 1931	C	2	N	Hills, Carla (politician)	Jan 3, 1934	O	D	1
Hagen, Uta (actress)	Jun 12, 1919	H	E	U	Hines, James (sprinter)	Sep 10, 1946	A	R	F
Haggard, Merle (songwriter)	Apr 6, 1937	G	R	2	Hines, Jerome (basso)	Nov 8, 1921	O	R	J
Haig Jr., Alexander Meigs (General)	Dec 2, 1924	G	R	G	Hingle, Pat (actor)	Jul 19, 1924	J	V	C
Hailey, Arthur (novelist)	Apr 5, 1920	G	X	V	Hirohito (Emperor)	Apr 29, 1901	O	X	B
Haise Jr., Fred W. (astronaut)	Nov 14, 1933	K	K	J	Hirschfeld, Al (cartoonist)	Jun 21, 1903	P	W	1
Halas, George (football)	Feb 2, 1895	O	O	B	Hirt, Al (trumpeter)	Nov 7, 1922	K	R	K
Halberstam, David (journalist)	Apr 10, 1934	T	R	Y	Hiss, Alger	Nov 11, 1904	S	2	G
Hall, Albert W. (weight thrower)	Aug 2, 1934	S	T	F	Hitchcock, Alfred J. (director)	Aug 13, 1899	L	P	E
Hall, Gary (swimming)	Aug 7, 1951	W	R	Q	Hodges, Eddie (actor)	Mar 5, 1947	Q	Z	R
Hamill, Pete (journalist)	Jun 24, 1935	W	J	B	Hoffa, James (labor leader)	Feb 14, 1913	W	U	V
Hammond, Kathy (runner)	Nov 2, 1951	R	U	D	Hoffman, Dustin (actor)	Aug 8, 1937	Q	A	T
Hampton, Lionel (band leader)	Apr 20, 1914	P	B	W	Hogan, Ben (golf)	Aug 13, 1912	V	C	A
Hanson, Howard (conductor)	Oct 28, 1896	D	D	J	Holbrook, Hal (actor)	Feb 17, 1925	P	K	S
Harding, Ann (actress)	Aug 7, 1902	T	M	E	Holden, William (actor)	Apr 17, 1918	A	D	3
Harnick, Sheldon (songwriter)	Apr 30, 1924	V	Z	W	Holder, Geoffrey (dancer)	Aug 1, 1930	E	N	4
Harriman, W. (ex-Governor)	Nov 15, 1891	M	P	P	Holloway, Stanley (actor)	Oct 1, 1890	Q	Z	A
Harris, Fred (ex-Senator)	Nov 13, 1930	R	E	A	Holm Celeste (actress)	Apr 29, 1919	K	R	J
Harris, Jed (producer)	Feb 25, 1900	X	P	C	Holtz, Lou (comedian)	Apr 11, 1898	E	B	L
Harris, Julie (actress)	Dec 2, 1925	D	S	J	Home, Lord (diplomat)	Jul 2, 1903	C	E	D
Harris, Phil (actor)	Jun 24, 1906	K	A	C	Hook, Sidney (philosopher)	Dec 20, 1902	Q	G	H
Harris, Richard (actor)	Oct 1, 1933	M	W	6	Hope, Bob (comedian)	May 29, 1903	P	2	C
Harris, Roy (composer)	Feb 12, 1898	Q	3	T	Hopper, Dennis (actor)	May 17, 1936	E	A	8
Harrison, George (singer)	Feb 25, 1943	T	M	8	Horne, Lena (singer)	Jun 30, 1917	J	V	A
Harrison, Noel (actor)	Jan 29, 1936	L	D	X	Horne, Marilyn (soprano)	Jan 16, 1934	D	R	F
Harrison, Rex (actor)	Mar 5, 1908	J	E	4	Hornung, Paul (football)	Dec 23, 1935	U	X	T
Hartford, Huntington (heir)	Apr 18, 1911	V	Y	N	Horowitz, Vladmir (pianist)	Oct 1, 1904	X	O	7
Hartman, Elizabeth (actress)	Dec 23, 1941	D	C	8	Hough, Lawrence A. (rowing)	Apr 4, 1944	J	Y	H
Hartz, Jim (newscaster)	Feb 3, 1940	E	O	D	Houk, Ralph (baseball)	Aug 9, 1919	U	G	M
Harvey, Doug (hockey)	Mar 13, 1930	B	M	U	Houseman, John (producer)	Sep 22, 1902	T	B	S

NAME	DATE OF BIRTH	CODE	NAME	DATE OF BIRTH	CODE
Howard, Elston (baseball)	Feb 23, 1930	G W B	Jourdan, Louis (actor)	Jun 19, 1920	N O 5
Howard, Trevor (actor)	Aug 29, 1916	C Y 1	Juliana (Queen)	Apr 30, 1909	Q F V
Howe, Gordon (hockey)	Mar 31, 1928	C 3 A	Jurgensen, Sonny (football)	Aug 23, 1934	Q M 2
Howell, Jim Lee (football)	Sep 27, 1914	O W R	Kabalevsky, Dmitri (composer)	Dec 30, 1904	V U X
Howes, Sally Ann (actress)	Jul 20, 1934	E F 1	Kaline, Al (baseball)	Dec 19, 1934	T S N
Hubbell, Carl (baseball)	Jun 22, 1903	Q X 2	Kanin, Garson (playwright)	Nov 24, 1912	J W E
Hudson, Rock (actor)	Nov 17, 1925	M C 2	Kantor, MacKinlay (novelist)	Feb 4, 1904	N 1 X
Huff, Sam (football)	Oct 4, 1934	M 1 C	Karajan, Herbert von (conductor)	Apr 5, 1908	R H 2
Hughes, Harold (politician)	Feb 10, 1922	Q 2 D	Kaye, Danny (comedian)	Jan 18, 1913	S V 2
Hughes, Howard (industrialist)	Dec 24, 1905	M P T	Kaye, Sammy (band leader)	Mar 13, 1910	L P H
Hull, Bobby (hockey)	Jan 3, 1939	X K D	Kazan, Elia (director)	Sep 7, 1909	H Y T
Humperdinck, Engelbert (singer)	May 2, 1936	N O S	Keach, Stacy (actor)	Jun 2, 1941	G X 2
Humphrey, Hubert (U.S. Senator)	May 27, 1911	O G T	Keel, Howard (singer)	Apr 13, 1919	R A 1
Hunt, Marsha (actress)	Oct 17, 1917	C S L	Keeler, Ruby (actress)	Aug 25, 1910	P M H
Hunter, Kim (actress)	Nov 12, 1922	P W P	Keith, Brian (actor)	Nov 14, 1921	U X P
Hunter, Tab (actor)	Jul 11, 1931	D V K	Kellerman, Sally (actress)	Jun 2, 1938	P T U
Hussein I (King)	May 2, 1935	P M P	Kelley, Clarence M.	Oct 24, 1911	C R D
Huston, John (director)	Aug 5, 1906	F P M	Kelley, Emmett (clown)	Dec 9, 1898	R U W
Hutchins, Robert M. (educator)	Jan 17, 1899	K C 3	Kelly, Gene (dancer)	Aug 23, 1912	H N L
Hutson, Donald (football)	Jan 31, 1913	H F G	Kelly, Grace (actress, Princess)	Nov 12, 1929	T C 6
Hutton, Barbara (heiress)	Nov 14, 1912	W M 3	Kelly, Patsy (actress)	Jan 12, 1910	U L O
Hutton, Betty (actress)	Feb 26, 1921	M O S	Kelly, Red (hockey)	Jul 9, 1927	N O 7
Inouye, Daniel (U.S. Senator)	Sep 7, 1924	N P U	Kennan, George F. (diplomat)	Feb 16, 1904	B K B
Insko, Del (harness racing)	Jul 10, 1931	C U J	Kennedy, Arthur (actor)	Feb 17, 1914	W Y 1
Ionesco, Eugene (playwright)	Nov 26, 1912	L Y G	Kennedy, Edward (U.S. Senator)	Feb 22, 1932	X X E
Ireland, John (actor)	Jan 30, 1915	A G K	Kennedy, George (actor)	Feb 18, 1925	Q L T
Isherwood, Christopher (novelist)	Aug 26, 1904	K F 4	Kennedy, Rose (President's mother)	Jul 22, 1890	O K 4
Iturbi, Jose (pianist)	Nov 28, 1895	O E D	Kenton, Stan (musician)	Feb 19, 1912	F X X
Ives, Burl (singer)	Jun 14, 1909	P X 8	Kerr, Deborah (actress)	Sep 30, 1921	V F C
Jackson, Anne (actress)	Sep 3, 1926	C N U	Kerr, Walter (columnist, author)	Jul 8, 1913	E Y 8
Jackson, Henry (U.S. Senator)	May 31, 1912	Q N 1	Keyes, Frances (novelist)	Jul 21, 1885	D C R
Jackson, Rev. Jesse (leader)	Oct 8, 1941	U L X	Khachaturian, Aram (composer)	Jun 6, 1903	X G L
Jacobi, Lou (actor)	Dec 28, 1913	R A H	Kheel, Theodore (politician)	May 9, 1914	L V H
Jaffe, Sam (actor)	Mar 8, 1898	R Y K	Kieran, John (columnist)	Aug 2, 1892	U Y M
Jagger, Dean (actor)	Nov 7, 1903	Q V 8	Kiesinger, Kurt (diplomat)	Apr 6, 1904	F D T
Jagger, Mick (singer)	Jul 26, 1944	G Z W	Kiley, Richard (actor)	Mar 31, 1922	T U U
James, Harry (trumpeter)	Mar 15, 1916	U Z Y	Killebrew, Harmon (baseball)	Jun 29, 1936	B Q K
Janis, Byron (pianist)	Mar 24, 1928	T V 2	Killy, Jean Claude (skiing)	Aug 30, 1943	V B V
Janssen, David (actor)	Mar 27, 1930	Q 1 A	King, Alan (entertainer)	Dec 26, 1927	W Q D
Javits, Jacob K. (U.S. Senator)	May 18, 1904	B S 3	King, Carole (singer)	Feb 9, 1941	J W N
Jeanmaire, Renee (dancer)	Apr 29, 1924	U Y V	King, Coretta Scott (civil rights leader)	Apr 27, 1927	J Z Z
Jessel, George (entertainer)	Apr 3, 1898	U W C	King, Harriet (fencing)	Sep 22, 1935	U P 1
Jessup, Philip C. (jurist)	Jan 5, 1897	D R M	King, Micki (diving)	Jul 26, 1944	G Z W
Joffrey, Robert (choreographer)	Dec 24, 1930	M S J	Kinglsey, Sidney (playwright)	Oct 18, 1906	L E U
John, Elton (singer)	Mar 25, 1947	N R D	Kinsella, John (swimming)	Aug 26, 1952	Q K E
Johns, Glynis (actress)	Oct 5, 1923	U N M	Kipnis, Alexander (basso)	Feb 1, 1891	A H Z
Johns, Jasper (painter)	May 15, 1930	T T R	Kirk, Grayson (educator)	Oct 12, 1903	N X G
Johnson, Anthony (rowing)	Nov 16, 1940	Q V 2	Kirk, Phyllis (actress)	Sep 18, 1930	G E L
Johnson, Lady Bird	Dec 22, 1912	O W 8	Kirkpatrick, Ralph (harpsichordist)	Jun 10, 1911	E V 8
Johnson, Luci Baines	Jul 2, 1947	U D D	Kirsten, Dorothy (soprano)	Jul 6, 1919	J A L
Johnson, Lynda Bird	Mar 19, 1944	Q H Z	Kissinger, Henry (politician)	May 27, 1923	D W N
Johnson, Rafer (decathlon)	Aug 18, 1935	H H Y	Kitt, Eartha (singer)	Jan 26, 1928	G T B
Johnson, Van (actor)	Aug 20, 1916	R P R	Klein, Herbert (politician)	Apr 1, 1928	D A B
Jones, Carolyn (actress)	Apr 28, 1933	R F G	Klemperer, Werner (actor)	Mar 22, 1920	Q J G
Jones, Dean (actor)	Jan 25, 1935	K 2 R	Kleindeinst, Richard (politician)	Aug 5, 1923	E H R
Jones, James (novelist)	Nov 6, 1921	M P G	Knievel, Evel (daredevil)	Oct 17, 1938	O Q Z
Jones, James Earl (actor)	Jan 17, 1931	N O 8	Knight, Gladys (singer)	May 28, 1944	R W 4
Jones, Jennifer (actress)	Mar 2, 1919	V P R	Knight, John S. (publisher)	Oct 26, 1894	G 2 B
Jones, Shirley (singer, actress)	Mar 31, 1934	J G O	Knopf, Alfred A. (publisher)	Sep 12, 1892	P J U
Jones, Tom (singer)	Jun 7, 1940	P 2 5			
Joplin, Janis (singer)	Jan 19, 1943	E C 4			
Jory, Victor (actor)	Nov 23, 1903	J J Q			

113

NAME	DATE OF BIRTH	CODE			NAME	DATE OF BIRTH	CODE		
Knotts, Don (actor)	Jul 21, 1924	L	X	E	Lewis, Shari (puppeteer)	Jan 17, 1934	E	S	G
Koestler, Arthur (novelist)	Sep 5, 1905	R	R	H	Liberace (pianist)	May 16, 1919	D	F	1
Kokoschka, Oskar (painter)	Mar 1, 1886	U	B	J	Lichtenstein, Roy (painter)	Oct 27, 1923	T	G	A
Kostelanetz, Andre (conductor)	Dec 22, 1901	V	H	H	Lillie, Beatrice (actress)	May 29, 1898	G	W	1
Kosygin, Aleksei, N. (Premier)	Feb 20, 1904	F	O	F	Lilly, Robert (football)	Jul 26, 1939	U	S	K
Koufax, Sandy (baseball)	Dec 30, 1935	D	B	1	Lin Yutang (author)	Oct 10, 1895	L	M	V
Kramer, Jack (tennis)	Aug 1, 1921	G	B	J	Lindbergh, Charles A. (aviator)	Feb 4, 1902	T	Y	T
Kramer, Stanley E. (producer)	Sep 29, 1913	T	X	R	Linden, Hal (actor)	Mar 20, 1931	F	U	4
Kristofferson, Kris (singer)	Jun 22, 1936	S	J	C	Lindfors, Viveca (actress)	Dec 29, 1920	W	L	Z
Kruger, Otto (actor)	Sep 6, 1885	E	W	6	Lindsay, John (ex-Mayor)	Nov 24, 1921	G	E	Z
Kubelik, Rafael (conductor)	Jun 29, 1914	Q	Q	1	Linkletter, Art (TV personality)	Jul 17, 1912	R	D	G
Kubrick, Stanley (producer)	Jul 26, 1928	E	E	T	Liquori, Marty (runner)	Sep 11, 1949	R	W	O
Kuhn, Bowie Kent (baseball)	Oct 28, 1926	M	M	J	Little, Lou (football)	Dec 6, 1893	E	L	H
Kurosawa, Akira (director)	Mar 23, 1910	V	Z	S	Little, Rich (comedian)	Dec 26, 1938	P	B	4
Kurtz, Efrem (conductor)	Nov 7, 1900	B	S	2	Livesey, Roger (actor)	Jun 25, 1906	L	B	D
Ky, Nguyen Cao (ex-Pres. of Vietnam)	Sep 8, 1930	U	X	A	Lockhart, June (actress)	Jun 25, 1925	E	1	O
Laine, Frankie (singer)	Mar 30, 1913	U	H	7	Lockwood, Margaret (actress)	Sep 15, 1916	U	N	K
Laird, Melvin R. (politician)	Sep 1, 1922	M	F	J	Lodge Jr., Henry Cabot (diplomat)	Jul 5, 1902	J	G	E
Laird, Ronald (walker)	May 31, 1935	V	N	L	Loewe, Frederick (composer)	Jun 10, 1904	B	N	S
Lamas, Fernando (actor)	Jan 9, 1915	C	O	W	Logan, Joshua (director)	Oct 10, 1908	V	3	R
Lamour, Dorothy (actress)	Oct 10, 1914	D	G	5	Lombardo, Guy (band leader)	Jun 19, 1902	Q	T	W
Lancaster, Burt (actor)	Nov 2, 1913	G	A	S	London, George (baritone)	May 30, 1920	Q	W	K
Lanchester, Elsa (actress)	Oct 28, 1902	J	K	V	London, Julie (singer)	Sep 26, 1926	C	H	K
Landers, Ann (columnist)	Jul 14, 1918	U	H	R	Long, Russell B. (U.S. Senator)	Nov 3, 1918	R	H	5
Landon, Alfred (politician)	Sep 9, 1887	B	2	E	Longden, Johnny (horse racing)	Feb 14, 1907	P	M	G
Landry, Tom (football)	Sep 11, 1924	R	T	Y	Loos, Anita (novelist)	Apr 26, 1893	L	L	P
Landy, John (runner)	Apr 4, 1930	A	F	J	Lopez, Trini (singer)	May 15, 1937	X	3	8
Lang, Fritz (director)	Dec 5, 1890	M	F	8	Lord, Jack (actor)	Dec 30, 1930	S	Y	P
Lang, Paul Henry (critic)	Aug 28, 1901	U	D	Y	Loren, Sophia (actress)	Sep 20, 1934	V	M	W
Lange, Hope (actress)	Nov 28, 1933	A	Y	X	Louis, Joe (boxing)	May 13, 1914	P	Z	M
Langford, Frances (singer)	Apr 4, 1913	B	N	D	Louise, Tina (actress)	Feb 11, 1937	W	T	F
Lansbury, Angela (actress)	Oct 16, 1925	C	2	3	Lovell Jr., James A. (astronaut)	Mar 25, 1928	U	W	3
Lansing, Robert (actor)	Jun 5, 1929	U	L	C	Lowell, Robert (poet)	Mar 1, 1917	C	M	M
Larrieu, Francie (runner)	Nov 23, 1952	N	P	3	Lowenstein, Allard (politician)	Jan 16, 1929	S	L	3
Laurents, Arthur (playwright)	Jul 14, 1918	U	H	R	Loy, Myrna (actress)	Aug 2, 1905	F	L	G
Laurie, Piper (actress)	Jan 22, 1932	P	U	G	Luce, Clare Boothe (playwright)	Apr 10, 1903	M	F	U
Lawford, Peter (actor)	Sep 7, 1923	P	N	R	Lumet, Sidney (director)	Jun 25, 1924	H	Z	M
Lawrence, Carol (dancer)	Sep 5, 1932	M	X	C	Lunt, Alfred (actor)	Aug 19, 1892	O	N	4
Lawrence, Marjorie (singer)	Feb 17, 1909	N	S	P	Lupino, Ida (actress)	Feb 4, 1918	V	Q	W
Lawrence, Steve (singer)	Jul 8, 1935	N	X	Q	Lynde, Paul (comedian)	Jun 13, 1926	N	P	D
Leachman, Cloris (actress)	Apr 30, 1930	D	D	B	Lynley, Carol (actress)	Feb 13, 1942	K	2	T
Lean, David (director)	Mar 25, 1908	F	Z	Q	Lynn, Janet (skating)	Apr 6, 1953	J	J	5
Le Carre, John (novelist)	Oct 19, 1931	M	J	L	Lynn, Loretta (singer)	Apr 14, 1932	F	T	Y
Lederer, Francis (actor)	Nov 6, 1906	G	Y	F	Maazel, Lorin (conductor)	Mar 5, 1930	R	D	M
Lee, Peggy (singer)	May 26, 1920	M	S	F	MacArthur, James (actor)	Dec 8, 1937	X	L	J
Le Gallienne, Eva (actress)	Jan 11, 1899	D	Z	W	MacDermot, Glat (composer)	Dec 19, 1928	N	L	8
Lehmann, Lotte (soprano)	Feb 27, 1888	M	B	L	MacGraw, Ali (actress)	Apr 1, 1939	T	O	1
Leigh, Janet (actress)	Jul 6, 1927	K	L	4	MacGregor, Clark (politician)	Jul 12, 1922	G	L	Y
Leighton, Margaret (actress)	Feb 26, 1922	J	P	U	Mack, Ted (TV personality)	Feb 12, 1904	V	F	6
Leinsdorf, Erich (conductor)	Feb 4, 1912	O	H	H	MacKenzie, Gisele (singer)	Jan 10, 1927	R	B	R
Lemmon, Jack (actor)	Feb 8, 1925	F	A	J	MacLaine, Shirley (actress)	Apr 24, 1934	K	C	E
Lemnitzer, Lyman L. (General)	Aug 29, 1899	D	C	V	MacLeish, Archibald (poet)	May 7, 1892	B	V	Y
Lennon, John (singer)	Oct 9, 1940	A	L	W	Macmillan, Harold (ex-Prime Minister)	Feb 10, 1894	B	V	H
Leonard, Sheldon (actor)	Feb 22, 1907	X	U	P	MacMurray, Fred (actor)	Aug 30, 1908	C	P	J
Lerner, Alan Jay (lyricist)	Aug 31, 1918	W	3	7	MacRae, Gordon (singer)	Mar 12, 1921	C	3	7
Lerner, Max (columnist)	Dec 20, 1902	Q	G	H	MacRae, Sheila (comedienne)	Sep 24, 1924	G	D	D
Le Roy, Mervyn (producer)	Oct 15, 1900	B	X	D	Maddox, Lester (politician)	Sep 30, 1915	O	1	W
Leslie, Joan (actress)	Jan 26, 1925	Q	Q	4	Madison, Guy (actor)	Jan 19, 1922	R	E	P
Lessing, Doris (novelist)	Oct 22, 1919	B	Z	U	Mailer, Norman (novelist)	Jan 31, 1923	C	S	4
Levene, Sam (actor)	Aug 28, 1905	J	J	8	Mainbocher (designer)	Oct 24, 1890	Q	U	Y
Levenson, Sam (humorist)	Dec 28, 1911	W	1	C	Makarova, Natalia (ballerina)	Nov 21, 1940	V	1	7
Levi, Carlo (novelist)	Nov 29, 1902	S	O	U	Makeba, Miriam (singer)	Mar 4, 1932	L	F	Q
Levi, Edward (professor)	Jun 26, 1911	V	J	Q	Malamud, Bernard (novelist)	Apr 26, 1914	V	H	3
Lewis, Jerry (comedian)	Mar 16, 1926	Q	K	O					

114

NAME	DATE OF BIRTH	CODE	NAME	DATE OF BIRTH	CODE
Malden, Karl (actor)	Mar 22, 1914	J A 1	McDivitt, James Alton (astronaut)	Jun 10, 1929	B Q H
Malone, Dorothy (actress)	Jan 30, 1925	U U 8	McDowall, Roddy (actor)	Sep 17, 1928	M B F
Malraux, Andre (author)	Nov 3, 1901	S P Z	McDowell, Malcolm (actor)	Jun 19, 1943	S O P
Manchester, William (historian)	Apr 1, 1922	U V V	McGavin, Darren (actor)	May 7, 1922	K A Y
Mancini, Henry (composer)	Apr 16, 1924	G L H	McGee, Fibber (radio personality)	Nov 16, 1896	X X 3
Mangano, Silvana (actress)	Apr 21, 1930	S X 1	McGinley, Phyllis (poet)	Mar 21, 1905	K R E
Mankiewicz, Frank F. (columnist)	May 16, 1924	O N E	McGovern, George (U.S. Senator)	Jul 19, 1922	O S 6
Mankiewicz, Joseph L. (writer)	Feb 11, 1909	G M J	McGuire, Dorothy (actress)	Jun 14, 1919	K G W
Mann, Carol (golf)	Feb 3, 1941	C Q G	McHugh, Frank (actor)	May 23, 1898	A Q U
Mannes, Marya (author)	Nov 14, 1904	V B K	McKenna, Siobhan (actress)	May 24, 1923	A T K
Manning, Madeline (runner)	Jan 11, 1948	F A 7	McKuen, Rod (composer)	Apr 29, 1933	S G H
Mansfield, Mike (politician)	Mar 16, 1903	K J 3	McLean, Don (singer)	Oct 2, 1945	C K 1
Mantle, Mickey (baseball)	Oct 20, 1931	N K M	McLuhan, Marshall (writer)	Jul 21, 1911	X F H
Marceau, Marcel (mime)	Mar 22, 1923	G M N	McNamara, Robert S. (politician)	Jun 9, 1916	O 2 L
Marchi, John (politician)	May 20, 1921	C N B	Mead, Margaret (anthropologist)	Dec 16, 1901	P B B
Marcuse, Herbert (philosopher)	Jul 19, 1898	M R L	Meadows, Jayne (actress)	Sep 27, 1926	D J L
Margaret Rose (Princess)	Aug 21, 1930	B E Q	Meany, George (labor leader)	Aug 16, 1894	E M 5
Margrethe II (Queen)	Apr 16, 1940	J C L	Medina, Harold R. (jurist)	Feb 16, 1888	A T 8
Marichal, Juan (baseball)	Oct 20, 1937	U S 1	Meeker, Ralph (actor)	Nov 21, 1920	G A U
Maris, Roger (baseball)	Sep 10, 1934	L B M	Mehta, Zubin (conductor)	Apr 29, 1936	K L P
Markova, Dame Alicia (ballerina)	Dec 1, 1910	V 1 G	Meir, Golda (ex-Premier of Israel)	May 3, 1898	S Y 8
Marshall, E. G. (actor)	Jun 18, 1910	Q 3 F	Mendes-France, Pierre (ex-Premier)	Jan 11, 1905	K D B
Marshall, Thurgood (judge)	Jul 2, 1908	N M Q	Mennin, Peter (composer)	May 17, 1923	R M C
Martin, Billy (baseball)	May 16, 1928	C S O	Menotti, Gian (composer)	Jul 7, 1911	J U 2
Martin, Dean (singer)	Jun 17, 1917	T H V	Menuhin, Yehudi (violinist)	Apr 22, 1916	M G 4
Martin, Mary (singer)	Dec 1, 1914	K C Q	Menzies, Robert (ex-Prime Minister)	Dec 20, 1894	Q 1 Y
Martin, Tony (singer)	Dec 25, 1914	L 2 G	Mercer, Johnny (song writer)	Nov 18, 1909	L M Z
Martin, William (Fed. Reserve)	Dec 17, 1906	B J O	Mercouri, Melina (actress)	Oct 18, 1925	E A 5
Marvin, Lee (actor)	Feb 19, 1924	T K R	Meredith, Burgess (actor)	Nov 16, 1908	M J V
Marx, Groucho (comedian)	Oct 2, 1890	R 1 B	Merkel, Una (actress)	Dec 10, 1903	C 1 8
Marx, Zeppo (comedian)	Feb 25, 1901	U Q E	Merman, Ethel (singer)	Jan 16, 1909	D O Q
Mason, James (actor)	May 15, 1909	H V C	Merrick, David (producer)	Nov 27, 1912	M Z H
Massell, Sam	Aug 26, 1927	P F O	Merrill, Dina (actress)	Dec 9, 1925	L Z Q
Massey, Raymond (actor)	Aug 30, 1896	O A Q	Merrill, Gary (actor)	Aug 2, 1914	D W 2
Massine, Leonide (choreographer)	Aug 9, 1896	Q H 3	Merrill, Robert (baritone)	Jun 4, 1919	X Z M
Mastroianni, Marcello (actor)	Sep 28, 1924	L H H	Meyer, Deborah (swimming)	Aug 14, 1952	D 1 1
Mathis, Johnny (singer)	Sep 30, 1935	E X A	Michener, James A. (novelist)	Feb 3, 1907	D A 4
Matson, Randy (shot putter)	Mar 5, 1945	W X N	Middlecoff, Cary (golf)	Jan 6, 1921	G T 8
Matthau, Walter (actor)	Oct 1, 1920	B F B	Mielziner, Jo (designer)	Mar 19, 1901	T K 2
Mature, Victor (actor)	Jan 19, 1916	K Z A	Mikoyan, Anastas I. (diplomat)	Nov 25, 1895	L B A
Mauldin, Bill (cartoonist)	Oct 29, 1921	D G 7	Milanov, Zinka (soprano)	May 17, 1908	N W C
May, Rollo (psychologist)	Apr 21, 1909	G Z M	Milburn Jr., Rodney (hurdler)	May 18, 1950	N T 7
Maynard, Don (football)	Jan 25, 1937	E B W	Miles, Sarah (actress)	Dec 31, 1943	F N M
Maynor, Dorothy (soprano)	Sep 3, 1910	A V R	Miles, Sylvia (actress)	Sep 9, 1932	Q 2 G
Mays, Willie (baseball)	May 6, 1931	G L K	Miles, Vera (actress)	Aug 23, 1929	G F Q
McBride, Mary (radio personality)	Nov 16, 1899	O 1 A	Milland, Ray (actor)	Jan 3, 1907	T 1 6
McBride, Patricia (ballerina)	Aug 23, 1942	R W M	Miller, Ann (dancer)	Apr 12, 1919	Q 3 Z
McCallum, David (actor)	Sep 19, 1933	X K T	Miller, Arthur (playwright)	Oct 17, 1915	H P F
McCambridge, Mercedes (actress)	Mar 17, 1918	Q A 5	Miller, Henry (novelist)	Dec 26, 1891	G 3 X
McCarthy, Eugene J. (Senator)	Mar 29, 1916	L L E	Miller, Johnny (golf)	Apr 29, 1947	B Y F
McCarthy, Mary (novelist)	Jun 21, 1912	O F O	Miller, Mitch (musician)	Jul 4, 1911	F R Y
McCartney, Paul (singer)	Jun 18, 1942	U M M	Millett, Kate (feminist)	Sep 14, 1934	P F Q
McClellan, John J. (U.S. Senator)	Feb 25, 1896	L K 2	Milliken, William	Mar 26, 1922	O P P
McCloskey, Paul (U.S. Senator)	Sep 29, 1927	C M P	Mills, Hayley (actress)	Apr 18, 1946	R M 1
McCloy, John J. (lawyer)	Mar 31, 1895	B P 1	Mills, John (actor)	Feb 22, 1908	U V R
McClure, Doug (actor)	May 11, 1938	Q Z 6	Mills, Wilbur (politician)	May 24, 1909	R B M
McCormack, John W. (politian)	Dec 21, 1891	B X S	Milstein, Nathan (violinist)	Dec 31, 1904	W V Y
McCormack, Patty (actress)	Aug 21, 1945	G Y R	Mimieux, Yvette (actress)	Jan 8, 1941	X S O
McCrea, Joel (actor)	Nov 5, 1906	F X E	Minnelli, Liza (singer, actress)	Mar 12, 1946	C C W

115

NAME	DATE OF BIRTH	CODE	NAME	DATE OF BIRTH	CODE
Minnelli, Vincente (director)	Feb 28, 1913	N F B	Nevelson, Louise (sculptor)	Sep 23, 1900	C A P
Miro, Joan (painter)	Apr 20, 1893	E E J	Newhart, Bob (entertainer)	Sep 5, 1929	U T 4
Mitchell, Cameron (actor)	Apr 11, 1918	S 1 W	Newhouse, Samuel I. (publisher)	May 24, 1895	K N O
Mitchell, Guy (actor)	Feb 27, 1927	T W 7	Newley, Anthony (actor)	Sep 24, 1931	K M T
Mitchell, John N. (politician)	Sep 15, 1913	E J C	Newman, Paul (actor)	Jan 26, 1925	Q Q 4
Mitchell, Joni (singer)	Nov 7, 1943	V P Y	Newton, Wayne (singer)	Apr 3, 1942	N U B
Mitchum, Robert (actor)	Aug 6, 1917	X B E	Nichols, Mike (director)	Nov 6, 1931	G 2 4
Moffo, Anna (soprano)	Jun 27, 1934	E L C	Nicholson, Jack (actor)	Apr 22, 1937	X E K
Mollet, Guy (ex-Premier)	Dec 31, 1905	T W 1	Nilsson, Birgit (soprano)	May 17, 1923	R M C
Molotov, Vyacheslav M. (diplomat)	Mar 9, 1890	R P 1	Niven, David (actor)	Mar 1, 1910	W C 4
Mondale, Walter (Vice-President)	Jan 5, 1928	J 1 O	Nixon, Julie	Jul 5, 1948	V J K
			Nixon, Patricia	Mar 16, 1912	J V Q
Monk, Thelonious (pianist)	Oct 10, 1918	Q M F	Nixon, Richard M. (ex-President)	Jan 9, 1913	J M S
Monsarret, Nicholas (novelist)	Mar 22, 1910	U Y R	Nixon, Tricia	Feb 21, 1946	G M C
Montalban, Ricardo (actor)	Nov 25, 1920	L E Y	Nizer, Louis (lawyer)	Feb 6, 1902	V 1 V
Montand, Yves (actor)	Oct 13, 1921	L T Q	Noguchi, Isamu (sculptor)	Nov 7, 1904	X O C
Montgomery, Elizabeth (actress)	Apr 15, 1933	D V 2	Nolan, Lloyd (actor)	Aug 11, 1902	X Q J
Montgomery, Robert (actor)	May 21, 1904	E V 6	Norstad, Gen (ex-Comm. of NATO)	Mar 24, 1907	G W M
Montgomery of Alamein (military)	Nov 17, 1887	B M H	North, John (circus director)	Aug 14, 1903	X U O
Montoya, Carlos (guitarist)	Dec 13, 1903	F A C	North, Lowell (yachting)	Dec 2, 1929	Q X S
Moore, Archie (boxing)	Dec 13, 1916	R S 8	North, Sheree (actress)	Jan 17, 1933	H R R
Moore, Garry (TV personality)	Jan 31, 1915	B H L	Novaes, Guiomar (pianist)	Feb 28, 1895	R M 3
Moore, Henry (sculptor)	Jul 30, 1898	X 3 W	Novak, Kim (actress)	Feb 13, 1933	M Q 7
Moore, Mary Tyler (actress)	Dec 29, 1937	V D 5	Nugent, Elliott (actor)	Sep 20, 1899	C Z K
Moore, Melba (singer)	Oct 27, 1945	E G S	Nureyev, Rudolf (ballet dancer)	Mar 17, 1938	G 1 J
Moreau, Jeanne (actress)	Jan 23, 1928	D Q 7	Nuyen, France (actress)	Jul 31, 1939	B X P
Moreno, Rita (actress)	Dec 11, 1931	T F 6	Oakie, Jack (actor)	Nov 12, 1903	V 1 E
Morgan, Dennis (actor)	Dec 10, 1920	C U F	Oates, Joyce Carol (novelist)	Jun 16, 1938	F E A
Morgan, Henry (comedian)	Mar 31, 1915	P L D	Oberon, Merle (actress)	Feb 19, 1911	J W V
Morini, Erica (violinist)	Jan 5, 1910	N D G	O'Brian, Hugh (actor)	Apr 19, 1930	Q V Y
Morison, Samuel Eliot (historian)	Jul 9, 1887	J V J	O'Brian, Edmond (actor)	Sep 10, 1915	R F B
Morley, Robert (actor)	May 26, 1908	W C M	O'Brien, Lawrence F. (politician)	Jul 7, 1917	Q 3 H
Morse, Robert (actor)	May 18, 1931	T X W	O'Brien, Margaret (actress)	Jan 15, 1937	S U M
Morse, Wayne (politician)	Oct 20, 1900	G 3 J	O'Brien, Pat (actor)	Nov 11, 1899	J V 4
Morton, Rogers (politician)	Sep 19, 1914	F O J	O'Connor, Carroll (actor)	Aug 2, 1924	X G R
Morton, Thurston	Aug 19, 1907	R B 3	O'Connor, Donald (actor)	Aug 28, 1925	X F M
Mosconi, Willie (billiards)	Jun 27, 1913	R N W	Odetta (folk singer)	Dec 31, 1930	T Z Q
Moses, Robert (urban planner)	Dec 18, 1888	H R J	Oerter, Al (discus thrower)	Sep 19, 1936	P O I
Mostel, Zero (actor)	Feb 28, 1915	G H F	O'Hara, Maureen (actress)	Aug 17, 1921	X S Z
Moyers, Bill D. (journalist)	Jun 5, 1934	F R O	O'Keefe, Georgia (painter)	Nov 15, 1887	X K F
Moynihan, Daniel P. (U.S. Senator)	Mar 16, 1927	N L Q	Olav V (King of Norway)	Jul 2, 1903	C E D
Mudd, Roger (broadcaster)	Feb 9, 1928	V E Q	Olivier, Lord Laurence (actor)	May 22, 1907	U Z E
Mumford, Lewis (city planner)	Oct 19, 1895	U V 5	Olsen Merlin Jay (football)	Sep 15, 1940	X P 6
Munsel, Patrice (soprano)	May 14, 1925	J M E	O'Malley, Walter (baseball)	Oct 9, 1903	K U D
Murphy, George (actor)	Jul 4, 1904	C J J	Onassis, Jacqueline Kennedy	July 28, 1929	D H X
Murray, Arthur (dance teacher)	Apr 4, 1895	F T 5	O'Neal, Ryan (actor)	Apr 20, 1941	K H R
Murray, Ken (producer)	Jul 14, 1903	P R Q	O'Neill, Jennifer (actress)	Feb 20, 1949	V P J
Musial, Stan (baseball)	Nov 21, 1920	G A U	Ormandy, Eugene (conductor)	Nov 18, 1899	Q 3 C
Muskie, Edmund (U.S. Senator)	Mar 28, 1914	P G 7	Osborn, Paul (playwright)	Sep 4, 1901	D L 6
Myrdal, Gunnar (sociologist)	Dec 6, 1898	O R T	Osborne, John (playwright)	Dec 12, 1929	C E 3
Nabokov, Vladimir (novelist)	Apr 23, 1899	O P Z	O'Sullivan, Maureen (actress)	May 17, 1911	D Z J
Nabors, Jim (actor)	Jun 12, 1933	Q X T	O'Toole, Peter (actor)	Aug 2, 1933	V S D
Nader, Ralph (consumer advocate)	Feb 27, 1934	X C P	Owens, Jesse (sprinter)	Sep 12, 1918	L M L
			Paar, Jack (TV performer)	May 1, 1918	P S J
Natwick, Mildred (actress)	Jun 19, 1908	X 2 C	Pacino, Al (actor)	April 25, 1940	S M U
Neal, Patricia (actress)	Jan 20, 1926	G L Z	Packard, Vance (author)	May 22, 1914	A F V
Nelson, David (actor)	Oct 24, 1936	D V 3	Page, Geraldine (actress)	Nov 22, 1924	U G 5
Nelson, Ricky (singer)	May 8, 1940	H Z 8	Page, Patti (singer)	Nov 8, 1927	U Y W
Nenni, Pietro (Socialist)	Feb 9, 1891	J Q 8	Paige, Janis (actress)	Sep 16, 1922	D V Y
Nero, Peter (pianist)	May 22, 1934	P C 8	Palance, Jack (actor)	Feb 18, 1920	F D G
Nesson, Ron (press)	May 25, 1934	S F C	Paley, William S. (broadcasting)	Sep 28, 1901	E G W
			Palmer, Lilli (actress)	May 24, 1914	C H X

NAME	DATE OF BIRTH	CODE		
Papp, Joseph (producer)	Jun 22, 1921	N	S	B
Park, Chung Hee				
(Pres. So. Korea)	Sep 30, 1917	J	A	2
Parker, Eleanor (actress)	Jun 26, 1922	O	X	H
Parker, Suzy (model)	Oct 28, 1933	Q	V	Z
Parkinson, C. (historian)	Jul 30, 1909	P	N	N
Parks, Bert (entertainer)	Dec 30, 1914	Q	D	M
Parks, Gordon (director)	Nov 30, 1912	P	3	L
Parnis, Mollie (designer)	Mar 18, 1905	G	O	B
Parseghian, Ara (football)	May 21, 1923	V	Q	3
Parsons, Estelle (actress)	Nov 20, 1927	J	H	A
Parton, Dolly (singer)	Jan 19, 1946	U	G	C
Pasternak, Joseph (producer)	Sep 19, 1901	T	1	N
Patterson, Floyd (boxing)	Jan 4, 1935	M	F	4
Paul VI (Pope)	Sep 26, 1897	P	A	M
Pauling, Linus (chemist)	Feb 28, 1901	X	T	H
Pavan, Marisa (actress)	Jun 19, 1932	C	A	Y
Peale, Norman (clergyman)	May 31, 1898	J	Y	3
Pearl, Minnie (commedienne)	Oct 25, 1912	B	U	H
Peckinpah, Sam (director)	Feb 21, 1925	T	O	W
Peck, Gregory (actor)	Apr 5, 1916	S	S	M
Pele (soccer)	Oct 23, 1940	P	Z	C
Penn, Arthur (director)	Sep 27, 1922	P	D	B
Pennel, John (pole vaulter)	Jul 25, 1940	R	T	M
Peppard, George (actor)	Oct 1, 1928	C	Q	U
Percy, Charles H. (U.S.Senator)	Sep 27, 1919	X	3	3
Perelman, S.J. (humorist)	Feb 1, 1904	K	X	U
Perkins, Tony (actor)	Apr 14, 1932	F	T	Y
Peron, Isabel (chief of State)	Feb 4, 1931	H	D	S
Peters, Jean (actress)	Oct 15, 1926	W	2	4
Peters, Roberta (soprano)	May 4, 1930	H	H	F
Petty, Richard Lee (auto racing)	Jul 2, 1937	B	U	P
Phillip (Duke of Edinburgh)	Jun 10, 1921	A	F	X
Piatigorsky, Gregor (cellist)	Apr 17, 1903	T	N	2
Piazza, Ben (actor)	Jul 30, 1934	P	Q	C
Piazza, Marguerite (soprano)	May 6, 1926	V	E	7
Pickford, Mary (actress)	Apr 8, 1893	Q	V	5
Picon, Molly (actress)	Jun 1, 1898	K	Z	4
Pidgeon, Walter (actor)	Sep 23, 1898	J	2	L
Pinter, Harold (playwright)	Oct 10, 1930	F	2	8
Piston, Walter (composer)	Jan 20, 1894	D	3	U
Pleasence, Donald (actor)	Oct 5, 1919	H	H	C
Pleshette, Suzanne (actress)	Jan 31, 1937	L	H	3
Plimpton, George (author)	Mar 18, 1927	P	N	S
Plowright, Joan (actress)	Oct 28, 1929	D	Q	Q
Plummer, Christopher (actor)	Dec 13, 1929	D	F	4
Plunkett, Jim (football)	Dec 5, 1947	P	U	3
Podhoretz, Norman (author)	Jan 16, 1930	P	M	5
Poitier, Sidney (actor)	Feb 20, 1924	U	L	S
Polanski, Roman (director)	Aug 18, 1933	O	F	U
Pollard, Michael J. (actor)	May 30, 1939	J	R	T
Pons, Lily (soprano)	Apr 13, 1904	N	L	1
Porter, Katherine (novelist)	May 15, 1894	D	C	C
Poston, Tom (actor)	Oct 17, 1927	V	B	8
Potok, Chaim (author)	Feb 17, 1929	D	P	2
Potter, Cynthia (diving)	Aug 27, 1950	W	H	A
Powell, Boog (baseball)	Aug 17, 1941	O	P	D
Powell, Eleanor (actress)	Nov 21, 1912	F	T	B
Powell, Jane (actress)	Apr 1, 1929	A	B	D
Powell, Lewis F. (judge)	Sep 19, 1907	B	E	1
Powell, William (actor)	Jul 29, 1892	Q	U	H
Powers, Stephanie (actress)	Nov 12, 1942	F	T	2
Preminger, Otto (director)	Dec 5, 1906	N	Z	B
Presley, Elvis (singer)	Jan 8, 1935	Q	K	8
Preston, Robert (actor)	Jun 8, 1918	G	3	O
Previn, Andre (conductor)	Apr 6, 1929	F	G	J
Price, Leontyne (soprano)	Feb 10, 1927	B	E	P
Price, Ray (country music)	Jan 12, 1926	W	C	R
Price, Vincent (actor)	May 27, 1911	O	G	T
Pride, Charley (singer)	Mar 18, 1938	H	2	K
Priestley, J.B. (author)	Sep 13, 1894	K	M	Z
Primrose, William (violinist)	Aug 23, 1904	G	C	1
Prince, Harold (producer)	Jan 30, 1928	L	X	F
Pritchett, V.S. (literary critic)	Dec 16, 1900	S	A	8
Proell, Annemarie Moser (skier)	Mar 27, 1953	W	2	U
Provine, Dorothy (actress)	Jan 20, 1937	X	Z	R
Prowse, Juliet (actress)	Sep 25, 1936	V	U	7
Proxmire, William (U.S. Senator)	Jan 11, 1915	E	Q	Y
Pucci, Emilio (designer)	Nov 20, 1914	W	U	E
Pusey, Nathan M. (educator)	Apr 4, 1907	S	E	X
Puzo, Mario (novelist)	Oct 15, 1921	N	V	S
Pynchon, Thomas (novelist)	May 8, 1937	Q	V	1
Quayle, Anthony (actor)	Sep 7, 1913	U	A	3
Quinn, Anthony (actor)	Apr 21, 1916	L	F	3
Rabe, David (playwright)	Mar 10, 1940	S	W	G
Rabi, I.I. (physicist)	Jul 29, 1898	W	2	V
Raft, George (actor)	Sep 27, 1896	T	A	L
Rainer III (Prince)	May 31, 1923	H	1	R
Rallins, Mamie (hurdler)	Jul 8, 1941	U	C	5
Randall, Tony (actor)	Feb 26, 1924	C	R	Y
Randolph, Asa (labor leader)	Apr 15, 1889	L	X	3
Rattigan, Terence (playwright)	Jun 10, 1911	E	V	8
Rawls, Betsy (swimming)	May 4, 1928	O	F	B
Ray, Satyajat (producer)	May 2, 1922	E	Y	T
Rayburn, Gene (TV personality)	Dec 22, 1917	X	3	L
Raye, Martha (actress)	Aug 27, 1916	A	W	Y
Raymond, Gene (actor)	Aug 13, 1908	J	1	Z
Reagan, Ronald (politician)	Feb 6, 1911	T	J	H
Reasoner, Harry (TV commentator)	Apr 17, 1923	K	K	F
Reddy, Helen (singer)	Oct 25, 1941	O	3	G
Redford, Robert (actor)	Aug 18, 1937	C	L	4
Redgrave, Lynn (actress)	Mar 8, 1943	G	X	L
Redgrave, Sir Michael (actor)	Mar 20, 1908	A	U	L
Redgrave, Vanessa (actress)	Jan 30, 1937	K	G	2
Reed, Donna (actress)	Jan 27, 1921	E	M	V
Reed, Rex (critic)	Oct 2, 1940	R	D	P
Reed, Willis (basketball)	Jun 25, 1942	D	T	T
Reese, Della (singer)	Jul 6, 1932	U	S	H
Reese, Pee Wee (baseball)	Jul 23, 1919	C	S	3
Rehnquist, William (judge)	Oct 1, 1924	O	L	L
Reiner, Carl (actor)	Mar 20, 1922	H	J	J
Remick, Lee (actress)	Dec 14, 1935	L	O	K
Renoir, Jean (director)	Sep 15, 1894	M	O	2
Resnais, Alain (director)	Jun 3, 1922	O	3	S
Resnik, Regina (mezzo-soprano)	Aug 30, 1922	K	D	G
Reston, James (journalist)	Nov 3, 1909	T	Z	K
Reynolds, Burt (actor)	Feb 11, 1936	A	R	C
Reynolds, Debbie (actress)	Apr 1, 1932	Q	F	L
Rhodes, John (congressman)	Sep 18, 1916	X	Q	N
Ribicoff, Abe (U.S. Senator)	Apr 9, 1910	P	O	B
Rich, Buddy (drummer)	Jun 30, 1917	J	V	A
Richardson, Elliot L. (diplomat)	Jul 20, 1921	S	S	5
Richardson, Sir Ralph (actor)	Dec 19, 1902	P	F	G
Richardson, Tony (director)	Jun 5, 1928	X	K	A
Richter, Sviatoslav (pianist)	Mar 20, 1914	G	2	Y
Rickles, Don (comedian)	May 8, 1926	X	G	A
Rickover, Vice Adm. (atomic energy)	Jan 27, 1900	R	O	G
Riddle, Nelson (composer)	Jun 1, 1921	P	Z	O

NAME	DATE OF BIRTH	CODE	NAME	DATE OF BIRTH	CODE
Ridgway, Gen. (ex-Army Chief)	Mar 3, 1895	U P 6	Rule, Janice (actress)	Aug 15, 1931	Q 3 M
Rigg, Diana (actress)	Jul 20, 1938	R L B	Rumsfeld, Donald (politician)	Jul 9, 1932	X V L
Rigney, William (baseball)	Jan 29, 1918	P K Q	Rusk, Dean (ex-Sec. of State)	Feb 9, 1909	E K G
Ritchard, Cyril (actor)	Dec 1, 1898	J M O	Russell, Bill (basketball)	Feb 12, 1934	H Q 8
Rivers, Larry (painter)	Aug 17, 1923	R U 4	Russell, Jane (actress)	Jun 21, 1921	M R A
Rizzuto, Phil (baseball)	Sep 25, 1918	A Z Y	Russell, Rosalind (actress)	Jun 4, 1912	U R 5
Roark, Helen (tennis)	Oct 6, 1922	A N L	Ryun, Jim (runner)	Apr 29, 1947	B Y F
Robards, Jr., Jason (actor)	Jul 26, 1922	V Z E	Sabin, Albert B. (researcher)	Aug 26, 1906	D H 8
Robbins, Harold (novelist)	May 21, 1916	S H Z	Sadat, Anwar (President)	Dec 25, 1918	X D Q
Robbins, Jerome (choreographer)	Oct 11, 1918	R N G	Safire, William (journalist)	Dec 17, 1929	H K 8
Roberts, Rev. Oral (evangelist)	Jan 24, 1918	K E L	Sagan, Francoise (novelist)	Jun 21, 1935	T F 7
Robertson, Cliff (actor)	Sep 9, 1925	M S Y	Sahl, Mort (comedian)	May 11, 1927	X L F
Robeson, Paul (singer)	Apr 9, 1898	C 3 J	Saint, Eva Marie (actress)	Jul 4, 1924	R F V
Robinson, Frank (baseball)	Aug 31, 1935	V V D	St. John, Jill (actress)	Aug 19, 1940	T Q D
Robinson, Brooks (baseball)	May 18, 1937	C C C	Saint-Laurent, Yves (designer)	Aug 1, 1936	M V K
Robson, Dame (actress)	Mar 28, 1902	B U E	Salinger, J. D. (novelist)	Jan 1, 1919	G L X
Robinson, Ray (boxing)	May 3, 1920	M X Q	Salinger, Pierre (journalist)	Jun 14, 1925	R P C
Rochester (actor)	Sep 18, 1905	G B V	Salisbury, Harrison (journalist)	Nov 14, 1908	K G T
Rockefeller, David (banker)	Jun 12, 1915	T 3 L	Salk, Jonas (polio researcher)	Oct 28, 1914	W Z P
Rockefeller 3rd, John D. (banker)	Mar 21, 1906	G S G	Samuelson, Paul A. (economist)	May 15, 1915	O 3 Q
Rockefeller, Laurence S.	May 26, 1910	Q E Q	Sands, Tommy (singer)	Aug 27, 1937	M U E
Rockefeller, Nelson A. (politician)	Jul 8, 1908	T S W	Santana, Manuel (tennis)	May 10, 1938	P Y 5
Rockwell, Martha (skiing)	Apr 26, 1944	H S 5	Saroyan, William (novelist)	Aug 31, 1908	D Q K
Rockwell, Norman (painter)	Feb 3, 1894	S O A	Sarrazin, Michael (actor)	May 22, 1940	W L O
Rodgers, Richard (composer)	Jun 28, 1902	B 3 6	Sartre, Jean-Paul (writer)	Jun 21, 1905	K Z 6
Rodino, Peter (congressman)	Jun 7, 1909	H Q 1	Savalas, Telly (actor)	Jan 21, 1927	E N 3
Rogers, Buddy (actor)	Aug 13, 1904	U V Q	Sayao, Bidu (soprano)	May 11, 1906	M N Z
Rogers, Ginger (dancer)	Jul 16, 1911	S A C	Scali, John (journalist)	Apr 27, 1918	L O E
Rogers, Roy (actor)	Nov 5, 1912	N C T	Schary, Dore (producer)	Aug 31, 1905	M M C
Rogers, Jr., Will (actor)	Oct 20, 1911	W N 8	Schell, Maria (actress)	Jan 15, 1926	B F U
Rogers, William P. (ex-Sec. State)	Jun 23, 1913	N J S	Schell, Maximilian (actor)	Dec 8, 1930	T B 1
Roland, Gilbert (actor)	Dec 11, 1905	W B F	Schiff, Dorothy (publisher)	Mar 11, 1903	E D X
Rome, Harold (composer)	May 27, 1908	X D N	Schippers, Thomas (conductor)	Mar 9, 1930	V H Q
Romero, Cesar (actor)	Feb 15, 1907	Q N H	Schirra, Walter (astronaut)	Mar 12, 1923	U B C
Romney, George W. (Sec. of HUD)	Jul 8, 1907	V Q T	Schisgal, Murray (playwright)	Nov 25, 1926	R M D
Romulo, Carlos P. (diplomat)	Jan 14, 1899	G 3 Z	Schlesinger, Arthur (historian)	Oct 15, 1917	A Q J
Rooney, Mickey (actor)	Sep 23, 1922	L 3 6	Schlesinger, James (politician)	Feb 15, 1929	B N Z
Rosenbloom, Maxie (boxing)	Sep 6, 1904	V R G	Schneider, Romy (actress)	Sep 23, 1938	N U A
Rosenstock, Joseph (conductor)	Jan 27, 1895	H H 4	Schoendienst, Al (baseball)	Feb 2, 1923	E U 6
Roosevelt, Elliot	Sep 23, 1910	V N D	Schollander, Donald (swimming)	Apr 30, 1946	F Y E
Roosevelt, Franklin D.	Jan 30, 1882	A X C	Schulberg, Budd (novelist)	Mar 27, 1914	O F 6
Roosevelt Jr., Franklin D.	Aug 17, 1914	T J J	Schulz, Charles (cartoonist)	Nov 26, 1922	F H 4
Ross, Diana (singer)	Mar 26, 1944	X P 7	Schuman, William (composer)	Aug 4, 1910	R T U
Ross, Katharine (actress)	Jan 29, 1943	P N F	Schwarzkopf, Elisabeth (soprano)	Dec 9, 1915	P M 1
Rossellini, Roberto (director)	May 8, 1906	J K W	Schweikart, Russell (astronaut)	Oct 25, 1935	G U 1
Rostow, Walt Whitman (economist)	Oct 7, 1916	T G 7	Scofield, Paul (actor)	Jan 21, 1922	T G R
Roth, Lillian (singer)	Dec 13, 1910	K K T	Scott, David (astronaut)	Jun 6, 1932	N Q L
Roth, Phillip (novelist)	Mar 19, 1933	X W 8	Scott, George C. (actor)	Oct 18, 1927	W C A
Rothhammer, Keena (swimming)	Feb 26, 1957	E C 8	Scott, Hugh (politician)	Nov 11, 1900	F W 6
Roundtree, Richard (actor)	Sep 7, 1942	J J 2	Scott, Martha (actress)	Sep 22, 1914	J R M
Rowan, Dan (comedian)	Jul 2, 1922	U A O	Scott, Randolph (actor)	Jan 23, 1903	D N J
Rowlands, Gena (actress)	Jun 19, 1936	P F 8	Scranton, William W. (politician)	Jul 19, 1917	E M U
Rozelle, Pete (football)	Mar 1, 1926	A X 7	Seagren, Bob (pole vaulter)	Oct 17, 1946	P 1 K
Rubinstein, Artur (pianist)	Jan 28, 1899	V O F	Sebastian, John (composer)	Mar 17, 1944	O F X
Ruckelshaus, William (politician)	Jul 24, 1932	P H 1	Seberg, Jean (actress)	Nov 13, 1938	S P T
Rudel, Julius (conductor)	Mar 6, 1921	U W 1	Seaborg, Glenn T.	Apr 19, 1912	U 2 R
Rudolph, Wilma Glodean (sprinter)	Jun 23, 1940	H P N	Seeger, Pete (folk singer)	May 3, 1919	O V N
			Segal, Erich (novelist)	Jun 16, 1937	J D 7
			Segal, George (actor)	Feb 13, 1934	J R A
			Segovia, Andres (guitarist)	Feb 18, 1894	K A Q
			Sellers, Peter (actor)	Sep 8, 1925	L R X
			Serkin, Rudolf (pianist)	Mar 28, 1903	W V G

NAME	DATE OF BIRTH	CODE	NAME	DATE OF BIRTH	CODE
Sessions, Roger (composer)	Dec 28, 1896	T J D	Smoke, Marcia (canoeing)	Jul 18, 1941	G N G
Seuss, Dr. (author)	Mar 2, 1904	R Z R	Smothers, Dick (comedian)	Nov 20, 1939	W X 3
Sevareid, Eric (TV commentator)	Nov 26, 1912	L Y G	Smothers, Tom (comedian)	Feb 2, 1937	N K 5
Shankar, Ravi (sitar player)	Apr 7, 1920	J Z X	Snow, Lord (author)	Oct 15, 1905	L A P
Shanker, Albert (labor leader)	Sep 14, 1928	J 2 C	Snyder, Tom (news)	May 12, 1936	X Y 3
Sharif, Omar (actor)	Apr 10, 1932	B P U	Solzhenitsyn, Aleksandr (novelist)	Dec 11, 1918	J S B
Shatner, William (actor)	Mar 22, 1931	H W 6	Sommer, Elke (actress)	Nov 5, 1942	W M U
Shaw, Artie (band leader)	May 23, 1910	N B N	Sondheim, Stephen (composer)	Mar 22, 1930	L V 4
Shaw, Irwin (novelist)	Feb 27, 1913	M E A	Sontag, Susan (author)	Jan 28, 1933	T 3 Q
Shaw, Robert (actor)	Aug 9, 1927	V R 5	Sorenson, Theodore (politician)	May 8, 1928	S K F
Shaw, Robert (conductor)	Apr 30, 1916	U P D	Sothern, Ann (actress)	Jan 22, 1911	D W 1
Shearer, Moira (ballerina)	Jan 17, 1926	D H W	Soyer, Raphael (painter)	Dec 25, 1899	G J G
Shearing, George (pianist)	Aug 13, 1920	W N T	Spassky, Boris (chess)	Jan 30, 1937	K G 2
Sheen, Fulton J. (R.C. Bishop)	May 8, 1895	R Z 6	Spender, Stephen (poet)	Feb 28, 1909	A A 1
Shepard, Jr., Alan B. (astronaut)	Nov 18, 1923	S A X	Spiegel, Sam (producer)	Nov 11, 1901	C X 8
Sheriff, Robert (playwright)	Jun 6, 1896	V 3 5	Spillane, Mickey (writer)	Mar 9, 1918	H V W
Shirer, William L. (journalist)	Feb 23, 1904	J R J	Spitz, Mark (swimming)	Feb 10, 1950	H F A
Sholokhov, Mikhail (novelist)	May 24, 1905	E Z C	Spock, Benjamin (pediatrician)	May 2, 1903	L 3 J
Shore, Dinah (singer)	Mar 1, 1917	C M M	Sproul, Robert G. (educator)	May 22, 1891	T F C
Short, Bobby (singer)	Sep 15, 1924	V X 3	Stack, Robert (actor)	Jan 13, 1919	T X B
Shorter, Frank (runner)	Oct 31, 1947	C N 1	Stafford, Thomas (astronaut)	Sep 17, 1930	F D K
Shriver, Sargent (business executive)	Nov 9, 1915	H K 4	Stalina, Svetlana (Stalin child)	Feb 28, 1926	X W 6
Shula, Don (football)	Jan 4, 1930	C 3 S	Stanley, Kim (actress)	Feb 11, 1925	J D M
Shulman, Max (novelist)	Mar 14, 1919	K 2 4	Stans, Maurice H. (politician)	Mar 22, 1908	C W N
Shultz, George (politician)	Dec 13, 1920	F X J	Stanton, Frank (broadcasting)	Mar 20, 1908	A U L
Shumlin, Herman (producer)	Dec 6, 1898	O R T	Stanwyck, Barbara (actress)	July 16, 1907	F Y 2
Sidney, Sylvia (actress)	Aug 8, 1910	V X Y	Stapleton, Jean (actress)	Jan 19, 1923	O F R
Siepi, Cesare (basso)	Feb 14, 1923	R D K	Stapleton, Maureen (actress)	Jun 21, 1925	A W K
Signoret, Simone (actress)	Mar 25, 1921	Q N M	Starker, Janos (cellist)	July 5, 1926	M J 1
Sills, Beverly (soprano)	May 25, 1929	J 3 Z	Starr, Bart (football)	Jan 9, 1934	U K 7
Silone, Ignazio (novelist)	May 1, 1900	T Y B	Starr, Kay (singer)	Jul 21, 1922	Q U 8
Silvers, Phil (comedian)	May 11, 1912	T V F	Starr, Ringo (singer)	Jul 7, 1940	W A 2
Silvester, Jay (discus thrower)	Feb 27, 1937	P G W	Stassen, Harold (politician)	Apr 13, 1907	D O 7
Sims, Alastair (actor)	Oct 9, 1900	T R 6	Steber, Eleanor (soprano)	Jul 17, 1916	F J Q
Simenon, Georges (writer)	Feb 13, 1903	D F 5	Steegmuller, Francis (biographer)	Jul 3, 1906	T K M
Simmons, Jean (actress)	Jan 31, 1929	K 1 K	Steele, Tommy (singer)	Dec 17, 1936	M T Q
Simon, Neil (playwright)	Jul 4, 1927	H J 2	Steiger, Rod (actor)	Apr 14, 1925	B K H
Simon, Norton (business executive)	Feb 5, 1907	F C 6	Steinberg, William (conductor)	Aug 1, 1899	W C 1
Simon, Simone (actress)	Apr 23, 1914	S E Z	Steinem, Gloria (feminist)	Mar 25, 1934	C A H
Simone, Nina (singer)	Feb 21, 1933	U Y G	Steinkraus, William C. (equestrian)	Oct 12, 1925	W X Y
Simpson, Adele (designer)	Dec 8, 1903	A Y 6	Stenmark, Ingemar (skier)	Mar 18, 1956	E W S
Sinatra, Frank (singer)	Dec 12, 1915	S P 4	Stern, Isaac (violinist)	Jul 21, 1920	W S 4
Sinatra, Nancy (singer)	Jun 8, 1940	Q 3 6	Stevens, Connie (singer)	Aug 8, 1938	N B V
Singer, Isaac (novelist)	Jul 14, 1904	N T T	Stevens, Rise (soprano)	Jun 11, 1913	A Z F
Sirica, John J. (judge)	Mar 19, 1904	L O A	Stevens, Roger L. (producer)	Mar 12, 1910	K O G
Skelton, Red (comedian)	Jul 18, 1913	P F K	Stevens, Stella (actress)	Oct 1, 1936	D 1 E
Skinner, B.F. (psychologist)	Mar 20, 1904	M P B	Stevenson, Adlai (U.S. Senator)	Oct 10, 1930	F 2 8
Skinner, Cornelia Otis (writer)	May 30, 1901	W 1 8	Stewart, James (actor)	May 20, 1908	Q Z F
Slayton, Donald K. (astronaut)	Mar 1, 1924	G V 3	Stewart, Potter (judge)	Jan 23, 1915	R 3 C
Slezak, Walter (actor)	May 3, 1902	P 3 H	Stickney, Dorothy (actress)	Jun 21, 1900	A T U
Smith, Alexis (actress)	Jun 8, 1921	W D V	Stokes, Carl (newscaster)	Jun 21, 1927	S Y O
Smith, Bubba (football)	Feb 28, 1945	R S H	Stokowski, Leopold (conductor)	Apr 18, 1882	K R P
Smith, H. Allen (humorist)	Dec 19, 1907	A M S	Stone, Edward (architect)	Mar 9, 1902	F A T
Smith, Howard K. (TV commentator)	May 12, 1914	O Y L	Stone, Ezra (actor)	Dec 2, 1917	C H Y
Smith, Kate (singer)	May 1, 1909	R G W	Stone, I. F. (journalist)	Dec 24, 1907	F R X
Smith, Maggie, (actress)	Dec 28, 1934	E 2 W	Stone, Irving (novelist)	Jul 14, 1903	P R Q
Smith, Margaret Chase (politician)	Dec 14, 1897	B Y Z	Stout, Rex (writer)	Dec 1, 1886	T Z U
Smith, Red (sports columnist)	Sep 25, 1905	O J 3	Strasberg, Lee (director)	Nov 17, 1901	J A F
Smith, Ronnie Ray (sprinter)	Mar 28, 1949	L X M	Strasberg, Susan (actress)	May 22, 1938	D H J
Smith, Tommie (sprinter)	Jun 5, 1944	B B D	Streisand, Barbra (singer)	Apr 24, 1942	L N X
Smith, Tracy (runner)	Mar 15, 1945	J E X	Stritch, Elaine (actress)	Feb 2, 1928	O 1 J
			Struthers, Sally (actress)	Jul 28, 1948	V D 8

119

NAME	DATE OF BIRTH	CODE		
Styron, William (novelist)	Jun 11, 1925	O	M	8
Sullivan, Barry (actor)	Aug 29, 1912	O	T	R
Sullivan, Frank (humorist)	Sep 22, 1892	B	T	5
Sulzberger, Arthur (publisher)	Feb 5, 1926	X	2	H
Sumac, Yma (singer)	Sep 10, 1927	G	V	4
Susskind, David (TV producer)	Dec. 19, 1920	M	A	P
Sutherland, Joan (soprano)	Nov 7, 1929	O	1	1
Swanson, Gloria (actress)	Mar 27, 1899	K	Q	6
Swayze, John Cameron (commentator)	Apr 4, 1906	V	D	V
Swigert, John (astronaut)	Aug 30, 1931	H	P	2
Symington, Stuart (U.S. Senator)	Jun 26, 1901	C	Z	2
Taft Jr., Robert (U.S. Senator)	Feb 26, 1917	X	J	J
Tallchief, Maria (ballerina)	Jan 24, l925	O	O	2
Talmadge, Herman (U.S. Senator)	Aug 9, 1913	O	3	7
Tandy, Jessica (actress)	Jun 7, 1909	H	Q	1
Tate, Allen (poet)	Nov 19, 1899	R	A	D
Tati, Jacques (actor)	Oct 9, 1908	U	2	Q
Taylor, Elizabeth (actress)	Feb 27, 1932	E	3	K
Taylor, Harold (educator)	Sep 28, 1914	P	X	S
Taylor, James (musician)	Mar 12, 1948	V	F	2
Taylor, Gen. Maxwell (ex-Army Chief)	Aug 26, 1901	S	B	W
Taylor, Rod (actor)	Jan 11, 1930	K	G	Z
Tebaldi, Renata (soprano)	Jan 2, 1922	X	Q	6
Teller, Edward (physicist)	Jan 15, 1908	E	L	M
Tereshkova, Valentina (cosmonaut)	Mar 6, 1937	W	O	4
Terry-Thomas (actor)	Jul 14, 1911	Q	2	A
Thebom, Blanche (soprano)	Sep 19, 1919	P	U	U
Thieu, Nguyen Van (Pres. of Vietnam)	Apr 5, 1923	V	1	2
Theoni, Gustavo (skier)	Feb 28, 1951	X	Z	V
Thomas, Danny (entertainer)	Jan 6, 1914	C	K	R
Thomas, Helen (journalist)	Aug 4, 1920	N	D	K
Thomas, Lowell (explorer)	Apr 6, 1892	R	S	1
Thomas, Marlo (actress)	Nov 21, 1943	M	A	E
Thomas, Michael (conductor)	Dec. 21, 1944	R	E	E
Thorndike, Dame (actress)	Oct 24, 1882	P	K	F
Thurmond, J. Strom (U.S. Senator)	Dec 5, 1902	A	U	l
Tierney, Gene (actress)	Oct 20, 1920	V	Z	V
Tiffin, Pamela (actress)	Oct 13, 1942	W	R	5
Tillstrom, Burr (puppeteer)	Oct 13, 1917	W	O	G
Tiomkin, Dmitri (composer)	May 10, 1899	H	D	J
Tittle, Y.A. (football)	Oct 24, 1926	H	H	E
Tito (Pres. of Yugoslavia)	May 25, 1892	U	L	J
Titov, Gerhman (cosmonaut)	Sep 11, 1935	J	D	P
Toomey, William (decathlon)	Jan 10, 1939	G	R	L
Torme, Mel (singer)	Sep 13, 1925	Q	W	3
Tower, John (U.S. Senator)	Sep 29, 1925	J	K	L
Toynbee, Arnold (historian)	Apr 14, 1889	K	W	2
Trigere, Pauline (designer)	Nov 4, 1912	M	B	S
Trilling, Lionel (author)	Jul 4, 1905	X	K	L
Trudeau, Pierre (Prime Minister)	Oct 18, 1919	V	V	Q
Truffaut, Francois (director)	Feb 6, 1932	G	G	W
Truman, Harry S.	May 8, 1884	B	M	G
Truman, Mrs. Harry	Feb 13, 1885	G	N	Y
Truman, Margaret (author)	Feb 17, 1924	R	H	P
Tryon, Thomas (actor)	Jan 14, 1926	A	E	T
Tuchman, Barbara (author)	Jan 30, 1912	J	C	C
Tucker, Forrest (actor)	Feb 12, 1919	C	Z	7
Tudor, Antony (choreographer)	Apr 4, 1909	N	H	3
Tunney, Gene (boxing)	May 25, 1920	L	R	E
Tunney, John V. (politician)	Jun 26, 1934	D	K	B
Turner, Lana (actress)	Feb 8, 1920	T	W	5
Tushingham, Rita (actress)	Mar 14, 1942	Q	3	P
Twiggy (model)	Sep 19, 1949	B	B	W
Twining, Gen. (Air Force Chief)	Oct 11, 1897	G	Q	2
Tyus, Wyomia (runner)	Aug 29, 1945	P	D	Z
Udall, Morris (congressman)	Jun 15, 1922	C	M	5
Udall, Stewart (ex-Sec. of Inter.)	Jan 31, 1920	L	O	W
Uggams, Leslie (singer)	May 25, 1943	Q	R	X
Ulanova, Galina (ballerina)	Jan 10, 1910	S	J	M
Ullman, Liv (actress)	Dec 16, 1939	B	V	V
Unitas, John (football)	May 7, 1933	C	P	Q
Untermeyer, Louis (anthologist)	Oct 1, 1885	G	T	X
Updike, John (novelist)	Mar 18, 1932	B	U	5
Urey, Harold C. (physicist)	Apr 29, 1893	O	O	S
Uris, Leon (novelist)	Aug 3, 1924	A	H	S
Ustinov, Peter (actor)	Apr 16, 1921	P	G	A
Vaccaro, Brenda (actress)	Nov 18, 1939	U	V	1
Valentino (designer)	May 11, 1932	K	S	S
Vallee, Rudy (singer)	Jul 28, 1901	M	A	1
Van Allen, James (physicist)	Sep 7, 1914	R	B	5
Van Brocklin, Norm (football)	Mar 15, 1926	P	J	N
Van Buren, Abigail (columnist)	Jul 14, 1918	U	H	R
Vanderbilt, Alfred (sportsman)	Sep 22, 1912	P	P	H
Van Dyke, Dick (actor)	Dec 13, 1925	P	A	U
Van Heusen, Jimmy (songwriter)	Jan 26, 1913	C	A	B
Van Peebles, Melvin (playwright)	Sep 21, 1932	E	L	T
Vaughn, Robert (actor)	Nov 22, 1932	V	R	P
Vaughan, Sarah (singer)	Mar 27, 1924	K	T	V
Veeck, Bill (baseball executive)	Feb 9, 1914	O	Q	S
Verdon, Gwen (actress)	Jan 13, 1926	X	D	S
Vereen, Ben (actor)	Oct 10, 1946	H	T	C
Verrett, Shirley (singer)	May 31, 1933	D	L	G
Vickers, Jon (tenor)	Oct 29, 1926	N	N	K
Vidal, Gore (novelist)	Oct 3, 1925	N	O	P
Vidor, King (director)	Feb 8, 1895	U	U	H
Villella, Edward (ballet dancer)	Oct 1, 1936	D	1	E
Voight, Jon (actor)	Dec 29, 1938	S	E	7
Volpe, John	Dec 8, 1908	L	C	K
von Furstenberg, Betsy (actress)	Aug 16, 1935	F	F	W
Vonnegut Jr., Kurt (novelist)	Nov 11, 1922	O	V	O
Von Sydow, Max (actor)	Jul 10, 1929	J	S	E
Vorster, Balthazar (Prime Minister)	Dec 13, 1915	T	Q	5
Wagner, Robert (actor)	Feb 10, 1930	R	J	W
Walcott, Jersey Joe (boxing)	Jan 31, 1914	E	G	J
Wagner, Robert F. (ex-Mayor of N.Y.)	Apr 20, 1910	C	Z	N
Waldheim, Kurt (U.N. Sec.)	Dec 21, 1918	T	3	M
Walker, Clint (actor)	May 30, 1927	T	B	Z
Walker, Mickey (boxing)	Jul 13, 1901	U	O	L
Walker, Nancy (actress)	May 10, 1922	N	D	2
Wallace, DeWitt (publisher)	Nov 12, 1889	P	K	H
Wallace, George C. (ex-Governor)	Aug 25, 1919	N	X	3
Wallace, Irving (novelist)	Mar 19, 1916	A	A	3
Wallace, Mike (commentator)	May 9, 1918	X	1	R
Wallach, Eli (actor)	Dec 7, 1915	N	K	Y
Wallis, Hal (producer)	Sep 14, 1899	U	T	D
Waltari, Mika (novelist)	Sep 19, 1908	X	G	4
Walters, Barbara (newscaster)	Sep 25, 1931	L	N	U
Wambaugh, Joseph (novelist)	Jan 22, 1937	B	2	T

NAME	DATE OF BIRTH	CODE		
Ward, Barbara (economist)	May 23, 1914	B	G	W
Warhol, Andy (artist)	Aug 8, 1931	J	V	E
Waring, Fred (band leader)	Jun 9, 1900	M	G	H
Warren, Robert Penn (novelist)	Apr 24, 1905	V	X	F
Waters, Ethel (actress)	Oct 31, 1900	S	L	U
Watts, Andre (pianist)	Jun 20, 1946	L	T	X
Waugh, Alex (novelist)	Jul 8, 1898	A	F	8
Wayne, David (actor)	Jan 30, 1914	D	F	H
Wayne, John (actor)	May 26, 1907	A	A	J
Weaver, Dennis (actor)	Jun 14, 1925	R	P	C
Weaver, Earl (baseball)	Aug 14, 1930	S	1	J
Weaver, Fritz (actor)	Jan 19, 1926	F	K	Y
Webb, Jack (actor)	Apr 2, 1920	D	U	S
Webster, Alex (football)	Apr 19, 1931	N	W	1
Weicker, Lowell (U.S. Senator)	May 16, 1931	R	V	U
Weinberger, Casper (politician)	Aug 18, 1917	M	O	R
Weissmuller, Johnny (swimmer)	Jun 2, 1904	R	E	K
Welch, Raquel (actress)	Sep 5, 1942	G	G	Z
Weld, Tuesday (actress)	Aug 27, 1943	S	2	S
Welk, Lawrence (band leader)	Mar 11, 1903	E	D	X
Welles, Orson (actor)	May 6, 1915	E	T	G
Welty, Eudora (novelist)	Apr 13, 1909	W	R	D
Werner, Oskar (actor)	Nov 13, 1922	Q	X	P
West, Dame Rebecca (novelist)	Dec 25, 1892	D	A	Z
West, Jerry (basketball)	May 28, 1938	K	O	P
West, Mae (actress)	Aug 17, 1892	M	L	2
Westmoreland, William (Army Chief)	Mar 26, 1914	N	E	5
White, Byron R. (judge)	Jun 8, 1917	K	2	M
White, E.B. (author)	Jul 11, 1899	A	K	E
White, Paul Dudley	Jun 6, 1886	B	P	G
White, Theodore (historian)	May 6, 1915	E	T	G
White, Willy (long jumper)	Jan 1, 1936	F	D	3
Whitmore, James (actor)	Oct 1, 1921	W	G	D
Whitney, Cornelius (sportsman)	Feb 20, 1899	V	J	4
Whitney, John Hay (publisher)	Aug 17, 1904	A	Z	U
Whitworth, Kathy (golf)	Sep 27, 1939	O	Z	G
Wicker, Tom (columnist)	Jun 18, 1926	S	U	J
Widmark, Richard (actor)	Dec 26, 1914	M	3	H
Wiesel, Elie (author)	Sep 30, 1928	B	P	T
Wilbur, Doreen (archery)	Jan 8, 1930	G	D	W
Wilbur, Richard (poet)	Mar 1, 1921	P	R	V
Wilde, Cornel (actor)	Oct 13, 1918	T	P	J
Wilder, Billy (producer)	Jun 22, 1906	H	2	A
Wilder, Thornton (author)	Apr 17, 1897	O	G	P
Wilding, Michael (actor)	Jul 23, 1912	X	K	N
Wilkins, Roy (civil rights leader)	Aug 30, 1901	W	F	1
Williams, Andy (singer)	Dec 3, 1930	O	Z	V
Williams, Dick (baseball)	May 7, 1929	O	K	G

NAME	DATE OF BIRTH	CODE		
Williams, Edward Bennett (law)	May 31, 1920	R	X	L
Williams, Emlyn (actor)	Nov 26, 1905	G	P	Y
Williams, Esther (actress)	Aug 8, 1923	H	L	U
Williams, Gluyas (cartoonist)	Jul 23, 1888	V	J	1
Williams, Ted (baseball)	Aug 30, 1918	V	2	6
Williams, Tennessee (playwright)	Mar 26, 1914	N	E	5
Wilson, Flip (comedian)	Dec 8, 1933	L	F	8
Wilson, Harold (Prime Minister)	Mar 11, 1916	Q	V	U
Wilson, Meredith (composer)	May 18, 1902	G	P	X
Wilson, Nancy (singer)	Feb 20, 1937	H	3	P
Wilson, Sloan (novelist)	May 8, 1920	R	3	V
Windsor, Duchess of	Jun 19, 1896	L	N	K
Winters, Jonathan (actor)	Nov 11, 1925	F	Z	V
Winters, Shelley (actress)	Aug 18, 1922	V	U	3
Wohlhuter, Richard C. (runner)	Dec 23, 1945	Q	H	J
Wolfe, Tom (journalist)	Mar 2, 1931	L	B	L
Wonder, Stevie (singer)	May 13, 1950	H	O	2
Wood, Natalie (actress)	Jul 20, 1938	R	L	B
Woodcock, Leonard (union leader)	Feb 5, 1911	S	H	G
Woodward, Bob (journalist)	Mar 26, 1943	B	N	4
Woodward, Joanne (actress)	Feb 27, 1930	L	1	F
Worley, Jo Anne (actress)	Sep 6, 1937	W	B	P
Wottle, David James (runner)	Aug 7, 1950	B	Q	O
Wouk, Herman (novelist)	May 27, 1915	C	M	3
Wright, Teresa (actress)	Oct 27, 1918	K	A	X
Wyatt, Jane (actress)	Aug 12, 1912	U	B	8
Wyeth, Andrew (painter)	Jul 12, 1917	V	E	N
Wyler, William (director)	Jul 1, 1902	E	C	A
Wyman, Jane (actress)	Jan 4, 1914	A	H	P
Wynn, Keenan (actor)	Jul 27, 1916	Q	T	1
Wynter, Dana (actress)	Jun 8, 1930	U	P	H
York, Michael (actor)	Mar 7, 1942	J	V	H
York, Susannah (actress)	Jan 9, 1942	V	U	R
Yorty, Samuel W. (ex-Mayor: L.A.)	Oct 1, 1909	J	U	K
Young, Alan (actor)	Nov 19, 1919	G	Z	P
Young, Gig (actor)	Nov 4, 1917	V	H	4
Young, John Watts (astronaut)	Sep 24, 1930	N	L	R
Young, Loretta (actress)	Jan 6, 1913	F	J	P
Young, Robert (actor)	Feb 22, 1907	X	U	P
Young, Sheila (skater)	Oct 14, 1950	A	3	Q
Zanuck, Darryl F. (producer)	Sep 5, 1902	B	N	A
Zeffirelli, Franco (director)	Feb 12, 1923	P	B	H
Ziegler, Ronald (politician)	May 12, 1939	O	2	A
Zimbalist, Efrem (violinist)	Apr 9, 1889	E	R	W
Zimbalist Jr., Efrem (actor)	Nov 30, 1923	G	N	B

1895   1895

Day	...JANUARY.. P--E--I	..FEBRUARY.. P--E--I	...MARCH... P--E--I	...APRIL... P--E--I	....MAY.... P--E--I	....JUNE.... P--E--I
1)	E..K..C	N..N..A	S..N..4	C..Q..2	K..S..Y	S..V..W
2)	F..L..D	O..O..B	T..O..5	D..R..3	L..T..Z	T..W..X
3)	G..M..E	P..P..C	U..P..6	E..S..4	M..U..1	U..X..Y
4)	H..N..F	Q..Q..D	V..Q..7	F..T..5	N..V..2	V..Y..Z
5)	J..O..G	R..R..E	W..R..8	G..U..6	O..W..3	W..Z..1
6)	K..P..H	S..S..F	X..S..A	H..V..7	P..X..4	X..1..2
7)	L..Q..J	T..T..G	A..T..B	J..W..8	Q..Y..5	A..2..3
8)	M..R..K	U..U..H	B..U..C	K..X..A	R..Z..6	B..3..4
9)	N..S..L	V..V..J	C..V..D	L..Y..B	S..1..7	C..A..5
10)	O..T..M	W..W..K	D..W..E	M..Z..C	T..2..8	D..B..6
11)	P..U..N	X..X..L	E..X..F	N..1..D	U..3..A	E..C..7
12)	Q..V..O	A..Y..M	F..Y..G	O..2..E	V..A..B	F..D..8
13)	R..W..P	B..Z..N	G..Z..H	P..3..F	W..B..C	G..E..A
14)	S..X..Q	C..1..O	H..1..J	Q..A..G	X..C..D	H..F..B
15)	T..Y..R	D..2..P	J..2..K	R..B..H	A..D..E	J..G..C
16)	U..Z..S	E..3..Q	K..3..L	S..C..J	B..E..F	K..H..D
17)	V..1..T	F..A..R	L..A..M	T..D..K	C..F..G	L..J..E
18)	W..2..U	G..B..S	M..B..N	U..E..L	D..G..H	M..K..F
19)	X..3..V	H..C..T	N..C..O	V..F..M	E..H..J	N..L..G
20)	A..A..W	J..D..U	O..D..P	W..G..N	F..J..K	O..M..H
21)	B..B..X	K..E..V	P..E..Q	X..H..O	G..K..L	P..N..J
22)	C..C..Y	L..F..W	Q..F..R	A..J..P	H..L..M	Q..O..K
23)	D..D..Z	M..G..X	R..G..S	B..K..Q	J..M..N	R..P..L
24)	E..E..1	N..H..Y	S..H..T	C..L..R	K..N..O	S..Q..M
25)	F..F..2	O..J..Z	T..J..U	D..M..S	L..O..P	T..R..N
26)	G..G..3	P..K..1	U..K..V	E..N..T	M..P..Q	U..S..O
27)	H..H..4	Q..L..2	V..L..W	F..O..U	N..Q..R	V..T..P
28)	J..J..5	R..M..3	W..M..X	G..P..V	O..R..S	W..U..Q
29)	K..K..6		X..N..Y	H..Q..W	P..S..T	X..V..R
30)	L..L..7		A..O..Z	J..R..X	Q..T..U	A..W..S
31)	M..M..8		B..P..1		R..U..V	

1895   1895

Day	...JULY.... P--E--I	...AUGUST... P--E--I	..SEPTEMBER. P--E--I	..OCTOBER... P--E--I	..NOVEMBER.. P--E--I	..DECEMBER.. P--E--I
1)	B..X..T	K..1..R	S..A..P	B..C..M	K..F..K	R..H..G
2)	C..Y..U	L..2..S	T..B..Q	C..D..N	L..G..L	S..J..H
3)	D..Z..V	M..3..T	U..C..R	D..E..O	M..H..M	T..K..J
4)	E..1..W	N..A..U	V..D..S	E..F..P	N..J..N	U..L..K
5)	F..2..X	O..B..V	W..E..T	F..G..Q	O..K..O	V..M..L
6)	G..3..Y	P..C..W	X..F..U	G..H..R	P..L..P	W..N..M
7)	H..A..Z	Q..D..X	A..G..V	H..J..S	Q..M..Q	X..O..N
8)	J..B..1	R..E..Y	B..H..W	J..K..T	R..N..R	A..P..O
9)	K..C..2	S..F..Z	C..J..X	K..L..U	S..O..S	B..Q..P
10)	L..D..3	T..G..1	D..K..Y	L..M..V	T..P..T	C..R..Q
11)	M..E..4	U..H..2	E..L..Z	M..N..W	U..Q..U	D..S..R
12)	N..F..5	V..J..3	F..M..1	N..O..X	V..R..V	E..T..S
13)	O..G..6	W..K..4	G..N..2	O..P..Y	W..S..W	F..U..T
14)	P..H..7	X..L..5	H..O..3	P..Q..Z	X..T..X	G..V..U
15)	Q..J..8	A..M..6	J..P..4	Q..R..1	A..U..Y	H..W..V
16)	R..K..A	B..N..7	K..Q..5	R..S..2	B..V..Z	J..X..W
17)	S..L..B	C..O..8	L..R..6	S..T..3	C..W..1	K..Y..X
18)	T..M..C	D..P..A	M..S..7	T..U..4	D..X..2	L..Z..Y
19)	U..N..D	E..Q..B	N..T..8	U..V..5	E..Y..3	M..1..Z
20)	V..O..E	F..R..C	O..U..A	V..W..6	F..Z..4	N..2..1
21)	W..P..F	G..S..D	P..V..B	W..X..7	G..1..5	O..3..2
22)	X..Q..G	H..T..E	Q..W..C	X..Y..8	H..2..6	P..A..3
23)	A..R..H	J..U..F	R..X..D	A..Z..A	J..3..7	Q..B..4
24)	B..S..J	K..V..G	S..Y..E	B..1..B	K..A..8	R..C..5
25)	C..T..K	L..W..H	T..Z..F	C..2..C	L..B..A	S..D..6
26)	D..U..L	M..X..J	U..1..G	D..3..D	M..C..B	T..E..7
27)	E..V..M	N..Y..K	V..2..H	E..A..E	N..D..C	U..F..8
28)	F..W..N	O..Z..L	W..3..J	F..B..F	O..E..D	V..G..A
29)	G..X..O	P..1..M	X..A..K	G..C..G	P..F..E	W..H..B
30)	H..Y..P	Q..2..N	A..B..L	H..D..H	Q..G..F	X..J..C
31)	J..Z..Q	R..3..O		J..E..J		A..K..D

CODES: P-PHYSICAL BIORHYTHM CURVE, E-EMOTIONAL BIORHYTHM CURVE, I-INTELLECTUAL BIORHYTHM CURVE

...JANUARY.. ..FEBRUARY.. ...MARCH... ...APRIL... ....MAY.... ...JUNE....

	JANUARY P--E--I	FEBRUARY P--E--I	MARCH P--E--I	APRIL P--E--I	MAY P--E--I	JUNE P--E--I
1)	B..L..E	K..O..C	Q..P..7	A..S..5	H..U..2	Q..X..Z
2)	C..M..F	L..P..D	R..Q..8	B..T..6	J..V..3	R..Y..1
3)	D..N..G	M..Q..E	S..R..A	C..U..7	K..W..4	S..Z..2
4)	E..O..H	N..R..F	T..S..B	D..V..8	L..X..5	T..1..3
5)	F..P..J	O..S..G	U..T..C	E..W..A	M..Y..6	U..2..4
6)	G..Q..K	P..T..H	V..U..D	F..X..B	N..Z..7	V..3..5
7)	H..R..L	Q..U..J	W..V..E	G..Y..C	O..1..8	W..A..6
8)	J..S..M	R..V..K	X..W..F	H..Z..D	P..2..A	X..B..7
9)	K..T..N	S..W..L	A..X..G	J..1..E	Q..3..B	A..C..8
10)	L..U..O	T..X..M	B..Y..H	K..2..F	R..A..C	B..D..A
11)	M..V..P	U..Y..N	C..Z..J	L..3..G	S..B..D	C..E..B
12)	N..W..Q	V..Z..O	D..1..K	M..A..H	T..C..E	D..F..C
13)	O..X..R	W..1..P	E..2..L	N..B..J	U..D..F	E..G..D
14)	P..Y..S	X..2..Q	F..3..M	O..C..K	V..E..G	F..H..E
15)	Q..Z..T	A..3..R	G..A..N	P..D..L	W..F..H	G..J..F
16)	R..1..U	B..A..S	H..B..O	Q..E..M	X..G..J	H..K..G
17)	S..2..V	C..B..T	J..C..P	R..F..N	A..H..K	J..L..H
18)	T..3..W	D..C..U	K..D..Q	S..G..O	B..J..L	K..M..J
19)	U..A..X	E..D..V	L..E..R	T..H..P	C..K..M	L..N..K
20)	V..B..Y	F..E..W	M..F..S	U..J..Q	D..L..N	M..O..L
21)	W..C..Z	G..F..X	N..G..T	V..K..R	E..M..O	N..P..M
22)	X..D..1	H..G..Y	O..H..U	W..L..S	F..N..P	O..Q..N
23)	A..E..2	J..H..Z	P..J..V	X..M..T	G..O..Q	P..R..O
24)	B..F..3	K..J..1	Q..K..W	A..N..U	H..P..R	Q..S..P
25)	C..G..4	L..K..2	R..L..X	B..O..V	J..Q..S	R..T..Q
26)	D..H..5	M..L..3	S..M..Y	C..P..W	K..R..T	S..U..R
27)	E..J..6	N..M..4	T..N..Z	D..Q..X	L..S..U	T..V..S
28)	F..K..7	O..N..5	U..O..1	E..R..Y	M..T..V	U..W..T
29)	G..L..8	P..O..6	V..P..2	F..S..Z	N..U..W	V..X..U
30)	H..M..A		W..Q..3	G..T..1	O..V..X	W..Y..V
31)	J..N..B		X..R..4		P..W..Y	

....JULY.... ...AUGUST... ..SEPTEMBER. ..OCTOBER... ..NOVEMBER.. ..DECEMBER..

	JULY P--E--I	AUGUST P--E--I	SEPTEMBER P--E--I	OCTOBER P--E--I	NOVEMBER P--E--I	DECEMBER P--E--I
1)	X..Z..W	H..3..U	Q..C..S	X..E..P	H..H..N	P..K..K
2)	A..1..X	J..A..V	R..D..T	A..F..Q	J..J..O	Q..L..L
3)	B..2..Y	K..B..W	S..E..U	B..G..R	K..K..P	R..M..M
4)	C..3..Z	L..C..X	T..F..V	C..H..S	L..L..Q	S..N..N
5)	D..A..1	M..D..Y	U..G..W	D..J..T	M..M..R	T..O..O
6)	E..B..2	N..E..Z	V..H..X	E..K..U	N..N..S	U..P..P
7)	F..C..3	O..F..1	W..J..Y	F..L..V	O..O..T	V..Q..Q
8)	G..D..4	P..G..2	X..K..Z	G..M..W	P..P..U	W..R..R
9)	H..E..5	Q..H..3	A..L..1	H..N..X	Q..Q..V	X..S..S
10)	J..F..6	R..J..4	B..M..2	J..O..Y	R..R..W	A..T..T
11)	K..G..7	S..K..5	C..N..3	K..P..Z	S..S..X	B..U..U
12)	L..H..8	T..L..6	D..O..4	L..Q..1	T..T..Y	C..V..V
13)	M..J..A	U..M..7	E..P..5	M..R..2	U..U..Z	D..W..W
14)	N..K..B	V..N..8	F..Q..6	N..S..3	V..V..1	E..X..X
15)	O..L..C	W..O..A	G..R..7	O..T..4	W..W..2	F..Y..Y
16)	P..M..D	X..P..B	H..S..8	P..U..5	X..X..3	G..Z..Z
17)	Q..N..E	A..Q..C	J..T..A	Q..V..6	A..Y..4	H..1..1
18)	R..O..F	B..R..D	K..U..B	R..W..7	B..Z..5	J..2..2
19)	S..P..G	C..S..E	L..V..C	S..X..8	C..1..6	K..3..3
20)	T..Q..H	D..T..F	M..W..D	T..Y..A	D..2..7	L..A..4
21)	U..R..J	E..U..G	N..X..E	U..Z..B	E..3..8	M..B..5
22)	V..S..K	F..V..H	O..Y..F	V..1..C	F..A..A	N..C..6
23)	W..T..L	G..W..J	P..Z..G	W..2..D	G..B..B	O..D..7
24)	X..U..M	H..X..K	Q..1..H	X..3..E	H..C..C	P..E..8
25)	A..V..N	J..Y..L	R..2..J	A..A..F	J..D..D	Q..F..A
26)	B..W..O	K..Z..M	S..3..K	B..B..G	K..E..E	R..G..B
27)	C..X..P	L..1..N	T..A..L	C..C..H	L..F..F	S..H..C
28)	D..Y..Q	M..2..O	U..B..M	D..D..J	M..G..G	T..J..D
29)	E..Z..R	N..3..P	V..C..N	E..E..K	N..H..H	U..K..E
30)	F..1..S	O..A..Q	W..D..O	F..F..L	O..J..J	V..L..F
31)	G..2..T	P..B..R		G..G..M		W..M..G

CODES: P-PHYSICAL BIORHYTHM CURVE,E-EMOTIONAL BIORHYTHM CURVE,I-INTELLECTUAL BIORHYTHM CURVE

```
    ...JANUARY..      .FEBRUARY..      ...MARCH...       ...APRIL...       ....MAY....       ....JUNE....

        P--E--I           P--E--I           P--E--I           P--E--I           P--E--I           P--E--I

 1)  X..N..H       1)  H..Q..F       1)  N..Q..A       1)  V..T..7       1)  E..V..4       1)  N..Y..2
 2)  A..O..J       2)  J..R..G       2)  O..R..B       2)  W..U..8       2)  F..W..5       2)  O..Z..3
 3)  B..P..K       3)  K..S..H       3)  P..S..C       3)  X..V..A       3)  G..X..6       3)  P..1..4
 4)  C..Q..L       4)  L..T..J       4)  Q..T..D       4)  A..W..B       4)  H..Y..7       4)  Q..2..5
 5)  D..R..M       5)  M..U..K       5)  R..U..E       5)  B..X..C       5)  J..Z..8       5)  R..3..6
 6)  E..S..N       6)  N..V..L       6)  S..V..F       6)  C..Y..D       6)  K..1..A       6)  S..A..7
 7)  F..T..O       7)  O..W..M       7)  T..W..G       7)  D..Z..E       7)  L..2..B       7)  T..B..8
 8)  G..U..P       8)  P..X..N       8)  U..X..H       8)  E..1..F       8)  M..3..C       8)  U..C..A
 9)  H..V..Q       9)  Q..Y..O       9)  V..Y..J       9)  F..2..G       9)  N..A..D       9)  V..D..B
10)  J..W..R      10)  R..Z..P      10)  W..Z..K      10)  G..3..H      10)  O..B..E      10)  W..E..C
11)  K..X..S      11)  S..1..Q      11)  X..1..L      11)  H..A..J      11)  P..C..F      11)  X..F..D
12)  L..Y..T      12)  T..2..R      12)  A..2..M      12)  J..B..K      12)  Q..D..G      12)  A..G..E
13)  M..Z..U      13)  U..3..S      13)  B..3..N      13)  K..C..L      13)  R..E..H      13)  B..H..F
14)  N..1..V      14)  V..A..T      14)  C..A..O      14)  L..D..M      14)  S..F..J      14)  C..J..G
15)  O..2..W      15)  W..B..U      15)  D..B..P      15)  M..E..N      15)  T..G..K      15)  D..K..H
16)  P..3..X      16)  X..C..V      16)  E..C..Q      16)  N..F..O      16)  U..H..L      16)  E..L..J
17)  Q..A..Y      17)  A..D..W      17)  F..D..R      17)  O..G..P      17)  V..J..M      17)  F..M..K
18)  R..B..Z      18)  B..E..X      18)  G..E..S      18)  P..H..Q      18)  W..K..N      18)  G..N..L
19)  S..C..1      19)  C..F..Y      19)  H..F..T      19)  Q..J..R      19)  X..L..O      19)  H..O..M
20)  T..D..2      20)  D..G..Z      20)  J..G..U      20)  R..K..S      20)  A..M..P      20)  J..P..N
21)  U..E..3      21)  E..H..1      21)  K..H..V      21)  S..L..T      21)  B..N..Q      21)  K..Q..O
22)  V..F..4      22)  F..J..2      22)  L..J..W      22)  T..M..U      22)  C..O..R      22)  L..R..P
23)  W..G..5      23)  G..K..3      23)  M..K..X      23)  U..N..V      23)  D..P..S      23)  M..S..Q
24)  X..H..6      24)  H..L..4      24)  N..L..Y      24)  V..O..W      24)  E..Q..T      24)  N..T..R
25)  A..J..7      25)  J..M..5      25)  O..M..Z      25)  W..P..X      25)  F..R..U      25)  O..U..S
26)  B..K..8      26)  K..N..6      26)  P..N..1      26)  X..Q..Y      26)  G..S..V      26)  P..V..T
27)  C..L..A      27)  L..O..7      27)  Q..O..2      27)  A..R..Z      27)  H..T..W      27)  Q..W..U
28)  D..M..B      28)  M..P..8      28)  R..P..3      28)  B..S..1      28)  J..U..X      28)  R..X..V
29)  E..N..C                        29)  S..Q..4      29)  C..T..2      29)  K..V..Y      29)  S..Y..W
30)  F..O..D                        30)  T..R..5      30)  D..U..3      30)  L..W..Z      30)  T..Z..X
31)  G..P..E                        31)  U..S..6                        31)  M..X..1
```

```
    ....JULY....      ...AUGUST...      .SEPTEMBER.       ..OCTOBER...      .NOVEMBER..       .DECEMBER..

        P--E--I           P--E--I           P--E--I           P--E--I           P--E--I           P--E--I

 1)  U..1..Y       1)  E..A..W       1)  N..D..U       1)  U..F..R       1)  E..J..P       1)  M..L..M
 2)  V..2..Z       2)  F..B..X       2)  O..E..V       2)  V..G..S       2)  F..K..Q       2)  N..M..N
 3)  W..3..1       3)  G..C..Y       3)  P..F..W       3)  W..H..T       3)  G..L..R       3)  O..N..O
 4)  X..A..2       4)  H..D..Z       4)  Q..G..X       4)  X..J..U       4)  H..M..S       4)  P..O..P
 5)  A..B..3       5)  J..E..1       5)  R..H..Y       5)  A..K..V       5)  J..N..T       5)  Q..P..Q
 6)  B..C..4       6)  K..F..2       6)  S..J..Z       6)  B..L..W       6)  K..O..U       6)  R..Q..R
 7)  C..D..5       7)  L..G..3       7)  T..K..1       7)  C..M..X       7)  L..P..V       7)  S..R..S
 8)  D..E..6       8)  M..H..4       8)  U..L..2       8)  D..N..Y       8)  M..Q..W       8)  T..S..T
 9)  E..F..7       9)  N..J..5       9)  V..M..3       9)  E..O..Z       9)  N..R..X       9)  U..T..U
10)  F..G..8      10)  O..K..6      10)  W..N..4      10)  F..P..1      10)  O..S..Y      10)  V..U..V
11)  G..H..A      11)  P..L..7      11)  X..O..5      11)  G..Q..2      11)  P..T..Z      11)  W..V..W
12)  H..J..B      12)  Q..M..8      12)  A..P..6      12)  H..R..3      12)  Q..U..1      12)  X..W..X
13)  J..K..C      13)  R..N..A      13)  B..Q..7      13)  J..S..4      13)  R..V..2      13)  A..X..Y
14)  K..L..D      14)  S..O..B      14)  C..R..8      14)  K..T..5      14)  S..W..3      14)  B..Y..Z
15)  L..M..E      15)  T..P..C      15)  D..S..A      15)  L..U..6      15)  T..X..4      15)  C..Z..1
16)  M..N..F      16)  U..Q..D      16)  E..T..B      16)  M..V..7      16)  U..Y..5      16)  D..1..2
17)  N..O..G      17)  V..R..E      17)  F..U..C      17)  N..W..8      17)  V..Z..6      17)  E..2..3
18)  O..P..H      18)  W..S..F      18)  G..V..D      18)  O..X..A      18)  W..1..7      18)  F..3..4
19)  P..Q..J      19)  X..T..G      19)  H..W..E      19)  P..Y..B      19)  X..2..8      19)  G..A..5
20)  Q..R..K      20)  A..U..H      20)  J..X..F      20)  Q..Z..C      20)  A..3..A      20)  H..B..6
21)  R..S..L      21)  B..V..J      21)  K..Y..G      21)  R..1..D      21)  B..A..B      21)  J..C..7
22)  S..T..M      22)  C..W..K      22)  L..Z..H      22)  S..2..E      22)  C..B..C      22)  K..D..8
23)  T..U..N      23)  D..X..L      23)  M..1..J      23)  T..3..F      23)  D..C..D      23)  L..E..A
24)  U..V..O      24)  E..Y..M      24)  N..2..K      24)  U..A..G      24)  E..D..E      24)  M..F..B
25)  V..W..P      25)  F..Z..N      25)  O..3..L      25)  V..B..H      25)  F..E..F      25)  N..G..C
26)  W..X..Q      26)  G..1..O      26)  P..A..M      26)  W..C..J      26)  G..F..G      26)  O..H..D
27)  X..Y..R      27)  H..2..P      27)  Q..B..N      27)  X..D..K      27)  H..G..H      27)  P..J..E
28)  A..Z..S      28)  J..3..Q      28)  R..C..O      28)  A..E..L      28)  J..H..J      28)  Q..K..F
29)  B..1..T      29)  K..A..R      29)  S..D..P      29)  B..F..M      29)  K..J..K      29)  R..L..G
30)  C..2..U      30)  L..B..S      30)  T..E..Q      30)  C..G..N      30)  L..K..L      30)  S..M..H
31)  D..3..V      31)  M..C..T                        31)  D..H..O                        31)  T..N..J
```

CODES: P-PHYSICAL BIORHYTHM CURVE, E-EMOTIONAL BIORHYTHM CURVE, I-INTELLECTUAL BIORHYTHM CURVE

	...JANUARY.. P--E--I		..FEBRUARY.. P--E--I		...MARCH... P--E--I		...APRIL... P--E--I		....MAY.... P--E--I		....JUNE.... P--E--I
1)	U..O..K	1)	E..R..H	1)	K..R..C	1)	S..U..A	1)	B..W..6	1)	K..Z..4
2)	V..P..L	2)	F..S..J	2)	L..S..D	2)	T..V..B	2)	C..X..7	2)	L..1..5
3)	W..Q..M	3)	G..T..K	3)	M..T..E	3)	U..W..C	3)	D..Y..8	3)	M..2..6
4)	X..R..N	4)	H..U..L	4)	N..U..F	4)	V..X..D	4)	E..Z..A	4)	N..3..7
5)	A..S..O	5)	J..V..M	5)	O..V..G	5)	W..Y..E	5)	F..1..B	5)	O..A..8
6)	B..T..P	6)	K..W..N	6)	P..W..H	6)	X..Z..F	6)	G..2..C	6)	P..B..A
7)	C..U..Q	7)	L..X..O	7)	Q..X..J	7)	A..1..G	7)	H..3..D	7)	Q..C..B
8)	D..V..R	8)	M..Y..P	8)	R..Y..K	8)	B..2..H	8)	J..A..E	8)	R..D..C
9)	E..W..S	9)	N..Z..Q	9)	S..Z..L	9)	C..3..J	9)	K..B..F	9)	S..E..D
10)	F..X..T	10)	O..1..R	10)	T..1..M	10)	D..A..K	10)	L..C..G	10)	T..F..E
11)	G..Y..U	11)	P..2..S	11)	U..2..N	11)	E..B..L	11)	M..D..H	11)	U..G..F
12)	H..Z..V	12)	Q..3..T	12)	V..3..O	12)	F..C..M	12)	N..E..J	12)	V..H..G
13)	J..1..W	13)	R..A..U	13)	W..A..P	13)	G..D..N	13)	O..F..K	13)	W..J..H
14)	K..2..X	14)	S..B..V	14)	X..B..Q	14)	H..E..O	14)	P..G..L	14)	X..K..J
15)	L..3..Y	15)	T..C..W	15)	A..C..R	15)	J..F..P	15)	Q..H..M	15)	A..L..K
16)	M..A..Z	16)	U..D..X	16)	B..D..S	16)	K..G..Q	16)	R..J..N	16)	B..M..L
17)	N..B..1	17)	V..E..Y	17)	C..E..T	17)	L..H..R	17)	S..K..O	17)	C..N..M
18)	O..C..2	18)	W..F..Z	18)	D..F..U	18)	M..J..S	18)	T..L..P	18)	D..O..N
19)	P..D..3	19)	X..G..1	19)	E..G..V	19)	N..K..T	19)	U..M..Q	19)	E..P..O
20)	Q..E..4	20)	A..H..2	20)	F..H..W	20)	O..L..U	20)	V..N..R	20)	F..Q..P
21)	R..F..5	21)	B..J..3	21)	G..J..X	21)	P..M..V	21)	W..O..S	21)	G..R..Q
22)	S..G..6	22)	C..K..4	22)	H..K..Y	22)	Q..N..W	22)	X..P..T	22)	H..S..R
23)	T..H..7	23)	D..L..5	23)	J..L..Z	23)	R..O..X	23)	A..Q..U	23)	J..T..S
24)	U..J..8	24)	E..M..6	24)	K..M..1	24)	S..P..Y	24)	B..R..V	24)	K..U..T
25)	V..K..A	25)	F..N..7	25)	L..N..2	25)	T..Q..Z	25)	C..S..W	25)	L..V..U
26)	W..L..B	26)	G..O..8	26)	M..O..3	26)	U..R..1	26)	D..T..X	26)	M..W..V
27)	X..M..C	27)	H..P..A	27)	N..P..4	27)	V..S..2	27)	E..U..Y	27)	N..X..W
28)	A..N..D	28)	J..Q..B	28)	O..Q..5	28)	W..T..3	28)	F..V..Z	28)	O..Y..X
29)	B..O..E			29)	P..R..6	29)	X..U..4	29)	G..W..1	29)	P..Z..Y
30)	C..P..F			30)	Q..S..7	30)	A..V..5	30)	H..X..2	30)	Q..1..Z
31)	D..Q..G			31)	R..T..8			31)	J..Y..3		

	....JULY.... P--E--I		...AUGUST... P--E--I		..SEPTEMBER. P--E--I		..OCTOBER... P--E--I		..NOVEMBER.. P--E--I		..DECEMBER.. P--E--I
1)	R..2..1	1)	B..B..Y	1)	K..E..W	1)	R..G..T	1)	B..K..R	1)	J..M..O
2)	S..3..2	2)	C..C..Z	2)	L..F..X	2)	S..H..U	2)	C..L..S	2)	K..N..P
3)	T..A..3	3)	D..D..1	3)	M..G..Y	3)	T..J..V	3)	D..M..T	3)	L..O..Q
4)	U..B..4	4)	E..E..2	4)	N..H..Z	4)	U..K..W	4)	E..N..U	4)	M..P..R
5)	V..C..5	5)	F..F..3	5)	O..J..1	5)	V..L..X	5)	F..O..V	5)	N..Q..S
6)	W..D..6	6)	G..G..4	6)	P..K..2	6)	W..M..Y	6)	G..P..W	6)	O..R..T
7)	X..E..7	7)	H..H..5	7)	Q..L..3	7)	X..N..Z	7)	H..Q..X	7)	P..S..U
8)	A..F..8	8)	J..J..6	8)	R..M..4	8)	A..O..1	8)	J..R..Y	8)	Q..T..V
9)	B..G..A	9)	K..K..7	9)	S..N..5	9)	B..P..2	9)	K..S..Z	9)	R..U..W
10)	C..H..B	10)	L..L..8	10)	T..O..6	10)	C..Q..3	10)	L..T..1	10)	S..V..X
11)	D..J..C	11)	M..M..A	11)	U..P..7	11)	D..R..4	11)	M..U..2	11)	T..W..Y
12)	E..K..D	12)	N..N..B	12)	V..Q..8	12)	E..S..5	12)	N..V..3	12)	U..X..Z
13)	F..L..E	13)	O..O..C	13)	W..R..A	13)	F..T..6	13)	O..W..4	13)	V..Y..1
14)	G..M..F	14)	P..P..D	14)	X..S..B	14)	G..U..7	14)	P..X..5	14)	W..Z..2
15)	H..N..G	15)	Q..Q..E	15)	A..T..C	15)	H..V..8	15)	Q..Y..6	15)	X..1..3
16)	J..O..H	16)	R..R..F	16)	B..U..D	16)	J..W..A	16)	R..Z..7	16)	A..2..4
17)	K..P..J	17)	S..S..G	17)	C..V..E	17)	K..X..B	17)	S..1..8	17)	B..3..5
18)	L..Q..K	18)	T..T..H	18)	D..W..F	18)	L..Y..C	18)	T..2..A	18)	C..A..6
19)	M..R..L	19)	U..U..J	19)	E..X..G	19)	M..Z..D	19)	U..3..B	19)	D..B..7
20)	N..S..M	20)	V..V..K	20)	F..Y..H	20)	N..1..E	20)	V..A..C	20)	E..C..8
21)	O..T..N	21)	W..W..L	21)	G..Z..J	21)	O..2..F	21)	W..B..D	21)	F..D..A
22)	P..U..O	22)	X..X..M	22)	H..1..K	22)	P..3..G	22)	X..C..E	22)	G..E..B
23)	Q..V..P	23)	A..Y..N	23)	J..2..L	23)	Q..A..H	23)	A..D..F	23)	H..F..C
24)	R..W..Q	24)	B..Z..O	24)	K..3..M	24)	R..B..J	24)	B..E..G	24)	J..G..D
25)	S..X..R	25)	C..1..P	25)	L..A..N	25)	S..C..K	25)	C..F..H	25)	K..H..E
26)	T..Y..S	26)	D..2..Q	26)	M..B..O	26)	T..D..L	26)	D..G..J	26)	L..J..F
27)	U..Z..T	27)	E..3..R	27)	N..C..P	27)	U..E..M	27)	E..H..K	27)	M..K..G
28)	V..1..U	28)	F..A..S	28)	O..D..Q	28)	V..F..N	28)	F..J..L	28)	N..L..H
29)	W..2..V	29)	G..B..T	29)	P..E..R	29)	W..G..O	29)	G..K..M	29)	O..M..J
30)	X..3..W	30)	H..C..U	30)	Q..F..S	30)	X..H..P	30)	H..L..N	30)	P..N..K
31)	A..A..X	31)	J..D..V			31)	A..J..Q			31)	Q..O..L

CODES: P-PHYSICAL BIORHYTHM CURVE,E-EMOTIONAL BIORHYTHM CURVE,I-INTELLECTUAL BIORHYTHM CURVE

1899

	...JANUARY.. P--E--I		..FEBRUARY.. P--E--I		...MARCH... P--E--I		...APRIL... P--E--I		....MAY.... P--E--I		....JUNE.... P--E--I
1)	R..P..M	1)	B..S..K	1)	G..S..E	1)	P..V..C	1)	W..X..8	1)	G..1..6
2)	S..Q..N	2)	C..T..L	2)	H..T..F	2)	Q..W..D	2)	X..Y..A	2)	H..2..7
3)	T..R..O	3)	D..U..M	3)	J..U..G	3)	R..X..E	3)	A..Z..B	3)	J..3..8
4)	U..S..P	4)	E..V..N	4)	K..V..H	4)	S..Y..F	4)	B..1..C	4)	K..A..A
5)	V..T..Q	5)	F..W..O	5)	L..W..J	5)	T..Z..G	5)	C..2..D	5)	L..B..B
6)	W..U..R	6)	G..X..P	6)	M..X..K	6)	U..1..H	6)	D..3..E	6)	M..C..C
7)	X..V..S	7)	H..Y..Q	7)	N..Y..L	7)	V..2..J	7)	E..A..F	7)	N..D..D
8)	A..W..T	8)	J..Z..R	8)	O..Z..M	8)	W..3..K	8)	F..B..G	8)	O..E..E
9)	B..X..U	9)	K..1..S	9)	P..1..N	9)	X..A..L	9)	G..C..H	9)	P..F..F
10)	C..Y..V	10)	L..2..T	10)	Q..2..O	10)	A..B..M	10)	H..D..J	10)	Q..G..G
11)	D..Z..W	11)	M..3..U	11)	R..3..P	11)	B..C..N	11)	J..E..K	11)	R..H..H
12)	E..1..X	12)	N..A..V	12)	S..A..Q	12)	C..D..O	12)	K..F..L	12)	S..J..J
13)	F..2..Y	13)	O..B..W	13)	T..B..R	13)	D..E..P	13)	L..G..M	13)	T..K..K
14)	G..3..Z	14)	P..C..X	14)	U..C..S	14)	E..F..Q	14)	M..H..N	14)	U..L..L
15)	H..A..1	15)	Q..D..Y	15)	V..D..T	15)	F..G..R	15)	N..J..O	15)	V..M..M
16)	J..B..2	16)	R..E..Z	16)	W..E..U	16)	G..H..S	16)	O..K..P	16)	W..N..N
17)	K..C..3	17)	S..F..1	17)	X..F..V	17)	H..J..T	17)	P..L..Q	17)	X..O..O
18)	L..D..4	18)	T..G..2	18)	A..G..W	18)	J..K..U	18)	Q..M..R	18)	A..P..P
19)	M..E..5	19)	U..H..3	19)	B..H..X	19)	K..L..V	19)	R..N..S	19)	B..Q..Q
20)	N..F..6	20)	V..J..4	20)	C..J..Y	20)	L..M..W	20)	S..O..T	20)	C..R..R
21)	O..G..7	21)	W..K..5	21)	D..K..Z	21)	M..N..X	21)	T..P..U	21)	D..S..S
22)	P..H..8	22)	X..L..6	22)	E..L..1	22)	N..O..Y	22)	U..Q..V	22)	E..T..T
23)	Q..J..A	23)	A..M..7	23)	F..M..2	23)	O..P..Z	23)	V..R..W	23)	F..U..U
24)	R..K..B	24)	B..N..8	24)	G..N..3	24)	P..Q..1	24)	W..S..X	24)	G..V..V
25)	S..L..C	25)	C..O..A	25)	H..O..4	25)	Q..R..2	25)	X..T..Y	25)	H..W..W
26)	T..M..D	26)	D..P..B	26)	J..P..5	26)	R..S..3	26)	A..U..Z	26)	J..X..X
27)	U..N..E	27)	E..Q..C	27)	K..Q..6	27)	S..T..4	27)	B..V..1	27)	K..Y..Y
28)	V..O..F	28)	F..R..D	28)	L..R..7	28)	T..U..5	28)	C..W..2	28)	L..Z..Z
29)	W..P..G			29)	M..S..8	29)	U..V..6	29)	D..X..3	29)	M..1..1
30)	X..Q..H			30)	N..T..A	30)	V..W..7	30)	E..Y..4	30)	N..2..2
31)	A..R..J			31)	O..U..B			31)	F..Z..5		

1899

	...JULY.... P--E--I		...AUGUST... P--E--I		.SEPTEMBER. P--E--I		..OCTOBER... P--E--I		.NOVEMBER.. P--E--I		.DECEMBER.. P--E--I
1)	O..3..3	1)	W..C..1	1)	G..F..Y	1)	O..H..V	1)	W..L..T	1)	F..N..Q
2)	P..A..4	2)	X..D..2	2)	H..G..Z	2)	P..J..W	2)	X..M..U	2)	G..O..R
3)	Q..B..5	3)	A..E..3	3)	J..H..1	3)	Q..K..X	3)	A..N..V	3)	H..P..S
4)	R..C..6	4)	B..F..4	4)	K..J..2	4)	R..L..Y	4)	B..O..W	4)	J..Q..T
5)	S..D..7	5)	C..G..5	5)	L..K..3	5)	S..M..Z	5)	C..P..X	5)	K..R..U
6)	T..E..8	6)	D..H..6	6)	M..L..4	6)	T..N..1	6)	D..Q..Y	6)	L..S..V
7)	U..F..A	7)	E..J..7	7)	N..M..5	7)	U..O..2	7)	E..R..Z	7)	M..T..W
8)	V..G..B	8)	F..K..8	8)	O..N..6	8)	V..P..3	8)	F..S..1	8)	N..U..X
9)	W..H..C	9)	G..L..A	9)	P..O..7	9)	W..Q..4	9)	G..T..2	9)	O..V..Y
10)	X..J..D	10)	H..M..B	10)	Q..P..8	10)	X..R..5	10)	H..U..3	10)	P..W..Z
11)	A..K..E	11)	J..N..C	11)	R..Q..A	11)	A..S..6	11)	J..V..4	11)	Q..X..1
12)	B..L..F	12)	K..O..D	12)	S..R..B	12)	B..T..7	12)	K..W..5	12)	R..Y..2
13)	C..M..G	13)	L..P..E	13)	T..S..C	13)	C..U..8	13)	L..X..6	13)	S..Z..3
14)	D..N..H	14)	M..Q..F	14)	U..T..D	14)	D..V..A	14)	M..Y..7	14)	T..1..4
15)	E..O..J	15)	N..R..G	15)	V..U..E	15)	E..W..B	15)	N..Z..8	15)	U..2..5
16)	F..P..K	16)	O..S..H	16)	W..V..F	16)	F..X..C	16)	O..1..A	16)	V..3..6
17)	G..Q..L	17)	P..T..J	17)	X..W..G	17)	G..Y..D	17)	P..2..B	17)	W..A..7
18)	H..R..M	18)	Q..U..K	18)	A..X..H	18)	H..Z..E	18)	Q..3..C	18)	X..B..8
19)	J..S..N	19)	R..V..L	19)	B..Y..J	19)	J..1..F	19)	R..A..D	19)	A..C..A
20)	K..T..O	20)	S..W..M	20)	C..Z..K	20)	K..2..G	20)	S..B..E	20)	B..D..B
21)	L..U..P	21)	T..X..N	21)	D..1..L	21)	L..3..H	21)	T..C..F	21)	C..E..C
22)	M..V..Q	22)	U..Y..O	22)	E..2..M	22)	M..A..J	22)	U..D..G	22)	D..F..D
23)	N..W..R	23)	V..Z..P	23)	F..3..N	23)	N..B..K	23)	V..E..H	23)	E..G..E
24)	O..X..S	24)	W..1..Q	24)	G..A..O	24)	O..C..L	24)	W..F..J	24)	F..H..F
25)	P..Y..T	25)	X..2..R	25)	H..B..P	25)	P..D..M	25)	X..G..K	25)	G..J..G
26)	Q..Z..U	26)	A..3..S	26)	J..C..Q	26)	Q..E..N	26)	A..H..L	26)	H..K..H
27)	R..1..V	27)	B..A..T	27)	K..D..R	27)	R..F..O	27)	B..J..M	27)	J..L..J
28)	S..2..W	28)	C..B..U	28)	L..E..S	28)	S..G..P	28)	C..K..N	28)	K..M..K
29)	T..3..X	29)	D..C..V	29)	M..F..T	29)	T..H..Q	29)	D..L..O	29)	L..N..L
30)	U..A..Y	30)	E..D..W	30)	N..G..U	30)	U..J..R	30)	E..M..P	30)	M..O..M
31)	V..B..Z	31)	F..E..X			31)	V..K..S			31)	N..P..N

CODES: P-PHYSICAL BIORHYTHM CURVE, E-EMOTIONAL BIORHYTHM CURVE, I-INTELLECTUAL BIORHYTHM CURVE

	...JANUARY..	..FEBRUARY..	...MARCH...	...APRIL...	.....MAY....	....JUNE....
	P--E--I	P--E--I	P--E--I	P--E--I	P--E--I	P--E--I
1)	O..Q..O	W..T..M	D..T..G	M..W..E	T..Y..B	D..2..8
2)	P..R..P	X..U..N	E..U..H	N..X..F	U..Z..C	E..3..A
3)	Q..S..Q	A..V..O	F..V..J	O..Y..G	V..1..D	F..A..B
4)	R..T..R	B..W..P	G..W..K	P..Z..H	W..2..E	G..B..C
5)	S..U..S	C..X..Q	H..X..L	Q..1..J	X..3..F	H..C..D
6)	T..V..T	D..Y..R	J..Y..M	R..2..K	A..A..G	J..D..E
7)	U..W..U	E..Z..S	K..Z..N	S..3..L	B..B..H	K..E..F
8)	V..X..V	F..1..T	L..1..O	T..A..M	C..C..J	L..F..G
9)	W..Y..W	G..2..U	M..2..P	U..B..N	D..D..K	M..G..H
10)	X..Z..X	H..3..V	N..3..Q	V..C..O	E..E..L	N..H..J
11)	A..1..Y	J..A..W	O..A..R	W..D..P	F..F..M	O..J..K
12)	B..2..Z	K..B..X	P..B..S	X..E..Q	G..G..N	P..K..L
13)	C..3..1	L..C..Y	Q..C..T	A..F..R	H..H..O	Q..L..M
14)	D..A..2	M..D..Z	R..D..U	B..G..S	J..J..P	R..M..N
15)	E..B..3	N..E..1	S..E..V	C..H..T	K..K..Q	S..N..O
16)	F..C..4	O..F..2	T..F..W	D..J..U	L..L..R	T..O..P
17)	G..D..5	P..G..3	U..G..X	E..K..V	M..M..S	U..P..Q
18)	H..E..6	Q..H..4	V..H..Y	F..L..W	N..N..T	V..Q..R
19)	J..F..7	R..J..5	W..J..Z	G..M..X	O..O..U	W..R..S
20)	K..G..8	S..K..6	X..K..1	H..N..Y	P..P..V	X..S..T
21)	L..H..A	T..L..7	A..L..2	J..O..Z	Q..Q..W	A..T..U
22)	M..J..B	U..M..8	B..M..3	K..P..1	R..R..X	B..U..V
23)	N..K..C	V..N..A	C..N..4	L..Q..2	S..S..Y	C..V..W
24)	O..L..D	W..O..B	D..O..5	M..R..3	T..T..Z	D..W..X
25)	P..M..E	X..P..C	E..P..6	N..S..4	U..U..1	E..X..Y
26)	Q..N..F	A..Q..D	F..Q..7	O..T..5	V..V..2	F..Y..Z
27)	R..O..G	B..R..E	G..R..8	P..U..6	W..W..3	G..Z..1
28)	S..P..H	C..S..F	H..S..A	Q..V..7	X..X..4	H..1..2
29)	T..Q..J		J..T..B	R..W..8	A..Y..5	J..2..3
30)	U..R..K		K..U..C	S..X..A	B..Z..6	K..3..4
31)	V..S..L		L..V..D		C..1..7	

	....JULY....	...AUGUST...	..SEPTEMBER.	..OCTOBER...	..NOVEMBER..	..DECEMBER..
	P--E--I	P--E--I	P--E--I	P--E--I	P--E--I	P--E--I
1)	L..A..5	T..D..3	D..G..1	L..J..X	T..M..V	C..O..S
2)	M..B..6	U..E..4	E..H..2	M..K..Y	U..N..W	D..P..T
3)	N..C..7	V..F..5	F..J..3	N..L..Z	V..O..X	E..Q..U
4)	O..D..8	W..G..6	G..K..4	O..M..1	W..P..Y	F..R..V
5)	P..E..A	X..H..7	H..L..5	P..N..2	X..Q..Z	G..S..W
6)	Q..F..B	A..J..8	J..M..6	Q..O..3	A..R..1	H..T..X
7)	R..G..C	B..K..A	K..N..7	R..P..4	B..S..2	J..U..Y
8)	S..H..D	C..L..B	L..O..8	S..Q..5	C..T..3	K..V..Z
9)	T..J..E	D..M..C	M..P..A	T..R..6	D..U..4	L..W..1
10)	U..K..F	E..N..D	N..Q..B	U..S..7	E..V..5	M..X..2
11)	V..L..G	F..O..E	O..R..C	V..T..8	F..W..6	N..Y..3
12)	W..M..H	G..P..F	P..S..D	W..U..A	G..X..7	O..Z..4
13)	X..N..J	H..Q..G	Q..T..E	X..V..B	H..Y..8	P..1..5
14)	A..O..K	J..R..H	R..U..F	A..W..C	J..Z..A	Q..2..6
15)	B..P..L	K..S..J	S..V..G	B..X..D	K..1..B	R..3..7
16)	C..Q..M	L..T..K	T..W..H	C..Y..E	L..2..C	S..A..8
17)	D..R..N	M..U..L	U..X..J	D..Z..F	M..3..D	T..B..A
18)	E..S..O	N..V..M	V..Y..K	E..1..G	N..A..E	U..C..B
19)	F..T..P	O..W..N	W..Z..L	F..2..H	O..B..F	V..D..C
20)	G..U..Q	P..X..O	X..1..M	G..3..J	P..C..G	W..E..D
21)	H..V..R	Q..Y..P	A..2..N	H..A..K	Q..D..H	X..F..E
22)	J..W..S	R..Z..Q	B..3..O	J..B..L	R..E..J	A..G..F
23)	K..X..T	S..1..R	C..A..P	K..C..M	S..F..K	B..H..G
24)	L..Y..U	T..2..S	D..B..Q	L..D..N	T..G..L	C..J..H
25)	M..Z..V	U..3..T	E..C..R	M..E..O	U..H..M	D..K..J
26)	N..1..W	V..A..U	F..D..S	N..F..P	V..J..N	E..L..K
27)	O..2..X	W..B..V	G..E..T	O..G..Q	W..K..O	F..M..L
28)	P..3..Y	X..C..W	H..F..U	P..H..R	X..L..P	G..N..M
29)	Q..A..Z	A..D..X	J..G..V	Q..J..S	A..M..Q	H..O..N
30)	R..B..1	B..E..Y	K..H..W	R..K..T	B..N..R	J..P..O
31)	S..C..2	C..F..Z		S..L..U		K..Q..P

CODES: P-PHYSICAL BIORHYTHM CURVE,E-EMOTIONAL BIORHYTHM CURVE,I-INTELLECTUAL BIORHYTHM CURVE

127

	...JANUARY..	..FEBRUARY..	...MARCH...	...APRIL...	....MAY....	....JUNE....
	P--E--I	P--E--I	P--E--I	P--E--I	P--E--I	P--E--I
1)	L..R..Q	T..U..O	A..U..J	J..X..G	Q..Z..D	A..3..B
2)	M..S..R	U..V..P	B..V..K	K..Y..H	R..1..E	B..A..C
3)	N..T..S	V..W..Q	C..W..L	L..Z..J	S..2..F	C..B..D
4)	O..U..T	W..X..R	D..X..M	M..1..K	T..3..G	D..C..E
5)	P..V..U	X..Y..S	E..Y..N	N..2..L	U..A..H	E..D..F
6)	Q..W..V	A..Z..T	F..Z..O	O..3..M	V..B..J	F..E..G
7)	R..X..W	B..1..U	G..1..P	P..A..N	W..C..K	G..F..H
8)	S..Y..X	C..2..V	H..2..Q	Q..B..O	X..D..L	H..G..J
9)	T..Z..Y	D..3..W	J..3..R	R..C..P	A..E..M	J..H..K
10)	U..1..Z	E..A..X	K..A..S	S..D..Q	B..F..N	K..J..L
11)	V..2..1	F..B..Y	L..B..T	T..E..R	C..G..O	L..K..M
12)	W..3..2	G..C..Z	M..C..U	U..F..S	D..H..P	M..L..N
13)	X..A..3	H..D..1	N..D..V	V..G..T	E..J..Q	N..M..O
14)	A..B..4	J..E..2	O..E..W	W..H..U	F..K..R	O..N..P
15)	B..C..5	K..F..3	P..F..X	X..J..V	G..L..S	P..O..Q
16)	C..D..6	L..G..4	Q..G..Y	A..K..W	H..M..T	Q..P..R
17)	D..E..7	M..H..5	R..H..Z	B..L..X	J..N..U	R..Q..S
18)	E..F..8	N..J..6	S..J..1	C..M..Y	K..O..V	S..R..T
19)	F..G..A	O..K..7	T..K..2	D..N..Z	L..P..W	T..S..U
20)	G..H..B	P..L..8	U..L..3	E..O..1	M..Q..X	U..T..V
21)	H..J..C	Q..M..A	V..M..4	F..P..2	N..R..Y	V..U..W
22)	J..K..D	R..N..B	W..N..5	G..Q..3	O..S..Z	W..V..X
23)	K..L..E	S..O..C	X..O..6	H..R..4	P..T..1	X..W..Y
24)	L..M..F	T..P..D	A..P..7	J..S..5	Q..U..2	A..X..Z
25)	M..N..G	U..Q..E	B..Q..8	K..T..6	R..V..3	B..Y..1
26)	N..O..H	V..R..F	C..R..A	L..U..7	S..W..4	C..Z..2
27)	O..P..J	W..S..G	D..S..B	M..V..8	T..X..5	D..1..3
28)	P..Q..K	X..T..H	E..T..C	N..W..A	U..Y..6	E..2..4
29)	Q..R..L		F..U..D	O..X..B	V..Z..7	F..3..5
30)	R..S..M		G..V..E	P..Y..C	W..1..8	G..A..6
31)	S..T..N		H..W..F		X..2..A	

	....JULY....	...AUGUST...	.SEPTEMBER.	.OCTOBER...	.NOVEMBER..	.DECEMBER..
	P--E--I	P--E--I	P--E--I	P--E--I	P--E--I	P--E--I
1)	H..B..7	Q..E..5	A..H..3	H..K..Z	Q..N..X	X..P..U
2)	J..C..8	R..F..6	B..J..4	J..L..1	R..O..Y	A..Q..V
3)	K..D..A	S..G..7	C..K..5	K..M..2	S..P..Z	B..R..W
4)	L..E..B	T..H..8	D..L..6	L..N..3	T..Q..1	C..S..X
5)	M..F..C	U..J..A	E..M..7	M..O..4	U..R..2	D..T..Y
6)	N..G..D	V..K..B	F..N..8	N..P..5	V..S..3	E..U..Z
7)	O..H..E	W..L..C	G..O..A	O..Q..6	W..T..4	F..V..1
8)	P..J..F	X..M..D	H..P..B	P..R..7	X..U..5	G..W..2
9)	Q..K..G	A..N..E	J..Q..C	Q..S..8	A..V..6	H..X..3
10)	R..L..H	B..O..F	K..R..D	R..T..A	B..W..7	J..Y..4
11)	S..M..J	C..P..G	L..S..E	S..U..B	C..X..8	K..Z..5
12)	T..N..K	D..Q..H	M..T..F	T..V..C	D..Y..A	L..1..6
13)	U..O..L	E..R..J	N..U..G	U..W..D	E..Z..B	M..2..7
14)	V..P..M	F..S..K	O..V..H	V..X..E	F..1..C	N..3..8
15)	W..Q..N	G..T..L	P..W..J	W..Y..F	G..2..D	O..A..B
16)	X..R..O	H..U..M	Q..X..K	X..Z..G	H..3..E	P..B..B
17)	A..S..P	J..V..N	R..Y..L	A..1..H	J..A..F	Q..C..C
18)	B..T..Q	K..W..O	S..Z..M	B..2..J	K..B..G	R..D..D
19)	C..U..R	L..X..P	T..1..N	C..3..K	L..C..H	S..E..E
20)	D..V..S	M..Y..Q	U..2..O	D..A..L	M..D..J	T..F..F
21)	E..W..T	N..Z..R	V..3..P	E..B..M	N..E..K	U..G..G
22)	F..X..U	O..1..S	W..A..Q	F..C..N	O..F..L	V..H..H
23)	G..Y..V	P..2..T	X..B..R	G..D..O	P..G..M	W..J..J
24)	H..Z..W	Q..3..U	A..C..S	H..E..P	Q..H..N	X..K..K
25)	J..1..X	R..A..V	B..D..T	J..F..Q	R..J..O	A..L..L
26)	K..2..Y	S..B..W	C..E..U	K..G..R	S..K..P	B..M..M
27)	L..3..Z	T..C..X	D..F..V	L..H..S	T..L..Q	C..N..N
28)	M..A..1	U..D..Y	E..G..W	M..J..T	U..M..R	D..O..O
29)	N..B..2	V..E..Z	F..H..X	N..K..U	V..N..S	E..P..P
30)	O..C..3	W..F..1	G..J..Y	O..L..V	W..O..T	F..Q..Q
31)	P..D..4	X..G..2		P..M..W		G..R..R

CODES: P-PHYSICAL BIORHYTHM CURVE,E-EMOTIONAL BIORHYTHM CURVE,I-INTELLECTUAL BIORHYTHM CURVE

```
...JANUARY..      ..FEBRUARY..      ...MARCH...       ...APRIL...       ....MAY....       ....JUNE....

   P--E--I           P--E--I           P--E--I           P--E--I           P--E--I           P--E--I

 1)  H..S..S      1)  Q..V..Q      1)  V..V..L      1)  F..Y..J      1)  N..1..F      1)  V..A..D
 2)  J..T..T      2)  R..W..R      2)  W..W..M      2)  G..Z..K      2)  O..2..G      2)  W..B..E
 3)  K..U..U      3)  S..X..S      3)  X..X..N      3)  H..1..L      3)  P..3..H      3)  X..C..F
 4)  L..V..V      4)  T..Y..T      4)  A..Y..O      4)  J..2..M      4)  Q..A..J      4)  A..D..G
 5)  M..W..W      5)  U..Z..U      5)  B..Z..P      5)  K..3..N      5)  R..B..K      5)  B..E..H
 6)  N..X..X      6)  V..1..V      6)  C..1..Q      6)  L..A..O      6)  S..C..L      6)  C..F..J
 7)  O..Y..Y      7)  W..2..W      7)  D..2..R      7)  M..B..P      7)  T..D..M      7)  D..G..K
 8)  P..Z..Z      8)  X..3..X      8)  E..3..S      8)  N..C..Q      8)  U..E..N      8)  E..H..L
 9)  Q..1..1      9)  A..A..Y      9)  F..A..T      9)  O..D..R      9)  V..F..O      9)  F..J..M
10)  R..2..2     10)  B..B..Z     10)  G..B..U     10)  P..E..S     10)  W..G..P     10)  G..K..N
11)  S..3..3     11)  C..C..1     11)  H..C..V     11)  Q..F..T     11)  X..H..Q     11)  H..L..O
12)  T..A..4     12)  D..D..2     12)  J..D..W     12)  R..G..U     12)  A..J..R     12)  J..M..P
13)  U..B..5     13)  E..E..3     13)  K..E..X     13)  S..H..V     13)  B..K..S     13)  K..N..Q
14)  V..C..6     14)  F..F..4     14)  L..F..Y     14)  T..J..W     14)  C..L..T     14)  L..O..R
15)  W..D..7     15)  G..G..5     15)  M..G..Z     15)  U..K..X     15)  D..M..U     15)  M..P..S
16)  X..E..8     16)  H..H..6     16)  N..H..1     16)  V..L..Y     16)  E..N..V     16)  N..Q..T
17)  A..F..A     17)  J..J..7     17)  O..J..2     17)  W..M..Z     17)  F..O..W     17)  O..R..U
18)  B..G..B     18)  K..K..8     18)  P..K..3     18)  X..N..1     18)  G..P..X     18)  P..S..V
19)  C..H..C     19)  L..L..A     19)  Q..L..4     19)  A..O..2     19)  H..Q..Y     19)  Q..T..W
20)  D..J..D     20)  M..M..B     20)  R..M..5     20)  B..P..3     20)  J..R..Z     20)  R..U..X
21)  E..K..E     21)  N..N..C     21)  S..N..6     21)  C..Q..4     21)  K..S..1     21)  S..V..Y
22)  F..L..F     22)  O..O..D     22)  T..O..7     22)  D..R..5     22)  L..T..2     22)  T..W..Z
23)  G..M..G     23)  P..P..E     23)  U..P..8     23)  E..S..6     23)  M..U..3     23)  U..X..1
24)  H..N..H     24)  Q..Q..F     24)  V..Q..A     24)  F..T..7     24)  N..V..4     24)  V..Y..2
25)  J..O..J     25)  R..R..G     25)  W..R..B     25)  G..U..8     25)  O..W..5     25)  W..Z..3
26)  K..P..K     26)  S..S..H     26)  X..S..C     26)  H..V..A     26)  P..X..6     26)  X..1..4
27)  L..Q..L     27)  T..T..J     27)  A..T..D     27)  J..W..B     27)  Q..Y..7     27)  A..2..5
28)  M..R..M     28)  U..U..K     28)  B..U..E     28)  K..X..C     28)  R..Z..8     28)  B..3..6
29)  N..S..N                      29)  C..V..F     29)  L..Y..D     29)  S..1..A     29)  C..A..7
30)  O..T..O                      30)  D..W..G     30)  M..Z..E     30)  T..2..B     30)  D..B..8
31)  P..U..P                      31)  E..X..H                      31)  U..3..C
```

```
....JULY....      ...AUGUST...      .SEPTEMBER.       ..OCTOBER...      .NOVEMBER..       .DECEMBER..

   P--E--I           P--E--I           P--E--I           P--E--I           P--E--I           P--E--I

 1)  E..C..A      1)  N..F..7      1)  V..J..5      1)  E..L..2      1)  N..O..Z      1)  U..Q..W
 2)  F..D..B      2)  O..G..8      2)  W..K..6      2)  F..M..3      2)  O..P..1      2)  V..R..X
 3)  G..E..C      3)  P..H..A      3)  X..L..7      3)  G..N..4      3)  P..Q..2      3)  W..S..Y
 4)  H..F..D      4)  Q..J..B      4)  A..M..8      4)  H..O..5      4)  Q..R..3      4)  X..T..Z
 5)  J..G..E      5)  R..K..C      5)  B..N..A      5)  J..P..6      5)  R..S..4      5)  A..U..1
 6)  K..H..F      6)  S..L..D      6)  C..O..B      6)  K..Q..7      6)  S..T..5      6)  B..V..2
 7)  L..J..G      7)  T..M..E      7)  D..P..C      7)  L..R..8      7)  T..U..6      7)  C..W..3
 8)  M..K..H      8)  U..N..F      8)  E..Q..D      8)  M..S..A      8)  U..V..7      8)  D..X..4
 9)  N..L..J      9)  V..O..G      9)  F..R..E      9)  N..T..B      9)  V..W..8      9)  E..Y..5
10)  O..M..K     10)  W..P..H     10)  G..S..F     10)  O..U..C     10)  W..X..A     10)  F..Z..6
11)  P..N..L     11)  X..Q..J     11)  H..T..G     11)  P..V..D     11)  X..Y..B     11)  G..1..7
12)  Q..O..M     12)  A..R..K     12)  J..U..H     12)  Q..W..E     12)  A..Z..C     12)  H..2..8
13)  R..P..N     13)  B..S..L     13)  K..V..J     13)  R..X..F     13)  B..1..D     13)  J..3..A
14)  S..Q..O     14)  C..T..M     14)  L..W..K     14)  S..Y..G     14)  C..2..E     14)  K..A..B
15)  T..R..P     15)  D..U..N     15)  M..X..L     15)  T..Z..H     15)  D..3..F     15)  L..B..C
16)  U..S..Q     16)  E..V..O     16)  N..Y..M     16)  U..1..J     16)  E..A..G     16)  M..C..D
17)  V..T..R     17)  F..W..P     17)  O..Z..N     17)  V..2..K     17)  F..B..H     17)  N..D..E
18)  W..U..S     18)  G..X..Q     18)  P..1..O     18)  W..3..L     18)  G..C..J     18)  O..E..F
19)  X..V..T     19)  H..Y..R     19)  Q..2..P     19)  X..A..M     19)  H..D..K     19)  P..F..G
20)  A..W..U     20)  J..Z..S     20)  R..3..Q     20)  A..B..N     20)  J..E..L     20)  Q..G..H
21)  B..X..V     21)  K..1..T     21)  S..A..R     21)  B..C..O     21)  K..F..M     21)  R..H..J
22)  C..Y..W     22)  L..2..U     22)  T..B..S     22)  C..D..P     22)  L..G..N     22)  S..J..K
23)  D..Z..X     23)  M..3..V     23)  U..C..T     23)  D..E..Q     23)  M..H..O     23)  T..K..L
24)  E..1..Y     24)  N..A..W     24)  V..D..U     24)  E..F..R     24)  N..J..P     24)  U..L..M
25)  F..2..Z     25)  O..B..X     25)  W..E..V     25)  F..G..S     25)  O..K..Q     25)  V..M..N
26)  G..3..1     26)  P..C..Y     26)  X..F..W     26)  G..H..T     26)  P..L..R     26)  W..N..O
27)  H..A..2     27)  Q..D..Z     27)  A..G..X     27)  H..J..U     27)  Q..M..S     27)  X..O..P
28)  J..B..3     28)  R..E..1     28)  B..H..Y     28)  J..K..V     28)  R..N..T     28)  A..P..Q
29)  K..C..4     29)  S..F..2     29)  C..J..Z     29)  K..L..W     29)  S..O..U     29)  B..Q..R
30)  L..D..5     30)  T..G..3     30)  D..K..1     30)  L..M..X     30)  T..P..V     30)  C..R..S
31)  M..E..6     31)  U..H..4                      31)  M..N..Y                      31)  D..S..T
```

CODES: P-PHYSICAL BIORHYTHM CURVE,E-EMOTIONAL BIORHYTHM CURVE,I-INTELLECTUAL BIORHYTHM CURVE

	...JANUARY..	..FEBRUARY..	...MARCH...	...APRIL...	....MAY....	...JUNE....
	P--E--I	P--E--I	P--E--I	P--E--I	P--E--I	P--E--I
1)	E..T..U	N..W..S	S..W..N	C..Z..L	K..2..H	S..B..F
2)	F..U..V	O..X..T	T..X..O	D..1..M	L..3..J	T..C..G
3)	G..V..W	P..Y..U	U..Y..P	E..2..N	M..A..K	U..D..H
4)	H..W..X	Q..Z..V	V..Z..Q	F..3..O	N..B..L	V..E..J
5)	J..X..Y	R..1..W	W..1..R	G..A..P	O..C..M	W..F..K
6)	K..Y..Z	S..2..X	X..2..S	H..B..Q	P..D..N	X..G..L
7)	L..Z..1	T..3..Y	A..3..T	J..C..R	Q..E..O	A..H..M
8)	M..1..2	U..A..Z	B..A..U	K..D..S	R..F..P	B..J..N
9)	N..2..3	V..B..1	C..B..V	L..E..T	S..G..Q	C..K..O
10)	O..3..4	W..C..2	D..C..W	M..F..U	T..H..R	D..L..P
11)	P..A..5	X..D..3	E..D..X	N..G..V	U..J..S	E..M..Q
12)	Q..B..6	A..E..4	F..E..Y	O..H..W	V..K..T	F..N..R
13)	R..C..7	B..F..5	G..F..Z	P..J..X	W..L..U	G..O..S
14)	S..D..8	C..G..6	H..G..1	Q..K..Y	X..M..V	H..P..T
15)	T..E..A	D..H..7	J..H..2	R..L..Z	A..N..W	J..Q..U
16)	U..F..B	E..J..8	K..J..3	S..M..1	B..O..X	K..R..V
17)	V..G..C	F..K..A	L..K..4	T..N..2	C..P..Y	L..S..W
18)	W..H..D	G..L..B	M..L..5	U..O..3	D..Q..Z	M..T..X
19)	X..J..E	H..M..C	N..M..6	V..P..4	E..R..1	N..U..Y
20)	A..K..F	J..N..D	O..N..7	W..Q..5	F..S..2	O..V..Z
21)	B..L..G	K..O..E	P..O..8	X..R..6	G..T..3	P..W..1
22)	C..M..H	L..P..F	Q..P..A	A..S..7	H..U..4	Q..X..2
23)	D..N..J	M..Q..G	R..Q..B	B..T..8	J..V..5	R..Y..3
24)	E..O..K	N..R..H	S..R..C	C..U..A	K..W..6	S..Z..4
25)	F..P..L	O..S..J	T..S..D	D..V..B	L..X..7	T..1..5
26)	G..Q..M	P..T..K	U..T..E	E..W..C	M..Y..8	U..2..6
27)	H..R..N	Q..U..L	V..U..F	F..X..D	N..Z..A	V..3..7
28)	J..S..O	R..V..M	W..V..G	G..Y..E	O..1..B	W..A..8
29)	K..T..P		X..W..H	H..Z..F	P..2..C	X..B..A
30)	L..U..Q		A..X..J	J..1..G	Q..3..D	A..C..B
31)	M..V..R		B..Y..K		R..A..E	

	....JULY....	...AUGUST...	..SEPTEMBER	..OCTOBER...	..NOVEMBER..	..DECEMBER..
	P--E--I	P--E--I	P--E--I	P--E--I	P--E--I	P--E--I
1)	B..D..C	K..G..A	S..K..7	B..M..4	K..P..2	R..R..Y
2)	C..E..D	L..H..B	T..L..8	C..N..5	L..Q..3	S..S..Z
3)	D..F..E	M..J..C	U..M..A	D..O..6	M..R..4	T..T..1
4)	E..G..F	N..K..D	V..N..B	E..P..7	N..S..5	U..U..2
5)	F..H..G	O..L..E	W..O..C	F..Q..8	O..T..6	V..V..3
6)	G..J..H	P..M..F	X..P..D	G..R..A	P..U..7	W..W..4
7)	H..K..J	Q..N..G	A..Q..E	H..S..B	Q..V..8	X..X..5
8)	J..L..K	R..O..H	B..R..F	J..T..C	R..W..A	A..Y..6
9)	K..M..L	S..P..J	C..S..G	K..U..D	S..X..B	B..Z..7
10)	L..N..M	T..Q..K	D..T..H	L..V..E	T..Y..C	C..1..8
11)	M..O..N	U..R..L	E..U..J	M..W..F	U..Z..D	D..2..A
12)	N..P..O	V..S..M	F..V..K	N..X..G	V..1..E	E..3..B
13)	O..Q..P	W..T..N	G..W..L	O..Y..H	W..2..F	F..A..C
14)	P..R..Q	X..U..O	H..X..M	P..Z..J	X..3..G	G..B..D
15)	Q..S..R	A..V..P	J..Y..N	Q..1..K	A..A..H	H..C..E
16)	R..T..S	B..W..Q	K..Z..O	R..2..L	B..B..J	J..D..F
17)	S..U..T	C..X..R	L..1..P	S..3..M	C..C..K	K..E..G
18)	T..V..U	D..Y..S	M..2..Q	T..A..N	D..D..L	L..F..H
19)	U..W..V	E..Z..T	N..3..R	U..B..O	E..E..M	M..G..J
20)	V..X..W	F..1..U	O..A..S	V..C..P	F..F..N	N..H..K
21)	W..Y..X	G..2..V	P..B..T	W..D..Q	G..G..O	O..J..L
22)	X..Z..Y	H..3..W	Q..C..U	X..E..R	H..H..P	P..K..M
23)	A..1..Z	J..A..X	R..D..V	A..F..S	J..J..Q	Q..L..N
24)	B..2..1	K..B..Y	S..E..W	B..G..T	K..K..R	R..M..O
25)	C..3..2	L..C..Z	T..F..X	C..H..U	L..L..S	S..N..P
26)	D..A..3	M..D..1	U..G..Y	D..J..V	M..M..T	T..O..Q
27)	E..B..4	N..E..2	V..H..Z	E..K..W	N..N..U	U..P..R
28)	F..C..5	O..F..3	W..J..1	F..L..X	O..O..V	V..Q..S
29)	G..D..6	P..G..4	X..K..2	G..M..Y	P..P..W	W..R..T
30)	H..E..7	Q..H..5	A..L..3	H..N..Z	Q..Q..X	X..S..U
31)	J..F..8	R..J..6		J..O..1		A..T..V

CODES: P-PHYSICAL BIORHYTHM CURVE, E-EMOTIONAL BIORHYTHM CURVE, I-INTELLECTUAL BIORHYTHM CURVE

...JANUARY..	..FEBRUARY..	....MARCH...	...APRIL...	.....MAY....	....JUNE....
P--E--I	P--E--I	P--E--I·	P--E--I	P--E--I	P--E--I
1) B..U..W	1) K..X..U	1) Q..Y..Q	1) A..2..O	1) H..A..L	1) Q..D..J
2) C..V..X	2) L..Y..V	2) R..Z..R	2) B..3..P	2) J..B..M	2) R..E..K
3) D..W..Y	3) M..Z..W	3) S..1..S	3) C..A..Q	3) K..C..N	3) S..F..L
4) E..X..Z	4) N..1..X	4) T..2..T	4) D..B..R	4) L..D..O	4) T..G..M
5) F..Y..1	5) O..2..Y	5) U..3..U	5) E..C..S	5) M..E..P	5) U..H..N
6) G..Z..2	6) P..3..Z	6) V..A..V	6) F..D..T	6) N..F..Q	6) V..J..O
7) H..1..3	7) Q..A..1	7) W..B..W	7) G..E..U	7) O..G..R	7) W..K..P
8) J..2..4	8) R..B..2	8) X..C..X	8) H..F..V	8) P..H..S	8) X..L..Q
9) K..3..5	9) S..C..3	9) A..D..Y	9) J..G..W	9) Q..J..T	9) A..M..R
10) L..A..6	10) T..D..4	10) B..E..Z	10) K..H..X	10) R..K..U	10) B..N..S
11) M..B..7	11) U..E..5	11) C..F..1	11) L..J..Y	11) S..L..V	11) C..O..T
12) N..C..8	12) V..F..6	12) D..G..2	12) M..K..Z	12) T..M..W	12) D..P..U
13) O..D..A	13) W..G..7	13) E..H..3	13) N..L..1	13) U..N..X	13) E..Q..V
14) P..E..B	14) X..H..8	14) F..J..4	14) O..M..2	14) V..O..Y	14) F..R..W
15) Q..F..C	15) A..J..A	15) G..K..5	15) P..N..3	15) W..P..Z	15) G..S..X
16) R..G..D	16) B..K..B	16) H..L..6	16) Q..O..4	16) X..Q..1	16) H..T..Y
17) S..H..E	17) C..L..C	17) J..M..7	17) R..P..5	17) A..R..2	17) J..U..Z
18) T..J..F	18) D..M..D	18) K..N..8	18) S..Q..6	18) B..S..3	18) K..V..1
19) U..K..G	19) E..N..E	19) L..O..A	19) T..R..7	19) C..T..4	19) L..W..2
20) V..L..H	20) F..O..F	20) M..P..B	20) U..S..8	20) D..U..5	20) M..X..3
21) W..M..J	21) G..P..G	21) N..Q..C	21) V..T..A	21) E..V..6	21) N..Y..4
22) X..N..K	22) H..Q..H	22) O..R..D	22) W..U..B	22) F..W..7	22) O..Z..5
23) A..O..L	23) J..R..J	23) P..S..E	23) X..V..C	23) G..X..8	23) P..1..6
24) B..P..M	24) K..S..K	24) Q..T..F	24) A..W..D	24) H..Y..A	24) Q..2..7
25) C..Q..N	25) L..T..L	25) R..U..G	25) B..X..E	25) J..Z..B	25) R..3..8
26) D..R..O	26) M..U..M	26) S..V..H	26) C..Y..F	26) K..1..C	26) S..A..A
27) E..S..P	27) N..V..N	27) T..W..J	27) D..Z..G	27) L..2..D	27) T..B..B
28) F..T..Q	28) O..W..O	28) U..X..K	28) E..1..H	28) M..3..E	28) U..C..C
29) G..U..R	29) P..X..P	29) V..Y..L	29) F..2..J	29) N..A..F	29) V..D..D
30) H..V..S		30) W..Z..M	30) G..3..K	30) O..B..G	30) W..E..E
31) J..W..T		31) X..1..N		31) P..C..H	

....JULY....	...AUGUST...	..SEPTEMBER.	..OCTOBER...	..NOVEMBER..	.DECEMBER..
P--E--I	P--E--I	P-E--I	P--E--I	P--E--I	P--E--I
1) X..F..F	1) H..J..D	1) Q..M..B	1) X..O..7	1) H..R..5	1) P..T..2
2) A..G..G	2) J..K..E	2) R..N..C	2) A..P..8	2) J..S..6	2) Q..U..3
3) B..H..H	3) K..L..F	3) S..O..D	3) B..Q..A	3) K..T..7	3) R..V..4
4) C..J..J	4) L..M..G	4) T..P..E	4) C..R..B	4) L..U..8	4) S..W..5
5) D..K..K	5) M..N..H	5) U..Q..F	5) D..S..C	5) M..V..A	5) T..X..6
6) E..L..L	6) N..O..J	6) V..R..G	6) E..T..D	6) N..W..B	6) U..Y..7
7) F..M..M	7) O..P..K	7) W..S..H	7) F..U..E	7) O..X..C	7) V..Z..8
8) G..N..N	8) P..Q..L	8) X..T..J	8) G..V..F	8) P..Y..D	8) W..1..A
9) H..O..O	9) Q..R..M	9) A..U..K	9) H..W..G	9) Q..Z..E	9) X..2..B
10) J..P..P	10) R..S..N	10) B..V..L	10) J..X..H	10) R..1..F	10) A..3..C
11) K..Q..Q	11) S..T..O	11) C..W..M	11) K..Y..J	11) S..2..G	11) B..A..D
12) L..R..R	12) T..U..P	12) D..X..N	12) L..Z..K	12) T..3..H	12) C..B..E
13) M..S..S	13) U..V..Q	13) E..Y..O	13) M..1..L	13) U..A..J	13) D..C..F
14) N..T..T	14) V..W..R	14) F..Z..P	14) N..2..M	14) V..B..K	14) E..D..G
15) O..U..U	15) W..X..S	15) G..1..Q	15) O..3..N	15) W..C..L	15) F..E..H
16) P..V..V	16) X..Y..T	16) H..2..R	16) P..A..O	16) X..D..M	16) G..F..J
17) Q..W..W	17) A..Z..U	17) J..3..S	17) Q..B..P	17) A..E..N	17) H..G..K
18) R..X..X	18) B..1..V	18) K..A..T	18) R..C..Q	18) B..F..O	18) J..H..L
19) S..Y..Y	19) C..2..W	19) L..B..U	19) S..D..R	19) C..G..P	19) K..J..M
20) T..Z..Z	20) D..3..X	20) M..C..V	20) T..E..S	20) D..H..Q	20) L..K..N
21) U..1..1	21) E..A..Y	21) N..D..W	21) U..F..T	21) E..J..R	21) M..L..O
22) V..2..2	22) F..B..Z	22) O..E..X	22) V..G..U	22) F..K..S	22) N..M..P
23) W..3..3	23) G..C..1	23) P..F..Y	23) W..H..V	23) G..L..T	23) O..N..Q
24) X..A..4	24) H..D..2	24) Q..G..Z	24) X..J..W	24) H..M..U	24) P..O..R
25) A..B..5	25) J..E..3	25) R..H..1	25) A..K..X	25) J..N..V	25) Q..P..S
26) B..C..6	26) K..F..4	26) S..J..2	26) B..L..Y	26) K..O..W	26) R..Q..T
27) C..D..7	27) L..G..5	27) T..K..3	27) C..M..Z	27) L..P..X	27) S..R..U
28) D..E..8	28) M..H..6	28) U..L..4	28) D..N..1	28) M..Q..Y	28) T..S..V
29) E..F..A	29) N..J..7	29) V..M..5	29) E..O..2	29) N..R..Z	29) U..T..W
30) F..G..B	30) O..K..8	30) W..N..6	30) F..P..3	30) O..S..1	30) V..U..X
31) G..H..C	31) P..L..A		31) G..Q..4		31) W..V..Y

CODES: P-PHYSICAL BIORHYTHM CURVE, E-EMOTIONAL BIORHYTHM CURVE, I-INTELLECTUAL BIORHYTHM CURVE

	..JANUARY..		..FEBRUARY..		...MARCH...		...APRIL...		....MAY....		....JUNE....
	P--E--I		P--E--I		P--E--I		P--E--I		P--E--I		P--E--I
1)	X..W..Z	1)	H..Z..X	1)	N..Z..S	1)	V..3..Q	1)	E..B..N	1)	N..E..L
2)	A..X..1	2)	J..1..Y	2)	O..1..T	2)	W..A..R	2)	F..C..O	2)	O..F..M
3)	B..Y..2	3)	K..2..Z	3)	P..2..U	3)	X..B..S	3)	G..D..P	3)	P..G..N
4)	C..Z..3	4)	L..3..1	4)	Q..3..V	4)	A..C..T	4)	H..E..Q	4)	Q..H..O
5)	D..1..4	5)	M..A..2	5)	R..A..W	5)	B..D..U	5)	J..F..R	5)	R..J..P
6)	E..2..5	6)	N..B..3	6)	S..B..X	6)	C..E..V	6)	K..G..S	6)	S..K..Q
7)	F..3..6	7)	O..C..4	7)	T..C..Y	7)	D..F..W	7)	L..H..T	7)	T..L..R
8)	G..A..7	8)	P..D..5	8)	U..D..Z	8)	E..G..X	8)	M..J..U	8)	U..M..S
9)	H..B..8	9)	Q..E..6	9)	V..E..1	9)	F..H..Y	9)	N..K..V	9)	V..N..T
10)	J..C..A	10)	R..F..7	10)	W..F..2	10)	G..J..Z	10)	O..L..W	10)	W..O..U
11)	K..D..B	11)	S..G..8	11)	X..G..3	11)	H..K..1	11)	P..M..X	11)	X..P..V
12)	L..E..C	12)	T..H..A	12)	A..H..4	12)	J..L..2	12)	Q..N..Y	12)	A..Q..W
13)	M..F..D	13)	U..J..B	13)	B..J..5	13)	K..M..3	13)	R..O..Z	13)	B..R..X
14)	N..G..E	14)	V..K..C	14)	C..K..6	14)	L..N..4	14)	S..P..1	14)	C..S..Y
15)	O..H..F	15)	W..L..D	15)	D..L..7	15)	M..O..5	15)	T..Q..2	15)	D..T..Z
16)	P..J..G	16)	X..M..E	16)	E..M..8	16)	N..P..6	16)	U..R..3	16)	E..U..1
17)	Q..K..H	17)	A..N..F	17)	F..N..A	17)	O..Q..7	17)	V..S..4	17)	F..V..2
18)	R..L..J	18)	B..O..G	18)	G..O..B	18)	P..R..8	18)	W..T..5	18)	G..W..3
19)	S..M..K	19)	C..P..H	19)	H..P..C	19)	Q..S..A	19)	X..U..6	19)	H..X..4
20)	T..N..L	20)	D..Q..J	20)	J..Q..D	20)	R..T..B	20)	A..V..7	20)	J..Y..5
21)	U..O..M	21)	E..R..K	21)	K..R..E	21)	S..U..C	21)	B..W..8	21)	K..Z..6
22)	V..P..N	22)	F..S..L	22)	L..S..F	22)	T..V..D	22)	C..X..A	22)	L..1..7
23)	W..Q..O	23)	G..T..M	23)	M..T..G	23)	U..W..E	23)	D..Y..B	23)	M..2..8
24)	X..R..P	24)	H..U..N	24)	N..U..H	24)	V..X..F	24)	E..Z..C	24)	N..3..A
25)	A..S..Q	25)	J..V..O	25)	O..V..J	25)	W..Y..G	25)	F..1..D	25)	O..A..B
26)	B..T..R	26)	K..W..P	26)	P..W..K	26)	X..Z..H	26)	G..2..E	26)	P..B..C
27)	C..U..S	27)	L..X..Q	27)	Q..X..L	27)	A..1..J	27)	H..3..F	27)	Q..C..D
28)	D..V..T	28)	M..Y..R	28)	R..Y..M	28)	B..2..K	28)	J..A..G	28)	R..D..E
29)	E..W..U			29)	S..Z..N	29)	C..3..L	29)	K..B..H	29)	S..E..F
30)	F..X..V			30)	T..1..O	30)	D..A..M	30)	L..C..J	30)	T..F..G
31)	G..Y..W			31)	U..2..P			31)	M..D..K		

	....JULY....		...AUGUST...		.SEPTEMBER.		..OCTOBER...		..NOVEMBER..		.DECEMBER..
	P--E--I		P--E--I		P--E--I		P--E--I		P--E--I		P--E--I
1)	U..G..H	1)	E..K..F	1)	N..N..D	1)	U..P..A	1)	E..S..7	1)	M..U..4
2)	V..H..J	2)	F..L..G	2)	O..O..E	2)	V..Q..B	2)	F..T..8	2)	N..V..5
3)	W..J..K	3)	G..M..H	3)	P..P..F	3)	W..R..C	3)	G..U..A	3)	O..W..6
4)	X..K..L	4)	H..N..J	4)	Q..Q..G	4)	X..S..D	4)	H..V..B	4)	P..X..7
5)	A..L..M	5)	J..O..K	5)	R..R..H	5)	A..T..E	5)	J..W..C	5)	Q..Y..8
6)	B..M..N	6)	K..P..L	6)	S..S..J	6)	B..U..F	6)	K..X..D	6)	R..Z..A
7)	C..N..O	7)	L..Q..M	7)	T..T..K	7)	C..V..G	7)	L..Y..E	7)	S..1..B
8)	D..O..P	8)	M..R..N	8)	U..U..L	8)	D..W..H	8)	M..Z..F	8)	T..2..C
9)	E..P..Q	9)	N..S..O	9)	V..V..M	9)	E..X..J	9)	N..1..G	9)	U..3..D
10)	F..Q..R	10)	O..T..P	10)	W..W..N	10)	F..Y..K	10)	O..2..H	10)	V..A..E
11)	G..R..S	11)	P..U..Q	11)	X..X..O	11)	G..Z..L	11)	P..3..J	11)	W..B..F
12)	H..S..T	12)	Q..V..R	12)	A..Y..P	12)	H..1..M	12)	Q..A..K	12)	X..C..G
13)	J..T..U	13)	R..W..S	13)	B..Z..Q	13)	J..2..N	13)	R..B..L	13)	A..D..H
14)	K..U..V	14)	S..X..T	14)	C..1..R	14)	K..3..O	14)	S..C..M	14)	B..E..J
15)	L..V..W	15)	T..Y..U	15)	D..2..S	15)	L..A..P	15)	T..D..N	15)	C..F..K
16)	M..W..X	16)	U..Z..V	16)	E..3..T	16)	M..B..Q	16)	U..E..O	16)	D..G..L
17)	N..X..Y	17)	V..1..W	17)	F..A..U	17)	N..C..R	17)	V..F..P	17)	E..H..M
18)	O..Y..Z	18)	W..2..X	18)	G..B..V	18)	O..D..S	18)	W..G..Q	18)	F..J..N
19)	P..Z..1	19)	X..3..Y	19)	H..C..W	19)	P..E..T	19)	X..H..R	19)	G..K..O
20)	Q..1..2	20)	A..A..Z	20)	J..D..X	20)	Q..F..U	20)	A..J..S	20)	H..L..P
21)	R..2..3	21)	B..B..1	21)	K..E..Y	21)	R..G..V	21)	B..K..T	21)	J..M..Q
22)	S..3..4	22)	C..C..2	22)	L..F..Z	22)	S..H..W	22)	C..L..U	22)	K..N..R
23)	T..A..5	23)	D..D..3	23)	M..G..1	23)	T..J..X	23)	D..M..V	23)	L..O..S
24)	U..B..6	24)	E..E..4	24)	N..H..2	24)	U..K..Y	24)	E..N..W	24)	M..P..T
25)	V..C..7	25)	F..F..5	25)	O..J..3	25)	V..L..Z	25)	F..O..X	25)	N..Q..U
26)	W..D..8	26)	G..G..6	26)	P..K..4	26)	W..M..1	26)	G..P..Y	26)	O..R..V
27)	X..E..A	27)	H..H..7	27)	Q..L..5	27)	X..N..2	27)	H..Q..Z	27)	P..S..W
28)	A..F..B	28)	J..J..8	28)	R..M..6	28)	A..O..3	28)	J..R..1	28)	Q..T..X
29)	B..G..C	29)	K..K..A	29)	S..N..7	29)	B..P..4	29)	K..S..2	29)	R..U..Y
30)	C..H..D	30)	L..L..B	30)	T..O..8	30)	C..Q..5	30)	L..T..3	30)	S..V..Z
31)	D..J..E	31)	M..M..C			31)	D..R..6			31)	T..W..1

CODES: P-PHYSICAL BIORHYTHM CURVE, E-EMOTIONAL BIORHYTHM CURVE, I-INTELLECTUAL BIORHYTHM CURVE

	...JANUARY..	..FEBRUARY..	...MARCH...	...APRIL...	....MAY....	...JUNE....
	P--E--I	P--E--I	P--E--I	P--E--I	P--E--I	P--E--I
1)	U..X..2	E..1..Z	K..1..U	S..A..S	B..C..P	K..F..N
2)	V..Y..3	F..2..1	L..2..V	T..B..T	C..D..Q	L..G..O
3)	W..Z..4	G..3..2	M..3..W	U..C..U	D..E..R	M..H..P
4)	X..1..5	H..A..3	N..A..X	V..D..V	E..F..S	N..J..Q
5)	A..2..6	J..B..4	O..B..Y	W..E..W	F..G..T	O..K..R
6)	B..3..7	K..C..5	P..C..Z	X..F..X	G..H..U	P..L..S
7)	C..A..8	L..D..6	Q..D..1	A..G..Y	H..J..V	Q..M..T
8)	D..B..A	M..E..7	R..E..2	B..H..Z	J..K..W	R..N..U
9)	E..C..B	N..F..8	S..F..3	C..J..1	K..L..X	S..O..V
10)	F..D..C	O..G..A	T..G..4	D..K..2	L..M..Y	T..P..W
11)	G..E..D	P..H..B	U..H..5	E..L..3	M..N..Z	U..Q..X
12)	H..F..E	Q..J..C	V..J..6	F..M..4	N..O..1	V..R..Y
13)	J..G..F	R..K..D	W..K..7	G..N..5	O..P..2	W..S..Z
14)	K..H..G	S..L..E	X..L..8	H..O..6	P..Q..3	X..T..1
15)	L..J..H	T..M..F	A..M..A	J..P..7	Q..R..4	A..U..2
16)	M..K..J	U..N..G	B..N..B	K..Q..8	R..S..5	B..V..3
17)	N..L..K	V..O..H	C..O..C	L..R..A	S..T..6	C..W..4
18)	O..M..L	W..P..J	D..P..D	M..S..B	T..U..7	D..X..5
19)	P..N..M	X..Q..K	E..Q..E	N..T..C	U..V..8	E..Y..6
20)	Q..O..N	A..R..L	F..R..F	O..U..D	V..W..A	F..Z..7
21)	R..P..O	B..S..M	G..S..G	P..V..E	W..X..B	G..1..8
22)	S..Q..P	C..T..N	H..T..H	Q..W..F	X..Y..C	H..2..A
23)	T..R..Q	D..U..O	J..U..J	R..X..G	A..Z..D	J..3..B
24)	U..S..R	E..V..P	K..V..K	S..Y..H	B..1..E	K..A..C
25)	V..T..S	F..W..Q	L..W..L	T..Z..J	C..2..F	L..B..D
26)	W..U..T	G..X..R	M..X..M	U..1..K	D..3..G	M..C..E
27)	X..V..U	H..Y..S	N..Y..N	V..2..L	E..A..H	N..D..F
28)	A..W..V	J..Z..T	O..Z..O	W..3..M	F..B..J	O..E..G
29)	B..X..W		P..1..P	X..A..N	G..C..K	P..F..H
30)	C..Y..X		Q..2..Q	A..B..O	H..D..L	Q..G..J
31)	D..Z..Y		R..3..R		J..E..M	

	....JULY....	...AUGUST...	..SEPTEMBER.	..OCTOBER...	..NOVEMBER..	..DECEMBER..
	P--E--I	P--E--I	P--E--I	P--E--I	P--E--I	P--E--I
1)	R..H..K	B..L..H	K..O..F	R..Q..C	B..T..A	J..V..6
2)	S..J..L	C..M..J	L..P..G	S..R..D	C..U..B	K..W..7
3)	T..K..M	D..N..K	M..Q..H	T..S..E	D..V..C	L..X..8
4)	U..L..N	E..O..L	N..R..J	U..T..F	E..W..D	M..Y..A
5)	V..M..O	F..P..M	O..S..K	V..U..G	F..X..E	N..Z..B
6)	W..N..P	G..Q..N	P..T..L	W..V..H	G..Y..F	O..1..C
7)	X..O..Q	H..R..O	Q..U..M	X..W..J	H..Z..G	P..2..D
8)	A..P..R	J..S..P	R..V..N	A..X..K	J..1..H	Q..3..E
9)	B..Q..S	K..T..Q	S..W..O	B..Y..L	K..2..J	R..A..F
10)	C..R..T	L..U..R	T..X..P	C..Z..M	L..3..K	S..B..G
11)	D..S..U	M..V..S	U..Y..Q	D..1..N	M..A..L	T..C..H
12)	E..T..V	N..W..T	V..Z..R	E..2..O	N..B..M	U..D..J
13)	F..U..W	O..X..U	W..1..S	F..3..P	O..C..N	V..E..K
14)	G..V..X	P..Y..V	X..2..T	G..A..Q	P..D..O	W..F..L
15)	H..W..Y	Q..Z..W	A..3..U	H..B..R	Q..E..P	X..G..M
16)	J..X..Z	R..1..X	B..A..V	J..C..S	R..F..Q	A..H..N
17)	K..Y..1	S..2..Y	C..B..W	K..D..T	S..G..R	B..J..O
18)	L..Z..2	T..3..Z	D..C..X	L..E..U	T..H..S	C..K..P
19)	M..1..3	U..A..1	E..D..Y	M..F..V	U..J..T	D..L..Q
20)	N..2..4	V..B..2	F..E..Z	N..G..W	V..K..U	E..M..R
21)	O..3..5	W..C..3	G..F..1	O..H..X	W..L..V	F..N..S
22)	P..A..6	X..D..4	H..G..2	P..J..Y	X..M..W	G..O..T
23)	Q..B..7	A..E..5	J..H..3	Q..K..Z	A..N..X	H..P..U
24)	R..C..8	B..F..6	K..J..4	R..L..1	B..O..Y	J..Q..V
25)	S..D..A	C..G..7	L..K..5	S..M..2	C..P..Z	K..R..W
26)	T..E..B	D..H..8	M..L..6	T..N..3	D..Q..1	L..S..X
27)	U..F..C	E..J..A	N..M..7	U..O..4	E..R..2	M..T..Y
28)	V..G..D	F..K..B	O..N..8	V..P..5	F..S..3	N..U..Z
29)	W..H..E	G..L..C	P..O..A	W..Q..6	G..T..4	O..V..1
30)	X..J..F	H..M..D	Q..P..B	X..R..7	H..U..5	P..W..2
31)	A..K..G	J..N..E		A..S..8		Q..X..3

CODES: P-PHYSICAL BIORHYTHM CURVE,E-EMOTIONAL BIORHYTHM CURVE,I-INTELLECTUAL BIORHYTHM CURVE

	...JANUARY..		.FEBRUARY..		...MARCH...		..APRIL...		....MAY....		...JUNE....
	P--E--I		P--E--I		P--E--I		P--E--I		P--E--I		P--E--I
1)	R..Y..4	1)	B..2..2	1)	G..2..W	1)	P..B..U	1)	W..D..R	1)	G..G..P
2)	S..Z..5	2)	C..3..3	2)	H..3..X	2)	Q..C..V	2)	X..E..S	2)	H..H..Q
3)	T..1..6	3)	D..A..4	3)	J..A..Y	3)	R..D..W	3)	A..F..T	3)	J..J..R
4)	U..2..7	4)	E..B..5	4)	K..B..Z	4)	S..E..X	4)	B..G..U	4)	K..K..S
5)	V..3..8	5)	F..C..6	5)	L..C..1	5)	T..F..Y	5)	C..H..V	5)	L..L..T
6)	W..A..A	6)	G..D..7	6)	M..D..2	6)	U..G..Z	6)	D..J..W	6)	M..M..U
7)	X..B..B	7)	H..E..8	7)	N..E..3	7)	V..H..1	7)	E..K..X	7)	N..N..V
8)	A..C..C	8)	J..F..A	8)	O..F..4	8)	W..J..2	8)	F..L..Y	8)	O..O..W
9)	B..D..D	9)	K..G..B	9)	P..G..5	9)	X..K..3	9)	G..M..Z	9)	P..P..X
10)	C..E..E	10)	L..H..C	10)	Q..H..6	10)	A..L..4	10)	H..N..1	10)	Q..Q..Y
11)	D..F..F	11)	M..J..D	11)	R..J..7	11)	B..M..5	11)	J..O..2	11)	R..R..Z
12)	E..G..G	12)	N..K..E	12)	S..K..8	12)	C..N..6	12)	K..P..3	12)	S..S..1
13)	F..H..H	13)	O..L..F	13)	T..L..A	13)	D..O..7	13)	L..Q..4	13)	T..T..2
14)	G..J..J	14)	P..M..G	14)	U..M..B	14)	E..P..8	14)	M..R..5	14)	U..U..3
15)	H..K..K	15)	Q..N..H	15)	V..N..C	15)	F..Q..A	15)	N..S..6	15)	V..V..4
16)	J..L..L	16)	R..O..J	16)	W..O..D	16)	G..R..B	16)	O..T..7	16)	W..W..5
17)	K..M..M	17)	S..P..K	17)	X..P..E	17)	H..S..C	17)	P..U..8	17)	X..X..6
18)	L..N..N	18)	T..Q..L	18)	A..Q..F	18)	J..T..D	18)	Q..V..A	18)	A..Y..7
19)	M..O..O	19)	U..R..M	19)	B..R..G	19)	K..U..E	19)	R..W..B	19)	B..Z..8
20)	N..P..P	20)	V..S..N	20)	C..S..H	20)	L..V..F	20)	S..X..C	20)	C..1..A
21)	O..Q..Q	21)	W..T..O	21)	D..T..J	21)	M..W..G	21)	T..Y..D	21)	D..2..B
22)	P..R..R	22)	X..U..P	22)	E..U..K	22)	N..X..H	22)	U..Z..E	22)	E..3..C
23)	Q..S..S	23)	A..V..Q	23)	F..V..L	23)	O..Y..J	23)	V..1..F	23)	F..A..D
24)	R..T..T	24)	B..W..R	24)	G..W..M	24)	P..Z..K	24)	W..2..G	24)	G..B..E
25)	S..U..U	25)	C..X..S	25)	H..X..N	25)	Q..1..L	25)	X..3..H	25)	H..C..F
26)	T..V..V	26)	D..Y..T	26)	J..Y..O	26)	R..2..M	26)	A..A..J	26)	J..D..G
27)	U..W..W	27)	E..Z..U	27)	K..Z..P	27)	S..3..N	27)	B..B..K	27)	K..E..H
28)	V..X..X	28)	F..1..V	28)	L..1..Q	28)	T..A..O	28)	C..C..L	28)	L..F..J
29)	W..Y..Y			29)	M..2..R	29)	U..B..P	29)	D..D..M	29)	M..G..K
30)	X..Z..Z			30)	N..3..S	30)	V..C..Q	30)	E..E..N	30)	N..H..L
31)	A..1..1			31)	O..A..T			31)	F..F..O		

	....JULY....		...AUGUST...		.SEPTEMBER.		..OCTOBER...		.NOVEMBER..		.DECEMBER..
	P--E--I		P--E--I		P--E--I		P--E--I		P--E--I		P--E--I
1)	O..J..M	1)	W..M..K	1)	G..P..H	1)	O..R..E	1)	W..U..C	1)	F..W..8
2)	P..K..N	2)	X..N..L	2)	H..Q..J	2)	P..S..F	2)	X..V..D	2)	G..X..A
3)	Q..L..O	3)	A..O..M	3)	J..R..K	3)	Q..T..G	3)	A..W..E	3)	H..Y..B
4)	R..M..P	4)	B..P..N	4)	K..S..L	4)	R..U..H	4)	B..X..F	4)	J..Z..C
5)	S..N..Q	5)	C..Q..O	5)	L..T..M	5)	S..V..J	5)	C..Y..G	5)	K..1..D
6)	T..O..R	6)	D..R..P	6)	M..U..N	6)	T..W..K	6)	D..Z..H	6)	L..2..E
7)	U..P..S	7)	E..S..Q	7)	N..V..O	7)	U..X..L	7)	E..1..J	7)	M..3..F
8)	V..Q..T	8)	F..T..R	8)	O..W..P	8)	V..Y..M	8)	F..2..K	8)	N..A..G
9)	W..R..U	9)	G..U..S	9)	P..X..Q	9)	W..Z..N	9)	G..3..L	9)	O..B..H
10)	X..S..V	10)	H..V..T	10)	Q..Y..R	10)	X..1..O	10)	H..A..M	10)	P..C..J
11)	A..T..W	11)	J..W..U	11)	R..Z..S	11)	A..2..P	11)	J..B..N	11)	Q..D..K
12)	B..U..X	12)	K..X..V	12)	S..1..T	12)	B..3..Q	12)	K..C..O	12)	R..E..L
13)	C..V..Y	13)	L..Y..W	13)	T..2..U	13)	C..A..R	13)	L..D..P	13)	S..F..M
14)	D..W..Z	14)	M..Z..X	14)	U..3..V	14)	D..B..S	14)	M..E..Q	14)	T..G..N
15)	E..X..1	15)	N..1..Y	15)	V..A..W	15)	E..C..T	15)	N..F..R	15)	U..H..O
16)	F..Y..2	16)	O..2..Z	16)	W..B..X	16)	F..D..U	16)	O..G..S	16)	V..J..P
17)	G..Z..3	17)	P..3..1	17)	X..C..Y	17)	G..E..V	17)	P..H..T	17)	W..K..Q
18)	H..1..4	18)	Q..A..2	18)	A..D..Z	18)	H..F..W	18)	Q..J..U	18)	X..L..R
19)	J..2..5	19)	R..B..3	19)	B..E..1	19)	J..G..X	19)	R..K..V	19)	A..M..S
20)	K..3..6	20)	S..C..4	20)	C..F..2	20)	K..H..Y	20)	S..L..W	20)	B..N..T
21)	L..A..7	21)	T..D..5	21)	D..G..3	21)	L..J..Z	21)	T..M..X	21)	C..O..U
22)	M..B..8	22)	U..E..6	22)	E..H..4	22)	M..K..1	22)	U..N..Y	22)	D..P..V
23)	N..C..A	23)	V..F..7	23)	F..J..5	23)	N..L..2	23)	V..O..Z	23)	E..Q..W
24)	O..D..B	24)	W..G..8	24)	G..K..6	24)	O..M..3	24)	W..P..1	24)	F..R..X
25)	P..E..C	25)	X..H..A	25)	H..L..7	25)	P..N..4	25)	X..Q..2	25)	G..S..Y
26)	Q..F..D	26)	A..J..B	26)	J..M..8	26)	Q..O..5	26)	A..R..3	26)	H..T..Z
27)	R..G..E	27)	B..K..C	27)	K..N..A	27)	R..P..6	27)	B..S..4	27)	J..U..1
28)	S..H..F	28)	C..L..D	28)	L..O..B	28)	S..Q..7	28)	C..T..5	28)	K..V..2
29)	T..J..G	29)	D..M..E	29)	M..P..C	29)	T..R..8	29)	D..U..6	29)	L..W..3
30)	U..K..H	30)	E..N..F	30)	N..Q..D	30)	U..S..A	30)	E..V..7	30)	M..X..4
31)	V..L..J	31)	F..O..G			31)	V..T..B			31)	N..Y..5

CODES: P-PHYSICAL BIORHYTHM CURVE,E-EMOTIONAL BIORHYTHM CURVE,I-INTELLECTUAL BIORHYTHM CURVE

...JANUARY..	..FEBRUARY..	...MARCH...	...APRIL...	....MAY....	....JUNE....
P--E--I	P--E--I	P--E--I	P--E--I	P--E--I	P--E--I
1) O..Z..6	1) W..3..4	1) E..A..Z	1) N..D..X	1) U..F..U	1) E..J..S
2) P..1..7	2) X..A..5	2) F..B..1	2) O..E..Y	2) V..G..V	2) F..K..T
3) Q..2..8	3) A..B..6	3) G..C..2	3) P..F..Z	3) W..H..W	3) G..L..U
4) R..3..A	4) B..C..7	4) H..D..3	4) Q..G..1	4) X..J..X	4) H..M..V
5) S..A..B	5) C..D..8	5) J..E..4	5) R..H..2	5) A..K..Y	5) J..N..W
6) T..B..C	6) D..E..A	6) K..F..5	6) S..J..3	6) B..L..Z	6) K..O..X
7) U..C..D	7) E..F..B	7) L..G..6	7) T..K..4	7) C..M..1	7) L..P..Y
8) V..D..E	8) F..G..C	8) M..H..7	8) U..L..5	8) D..N..2	8) M..Q..Z
9) W..E..F	9) G..H..D	9) N..J..8	9) V..M..6	9) E..O..3	9) N..R..1
10) X..F..G	10) H..J..E	10) O..K..A	10) W..N..7	10) F..P..4	10) O..S..2
11) A..G..H	11) J..K..F	11) P..L..B	11) X..O..8	11) G..Q..5	11) P..T..3
12) B..H..J	12) K..L..G	12) Q..M..C	12) A..P..A	12) H..R..6	12) Q..U..4
13) C..J..K	13) L..M..H	13) R..N..D	13) B..Q..B	13) J..S..7	13) R..V..5
14) D..K..L	14) M..N..J	14) S..O..E	14) C..R..C	14) K..T..8	14) S..W..6
15) E..L..M	15) N..O..K	15) T..P..F	15) D..S..D	15) L..U..A	15) T..X..7
16) F..M..N	16) O..P..L	16) U..Q..G	16) E..T..E	16) M..V..B	16) U..Y..8
17) G..N..O	17) P..Q..M	17) V..R..H	17) F..U..F	17) N..W..C	17) V..Z..A
18) H..O..P	18) Q..R..N	18) W..S..J	18) G..V..G	18) O..X..D	18) W..1..B
19) J..P..Q	19) R..S..O	19) X..T..K	19) H..W..H	19) P..Y..E	19) X..2..C
20) K..Q..R	20) S..T..P	20) A..U..L	20) J..X..J	20) Q..Z..F	20) A..3..D
21) L..R..S	21) T..U..Q	21) B..V..M	21) K..Y..K	21) R..1..G	21) B..A..E
22) M..S..T	22) U..V..R	22) C..W..N	22) L..Z..L	22) S..2..H	22) C..B..F
23) N..T..U	23) V..W..S	23) D..X..O	23) M..1..M	23) T..3..J	23) D..C..G
24) O..U..V	24) W..X..T	24) E..Y..P	24) N..2..N	24) U..A..K	24) E..D..H
25) P..V..W	25) X..Y..U	25) F..Z..Q	25) O..3..O	25) V..B..L	25) F..E..J
26) Q..W..X	26) A..Z..V	26) G..1..R	26) P..A..P	26) W..C..M	26) G..F..K
27) R..X..Y	27) B..1..W	27) H..2..S	27) Q..B..Q	27) X..D..N	27) H..G..L
28) S..Y..Z	28) C..2..X	28) J..3..T	28) R..C..R	28) A..E..O	28) J..H..M
29) T..Z..1	29) D..3..Y	29) K..A..U	29) S..D..S	29) B..F..P	29) K..J..N
30) U..1..2		30) L..B..V	30) T..E..T	30) C..G..Q	30) L..K..O
31) V..2..3		31) M..C..W		31) D..H..R	

....JULY....	...AUGUST...	..SEPTEMBER.	..OCTOBER...	..NOVEMBER..	..DECEMBER..
P--E--I	P--E--I	P--E--I	P--E--I	P--E--I	P--E--I
1) M..L..P	1) U..O..N	1) E..R..L	1) M..T..H	1) U..W..F	1) D..Y..C
2) N..M..Q	2) V..P..O	2) F..S..M	2) N..U..J	2) V..X..G	2) E..Z..D
3) O..N..R	3) W..Q..P	3) G..T..N	3) O..V..K	3) W..Y..H	3) F..1..E
4) P..O..S	4) X..R..Q	4) H..U..O	4) P..W..L	4) X..Z..J	4) G..2..F
5) Q..P..T	5) A..S..R	5) J..V..P	5) Q..X..M	5) A..1..K	5) H..3..G
6) R..Q..U	6) B..T..S	6) K..W..Q	6) R..Y..N	6) B..2..L	6) J..A..H
7) S..R..V	7) C..U..T	7) L..X..R	7) S..Z..O	7) C..3..M	7) K..B..J
8) T..S..W	8) D..V..U	8) M..Y..S	8) T..1..P	8) D..A..N	8) L..C..K
9) U..T..X	9) E..W..V	9) N..Z..T	9) U..2..Q	9) E..B..O	9) M..D..L
10) V..U..Y	10) F..X..W	10) O..1..U	10) V..3..R	10) F..C..P	10) N..E..M
11) W..V..Z	11) G..Y..X	11) P..2..V	11) W..A..S	11) G..D..Q	11) O..F..N
12) X..W..1	12) H..Z..Y	12) Q..3..W	12) X..B..T	12) H..E..R	12) P..G..O
13) A..X..2	13) J..1..Z	13) R..A..X	13) A..C..U	13) J..F..S	13) Q..H..P
14) B..Y..3	14) K..2..1	14) S..B..Y	14) B..D..V	14) K..G..T	14) R..J..Q
15) C..Z..4	15) L..3..2	15) T..C..Z	15) C..E..W	15) L..H..U	15) S..K..R
16) D..1..5	16) M..A..3	16) U..D..1	16) D..F..X	16) M..J..V	16) T..L..S
17) E..2..6	17) N..B..4	17) V..E..2	17) E..G..Y	17) N..K..W	17) U..M..T
18) F..3..7	18) O..C..5	18) W..F..3	18) F..H..Z	18) O..L..X	18) V..N..U
19) G..A..8	19) P..D..6	19) X..G..4	19) G..J..1	19) P..M..Y	19) W..O..V
20) H..B..A	20) Q..E..7	20) A..H..5	20) H..K..2	20) Q..N..Z	20) X..P..W
21) J..C..B	21) R..F..8	21) B..J..6	21) J..L..3	21) R..O..1	21) A..Q..X
22) K..D..C	22) S..G..A	22) C..K..7	22) K..M..4	22) S..P..2	22) B..R..Y
23) L..E..D	23) T..H..B	23) D..L..8	23) L..N..5	23) T..Q..3	23) C..S..Z
24) M..F..E	24) U..J..C	24) E..M..A	24) M..O..6	24) U..R..4	24) D..T..1
25) N..G..F	25) V..K..D	25) F..N..B	25) N..P..7	25) V..S..5	25) E..U..2
26) O..H..G	26) W..L..E	26) G..O..C	26) O..Q..8	26) W..T..6	26) F..V..3
27) P..J..H	27) X..M..F	27) H..P..D	27) P..R..A	27) X..U..7	27) G..W..4
28) Q..K..J	28) A..N..G	28) J..Q..E	28) Q..S..B	28) A..V..8	28) H..X..5
29) R..L..K	29) B..O..H	29) K..R..F	29) R..T..C	29) B..W..A	29) J..Y..6
30) S..M..L	30) C..P..J	30) L..S..G	30) S..U..D	30) C..X..B	30) K..Z..7
31) T..N..M	31) D..Q..K		31) T..V..E		31) L..1..8

CODES: P-PHYSICAL BIORHYTHM CURVE, E-EMOTIONAL BIORHYTHM CURVE, I-INTELLECTUAL BIORHYTHM CURVE

	...JANUARY..	.FEBRUARY..	...MARCH...	...APRIL...	....MAY....	....JUNE....
	P--E--I	P--E--I	P--E--I	P--E--I	P--E--I	P--E--I
1)	M..2..A	U..B..7	B..B..2	K..E..Z	R..G..W	B..K..U
2)	N..3..B	V..C..8	C..C..3	L..F..1	S..H..X	C..L..V
3)	O..A..C	W..D..A	D..D..4	M..G..2	T..J..Y	D..M..W
4)	P..B..D	X..E..B	E..E..5	N..H..3	U..K..Z	E..N..X
5)	Q..C..E	A..F..C	F..F..6	O..J..4	V..L..1	F..O..Y
6)	R..D..F	B..G..D	G..G..7	P..K..5	W..M..2	G..P..Z
7)	S..E..G	C..H..E	H..H..8	Q..L..6	X..N..3	H..Q..1
8)	T..F..H	D..J..F	J..J..A	R..M..7	A..O..4	J..R..2
9)	U..G..J	E..K..G	K..K..B	S..N..8	B..P..5	K..S..3
10)	V..H..K	F..L..H	L..L..C	T..O..A	C..Q..6	L..T..4
11)	W..J..L	G..M..J	M..M..D	U..P..B	D..R..7	M..U..5
12)	X..K..M	H..N..K	N..N..E	V..Q..C	E..S..8	N..V..6
13)	A..L..N	J..O..L	O..O..F	W..R..D	F..T..A	O..W..7
14)	B..M..O	K..P..M	P..P..G	X..S..E	G..U..B	P..X..8
15)	C..N..P	L..Q..N	Q..Q..H	A..T..F	H..V..C	Q..Y..A
16)	D..O..Q	M..R..O	R..R..J	B..U..G	J..W..D	R..Z..B
17)	E..P..R	N..S..P	S..S..K	C..V..H	K..X..E	S..1..C
18)	F..Q..S	O..T..Q	T..T..L	D..W..J	L..Y..F	T..2..D
19)	G..R..T	P..U..R	U..U..M	E..X..K	M..Z..G	U..3..E
20)	H..S..U	Q..V..S	V..V..N	F..Y..L	N..1..H	V..A..F
21)	J..T..V	R..W..T	W..W..O	G..Z..M	O..2..J	W..B..G
22)	K..U..W	S..X..U	X..X..P	H..1..N	P..3..K	X..C..H
23)	L..V..X	T..Y..V	A..Y..Q	J..2..O	Q..A..L	A..D..J
24)	M..W..Y	U..Z..W	B..Z..R	K..3..P	R..B..M	B..E..K
25)	N..X..Z	V..1..X	C..1..S	L..A..Q	S..C..N	C..F..L
26)	O..Y..1	W..2..Y	D..2..T	M..B..R	T..D..O	D..G..M
27)	P..Z..2	X..3..Z	E..3..U	N..C..S	U..E..P	E..H..N
28)	Q..1..3	A..A..1	F..A..V	O..D..T	V..F..Q	F..J..O
29)	R..2..4		G..B..W	P..E..U	W..G..R	G..K..P
30)	S..3..5		H..C..X	Q..F..V	X..H..S	H..L..Q
31)	T..A..6		J..D..Y		A..J..T	

	....JULY....	...AUGUST...	.SEPTEMBER.	..OCTOBER...	.NOVEMBER..	.DECEMBER..
	P--E--I	P--E--I	P--E--I	P--E--I	P--E--I	P--E--I
1)	J..M..R	R..P..P	B..S..N	J..U..K	R..X..H	A..Z..E
2)	K..N..S	S..Q..Q	C..T..O	K..V..L	S..Y..J	B..1..F
3)	L..O..T	T..R..R	D..U..P	L..W..M	T..Z..K	C..2..G
4)	M..P..U	U..S..S	E..V..Q	M..X..N	U..1..L	D..3..H
5)	N..Q..V	V..T..T	F..W..R	N..Y..O	V..2..M	E..A..J
6)	O..R..W	W..U..U	G..X..S	O..Z..P	W..3..N	F..B..K
7)	P..S..X	X..V..V	H..Y..T	P..1..Q	X..A..O	G..C..L
8)	Q..T..Y	A..W..W	J..Z..U	Q..2..R	A..B..P	H..D..M
9)	R..U..Z	B..X..X	K..1..V	R..3..S	B..C..Q	J..E..N
10)	S..V..1	C..Y..Y	L..2..W	S..A..T	C..D..R	K..F..O
11)	T..W..2	D..Z..Z	M..3..X	T..B..U	D..E..S	L..G..P
12)	U..X..3	E..1..1	N..A..Y	U..C..V	E..F..T	M..H..Q
13)	V..Y..4	F..2..2	O..B..Z	V..D..W	F..G..U	N..J..R
14)	W..Z..5	G..3..3	P..C..1	W..E..X	G..H..V	O..K..S
15)	X..1..6	H..A..4	Q..D..2	X..F..Y	H..J..W	P..L..T
16)	A..2..7	J..B..5	R..E..3	A..G..Z	J..K..X	Q..M..U
17)	B..3..8	K..C..6	S..F..4	B..H..1	K..L..Y	R..N..V
18)	C..A..A	L..D..7	T..G..5	C..J..2	L..M..Z	S..O..W
19)	D..B..B	M..E..8	U..H..6	D..K..3	M..N..1	T..P..X
20)	E..C..C	N..F..A	V..J..7	E..L..4	N..O..2	U..Q..Y
21)	F..D..D	O..G..B	W..K..8	F..M..5	O..P..3	V..R..Z
22)	G..E..E	P..H..C	X..L..A	G..N..6	P..Q..4	W..S..1
23)	H..F..F	Q..J..D	A..M..B	H..O..7	Q..R..5	X..T..2
24)	J..G..G	R..K..E	B..N..C	J..P..8	R..S..6	A..U..3
25)	K..H..H	S..L..F	C..O..D	K..Q..A	S..T..7	B..V..4
26)	L..J..J	T..M..G	D..P..E	L..R..B	T..U..8	C..W..5
27)	M..K..K	U..N..H	E..Q..F	M..S..C	U..V..A	D..X..6
28)	N..L..L	V..O..J	F..R..G	N..T..D	V..W..B	E..Y..7
29)	O..M..M	W..P..K	G..S..H	O..U..E	W..X..C	F..Z..8
30)	P..N..N	X..Q..L	H..T..J	P..V..F	X..Y..D	G..1..A
31)	Q..O..O	A..R..M		Q..W..G		H..2..B

CODES: P-PHYSICAL BIORHYTHM CURVE,E-EMOTIONAL BIORHYTHM CURVE,I-INTELLECTUAL BIORHYTHM CURVE

	...JANUARY..	..FEBRUARY..	...MARCH...	...APRIL...	....MAY....	...JUNE....
	P--E--I	P--E--I	P--E--I	P--E--I	P--E--I	P--E--I
1)	J..3..C	R..C..A	W..C..4	G..F..2	O..H..Y	W..L..W
2)	K..A..D	S..D..B	X..D..5	H..G..3	P..J..Z	X..M..X
3)	L..B..E	T..E..C	A..E..6	J..H..4	Q..K..1	A..N..Y
4)	M..C..F	U..F..D	B..F..7	K..J..5	R..L..2	B..O..Z
5)	N..D..G	V..G..E	C..G..8	L..K..6	S..M..3	C..P..1
6)	O..E..H	W..H..F	D..H..A	M..L..7	T..N..4	D..Q..2
7)	P..F..J	X..J..G	E..J..B	N..M..8	U..O..5	E..R..3
8)	Q..G..K	A..K..H	F..K..C	O..N..A	V..P..6	F..S..4
9)	R..H..L	B..L..J	G..L..D	P..O..B	W..Q..7	G..T..5
10)	S..J..M	C..M..K	H..M..E	Q..P..C	X..R..8	H..U..6
11)	T..K..N	D..N..L	J..N..F	R..Q..D	A..S..A	J..V..7
12)	U..L..O	E..O..M	K..O..G	S..R..E	B..T..B	K..W..8
13)	V..M..P	F..P..N	L..P..H	T..S..F	C..U..C	L..X..A
14)	W..N..Q	G..Q..O	M..Q..J	U..T..G	D..V..D	M..Y..B
15)	X..O..R	H..R..P	N..R..K	V..U..H	E..W..E	N..Z..C
16)	A..P..S	J..S..Q	O..S..L	W..V..J	F..X..F	O..1..D
17)	B..Q..T	K..T..R	P..T..M	X..W..K	G..Y..G	P..2..E
18)	C..R..U	L..U..S	Q..U..N	A..X..L	H..Z..H	Q..3..F
19)	D..S..V	M..V..T	R..V..O	B..Y..M	J..1..J	R..A..G
20)	E..T..W	N..W..U	S..W..P	C..Z..N	K..2..K	S..B..H
21)	F..U..X	O..X..V	T..X..Q	D..1..O	L..3..L	T..C..J
22)	G..V..Y	P..Y..W	U..Y..R	E..2..P	M..A..M	U..D..K
23)	H..W..Z	Q..Z..X	V..Z..S	F..3..Q	N..B..N	V..E..L
24)	J..X..1	R..1..Y	W..1..T	G..A..R	O..C..O	W..F..M
25)	K..Y..2	S..2..Z	X..2..U	H..B..S	P..D..P	X..G..N
26)	L..Z..3	T..3..1	A..3..V	J..C..T	Q..E..Q	A..H..O
27)	M..1..4	U..A..2	B..A..W	K..D..U	R..F..R	B..J..P
28)	N..2..5	V..B..3	C..B..X	L..E..V	S..G..S	C..K..Q
29)	O..3..6		D..C..Y	M..F..W	T..H..T	D..L..R
30)	P..A..7		E..D..Z	N..G..X	U..J..U	E..M..S
31)	Q..B..8		F..E..1		V..K..V	

	....JULY....	...AUGUST...	..SEPTEMBER.	..OCTOBER...	..NOVEMBER..	..DECEMBER..
	P--E--I	P--E--I	P--E--I	P--E--I	P--E--I	P--E--I
1)	F..N..T	O..Q..R	W..T..P	F..V..M	O..Y..K	V..1..G
2)	G..O..U	P..R..S	X..U..Q	G..W..N	P..Z..L	W..2..H
3)	H..P..V	Q..S..T	A..V..R	H..X..O	Q..1..M	X..3..J
4)	J..Q..W	R..T..U	B..W..S	J..Y..P	R..2..N	A..A..K
5)	K..R..X	S..U..V	C..X..T	K..Z..Q	S..3..O	B..B..L
6)	L..S..Y	T..V..W	D..Y..U	L..1..R	T..A..P	C..C..M
7)	M..T..Z	U..W..X	E..Z..V	M..2..S	U..B..Q	D..D..N
8)	N..U..1	V..X..Y	F..1..W	N..3..T	V..C..R	E..E..O
9)	O..V..2	W..Y..Z	G..2..X	O..A..U	W..D..S	F..F..P
10)	P..W..3	X..Z..1	H..3..Y	P..B..V	X..E..T	G..G..Q
11)	Q..X..4	A..1..2	J..A..Z	Q..C..W	A..F..U	H..H..R
12)	R..Y..5	B..2..3	K..B..1	R..D..X	B..G..V	J..J..S
13)	S..Z..6	C..3..4	L..C..2	S..E..Y	C..H..W	K..K..T
14)	T..1..7	D..A..5	M..D..3	T..F..Z	D..J..X	L..L..U
15)	U..2..8	E..B..6	N..E..4	U..G..1	E..K..Y	M..M..V
16)	V..3..A	F..C..7	O..F..5	V..H..2	F..L..Z	N..N..W
17)	W..A..B	G..D..8	P..G..6	W..J..3	G..M..1	O..O..X
18)	X..B..C	H..E..A	Q..H..7	X..K..4	H..N..2	P..P..Y
19)	A..C..D	J..F..B	R..J..8	A..L..5	J..O..3	Q..Q..Z
20)	B..D..E	K..G..C	S..K..A	B..M..6	K..P..4	R..R..1
21)	C..E..F	L..H..D	T..L..B	C..N..7	L..Q..5	S..S..2
22)	D..F..G	M..J..E	U..M..C	D..O..8	M..R..6	T..T..3
23)	E..G..H	N..K..F	V..N..D	E..P..A	N..S..7	U..U..4
24)	F..H..J	O..L..G	W..O..E	F..Q..B	O..T..8	V..V..5
25)	G..J..K	P..M..H	X..P..F	G..R..C	P..U..A	W..W..6
26)	H..K..L	Q..N..J	A..Q..G	H..S..D	Q..V..B	X..X..7
27)	J..L..M	R..O..K	B..R..H	J..T..E	R..W..C	A..Y..8
28)	K..M..N	S..P..L	C..S..J	K..U..F	S..X..D	B..Z..A
29)	L..N..O	T..Q..M	D..T..K	L..V..G	T..Y..E	C..1..B
30)	M..O..P	U..R..N	E..U..L	M..W..H	U..Z..F	D..2..C
31)	N..P..Q	V..S..O		N..X..J		E..3..D

CODES: P-PHYSICAL BIORHYTHM CURVE,E-EMOTIONAL BIORHYTHM CURVE,I-INTELLECTUAL BIORHYTHM CURVE

First half of 1911

	...JANUARY..	..FEBRUARY..	...MARCH...	...APRIL...	....MAY....	...JUNE....
	P--E--I	P--E--I	P--E--I	P--E--I	P--E--I	P--E--I
1)	F..A..E	O..D..C	T..D..6	D..G..4	L..J..1	T..M..Y
2)	G..B..F	P..E..D	U..E..7	E..H..5	M..K..2	U..N..Z
3)	H..C..G	Q..F..E	V..F..8	F..J..6	N..L..3	V..O..1
4)	J..D..H	R..G..F	W..G..A	G..K..7	O..M..4	W..P..2
5)	K..E..J	S..H..G	X..H..B	H..L..8	P..N..5	X..Q..3
6)	L..F..K	T..J..H	A..J..C	J..M..A	Q..O..6	A..R..4
7)	M..G..L	U..K..J	B..K..D	K..N..B	R..P..7	B..S..5
8)	N..H..M	V..L..K	C..L..E	L..O..C	S..Q..8	C..T..6
9)	O..J..N	W..M..L	D..M..F	M..P..D	T..R..A	D..U..7
10)	P..K..O	X..N..M	E..N..G	N..Q..E	U..S..B	E..V..8
11)	Q..L..P	A..O..N	F..O..H	O..R..F	V..T..C	F..W..A
12)	R..M..Q	B..P..O	G..P..J	P..S..G	W..U..D	G..X..B
13)	S..N..R	C..Q..P	H..Q..K	Q..T..H	X..V..E	H..Y..C
14)	T..O..S	D..R..Q	J..R..L	R..U..J	A..W..F	J..Z..D
15)	U..P..T	E..S..R	K..S..M	S..V..K	B..X..G	K..1..E
16)	V..Q..U	F..T..S	L..T..N	T..W..L	C..Y..H	L..2..F
17)	W..R..V	G..U..T	M..U..O	U..X..M	D..Z..J	M..3..G
18)	X..S..W	H..V..U	N..V..P	V..Y..N	E..1..K	N..A..H
19)	A..T..X	J..W..V	O..W..Q	W..Z..O	F..2..L	O..B..J
20)	B..U..Y	K..X..W	P..X..R	X..1..P	G..3..M	P..C..K
21)	C..V..Z	L..Y..X	Q..Y..S	A..2..Q	H..A..N	Q..D..L
22)	D..W..1	M..Z..Y	R..Z..T	B..3..R	J..B..O	R..E..M
23)	E..X..2	N..1..Z	S..1..U	C..A..S	K..C..P	S..F..N
24)	F..Y..3	O..2..1	T..2..V	D..B..T	L..D..Q	T..G..O
25)	G..Z..4	P..3..2	U..3..W	E..C..U	M..E..R	U..H..P
26)	H..1..5	Q..A..3	V..A..X	F..D..V	N..F..S	V..J..Q
27)	J..2..6	R..B..4	W..B..Y	G..E..W	O..G..T	W..K..R
28)	K..3..7	S..C..5	X..C..Z	H..F..X	P..H..U	X..L..S
29)	L..A..8		A..D..1	J..G..Y	Q..J..V	A..M..T
30)	M..B..A		B..E..2	K..H..Z	R..K..W	B..N..U
31)	N..C..B		C..F..3		S..L..X	

Second half of 1911

	....JULY....	...AUGUST...	.SEPTEMBER.	..OCTOBER...	.NOVEMBER..	.DECEMBER..
	P--E--I	P--E--I	P--E--I	P--E--I	P--E--I	P--E--I
1)	C..O..V	L..R..T	T..U..R	C..W..O	L..Z..M	S..2..J
2)	D..P..W	M..S..U	U..V..S	D..X..P	M..1..N	T..3..K
3)	E..Q..X	N..T..V	V..W..T	E..Y..Q	N..2..O	U..A..L
4)	F..R..Y	O..U..W	W..X..U	F..Z..R	O..3..P	V..B..M
5)	G..S..Z	P..V..X	X..Y..V	G..1..S	P..A..Q	W..C..N
6)	H..T..1	Q..W..Y	A..Z..W	H..2..T	Q..B..R	X..D..O
7)	J..U..2	R..X..Z	B..1..X	J..3..U	R..C..S	A..E..P
8)	K..V..3	S..Y..1	C..2..Y	K..A..V	S..D..T	B..F..Q
9)	L..W..4	T..Z..2	D..3..Z	L..B..W	T..E..U	C..G..R
10)	M..X..5	U..1..3	E..A..1	M..C..X	U..F..V	D..H..S
11)	N..Y..6	V..2..4	F..B..2	N..D..Y	V..G..W	E..J..T
12)	O..Z..7	W..3..5	G..C..3	O..E..Z	W..H..X	F..K..U
13)	P..1..8	X..A..6	H..D..4	P..F..1	X..J..Y	G..L..V
14)	Q..2..A	A..B..7	J..E..5	Q..G..2	A..K..Z	H..M..W
15)	R..3..B	B..C..8	K..F..6	R..H..3	B..L..1	J..N..X
16)	S..A..C	C..D..A	L..G..7	S..J..4	C..M..2	K..O..Y
17)	T..B..D	D..E..B	M..H..8	T..K..5	D..N..3	L..P..Z
18)	U..C..E	E..F..C	N..J..A	U..L..6	E..O..4	M..Q..1
19)	V..D..F	F..G..D	O..K..B	V..M..7	F..P..5	N..R..2
20)	W..E..G	G..H..E	P..L..C	W..N..8	G..Q..6	O..S..3
21)	X..F..H	H..J..F	Q..M..D	X..O..A	H..R..7	P..T..4
22)	A..G..J	J..K..G	R..N..E	A..P..B	J..S..8	Q..U..5
23)	B..H..K	K..L..H	S..O..F	B..Q..C	K..T..A	R..V..6
24)	C..J..L	L..M..J	T..P..G	C..R..D	L..U..B	S..W..7
25)	D..K..M	M..N..K	U..Q..H	D..S..E	M..V..C	T..X..8
26)	E..L..N	N..O..L	V..R..J	E..T..F	N..W..D	U..Y..A
27)	F..M..O	O..P..M	W..S..K	F..U..G	O..X..E	V..Z..B
28)	G..N..P	P..Q..N	X..T..L	G..V..H	P..Y..F	W..1..C
29)	H..O..Q	Q..R..O	A..U..M	H..W..J	Q..Z..G	X..2..D
30)	J..P..R	R..S..P	B..V..N	J..X..K	R..1..H	A..3..E
31)	K..Q..S	S..T..Q		K..Y..L		B..A..F

CODES: P-PHYSICAL BIORHYTHM CURVE,E-EMOTIONAL BIORHYTHM CURVE,I-INTELLECTUAL BIORHYTHM CURVE

.... JANUARY .. .. FEBRUARY .. ... MARCH ... . APRIL ... . MAY .... JUNE ....

	JANUARY P--E--I	FEBRUARY P--E--I	MARCH P--E--I	APRIL P--E--I	MAY P--E--I	JUNE P--E--I
1)	C..B..G	L..E..E	R..F..A	B..J..7	J..L..4	R..O..2
2)	D..C..H	M..F..F	S..G..B	C..K..8	K..M..5	S..P..3
3)	E..D..J	N..G..G	T..H..C	D..L..A	L..N..6	T..Q..4
4)	F..E..K	O..H..H	U..J..D	E..M..B	M..O..7	U..R..5
5)	G..F..L	P..J..J	V..K..E	F..N..C	N..P..8	V..S..6
6)	H..G..M	Q..K..K	W..L..F	G..O..D	O..Q..A	W..T..7
7)	J..H..N	R..L..L	X..M..G	H..P..E	P..R..B	X..U..8
8)	K..J..O	S..M..M	A..N..H	J..Q..F	Q..S..C	A..V..A
9)	L..K..P	T..N..N	B..O..J	K..R..G	R..T..D	B..W..B
10)	M..L..Q	U..O..O	C..P..K	L..S..H	S..U..E	C..X..C
11)	N..M..R	V..P..P	D..Q..L	M..T..J	T..V..F	D..Y..D
12)	O..N..S	W..Q..Q	E..R..M	N..U..K	U..W..G	E..Z..E
13)	P..O..T	X..R..R	F..S..N	O..V..L	V..X..H	F..1..F
14)	Q..P..U	A..S..S	G..T..O	P..W..M	W..Y..J	G..2..G
15)	R..Q..V	B..T..T	H..U..P	Q..X..N	X..Z..K	H..3..H
16)	S..R..W	C..U..U	J..V..Q	R..Y..O	A..1..L	J..A..J
17)	T..S..X	D..V..V	K..W..R	S..Z..P	B..2..M	K..B..K
18)	U..T..Y	E..W..W	L..X..S	T..1..Q	C..3..N	L..C..L
19)	V..U..Z	F..X..X	M..Y..T	U..2..R	D..A..O	M..D..M
20)	W..V..1	G..Y..Y	N..Z..U	V..3..S	E..B..P	N..E..N
21)	X..W..2	H..Z..Z	O..1..V	W..A..T	F..C..Q	O..F..O
22)	A..X..3	J..1..1	P..2..W	X..B..U	G..D..R	P..G..P
23)	B..Y..4	K..2..2	Q..3..X	A..C..V	H..E..S	Q..H..Q
24)	C..Z..5	L..3..3	R..A..Y	B..D..W	J..F..T	R..J..R
25)	D..1..6	M..A..4	S..B..Z	C..E..X	K..G..U	S..K..S
26)	E..2..7	N..B..5	T..C..1	D..F..Y	L..H..V	T..L..T
27)	F..3..8	O..C..6	U..D..2	E..G..Z	M..J..W	U..M..U
28)	G..A..A	P..D..7	V..E..3	F..H..1	N..K..X	V..N..V
29)	H..B..B	Q..E..8	W..F..4	G..J..2	O..L..Y	W..O..W
30)	J..C..C		X..G..5	H..K..3	P..M..Z	X..P..X
31)	K..D..D		A..H..6		Q..N..1	

.... JULY .... AUGUST ... .. SEPTEMBER . .. OCTOBER ... .. NOVEMBER .. .. DECEMBER ..

	JULY P--E--I	AUGUST P--E--I	SEPTEMBER P--E--I	OCTOBER P--E--I	NOVEMBER P--E--I	DECEMBER P--E--I
1)	A..Q..Y	J..T..W	R..W..U	A..Y..R	J..2..P	Q..A..M
2)	B..R..Z	K..U..X	S..X..V	B..Z..S	K..3..Q	R..B..N
3)	C..S..1	L..V..Y	T..Y..W	C..1..T	L..A..R	S..C..O
4)	D..T..2	M..W..Z	U..Z..X	D..2..U	M..B..S	T..D..P
5)	E..U..3	N..X..1	V..1..Y	E..3..V	N..C..T	U..E..Q
6)	F..V..4	O..Y..2	W..2..Z	F..A..W	O..D..U	V..F..R
7)	G..W..5	P..Z..3	X..3..1	G..B..X	P..E..V	W..G..S
8)	H..X..6	Q..1..4	A..A..2	H..C..Y	Q..F..W	X..H..T
9)	J..Y..7	R..2..5	B..B..3	J..D..Z	R..G..X	A..J..U
10)	K..Z..8	S..3..6	C..C..4	K..E..1	S..H..Y	B..K..V
11)	L..1..A	T..A..7	D..D..5	L..F..2	T..J..Z	C..L..W
12)	M..2..B	U..B..8	E..E..6	M..G..3	U..K..1	D..M..X
13)	N..3..C	V..C..A	F..F..7	N..H..4	V..L..2	E..N..Y
14)	O..A..D	W..D..B	G..G..8	O..J..5	W..M..3	F..O..Z
15)	P..B..E	X..E..C	H..H..A	P..K..6	X..N..4	G..P..1
16)	Q..C..F	A..F..D	J..J..B	Q..L..7	A..O..5	H..Q..2
17)	R..D..G	B..G..E	K..K..C	R..M..8	B..P..6	J..R..3
18)	S..E..H	C..H..F	L..L..D	S..N..A	C..Q..7	K..S..4
19)	T..F..J	D..J..G	M..M..E	T..O..B	D..R..8	L..T..5
20)	U..G..K	E..K..H	N..N..F	U..P..C	E..S..A	M..U..6
21)	V..H..L	F..L..J	O..O..G	V..Q..D	F..T..B	N..V..7
22)	W..J..M	G..M..K	P..P..H	W..R..E	G..U..C	O..W..8
23)	X..K..N	H..N..L	Q..Q..J	X..S..F	H..V..D	P..X..A
24)	A..L..O	J..O..M	R..R..K	A..T..G	J..W..E	Q..Y..B
25)	B..M..P	K..P..N	S..S..L	B..U..H	K..X..F	R..Z..C
26)	C..N..Q	L..Q..O	T..T..M	C..V..J	L..Y..G	S..1..D
27)	D..O..R	M..R..P	U..U..N	D..W..K	M..Z..H	T..2..E
28)	E..P..S	N..S..Q	V..V..O	E..X..L	N..1..J	U..3..F
29)	F..Q..T	O..T..R	W..W..P	F..Y..M	O..2..K	V..A..G
30)	G..R..U	P..U..S	X..X..Q	G..Z..N	P..3..L	W..B..H
31)	H..S..V	Q..V..T		H..1..O		X..C..J

CODES: P-PHYSICAL BIORHYTHM CURVE, E-EMOTIONAL BIORHYTHM CURVE, I-INTELLECTUAL BIORHYTHM CURVE

	...JANUARY..	..FEBRUARY..	...MARCH...	...APRIL...	....MAY....	...JUNE....
	P--E--I	P--E--I	P--E--I	P--E--I	P--E--I	P--E--I
1)	A..D..K	J..G..H	O..G..C	W..K..A	F..M..6	O..P..4
2)	B..E..L	K..H..J	P..H..D	X..L..B	G..N..7	P..Q..5
3)	C..F..M	L..J..K	Q..J..E	A..M..C	H..O..8	Q..R..6
4)	D..G..N	M..K..L	R..K..F	B..N..D	J..P..A	R..S..7
5)	E..H..O	N..L..M	S..L..G	C..O..E	K..Q..B	S..T..8
6)	F..J..P	O..M..N	T..M..H	D..P..F	L..R..C	T..U..A
7)	G..K..Q	P..N..O	U..N..J	E..Q..G	M..S..D	U..V..B
8)	H..L..R	Q..O..P	V..O..K	F..R..H	N..T..E	V..W..C
9)	J..M..S	R..P..Q	W..P..L	G..S..J	O..U..F	W..X..D
10)	K..N..T	S..Q..R	X..Q..M	H..T..K	P..V..G	X..Y..E
11)	L..O..U	T..R..S	A..R..N	J..U..L	Q..W..H	A..Z..F
12)	M..P..V	U..S..T	B..S..O	K..V..M	R..X..J	B..1..G
13)	N..Q..W	V..T..U	C..T..P	L..W..N	S..Y..K	C..2..H
14)	O..R..X	W..U..V	D..U..Q	M..X..O	T..Z..L	D..3..J
15)	P..S..Y	X..V..W	E..V..R	N..Y..P	U..1..M	E..A..K
16)	Q..T..Z	A..W..X	F..W..S	O..Z..Q	V..2..N	F..B..L
17)	R..U..1	B..X..Y	G..X..T	P..1..R	W..3..O	G..C..M
18)	S..V..2	C..Y..Z	H..Y..U	Q..2..S	X..A..P	H..D..N
19)	T..W..3	D..Z..1	J..Z..V	R..3..T	A..B..Q	J..E..O
20)	U..X..4	E..1..2	K..1..W	S..A..U	B..C..R	K..F..P
21)	V..Y..5	F..2..3	L..2..X	T..B..V	C..D..S	L..G..Q
22)	W..Z..6	G..3..4	M..3..Y	U..C..W	D..E..T	M..H..R
23)	X..1..7	H..A..5	N..A..Z	V..D..X	E..F..U	N..J..S
24)	A..2..8	J..B..6	O..B..1	W..E..Y	F..G..V	O..K..T
25)	B..3..A	K..C..7	P..C..2	X..F..Z	G..H..W	P..L..U
26)	C..A..B	L..D..8	Q..D..3	A..G..1	H..J..X	Q..M..V
27)	D..B..C	M..E..A	R..E..4	B..H..2	J..K..Y	R..N..W
28)	E..C..D	N..F..B	S..F..5	C..J..3	K..L..Z	S..O..X
29)	F..D..E		T..G..6	D..K..4	L..M..1	T..P..Y
30)	G..E..F		U..H..7	E..L..5	M..N..2	U..Q..Z
31)	H..F..G		V..J..8		N..O..3	

	....JULY....	...AUGUST...	.SEPTEMBER.	..OCTOBER...	.NOVEMBER..	.DECEMBER..
	P--E--I	P--E--I	P--E--I	P--E--I	P--E--I	P--E--I
1)	V..R..1	F..U..Y	O..X..W	V..Z..T	F..3..R	N..B..O
2)	W..S..2	G..V..Z	P..Y..X	W..1..U	G..A..S	O..C..P
3)	X..T..3	H..W..1	Q..Z..Y	X..2..V	H..B..T	P..D..Q
4)	A..U..4	J..X..2	R..1..Z	A..3..W	J..C..U	Q..E..R
5)	B..V..5	K..Y..3	S..2..1	B..A..X	K..D..V	R..F..S
6)	C..W..6	L..Z..4	T..3..2	C..B..Y	L..E..W	S..G..T
7)	D..X..7	M..1..5	U..A..3	D..C..Z	M..F..X	T..H..U
8)	E..Y..8	N..2..6	V..B..4	E..D..1	N..G..Y	U..J..V
9)	F..Z..A	O..3..7	W..C..5	F..E..2	O..H..Z	V..K..W
10)	G..1..B	P..A..8	X..D..6	G..F..3	P..J..1	W..L..X
11)	H..2..C	Q..B..A	A..E..7	H..G..4	Q..K..2	X..M..Y
12)	J..3..D	R..C..B	B..F..8	J..H..5	R..L..3	A..N..Z
13)	K..A..E	S..D..C	C..G..A	K..J..6	S..M..4	B..O..1
14)	L..B..F	T..E..D	D..H..B	L..K..7	T..N..5	C..P..2
15)	M..C..G	U..F..E	E..J..C	M..L..8	U..O..6	D..Q..3
16)	N..D..H	V..G..F	F..K..D	N..M..A	V..P..7	E..R..4
17)	O..E..J	W..H..G	G..L..E	O..N..B	W..Q..8	F..S..5
18)	P..F..K	X..J..H	H..M..F	P..O..C	X..R..A	G..T..6
19)	Q..G..L	A..K..J	J..N..G	Q..P..D	A..S..B	H..U..7
20)	R..H..M	B..L..K	K..O..H	R..Q..E	B..T..C	J..V..8
21)	S..J..N	C..M..L	L..P..J	S..R..F	C..U..D	K..W..A
22)	T..K..O	D..N..M	M..Q..K	T..S..G	D..V..E	L..X..B
23)	U..L..P	E..O..N	N..R..L	U..T..H	E..W..F	M..Y..C
24)	V..M..Q	F..P..O	O..S..M	V..U..J	F..X..G	N..Z..D
25)	W..N..R	G..Q..P	P..T..N	W..V..K	G..Y..H	O..1..E
26)	X..O..S	H..R..Q	Q..U..O	X..W..L	H..Z..J	P..2..F
27)	A..P..T	J..S..R	R..V..P	A..X..M	J..1..K	Q..3..G
28)	B..Q..U	K..T..S	S..W..Q	B..Y..N	K..2..L	R..A..H
29)	C..R..V	L..U..T	T..X..R	C..Z..O	L..3..M	S..B..J
30)	D..S..W	M..V..U	U..Y..S	D..1..P	M..A..N	T..C..K
31)	E..T..X	N..W..V		E..2..Q		U..D..L

CODES: P-PHYSICAL BIORHYTHM CURVE,E-EMOTIONAL BIORHYTHM CURVE,I-INTELLECTUAL BIORHYTHM CURVE

1914

	...JANUARY.. P--E--I		.FEBRUARY.. P--E--I		...MARCH... P--E--I		...APRIL... P--E--I		....MAY.... P--E--I		....JUNE.... P--E--I
1)	V..E..M	1)	F..H..K	1)	L..H..E	1)	T..L..C	1)	C..N..8	1)	L..Q..6
2)	W..F..N	2)	G..J..L	2)	M..J..F	2)	U..M..D	2)	D..O..A	2)	M..R..7
3)	X..G..O	3)	H..K..M	3)	N..K..G	3)	V..N..E	3)	E..P..B	3)	N..S..8
4)	A..H..P	4)	J..L..N	4)	O..L..H	4)	W..O..F	4)	F..Q..C	4)	O..T..A
5)	B..J..Q	5)	K..M..O	5)	P..M..J	5)	X..P..G	5)	G..R..D	5)	P..U..B
6)	C..K..R	6)	L..N..P	6)	Q..N..K	6)	A..Q..H	6)	H..S..E	6)	Q..V..C
7)	D..L..S	7)	M..O..Q	7)	R..O..L	7)	B..R..J	7)	J..T..F	7)	R..W..D
8)	E..M..T	8)	N..P..R	8)	S..P..M	8)	C..S..K	8)	K..U..G	8)	S..X..E
9)	F..N..U	9)	O..Q..S	9)	T..Q..N	9)	D..T..L	9)	L..V..H	9)	T..Y..F
10)	G..O..V	10)	P..R..T	10)	U..R..O	10)	E..U..M	10)	M..W..J	10)	U..Z..G
11)	H..P..W	11)	Q..S..U	11)	V..S..P	11)	F..V..N	11)	N..X..K	11)	V..1..H
12)	J..Q..X	12)	R..T..V	12)	W..T..Q	12)	G..W..O	12)	O..Y..L	12)	W..2..J
13)	K..R..Y	13)	S..U..W	13)	X..U..R	13)	H..X..P	13)	P..Z..M	13)	X..3..K
14)	L..S..Z	14)	T..V..X	14)	A..V..S	14)	J..Y..Q	14)	Q..1..N	14)	A..A..L
15)	M..T..1	15)	U..W..Y	15)	B..W..T	15)	K..Z..R	15)	R..2..O	15)	B..B..M
16)	N..U..2	16)	V..X..Z	16)	C..X..U	16)	L..1..S	16)	S..3..P	16)	C..C..N
17)	O..V..3	17)	W..Y..1	17)	D..Y..V	17)	M..2..T	17)	T..A..Q	17)	D..D..O
18)	P..W..4	18)	X..Z..2	18)	E..Z..W	18)	N..3..U	18)	U..B..R	18)	E..E..P
19)	Q..X..5	19)	A..1..3	19)	F..1..X	19)	O..A..V	19)	V..C..S	19)	F..F..Q
20)	R..Y..6	20)	B..2..4	20)	G..2..Y	20)	P..B..W	20)	W..D..T	20)	G..G..R
21)	S..Z..7	21)	C..3..5	21)	H..3..Z	21)	Q..C..X	21)	X..E..U	21)	H..H..S
22)	T..1..8	22)	D..A..6	22)	J..A..1	22)	R..D..Y	22)	A..F..V	22)	J..J..T
23)	U..2..A	23)	E..B..7	23)	K..B..2	23)	S..E..Z	23)	B..G..W	23)	K..K..U
24)	V..3..B	24)	F..C..8	24)	L..C..3	24)	T..F..1	24)	C..H..X	24)	L..L..V
25)	W..A..C	25)	G..D..A	25)	M..D..4	25)	U..G..2	25)	D..J..Y	25)	M..M..W
26)	X..B..D	26)	H..E..B	26)	N..E..5	26)	V..H..3	26)	E..K..Z	26)	N..N..X
27)	A..C..E	27)	J..F..C	27)	O..F..6	27)	W..J..4	27)	F..L..1	27)	O..O..Y
28)	B..D..F	28)	K..G..D	28)	P..G..7	28)	X..K..5	28)	G..M..2	28)	P..P..Z
29)	C..E..G			29)	Q..H..8	29)	A..L..6	29)	H..N..3	29)	Q..Q..1
30)	D..F..H			30)	R..J..A	30)	B..M..7	30)	J..O..4	30)	R..R..2
31)	E..G..J			31)	S..K..B			31)	K..P..5		

1914

	....JULY.... P--E--I		...AUGUST... P--E--I		..SEPTEMBER. P--E--I		..OCTOBER... P--E--I		..NOVEMBER.. P--E--I		..DECEMBER.. P--E--I
1)	S..S..3	1)	C..V..1	1)	L..Y..Y	1)	S..1..V	1)	C..A..T	1)	K..C..Q
2)	T..T..4	2)	D..W..2	2)	M..Z..Z	2)	T..2..W	2)	D..B..U	2)	L..D..R
3)	U..U..5	3)	E..X..3	3)	N..1..1	3)	U..3..X	3)	E..C..V	3)	M..E..S
4)	V..V..6	4)	F..Y..4	4)	O..2..2	4)	V..A..Y	4)	F..D..W	4)	N..F..T
5)	W..W..7	5)	G..Z..5	5)	P..3..3	5)	W..B..Z	5)	G..E..X	5)	O..G..U
6)	X..X..8	6)	H..1..6	6)	Q..A..4	6)	X..C..1	6)	H..F..Y	6)	P..H..V
7)	A..Y..A	7)	J..2..7	7)	R..B..5	7)	A..D..2	7)	J..G..Z	7)	Q..J..W
8)	B..Z..B	8)	K..3..8	8)	S..C..6	8)	B..E..3	8)	K..H..1	8)	R..K..X
9)	C..1..C	9)	L..A..A	9)	T..D..7	9)	C..F..4	9)	L..J..2	9)	S..L..Y
10)	D..2..D	10)	M..B..B	10)	U..E..8	10)	D..G..5	10)	M..K..3	10)	T..M..Z
11)	E..3..E	11)	N..C..C	11)	V..F..A	11)	E..H..6	11)	N..L..4	11)	U..N..1
12)	F..A..F	12)	O..D..D	12)	W..G..B	12)	F..J..7	12)	O..M..5	12)	V..O..2
13)	G..B..G	13)	P..E..E	13)	X..H..C	13)	G..K..8	13)	P..N..6	13)	W..P..3
14)	H..C..H	14)	Q..F..F	14)	A..J..D	14)	H..L..A	14)	Q..O..7	14)	X..Q..4
15)	J..D..J	15)	R..G..G	15)	B..K..E	15)	J..M..B	15)	R..P..8	15)	A..R..5
16)	K..E..K	16)	S..H..H	16)	C..L..F	16)	K..N..C	16)	S..Q..A	16)	B..S..6
17)	L..F..L	17)	T..J..J	17)	D..M..G	17)	L..O..D	17)	T..R..B	17)	C..T..7
18)	M..G..M	18)	U..K..K	18)	E..N..H	18)	M..P..E	18)	U..S..C	18)	D..U..8
19)	N..H..N	19)	V..L..L	19)	F..O..J	19)	N..Q..F	19)	V..T..D	19)	E..V..A
20)	O..J..O	20)	W..M..M	20)	G..P..K	20)	O..R..G	20)	W..U..E	20)	F..W..B
21)	P..K..P	21)	X..N..N	21)	H..Q..L	21)	P..S..H	21)	X..V..F	21)	G..X..C
22)	Q..L..Q	22)	A..O..O	22)	J..R..M	22)	Q..T..J	22)	A..W..G	22)	H..Y..D
23)	R..M..R	23)	B..P..P	23)	K..S..N	23)	R..U..K	23)	B..X..H	23)	J..Z..E
24)	S..N..S	24)	C..Q..Q	24)	L..T..O	24)	S..V..L	24)	C..Y..J	24)	K..1..F
25)	T..O..T	25)	D..R..R	25)	M..U..P	25)	T..W..M	25)	D..Z..K	25)	L..2..G
26)	U..P..U	26)	E..S..S	26)	N..V..Q	26)	U..X..N	26)	E..1..L	26)	M..3..H
27)	V..Q..V	27)	F..T..T	27)	O..W..R	27)	V..Y..O	27)	F..2..M	27)	N..A..J
28)	W..R..W	28)	G..U..U	28)	P..X..S	28)	W..Z..P	28)	G..3..N	28)	O..B..K
29)	X..S..X	29)	H..V..V	29)	Q..Y..T	29)	X..1..Q	29)	H..A..O	29)	P..C..L
30)	A..T..Y	30)	J..W..W	30)	R..Z..U	30)	A..2..R	30)	J..B..P	30)	Q..D..M
31)	B..U..Z	31)	K..X..X			31)	B..3..S			31)	R..E..N

CODES: P-PHYSICAL BIORHYTHM CURVE, E-EMOTIONAL BIORHYTHM CURVE, I-INTELLECTUAL BIORHYTHM CURVE

...JANUARY..

Day	P	E	I
1)	S	F	O
2)	T	G	P
3)	U	H	Q
4)	V	J	R
5)	W	K	S
6)	X	L	T
7)	A	M	U
8)	B	N	V
9)	C	O	W
10)	D	P	X
11)	E	Q	Y
12)	F	R	Z
13)	G	S	1
14)	H	T	2
15)	J	U	3
16)	K	V	4
17)	L	W	5
18)	M	X	6
19)	N	Y	7
20)	O	Z	8
21)	P	1	A
22)	Q	2	B
23)	R	3	C
24)	S	A	D
25)	T	B	E
26)	U	C	F
27)	V	D	G
28)	W	E	H
29)	X	F	J
30)	A	G	K
31)	B	H	L

..FEBRUARY..

Day	P	E	I
1)	C	J	M
2)	D	K	N
3)	E	L	O
4)	F	M	P
5)	G	N	Q
6)	H	O	R
7)	J	P	S
8)	K	Q	T
9)	L	R	U
10)	M	S	V
11)	N	T	W
12)	O	U	X
13)	P	V	Y
14)	Q	W	Z
15)	R	X	1
16)	S	Y	2
17)	T	Z	3
18)	U	1	4
19)	V	2	5
20)	W	3	6
21)	X	A	7
22)	A	B	8
23)	B	C	A
24)	C	D	B
25)	D	E	C
26)	E	F	D
27)	F	G	E
28)	G	H	F

...MARCH...

Day	P	E	I
1)	H	J	G
2)	J	K	H
3)	K	L	J
4)	L	M	K
5)	M	N	L
6)	N	O	M
7)	O	P	N
8)	P	Q	O
9)	Q	R	P
10)	R	S	Q
11)	S	T	R
12)	T	U	S
13)	U	V	T
14)	V	W	U
15)	W	X	V
16)	X	Y	W
17)	A	Z	X
18)	B	1	Y
19)	C	2	Z
20)	D	3	1
21)	E	A	2
22)	F	B	3
23)	G	C	4
24)	H	D	5
25)	J	E	6
26)	K	F	7
27)	L	G	8
28)	M	H	A
29)	N	J	B
30)	O	K	C
31)	P	L	D

...APRIL...

Day	P	E	I
1)	Q	M	E
2)	R	N	F
3)	S	O	G
4)	T	P	H
5)	U	Q	J
6)	V	R	K
7)	W	S	L
8)	X	T	M
9)	A	U	N
10)	B	V	O
11)	C	W	P
12)	D	X	Q
13)	E	Y	R
14)	F	Z	S
15)	G	1	T
16)	H	2	U
17)	J	3	V
18)	K	A	W
19)	L	B	X
20)	M	C	Y
21)	N	D	Z
22)	O	E	1
23)	P	F	2
24)	Q	G	3
25)	R	H	4
26)	S	J	5
27)	T	K	6
28)	U	L	7
29)	V	M	8
30)	W	N	A

....MAY....

Day	P	E	I
1)	X	O	B
2)	A	P	C
3)	B	Q	D
4)	C	R	E
5)	D	S	F
6)	E	T	G
7)	F	U	H
8)	G	V	J
9)	H	W	K
10)	J	X	L
11)	K	Y	M
12)	L	Z	N
13)	M	1	O
14)	N	2	P
15)	O	3	Q
16)	P	A	R
17)	Q	B	S
18)	R	C	T
19)	S	D	U
20)	T	E	V
21)	U	F	W
22)	V	G	X
23)	W	H	Y
24)	X	J	Z
25)	A	K	1
26)	B	L	2
27)	C	M	3
28)	D	N	4
29)	E	O	5
30)	F	P	6
31)	G	Q	7

....JUNE....

Day	P	E	I
1)	H	R	8
2)	J	S	A
3)	K	T	B
4)	L	U	C
5)	M	V	D
6)	N	W	E
7)	O	X	F
8)	P	Y	G
9)	Q	Z	H
10)	R	1	J
11)	S	2	K
12)	T	3	L
13)	U	A	M
14)	V	B	N
15)	W	C	O
16)	X	D	P
17)	A	E	Q
18)	B	F	R
19)	C	G	S
20)	D	H	T
21)	E	J	U
22)	F	K	V
23)	G	L	W
24)	H	M	X
25)	J	N	Y
26)	K	O	Z
27)	L	P	1
28)	M	Q	2
29)	N	R	3
30)	O	S	4

....JULY....

Day	P	E	I
1)	P	T	5
2)	Q	U	6
3)	R	V	7
4)	S	W	8
5)	T	X	A
6)	U	Y	B
7)	V	Z	C
8)	W	1	D
9)	X	2	E
10)	A	3	F
11)	B	A	G
12)	C	B	H
13)	D	C	J
14)	E	D	K
15)	F	E	L
16)	G	F	M
17)	H	G	N
18)	J	H	O
19)	K	J	P
20)	L	K	Q
21)	M	L	R
22)	N	M	S
23)	O	N	T
24)	P	O	U
25)	Q	P	V
26)	R	Q	W
27)	S	R	X
28)	T	S	Y
29)	U	T	Z
30)	V	U	1
31)	W	V	2

...AUGUST...

Day	P	E	I
1)	X	W	3
2)	A	X	4
3)	B	Y	5
4)	C	Z	6
5)	D	1	7
6)	E	2	8
7)	F	3	A
8)	G	A	B
9)	H	B	C
10)	J	C	D
11)	K	D	E
12)	L	E	F
13)	M	F	G
14)	N	G	H
15)	O	H	J
16)	P	J	K
17)	Q	K	L
18)	R	L	M
19)	S	M	N
20)	T	N	O
21)	U	O	P
22)	V	P	Q
23)	W	Q	R
24)	X	R	S
25)	A	S	T
26)	B	T	U
27)	C	U	V
28)	D	V	W
29)	E	W	X
30)	F	X	Y
31)	G	Y	Z

.SEPTEMBER.

Day	P	E	I
1)	H	Z	1
2)	J	1	2
3)	K	2	3
4)	L	3	4
5)	M	A	5
6)	N	B	6
7)	O	C	7
8)	P	D	8
9)	Q	E	A
10)	R	F	B
11)	S	G	C
12)	T	H	D
13)	U	J	E
14)	V	K	F
15)	W	L	G
16)	X	M	H
17)	A	N	J
18)	B	O	K
19)	C	P	L
20)	D	Q	M
21)	E	R	N
22)	F	S	O
23)	G	T	P
24)	H	U	Q
25)	J	V	R
26)	K	W	S
27)	L	X	T
28)	M	Y	U
29)	N	Z	V
30)	O	1	W

..OCTOBER...

Day	P	E	I
1)	P	2	X
2)	Q	3	Y
3)	R	A	Z
4)	S	B	1
5)	T	C	2
6)	U	D	3
7)	V	E	4
8)	W	F	5
9)	X	G	6
10)	A	H	7
11)	B	J	8
12)	C	K	A
13)	D	L	B
14)	E	M	C
15)	F	N	D
16)	G	O	E
17)	H	P	F
18)	J	Q	G
19)	K	R	H
20)	L	S	J
21)	M	T	K
22)	N	U	L
23)	O	V	M
24)	P	W	N
25)	Q	X	O
26)	R	Y	P
27)	S	Z	Q
28)	T	1	R
29)	U	2	S
30)	V	3	T
31)	W	A	U

.NOVEMBER..

Day	P	E	I
1)	X	B	V
2)	A	C	W
3)	B	D	X
4)	C	E	Y
5)	D	F	Z
6)	E	G	1
7)	F	H	2
8)	G	J	3
9)	H	K	4
10)	J	L	5
11)	K	M	6
12)	L	N	7
13)	M	O	8
14)	N	P	A
15)	O	Q	B
16)	P	R	C
17)	Q	S	D
18)	R	T	E
19)	S	U	F
20)	T	V	G
21)	U	W	H
22)	V	X	J
23)	W	Y	K
24)	X	Z	L
25)	A	1	M
26)	B	2	N
27)	C	3	O
28)	D	A	P
29)	E	B	Q
30)	F	C	R

.DECEMBER..

Day	P	E	I
1)	G	D	S
2)	H	E	T
3)	J	F	U
4)	K	G	V
5)	L	H	W
6)	M	J	X
7)	N	K	Y
8)	O	L	Z
9)	P	M	1
10)	Q	N	2
11)	R	O	3
12)	S	P	4
13)	T	Q	5
14)	U	R	6
15)	V	S	7
16)	W	T	8
17)	X	U	A
18)	A	V	B
19)	B	W	C
20)	C	X	D
21)	D	Y	E
22)	E	Z	F
23)	F	1	G
24)	G	2	H
25)	H	3	J
26)	J	A	K
27)	K	B	L
28)	L	C	M
29)	M	D	N
30)	N	E	O
31)	O	F	P

CODES: P-PHYSICAL BIORHYTHM CURVE, E-EMOTIONAL BIORHYTHM CURVE, I-INTELLECTUAL BIORHYTHM CURVE

	...JANUARY.. P--E--I	..FEBRUARY.. P--E--I	...MARCH... P--E--I	...APRIL... P--E--I	....MAY.... P--E--I	...JUNE.... P--E--I
1)	P..G..Q	X..K..O	F..L..K	O..O..H	V..Q..E	F..T..C
2)	Q..H..R	A..L..P	G..M..L	P..P..J	W..R..F	G..U..D
3)	R..J..S	B..M..Q	H..N..M	Q..Q..K	X..S..G	H..V..E
4)	S..K..T	C..N..R	J..O..N	R..R..L	A..T..H	J..W..F
5)	T..L..U	D..O..S	K..P..O	S..S..M	B..U..J	K..X..G
6)	U..M..V	E..P..T	L..Q..P	T..T..N	C..V..K	L..Y..H
7)	V..N..W	F..Q..U	M..R..Q	U..U..O	D..W..L	M..Z..J
8)	W..O..X	G..R..V	N..S..R	V..V..P	E..X..M	N..1..K
9)	X..P..Y	H..S..W	O..T..S	W..W..Q	F..Y..N	O..2..L
10)	A..Q..Z	J..T..X	P..U..T	X..X..R	G..Z..O	P..3..M
11)	B..R..1	K..U..Y	Q..V..U	A..Y..S	H..1..P	Q..A..N
12)	C..S..2	L..V..Z	R..W..V	B..Z..T	J..2..Q	R..B..O
13)	D..T..3	M..W..1	S..X..W	C..1..U	K..3..R	S..C..P
14)	E..U..4	N..X..2	T..Y..X	D..2..V	L..A..S	T..D..Q
15)	F..V..5	O..Y..3	U..Z..Y	E..3..W	M..B..T	U..E..R
16)	G..W..6	P..Z..4	V..1..Z	F..A..X	N..C..U	V..F..S
17)	H..X..7	Q..1..5	W..2..1	G..B..Y	O..D..V	W..G..T
18)	J..Y..8	R..2..6	X..3..2	H..C..Z	P..E..W	X..H..U
19)	K..Z..A	S..3..7	A..A..3	J..D..1	Q..F..X	A..J..V
20)	L..1..B	T..A..8	B..B..4	K..E..2	R..G..Y	B..K..W
21)	M..2..C	U..B..A	C..C..5	L..F..3	S..H..Z	C..L..X
22)	N..3..D	V..C..B	D..D..6	M..G..4	T..J..1	D..M..Y
23)	O..A..E	W..D..C	E..E..7	N..H..5	U..K..2	E..N..Z
24)	P..B..F	X..E..D	F..F..8	O..J..6	V..L..3	F..O..1
25)	Q..C..G	A..F..E	G..G..A	P..K..7	W..M..4	G..P..2
26)	R..D..H	B..G..F	H..H..B	Q..L..8	X..N..5	H..Q..3
27)	S..E..J	C..H..G	J..J..C	R..M..A	A..O..6	J..R..4
28)	T..F..K	D..J..H	K..K..D	S..N..B	B..P..7	K..S..5
29)	U..G..L	E..K..J	L..L..E	T..O..C	C..Q..8	L..T..6
30)	V..H..M		M..M..F	U..P..D	D..R..A	M..U..7
31)	W..J..N		N..N..G		E..S..B	

	....JULY.... P--E--I	...AUGUST... P--E--I	.SEPTEMBER. P--E--I	..OCTOBER... P--E--I	..NOVEMBER.. P--E--I	..DECEMBER.. P--E--I
1)	N..V..8	V..Y..6	F..2..4	N..A..1	V..D..Y	E..F..V
2)	O..W..A	W..Z..7	G..3..5	O..B..2	W..E..Z	F..G..W
3)	P..X..B	X..1..8	H..A..6	P..C..3	X..F..1	G..H..X
4)	Q..Y..C	A..2..A	J..B..7	Q..D..4	A..G..2	H..J..Y
5)	R..Z..D	B..3..B	K..C..8	R..E..5	B..H..3	J..K..Z
6)	S..1..E	C..A..C	L..D..A	S..F..6	C..J..4	K..L..1
7)	T..2..F	D..B..D	M..E..B	T..G..7	D..K..5	L..M..2
8)	U..3..G	E..C..E	N..F..C	U..H..8	E..L..6	M..N..3
9)	V..A..H	F..D..F	O..G..D	V..J..A	F..M..7	N..O..4
10)	W..B..J	G..E..G	P..H..E	W..K..B	G..N..8	O..P..5
11)	X..C..K	H..F..H	Q..J..F	X..L..C	H..O..A	P..Q..6
12)	A..D..L	J..G..J	R..K..G	A..M..D	J..P..B	Q..R..7
13)	B..E..M	K..H..K	S..L..H	B..N..E	K..Q..C	R..S..8
14)	C..F..N	L..J..L	T..M..J	C..O..F	L..R..D	S..T..A
15)	D..G..O	M..K..M	U..N..K	D..P..G	M..S..E	T..U..B
16)	E..H..P	N..L..N	V..O..L	E..Q..H	N..T..F	U..V..C
17)	F..J..Q	O..M..O	W..P..M	F..R..J	O..U..G	V..W..D
18)	G..K..R	P..N..P	X..Q..N	G..S..K	P..V..H	W..X..E
19)	H..L..S	Q..O..Q	A..R..O	H..T..L	Q..W..J	X..Y..F
20)	J..M..T	R..P..R	B..S..P	J..U..M	R..X..K	A..Z..G
21)	K..N..U	S..Q..S	C..T..Q	K..V..N	S..Y..L	B..1..H
22)	L..O..V	T..R..T	D..U..R	L..W..O	T..Z..M	C..2..J
23)	M..P..W	U..S..U	E..V..S	M..X..P	U..1..N	D..3..K
24)	N..Q..X	V..T..V	F..W..T	N..Y..Q	V..2..O	E..A..L
25)	O..R..Y	W..U..W	G..X..U	O..Z..R	W..3..P	F..B..M
26)	P..S..Z	X..V..X	H..Y..V	P..1..S	X..A..Q	G..C..N
27)	Q..T..1	A..W..Y	J..Z..W	Q..2..T	A..B..R	H..D..O
28)	R..U..2	B..X..Z	K..1..X	R..3..U	B..C..S	J..E..P
29)	S..V..3	C..Y..1	L..2..Y	S..A..V	C..D..T	K..F..Q
30)	T..W..4	D..Z..2	M..3..Z	T..B..W	D..E..U	L..G..R
31)	U..X..5	E..1..3		U..C..X		M..H..S

CODES: P-PHYSICAL BIORHYTHM CURVE,E-EMOTIONAL BIORHYTHM CURVE,I-INTELLECTUAL BIORHYTHM CURVE

	...JANUARY..	..FEBRUARY..	...MARCH...	...APRIL...	....MAY....	....JUNE....
	P--E--I	P--E--I	P--E--I	P--E--I	P--E--I	P--E--I
1)	N..J..T	V..M..R	C..M..M	L..P..K	S..R..G	C..U..E
2)	O..K..U	W..N..S	D..N..N	M..Q..L	T..S..H	D..V..F
3)	P..L..V	X..O..T	E..O..O	N..R..M	U..T..J	E..W..G
4)	Q..M..W	A..P..U	F..P..P	O..S..N	V..U..K	F..X..H
5)	R..N..X	B..Q..V	G..Q..Q	P..T..O	W..V..L	G..Y..J
6)	S..O..Y	C..R..W	H..R..R	Q..U..P	X..W..M	H..Z..K
7)	T..P..Z	D..S..X	J..S..S	R..V..Q	A..X..N	J..1..L
8)	U..Q..1	E..T..Y	K..T..T	S..W..R	B..Y..O	K..2..M
9)	V..R..2	F..U..Z	L..U..U	T..X..S	C..Z..P	L..3..N
10)	W..S..3	G..V..1	M..V..V	U..Y..T	D..1..Q	M..A..O
11)	X..T..4	H..W..2	N..W..W	V..Z..U	E..2..R	N..B..P
12)	A..U..5	J..X..3	O..X..X	W..1..V	F..3..S	O..C..Q
13)	B..V..6	K..Y..4	P..Y..Y	X..2..W	G..A..T	P..D..R
14)	C..W..7	L..Z..5	Q..Z..Z	A..3..X	H..B..U	Q..E..S
15)	D..X..8	M..1..6	R..1..1	B..A..Y	J..C..V	R..F..T
16)	E..Y..A	N..2..7	S..2..2	C..B..Z	K..D..W	S..G..U
17)	F..Z..B	O..3..8	T..3..3	D..C..1	L..E..X	T..H..V
18)	G..1..C	P..A..A	U..A..4	E..D..2	M..F..Y	U..J..W
19)	H..2..D	Q..B..B	V..B..5	F..E..3	N..G..Z	V..K..X
20)	J..3..E	R..C..C	W..C..6	G..F..4	O..H..1	W..L..Y
21)	K..A..F	S..D..D	X..D..7	H..G..5	P..J..2	X..M..Z
22)	L..B..G	T..E..E	A..E..8	J..H..6	Q..K..3	A..N..1
23)	M..C..H	U..F..F	B..F..A	K..J..7	R..L..4	B..O..2
24)	N..D..J	V..G..G	C..G..B	L..K..8	S..M..5	C..P..3
25)	O..E..K	W..H..H	D..H..C	M..L..A	T..N..6	D..Q..4
26)	P..F..L	X..J..J	E..J..D	N..M..B	U..O..7	E..R..5
27)	Q..G..M	A..K..K	F..K..E	O..N..C	V..P..8	F..S..6
28)	R..H..N	B..L..L	G..L..F	P..O..D	W..Q..A	G..T..7
29)	S..J..O		H..M..G	Q..P..E	X..R..B	H..U..8
30)	T..K..P		J..N..H	R..Q..F	A..S..C	J..V..A
31)	U..L..Q		K..O..J		B..T..D	

	....JULY....	...AUGUST...	..SEPTEMBER.	..OCTOBER...	..NOVEMBER..	..DECEMBER..
	P--E--I	P--E--I	P--E--I	P--E--I	P--E--I	P--E--I
1)	K..W..B	S..Z..8	C..3..6	K..B..3	S..E..1	B..G..X
2)	L..X..C	T..1..A	D..A..7	L..C..4	T..F..2	C..H..Y
3)	M..Y..D	U..2..B	E..B..8	M..D..5	U..G..3	D..J..Z
4)	N..Z..E	V..3..C	F..C..A	N..E..6	V..H..4	E..K..1
5)	O..1..F	W..A..D	G..D..B	O..F..7	W..J..5	F..L..2
6)	P..2..G	X..B..E	H..E..C	P..G..8	X..K..6	G..M..3
7)	Q..3..H	A..C..F	J..F..D	Q..H..A	A..L..7	H..N..4
8)	R..A..J	B..D..G	K..G..E	R..J..B	B..M..8	J..O..5
9)	S..B..K	C..E..H	L..H..F	S..K..C	C..N..A	K..P..6
10)	T..C..L	D..F..J	M..J..G	T..L..D	D..O..B	L..Q..7
11)	U..D..M	E..G..K	N..K..H	U..M..E	E..P..C	M..R..8
12)	V..E..N	F..H..L	O..L..J	V..N..F	F..Q..D	N..S..A
13)	W..F..O	G..J..M	P..M..K	W..O..G	G..R..E	O..T..B
14)	X..G..P	H..K..N	Q..N..L	X..P..H	H..S..F	P..U..C
15)	A..H..Q	J..L..O	R..O..M	A..Q..J	J..T..G	Q..V..D
16)	B..J..R	K..M..P	S..P..N	B..R..K	K..U..H	R..W..E
17)	C..K..S	L..N..Q	T..Q..O	C..S..L	L..V..J	S..X..F
18)	D..L..T	M..O..R	U..R..P	D..T..M	M..W..K	T..Y..G
19)	E..M..U	N..P..S	V..S..Q	E..U..N	N..X..L	U..Z..H
20)	F..N..V	O..Q..T	W..T..R	F..V..O	O..Y..M	V..1..J
21)	G..O..W	P..R..U	X..U..S	G..W..P	P..Z..N	W..2..K
22)	H..P..X	Q..S..V	A..V..T	H..X..Q	Q..1..O	X..3..L
23)	J..Q..Y	R..T..W	B..W..U	J..Y..R	R..2..P	A..A..M
24)	K..R..Z	S..U..X	C..X..V	K..Z..S	S..3..Q	B..B..N
25)	L..S..1	T..V..Y	D..Y..W	L..1..T	T..A..R	C..C..O
26)	M..T..2	U..W..Z	E..Z..X	M..2..U	U..B..S	D..D..P
27)	N..U..3	V..X..1	F..1..Y	N..3..V	V..C..T	E..E..Q
28)	O..V..4	W..Y..2	G..2..Z	O..A..W	W..D..U	F..F..R
29)	P..W..5	X..Z..3	H..3..1	P..B..X	X..E..V	G..G..S
30)	Q..X..6	A..1..4	J..A..2	Q..C..Y	A..F..W	H..H..T
31)	R..Y..7	B..2..5		R..D..Z		J..J..U

CODES: P-PHYSICAL BIORHYTHM CURVE, E-EMOTIONAL BIORHYTHM CURVE, I-INTELLECTUAL BIORHYTHM CURVE

```
...JANUARY..      ..FEBRUARY..     ...MARCH...      ...APRIL...      ....MAY....      ....JUNE....

    P--E--I          P--E--I          P--E--I          P--E--I          P--E--I          P--E--I

1)  K..K..V       1)  S..N..T       1)  X..N..O       1)  H..Q..M       1)  P..S..J       1)  X..V..G
2)  L..L..W       2)  T..O..U       2)  A..O..P       2)  J..R..N       2)  Q..T..K       2)  A..W..H
3)  M..M..X       3)  U..P..V       3)  B..P..Q       3)  K..S..O       3)  R..U..L       3)  B..X..J
4)  N..N..Y       4)  V..Q..W       4)  C..Q..R       4)  L..T..P       4)  S..V..M       4)  C..Y..K
5)  O..O..Z       5)  W..R..X       5)  D..R..S       5)  M..U..Q       5)  T..W..N       5)  D..Z..L
6)  P..P..1       6)  X..S..Y       6)  E..S..T       6)  N..V..R       6)  U..X..O       6)  E..1..M
7)  Q..Q..2       7)  A..T..Z       7)  F..T..U       7)  O..W..S       7)  V..Y..P       7)  F..2..N
8)  R..R..3       8)  B..U..1       8)  G..U..V       8)  P..X..T       8)  W..Z..Q       8)  G..3..O
9)  S..S..4       9)  C..V..2       9)  H..V..W       9)  Q..Y..U       9)  X..1..R       9)  H..A..P
10) T..T..5       10) D..W..3       10) J..W..X       10) R..Z..V       10) A..2..S       10) J..B..Q
11) U..U..6       11) E..X..4       11) K..X..Y       11) S..1..W       11) B..3..T       11) K..C..R
12) V..V..7       12) F..Y..5       12) L..Y..Z       12) T..2..X       12) C..A..U       12) L..D..S
13) W..W..8       13) G..Z..6       13) M..Z..1       13) U..3..Y       13) D..B..V       13) M..E..T
14) X..X..A       14) H..1..7       14) N..1..2       14) V..A..Z       14) E..C..W       14) N..F..U
15) A..Y..B       15) J..2..8       15) O..2..3       15) W..B..1       15) F..D..X       15) O..G..V
16) B..Z..C       16) K..3..A       16) P..3..4       16) X..C..2       16) G..E..Y       16) P..H..W
17) C..1..D       17) L..A..B       17) Q..A..5       17) A..D..3       17) H..F..Z       17) Q..J..X
18) D..2..E       18) M..B..C       18) R..B..6       18) B..E..4       18) J..G..1       18) R..K..Y
19) E..3..F       19) N..C..D       19) S..C..7       19) C..F..5       19) K..H..2       19) S..L..Z
20) F..A..G       20) O..D..E       20) T..D..8       20) D..G..6       20) L..J..3       20) T..M..1
21) G..B..H       21) P..E..F       21) U..E..A       21) E..H..7       21) M..K..4       21) U..N..2
22) H..C..J       22) Q..F..G       22) V..F..B       22) F..J..8       22) N..L..5       22) V..O..3
23) J..D..K       23) R..G..H       23) W..G..C       23) G..K..A       23) O..M..6       23) W..P..4
24) K..E..L       24) S..H..J       24) X..H..D       24) H..L..B       24) P..N..7       24) X..Q..5
25) L..F..M       25) T..J..K       25) A..J..E       25) J..M..C       25) Q..O..8       25) A..R..6
26) M..G..N       26) U..K..L       26) B..K..F       26) K..N..D       26) R..P..A       26) B..S..7
27) N..H..O       27) V..L..M       27) C..L..G       27) L..O..E       27) S..Q..B       27) C..T..8
28) O..J..P       28) W..M..N       28) D..M..H       28) M..P..F       28) T..R..C       28) D..U..A
29) P..K..Q                         29) E..N..J       29) N..Q..G       29) U..S..D       29) E..V..B
30) Q..L..R                         30) F..O..K       30) O..R..H       30) V..T..E       30) F..W..C
31) R..M..S                         31) G..P..L                         31) W..U..F
```

```
....JULY....      ...AUGUST...     .SEPTEMBER.      ..OCTOBER...     ..NOVEMBER..     ..DECEMBER..

    P--E--I          P--E--I          P--E--I          P--E--I          P--E--I          P--E--I

1)  G..X..D       1)  P..1..B       1)  X..A..8       1)  G..C..5       1)  P..F..3       1)  W..H..Z
2)  H..Y..E       2)  Q..2..C       2)  A..B..A       2)  H..D..6       2)  Q..G..4       2)  X..J..1
3)  J..Z..F       3)  R..3..D       3)  B..C..B       3)  J..E..7       3)  R..H..5       3)  A..K..2
4)  K..1..G       4)  S..A..E       4)  C..D..C       4)  K..F..8       4)  S..J..6       4)  B..L..3
5)  L..2..H       5)  T..B..F       5)  D..E..D       5)  L..G..A       5)  T..K..7       5)  C..M..4
6)  M..3..J       6)  U..C..G       6)  E..F..E       6)  M..H..B       6)  U..L..8       6)  D..N..5
7)  N..A..K       7)  V..D..H       7)  F..G..F       7)  N..J..C       7)  V..M..A       7)  E..O..6
8)  O..B..L       8)  W..E..J       8)  G..H..G       8)  O..K..D       8)  W..N..B       8)  F..P..7
9)  P..C..M       9)  X..F..K       9)  H..J..H       9)  P..L..E       9)  X..O..C       9)  G..Q..8
10) Q..D..N       10) A..G..L       10) J..K..J       10) Q..M..F       10) A..P..D       10) H..R..A
11) R..E..O       11) B..H..M       11) K..L..K       11) R..N..G       11) B..Q..E       11) J..S..B
12) S..F..P       12) C..J..N       12) L..M..L       12) S..O..H       12) C..R..F       12) K..T..C
13) T..G..Q       13) D..K..O       13) M..N..M       13) T..P..J       13) D..S..G       13) L..U..D
14) U..H..R       14) E..L..P       14) N..O..N       14) U..Q..K       14) E..T..H       14) M..V..E
15) V..J..S       15) F..M..Q       15) O..P..O       15) V..R..L       15) F..U..J       15) N..W..F
16) W..K..T       16) G..N..R       16) P..Q..P       16) W..S..M       16) G..V..K       16) O..X..G
17) X..L..U       17) H..O..S       17) Q..R..Q       17) X..T..N       17) H..W..L       17) P..Y..H
18) A..M..V       18) J..P..T       18) R..S..R       18) A..U..O       18) J..X..M       18) Q..Z..J
19) B..N..W       19) K..Q..U       19) S..T..S       19) B..V..P       19) K..Y..N       19) R..1..K
20) C..O..X       20) L..R..V       20) T..U..T       20) C..W..Q       20) L..Z..O       20) S..2..L
21) D..P..Y       21) M..S..W       21) U..V..U       21) D..X..R       21) M..1..P       21) T..3..M
22) E..Q..Z       22) N..T..X       22) V..W..V       22) E..Y..S       22) N..2..Q       22) U..A..N
23) F..R..1       23) O..U..Y       23) W..X..W       23) F..Z..T       23) O..3..R       23) V..B..O
24) G..S..2       24) P..V..Z       24) X..Y..X       24) G..1..U       24) P..A..S       24) W..C..P
25) H..T..3       25) Q..W..1       25) A..Z..Y       25) H..2..V       25) Q..B..T       25) X..D..Q
26) J..U..4       26) R..X..2       26) B..1..Z       26) J..3..W       26) R..C..U       26) A..E..R
27) K..V..5       27) S..Y..3       27) C..2..1       27) K..A..X       27) S..D..V       27) B..F..S
28) L..W..6       28) T..Z..4       28) D..3..2       28) L..B..Y       28) T..E..W       28) C..G..T
29) M..X..7       29) U..1..5       29) E..A..3       29) M..C..Z       29) U..F..X       29) D..H..U
30) N..Y..8       30) V..2..6       30) F..B..4       30) N..D..1       30) V..G..Y       30) E..J..V
31) O..Z..A       31) W..3..7                         31) O..E..2                         31) F..K..W
```

CODES: P-PHYSICAL BIORHYTHM CURVE, E-EMOTIONAL BIORHYTHM CURVE, I-INTELLECTUAL BIORHYTHM CURVE

	JANUARY P--E--I		FEBRUARY P--E--I		MARCH P--E--I		APRIL P--E--I		MAY P--E--I		JUNE P--E--I
1)	G..L..X	1)	P..O..V	1)	U..O..Q	1)	E..R..O	1)	M..T..L	1)	U..W..J
2)	H..M..Y	2)	Q..P..W	2)	V..P..R	2)	F..S..P	2)	N..U..M	2)	V..X..K
3)	J..N..Z	3)	R..Q..X	3)	W..Q..S	3)	G..T..Q	3)	O..V..N	3)	W..Y..L
4)	K..O..1	4)	S..R..Y	4)	X..R..T	4)	H..U..R	4)	P..W..O	4)	X..Z..M
5)	L..P..2	5)	T..S..Z	5)	A..S..U	5)	J..V..S	5)	Q..X..P	5)	A..1..N
6)	M..Q..3	6)	U..T..1	6)	B..T..V	6)	K..W..T	6)	R..Y..Q	6)	B..2..O
7)	N..R..4	7)	V..U..2	7)	C..U..W	7)	L..X..U	7)	S..Z..R	7)	C..3..P
8)	O..S..5	8)	W..V..3	8)	D..V..X	8)	M..Y..V	8)	T..1..S	8)	D..A..Q
9)	P..T..6	9)	X..W..4	9)	E..W..Y	9)	N..Z..W	9)	U..2..T	9)	E..B..R
10)	Q..U..7	10)	A..X..5	10)	F..X..Z	10)	O..1..X	10)	V..3..U	10)	F..C..S
11)	R..V..8	11)	B..Y..6	11)	G..Y..1	11)	P..2..Y	11)	W..A..V	11)	G..D..T
12)	S..W..A	12)	C..Z..7	12)	H..Z..2	12)	Q..3..Z	12)	X..B..W	12)	H..E..U
13)	T..X..B	13)	D..1..8	13)	J..1..3	13)	R..A..1	13)	A..C..X	13)	J..F..V
14)	U..Y..C	14)	E..2..A	14)	K..2..4	14)	S..B..2	14)	B..D..Y	14)	K..G..W
15)	V..Z..D	15)	F..3..B	15)	L..3..5	15)	T..C..3	15)	C..E..Z	15)	L..H..X
16)	W..1..E	16)	G..A..C	16)	M..A..6	16)	U..D..4	16)	D..F..1	16)	M..J..Y
17)	X..2..F	17)	H..B..D	17)	N..B..7	17)	V..E..5	17)	E..G..2	17)	N..K..Z
18)	A..3..G	18)	J..C..E	18)	O..C..8	18)	W..F..6	18)	F..H..3	18)	O..L..1
19)	B..A..H	19)	K..D..F	19)	P..D..A	19)	X..G..7	19)	G..J..4	19)	P..M..2
20)	C..B..J	20)	L..E..G	20)	Q..E..B	20)	A..H..8	20)	H..K..5	20)	Q..N..3
21)	D..C..K	21)	M..F..H	21)	R..F..C	21)	B..J..A	21)	J..L..6	21)	R..O..4
22)	E..D..L	22)	N..G..J	22)	S..G..D	22)	C..K..B	22)	K..M..7	22)	S..P..5
23)	F..E..M	23)	O..H..K	23)	T..H..E	23)	D..L..C	23)	L..N..8	23)	T..Q..6
24)	G..F..N	24)	P..J..L	24)	U..J..F	24)	E..M..D	24)	M..O..A	24)	U..R..7
25)	H..G..O	25)	Q..K..M	25)	V..K..G	25)	F..N..E	25)	N..P..B	25)	V..S..8
26)	J..H..P	26)	R..L..N	26)	W..L..H	26)	G..O..F	26)	O..Q..C	26)	W..T..A
27)	K..J..Q	27)	S..M..O	27)	X..M..J	27)	H..P..G	27)	P..R..D	27)	X..U..B
28)	L..K..R	28)	T..N..P	28)	A..N..K	28)	J..Q..H	28)	Q..S..E	28)	A..V..C
29)	M..L..S			29)	B..O..L	29)	K..R..J	29)	R..T..F	29)	B..W..D
30)	N..M..T			30)	C..P..M	30)	L..S..K	30)	S..U..G	30)	C..X..E
31)	O..N..U			31)	D..Q..N			31)	T..V..H		

	JULY P--E--I		AUGUST P--E--I		SEPTEMBER P--E--I		OCTOBER P--E--I		NOVEMBER P--E--I		DECEMBER P--E--I
1)	D..Y..F	1)	M..2..D	1)	U..B..B	1)	D..D..7	1)	M..G..5	1)	T..J..2
2)	E..Z..G	2)	N..3..E	2)	V..C..C	2)	E..E..8	2)	N..H..6	2)	U..K..3
3)	F..1..H	3)	O..A..F	3)	W..D..D	3)	F..F..A	3)	O..J..7	3)	V..L..4
4)	G..2..J	4)	P..B..G	4)	X..E..E	4)	G..G..B	4)	P..K..8	4)	W..M..5
5)	H..3..K	5)	Q..C..H	5)	A..F..F	5)	H..H..C	5)	Q..L..A	5)	X..N..6
6)	J..A..L	6)	R..D..J	6)	B..G..G	6)	J..J..D	6)	R..M..B	6)	A..O..7
7)	K..B..M	7)	S..E..K	7)	C..H..H	7)	K..K..E	7)	S..N..C	7)	B..P..8
8)	L..C..N	8)	T..F..L	8)	D..J..J	8)	L..L..F	8)	T..O..D	8)	C..Q..A
9)	M..D..O	9)	U..G..M	9)	E..K..K	9)	M..M..G	9)	U..P..E	9)	D..R..B
10)	N..E..P	10)	V..H..N	10)	F..L..L	10)	N..N..H	10)	V..Q..F	10)	E..S..C
11)	O..F..Q	11)	W..J..O	11)	G..M..M	11)	O..O..J	11)	W..R..G	11)	F..T..D
12)	P..G..R	12)	X..K..P	12)	H..N..N	12)	P..P..K	12)	X..S..H	12)	G..U..E
13)	Q..H..S	13)	A..L..Q	13)	J..O..O	13)	Q..Q..L	13)	A..T..J	13)	H..V..F
14)	R..J..T	14)	B..M..R	14)	K..P..P	14)	R..R..M	14)	B..U..K	14)	J..W..G
15)	S..K..U	15)	C..N..S	15)	L..Q..Q	15)	S..S..N	15)	C..V..L	15)	K..X..H
16)	T..L..V	16)	D..O..T	16)	M..R..R	16)	T..T..O	16)	D..W..M	16)	L..Y..J
17)	U..M..W	17)	E..P..U	17)	N..S..S	17)	U..U..P	17)	E..X..N	17)	M..Z..K
18)	V..N..X	18)	F..Q..V	18)	O..T..T	18)	V..V..Q	18)	F..Y..O	18)	N..1..L
19)	W..O..Y	19)	G..R..W	19)	P..U..U	19)	W..W..R	19)	G..Z..P	19)	O..2..M
20)	X..P..Z	20)	H..S..X	20)	Q..V..V	20)	X..X..S	20)	H..1..Q	20)	P..3..N
21)	A..Q..1	21)	J..T..Y	21)	R..W..W	21)	A..Y..T	21)	J..2..R	21)	Q..A..O
22)	B..R..2	22)	K..U..Z	22)	S..X..X	22)	B..Z..U	22)	K..3..S	22)	R..B..P
23)	C..S..3	23)	L..V..1	23)	T..Y..Y	23)	C..1..V	23)	L..A..T	23)	S..C..Q
24)	D..T..4	24)	M..W..2	24)	U..Z..Z	24)	D..2..W	24)	M..B..U	24)	T..D..R
25)	E..U..5	25)	N..X..3	25)	V..1..1	25)	E..3..X	25)	N..C..V	25)	U..E..S
26)	F..V..6	26)	O..Y..4	26)	W..2..2	26)	F..A..Y	26)	O..D..W	26)	V..F..T
27)	G..W..7	27)	P..Z..5	27)	X..3..3	27)	G..B..Z	27)	P..E..X	27)	W..G..U
28)	H..X..8	28)	Q..1..6	28)	A..A..4	28)	H..C..1	28)	Q..F..Y	28)	X..H..V
29)	J..Y..A	29)	R..2..7	29)	B..B..5	29)	J..D..2	29)	R..G..Z	29)	A..J..W
30)	K..Z..B	30)	S..3..8	30)	C..C..6	30)	K..E..3	30)	S..H..1	30)	B..K..X
31)	L..1..C	31)	T..A..A			31)	L..F..4			31)	C..L..Y

CODES: P-PHYSICAL BIORHYTHM CURVE, E-EMOTIONAL BIORHYTHM CURVE, I-INTELLECTUAL BIORHYTHM CURVE

	...JANUARY..	..FEBRUARY..	....MARCH...	...APRIL...	....MAY....	....JUNE....
	P--E--I	P--E--I	P--E--I	P--E--I	P--E--I	P--E--I
1)	D..M..Z	M..P..X	S..Q..T	C..T..R	K..V..O	S..Y..M
2)	E..N..1	N..Q..Y	T..R..U	D..U..S	L..W..P	T..Z..N
3)	F..O..2	O..R..Z	U..S..V	E..V..T	M..X..Q	U..1..O
4)	G..P..3	P..S..1	V..T..W	F..W..U	N..Y..R	V..2..P
5)	H..Q..4	Q..T..2	W..U..X	G..X..V	O..Z..S	W..3..Q
6)	J..R..5	R..U..3	X..V..Y	H..Y..W	P..1..T	X..A..R
7)	K..S..6	S..V..4	A..W..Z	J..Z..X	Q..2..U	A..B..S
8)	L..T..7	T..W..5	B..X..1	K..1..Y	R..3..V	B..C..T
9)	M..U..8	U..X..6	C..Y..2	L..2..Z	S..A..W	C..D..U
10)	N..V..A	V..Y..7	D..Z..3	M..3..1	T..B..X	D..E..V
11)	O..W..B	W..Z..8	E..1..4	N..A..2	U..C..Y	E..F..W
12)	P..X..C	X..1..A	F..2..5	O..B..3	V..D..Z	F..G..X
13)	Q..Y..D	A..2..B	G..3..6	P..C..4	W..E..1	G..H..Y
14)	R..Z..E	B..3..C	H..A..7	Q..D..5	X..F..2	H..J..Z
15)	S..1..F	C..A..D	J..B..8	R..E..6	A..G..3	J..K..1
16)	T..2..G	D..B..E	K..C..A	S..F..7	B..H..4	K..L..2
17)	U..3..H	E..C..F	L..D..B	T..G..8	C..J..5	L..M..3
18)	V..A..J	F..D..G	M..E..C	U..H..A	D..K..6	M..N..4
19)	W..B..K	G..E..H	N..F..D	V..J..B	E..L..7	N..O..5
20)	X..C..L	H..F..J	O..G..E	W..K..C	F..M..8	O..P..6
21)	A..D..M	J..G..K	P..H..F	X..L..D	G..N..A	P..Q..7
22)	B..E..N	K..H..L	Q..J..G	A..M..E	H..O..B	Q..R..8
23)	C..F..O	L..J..M	R..K..H	B..N..F	J..P..C	R..S..A
24)	D..G..P	M..K..N	S..L..J	C..O..G	K..Q..D	S..T..B
25)	E..H..Q	N..L..O	T..M..K	D..P..H	L..R..E	T..U..C
26)	F..J..R	O..M..P	U..N..L	E..Q..J	M..S..F	U..V..D
27)	G..K..S	P..N..Q	V..O..M	F..R..K	N..T..G	V..W..E
28)	H..L..T	Q..O..R	W..P..N	G..S..L	O..U..H	W..X..F
29)	J..M..U	R..P..S	X..Q..O	H..T..M	P..V..J	X..Y..G
30)	K..N..V		A..R..P	J..U..N	Q..W..K	A..Z..H
31)	L..O..W		B..S..Q		R..X..L	

	....JULY....	...AUGUST...	.SEPTEMBER.	..OCTOBER...	..NOVEMBER..	..DECEMBER..
	P--E--I	P--E--I	P--E--I	P--E--I	P--E--I	P--E--I
1)	B..1..J	K..A..G	S..D..E	B..F..B	K..J..8	R..L..5
2)	C..2..K	L..B..H	T..E..F	C..G..C	L..K..A	S..M..6
3)	D..3..L	M..C..J	U..F..G	D..H..D	M..L..B	T..N..7
4)	E..A..M	N..D..K	V..G..H	E..J..E	N..M..C	U..O..8
5)	F..B..N	O..E..L	W..H..J	F..K..F	O..N..D	V..P..A
6)	G..C..O	P..F..M	X..J..K	G..L..G	P..O..E	W..Q..B
7)	H..D..P	Q..G..N	A..K..L	H..M..H	Q..P..F	X..R..C
8)	J..E..Q	R..H..O	B..L..M	J..N..J	R..Q..G	A..S..D
9)	K..F..R	S..J..P	C..M..N	K..O..K	S..R..H	B..T..E
10)	L..G..S	T..K..Q	D..N..O	L..P..L	T..S..J	C..U..F
11)	M..H..T	U..L..R	E..O..P	M..Q..M	U..T..K	D..V..G
12)	N..J..U	V..M..S	F..P..Q	N..R..N	V..U..L	E..W..H
13)	O..K..V	W..N..T	G..Q..R	O..S..O	W..V..M	F..X..J
14)	P..L..W	X..O..U	H..R..S	P..T..P	X..W..N	G..Y..K
15)	Q..M..X	A..P..V	J..S..T	Q..U..Q	A..X..O	H..Z..L
16)	R..N..Y	B..Q..W	K..T..U	R..V..R	B..Y..P	J..1..M
17)	S..O..Z	C..R..X	L..U..V	S..W..S	C..Z..Q	K..2..N
18)	T..P..1	D..S..Y	M..V..W	T..X..T	D..1..R	L..3..O
19)	U..Q..2	E..T..Z	N..W..X	U..Y..U	E..2..S	M..A..P
20)	V..R..3	F..U..1	O..X..Y	V..Z..V	F..3..T	N..B..Q
21)	W..S..4	G..V..2	P..Y..Z	W..1..W	G..A..U	O..C..R
22)	X..T..5	H..W..3	Q..Z..1	X..2..X	H..B..V	P..D..S
23)	A..U..6	J..X..4	R..1..2	A..3..Y	J..C..W	Q..E..T
24)	B..V..7	K..Y..5	S..2..3	B..A..Z	K..D..X	R..F..U
25)	C..W..8	L..Z..6	T..3..4	C..B..1	L..E..Y	S..G..V
26)	D..X..A	M..1..7	U..A..5	D..C..2	M..F..Z	T..H..W
27)	E..Y..B	N..2..8	V..B..6	E..D..3	N..G..1	U..J..X
28)	F..Z..C	O..3..A	W..C..7	F..E..4	O..H..2	V..K..Y
29)	G..1..D	P..A..B	X..D..8	G..F..5	P..J..3	W..L..Z
30)	H..2..E	Q..B..C	A..E..A	H..G..6	Q..K..4	X..M..1
31)	J..3..F	R..C..D		J..H..7		A..N..2

CODES: P-PHYSICAL BIORHYTHM CURVE,E-EMOTIONAL BIORHYTHM CURVE,I-INTELLECTUAL BIORHYTHM CURVE

Day	...JANUARY..	..FEBRUARY..	...MARCH...	...APRIL...	....MAY....	...JUNE...
	P--E--I	P--E--I	P--E--I	P--E--I	P--E--I	P--E--I
1)	B..O..3	K..R..1	P..R..V	X..U..T	G..W..Q	P..Z..O
2)	C..P..4	L..S..2	Q..S..W	A..V..U	H..X..R	Q..1..P
3)	D..Q..5	M..T..3	R..T..X	B..W..V	J..Y..S	R..2..Q
4)	E..R..6	N..U..4	S..U..Y	C..X..W	K..Z..T	S..3..R
5)	F..S..7	O..V..5	T..V..Z	D..Y..X	L..1..U	T..A..S
6)	G..T..8	P..W..6	U..W..1	E..Z..Y	M..2..V	U..B..T
7)	H..U..A	Q..X..7	V..X..2	F..1..Z	N..3..W	V..C..U
8)	J..V..B	R..Y..8	W..Y..3	G..2..1	O..A..X	W..D..V
9)	K..W..C	S..Z..A	X..Z..4	H..3..2	P..B..Y	X..E..W
10)	L..X..D	T..1..B	A..1..5	J..A..3	Q..C..Z	A..F..X
11)	M..Y..E	U..2..C	B..2..6	K..B..4	R..D..1	B..G..Y
12)	N..Z..F	V..3..D	C..3..7	L..C..5	S..E..2	C..H..Z
13)	O..1..G	W..A..E	D..A..8	M..D..6	T..F..3	D..J..1
14)	P..2..H	X..B..F	E..B..A	N..E..7	U..G..4	E..K..2
15)	Q..3..J	A..C..G	F..C..B	O..F..8	V..H..5	F..L..3
16)	R..A..K	B..D..H	G..D..C	P..G..A	W..J..6	G..M..4
17)	S..B..L	C..E..J	H..E..D	Q..H..B	X..K..7	H..N..5
18)	T..C..M	D..F..K	J..F..E	R..J..C	A..L..8	J..O..6
19)	U..D..N	E..G..L	K..G..F	S..K..D	B..M..A	K..P..7
20)	V..E..O	F..H..M	L..H..G	T..L..E	C..N..B	L..Q..8
21)	W..F..P	G..J..N	M..J..H	U..M..F	D..O..C	M..R..A
22)	X..G..Q	H..K..O	N..K..J	V..N..G	E..P..D	N..S..B
23)	A..H..R	J..L..P	O..L..K	W..O..H	F..Q..E	O..T..C
24)	B..J..S	K..M..Q	P..M..L	X..P..J	G..R..F	P..U..D
25)	C..K..T	L..N..R	Q..N..M	A..Q..K	H..S..G	Q..V..E
26)	D..L..U	M..O..S	R..O..N	B..R..L	J..T..H	R..W..F
27)	E..M..V	N..P..T	S..P..O	C..S..M	K..U..J	S..X..G
28)	F..N..W	O..Q..U	T..Q..P	D..T..N	L..V..K	T..Y..H
29)	G..O..X		U..R..Q	E..U..O	M..W..L	U..Z..J
30)	H..P..Y		V..S..R	F..V..P	N..X..M	V..1..K
31)	J..Q..Z		W..T..S		O..Y..N	

Day	....JULY....	...AUGUST...	..SEPTEMBER.	..OCTOBER...	.NOVEMBER..	.DECEMBER..
	P--E--I	P--E--I	P--E--I	P--E--I	P--E--I	P--E--I
1)	W..2..L	G..B..J	P..E..G	W..G..D	G..K..B	O..M..7
2)	X..3..M	H..C..K	Q..F..H	X..H..E	H..L..C	P..N..8
3)	A..A..N	J..D..L	R..G..J	A..J..F	J..M..D	Q..O..A
4)	B..B..O	K..E..M	S..H..K	B..K..G	K..N..E	R..P..B
5)	C..C..P	L..F..N	T..J..L	C..L..H	L..O..F	S..Q..C
6)	D..D..Q	M..G..O	U..K..M	D..M..J	M..P..G	T..R..D
7)	E..E..R	N..H..P	V..L..N	E..N..K	N..Q..H	U..S..E
8)	F..F..S	O..J..Q	W..M..O	F..O..L	O..R..J	V..T..F
9)	G..G..T	P..K..R	X..N..P	G..P..M	P..S..K	W..U..G
10)	H..H..U	Q..L..S	A..O..Q	H..Q..N	Q..T..L	X..V..H
11)	J..J..V	R..M..T	B..P..R	J..R..O	R..U..M	A..W..J
12)	K..K..W	S..N..U	C..Q..S	K..S..P	S..V..N	B..X..K
13)	L..L..X	T..O..V	D..R..T	L..T..Q	T..W..O	C..Y..L
14)	M..M..Y	U..P..W	E..S..U	M..U..R	U..X..P	D..Z..M
15)	N..N..Z	V..Q..X	F..T..V	N..V..S	V..Y..Q	E..1..N
16)	O..O..1	W..R..Y	G..U..W	O..W..T	W..Z..R	F..2..O
17)	P..P..2	X..S..Z	H..V..X	P..X..U	X..1..S	G..3..P
18)	Q..Q..3	A..T..1	J..W..Y	Q..Y..V	A..2..T	H..A..Q
19)	R..R..4	B..U..2	K..X..Z	R..Z..W	B..3..U	J..B..R
20)	S..S..5	C..V..3	L..Y..1	S..1..X	C..A..V	K..C..S
21)	T..T..6	D..W..4	M..Z..2	T..2..Y	D..B..W	L..D..T
22)	U..U..7	E..X..5	N..1..3	U..3..Z	E..C..X	M..E..U
23)	V..V..8	F..Y..6	O..2..4	V..A..1	F..D..Y	N..F..V
24)	W..W..A	G..Z..7	P..3..5	W..B..2	G..E..Z	O..G..W
25)	X..X..B	H..1..8	Q..A..6	X..C..3	H..F..1	P..H..X
26)	A..Y..C	J..2..A	R..B..7	A..D..4	J..G..2	Q..J..Y
27)	B..Z..D	K..3..B	S..C..8	B..E..5	K..H..3	R..K..Z
28)	C..1..E	L..A..C	T..D..A	C..F..6	L..J..4	S..L..1
29)	D..2..F	M..B..D	U..E..B	D..G..7	M..K..5	T..M..2
30)	E..3..G	N..C..E	V..F..C	E..H..8	N..L..6	U..N..3
31)	F..A..H	O..D..F		F..J..A		V..O..4

CODES: P-PHYSICAL BIORHYTHM CURVE, E-EMOTIONAL BIORHYTHM CURVE, I-INTELLECTUAL BIORHYTHM CURVE

1922

...JANUARY..
```
   P--E--I
 1) W..P..5
 2) X..Q..6
 3) A..R..7
 4) B..S..8
 5) C..T..A
 6) D..U..B
 7) E..V..C
 8) F..W..D
 9) G..X..E
10) H..Y..F
11) J..Z..G
12) K..1..H
13) L..2..J
14) M..3..K
15) N..A..L
16) O..B..M
17) P..C..N
18) Q..D..O
19) R..E..P
20) S..F..Q
21) T..G..R
22) U..H..S
23) V..J..T
24) W..K..U
25) X..L..V
26) A..M..W
27) B..N..X
28) C..O..Y
29) D..P..Z
30) E..Q..1
31) F..R..2
```

..FEBRUARY..
```
   P--E--I
 1) G..S..3
 2) H..T..4
 3) J..U..5
 4) K..V..6
 5) L..W..7
 6) M..X..8
 7) N..Y..A
 8) O..Z..B
 9) P..1..C
10) Q..2..D
11) R..3..E
12) S..A..F
13) T..B..G
14) U..C..H
15) V..D..J
16) W..E..K
17) X..F..L
18) A..G..M
19) B..H..N
20) C..J..O
21) D..K..P
22) E..L..Q
23) F..M..R
24) G..N..S
25) H..O..T
26) J..P..U
27) K..Q..V
28) L..R..W
```

....MARCH...
```
   P--E--I
 1) M..S..X
 2) N..T..Y
 3) O..U..Z
 4) P..V..1
 5) Q..W..2
 6) R..X..3
 7) S..Y..4
 8) T..Z..5
 9) U..1..6
10) V..2..7
11) W..3..8
12) X..A..A
13) A..B..B
14) B..C..C
15) C..D..D
16) D..E..E
17) E..F..F
18) F..G..G
19) G..H..H
20) H..J..J
21) J..K..K
22) K..L..L
23) L..M..M
24) M..N..N
25) N..O..O
26) O..P..P
27) P..Q..Q
28) Q..R..R
29) R..S..S
30) S..T..T
31) T..U..U
```

...APRIL...
```
   P--E--I
 1) U..V..V
 2) V..W..W
 3) W..X..X
 4) X..Y..Y
 5) A..Z..Z
 6) B..1..1
 7) C..2..2
 8) D..3..3
 9) E..A..4
10) F..B..5
11) G..C..6
12) H..D..7
13) J..E..8
14) K..F..A
15) L..G..B
16) M..H..C
17) N..J..D
18) O..K..E
19) P..L..F
20) Q..M..G
21) R..N..H
22) S..O..J
23) T..P..K
24) U..Q..L
25) V..R..M
26) W..S..N
27) X..T..O
28) A..U..P
29) B..V..Q
30) C..W..R
```

....MAY....
```
   P--E--I
 1) D..X..S
 2) E..Y..T
 3) F..Z..U
 4) G..1..V
 5) H..2..W
 6) J..3..X
 7) K..A..Y
 8) L..B..Z
 9) M..C..1
10) N..D..2
11) O..E..3
12) P..F..4
13) Q..G..5
14) R..H..6
15) S..J..7
16) T..K..8
17) U..L..A
18) V..M..B
19) W..N..C
20) X..O..D
21) A..P..E
22) B..Q..F
23) C..R..G
24) D..S..H
25) E..T..J
26) F..U..K
27) G..V..L
28) H..W..M
29) J..X..N
30) K..Y..O
31) L..Z..P
```

....JUNE....
```
   P--E--I
 1) M..1..Q
 2) N..2..R
 3) O..3..S
 4) P..A..T
 5) Q..B..U
 6) R..C..V
 7) S..D..W
 8) T..E..X
 9) U..F..Y
10) V..G..Z
11) W..H..1
12) X..J..2
13) A..K..3
14) B..L..4
15) C..M..5
16) D..N..6
17) E..O..7
18) F..P..8
19) G..Q..A
20) H..R..B
21) J..S..C
22) K..T..D
23) L..U..E
24) M..V..F
25) N..W..G
26) O..X..H
27) P..Y..J
28) Q..Z..K
29) R..1..L
30) S..2..M
```

1922

....JULY....
```
   P--E--I
 1) T..3..N
 2) U..A..O
 3) V..B..P
 4) W..C..Q
 5) X..D..R
 6) A..E..S
 7) B..F..T
 8) C..G..U
 9) D..H..V
10) E..J..W
11) F..K..X
12) G..L..Y
13) H..M..Z
14) J..N..1
15) K..O..2
16) L..P..3
17) M..Q..4
18) N..R..5
19) O..S..6
20) P..T..7
21) Q..U..8
22) R..V..A
23) S..W..B
24) T..X..C
25) U..Y..D
26) V..Z..E
27) W..1..F
28) X..2..G
29) A..3..H
30) B..A..J
31) C..B..K
```

...AUGUST...
```
   P--E--I
 1) D..C..L
 2) E..D..M
 3) F..E..N
 4) G..F..O
 5) H..G..P
 6) J..H..Q
 7) K..J..R
 8) L..K..S
 9) M..L..T
10) N..M..U
11) O..N..V
12) P..O..W
13) Q..P..X
14) R..Q..Y
15) S..R..Z
16) T..S..1
17) U..T..2
18) V..U..3
19) W..V..4
20) X..W..5
21) A..X..6
22) B..Y..7
23) C..Z..8
24) D..1..A
25) E..2..B
26) F..3..C
27) G..A..D
28) H..B..E
29) J..C..F
30) K..D..G
31) L..E..H
```

..SEPTEMBER.
```
   P--E--I
 1) M..F..J
 2) N..G..K
 3) O..H..L
 4) P..J..M
 5) Q..K..N
 6) R..L..O
 7) S..M..P
 8) T..N..Q
 9) U..O..R
10) V..P..S
11) W..Q..T
12) X..R..U
13) A..S..V
14) B..T..W
15) C..U..X
16) D..V..Y
17) E..W..Z
18) F..X..1
19) G..Y..2
20) H..Z..3
21) J..1..4
22) K..2..5
23) L..3..6
24) M..A..7
25) N..B..8
26) O..C..A
27) P..D..B
28) Q..E..C
29) R..F..D
30) S..G..E
```

..OCTOBER...
```
   P--E--I
 1) T..H..F
 2) U..J..G
 3) V..K..H
 4) W..L..J
 5) X..M..K
 6) A..N..L
 7) B..O..M
 8) C..P..N
 9) D..Q..O
10) E..R..P
11) F..S..Q
12) G..T..R
13) H..U..S
14) J..V..T
15) K..W..U
16) L..X..V
17) M..Y..W
18) N..Z..X
19) O..1..Y
20) P..2..Z
21) Q..3..1
22) R..A..2
23) S..B..3
24) T..C..4
25) U..D..5
26) V..E..6
27) W..F..7
28) X..G..8
29) A..H..A
30) B..J..B
31) C..K..C
```

..NOVEMBER..
```
   P--E--I
 1) D..L..D
 2) E..M..E
 3) F..N..F
 4) G..O..G
 5) H..P..H
 6) J..Q..J
 7) K..R..K
 8) L..S..L
 9) M..T..M
10) N..U..N
11) O..V..O
12) P..W..P
13) Q..X..Q
14) R..Y..R
15) S..Z..S
16) T..1..T
17) U..2..U
18) V..3..V
19) W..A..W
20) X..B..X
21) A..C..Y
22) B..D..Z
23) C..E..1
24) D..F..2
25) E..G..3
26) F..H..4
27) G..J..5
28) H..K..6
29) J..L..7
30) K..M..8
```

..DECEMBER..
```
   P--E--I
 1) L..N..A
 2) M..O..B
 3) N..P..C
 4) O..Q..D
 5) P..R..E
 6) Q..S..F
 7) R..T..G
 8) S..U..H
 9) T..V..J
10) U..W..K
11) V..X..L
12) W..Y..M
13) X..Z..N
14) A..1..O
15) B..2..P
16) C..3..Q
17) D..A..R
18) E..B..S
19) F..C..T
20) G..D..U
21) H..E..V
22) J..F..W
23) K..G..X
24) L..H..Y
25) M..J..Z
26) N..K..1
27) O..L..2
28) P..M..3
29) Q..N..4
30) R..O..5
31) S..P..6
```

CODES: P-PHYSICAL BIORHYTHM CURVE, E-EMOTIONAL BIORHYTHM CURVE, I-INTELLECTUAL BIORHYTHM CURVE

	...JANUARY..		..FEBRUARY..		...MARCH...		...APRIL...		....MAY....		....JUNE....
	P--E--I		P--E--I		P--E--I		P--E--I		P--E--I		P--E--I
1)	T..Q..7	1)	D..T..5	1)	J..T..Z	1)	R..W..X	1)	A..Y..U	1)	J..2..S
2)	U..R..8	2)	E..U..6	2)	K..U..1	2)	S..X..Y	2)	B..Z..V	2)	K..3..T
3)	V..S..A	3)	F..V..7	3)	L..V..2	3)	T..Y..Z	3)	C..1..W	3)	L..A..U
4)	W..T..B	4)	G..W..8	4)	M..W..3	4)	U..Z..1	4)	D..2..X	4)	M..B..V
5)	X..U..C	5)	H..X..A	5)	N..X..4	5)	V..1..2	5)	E..3..Y	5)	N..C..W
6)	A..V..D	6)	J..Y..B	6)	O..Y..5	6)	W..2..3	6)	F..A..Z	6)	O..D..X
7)	B..W..E	7)	K..Z..C	7)	P..Z..6	7)	X..3..4	7)	G..B..1	7)	P..E..Y
8)	C..X..F	8)	L..1..D	8)	Q..1..7	8)	A..A..5	8)	H..C..2	8)	Q..F..Z
9)	D..Y..G	9)	M..2..E	9)	R..2..8	9)	B..B..6	9)	J..D..3	9)	R..G..1
10)	E..Z..H	10)	N..3..F	10)	S..3..A	10)	C..C..7	10)	K..E..4	10)	S..H..2
11)	F..1..J	11)	O..A..G	11)	T..A..B	11)	D..D..8	11)	L..F..5	11)	T..J..3
12)	G..2..K	12)	P..B..H	12)	U..B..C	12)	E..E..A	12)	M..G..6	12)	U..K..4
13)	H..3..L	13)	Q..C..J	13)	V..C..D	13)	F..F..B	13)	N..H..7	13)	V..L..5
14)	J..A..M	14)	R..D..K	14)	W..D..E	14)	G..G..C	14)	O..J..8	14)	W..M..6
15)	K..B..N	15)	S..E..L	15)	X..E..F	15)	H..H..D	15)	P..K..A	15)	X..N..7
16)	L..C..O	16)	T..F..M	16)	A..F..G	16)	J..J..E	16)	Q..L..B	16)	A..O..8
17)	M..D..P	17)	U..G..N	17)	B..G..H	17)	K..K..F	17)	R..M..C	17)	B..P..A
18)	N..E..Q	18)	V..H..O	18)	C..H..J	18)	L..L..G	18)	S..N..D	18)	C..Q..B
19)	O..F..R	19)	W..J..P	19)	D..J..K	19)	M..M..H	19)	T..O..E	19)	D..R..C
20)	P..G..S	20)	X..K..Q	20)	E..K..L	20)	N..N..J	20)	U..P..F	20)	E..S..D
21)	Q..H..T	21)	A..L..R	21)	F..L..M	21)	O..O..K	21)	V..Q..G	21)	F..T..E
22)	R..J..U	22)	B..M..S	22)	G..M..N	22)	P..P..L	22)	W..R..H	22)	G..U..F
23)	S..K..V	23)	C..N..T	23)	H..N..O	23)	Q..Q..M	23)	X..S..J	23)	H..V..G
24)	T..L..W	24)	D..O..U	24)	J..O..P	24)	R..R..N	24)	A..T..K	24)	J..W..H
25)	U..M..X	25)	E..P..V	25)	K..P..Q	25)	S..S..O	25)	B..U..L	25)	K..X..J
26)	V..N..Y	26)	F..Q..W	26)	L..Q..R	26)	T..T..P	26)	C..V..M	26)	L..Y..K
27)	W..O..Z	27)	G..R..X	27)	M..R..S	27)	U..U..Q	27)	D..W..N	27)	M..Z..L
28)	X..P..1	28)	H..S..Y	28)	N..S..T	28)	V..V..R	28)	E..X..O	28)	N..1..M
29)	A..Q..2			29)	O..T..U	29)	W..W..S	29)	F..Y..P	29)	O..2..N
30)	B..R..3			30)	P..U..V	30)	X..X..T	30)	G..Z..Q	30)	P..3..O
31)	C..S..4			31)	Q..V..W			31)	H..1..R		

	....JULY....		...AUGUST...		..SEPTEMBER.		..OCTOBER...		..NOVEMBER..		..DECEMBER..
	P--E--I		P--E--I		P--E--I		P--E--I		P--E--I		P--E--I
1)	Q..A..P	1)	A..D..N	1)	J..G..L	1)	Q..J..H	1)	A..M..F	1)	H..O..C
2)	R..B..Q	2)	B..E..O	2)	K..H..M	2)	R..K..J	2)	B..N..G	2)	J..P..D
3)	S..C..R	3)	C..F..P	3)	L..J..N	3)	S..L..K	3)	C..O..H	3)	K..Q..E
4)	T..D..S	4)	D..G..Q	4)	M..K..O	4)	T..M..L	4)	D..P..J	4)	L..R..F
5)	U..E..T	5)	E..H..R	5)	N..L..P	5)	U..N..M	5)	E..Q..K	5)	M..S..G
6)	V..F..U	6)	F..J..S	6)	O..M..Q	6)	V..O..N	6)	F..R..L	6)	N..T..H
7)	W..G..V	7)	G..K..T	7)	P..N..R	7)	W..P..O	7)	G..S..M	7)	O..U..J
8)	X..H..W	8)	H..L..U	8)	Q..O..S	8)	X..Q..P	8)	H..T..N	8)	P..V..K
9)	A..J..X	9)	J..M..V	9)	R..P..T	9)	A..R..Q	9)	J..U..O	9)	Q..W..L
10)	B..K..Y	10)	K..N..W	10)	S..Q..U	10)	B..S..R	10)	K..V..P	10)	R..X..M
11)	C..L..Z	11)	L..O..X	11)	T..R..V	11)	C..T..S	11)	L..W..Q	11)	S..Y..N
12)	D..M..1	12)	M..P..Y	12)	U..S..W	12)	D..U..T	12)	M..X..R	12)	T..Z..O
13)	E..N..2	13)	N..Q..Z	13)	V..T..X	13)	E..V..U	13)	N..Y..S	13)	U..1..P
14)	F..O..3	14)	O..R..1	14)	W..U..Y	14)	F..W..V	14)	O..Z..T	14)	V..2..Q
15)	G..P..4	15)	P..S..2	15)	X..V..Z	15)	G..X..W	15)	P..1..U	15)	W..3..R
16)	H..Q..5	16)	Q..T..3	16)	A..W..1	16)	H..Y..X	16)	Q..2..V	16)	X..A..S
17)	J..R..6	17)	R..U..4	17)	B..X..2	17)	J..Z..Y	17)	R..3..W	17)	A..B..T
18)	K..S..7	18)	S..V..5	18)	C..Y..3	18)	K..1..Z	18)	S..A..X	18)	B..C..U
19)	L..T..8	19)	T..W..6	19)	D..Z..4	19)	L..2..1	19)	T..B..Y	19)	C..D..V
20)	M..U..A	20)	U..X..7	20)	E..1..5	20)	M..3..2	20)	U..C..Z	20)	D..E..W
21)	N..V..B	21)	V..Y..8	21)	F..2..6	21)	N..A..3	21)	V..D..1	21)	E..F..X
22)	O..W..C	22)	W..Z..A	22)	G..3..7	22)	O..B..4	22)	W..E..2	22)	F..G..Y
23)	P..X..D	23)	X..1..B	23)	H..A..8	23)	P..C..5	23)	X..F..3	23)	G..H..Z
24)	Q..Y..E	24)	A..2..C	24)	J..B..A	24)	Q..D..6	24)	A..G..4	24)	H..J..1
25)	R..Z..F	25)	B..3..D	25)	K..C..B	25)	R..E..7	25)	B..H..5	25)	J..K..2
26)	S..1..G	26)	C..A..E	26)	L..D..C	26)	S..F..8	26)	C..J..6	26)	K..L..3
27)	T..2..H	27)	D..B..F	27)	M..E..D	27)	T..G..A	27)	D..K..7	27)	L..M..4
28)	U..3..J	28)	E..C..G	28)	N..F..E	28)	U..H..B	28)	E..L..8	28)	M..N..5
29)	V..A..K	29)	F..D..H	29)	O..G..F	29)	V..J..C	29)	F..M..A	29)	N..O..6
30)	W..B..L	30)	G..E..J	30)	P..H..G	30)	W..K..D	30)	G..N..B	30)	O..P..7
31)	X..C..M	31)	H..F..K			31)	X..L..E			31)	P..Q..8

CODES: P-PHYSICAL BIORHYTHM CURVE,E-EMOTIONAL BIORHYTHM CURVE,I-INTELLECTUAL BIORHYTHM CURVE

	...JANUARY..	..FEBRUARY..	....MARCH...	....APRIL...	....MAY....	....JUNE....
	P--E--I	P--E--I	P--E--I	P--E--I	P--E--I	P--E--I
1)	Q..R..A	A..U..7	G..V..3	P..Y..1	W..1..X	G..A..V
2)	R..S..B	B..V..8	H..W..4	Q..Z..2	X..2..Y	H..B..W
3)	S..T..C	C..W..A	J..X..5	R..1..3	A..3..Z	J..C..X
4)	T..U..D	D..X..B	K..Y..6	S..2..4	B..A..1	K..D..Y
5)	U..V..E	E..Y..C	L..Z..7	T..3..5	C..B..2	L..E..Z
6)	V..W..F	F..Z..D	M..1..8	U..A..6	D..C..3	M..F..1
7)	W..X..G	G..1..E	N..2..A	V..B..7	E..D..4	N..G..2
8)	X..Y..H	H..2..F	O..3..B	W..C..8	F..E..5	O..H..3
9)	A..Z..J	J..3..G	P..A..C	X..D..A	G..F..6	P..J..4
10)	B..1..K	K..A..H	Q..B..D	A..E..B	H..G..7	Q..K..5
11)	C..2..L	L..B..J	R..C..E	B..F..C	J..H..8	R..L..6
12)	D..3..M	M..C..K	S..D..F	C..G..D	K..J..A	S..M..7
13)	E..A..N	N..D..L	T..E..G	D..H..E	L..K..B	T..N..8
14)	F..B..O	O..E..M	U..F..H	E..J..F	M..L..C	U..O..A
15)	G..C..P	P..F..N	V..G..J	F..K..G	N..M..D	V..P..B
16)	H..D..Q	Q..G..O	W..H..K	G..L..H	O..N..E	W..Q..C
17)	J..E..R	R..H..P	X..J..L	H..M..J	P..O..F	X..R..D
18)	K..F..S	S..J..Q	A..K..M	J..N..K	Q..P..G	A..S..E
19)	L..G..T	T..K..R	B..L..N	K..O..L	R..Q..H	B..T..F
20)	M..H..U	U..L..S	C..M..O	L..P..M	S..R..J	C..U..G
21)	N..J..V	V..M..T	D..N..P	M..Q..N	T..S..K	D..V..H
22)	O..K..W	W..N..U	E..O..Q	N..R..O	U..T..L	E..W..J
23)	P..L..X	X..O..V	F..P..R	O..S..P	V..U..M	F..X..K
24)	Q..M..Y	A..P..W	G..Q..S	P..T..Q	W..V..N	G..Y..L
25)	R..N..Z	B..Q..X	H..R..T	Q..U..R	X..W..O	H..Z..M
26)	S..O..1	C..R..Y	J..S..U	R..V..S	A..X..P	J..1..N
27)	T..P..2	D..S..Z	K..T..V	S..W..T	B..Y..Q	K..2..O
28)	U..Q..3	E..T..1	L..U..W	T..X..U	C..Z..R	L..3..P
29)	V..R..4	F..U..2	M..V..X	U..Y..V	D..1..S	M..A..Q
30)	W..S..5		N..W..Y	V..Z..W	E..2..T	N..B..R
31)	X..T..6		O..X..Z		F..3..U	

	....JULY....	...AUGUST...	.SEPTEMBER.	..OCTOBER...	..NOVEMBER..	..DECEMBER..
	P--E--I	P--E--I	P--E--I	P--E--I	P--E--I	P--E--I
1)	O..C..S	W..F..Q	G..J..O	O..L..L	W..O..J	F..Q..F
2)	P..D..T	X..G..R	H..K..P	P..M..M	X..P..K	G..R..G
3)	Q..E..U	A..H..S	J..L..Q	Q..N..N	A..Q..L	H..S..H
4)	R..F..V	B..J..T	K..M..R	R..O..O	B..R..M	J..T..J
5)	S..G..W	C..K..U	L..N..S	S..P..P	C..S..N	K..U..K
6)	T..H..X	D..L..V	M..O..T	T..Q..Q	D..T..O	L..V..L
7)	U..J..Y	E..M..W	N..P..U	U..R..R	E..U..P	M..W..M
8)	V..K..Z	F..N..X	O..Q..V	V..S..S	F..V..Q	N..X..N
9)	W..L..1	G..O..Y	P..R..W	W..T..T	G..W..R	O..Y..O
10)	X..M..2	H..P..Z	Q..S..X	X..U..U	H..X..S	P..Z..P
11)	A..N..3	J..Q..1	R..T..Y	A..V..V	J..Y..T	Q..1..Q
12)	B..O..4	K..R..2	S..U..Z	B..W..W	K..Z..U	R..2..R
13)	C..P..5	L..S..3	T..V..1	C..X..X	L..1..V	S..3..S
14)	D..Q..6	M..T..4	U..W..2	D..Y..Y	M..2..W	T..A..T
15)	E..R..7	N..U..5	V..X..3	E..Z..Z	N..3..X	U..B..U
16)	F..S..8	O..V..6	W..Y..4	F..1..1	O..A..Y	V..C..V
17)	G..T..A	P..W..7	X..Z..5	G..2..2	P..B..Z	W..D..W
18)	H..U..B	Q..X..8	A..1..6	H..3..3	Q..C..1	X..E..X
19)	J..V..C	R..Y..A	B..2..7	J..A..4	R..D..2	A..F..Y
20)	K..W..D	S..Z..B	C..3..8	K..B..5	S..E..3	B..G..Z
21)	L..X..E	T..1..C	D..A..A	L..C..6	T..F..4	C..H..1
22)	M..Y..F	U..2..D	E..B..B	M..D..7	U..G..5	D..J..2
23)	N..Z..G	V..3..E	F..C..C	N..E..8	V..H..6	E..K..3
24)	O..1..H	W..A..F	G..D..D	O..F..A	W..J..7	F..L..4
25)	P..2..J	X..B..G	H..E..E	P..G..B	X..K..8	G..M..5
26)	Q..3..K	A..C..H	J..F..F	Q..H..C	A..L..A	H..N..6
27)	R..A..L	B..D..J	K..G..G	R..J..D	B..M..B	J..O..7
28)	S..B..M	C..E..K	L..H..H	S..K..E	C..N..C	K..P..8
29)	T..C..N	D..F..L	M..J..J	T..L..F	D..O..D	L..Q..A
30)	U..D..O	E..G..M	N..K..K	U..M..G	E..P..E	M..R..B
31)	V..E..P	F..H..N		V..N..H		N..S..C

CODES: P-PHYSICAL BIORHYTHM CURVE,E-EMOTIONAL BIORHYTHM CURVE,I-INTELLECTUAL BIORHYTHM CURVE

	...JANUARY..	..FEBRUARY..	...MARCH...	...APRIL...	....MAY....	...JUNE....
	P--E--I	P--E--I	P--E--I	P--E--I	P--E--I	P--E--I
1)	O..T..D	W..W..B	D..W..5	M..Z..3	T..2..Z	D..B..X
2)	P..U..E	X..X..C	E..X..6	N..1..4	U..3..1	E..C..Y
3)	Q..V..F	A..Y..D	F..Y..7	O..2..5	V..A..2	F..D..Z
4)	R..W..G	B..Z..E	G..Z..8	P..3..6	W..B..3	G..E..1
5)	S..X..H	C..1..F	H..1..A	Q..A..7	X..C..4	H..F..2
6)	T..Y..J	D..2..G	J..2..B	R..B..8	A..D..5	J..G..3
7)	U..Z..K	E..3..H	K..3..C	S..C..A	B..E..6	K..H..4
8)	V..1..L	F..A..J	L..A..D	T..D..B	C..F..7	L..J..5
9)	W..2..M	G..B..K	M..B..E	U..E..C	D..G..8	M..K..6
10)	X..3..N	H..C..L	N..C..F	V..F..D	E..H..A	N..L..7
11)	A..A..O	J..D..M	O..D..G	W..G..E	F..J..B	O..M..8
12)	B..B..P	K..E..N	P..E..H	X..H..F	G..K..C	P..N..A
13)	C..C..Q	L..F..O	Q..F..J	A..J..G	H..L..D	Q..O..B
14)	D..D..R	M..G..P	R..G..K	B..K..H	J..M..E	R..P..C
15)	E..E..S	N..H..Q	S..H..L	C..L..J	K..N..F	S..Q..D
16)	F..F..T	O..J..R	T..J..M	D..M..K	L..O..G	T..R..E
17)	G..G..U	P..K..S	U..K..N	E..N..L	M..P..H	U..S..F
18)	H..H..V	Q..L..T	V..L..O	F..O..M	N..Q..J	V..T..G
19)	J..J..W	R..M..U	W..M..P	G..P..N	O..R..K	W..U..H
20)	K..K..X	S..N..V	X..N..Q	H..Q..O	P..S..L	X..V..J
21)	L..L..Y	T..O..W	A..O..R	J..R..P	Q..T..M	A..W..K
22)	M..M..Z	U..P..X	B..P..S	K..S..Q	R..U..N	B..X..L
23)	N..N..1	V..Q..Y	C..Q..T	L..T..R	S..V..O	C..Y..M
24)	O..O..2	W..R..Z	D..R..U	M..U..S	T..W..P	D..Z..N
25)	P..P..3	X..S..1	E..S..V	N..V..T	U..X..Q	E..1..O
26)	Q..Q..4	A..T..2	F..T..W	O..W..U	V..Y..R	F..2..P
27)	R..R..5	B..U..3	G..U..X	P..X..V	W..Z..S	G..3..Q
28)	S..S..6	C..V..4	H..V..Y	Q..Y..W	X..1..T	H..A..R
29)	T..T..7		J..W..Z	R..Z..X	A..2..U	J..B..S
30)	U..U..8		K..X..1	S..1..Y	B..3..V	K..C..T
31)	V..V..A		L..Y..2		C..A..W	

	....JULY....	...AUGUST...	..SEPTEMBER.	..OCTOBER...	..NOVEMBER..	..DECEMBER..
	P--E--I	P--E--I	P--E--I	P--E--I	P--E--I	P--E--I
1)	L..D..U	T..G..S	D..K..Q	L..M..N	T..P..L	C..R..H
2)	M..E..V	U..H..T	E..L..R	M..N..O	U..Q..M	D..S..J
3)	N..F..W	V..J..U	F..M..S	N..O..P	V..R..N	E..T..K
4)	O..G..X	W..K..V	G..N..T	O..P..Q	W..S..O	F..U..L
5)	P..H..Y	X..L..W	H..O..U	P..Q..R	X..T..P	G..V..M
6)	Q..J..Z	A..M..X	J..P..V	Q..R..S	A..U..Q	H..W..N
7)	R..K..1	B..N..Y	K..Q..W	R..S..T	B..V..R	J..X..O
8)	S..L..2	C..O..Z	L..R..X	S..T..U	C..W..S	K..Y..P
9)	T..M..3	D..P..1	M..S..Y	T..U..V	D..X..T	L..Z..Q
10)	U..N..4	E..Q..2	N..T..Z	U..V..W	E..Y..U	M..1..R
11)	V..O..5	F..R..3	O..U..1	V..W..X	F..Z..V	N..2..S
12)	W..P..6	G..S..4	P..V..2	W..X..Y	G..1..W	O..3..T
13)	X..Q..7	H..T..5	Q..W..3	X..Y..Z	H..2..X	P..A..U
14)	A..R..8	J..U..6	R..X..4	A..Z..1	J..3..Y	Q..B..V
15)	B..S..A	K..V..7	S..Y..5	B..1..2	K..A..Z	R..C..W
16)	C..T..B	L..W..8	T..Z..6	C..2..3	L..B..1	S..D..X
17)	D..U..C	M..X..A	U..1..7	D..3..4	M..C..2	T..E..Y
18)	E..V..D	N..Y..B	V..2..8	E..A..5	N..D..3	U..F..Z
19)	F..W..E	O..Z..C	W..3..A	F..B..6	O..E..4	V..G..1
20)	G..X..F	P..1..D	X..A..B	G..C..7	P..F..5	W..H..2
21)	H..Y..G	Q..2..E	A..B..C	H..D..8	Q..G..6	X..J..3
22)	J..Z..H	R..3..F	B..C..D	J..E..A	R..H..7	A..K..4
23)	K..1..J	S..A..G	C..D..E	K..F..B	S..J..8	B..L..5
24)	L..2..K	T..B..H	D..E..F	L..G..C	T..K..A	C..M..6
25)	M..3..L	U..C..J	E..F..G	M..H..D	U..L..B	D..N..7
26)	N..A..M	V..D..K	F..G..H	N..J..E	V..M..C	E..O..8
27)	O..B..N	W..E..L	G..H..J	O..K..F	W..N..D	F..P..A
28)	P..C..O	X..F..M	H..J..K	P..L..G	X..O..E	G..Q..B
29)	Q..D..P	A..G..N	J..K..L	Q..M..H	A..P..F	H..R..C
30)	R..E..Q	B..H..O	K..L..M	R..N..J	B..Q..G	J..S..D
31)	S..F..R	C..J..P		S..O..K		K..T..E

CODES: P-PHYSICAL BIORHYTHM CURVE,E-EMOTIONAL BIORHYTHM CURVE,I-INTELLECTUAL BIORHYTHM CURVE

	...JANUARY..	..FEBRUARY..	...MARCH...	...APRIL...	....MAY....	...JUNE....
	P--E--I	P--E--I	P--E--I	P--E--I	P--E--I	P--E--I
1)	L..U..F	T..X..D	A..X..7	J..1..5	Q..3..2	A..C..Z
2)	M..V..G	U..Y..E	B..Y..8	K..2..6	R..A..3	B..D..1
3)	N..W..H	V..Z..F	C..Z..A	L..3..7	S..B..4	C..E..2
4)	O..X..J	W..1..G	D..1..B	M..A..8	T..C..5	D..F..3
5)	P..Y..K	X..2..H	E..2..C	N..B..A	U..D..6	E..G..4
6)	Q..Z..L	A..3..J	F..3..D	O..C..B	V..E..7	F..H..5
7)	R..1..M	B..A..K	G..A..E	P..D..C	W..F..8	G..J..6
8)	S..2..N	C..B..L	H..B..F	Q..E..D	X..G..A	H..K..7
9)	T..3..O	D..C..M	J..C..G	R..F..E	A..H..B	J..L..8
10)	U..A..P	E..D..N	K..D..H	S..G..F	B..J..C	K..M..A
11)	V..B..Q	F..E..O	L..E..J	T..H..G	C..K..D	L..N..B
12)	W..C..R	G..F..P	M..F..K	U..J..H	D..L..E	M..O..C
13)	X..D..S	H..G..Q	N..G..L	V..K..J	E..M..F	N..P..D
14)	A..E..T	J..H..R	O..H..M	W..L..K	F..N..G	O..Q..E
15)	B..F..U	K..J..S	P..J..N	X..M..L	G..O..H	P..R..F
16)	C..G..V	L..K..T	Q..K..O	A..N..M	H..P..J	Q..S..G
17)	D..H..W	M..L..U	R..L..P	B..O..N	J..Q..K	R..T..H
18)	E..J..X	N..M..V	S..M..Q	C..P..O	K..R..L	S..U..J
19)	F..K..Y	O..N..W	T..N..R	D..Q..P	L..S..M	T..V..K
20)	G..L..Z	P..O..X	U..O..S	E..R..Q	M..T..N	U..W..L
21)	H..M..1	Q..P..Y	V..P..T	F..S..R	N..U..O	V..X..M
22)	J..N..2	R..Q..Z	W..Q..U	G..T..S	O..V..P	W..Y..N
23)	K..O..3	S..R..1	X..R..V	H..U..T	P..W..Q	X..Z..O
24)	L..P..4	T..S..2	A..S..W	J..V..U	Q..X..R	A..1..P
25)	M..Q..5	U..T..3	B..T..X	K..W..V	R..Y..S	B..2..Q
26)	N..R..6	V..U..4	C..U..Y	L..X..W	S..Z..T	C..3..R
27)	O..S..7	W..V..5	D..V..Z	M..Y..X	T..1..U	D..A..S
28)	P..T..8	X..W..6	E..W..1	N..Z..Y	U..2..V	E..B..T
29)	Q..U..A		F..X..2	O..1..Z	V..3..W	F..C..U
30)	R..V..B		G..Y..3	P..2..1	W..A..X	G..D..V
31)	S..W..C		H..Z..4		X..B..Y	

	....JULY....	...AUGUST...	.SEPTEMBER.	..OCTOBER...	..NOVEMBER..	..DECEMBER..
	P--E--I	P--E--I	P--E--I	P--E--I	P--E--I	P--E--I
1)	H..E..W	Q..H..U	A..L..S	H..N..P	Q..Q..N	X..S..K
2)	J..F..X	R..J..V	B..M..T	J..O..Q	R..R..O	A..T..L
3)	K..G..Y	S..K..W	C..N..U	K..P..R	S..S..P	B..U..M
4)	L..H..Z	T..L..X	D..O..V	L..Q..S	T..T..Q	C..V..N
5)	M..J..1	U..M..Y	E..P..W	M..R..T	U..U..R	D..W..O
6)	N..K..2	V..N..Z	F..Q..X	N..S..U	V..V..S	E..X..P
7)	O..L..3	W..O..1	G..R..Y	O..T..V	W..W..T	F..Y..Q
8)	P..M..4	X..P..2	H..S..Z	P..U..W	X..X..U	G..Z..R
9)	Q..N..5	A..Q..3	J..T..1	Q..V..X	A..Y..V	H..1..S
10)	R..O..6	B..R..4	K..U..2	R..W..Y	B..Z..W	J..2..T
11)	S..P..7	C..S..5	L..V..3	S..X..Z	C..1..X	K..3..U
12)	T..Q..8	D..T..6	M..W..4	T..Y..1	D..2..Y	L..A..V
13)	U..R..A	E..U..7	N..X..5	U..Z..2	E..3..Z	M..B..W
14)	V..S..B	F..V..8	O..Y..6	V..1..3	F..A..1	N..C..X
15)	W..T..C	G..W..A	P..Z..7	W..2..4	G..B..2	O..D..Y
16)	X..U..D	H..X..B	Q..1..8	X..3..5	H..C..3	P..E..Z
17)	A..V..E	J..Y..C	R..2..A	A..A..6	J..D..4	Q..F..1
18)	B..W..F	K..Z..D	S..3..B	B..B..7	K..E..5	R..G..2
19)	C..X..G	L..1..E	T..A..C	C..C..8	L..F..6	S..H..3
20)	D..Y..H	M..2..F	U..B..D	D..D..A	M..G..7	T..J..4
21)	E..Z..J	N..3..G	V..C..E	E..E..B	N..H..8	U..K..5
22)	F..1..K	O..A..H	W..D..F	F..F..C	O..J..A	V..L..6
23)	G..2..L	P..B..J	X..E..G	G..G..D	P..K..B	W..M..7
24)	H..3..M	Q..C..K	A..F..H	H..H..E	Q..L..C	X..N..8
25)	J..A..N	R..D..L	B..G..J	J..J..F	R..M..D	A..O..A
26)	K..B..O	S..E..M	C..H..K	K..K..G	S..N..E	B..P..B
27)	L..C..P	T..F..N	D..J..L	L..L..H	T..O..F	C..Q..C
28)	M..D..Q	U..G..O	E..K..M	M..M..J	U..P..G	D..R..D
29)	N..E..R	V..H..P	F..L..N	N..N..K	V..Q..H	E..S..E
30)	O..F..S	W..J..Q	G..M..O	O..O..L	W..R..J	F..T..F
31)	P..G..T	X..K..R		P..P..M		G..U..G

CODES: P-PHYSICAL BIORHYTHM CURVE, E-EMOTIONAL BIORHYTHM CURVE, I-INTELLECTUAL BIORHYTHM CURVE

	...JANUARY..	..FEBRUARY..	....MARCH...	...APRIL...	....MAY....	....JUNE....
	P--E--I	P--E--I	P--E--I	P--E--I	P--E--I	P--E--I
1)	H..V..H	Q..Y..F	V..Y..A	F..2..7	N..A..4	V..D..2
2)	J..W..J	R..Z..G	W..Z..B	G..3..8	O..B..5	W..E..3
3)	K..X..K	S..1..H	X..1..C	H..A..A	P..C..6	X..F..4
4)	L..Y..L	T..2..J	A..2..D	J..B..B	Q..D..7	A..G..5
5)	M..Z..M	U..3..K	B..3..E	K..C..C	R..E..8	B..H..6
6)	N..1..N	V..A..L	C..A..F	L..D..D	S..F..A	C..J..7
7)	O..2..O	W..B..M	D..B..G	M..E..E	T..G..B	D..K..8
8)	P..3..P	X..C..N	E..C..H	N..F..F	U..H..C	E..L..A
9)	Q..A..Q	A..D..O	F..D..J	O..G..G	V..J..D	F..M..B
10)	R..B..R	B..E..P	G..E..K	P..H..H	W..K..E	G..N..C
11)	S..C..S	C..F..Q	H..F..L	Q..J..J	X..L..F	H..O..D
12)	T..D..T	D..G..R	J..G..M	R..K..K	A..M..G	J..P..E
13)	U..E..U	E..H..S	K..H..N	S..L..L	B..N..H	K..Q..F
14)	V..F..V	F..J..T	L..J..O	T..M..M	C..O..J	L..R..G
15)	W..G..W	G..K..U	M..K..P	U..N..N	D..P..K	M..S..H
16)	X..H..X	H..L..V	N..L..Q	V..O..O	E..Q..L	N..T..J
17)	A..J..Y	J..M..W	O..M..R	W..P..P	F..R..M	O..U..K
18)	B..K..Z	K..N..X	P..N..S	X..Q..Q	G..S..N	P..V..L
19)	C..L..1	L..O..Y	Q..O..T	A..R..R	H..T..O	Q..W..M
20)	D..M..2	M..P..Z	R..P..U	B..S..S	J..U..P	R..X..N
21)	E..N..3	N..Q..1	S..Q..V	C..T..T	K..V..Q	S..Y..O
22)	F..O..4	O..R..2	T..R..W	D..U..U	L..W..R	T..Z..P
23)	G..P..5	P..S..3	U..S..X	E..V..V	M..X..S	U..1..Q
24)	H..Q..6	Q..T..4	V..T..Y	F..W..W	N..Y..T	V..2..R
25)	J..R..7	R..U..5	W..U..Z	G..X..X	O..Z..U	W..3..S
26)	K..S..8	S..V..6	X..V..1	H..Y..Y	P..1..V	X..A..T
27)	L..T..A	T..W..7	A..W..2	J..Z..Z	Q..2..W	A..B..U
28)	M..U..B	U..X..8	B..X..3	K..1..1	R..3..X	B..C..V
29)	N..V..C		C..Y..4	L..2..2	S..A..Y	C..D..W
30)	O..W..D		D..Z..5	M..3..3	T..B..Z	D..E..X
31)	P..X..E		E..1..6		U..C..1	

	....JULY....	...AUGUST...	.SEPTEMBER.	..OCTOBER...	..NOVEMBER..	.DECEMBER..
	P--E--I	P--E--I	P--E--I	P--E--I	P--E--I	P--E--I
1)	E..F..Y	N..J..W	V..M..U	E..O..R	N..R..P	U..T..M
2)	F..G..Z	O..K..X	W..N..V	F..P..S	O..S..Q	V..U..N
3)	G..H..1	P..L..Y	X..O..W	G..Q..T	P..T..R	W..V..O
4)	H..J..2	Q..M..Z	A..P..X	H..R..U	Q..U..S	X..W..P
5)	J..K..3	R..N..1	B..Q..Y	J..S..V	R..V..T	A..X..Q
6)	K..L..4	S..O..2	C..R..Z	K..T..W	S..W..U	B..Y..R
7)	L..M..5	T..P..3	D..S..1	L..U..X	T..X..V	C..Z..S
8)	M..N..6	U..Q..4	E..T..2	M..V..Y	U..Y..W	D..1..T
9)	N..O..7	V..R..5	F..U..3	N..W..Z	V..Z..X	E..2..U
10)	O..P..8	W..S..6	G..V..4	O..X..1	W..1..Y	F..3..V
11)	P..Q..A	X..T..7	H..W..5	P..Y..2	X..2..Z	G..A..W
12)	Q..R..B	A..U..8	J..X..6	Q..Z..3	A..3..1	H..B..X
13)	R..S..C	B..V..A	K..Y..7	R..1..4	B..A..2	J..C..Y
14)	S..T..D	C..W..B	L..Z..8	S..2..5	C..B..3	K..D..Z
15)	T..U..E	D..X..C	M..1..A	T..3..6	D..C..4	L..E..1
16)	U..V..F	E..Y..D	N..2..B	U..A..7	E..D..5	M..F..2
17)	V..W..G	F..Z..E	O..3..C	V..B..8	F..E..6	N..G..3
18)	W..X..H	G..1..F	P..A..D	W..C..A	G..F..7	O..H..4
19)	X..Y..J	H..2..G	Q..B..E	X..D..B	H..G..8	P..J..5
20)	A..Z..K	J..3..H	R..C..F	A..E..C	J..H..A	Q..K..6
21)	B..1..L	K..A..J	S..D..G	B..F..D	K..J..B	R..L..7
22)	C..2..M	L..B..K	T..E..H	C..G..E	L..K..C	S..M..8
23)	D..3..N	M..C..L	U..F..J	D..H..F	M..L..D	T..N..A
24)	E..A..O	N..D..M	V..G..K	E..J..G	N..M..E	U..O..B
25)	F..B..P	O..E..N	W..H..L	F..K..H	O..N..F	V..P..C
26)	G..C..Q	P..F..O	X..J..M	G..L..J	P..O..G	W..Q..D
27)	H..D..R	Q..G..P	A..K..N	H..M..K	Q..P..H	X..R..E
28)	J..E..S	R..H..Q	B..L..O	J..N..L	R..Q..J	A..S..F
29)	K..F..T	S..J..R	C..M..P	K..O..M	S..R..K	B..T..G
30)	L..G..U	T..K..S	D..N..Q	L..P..N	T..S..L	C..U..H
31)	M..H..V	U..L..T		M..Q..O		D..V..J

CODES: P-PHYSICAL BIORHYTHM CURVE, E-EMOTIONAL BIORHYTHM CURVE, I-INTELLECTUAL BIORHYTHM CURVE

```
  ...JANUARY..    ..FEBRUARY..    ....MARCH...    ....APRIL...    ....MAY....    ....JUNE....

     P--E--I          P--E--I          P--E--I          P--E--I          P--E--I          P--E--I

 1)  E..W..K      1)  N..Z..H      1)  T..1..D      1)  D..A..B      1)  L..C..7      1)  T..F..5
 2)  F..X..L      2)  O..1..J      2)  U..2..E      2)  E..B..C      2)  M..D..8      2)  U..G..6
 3)  G..Y..M      3)  P..2..K      3)  V..3..F      3)  F..C..D      3)  N..E..A      3)  V..H..7
 4)  H..Z..N      4)  Q..3..L      4)  W..A..G      4)  G..D..E      4)  O..F..B      4)  W..J..8
 5)  J..1..O      5)  R..A..M      5)  X..B..H      5)  H..E..F      5)  P..G..C      5)  X..K..A
 6)  K..2..P      6)  S..B..N      6)  A..C..J      6)  J..F..G      6)  Q..H..D      6)  A..L..B
 7)  L..3..Q      7)  T..C..O      7)  B..D..K      7)  K..G..H      7)  R..J..E      7)  B..M..C
 8)  M..A..R      8)  U..D..P      8)  C..E..L      8)  L..H..J      8)  S..K..F      8)  C..N..D
 9)  N..B..S      9)  V..E..Q      9)  D..F..M      9)  M..J..K      9)  T..L..G      9)  D..O..E
10)  O..C..T     10)  W..F..R     10)  E..G..N     10)  N..K..L     10)  U..M..H     10)  E..P..F
11)  P..D..U     11)  X..G..S     11)  F..H..O     11)  O..L..M     11)  V..N..J     11)  F..Q..G
12)  Q..E..V     12)  A..H..T     12)  G..J..P     12)  P..M..N     12)  W..O..K     12)  G..R..H
13)  R..F..W     13)  B..J..U     13)  H..K..Q     13)  Q..N..O     13)  X..P..L     13)  H..S..J
14)  S..G..X     14)  C..K..V     14)  J..L..R     14)  R..O..P     14)  A..Q..M     14)  J..T..K
15)  T..H..Y     15)  D..L..W     15)  K..M..S     15)  S..P..Q     15)  B..R..N     15)  K..U..L
16)  U..J..Z     16)  E..M..X     16)  L..N..T     16)  T..Q..R     16)  C..S..O     16)  L..V..M
17)  V..K..1     17)  F..N..Y     17)  M..O..U     17)  U..R..S     17)  D..T..P     17)  M..W..N
18)  W..L..2     18)  G..O..Z     18)  N..P..V     18)  V..S..T     18)  E..U..Q     18)  N..X..O
19)  X..M..3     19)  H..P..1     19)  O..Q..W     19)  W..T..U     19)  F..V..R     19)  O..Y..P
20)  A..N..4     20)  J..Q..2     20)  P..R..X     20)  X..U..V     20)  G..W..S     20)  P..Z..Q
21)  B..O..5     21)  K..R..3     21)  Q..S..Y     21)  A..V..W     21)  H..X..T     21)  Q..1..R
22)  C..P..6     22)  L..S..4     22)  R..T..Z     22)  B..W..X     22)  J..Y..U     22)  R..2..S
23)  D..Q..7     23)  M..T..5     23)  S..U..1     23)  C..X..Y     23)  K..Z..V     23)  S..3..T
24)  E..R..8     24)  N..U..6     24)  T..V..2     24)  D..Y..Z     24)  L..1..W     24)  T..A..U
25)  F..S..A     25)  O..V..7     25)  U..W..3     25)  E..Z..1     25)  M..2..X     25)  U..B..V
26)  G..T..B     26)  P..W..8     26)  V..X..4     26)  F..1..2     26)  N..3..Y     26)  V..C..W
27)  H..U..C     27)  Q..X..A     27)  W..Y..5     27)  G..2..3     27)  O..A..Z     27)  W..D..X
28)  J..V..D     28)  R..Y..B     28)  X..Z..6     28)  H..3..4     28)  P..B..1     28)  X..E..Y
29)  K..W..E     29)  S..Z..C     29)  A..1..7     29)  J..A..5     29)  Q..C..2     29)  A..F..Z
30)  L..X..F                      30)  B..2..8     30)  K..B..6     30)  R..D..3     30)  B..G..1
31)  M..Y..G                      31)  C..3..A                      31)  S..E..4
```

```
  ....JULY....    ...AUGUST...    .SEPTEMBER.    ..OCTOBER...    .NOVEMBER..    .DECEMBER..

     P--E--I          P--E--I          P--E--I          P--E--I          P--E--I          P--E--I

 1)  C..H..2      1)  L..L..Z      1)  T..O..X      1)  C..Q..U      1)  L..T..S      1)  S..V..P
 2)  D..J..3      2)  M..M..1      2)  U..P..Y      2)  D..R..V      2)  M..U..T      2)  T..W..Q
 3)  E..K..4      3)  N..N..2      3)  V..Q..Z      3)  E..S..W      3)  N..V..U      3)  U..X..R
 4)  F..L..5      4)  O..O..3      4)  W..R..1      4)  F..T..X      4)  O..W..V      4)  V..Y..S
 5)  G..M..6      5)  P..P..4      5)  X..S..2      5)  G..U..Y      5)  P..X..W      5)  W..Z..T
 6)  H..N..7      6)  Q..Q..5      6)  A..T..3      6)  H..V..Z      6)  Q..Y..X      6)  X..1..U
 7)  J..O..8      7)  R..R..6      7)  B..U..4      7)  J..W..1      7)  R..Z..Y      7)  A..2..V
 8)  K..P..A      8)  S..S..7      8)  C..V..5      8)  K..X..2      8)  S..1..Z      8)  B..3..W
 9)  L..Q..B      9)  T..T..8      9)  D..W..6      9)  L..Y..3      9)  T..2..1      9)  C..A..X
10)  M..R..C     10)  U..U..A     10)  E..X..7     10)  M..Z..4     10)  U..3..2     10)  D..B..Y
11)  N..S..D     11)  V..V..B     11)  F..Y..8     11)  N..1..5     11)  V..A..3     11)  E..C..Z
12)  O..T..E     12)  W..W..C     12)  G..Z..A     12)  O..2..6     12)  W..B..4     12)  F..D..1
13)  P..U..F     13)  X..X..D     13)  H..1..B     13)  P..3..7     13)  X..C..5     13)  G..E..2
14)  Q..V..G     14)  A..Y..E     14)  J..2..C     14)  Q..A..8     14)  A..D..6     14)  H..F..3
15)  R..W..H     15)  B..Z..F     15)  K..3..D     15)  R..B..A     15)  B..E..7     15)  J..G..4
16)  S..X..J     16)  C..1..G     16)  L..A..E     16)  S..C..B     16)  C..F..8     16)  K..H..5
17)  T..Y..K     17)  D..2..H     17)  M..B..F     17)  T..D..C     17)  D..G..A     17)  L..J..6
18)  U..Z..L     18)  E..3..J     18)  N..C..G     18)  U..E..D     18)  E..H..B     18)  M..K..7
19)  V..1..M     19)  F..A..K     19)  O..D..H     19)  V..F..E     19)  F..J..C     19)  N..L..8
20)  W..2..N     20)  G..B..L     20)  P..E..J     20)  W..G..F     20)  G..K..D     20)  O..M..A
21)  X..3..O     21)  H..C..M     21)  Q..F..K     21)  X..H..G     21)  H..L..E     21)  P..N..B
22)  A..A..P     22)  J..D..N     22)  R..G..L     22)  A..J..H     22)  J..M..F     22)  Q..O..C
23)  B..B..Q     23)  K..E..O     23)  S..H..M     23)  B..K..J     23)  K..N..G     23)  R..P..D
24)  C..C..R     24)  L..F..P     24)  T..J..N     24)  C..L..K     24)  L..O..H     24)  S..Q..E
25)  D..D..S     25)  M..G..Q     25)  U..K..O     25)  D..M..L     25)  M..P..J     25)  T..R..F
26)  E..E..T     26)  N..H..R     26)  V..L..P     26)  E..N..M     26)  N..Q..K     26)  U..S..G
27)  F..F..U     27)  O..J..S     27)  W..M..Q     27)  F..O..N     27)  O..R..L     27)  V..T..H
28)  G..G..V     28)  P..K..T     28)  X..N..R     28)  G..P..O     28)  P..S..M     28)  W..U..J
29)  H..H..W     29)  Q..L..U     29)  A..O..S     29)  H..Q..P     29)  Q..T..N     29)  X..V..K
30)  J..J..X     30)  R..M..V     30)  B..P..T     30)  J..R..Q     30)  R..U..O     30)  A..W..L
31)  K..K..Y     31)  S..N..W                      31)  K..S..R                      31)  B..X..M
```

CODES: P-PHYSICAL BIORHYTHM CURVE,E-EMOTIONAL BIORHYTHM CURVE,I-INTELLECTUAL BIORHYTHM CURVE

	...JANUARY.. P--E--I		..FEBRUARY.. P--E--I		...MARCH... P--E--I		...APRIL... P--E--I		....MAY.... P--E--I		...JUNE.... P--E--I
1)	C..Y..N	1)	L..2..L	1)	Q..2..F	1)	A..B..D	1)	H..D..A	1)	Q..G..7
2)	D..Z..O	2)	M..3..M	2)	R..3..G	2)	B..C..E	2)	J..E..B	2)	R..H..8
3)	E..1..P	3)	N..A..N	3)	S..A..H	3)	C..D..F	3)	K..F..C	3)	S..J..A
4)	F..2..Q	4)	O..B..O	4)	T..B..J	4)	D..E..G	4)	L..G..D	4)	T..K..B
5)	G..3..R	5)	P..C..P	5)	U..C..K	5)	E..F..H	5)	M..H..E	5)	U..L..C
6)	H..A..S	6)	Q..D..Q	6)	V..D..L	6)	F..G..J	6)	N..J..F	6)	V..M..D
7)	J..B..T	7)	R..E..R	7)	W..E..M	7)	G..H..K	7)	O..K..G	7)	W..N..E
8)	K..C..U	8)	S..F..S	8)	X..F..N	8)	H..J..L	8)	P..L..H	8)	X..O..F
9)	L..D..V	9)	T..G..T	9)	A..G..O	9)	J..K..M	9)	Q..M..J	9)	A..P..G
10)	M..E..W	10)	U..H..U	10)	B..H..P	10)	K..L..N	10)	R..N..K	10)	B..Q..H
11)	N..F..X	11)	V..J..V	11)	C..J..Q	11)	L..M..O	11)	S..O..L	11)	C..R..J
12)	O..G..Y	12)	W..K..W	12)	D..K..R	12)	M..N..P	12)	T..P..M	12)	D..S..K
13)	P..H..Z	13)	X..L..X	13)	E..L..S	13)	N..O..Q	13)	U..Q..N	13)	E..T..L
14)	Q..J..1	14)	A..M..Y	14)	F..M..T	14)	O..P..R	14)	V..R..O	14)	F..U..M
15)	R..K..2	15)	B..N..Z	15)	G..N..U	15)	P..Q..S	15)	W..S..P	15)	G..V..N
16)	S..L..3	16)	C..O..1	16)	H..O..V	16)	Q..R..T	16)	X..T..Q	16)	H..W..O
17)	T..M..4	17)	D..P..2	17)	J..P..W	17)	R..S..U	17)	A..U..R	17)	J..X..P
18)	U..N..5	18)	E..Q..3	18)	K..Q..X	18)	S..T..V	18)	B..V..S	18)	K..Y..Q
19)	V..O..6	19)	F..R..4	19)	L..R..Y	19)	T..U..W	19)	C..W..T	19)	L..Z..R
20)	W..P..7	20)	G..S..5	20)	M..S..Z	20)	U..V..X	20)	D..X..U	20)	M..1..S
21)	X..Q..8	21)	H..T..6	21)	N..T..1	21)	V..W..Y	21)	E..Y..V	21)	N..2..T
22)	A..R..A	22)	J..U..7	22)	O..U..2	22)	W..X..Z	22)	F..Z..W	22)	O..3..U
23)	B..S..B	23)	K..V..8	23)	P..V..3	23)	X..Y..1	23)	G..1..X	23)	P..A..V
24)	C..T..C	24)	L..W..A	24)	Q..W..4	24)	A..Z..2	24)	H..2..Y	24)	Q..B..W
25)	D..U..D	25)	M..X..B	25)	R..X..5	25)	B..1..3	25)	J..3..Z	25)	R..C..X
26)	E..V..E	26)	N..Y..C	26)	S..Y..6	26)	C..2..4	26)	K..A..1	26)	S..D..Y
27)	F..W..F	27)	O..Z..D	27)	T..Z..7	27)	D..3..5	27)	L..B..2	27)	T..E..Z
28)	G..X..G	28)	P..1..E	28)	U..1..8	28)	E..A..6	28)	M..C..3	28)	U..F..1
29)	H..Y..H			29)	V..2..A	29)	F..B..7	29)	N..D..4	29)	V..G..2
30)	J..Z..J			30)	W..3..B	30)	G..C..8	30)	O..E..5	30)	W..H..3
31)	K..1..K			31)	X..A..C			31)	P..F..6		

	....JULY.... P--E--I		...AUGUST... P--E--I		..SEPTEMBER. P--E--I		..OCTOBER... P--E--I		..NOVEMBER.. P--E--I		..DECEMBER.. P--E--I
1)	X..J..4	1)	H..M..2	1)	Q..P..Z	1)	X..R..W	1)	H..U..U	1)	P..W..R
2)	A..K..5	2)	J..N..3	2)	R..Q..1	2)	A..S..X	2)	J..V..V	2)	Q..X..S
3)	B..L..6	3)	K..O..4	3)	S..R..2	3)	B..T..Y	3)	K..W..W	3)	R..Y..T
4)	C..M..7	4)	L..P..5	4)	T..S..3	4)	C..U..Z	4)	L..X..X	4)	S..Z..U
5)	D..N..8	5)	M..Q..6	5)	U..T..4	5)	D..V..1	5)	M..Y..Y	5)	T..1..V
6)	E..O..A	6)	N..R..7	6)	V..U..5	6)	E..W..2	6)	N..Z..Z	6)	U..2..W
7)	F..P..B	7)	O..S..8	7)	W..V..6	7)	F..X..3	7)	O..1..1	7)	V..3..X
8)	G..Q..C	8)	P..T..A	8)	X..W..7	8)	G..Y..4	8)	P..2..2	8)	W..A..Y
9)	H..R..D	9)	Q..U..B	9)	A..X..8	9)	H..Z..5	9)	Q..3..3	9)	X..B..Z
10)	J..S..E	10)	R..V..C	10)	B..Y..A	10)	J..1..6	10)	R..A..4	10)	A..C..1
11)	K..T..F	11)	S..W..D	11)	C..Z..B	11)	K..2..7	11)	S..B..5	11)	B..D..2
12)	L..U..G	12)	T..X..E	12)	D..1..C	12)	L..3..8	12)	T..C..6	12)	C..E..3
13)	M..V..H	13)	U..Y..F	13)	E..2..D	13)	M..A..A	13)	U..D..7	13)	D..F..4
14)	N..W..J	14)	V..Z..G	14)	F..3..E	14)	N..B..B	14)	V..E..8	14)	E..G..5
15)	O..X..K	15)	W..1..H	15)	G..A..F	15)	O..C..C	15)	W..F..A	15)	F..H..6
16)	P..Y..L	16)	X..2..J	16)	H..B..G	16)	P..D..D	16)	X..G..B	16)	G..J..7
17)	Q..Z..M	17)	A..3..K	17)	J..C..H	17)	Q..E..E	17)	A..H..C	17)	H..K..8
18)	R..1..N	18)	B..A..L	18)	K..D..J	18)	R..F..F	18)	B..J..D	18)	J..L..A
19)	S..2..O	19)	C..B..M	19)	L..E..K	19)	S..G..G	19)	C..K..E	19)	K..M..B
20)	T..3..P	20)	D..C..N	20)	M..F..L	20)	T..H..H	20)	D..L..F	20)	L..N..C
21)	U..A..Q	21)	E..D..O	21)	N..G..M	21)	U..J..J	21)	E..M..G	21)	M..O..D
22)	V..B..R	22)	F..E..P	22)	O..H..N	22)	V..K..K	22)	F..N..H	22)	N..P..E
23)	W..C..S	23)	G..F..Q	23)	P..J..O	23)	W..L..L	23)	G..O..J	23)	O..Q..F
24)	X..D..T	24)	H..G..R	24)	Q..K..P	24)	X..M..M	24)	H..P..K	24)	P..R..G
25)	A..E..U	25)	J..H..S	25)	R..L..Q	25)	A..N..N	25)	J..Q..L	25)	Q..S..H
26)	B..F..V	26)	K..J..T	26)	S..M..R	26)	B..O..O	26)	K..R..M	26)	R..T..J
27)	C..G..W	27)	L..K..U	27)	T..N..S	27)	C..P..P	27)	L..S..N	27)	S..U..K
28)	D..H..X	28)	M..L..V	28)	U..O..T	28)	D..Q..Q	28)	M..T..O	28)	T..V..L
29)	E..J..Y	29)	N..M..W	29)	V..P..U	29)	E..R..R	29)	N..U..P	29)	U..W..M
30)	F..K..Z	30)	O..N..X	30)	W..Q..V	30)	F..S..S	30)	O..V..Q	30)	V..X..N
31)	G..L..1	31)	P..O..Y			31)	G..T..T			31)	W..Y..O

CODES: P-PHYSICAL BIORHYTHM CURVE,E-EMOTIONAL BIORHYTHM CURVE,I-INTELLECTUAL BIORHYTHM CURVE

```
   ...JANUARY..     ..FEBRUARY..     ...MARCH...      ...APRIL...      .....MAY....     ...JUNE....

       P--E--I          P--E--I          P--E--I          P--E--I          P--E--I          P--E--I

 1)    X..Z..P     1)  H..3..N     1)  N..3..H     1)  V..C..F     1)  E..E..C     1)  N..H..A
 2)    A..1..Q     2)  J..A..O     2)  O..A..J     2)  W..D..G     2)  F..F..D     2)  O..J..B
 3)    B..2..R     3)  K..B..P     3)  P..B..K     3)  X..E..H     3)  G..G..E     3)  P..K..C
 4)    C..3..S     4)  L..C..Q     4)  Q..C..L     4)  A..F..J     4)  H..H..F     4)  Q..L..D
 5)    D..A..T     5)  M..D..R     5)  R..D..M     5)  B..G..K     5)  J..J..G     5)  R..M..E
 6)    E..B..U     6)  N..E..S     6)  S..E..N     6)  C..H..L     6)  K..K..H     6)  S..N..F
 7)    F..C..V     7)  O..F..T     7)  T..F..O     7)  D..J..M     7)  L..L..J     7)  T..O..G
 8)    G..D..W     8)  P..G..U     8)  U..G..P     8)  E..K..N     8)  M..M..K     8)  U..P..H
 9)    H..E..X     9)  Q..H..V     9)  V..H..Q     9)  F..L..O     9)  N..N..L     9)  V..Q..J
10)    J..F..Y    10)  R..J..W    10)  W..J..R    10)  G..M..P    10)  O..O..M    10)  W..R..K
11)    K..G..Z    11)  S..K..X    11)  X..K..S    11)  H..N..Q    11)  P..P..N    11)  X..S..L
12)    L..H..1    12)  T..L..Y    12)  A..L..T    12)  J..O..R    12)  Q..Q..O    12)  A..T..M
13)    M..J..2    13)  U..M..Z    13)  B..M..U    13)  K..P..S    13)  R..R..P    13)  B..U..N
14)    N..K..3    14)  V..N..1    14)  C..N..V    14)  L..Q..T    14)  S..S..Q    14)  C..V..O
15)    O..L..4    15)  W..O..2    15)  D..O..W    15)  M..R..U    15)  T..T..R    15)  D..W..P
16)    P..M..5    16)  X..P..3    16)  E..P..X    16)  N..S..V    16)  U..U..S    16)  E..X..Q
17)    Q..N..6    17)  A..Q..4    17)  F..Q..Y    17)  O..T..W    17)  V..V..T    17)  F..Y..R
18)    R..O..7    18)  B..R..5    18)  G..R..Z    18)  P..U..X    18)  W..W..U    18)  G..Z..S
19)    S..P..8    19)  C..S..6    19)  H..S..1    19)  Q..V..Y    19)  X..X..V    19)  H..1..T
20)    T..Q..A    20)  D..T..7    20)  J..T..2    20)  R..W..Z    20)  A..Y..W    20)  J..2..U
21)    U..R..B    21)  E..U..8    21)  K..U..3    21)  S..X..1    21)  B..Z..X    21)  K..3..V
22)    V..S..C    22)  F..V..A    22)  L..V..4    22)  T..Y..2    22)  C..1..Y    22)  L..A..W
23)    W..T..D    23)  G..W..B    23)  M..W..5    23)  U..Z..3    23)  D..2..Z    23)  M..B..X
24)    X..U..E    24)  H..X..C    24)  N..X..6    24)  V..1..4    24)  E..3..1    24)  N..C..Y
25)    A..V..F    25)  J..Y..D    25)  O..Y..7    25)  W..2..5    25)  F..A..2    25)  O..D..Z
26)    B..W..G    26)  K..Z..E    26)  P..Z..8    26)  X..3..6    26)  G..B..3    26)  P..E..1
27)    C..X..H    27)  L..1..F    27)  Q..1..A    27)  A..A..7    27)  H..C..4    27)  Q..F..2
28)    D..Y..J    28)  M..2..G    28)  R..2..B    28)  B..B..8    28)  J..D..5    28)  R..G..3
29)    E..Z..K                    29)  S..3..C    29)  C..C..A    29)  K..E..6    29)  S..H..4
30)    F..1..L                    30)  T..A..D    30)  D..D..B    30)  L..F..7    30)  T..J..5
31)    G..2..M                    31)  U..B..E                    31)  M..G..8
```

```
   ....JULY....     ...AUGUST...     ..SEPTEMBER.     .OCTOBER...      .NOVEMBER..      ..DECEMBER..

       P--E--I          P--E--I          P--E--I          P--E--I          P--E--I          P--E--I

 1)    U..K..6     1)  E..N..4     1)  N..Q..2     1)  U..S..Y     1)  E..V..W     1)  M..X..T
 2)    V..L..7     2)  F..O..5     2)  O..R..3     2)  V..T..Z     2)  F..W..X     2)  N..Y..U
 3)    W..M..8     3)  G..P..6     3)  P..S..4     3)  W..U..1     3)  G..X..Y     3)  O..Z..V
 4)    X..N..A     4)  H..Q..7     4)  Q..T..5     4)  X..V..2     4)  H..Y..Z     4)  P..1..W
 5)    A..O..B     5)  J..R..8     5)  R..U..6     5)  A..W..3     5)  J..Z..1     5)  Q..2..X
 6)    B..P..C     6)  K..S..A     6)  S..V..7     6)  B..X..4     6)  K..1..2     6)  R..3..Y
 7)    C..Q..D     7)  L..T..B     7)  T..W..8     7)  C..Y..5     7)  L..2..3     7)  S..A..Z
 8)    D..R..E     8)  M..U..C     8)  U..X..A     8)  D..Z..6     8)  M..3..4     8)  T..B..1
 9)    E..S..F     9)  N..V..D     9)  V..Y..B     9)  E..1..7     9)  N..A..5     9)  U..C..2
10)    F..T..G    10)  O..W..E    10)  W..Z..C    10)  F..2..8    10)  O..B..6    10)  V..D..3
11)    G..U..H    11)  P..X..F    11)  X..1..D    11)  G..3..A    11)  P..C..7    11)  W..E..4
12)    H..V..J    12)  Q..Y..G    12)  A..2..E    12)  H..A..B    12)  Q..D..8    12)  X..F..5
13)    J..W..K    13)  R..Z..H    13)  B..3..F    13)  J..B..C    13)  R..E..A    13)  A..G..6
14)    K..X..L    14)  S..1..J    14)  C..A..G    14)  K..C..D    14)  S..F..B    14)  B..H..7
15)    L..Y..M    15)  T..2..K    15)  D..B..H    15)  L..D..E    15)  T..G..C    15)  C..J..8
16)    M..Z..N    16)  U..3..L    16)  E..C..J    16)  M..E..F    16)  U..H..D    16)  D..K..A
17)    N..1..O    17)  V..A..M    17)  F..D..K    17)  N..F..G    17)  V..J..E    17)  E..L..B
18)    O..2..P    18)  W..B..N    18)  G..E..L    18)  O..G..H    18)  W..K..F    18)  F..M..C
19)    P..3..Q    19)  X..C..O    19)  H..F..M    19)  P..H..J    19)  X..L..G    19)  G..N..D
20)    Q..A..R    20)  A..D..P    20)  J..G..N    20)  Q..J..K    20)  A..M..H    20)  H..O..E
21)    R..B..S    21)  B..E..Q    21)  K..H..O    21)  R..K..L    21)  B..N..J    21)  J..P..F
22)    S..C..T    22)  C..F..R    22)  L..J..P    22)  S..L..M    22)  C..O..K    22)  K..Q..G
23)    T..D..U    23)  D..G..S    23)  M..K..Q    23)  T..M..N    23)  D..P..L    23)  L..R..H
24)    U..E..V    24)  E..H..T    24)  N..L..R    24)  U..N..O    24)  E..Q..M    24)  M..S..J
25)    V..F..W    25)  F..J..U    25)  O..M..S    25)  V..O..P    25)  F..R..N    25)  N..T..K
26)    W..G..X    26)  G..K..V    26)  P..N..T    26)  W..P..Q    26)  G..S..O    26)  O..U..L
27)    X..H..Y    27)  H..L..W    27)  Q..O..U    27)  X..Q..R    27)  H..T..P    27)  P..V..M
28)    A..J..Z    28)  J..M..X    28)  R..P..V    28)  A..R..S    28)  J..U..Q    28)  Q..W..N
29)    B..K..1    29)  K..N..Y    29)  S..Q..W    29)  B..S..T    29)  K..V..R    29)  R..X..O
30)    C..L..2    30)  L..O..Z    30)  T..R..X    30)  C..T..U    30)  L..W..S    30)  S..Y..P
31)    D..M..3    31)  M..P..1                    31)  D..U..V                    31)  T..Z..Q
```

CODES: P-PHYSICAL BIORHYTHM CURVE,E-EMOTIONAL BIORHYTHM CURVE,I-INTELLECTUAL BIORHYTHM CURVE

```
        ...JANUARY..    ..FEBRUARY..    ...MARCH...     ...APRIL...     ...MAY....      ...JUNE....

           P--E--I         P--E--I         P--E--I         P--E--I         P--E--I         P--E--I

     1)    U..1..R    1)  E..A..P    1)  K..A..K    1)  S..D..H    1)  B..F..E    1)  K..J..C
     2)    V..2..S    2)  F..B..Q    2)  L..B..L    2)  T..E..J    2)  C..G..F    2)  L..K..D
     3)    W..3..T    3)  G..C..R    3)  M..C..M    3)  U..F..K    3)  D..H..G    3)  M..L..E
     4)    X..A..U    4)  H..D..S    4)  N..D..N    4)  V..G..L    4)  E..J..H    4)  N..M..F
     5)    A..B..V    5)  J..E..T    5)  O..E..O    5)  W..H..M    5)  F..K..J    5)  O..N..G
     6)    B..C..W    6)  K..F..U    6)  P..F..P    6)  X..J..N    6)  G..L..K    6)  P..O..H
     7)    C..D..X    7)  L..G..V    7)  Q..G..Q    7)  A..K..O    7)  H..M..L    7)  Q..P..J
     8)    D..E..Y    8)  M..H..W    8)  R..H..R    8)  B..L..P    8)  J..N..M    8)  R..Q..K
     9)    E..F..Z    9)  N..J..X    9)  S..J..S    9)  C..M..Q    9)  K..O..N    9)  S..R..L
    10)    F..G..1   10)  O..K..Y   10)  T..K..T   10)  D..N..R   10)  L..P..O   10)  T..S..M
    11)    G..H..2   11)  P..L..Z   11)  U..L..U   11)  E..O..S   11)  M..Q..P   11)  U..T..N
    12)    H..J..3   12)  Q..M..1   12)  V..M..V   12)  F..P..T   12)  N..R..Q   12)  V..U..O
    13)    J..K..4   13)  R..N..2   13)  W..N..W   13)  G..Q..U   13)  O..S..R   13)  W..V..P
    14)    K..L..5   14)  S..O..3   14)  X..O..X   14)  H..R..V   14)  P..T..S   14)  X..W..Q
    15)    L..M..6   15)  T..P..4   15)  A..P..Y   15)  J..S..W   15)  Q..U..T   15)  A..X..R
    16)    M..N..7   16)  U..Q..5   16)  B..Q..Z   16)  K..T..X   16)  R..V..U   16)  B..Y..S
    17)    N..O..8   17)  V..R..6   17)  C..R..1   17)  L..U..Y   17)  S..W..V   17)  C..Z..T
    18)    O..P..A   18)  W..S..7   18)  D..S..2   18)  M..V..Z   18)  T..X..W   18)  D..1..U
    19)    P..Q..B   19)  X..T..8   19)  E..T..3   19)  N..W..1   19)  U..Y..X   19)  E..2..V
    20)    Q..R..C   20)  A..U..A   20)  F..U..4   20)  O..X..2   20)  V..Z..Y   20)  F..3..W
    21)    R..S..D   21)  B..V..B   21)  G..V..5   21)  P..Y..3   21)  W..1..Z   21)  G..A..X
    22)    S..T..E   22)  C..W..C   22)  H..W..6   22)  Q..Z..4   22)  X..2..1   22)  H..B..Y
    23)    T..U..F   23)  D..X..D   23)  J..X..7   23)  R..1..5   23)  A..3..2   23)  J..C..Z
    24)    U..V..G   24)  E..Y..E   24)  K..Y..8   24)  S..2..6   24)  B..A..3   24)  K..D..1
    25)    V..W..H   25)  F..Z..F   25)  L..Z..A   25)  T..3..7   25)  C..B..4   25)  L..E..2
    26)    W..X..J   26)  G..1..G   26)  M..1..B   26)  U..A..8   26)  D..C..5   26)  M..F..3
    27)    X..Y..K   27)  H..2..H   27)  N..2..C   27)  V..B..A   27)  E..D..6   27)  N..G..4
    28)    A..Z..L   28)  J..3..J   28)  O..3..D   28)  W..C..B   28)  F..E..7   28)  O..H..5
    29)    B..1..M                  29)  P..A..E   29)  X..D..C   29)  G..F..8   29)  P..J..6
    30)    C..2..N                  30)  Q..B..F   30)  A..E..D   30)  H..G..A   30)  Q..K..7
    31)    D..3..O                  31)  R..C..G                  31)  J..H..B
```

```
        ....JULY....    ...AUGUST...    .SEPTEMBER.     ..OCTOBER...    ..NOVEMBER..    ..DECEMBER..

           P--E--I         P--E--I         P--E--I         P--E--I         P--E--I         P--E--I

     1)    R..L..8    1)  B..O..6    1)  K..R..4    1)  R..T..1    1)  B..W..Y    1)  J..Y..V
     2)    S..M..A    2)  C..P..7    2)  L..S..5    2)  S..U..2    2)  C..X..Z    2)  K..Z..W
     3)    T..N..B    3)  D..Q..8    3)  M..T..6    3)  T..V..3    3)  D..Y..1    3)  L..1..X
     4)    U..O..C    4)  E..R..A    4)  N..U..7    4)  U..W..4    4)  E..Z..2    4)  M..2..Y
     5)    V..P..D    5)  F..S..B    5)  O..V..8    5)  V..X..5    5)  F..1..3    5)  N..3..Z
     6)    W..Q..E    6)  G..T..C    6)  P..W..A    6)  W..Y..6    6)  G..2..4    6)  O..A..1
     7)    X..R..F    7)  H..U..D    7)  Q..X..B    7)  X..Z..7    7)  H..3..5    7)  P..B..2
     8)    A..S..G    8)  J..V..E    8)  R..Y..C    8)  A..1..8    8)  J..A..6    8)  Q..C..3
     9)    B..T..H    9)  K..W..F    9)  S..Z..D    9)  B..2..A    9)  K..B..7    9)  R..D..4
    10)    C..U..J   10)  L..X..G   10)  T..1..E   10)  C..3..B   10)  L..C..8   10)  S..E..5
    11)    D..V..K   11)  M..Y..H   11)  U..2..F   11)  D..A..C   11)  M..D..A   11)  T..F..6
    12)    E..W..L   12)  N..Z..J   12)  V..3..G   12)  E..B..D   12)  N..E..B   12)  U..G..7
    13)    F..X..M   13)  O..1..K   13)  W..A..H   13)  F..C..E   13)  O..F..C   13)  V..H..8
    14)    G..Y..N   14)  P..2..L   14)  X..B..J   14)  G..D..F   14)  P..G..D   14)  W..J..A
    15)    H..Z..O   15)  Q..3..M   15)  A..C..K   15)  H..E..G   15)  Q..H..E   15)  X..K..B
    16)    J..1..P   16)  R..A..N   16)  B..D..L   16)  J..F..H   16)  R..J..F   16)  A..L..C
    17)    K..2..Q   17)  S..B..O   17)  C..E..M   17)  K..G..J   17)  S..K..G   17)  B..M..D
    18)    L..3..R   18)  T..C..P   18)  D..F..N   18)  L..H..K   18)  T..L..H   18)  C..N..E
    19)    M..A..S   19)  U..D..Q   19)  E..G..O   19)  M..J..L   19)  U..M..J   19)  D..O..F
    20)    N..B..T   20)  V..E..R   20)  F..H..P   20)  N..K..M   20)  V..N..K   20)  E..P..G
    21)    O..C..U   21)  W..F..S   21)  G..J..Q   21)  O..L..N   21)  W..O..L   21)  F..Q..H
    22)    P..D..V   22)  X..G..T   22)  H..K..R   22)  P..M..O   22)  X..P..M   22)  G..R..J
    23)    Q..E..W   23)  A..H..U   23)  J..L..S   23)  Q..N..P   23)  A..Q..N   23)  H..S..K
    24)    R..F..X   24)  B..J..V   24)  K..M..T   24)  R..O..Q   24)  B..R..O   24)  J..T..L
    25)    S..G..Y   25)  C..K..W   25)  L..N..U   25)  S..P..R   25)  C..S..P   25)  K..U..M
    26)    T..H..Z   26)  D..L..X   26)  M..O..V   26)  T..Q..S   26)  D..T..Q   26)  L..V..N
    27)    U..J..1   27)  E..M..Y   27)  N..P..W   27)  U..R..T   27)  E..U..R   27)  M..W..O
    28)    V..K..2   28)  F..N..Z   28)  O..Q..X   28)  V..S..U   28)  F..V..S   28)  N..X..P
    29)    W..L..3   29)  G..O..1   29)  P..R..Y   29)  W..T..V   29)  G..W..T   29)  O..Y..Q
    30)    X..M..4   30)  H..P..2   30)  Q..S..Z   30)  X..U..W   30)  H..X..U   30)  P..Z..R
    31)    A..N..5   31)  J..Q..3                  31)  A..V..X                  31)  Q..1..S
```

CODES: P-PHYSICAL BIORHYTHM CURVE, E-EMOTIONAL BIORHYTHM CURVE, I-INTELLECTUAL BIORHYTHM CURVE

	...JANUARY..	..FEBRUARY..	....MARCH...	....APRIL...	.....MAY....	....JUNE....
	P--E--I	P--E--I	P--E--I	P--E--I	P--E--I	P--E--I
1)	R..2..T	B..B..R	H..C..N	Q..F..L	X..H..H	H..L..F
2)	S..3..U	C..C..S	J..D..O	R..G..M	A..J..J	J..M..G
3)	T..A..V	D..D..T	K..E..P	S..H..N	B..K..K	K..N..H
4)	U..B..W	E..E..U	L..F..Q	T..J..O	C..L..L	L..O..J
5)	V..C..X	F..F..V	M..G..R	U..K..P	D..M..M	M..P..K
6)	W..D..Y	G..G..W	N..H..S	V..L..Q	E..N..N	N..Q..L
7)	X..E..Z	H..H..X	O..J..T	W..M..R	F..O..O	O..R..M
8)	A..F..1	J..J..Y	P..K..U	X..N..S	G..P..P	P..S..N
9)	B..G..2	K..K..Z	Q..L..V	A..O..T	H..Q..Q	Q..T..O
10)	C..H..3	L..L..1	R..M..W	B..P..U	J..R..R	R..U..P
11)	D..J..4	M..M..2	S..N..X	C..Q..V	K..S..S	S..V..Q
12)	E..K..5	N..N..3	T..O..Y	D..R..W	L..T..T	T..W..R
13)	F..L..6	O..O..4	U..P..Z	E..S..X	M..U..U	U..X..S
14)	G..M..7	P..P..5	V..Q..1	F..T..Y	N..V..V	V..Y..T
15)	H..N..8	Q..Q..6	W..R..2	G..U..Z	O..W..W	W..Z..U
16)	J..O..A	R..R..7	X..S..3	H..V..1	P..X..X	X..1..V
17)	K..P..B	S..S..8	A..T..4	J..W..2	Q..Y..Y	A..2..W
18)	L..Q..C	T..T..A	B..U..5	K..X..3	R..Z..Z	B..3..X
19)	M..R..D	U..U..B	C..V..6	L..Y..4	S..1..1	C..A..Y
20)	N..S..E	V..V..C	D..W..7	M..Z..5	T..2..2	D..B..Z
21)	O..T..F	W..W..D	E..X..8	N..1..6	U..3..3	E..C..1
22)	P..U..G	X..X..E	F..Y..A	O..2..7	V..A..4	F..D..2
23)	Q..V..H	A..Y..F	G..Z..B	P..3..8	W..B..5	G..E..3
24)	R..W..J	B..Z..G	H..1..C	Q..A..A	X..C..6	H..F..4
25)	S..X..K	C..1..H	J..2..D	R..B..B	A..D..7	J..G..5
26)	T..Y..L	D..2..J	K..3..E	S..C..C	B..E..8	K..H..6
27)	U..Z..M	E..3..K	L..A..F	T..D..D	C..F..A	L..J..7
28)	V..1..N	F..A..L	M..B..G	U..E..E	D..G..B	M..K..8
29)	W..2..O	G..B..M	N..C..H	V..F..F	E..H..C	N..L..A
30)	X..3..P		O..D..J	W..G..G	F..J..D	O..M..B
31)	A..A..Q		P..E..K		G..K..E	

	....JULY....	...AUGUST...	..SEPTEMBER.	..OCTOBER...	..NOVEMBER..	..DECEMBER..
	P--E--I	P--E--I	P--E--I	P--E--I	P--E--I	P--E--I
1)	P..N..C	X..Q..A	H..T..7	P..V..4	X..Y..2	G..1..Y
2)	Q..O..D	A..R..B	J..U..8	Q..W..5	A..Z..3	H..2..Z
3)	R..P..E	B..S..C	K..V..A	R..X..6	B..1..4	J..3..1
4)	S..Q..F	C..T..D	L..W..B	S..Y..7	C..2..5	K..A..2
5)	T..R..G	D..U..E	M..X..C	T..Z..8	D..3..6	L..B..3
6)	U..S..H	E..V..F	N..Y..D	U..1..A	E..A..7	M..C..4
7)	V..T..J	F..W..G	O..Z..E	V..2..B	F..B..8	N..D..5
8)	W..U..K	G..X..H	P..1..F	W..3..C	G..C..A	O..E..6
9)	X..V..L	H..Y..J	Q..2..G	X..A..D	H..D..B	P..F..7
10)	A..W..M	J..Z..K	R..3..H	A..B..E	J..E..C	Q..G..8
11)	B..X..N	K..1..L	S..A..J	B..C..F	K..F..D	R..H..A
12)	C..Y..O	L..2..M	T..B..K	C..D..G	L..G..E	S..J..B
13)	D..Z..P	M..3..N	U..C..L	D..E..H	M..H..F	T..K..C
14)	E..1..Q	N..A..O	V..D..M	E..F..J	N..J..G	U..L..D
15)	F..2..R	O..B..P	W..E..N	F..G..K	O..K..H	V..M..E
16)	G..3..S	P..C..Q	X..F..O	G..H..L	P..L..J	W..N..F
17)	H..A..T	Q..D..R	A..G..P	H..J..M	Q..M..K	X..O..G
18)	J..B..U	R..E..S	B..H..Q	J..K..N	R..N..L	A..P..H
19)	K..C..V	S..F..T	C..J..R	K..L..O	S..O..M	B..Q..J
20)	L..D..W	T..G..U	D..K..S	L..M..P	T..P..N	C..R..K
21)	M..E..X	U..H..V	E..L..T	M..N..Q	U..Q..O	D..S..L
22)	N..F..Y	V..J..W	F..M..U	N..O..R	V..R..P	E..T..M
23)	O..G..Z	W..K..X	G..N..V	O..P..S	W..S..Q	F..U..N
24)	P..H..1	X..L..Y	H..O..W	P..Q..T	X..T..R	G..V..O
25)	Q..J..2	A..M..Z	J..P..X	Q..R..U	A..U..S	H..W..P
26)	R..K..3	B..N..1	K..Q..Y	R..S..V	B..V..T	J..X..Q
27)	S..L..4	C..O..2	L..R..Z	S..T..W	C..W..U	K..Y..R
28)	T..M..5	D..P..3	M..S..1	T..U..X	D..X..V	L..Z..S
29)	U..N..6	E..Q..4	N..T..2	U..V..Y	E..Y..W	M..1..T
30)	V..O..7	F..R..5	O..U..3	V..W..Z	F..Z..X	N..2..U
31)	W..P..8	G..S..6		W..X..1		O..3..V

CODES: P-PHYSICAL BIORHYTHM CURVE, E-EMOTIONAL BIORHYTHM CURVE, I-INTELLECTUAL BIORHYTHM CURVE

	JANUARY P--E--I	FEBRUARY P--E--I	MARCH P--E--I	APRIL P--E--I	MAY P--E--I	JUNE P--E--I
1)	P..A..W	X..D..U	E..D..P	N..G..N	U..J..K	E..M..H
2)	Q..B..X	A..E..V	F..E..Q	O..H..O	V..K..L	F..N..J
3)	R..C..Y	B..F..W	G..F..R	P..J..P	W..L..M	G..O..K
4)	S..D..Z	C..G..X	H..G..S	Q..K..Q	X..M..N	H..P..L
5)	T..E..1	D..H..Y	J..H..T	R..L..R	A..N..O	J..Q..M
6)	U..F..2	E..J..Z	K..J..U	S..M..S	B..O..P	K..R..N
7)	V..G..3	F..K..1	L..K..V	T..N..T	C..P..Q	L..S..O
8)	W..H..4	G..L..2	M..L..W	U..O..U	D..Q..R	M..T..P
9)	X..J..5	H..M..3	N..M..X	V..P..V	E..R..S	N..U..Q
10)	A..K..6	J..N..4	O..N..Y	W..Q..W	F..S..T	O..V..R
11)	B..L..7	K..O..5	P..O..Z	X..R..X	G..T..U	P..W..S
12)	C..M..8	L..P..6	Q..P..1	A..S..Y	H..U..V	Q..X..T
13)	D..N..A	M..Q..7	R..Q..2	B..T..Z	J..V..W	R..Y..U
14)	E..O..B	N..R..8	S..R..3	C..U..1	K..W..X	S..Z..V
15)	F..P..C	O..S..A	T..S..4	D..V..2	L..X..Y	T..1..W
16)	G..Q..D	P..T..B	U..T..5	E..W..3	M..Y..Z	U..2..X
17)	H..R..E	Q..U..C	V..U..6	F..X..4	N..Z..1	V..3..Y
18)	J..S..F	R..V..D	W..V..7	G..Y..5	O..1..2	W..A..Z
19)	K..T..G	S..W..E	X..W..8	H..Z..6	P..2..3	X..B..1
20)	L..U..H	T..X..F	A..X..A	J..1..7	Q..3..4	A..C..2
21)	M..V..J	U..Y..G	B..Y..B	K..2..8	R..A..5	B..D..3
22)	N..W..K	V..Z..H	C..Z..C	L..3..A	S..B..6	C..E..4
23)	O..X..L	W..1..J	D..1..D	M..A..B	T..C..7	D..F..5
24)	P..Y..M	X..2..K	E..2..E	N..B..C	U..D..8	E..G..6
25)	Q..Z..N	A..3..L	F..3..F	O..C..D	V..E..A	F..H..7
26)	R..1..O	B..A..M	G..A..G	P..D..E	W..F..B	G..J..8
27)	S..2..P	C..B..N	H..B..H	Q..E..F	X..G..C	H..K..A
28)	T..3..Q	D..C..O	J..C..J	R..F..G	A..H..D	J..L..B
29)	U..A..R		K..D..K	S..G..H	B..J..E	K..M..C
30)	V..B..S		L..E..L	T..H..J	C..K..F	L..N..D
31)	W..C..T		M..F..M		D..L..G	

	JULY P--E--I	AUGUST P--E--I	SEPTEMBER P--E--I	OCTOBER P--E--I	NOVEMBER P--E--I	DECEMBER P--E--I
1)	M..O..E	U..R..C	E..U..A	M..W..6	U..Z..4	D..2..1
2)	N..P..F	V..S..D	F..V..B	N..X..7	V..1..5	E..3..2
3)	O..Q..G	W..T..E	G..W..C	O..Y..8	W..2..6	F..A..3
4)	P..R..H	X..U..F	H..X..D	P..Z..A	X..3..7	G..B..4
5)	Q..S..J	A..V..G	J..Y..E	Q..1..B	A..A..8	H..C..5
6)	R..T..K	B..W..H	K..Z..F	R..2..C	B..B..A	J..D..6
7)	S..U..L	C..X..J	L..1..G	S..3..D	C..C..B	K..E..7
8)	T..V..M	D..Y..K	M..2..H	T..A..E	D..D..C	L..F..8
9)	U..W..N	E..Z..L	N..3..J	U..B..F	E..E..D	M..G..A
10)	V..X..O	F..1..M	O..A..K	V..C..G	F..F..E	N..H..B
11)	W..Y..P	G..2..N	P..B..L	W..D..H	G..G..F	O..J..C
12)	X..Z..Q	H..3..O	Q..C..M	X..E..J	H..H..G	P..K..D
13)	A..1..R	J..A..P	R..D..N	A..F..K	J..J..H	Q..L..E
14)	B..2..S	K..B..Q	S..E..O	B..G..L	K..K..J	R..M..F
15)	C..3..T	L..C..R	T..F..P	C..H..M	L..L..K	S..N..G
16)	D..A..U	M..D..S	U..G..Q	D..J..N	M..M..L	T..O..H
17)	E..B..V	N..E..T	V..H..R	E..K..O	N..N..M	U..P..J
18)	F..C..W	O..F..U	W..J..S	F..L..P	O..O..N	V..Q..K
19)	G..D..X	P..G..V	X..K..T	G..M..Q	P..P..O	W..R..L
20)	H..E..Y	Q..H..W	A..L..U	H..N..R	Q..Q..P	X..S..M
21)	J..F..Z	R..J..X	B..M..V	J..O..S	R..R..Q	A..T..N
22)	K..G..1	S..K..Y	C..N..W	K..P..T	S..S..R	B..U..O
23)	L..H..2	T..L..Z	D..O..X	L..Q..U	T..T..S	C..V..P
24)	M..J..3	U..M..1	E..P..Y	M..R..V	U..U..T	D..W..Q
25)	N..K..4	V..N..2	F..Q..Z	N..S..W	V..V..U	E..X..R
26)	O..L..5	W..O..3	G..R..1	O..T..X	W..W..V	F..Y..S
27)	P..M..6	X..P..4	H..S..2	P..U..Y	X..X..W	G..Z..T
28)	Q..N..7	A..Q..5 (28*)	J..T..3	Q..V..Z	A..Y..X	H..1..U
29)	R..O..8	B..R..6	K..U..4	R..W..1	B..Z..Y	J..2..V
30)	S..P..A	C..S..7	L..V..5	S..X..2	C..1..Z	K..3..W
31)	T..Q..B	D..T..8		T..Y..3		L..A..X

CODES: P-PHYSICAL BIORHYTHM CURVE, E-EMOTIONAL BIORHYTHM CURVE, I-INTELLECTUAL BIORHYTHM CURVE

	...JANUARY..		..FEBRUARY..		...MARCH...		...APRIL...		....MAY....		...JUNE....
	P--E--I		P--E--I		P--E--I		P--E--I		P--E--I		P--E--I
1)	M..B..Y	1)	U..E..W	1)	B..E..R	1)	K..H..P	1)	R..K..M	1)	B..N..K
2)	N..C..Z	2)	V..F..X	2)	C..F..S	2)	L..J..Q	2)	S..L..N	2)	C..O..L
3)	O..D..1	3)	W..G..Y	3)	D..G..T	3)	M..K..R	3)	T..M..O	3)	D..P..M
4)	P..E..2	4)	X..H..Z	4)	E..H..U	4)	N..L..S	4)	U..N..P	4)	E..Q..N
5)	Q..F..3	5)	A..J..1	5)	F..J..V	5)	O..M..T	5)	V..O..Q	5)	F..R..O
6)	R..G..4	6)	B..K..2	6)	G..K..W	6)	P..N..U	6)	W..P..R	6)	G..S..P
7)	S..H..5	7)	C..L..3	7)	H..L..X	7)	Q..O..V	7)	X..Q..S	7)	H..T..Q
8)	T..J..6	8)	D..M..4	8)	J..M..Y	8)	R..P..W	8)	A..R..T	8)	J..U..R
9)	U..K..7	9)	E..N..5	9)	K..N..Z	9)	S..Q..X	9)	B..S..U	9)	K..V..S
10)	V..L..8	10)	F..O..6	10)	L..O..1	10)	T..R..Y	10)	C..T..V	10)	L..W..T
11)	W..M..A	11)	G..P..7	11)	M..P..2	11)	U..S..Z	11)	D..U..W	11)	M..X..U
12)	X..N..B	12)	H..Q..8	12)	N..Q..3	12)	V..T..1	12)	E..V..X	12)	N..Y..V
13)	A..O..C	13)	J..R..A	13)	O..R..4	13)	W..U..2	13)	F..W..Y	13)	O..Z..W
14)	B..P..D	14)	K..S..B	14)	P..S..5	14)	X..V..3	14)	G..X..Z	14)	P..1..X
15)	C..Q..E	15)	L..T..C	15)	Q..T..6	15)	A..W..4	15)	H..Y..1	15)	Q..2..Y
16)	D..R..F	16)	M..U..D	16)	R..U..7	16)	B..X..5	16)	J..Z..2	16)	R..3..Z
17)	E..S..G	17)	N..V..E	17)	S..V..8	17)	C..Y..6	17)	K..1..3	17)	S..A..1
18)	F..T..H	18)	O..W..F	18)	T..W..A	18)	D..Z..7	18)	L..2..4	18)	T..B..2
19)	G..U..J	19)	P..X..G	19)	U..X..B	19)	E..1..8	19)	M..3..5	19)	U..C..3
20)	H..V..K	20)	Q..Y..H	20)	V..Y..C	20)	F..2..A	20)	N..A..6	20)	V..D..4
21)	J..W..L	21)	R..Z..J	21)	W..Z..D	21)	G..3..B	21)	O..B..7	21)	W..E..5
22)	K..X..M	22)	S..1..K	22)	X..1..E	22)	H..A..C	22)	P..C..8	22)	X..F..6
23)	L..Y..N	23)	T..2..L	23)	A..2..F	23)	J..B..D	23)	Q..D..A	23)	A..G..7
24)	M..Z..O	24)	U..3..M	24)	B..3..G	24)	K..C..E	24)	R..E..B	24)	B..H..8
25)	N..1..P	25)	V..A..N	25)	C..A..H	25)	L..D..F	25)	S..F..C	25)	C..J..A
26)	O..2..Q	26)	W..B..O	26)	D..B..J	26)	M..E..G	26)	T..G..D	26)	D..K..B
27)	P..3..R	27)	X..C..P	27)	E..C..K	27)	N..F..H	27)	U..H..E	27)	E..L..C
28)	Q..A..S	28)	A..D..Q	28)	F..D..L	28)	O..G..J	28)	V..J..F	28)	F..M..D
29)	R..B..T			29)	G..E..M	29)	P..H..K	29)	W..K..G	29)	G..N..E
30)	S..C..U			30)	H..F..N	30)	Q..J..L	30)	X..L..H	30)	H..O..F
31)	T..D..V			31)	J..G..O			31)	A..M..J		

	....JULY....		...AUGUST...		.SEPTEMBER.		..OCTOBER...		.NOVEMBER..		.DECEMBER..
	P--E--I		P--E--I		P--E--I		P--E--I		P--E--I		P--E--I
1)	J..P..G	1)	R..S..E	1)	B..V..C	1)	J..X..8	1)	R..1..6	1)	A..3..3
2)	K..Q..H	2)	S..T..F	2)	C..W..D	2)	K..Y..A	2)	S..2..7	2)	B..A..4
3)	L..R..J	3)	T..U..G	3)	D..X..E	3)	L..Z..B	3)	T..3..8	3)	C..B..5
4)	M..S..K	4)	U..V..H	4)	E..Y..F	4)	M..1..C	4)	U..A..A	4)	D..C..6
5)	N..T..L	5)	V..W..J	5)	F..Z..G	5)	N..2..D	5)	V..B..B	5)	E..D..7
6)	O..U..M	6)	W..X..K	6)	G..1..H	6)	O..3..E	6)	W..C..C	6)	F..E..8
7)	P..V..N	7)	X..Y..L	7)	H..2..J	7)	P..A..F	7)	X..D..D	7)	G..F..A
8)	Q..W..O	8)	A..Z..M	8)	J..3..K	8)	Q..B..G	8)	A..E..E	8)	H..G..B
9)	R..X..P	9)	B..1..N	9)	K..A..L	9)	R..C..H	9)	B..F..F	9)	J..H..C
10)	S..Y..Q	10)	C..2..O	10)	L..B..M	10)	S..D..J	10)	C..G..G	10)	K..J..D
11)	T..Z..R	11)	D..3..P	11)	M..C..N	11)	T..E..K	11)	D..H..H	11)	L..K..E
12)	U..1..S	12)	E..A..Q	12)	N..D..O	12)	U..F..L	12)	E..J..J	12)	M..L..F
13)	V..2..T	13)	F..B..R	13)	O..E..P	13)	V..G..M	13)	F..K..K	13)	N..M..G
14)	W..3..U	14)	G..C..S	14)	P..F..Q	14)	W..H..N	14)	G..L..L	14)	O..N..H
15)	X..A..V	15)	H..D..T	15)	Q..G..R	15)	X..J..O	15)	H..M..M	15)	P..O..J
16)	A..B..W	16)	J..E..U	16)	R..H..S	16)	A..K..P	16)	J..N..N	16)	Q..P..K
17)	B..C..X	17)	K..F..V	17)	S..J..T	17)	B..L..Q	17)	K..O..O	17)	R..Q..L
18)	C..D..Y	18)	L..G..W	18)	T..K..U	18)	C..M..R	18)	L..P..P	18)	S..R..M
19)	D..E..Z	19)	M..H..X	19)	U..L..V	19)	D..N..S	19)	M..Q..Q	19)	T..S..N
20)	E..F..1	20)	N..J..Y	20)	V..M..W	20)	E..O..T	20)	N..R..R	20)	U..T..O
21)	F..G..2	21)	O..K..Z	21)	W..N..X	21)	F..P..U	21)	O..S..S	21)	V..U..P
22)	G..H..3	22)	P..L..1	22)	X..O..Y	22)	G..Q..V	22)	P..T..T	22)	W..V..Q
23)	H..J..4	23)	Q..M..2	23)	A..P..Z	23)	H..R..W	23)	Q..U..U	23)	X..W..R
24)	J..K..5	24)	R..N..3	24)	B..Q..1	24)	J..S..X	24)	R..V..V	24)	A..X..S
25)	K..L..6	25)	S..O..4	25)	C..R..2	25)	K..T..Y	25)	S..W..W	25)	B..Y..T
26)	L..M..7	26)	T..P..5	26)	D..S..3	26)	L..U..Z	26)	T..X..X	26)	C..Z..U
27)	M..N..8	27)	U..Q..6	27)	E..T..4	27)	M..V..1	27)	U..Y..Y	27)	D..1..V
28)	N..O..A	28)	V..R..7	28)	F..U..5	28)	N..W..2	28)	V..Z..Z	28)	E..2..W
29)	O..P..B	29)	W..S..8	29)	G..V..6	29)	O..X..3	29)	W..1..1	29)	F..3..X
30)	P..Q..C	30)	X..T..A	30)	H..W..7	30)	P..Y..4	30)	X..2..2	30)	G..A..Y
31)	Q..R..D	31)	A..U..B			31)	Q..Z..5			31)	H..B..Z

CODES: P-PHYSICAL BIORHYTHM CURVE, E-EMOTIONAL BIORHYTHM CURVE, I-INTELLECTUAL BIORHYTHM CURVE

1935 — JANUARY–JUNE

Day	JANUARY P–E–I	FEBRUARY P–E–I	MARCH P–E–I	APRIL P–E–I	MAY P–E–I	JUNE P–E–I
1)	J..C..1	R..F..Y	W..F..T	G..J..R	O..L..O	W..O..M
2)	K..D..2	S..G..Z	X..G..U	H..K..S	P..M..P	X..P..N
3)	L..E..3	T..H..1	A..H..V	J..L..T	Q..N..Q	A..Q..O
4)	M..F..4	U..J..2	B..J..W	K..M..U	R..O..R	B..R..P
5)	N..G..5	V..K..3	C..K..X	L..N..V	S..P..S	C..S..Q
6)	O..H..6	W..L..4	D..L..Y	M..O..W	T..Q..T	D..T..R
7)	P..J..7	X..M..5	E..M..Z	N..P..X	U..R..U	E..U..S
8)	Q..K..8	A..N..6	F..N..1	O..Q..Y	V..S..V	F..V..T
9)	R..L..A	B..O..7	G..O..2	P..R..Z	W..T..W	G..W..U
10)	S..M..B	C..P..8	H..P..3	Q..S..1	X..U..X	H..X..V
11)	T..N..C	D..Q..A	J..Q..4	R..T..2	A..V..Y	J..Y..W
12)	U..O..D	E..R..B	K..R..5	S..U..3	B..W..Z	K..Z..X
13)	V..P..E	F..S..C	L..S..6	T..V..4	C..X..1	L..1..Y
14)	W..Q..F	G..T..D	M..T..7	U..W..5	D..Y..2	M..2..Z
15)	X..R..G	H..U..E	N..U..8	V..X..6	E..Z..3	N..3..1
16)	A..S..H	J..V..F	O..V..A	W..Y..7	F..1..4	O..A..2
17)	B..T..J	K..W..G	P..W..B	X..Z..8	G..2..5	P..B..3
18)	C..U..K	L..X..H	Q..X..C	A..1..A	H..3..6	Q..C..4
19)	D..V..L	M..Y..J	R..Y..D	B..2..B	J..A..7	R..D..5
20)	E..W..M	N..Z..K	S..Z..E	C..3..C	K..B..8	S..E..6
21)	F..X..N	O..1..L	T..1..F	D..A..D	L..C..A	T..F..7
22)	G..Y..O	P..2..M	U..2..G	E..B..E	M..D..B	U..G..8
23)	H..Z..P	Q..3..N	V..3..H	F..C..F	N..E..C	V..H..A
24)	J..1..Q	R..A..O	W..A..J	G..D..G	O..F..D	W..J..B
25)	K..2..R	S..B..P	X..B..K	H..E..H	P..G..E	X..K..C
26)	L..3..S	T..C..Q	A..C..L	J..F..J	Q..H..F	A..L..D
27)	M..A..T	U..D..R	B..D..M	K..G..K	R..J..G	B..M..E
28)	N..B..U	V..E..S	C..E..N	L..H..L	S..K..H	C..N..F
29)	O..C..V		D..F..O	M..J..M	T..L..J	D..O..G
30)	P..D..W		E..G..P	N..K..N	U..M..K	E..P..H
31)	Q..E..X		F..H..Q		V..N..L	

1935 — JULY–DECEMBER

Day	JULY P–E–I	AUGUST P–E–I	SEPTEMBER P–E–I	OCTOBER P–E–I	NOVEMBER P–E–I	DECEMBER P–E–I
1)	F..Q..J	O..T..G	W..W..E	F..Y..B	O..2..8	V..A..5
2)	G..R..K	P..U..H	X..X..F	G..Z..C	P..3..A	W..B..6
3)	H..S..L	Q..V..J	A..Y..G	H..1..D	Q..A..B	X..C..7
4)	J..T..M	R..W..K	B..Z..H	J..2..E	R..B..C	A..D..8
5)	K..U..N	S..X..L	C..1..J	K..3..F	S..C..D	B..E..A
6)	L..V..O	T..Y..M	D..2..K	L..A..G	T..D..E	C..F..B
7)	M..W..P	U..Z..N	E..3..L	M..B..H	U..E..F	D..G..C
8)	N..X..Q	V..1..O	F..A..M	N..C..J	V..F..G	E..H..D
9)	O..Y..R	W..2..P	G..B..N	O..D..K	W..G..H	F..J..E
10)	P..Z..S	X..3..Q	H..C..O	P..E..L	X..H..J	G..K..F
11)	Q..1..T	A..A..R	J..D..P	Q..F..M	A..J..K	H..L..G
12)	R..2..U	B..B..S	K..E..Q	R..G..N	B..K..L	J..M..H
13)	S..3..V	C..C..T	L..F..R	S..H..O	C..L..M	K..N..J
14)	T..A..W	D..D..U	M..G..S	T..J..P	D..M..N	L..O..K
15)	U..B..X	E..E..V	N..H..T	U..K..Q	E..N..O	M..P..L
16)	V..C..Y	F..F..W	O..J..U	V..L..R	F..O..P	N..Q..M
17)	W..D..Z	G..G..X	P..K..V	W..M..S	G..P..Q	O..R..N
18)	X..E..1	H..H..Y	Q..L..W	X..N..T	H..Q..R	P..S..O
19)	A..F..2	J..J..Z	R..M..X	A..O..U	J..R..S	Q..T..P
20)	B..G..3	K..K..1	S..N..Y	B..P..V	K..S..T	R..U..Q
21)	C..H..4	L..L..2	T..O..Z	C..Q..W	L..T..U	S..V..R
22)	D..J..5	M..M..3	U..P..1	D..R..X	M..U..V	T..W..S
23)	E..K..6	N..N..4	V..Q..2	E..S..Y	N..V..W	U..X..T
24)	F..L..7	O..O..5	W..R..3	F..T..Z	O..W..X	V..Y..U
25)	G..M..8	P..P..6	X..S..4	G..U..1	P..X..Y	W..Z..V
26)	H..N..A	Q..Q..7	A..T..5	H..V..2	Q..Y..Z	X..1..W
27)	J..O..B	R..R..8	B..U..6	J..W..3	R..Z..1	A..2..X
28)	K..P..C	S..S..A	C..V..7	K..X..4	S..1..2	B..3..Y
29)	L..Q..D	T..T..B	D..W..8	L..Y..5	T..2..3	C..A..Z
30)	M..R..E	U..U..C	E..X..A	M..Z..6	U..3..4	D..B..1
31)	N..S..F	V..V..D		N..1..7		E..C..2

CODES: P-PHYSICAL BIORHYTHM CURVE, E-EMOTIONAL BIORHYTHM CURVE, I-INTELLECTUAL BIORHYTHM CURVE

	...JANUARY.. P--E--I	..FEBRUARY.. P--E--I	...MARCH... P--E--I	...APRIL... P--E--I	....MAY.... P--E--I	....JUNE.... P--E--I
1)	F..D..3	O..G..1	U..H..W	E..L..U	M..N..R	U..Q..P
2)	G..E..4	P..H..2	V..J..X	F..M..V	N..O..S	V..R..Q
3)	H..F..5	Q..J..3	W..K..Y	G..N..W	O..P..T	W..S..R
4)	J..G..6	R..K..4	X..L..Z	H..O..X	P..Q..U	X..T..S
5)	K..H..7	S..L..5	A..M..1	J..P..Y	Q..R..V	A..U..T
6)	L..J..8	T..M..6	B..N..2	K..Q..Z	R..S..W	B..V..U
7)	M..K..A	U..N..7	C..O..3	L..R..1	S..T..X	C..W..V
8)	N..L..B	V..O..8	D..P..4	M..S..2	T..U..Y	D..X..W
9)	O..M..C	W..P..A	E..Q..5	N..T..3	U..V..Z	E..Y..X
10)	P..N..D	X..Q..B	F..R..6	O..U..4	V..W..1	F..Z..Y
11)	Q..O..E	A..R..C	G..S..7	P..V..5	W..X..2	G..1..Z
12)	R..P..F	B..S..D	H..T..8	Q..W..6	X..Y..3	H..2..1
13)	S..Q..G	C..T..E	J..U..A	R..X..7	A..Z..4	J..3..2
14)	T..R..H	D..U..F	K..V..B	S..Y..8	B..1..5	K..A..3
15)	U..S..J	E..V..G	L..W..C	T..Z..A	C..2..6	L..B..4
16)	V..T..K	F..W..H	M..X..D	U..1..B	D..3..7	M..C..5
17)	W..U..L	G..X..J	N..Y..E	V..2..C	E..A..8	N..D..6
18)	X..V..M	H..Y..K	O..Z..F	W..3..D	F..B..A	O..E..7
19)	A..W..N	J..Z..L	P..1..G	X..A..E	G..C..B	P..F..8
20)	B..X..O	K..1..M	Q..2..H	A..B..F	H..D..C	Q..G..A
21)	C..Y..P	L..2..N	R..3..J	B..C..G	J..E..D	R..H..B
22)	D..Z..Q	M..3..O	S..A..K	C..D..H	K..F..E	S..J..C
23)	E..1..R	N..A..P	T..B..L	D..E..J	L..G..F	T..K..D
24)	F..2..S	O..B..Q	U..C..M	E..F..K	M..H..G	U..L..E
25)	G..3..T	P..C..R	V..D..N	F..G..L	N..J..H	V..M..F
26)	H..A..U	Q..D..S	W..E..O	G..H..M	O..K..J	W..N..G
27)	J..B..V	R..E..T	X..F..P	H..J..N	P..L..K	X..O..H
28)	K..C..W	S..F..U	A..G..Q	J..K..O	Q..M..L	A..P..J
29)	L..D..X	T..G..V	B..H..R	K..L..P	R..N..M	B..Q..K
30)	M..E..Y		C..J..S	L..M..Q	S..O..N	C..R..L
31)	N..F..Z		D..K..T		T..P..O	

	....JULY.... P--E--I	...AUGUST... P--E--I	.SEPTEMBER. P--E--I	..OCTOBER... P--E--I	..NOVEMBER.. P--E--I	.DECEMBER.. P--E--I
1)	D..S..M	M..V..K	U..Y..H	D..1..E	M..A..C	T..C..8
2)	E..T..N	N..W..L	V..Z..J	E..2..F	N..B..D	U..D..A
3)	F..U..O	O..X..M	W..1..K	F..3..G	O..C..E	V..E..B
4)	G..V..P	P..Y..N	X..2..L	G..A..H	P..D..F	W..F..C
5)	H..W..Q	Q..Z..O	A..3..M	H..B..J	Q..E..G	X..G..D
6)	J..X..R	R..1..P	B..A..N	J..C..K	R..F..H	A..H..E
7)	K..Y..S	S..2..Q	C..B..O	K..D..L	S..G..J	B..J..F
8)	L..Z..T	T..3..R	D..C..P	L..E..M	T..H..K	C..K..G
9)	M..1..U	U..A..S	E..D..Q	M..F..N	U..J..L	D..L..H
10)	N..2..V	V..B..T	F..E..R	N..G..O	V..K..M	E..M..J
11)	O..3..W	W..C..U	G..F..S	O..H..P	W..L..N	F..N..K
12)	P..A..X	X..D..V	H..G..T	P..J..Q	X..M..O	G..O..L
13)	Q..B..Y	A..E..W	J..H..U	Q..K..R	A..N..P	H..P..M
14)	R..C..Z	B..F..X	K..J..V	R..L..S	B..O..Q	J..Q..N
15)	S..D..1	C..G..Y	L..K..W	S..M..T	C..P..R	K..R..O
16)	T..E..2	D..H..Z	M..L..X	T..N..U	D..Q..S	L..S..P
17)	U..F..3	E..J..1	N..M..Y	U..O..V	E..R..T	M..T..Q
18)	V..G..4	F..K..2	O..N..Z	V..P..W	F..S..U	N..U..R
19)	W..H..5	G..L..3	P..O..1	W..Q..X	G..T..V	O..V..S
20)	X..J..6	H..M..4	Q..P..2	X..R..Y	H..U..W	P..W..T
21)	A..K..7	J..N..5	R..Q..3	A..S..Z	J..V..X	Q..X..U
22)	B..L..8	K..O..6	S..R..4	B..T..1	K..W..Y	R..Y..V
23)	C..M..A	L..P..7	T..S..5	C..U..2	L..X..Z	S..Z..W
24)	D..N..B	M..Q..8	U..T..6	D..V..3	M..Y..1	T..1..X
25)	E..O..C	N..R..A	V..U..7	E..W..4	N..Z..2	U..2..Y
26)	F..P..D	O..S..B	W..V..8	F..X..5	O..1..3	V..3..Z
27)	G..Q..E	P..T..C	X..W..A	G..Y..6	P..2..4	W..A..1
28)	H..R..F	Q..U..D	A..X..B	H..Z..7	Q..3..5	X..B..2
29)	J..S..G	R..V..E	B..Y..C	J..1..8	R..A..6	A..C..3
30)	K..T..H	S..W..F	C..Z..D	K..2..A	S..B..7	B..D..4
31)	L..U..J	T..X..G		L..3..B		C..E..5

CODES: P-PHYSICAL BIORHYTHM CURVE,E-EMOTIONAL BIORHYTHM CURVE,I-INTELLECTUAL BIORHYTHM CURVE

...JANUARY..	..FEBRUARY..	...MARCH...	...APRIL...	....MAY....	....JUNE....
P--E--I	P--E--I	P--E--I	P--E--I	P--E--I	P--E--I
1) D..F..6	1) M..J..4	1) R..J..Y	1) B..M..W	1) J..O..T	1) R..R..R
2) E..G..7	2) N..K..5	2) S..K..Z	2) C..N..X	2) K..P..U	2) S..S..S
3) F..H..8	3) O..L..6	3) T..L..1	3) D..O..Y	3) L..Q..V	3) T..T..T
4) G..J..A	4) P..M..7	4) U..M..2	4) E..P..Z	4) M..R..W	4) U..U..U
5) H..K..B	5) Q..N..8	5) V..N..3	5) F..Q..1	5) N..S..X	5) V..V..V
6) J..L..C	6) R..O..A	6) W..O..4	6) G..R..2	6) O..T..Y	6) W..W..W
7) K..M..D	7) S..P..B	7) X..P..5	7) H..S..3	7) P..U..Z	7) X..X..X
8) L..N..E	8) T..Q..C	8) A..Q..6	8) J..T..4	8) Q..V..1	8) A..Y..Y
9) M..O..F	9) U..R..D	9) B..R..7	9) K..U..5	9) R..W..2	9) B..Z..Z
10) N..P..G	10) V..S..E	10) C..S..8	10) L..V..6	10) S..X..3	10) C..1..1
11) O..Q..H	11) W..T..F	11) D..T..A	11) M..W..7	11) T..Y..4	11) D..2..2
12) P..R..J	12) X..U..G	12) E..U..B	12) N..X..8	12) U..Z..5	12) E..3..3
13) Q..S..K	13) A..V..H	13) F..V..C	13) O..Y..A	13) V..1..6	13) F..A..4
14) R..T..L	14) B..W..J	14) G..W..D	14) P..Z..B	14) W..2..7	14) G..B..5
15) S..U..M	15) C..X..K	15) H..X..E	15) Q..1..C	15) X..3..8	15) H..C..6
16) T..V..N	16) D..Y..L	16) J..Y..F	16) R..2..D	16) A..A..A	16) J..D..7
17) U..W..O	17) E..Z..M	17) K..Z..G	17) S..3..E	17) B..B..B	17) K..E..8
18) V..X..P	18) F..1..N	18) L..1..H	18) T..A..F	18) C..C..C	18) L..F..A
19) W..Y..Q	19) G..2..O	19) M..2..J	19) U..B..G	19) D..D..D	19) M..G..B
20) X..Z..R	20) H..3..P	20) N..3..K	20) V..C..H	20) E..E..E	20) N..H..C
21) A..1..S	21) J..A..Q	21) O..A..L	21) W..D..J	21) F..F..F	21) O..J..D
22) B..2..T	22) K..B..R	22) P..B..M	22) X..E..K	22) G..G..G	22) P..K..E
23) C..3..U	23) L..C..S	23) Q..C..N	23) A..F..L	23) H..H..H	23) Q..L..F
24) D..A..V	24) M..D..T	24) R..D..O	24) B..G..M	24) J..J..J	24) R..M..G
25) E..B..W	25) N..E..U	25) S..E..P	25) C..H..N	25) K..K..K	25) S..N..H
26) F..C..X	26) O..F..V	26) T..F..Q	26) D..J..O	26) L..L..L	26) T..O..J
27) G..D..Y	27) P..G..W	27) U..G..R	27) E..K..P	27) M..M..M	27) U..P..K
28) H..E..Z	28) Q..H..X	28) V..H..S	28) F..L..Q	28) N..N..N	28) V..Q..L
29) J..F..1		29) W..J..T	29) G..M..R	29) O..O..O	29) W..R..M
30) K..G..2		30) X..K..U	30) H..N..S	30) P..P..P	30) X..S..N
31) L..H..3		31) A..L..V		31) Q..Q..Q	

....JULY....	...AUGUST...	..SEPTEMBER.	..OCTOBER...	..NOVEMBER..	..DECEMBER..
P--E--I	P--E--I	P--E--I	P--E--I	P--E--I	P--E--I
1) A..T..O	1) J..W..M	1) R..Z..K	1) A..2..G	1) J..B..E	1) Q..D..B
2) B..U..P	2) K..X..N	2) S..1..L	2) B..3..H	2) K..C..F	2) R..E..C
3) C..V..Q	3) L..Y..O	3) T..2..M	3) C..A..J	3) L..D..G	3) S..F..D
4) D..W..R	4) M..Z..P	4) U..3..N	4) D..B..K	4) M..E..H	4) T..G..E
5) E..X..S	5) N..1..Q	5) V..A..O	5) E..C..L	5) N..F..J	5) U..H..F
6) F..Y..T	6) O..2..R	6) W..B..P	6) F..D..M	6) O..G..K	6) V..J..G
7) G..Z..U	7) P..3..S	7) X..C..Q	7) G..E..N	7) P..H..L	7) W..K..H
8) H..1..V	8) Q..A..T	8) A..D..R	8) H..F..O	8) Q..J..M	8) X..L..J
9) J..2..W	9) R..B..U	9) B..E..S	9) J..G..P	9) R..K..N	9) A..M..K
10) K..3..X	10) S..C..V	10) C..F..T	10) K..H..Q	10) S..L..O	10) B..N..L
11) L..A..Y	11) T..D..W	11) D..G..U	11) L..J..R	11) T..M..P	11) C..O..M
12) M..B..Z	12) U..E..X	12) E..H..V	12) M..K..S	12) U..N..Q	12) D..P..N
13) N..C..1	13) V..F..Y	13) F..J..W	13) N..L..T	13) V..O..R	13) E..Q..O
14) O..D..2	14) W..G..Z	14) G..K..X	14) O..M..U	14) W..P..S	14) F..R..P
15) P..E..3	15) X..H..1	15) H..L..Y	15) P..N..V	15) X..Q..T	15) G..S..Q
16) Q..F..4	16) A..J..2	16) J..M..Z	16) Q..O..W	16) A..R..U	16) H..T..R
17) R..G..5	17) B..K..3	17) K..N..1	17) R..P..X	17) B..S..V	17) J..U..S
18) S..H..6	18) C..L..4	18) L..O..2	18) S..Q..Y	18) C..T..W	18) K..V..T
19) T..J..7	19) D..M..5	19) M..P..3	19) T..R..Z	19) D..U..X	19) L..W..U
20) U..K..8	20) E..N..6	20) N..Q..4	20) U..S..1	20) E..V..Y	20) M..X..V
21) V..L..A	21) F..O..7	21) O..R..5	21) V..T..2	21) F..W..Z	21) N..Y..W
22) W..M..B	22) G..P..8	22) P..S..6	22) W..U..3	22) G..X..1	22) O..Z..X
23) X..N..C	23) H..Q..A	23) Q..T..7	23) X..V..4	23) H..Y..2	23) P..1..Y
24) A..O..D	24) J..R..B	24) R..U..8	24) A..W..5	24) J..Z..3	24) Q..2..Z
25) B..P..E	25) K..S..C	25) S..V..A	25) B..X..6	25) K..1..4	25) R..3..1
26) C..Q..F	26) L..T..D	26) T..W..B	26) C..Y..7	26) L..2..5	26) S..A..2
27) D..R..G	27) M..U..E	27) U..X..C	27) D..Z..8	27) M..3..6	27) T..B..3
28) E..S..H	28) N..V..F	28) V..Y..D	28) E..1..A	28) N..A..7	28) U..C..4
29) F..T..J	29) O..W..G	29) W..Z..E	29) F..2..B	29) O..B..8	29) V..D..5
30) G..U..K	30) P..X..H	30) X..1..F	30) G..3..C	30) P..C..A	30) W..E..6
31) H..V..L	31) Q..Y..J		31) H..A..D		31) X..F..7

CODES: P-PHYSICAL BIORHYTHM CURVE,E-EMOTIONAL BIORHYTHM CURVE,I-INTELLECTUAL BIORHYTHM CURVE

	...JANUARY.. P--E--I	..FEBRUARY.. P--E--I	...MARCH... P--E--I	...APRIL... P--E--I	....MAY.... P--E--I	...JUNE.... P--E--I
1)	A..G..8	J..K..6	O..K..1	W..N..Y	F..P..V	O..S..T
2)	B..H..A	K..L..7	P..L..2	X..O..Z	G..Q..W	P..T..U
3)	C..J..B	L..M..8	Q..M..3	A..P..1	H..R..X	Q..U..V
4)	D..K..C	M..N..A	R..N..4	B..Q..2	J..S..Y	R..V..W
5)	E..L..D	N..O..B	S..O..5	C..R..3	K..T..Z	S..W..X
6)	F..M..E	O..P..C	T..P..6	D..S..4	L..U..1	T..X..Y
7)	G..N..F	P..Q..D	U..Q..7	E..T..5	M..V..2	U..Y..Z
8)	H..O..G	Q..R..E	V..R..8	F..U..6	N..W..3	V..Z..1
9)	J..P..H	R..S..F	W..S..A	G..V..7	O..X..4	W..1..2
10)	K..Q..J	S..T..G	X..T..B	H..W..8	P..Y..5	X..2..3
11)	L..R..K	T..U..H	A..U..C	J..X..A	Q..Z..6	A..3..4
12)	M..S..L	U..V..J	B..V..D	K..Y..B	R..1..7	B..A..5
13)	N..T..M	V..W..K	C..W..E	L..Z..C	S..2..8	C..B..6
14)	O..U..N	W..X..L	D..X..F	M..1..D	T..3..A	D..C..7
15)	P..V..O	X..Y..M	E..Y..G	N..2..E	U..A..B	E..D..8
16)	Q..W..P	A..Z..N	F..Z..H	O..3..F	V..B..C	F..E..A
17)	R..X..Q	B..1..O	G..1..J	P..A..G	W..C..D	G..F..B
18)	S..Y..R	C..2..P	H..2..K	Q..B..H	X..D..E	H..G..C
19)	T..Z..S	D..3..Q	J..3..L	R..C..J	A..E..F	J..H..D
20)	U..1..T	E..A..R	K..A..M	S..D..K	B..F..G	K..J..E
21)	V..2..U	F..B..S	L..B..N	T..E..L	C..G..H	L..K..F
22)	W..3..V	G..C..T	M..C..O	U..F..M	D..H..J	M..L..G
23)	X..A..W	H..D..U	N..D..P	V..G..N	E..J..K	N..M..H
24)	A..B..X	J..E..V	O..E..Q	W..H..O	F..K..L	O..N..J
25)	B..C..Y	K..F..W	P..F..R	X..J..P	G..L..M	P..O..K
26)	C..D..Z	L..G..X	Q..G..S	A..K..Q	H..M..N	Q..P..L
27)	D..E..1	M..H..Y	R..H..T	B..L..R	J..N..O	R..Q..M
28)	E..F..2	N..J..Z	S..J..U	C..M..S	K..O..P	S..R..N
29)	F..G..3		T..K..V	D..N..T	L..P..Q	T..S..O
30)	G..H..4		U..L..W	E..O..U	M..Q..R	U..T..P
31)	H..J..5		V..M..X		N..R..S	

	...JULY.... P--E--I	...AUGUST... P--E--I	..SEPTEMBER. P--E--I	..OCTOBER... P--E--I	..NOVEMBER.. P--E--I	..DECEMBER.. P--E--I
1)	V..U..Q	F..X..O	O..1..M	V..3..J	F..C..G	N..E..D
2)	W..V..R	G..Y..P	P..2..N	W..A..K	G..D..H	O..F..E
3)	X..W..S	H..Z..Q	Q..3..O	X..B..L	H..E..J	P..G..F
4)	A..X..T	J..1..R	R..A..P	A..C..M	J..F..K	Q..H..G
5)	B..Y..U	K..2..S	S..B..Q	B..D..N	K..G..L	R..J..H
6)	C..Z..V	L..3..T	T..C..R	C..E..O	L..H..M	S..K..J
7)	D..1..W	M..A..U	U..D..S	D..F..P	M..J..N	T..L..K
8)	E..2..X	N..B..V	V..E..T	E..G..Q	N..K..O	U..M..L
9)	F..3..Y	O..C..W	W..F..U	F..H..R	O..L..P	V..N..M
10)	G..A..Z	P..D..X	X..G..V	G..J..S	P..M..Q	W..O..N
11)	H..B..1	Q..E..Y	A..H..W	H..K..T	Q..N..R	X..P..O
12)	J..C..2	R..F..Z	B..J..X	J..L..U	R..O..S	A..Q..P
13)	K..D..3	S..G..1	C..K..Y	K..M..V	S..P..T	B..R..Q
14)	L..E..4	T..H..2	D..L..Z	L..N..W	T..Q..U	C..S..R
15)	M..F..5	U..J..3	E..M..1	M..O..X	U..R..V	D..T..S
16)	N..G..6	V..K..4	F..N..2	N..P..Y	V..S..W	E..U..T
17)	O..H..7	W..L..5	G..O..3	O..Q..Z	W..T..X	F..V..U
18)	P..J..8	X..M..6	H..P..4	P..R..1	X..U..Y	G..W..V
19)	Q..K..A	A..N..7	J..Q..5	Q..S..2	A..V..Z	H..X..W
20)	R..L..B	B..O..8	K..R..6	R..T..3	B..W..1	J..Y..X
21)	S..M..C	C..P..A	L..S..7	S..U..4	C..X..2	K..Z..Y
22)	T..N..D	D..Q..B	M..T..8	T..V..5	D..Y..3	L..1..Z
23)	U..O..E	E..R..C	N..U..A	U..W..6	E..Z..4	M..2..1
24)	V..P..F	F..S..D	O..V..B	V..X..7	F..1..5	N..3..2
25)	W..Q..G	G..T..E	P..W..C	W..Y..8	G..2..6	O..A..3
26)	X..R..H	H..U..F	Q..X..D	X..Z..A	H..3..7	P..B..4
27)	A..S..J	J..V..G	R..Y..E	A..1..B	J..A..8	Q..C..5
28)	B..T..K	K..W..H	S..Z..F	B..2..C	K..B..A	R..D..6
29)	C..U..L	L..X..J	T..1..G	C..3..D	L..C..B	S..E..7
30)	D..V..M	M..Y..K	U..2..H	D..A..E	M..D..C	T..F..8
31)	E..W..N	N..Z..L		E..B..F		U..G..A

CODES: P-PHYSICAL BIORHYTHM CURVE, E-EMOTIONAL BIORHYTHM CURVE, I-INTELLECTUAL BIORHYTHM CURVE

...JANUARY..

Day	P	E	I
1)	V	H	B
2)	W	J	C
3)	X	K	D
4)	A	L	E
5)	B	M	F
6)	C	N	G
7)	D	O	H
8)	E	P	J
9)	F	Q	K
10)	G	R	L
11)	H	S	M
12)	J	T	N
13)	K	U	O
14)	L	V	P
15)	M	W	Q
16)	N	X	R
17)	O	Y	S
18)	P	Z	T
19)	Q	1	U
20)	R	2	V
21)	S	3	W
22)	T	A	X
23)	U	B	Y
24)	V	C	Z
25)	W	D	1
26)	X	E	2
27)	A	F	3
28)	B	G	4
29)	C	H	5
30)	D	J	6
31)	E	K	7

..FEBRUARY..

Day	P	E	I
1)	F	L	8
2)	G	M	A
3)	H	N	B
4)	J	O	C
5)	K	P	D
6)	L	Q	E
7)	M	R	F
8)	N	S	G
9)	O	T	H
10)	P	U	J
11)	Q	V	K
12)	R	W	L
13)	S	X	M
14)	T	Y	N
15)	U	Z	O
16)	V	1	P
17)	W	2	Q
18)	X	3	R
19)	A	A	S
20)	B	B	T
21)	C	C	U
22)	D	D	V
23)	E	E	W
24)	F	F	X
25)	G	G	Y
26)	H	H	Z
27)	J	J	1
28)	K	K	2

...MARCH...

Day	P	E	I
1)	L	L	3
2)	M	M	4
3)	N	N	5
4)	O	O	6
5)	P	P	7
6)	Q	Q	8
7)	R	R	A
8)	S	S	B
9)	T	T	C
10)	U	U	D
11)	V	V	E
12)	W	W	F
13)	X	X	G
14)	A	Y	H
15)	B	Z	J
16)	C	1	K
17)	D	2	L
18)	E	3	M
19)	F	A	N
20)	G	B	O
21)	H	C	P
22)	J	D	Q
23)	K	E	R
24)	L	F	S
25)	M	G	T
26)	N	H	U
27)	O	J	V
28)	P	K	W
29)	Q	L	X
30)	R	M	Y
31)	S	N	Z

...APRIL...

Day	P	E	I
1)	T	O	1
2)	U	P	2
3)	V	Q	3
4)	W	R	4
5)	X	S	5
6)	A	T	6
7)	B	U	7
8)	C	V	8
9)	D	W	A
10)	E	X	B
11)	F	Y	C
12)	G	Z	D
13)	H	1	E
14)	J	2	F
15)	K	3	G
16)	L	A	H
17)	M	B	J
18)	N	C	K
19)	O	D	L
20)	P	E	M
21)	Q	F	N
22)	R	G	O
23)	S	H	P
24)	T	J	Q
25)	U	K	R
26)	V	L	S
27)	W	M	T
28)	X	N	U
29)	A	O	V
30)	B	P	W

.....MAY....

Day	P	E	I
1)	C	Q	X
2)	D	R	Y
3)	E	S	Z
4)	F	T	1
5)	G	U	2
6)	H	V	3
7)	J	W	4
8)	K	X	5
9)	L	Y	6
10)	M	Z	7
11)	N	1	8
12)	O	2	A
13)	P	3	B
14)	Q	A	C
15)	R	B	D
16)	S	C	E
17)	T	D	F
18)	U	E	G
19)	V	F	H
20)	W	G	J
21)	X	H	K
22)	A	J	L
23)	B	K	M
24)	C	L	N
25)	D	M	O
26)	E	N	P
27)	F	O	Q
28)	G	P	R
29)	H	Q	S
30)	J	R	T
31)	K	S	U

....JUNE....

Day	P	E	I
1)	L	T	V
2)	M	U	W
3)	N	V	X
4)	O	W	Y
5)	P	X	Z
6)	Q	Y	1
7)	R	Z	2
8)	S	1	3
9)	T	2	4
10)	U	3	5
11)	V	A	6
12)	W	B	7
13)	X	C	8
14)	A	D	A
15)	B	E	B
16)	C	F	C
17)	D	G	D
18)	E	H	E
19)	F	J	F
20)	G	K	G
21)	H	L	H
22)	J	M	J
23)	K	N	K
24)	L	O	L
25)	M	P	M
26)	N	Q	N
27)	O	R	O
28)	P	S	P
29)	Q	T	Q
30)	R	U	R

....JULY....

Day	P	E	I
1)	S	V	S
2)	T	W	T
3)	U	X	U
4)	V	Y	V
5)	W	Z	W
6)	X	1	X
7)	A	2	Y
8)	B	3	Z
9)	C	A	1
10)	D	B	2
11)	E	C	3
12)	F	D	4
13)	G	E	5
14)	H	F	6
15)	J	G	7
16)	K	H	8
17)	L	J	A
18)	M	K	B
19)	N	L	C
20)	O	M	D
21)	P	N	E
22)	Q	O	F
23)	R	P	G
24)	S	Q	H
25)	T	R	J
26)	U	S	K
27)	V	T	L
28)	W	U	M
29)	X	V	N
30)	A	W	O
31)	B	X	P

...AUGUST...

Day	P	E	I
1)	C	Y	Q
2)	D	Z	R
3)	E	1	S
4)	F	2	T
5)	G	3	U
6)	H	A	V
7)	J	B	W
8)	K	C	X
9)	L	D	Y
10)	M	E	Z
11)	N	F	1
12)	O	G	2
13)	P	H	3
14)	Q	J	4
15)	R	K	5
16)	S	L	6
17)	T	M	7
18)	U	N	8
19)	V	O	A
20)	W	P	B
21)	X	Q	C
22)	A	R	D
23)	B	S	E
24)	C	T	F
25)	D	U	G
26)	E	V	H
27)	F	W	J
28)	G	X	K
29)	H	Y	L
30)	J	Z	M
31)	K	1	N

..SEPTEMBER.

Day	P	E	I
1)	L	2	O
2)	M	3	P
3)	N	A	Q
4)	O	B	R
5)	P	C	S
6)	Q	D	T
7)	R	E	U
8)	S	F	V
9)	T	G	W
10)	U	H	X
11)	V	J	Y
12)	W	K	Z
13)	X	L	1
14)	A	M	2
15)	B	N	3
16)	C	O	4
17)	D	P	5
18)	E	Q	6
19)	F	R	7
20)	G	S	8
21)	H	T	A
22)	J	U	B
23)	K	V	C
24)	L	W	D
25)	M	X	E
26)	N	Y	F
27)	O	Z	G
28)	P	1	H
29)	Q	2	J
30)	R	3	K

..OCTOBER...

Day	P	E	I
1)	S	A	L
2)	T	B	M
3)	U	C	N
4)	V	D	O
5)	W	E	P
6)	X	F	Q
7)	A	G	R
8)	B	H	S
9)	C	J	T
10)	D	K	U
11)	E	L	V
12)	F	M	W
13)	G	N	X
14)	H	O	Y
15)	J	P	Z
16)	K	Q	1
17)	L	R	2
18)	M	S	3
19)	N	T	4
20)	O	U	5
21)	P	V	6
22)	Q	W	7
23)	R	X	8
24)	S	Y	A
25)	T	Z	B
26)	U	1	C
27)	V	2	D
28)	W	3	E
29)	X	A	F
30)	A	B	G
31)	B	C	H

..NOVEMBER..

Day	P	E	I
1)	C	D	J
2)	D	E	K
3)	E	F	L
4)	F	G	M
5)	G	H	N
6)	H	J	O
7)	J	K	P
8)	K	L	Q
9)	L	M	R
10)	M	N	S
11)	N	O	T
12)	O	P	U
13)	P	Q	V
14)	Q	R	W
15)	R	S	X
16)	S	T	Y
17)	T	U	Z
18)	U	V	1
19)	V	W	2
20)	W	X	3
21)	X	Y	4
22)	A	Z	5
23)	B	1	6
24)	C	2	7
25)	D	3	8
26)	E	A	A
27)	F	B	B
28)	G	C	C
29)	H	D	D
30)	J	E	E

..DECEMBER..

Day	P	E	I
1)	K	F	F
2)	L	G	G
3)	M	H	H
4)	N	J	J
5)	O	K	K
6)	P	L	L
7)	Q	M	M
8)	R	N	N
9)	S	O	O
10)	T	P	P
11)	U	Q	Q
12)	V	R	R
13)	W	S	S
14)	X	T	T
15)	A	U	U
16)	B	V	V
17)	C	W	W
18)	D	X	X
19)	E	Y	Y
20)	F	Z	Z
21)	G	1	1
22)	H	2	2
23)	J	3	3
24)	K	4	4
25)	L	B	5
26)	M	C	6
27)	N	D	7
28)	O	E	8
29)	P	F	A
30)	Q	G	B
31)	R	H	C

CODES: P-PHYSICAL BIORHYTHM CURVE, E-EMOTIONAL BIORHYTHM CURVE, I-INTELLECTUAL BIORHYTHM CURVE

```
    ...JANUARY..      ..FEBRUARY..       ...MARCH...        ...APRIL...        ....MAY....       ....JUNE....

       P--E--I           P--E--I            P--E--I           P--E--I            P--E--I            P--E--I

  1)   S..J..D      1)   C..M..B       1)   J..N..6      1)   R..Q..4      1)   A..S..1       1)   J..V..Y
  2)   T..K..E      2)   D..N..C       2)   K..O..7      2)   S..R..5      2)   B..T..2       2)   K..W..Z
  3)   U..L..F      3)   E..O..D       3)   L..P..8      3)   T..S..6      3)   C..U..3       3)   L..X..1
  4)   V..M..G      4)   F..P..E       4)   M..Q..A      4)   U..T..7      4)   D..V..4       4)   M..Y..2
  5)   W..N..H      5)   G..Q..F       5)   N..R..B      5)   V..U..8      5)   E..W..5       5)   N..Z..3
  6)   X..O..J      6)   H..R..G       6)   O..S..C      6)   W..V..A      6)   F..X..6       6)   O..1..4
  7)   A..P..K      7)   J..S..H       7)   P..T..D      7)   X..W..B      7)   G..Y..7       7)   P..2..5
  8)   B..Q..L      8)   K..T..J       8)   Q..U..E      8)   A..X..C      8)   H..Z..8       8)   Q..3..6
  9)   C..R..M      9)   L..U..K       9)   R..V..F      9)   B..Y..D      9)   J..1..A       9)   R..A..7
 10)   D..S..N     10)   M..V..L      10)   S..W..G     10)   C..Z..E     10)   K..2..B      10)   S..B..8
 11)   E..T..O     11)   N..W..M      11)   T..X..H     11)   D..1..F     11)   L..3..C      11)   T..C..A
 12)   F..U..P     12)   O..X..N      12)   U..Y..J     12)   E..2..G     12)   M..A..D      12)   U..D..B
 13)   G..V..Q     13)   P..Y..O      13)   V..Z..K     13)   F..3..H     13)   N..B..E      13)   V..E..C
 14)   H..W..R     14)   Q..Z..P      14)   W..1..L     14)   G..A..J     14)   O..C..F      14)   W..F..D
 15)   J..X..S     15)   R..1..Q      15)   X..2..M     15)   H..B..K     15)   P..D..G      15)   X..G..E
 16)   K..Y..T     16)   S..2..R      16)   A..3..N     16)   J..C..L     16)   Q..E..H      16)   A..H..F
 17)   L..Z..U     17)   T..3..S      17)   B..A..O     17)   K..D..M     17)   R..F..J      17)   B..J..G
 18)   M..1..V     18)   U..A..T      18)   C..B..P     18)   L..E..N     18)   S..G..K      18)   C..K..H
 19)   N..2..W     19)   V..B..U      19)   D..C..Q     19)   M..F..O     19)   T..H..L      19)   D..L..J
 20)   O..3..X     20)   W..C..V      20)   E..D..R     20)   N..G..P     20)   U..J..M      20)   E..M..K
 21)   P..A..Y     21)   X..D..W      21)   F..E..S     21)   O..H..Q     21)   V..K..N      21)   F..N..L
 22)   Q..B..Z     22)   A..E..X      22)   G..F..T     22)   P..J..R     22)   W..L..O      22)   G..O..M
 23)   R..C..1     23)   B..F..Y      23)   H..G..U     23)   Q..K..S     23)   X..M..P      23)   H..P..N
 24)   S..D..2     24)   C..G..Z      24)   J..H..V     24)   R..L..T     24)   A..N..Q      24)   J..Q..O
 25)   T..E..3     25)   D..H..1      25)   K..J..W     25)   S..M..U     25)   B..O..R      25)   K..R..P
 26)   U..F..4     26)   E..J..2      26)   L..K..X     26)   T..N..V     26)   C..P..S      26)   L..S..Q
 27)   V..G..5     27)   F..K..3      27)   M..L..Y     27)   U..O..W     27)   D..Q..T      27)   M..T..R
 28)   W..H..6     28)   G..L..4      28)   N..M..Z     28)   V..P..X     28)   E..R..U      28)   N..U..S
 29)   X..J..7     29)   H..M..5      29)   O..N..1     29)   W..Q..Y     29)   F..S..V      29)   O..V..T
 30)   A..K..8                        30)   P..O..2     30)   X..R..Z     30)   G..T..W      30)   P..W..U
 31)   B..L..A                        31)   Q..P..3                       31)   H..U..X
```

```
    ....JULY....      ...AUGUST...      ..SEPTEMBER.       ..OCTOBER...       ..NOVEMBER..      ..DECEMBER..

       P--E--I           P--E--I            P--E--I           P--E--I            P--E--I            P--E--I

  1)   Q..X..V      1)   A..1..T       1)   J..A..R      1)   Q..C..O      1)   A..F..M       1)   H..H..J
  2)   R..Y..W      2)   B..2..U       2)   K..B..S      2)   R..D..P      2)   B..G..N       2)   J..J..K
  3)   S..Z..X      3)   C..3..V       3)   L..C..T      3)   S..E..Q      3)   C..H..O       3)   K..K..L
  4)   T..1..Y      4)   D..A..W       4)   M..D..U      4)   T..F..R      4)   D..J..P       4)   L..L..M
  5)   U..2..Z      5)   E..B..X       5)   N..E..V      5)   U..G..S      5)   E..K..Q       5)   M..M..N
  6)   V..3..1      6)   F..C..Y       6)   O..F..W      6)   V..H..T      6)   F..L..R       6)   N..N..O
  7)   W..A..2      7)   G..D..Z       7)   P..G..X      7)   W..J..U      7)   G..M..S       7)   O..O..P
  8)   X..B..3      8)   H..E..1       8)   Q..H..Y      8)   X..K..V      8)   H..N..T       8)   P..P..Q
  9)   A..C..4      9)   J..F..2       9)   R..J..Z      9)   A..L..W      9)   J..O..U       9)   Q..Q..R
 10)   B..D..5     10)   K..G..3      10)   S..K..1     10)   B..M..X     10)   K..P..V      10)   R..R..S
 11)   C..E..6     11)   L..H..4      11)   T..L..2     11)   C..N..Y     11)   L..Q..W      11)   S..S..T
 12)   D..F..7     12)   M..J..5      12)   U..M..3     12)   D..O..Z     12)   M..R..X      12)   T..T..U
 13)   E..G..8     13)   N..K..6      13)   V..N..4     13)   E..P..1     13)   N..S..Y      13)   U..U..V
 14)   F..H..A     14)   O..L..7      14)   W..O..5     14)   F..Q..2     14)   O..T..Z      14)   V..V..W
 15)   G..J..B     15)   P..M..8      15)   X..P..6     15)   G..R..3     15)   P..U..1      15)   W..W..X
 16)   H..K..C     16)   Q..N..A      16)   A..Q..7     16)   H..S..4     16)   Q..V..2      16)   X..X..Y
 17)   J..L..D     17)   R..O..B      17)   B..R..8     17)   J..T..5     17)   R..W..3      17)   A..Y..Z
 18)   K..M..E     18)   S..P..C      18)   C..S..A     18)   K..U..6     18)   S..X..4      18)   B..Z..1
 19)   L..N..F     19)   T..Q..D      19)   D..T..B     19)   L..V..7     19)   T..Y..5      19)   C..1..2
 20)   M..O..G     20)   U..R..E      20)   E..U..C     20)   M..W..8     20)   U..Z..6      20)   D..2..3
 21)   N..P..H     21)   V..S..F      21)   F..V..D     21)   N..X..A     21)   V..1..7      21)   E..3..4
 22)   O..Q..J     22)   W..T..G      22)   G..W..E     22)   O..Y..B     22)   W..2..8      22)   F..A..5
 23)   P..R..K     23)   X..U..H      23)   H..X..F     23)   P..Z..C     23)   X..3..A      23)   G..B..6
 24)   Q..S..L     24)   A..V..J      24)   J..Y..G     24)   Q..1..D     24)   A..A..B      24)   H..C..7
 25)   R..T..M     25)   B..W..K      25)   K..Z..H     25)   R..2..E     25)   B..B..C      25)   J..D..8
 26)   S..U..N     26)   C..X..L      26)   L..1..J     26)   S..3..F     26)   C..C..D      26)   K..E..A
 27)   T..V..O     27)   D..Y..M      27)   M..2..K     27)   T..A..G     27)   D..D..E      27)   L..F..B
 28)   U..W..P     28)   E..Z..N      28)   N..3..L     28)   U..B..H     28)   E..E..F      28)   M..G..C
 29)   V..X..Q     29)   F..1..O      29)   O..A..M     29)   V..C..J     29)   F..F..G      29)   N..H..D
 30)   W..Y..R     30)   G..2..P      30)   P..B..N     30)   W..D..K     30)   G..G..H      30)   O..J..E
 31)   X..Z..S     31)   H..3..Q                        31)   X..E..L                        31)   P..K..F
```

CODES: P-PHYSICAL BIORHYTHM CURVE,E-EMOTIONAL BIORHYTHM CURVE,I-INTELLECTUAL BIORHYTHM CURVE

...JANUARY..	.FEBRUARY..	...MARCH...	...APRIL...	....MAY....	....JUNE....
P--E--I	P--E--I	P--E--I	P--E--I	P--E--I	P--E--I
1) Q..L..G	1) A..O..E	1) F..O..8	1) O..R..6	1) V..T..3	1) F..W..1
2) R..M..H	2) B..P..F	2) G..P..A	2) P..S..7	2) W..U..4	2) G..X..2
3) S..N..J	3) C..Q..G	3) H..Q..B	3) Q..T..8	3) X..V..5	3) H..Y..3
4) T..O..K	4) D..R..H	4) J..R..C	4) R..U..A	4) A..W..6	4) J..Z..4
5) U..P..L	5) E..S..J	5) K..S..D	5) S..V..B	5) B..X..7	5) K..1..5
6) V..Q..M	6) F..T..K	6) L..T..E	6) T..W..C	6) C..Y..8	6) L..2..6
7) W..R..N	7) G..U..L	7) M..U..F	7) U..X..D	7) D..Z..A	7) M..3..7
8) X..S..O	8) H..V..M	8) N..V..G	8) V..Y..E	8) E..1..B	8) N..A..8
9) A..T..P	9) J..W..N	9) O..W..H	9) W..Z..F	9) F..2..C	9) O..B..A
10) B..U..Q	10) K..X..O	10) P..X..J	10) X..1..G	10) G..3..D	10) P..C..B
11) C..V..R	11) L..Y..P	11) Q..Y..K	11) A..2..H	11) H..A..E	11) Q..D..C
12) D..W..S	12) M..Z..Q	12) R..Z..L	12) B..3..J	12) J..B..F	12) R..E..D
13) E..X..T	13) N..1..R	13) S..1..M	13) C..A..K	13) K..C..G	13) S..F..E
14) F..Y..U	14) O..2..S	14) T..2..N	14) D..B..L	14) L..D..H	14) T..G..F
15) G..Z..V	15) P..3..T	15) U..3..O	15) E..C..M	15) M..E..J	15) U..H..G
16) H..1..W	16) Q..A..U	16) V..A..P	16) F..D..N	16) N..F..K	16) V..J..H
17) J..2..X	17) R..B..V	17) W..B..Q	17) G..E..O	17) O..G..L	17) W..K..J
18) K..3..Y	18) S..C..W	18) X..C..R	18) H..F..P	18) P..H..M	18) X..L..K
19) L..A..Z	19) T..D..X	19) A..D..S	19) J..G..Q	19) Q..J..N	19) A..M..L
20) M..B..1	20) U..E..Y	20) B..E..T	20) K..H..R	20) R..K..O	20) B..N..M
21) N..C..2	21) V..F..Z	21) C..F..U	21) L..J..S	21) S..L..P	21) C..O..N
22) O..D..3	22) W..G..1	22) D..G..V	22) M..K..T	22) T..M..Q	22) D..P..O
23) P..E..4	23) X..H..2	23) E..H..W	23) N..L..U	23) U..N..R	23) E..Q..P
24) Q..F..5	24) A..J..3	24) F..J..X	24) O..M..V	24) V..O..S	24) F..R..Q
25) R..G..6	25) B..K..4	25) G..K..Y	25) P..N..W	25) W..P..T	25) G..S..R
26) S..H..7	26) C..L..5	26) H..L..Z	26) Q..O..X	26) X..Q..U	26) H..T..S
27) T..J..8	27) D..M..6	27) J..M..1	27) R..P..Y	27) A..R..V	27) J..U..T
28) U..K..A	28) E..N..7	28) K..N..2	28) S..Q..Z	28) B..S..W	28) K..V..U
29) V..L..B		29) L..O..3	29) T..R..1	29) C..T..X	29) L..W..V
30) W..M..C		30) M..P..4	30) U..S..2	30) D..U..Y	30) M..X..W
31) X..N..D		31) N..Q..5		31) E..V..Z	

....JULY....	...AUGUST...	.SEPTEMBER.	..OCTOBER...	.NOVEMBER..	.DECEMBER..
P--E--I	P--E--I	P--E--I	P--E--I	P--E--I	P--E--I
1) N..Y..X	1) V..2..V	1) F..B..T	1) N..D..Q	1) V..G..O	1) E..J..L
2) O..Z..Y	2) W..3..W	2) G..C..U	2) O..E..R	2) W..H..P	2) F..K..M
3) P..1..Z	3) X..A..X	3) H..D..V	3) P..F..S	3) X..J..Q	3) G..L..N
4) Q..2..1	4) A..B..Y	4) J..E..W	4) Q..G..T	4) A..K..R	4) H..M..O
5) R..3..2	5) B..C..Z	5) K..F..X	5) R..H..U	5) B..L..S	5) J..N..P
6) S..A..3	6) C..D..1	6) L..G..Y	6) S..J..V	6) C..M..T	6) K..O..Q
7) T..B..4	7) D..E..2	7) M..H..Z	7) T..K..W	7) D..N..U	7) L..P..R
8) U..C..5	8) E..F..3	8) N..J..1	8) U..L..X	8) E..O..V	8) M..Q..S
9) V..D..6	9) F..G..4	9) O..K..2	9) V..M..Y	9) F..P..W	9) N..R..T
10) W..E..7	10) G..H..5	10) P..L..3	10) W..N..Z	10) G..Q..X	10) O..S..U
11) X..F..8	11) H..J..6	11) Q..M..4	11) X..O..1	11) H..R..Y	11) P..T..V
12) A..G..A	12) J..K..7	12) R..N..5	12) A..P..2	12) J..S..Z	12) Q..U..W
13) B..H..B	13) K..L..8	13) S..O..6	13) B..Q..3	13) K..T..1	13) R..V..X
14) C..J..C	14) L..M..A	14) T..P..7	14) C..R..4	14) L..U..2	14) S..W..Y
15) D..K..D	15) M..N..B	15) U..Q..8	15) D..S..5	15) M..V..3	15) T..X..Z
16) E..L..E	16) N..O..C	16) V..R..A	16) E..T..6	16) N..W..4	16) U..Y..1
17) F..M..F	17) O..P..D	17) W..S..B	17) F..U..7	17) O..X..5	17) V..Z..2
18) G..N..G	18) P..Q..E	18) X..T..C	18) G..V..8	18) P..Y..6	18) W..1..3
19) H..O..H	19) Q..R..F	19) A..U..D	19) H..W..A	19) Q..Z..7	19) X..2..4
20) J..P..J	20) R..S..G	20) B..V..E	20) J..X..B	20) R..1..8	20) A..3..5
21) K..Q..K	21) S..T..H	21) C..W..F	21) K..Y..C	21) S..2..A	21) B..A..6
22) L..R..L	22) T..U..J	22) D..X..G	22) L..Z..D	22) T..3..B	22) C..B..7
23) M..S..M	23) U..V..K	23) E..Y..H	23) M..1..E	23) U..A..C	23) D..C..8
24) N..T..N	24) V..W..L	24) F..Z..J	24) N..2..F	24) V..B..D	24) E..D..A
25) O..U..O	25) W..X..M	25) G..1..K	25) O..3..G	25) W..C..E	25) F..E..B
26) P..V..P	26) X..Y..N	26) H..2..L	26) P..A..H	26) X..D..F	26) G..F..C
27) Q..W..Q	27) A..Z..O	27) J..3..M	27) Q..B..J	27) A..E..G	27) H..G..D
28) R..X..R	28) B..1..P	28) K..A..N	28) R..C..K	28) B..F..H	28) J..H..E
29) S..Y..S	29) C..2..Q	29) L..B..O	29) S..D..L	29) C..G..J	29) K..J..F
30) T..Z..T	30) D..3..R	30) M..C..P	30) T..E..M	30) D..H..K	30) L..K..G
31) U..1..U	31) E..A..S		31) U..F..N		31) M..L..H

CODES: P-PHYSICAL BIORHYTHM CURVE,E-EMOTIONAL BIORHYTHM CURVE,I-INTELLECTUAL BIORHYTHM CURVE

...JANUARY..	..FEBRUARY..	...MARCH...	...APRIL...	....MAY....	...JUNE....
P--E--I	P--E--I	P--E--I	P--E--I	P--E--I	P--E--I
1) N..M..J	1) V..P..G	1) C..P..B	1) L..S..8	1) S..U..5	1) C..X..3
2) O..N..K	2) W..Q..H	2) D..Q..C	2) M..T..A	2) T..V..6	2) D..Y..4
3) P..O..L	3) X..R..J	3) E..R..D	3) N..U..B	3) U..W..7	3) E..Z..5
4) Q..P..M	4) A..S..K	4) F..S..E	4) O..V..C	4) V..X..8	4) F..1..6
5) R..Q..N	5) B..T..L	5) G..T..F	5) P..W..D	5) W..Y..A	5) G..2..7
6) S..R..O	6) C..U..M	6) H..U..G	6) Q..X..E	6) X..Z..B	6) H..B..8
7) T..S..P	7) D..V..N	7) J..V..H	7) R..Y..F	7) A..1..C	7) J..A..A
8) U..T..Q	8) E..W..O	8) K..W..J	8) S..Z..G	8) B..2..D	8) K..B..B
9) V..U..R	9) F..X..P	9) L..X..K	9) T..1..H	9) C..3..E	9) L..C..C
10) W..V..S	10) G..Y..Q	10) M..Y..L	10) U..2..J	10) D..A..F	10) M..D..D
11) X..W..T	11) H..Z..R	11) N..Z..M	11) V..3..K	11) E..B..G	11) N..E..E
12) A..X..U	12) J..1..S	12) O..1..N	12) W..A..L	12) F..C..H	12) O..F..F
13) B..Y..V	13) K..2..T	13) P..2..O	13) X..B..M	13) G..D..J	13) P..G..G
14) C..Z..W	14) L..3..U	14) Q..3..P	14) A..C..N	14) H..E..K	14) Q..H..H
15) D..1..X	15) M..A..V	15) R..A..Q	15) B..D..O	15) J..F..L	15) R..J..J
16) E..2..Y	16) N..B..W	16) S..B..R	16) C..E..P	16) K..G..M	16) S..K..K
17) F..3..Z	17) O..C..X	17) T..C..S	17) D..F..Q	17) L..H..N	17) T..L..L
18) G..A..1	18) P..D..Y	18) U..D..T	18) E..G..R	18) M..J..O	18) U..M..M
19) H..B..2	19) Q..E..Z	19) V..E..U	19) F..H..S	19) N..K..P	19) V..N..N
20) J..C..3	20) R..F..1	20) W..F..V	20) G..J..T	20) O..L..Q	20) W..O..O
21) K..D..4	21) S..G..2	21) X..G..W	21) H..K..U	21) P..M..R	21) X..P..P
22) L..E..5	22) T..H..3	22) A..H..X	22) J..L..V	22) Q..N..S	22) A..Q..Q
23) M..F..6	23) U..J..4	23) B..J..Y	23) K..M..W	23) R..O..T	23) B..R..R
24) N..G..7	24) V..K..5	24) C..K..Z	24) L..N..X	24) S..P..U	24) C..S..S
25) O..H..8	25) W..L..6	25) D..L..1	25) M..O..Y	25) T..Q..V	25) D..T..T
26) P..J..A	26) X..M..7	26) E..M..2	26) N..P..Z	26) U..R..W	26) E..U..U
27) Q..K..B	27) A..N..8	27) F..N..3	27) O..Q..1	27) V..S..X	27) F..V..V
28) R..L..C	28) B..O..A	28) G..O..4	28) P..R..2	28) W..T..Y	28) G..W..W
29) S..M..D		29) H..P..5	29) Q..S..3	29) X..U..Z	29) H..X..X
30) T..N..E		30) J..Q..6	30) R..T..4	30) A..V..1	30) J..Y..Y
31) U..O..F		31) K..R..7		31) B..W..2	

....JULY....	...AUGUST...	..SEPTEMBER.	..OCTOBER...	..NOVEMBER..	..DECEMBER..
P--E--I	P--E--I	P--E--I	P--E--I	P--E--I	P--E--I
1) K..Z..Z	1) S..3..X	1) C..C..V	1) K..E..S	1) S..H..Q	1) B..K..N
2) L..1..1	2) T..A..Y	2) D..D..W	2) L..F..T	2) T..J..R	2) C..L..O
3) M..2..2	3) U..B..Z	3) E..E..X	3) M..G..U	3) U..K..S	3) D..M..P
4) N..3..3	4) V..C..1	4) F..F..Y	4) N..H..V	4) V..L..T	4) E..N..Q
5) O..A..4	5) W..D..2	5) G..G..Z	5) O..J..W	5) W..M..U	5) F..O..R
6) P..B..5	6) X..E..3	6) H..H..1	6) P..K..X	6) X..N..V	6) G..P..S
7) Q..C..6	7) A..F..4	7) J..J..2	7) Q..L..Y	7) A..O..W	7) H..Q..T
8) R..D..7	8) B..G..5	8) K..K..3	8) R..M..Z	8) B..P..X	8) J..R..U
9) S..E..8	9) C..H..6	9) L..L..4	9) S..N..1	9) C..Q..Y	9) K..S..V
10) T..F..A	10) D..J..7	10) M..M..5	10) T..O..2	10) D..R..Z	10) L..T..W
11) U..G..B	11) E..K..8	11) N..N..6	11) U..P..3	11) E..S..1	11) M..U..X
12) V..H..C	12) F..L..A	12) O..O..7	12) V..Q..4	12) F..T..2	12) N..V..Y
13) W..J..D	13) G..M..B	13) P..P..8	13) W..R..5	13) G..U..3	13) O..W..Z
14) X..K..E	14) H..N..C	14) Q..Q..A	14) X..S..6	14) H..V..4	14) P..X..1
15) A..L..F	15) J..O..D	15) R..R..B	15) A..T..7	15) J..W..5	15) Q..Y..2
16) B..M..G	16) K..P..E	16) S..S..C	16) B..U..8	16) K..X..6	16) R..Z..3
17) C..N..H	17) L..Q..F	17) T..T..D	17) C..V..A	17) L..Y..7	17) S..1..4
18) D..O..J	18) M..R..G	18) U..U..E	18) D..W..B	18) M..Z..8	18) T..2..5
19) E..P..K	19) N..S..H	19) V..V..F	19) E..X..C	19) N..1..A	19) U..3..6
20) F..Q..L	20) O..T..J	20) W..W..G	20) F..Y..D	20) O..2..B	20) V..A..7
21) G..R..M	21) P..U..K	21) X..X..H	21) G..Z..E	21) P..3..C	21) W..B..8
22) H..S..N	22) Q..V..L	22) A..Y..J	22) H..1..F	22) Q..A..D	22) X..C..A
23) J..T..O	23) R..W..M	23) B..Z..K	23) J..2..G	23) R..B..E	23) A..D..B
24) K..U..P	24) S..X..N	24) C..1..L	24) K..3..H	24) S..C..F	24) B..E..C
25) L..V..Q	25) T..Y..O	25) D..2..M	25) L..A..J	25) T..D..G	25) C..F..D
26) M..W..R	26) U..Z..P	26) E..3..N	26) M..B..K	26) U..E..H	26) D..G..E
27) N..X..S	27) V..1..Q	27) F..A..O	27) N..C..L	27) V..F..J	27) E..H..F
28) O..Y..T	28) W..2..R	28) G..B..P	28) O..D..M	28) W..G..K	28) F..J..G
29) P..Z..U	29) X..3..S	29) H..C..Q	29) P..E..N	29) X..H..L	29) G..K..H
30) Q..1..V	30) A..A..T	30) J..D..R	30) Q..F..O	30) A..J..M	30) H..L..J
31) R..2..W	31) B..B..U		31) R..G..P		31) J..M..K

CODES: P-PHYSICAL BIORHYTHM CURVE,E-EMOTIONAL BIORHYTHM CURVE,I-INTELLECTUAL BIORHYTHM CURVE

JANUARY..

	P	E	I
1)	K	N	L
2)	L	O	M
3)	M	P	N
4)	N	Q	O
5)	O	R	P
6)	P	S	Q
7)	Q	T	R
8)	R	U	S
9)	S	V	T
10)	T	W	U
11)	U	X	V
12)	V	Y	W
13)	W	Z	X
14)	X	1	Y
15)	A	2	Z
16)	B	3	1
17)	C	A	2
18)	D	B	3
19)	E	C	4
20)	F	D	5
21)	G	E	6
22)	H	F	7
23)	J	G	8
24)	K	H	A
25)	L	J	B
26)	M	K	C
27)	N	L	D
28)	O	M	E
29)	P	N	F
30)	Q	O	G
31)	R	P	H

FEBRUARY..

	P	E	I
1)	S	Q	J
2)	T	R	K
3)	U	S	L
4)	V	T	M
5)	W	U	N
6)	X	V	O
7)	A	W	P
8)	B	X	Q
9)	C	Y	R
10)	D	Z	S
11)	E	1	T
12)	F	2	U
13)	G	3	V
14)	H	A	W
15)	J	B	X
16)	K	C	Y
17)	L	D	Z
18)	M	E	1
19)	N	F	2
20)	O	G	3
21)	P	H	4
22)	Q	J	5
23)	R	K	6
24)	S	L	7
25)	T	M	8
26)	U	N	A
27)	V	O	B
28)	W	P	C

MARCH...

	P	E	I
1)	X	Q	D
2)	A	R	E
3)	B	S	F
4)	C	T	G
5)	D	U	H
6)	E	V	J
7)	F	W	K
8)	G	X	L
9)	H	Y	M
10)	J	Z	N
11)	K	1	O
12)	L	2	P
13)	M	3	Q
14)	N	A	R
15)	O	B	S
16)	P	C	T
17)	Q	D	U
18)	R	E	V
19)	S	F	W
20)	T	G	X
21)	U	H	Y
22)	V	J	Z
23)	W	K	1
24)	X	L	2
25)	A	M	3
26)	B	N	4
27)	C	O	5
28)	D	P	6
29)	E	Q	7
30)	F	R	8
31)	G	S	A

APRIL...

	P	E	I
1)	H	T	B
2)	J	U	C
3)	K	V	D
4)	L	W	E
5)	M	X	F
6)	N	Y	G
7)	O	Z	H
8)	P	1	J
9)	Q	2	K
10)	R	3	L
11)	S	A	M
12)	T	B	N
13)	U	C	O
14)	V	D	P
15)	W	E	Q
16)	X	F	R
17)	A	G	S
18)	B	H	T
19)	C	J	U
20)	D	K	V
21)	E	L	W
22)	F	M	X
23)	G	N	Y
24)	H	O	Z
25)	J	P	1
26)	K	Q	2
27)	L	R	3
28)	M	S	4
29)	N	T	5
30)	O	U	6

MAY....

	P	E	I
1)	P	V	7
2)	Q	W	8
3)	R	X	A
4)	S	Y	B
5)	T	Z	C
6)	U	1	D
7)	V	2	E
8)	W	3	F
9)	X	A	G
10)	A	B	H
11)	B	C	J
12)	C	D	K
13)	D	E	L
14)	E	F	M
15)	F	G	N
16)	G	H	O
17)	H	J	P
18)	J	K	Q
19)	K	L	R
20)	L	M	S
21)	M	N	T
22)	N	O	U
23)	O	P	V
24)	P	Q	W
25)	Q	R	X
26)	R	S	Y
27)	S	T	Z
28)	T	U	1
29)	U	V	2
30)	V	W	3
31)	W	X	4

JUNE....

	P	E	I
1)	X	Y	5
2)	A	Z	6
3)	B	1	7
4)	C	2	8
5)	D	3	A
6)	E	A	B
7)	F	B	C
8)	G	C	D
9)	H	D	E
10)	J	E	F
11)	K	F	G
12)	L	G	H
13)	M	H	J
14)	N	J	K
15)	O	K	L
16)	P	L	M
17)	Q	M	N
18)	R	N	O
19)	S	O	P
20)	T	P	Q
21)	U	Q	R
22)	V	R	S
23)	W	S	T
24)	X	T	U
25)	A	U	V
26)	B	V	W
27)	C	W	X
28)	D	X	Y
29)	E	Y	Z
30)	F	Z	1

JULY....

	P	E	I
1)	G	1	2
2)	H	2	3
3)	J	3	4
4)	K	A	5
5)	L	B	6
6)	M	C	7
7)	N	D	8
8)	O	E	A
9)	P	F	B
10)	Q	G	C
11)	R	H	D
12)	S	J	E
13)	T	K	F
14)	U	L	G
15)	V	M	H
16)	W	N	J
17)	X	O	K
18)	A	P	L
19)	B	Q	M
20)	C	R	N
21)	D	S	O
22)	E	T	P
23)	F	U	Q
24)	G	V	R
25)	H	W	S
26)	J	X	T
27)	K	Y	U
28)	L	Z	V
29)	M	1	W
30)	N	2	X
31)	O	3	Y

AUGUST...

	P	E	I
1)	P	A	Z
2)	Q	B	1
3)	R	C	2
4)	S	D	3
5)	T	E	4
6)	U	F	5
7)	V	G	6
8)	W	H	7
9)	X	J	8
10)	A	K	A
11)	B	L	B
12)	C	M	C
13)	D	N	D
14)	E	O	E
15)	F	P	F
16)	G	Q	G
17)	H	R	H
18)	J	S	J
19)	K	T	K
20)	L	U	L
21)	M	V	M
22)	N	W	N
23)	O	X	O
24)	P	Y	P
25)	Q	Z	Q
26)	R	1	R
27)	S	2	S
28)	T	3	T
29)	U	A	U
30)	V	B	V
31)	W	C	W

SEPTEMBER.

	P	E	I
1)	X	D	X
2)	A	E	Y
3)	B	F	Z
4)	C	G	1
5)	D	H	2
6)	E	J	3
7)	F	K	4
8)	G	L	5
9)	H	M	6
10)	J	N	7
11)	K	O	8
12)	L	P	A
13)	M	Q	B
14)	N	R	C
15)	O	S	D
16)	P	T	E
17)	Q	U	F
18)	R	V	G
19)	S	W	H
20)	T	X	J
21)	U	Y	K
22)	V	Z	L
23)	W	1	M
24)	X	2	N
25)	A	3	O
26)	B	A	P
27)	C	B	Q
28)	D	C	R
29)	E	D	S
30)	F	E	T

OCTOBER...

	P	E	I
1)	G	F	U
2)	H	G	V
3)	J	H	W
4)	K	J	X
5)	L	K	Y
6)	M	L	Z
7)	N	M	1
8)	O	N	2
9)	P	O	3
10)	Q	P	4
11)	R	Q	5
12)	S	R	6
13)	T	S	7
14)	U	T	8
15)	V	U	A
16)	W	V	B
17)	X	W	C
18)	A	X	D
19)	B	Y	E
20)	C	Z	F
21)	D	1	G
22)	E	2	H
23)	F	3	J
24)	G	A	K
25)	H	B	L
26)	J	C	M
27)	K	D	N
28)	L	E	O
29)	M	F	P
30)	N	G	Q
31)	O	H	R

NOVEMBER..

	P	E	I
1)	P	J	S
2)	Q	K	T
3)	R	L	U
4)	S	M	V
5)	T	N	W
6)	U	O	X
7)	V	P	Y
8)	W	Q	Z
9)	X	R	1
10)	A	S	2
11)	B	T	3
12)	C	U	4
13)	D	V	5
14)	E	W	6
15)	F	X	7
16)	G	Y	8
17)	H	Z	A
18)	J	1	B
19)	K	2	C
20)	L	3	D
21)	M	A	E
22)	N	B	F
23)	O	C	G
24)	P	D	H
25)	Q	E	J
26)	R	F	K
27)	S	G	L
28)	T	H	M
29)	U	J	N
30)	V	K	O

DECEMBER..

	P	E	I
1)	W	L	P
2)	X	M	Q
3)	A	N	R
4)	B	O	S
5)	C	P	T
6)	D	Q	U
7)	E	R	V
8)	F	S	W
9)	G	T	X
10)	H	U	Y
11)	J	V	Z
12)	K	W	1
13)	L	X	2
14)	M	Y	3
15)	N	Z	4
16)	O	1	5
17)	P	2	6
18)	Q	3	7
19)	R	A	8
20)	S	B	A
21)	T	C	B
22)	U	D	C
23)	V	E	D
24)	W	F	E
25)	X	G	F
26)	A	H	G
27)	B	J	H
28)	C	K	J
29)	D	L	K
30)	E	M	L
31)	F	N	M

CODES: P-PHYSICAL BIORHYTHM CURVE, E-EMOTIONAL BIORHYTHM CURVE, I-INTELLECTUAL BIORHYTHM CURVE

...JANUARY..	.FEBRUARY..	...MARCH...	...APRIL...	....MAY....	...JUNE....
P--E--I	P--E--I	P--E--I	P--E--I	P--E--I	P--E--I
1) G..O..N	1) P..R..L	1) V..S..G	1) F..V..E	1) N..X..B	1) V..1..8
2) H..P..O	2) Q..S..M	2) W..T..H	2) G..W..F	2) O..Y..C	2) W..2..A
3) J..Q..P	3) R..T..N	3) X..U..J	3) H..X..G	3) P..Z..D	3) X..3..B
4) K..R..Q	4) S..U..O	4) A..V..K	4) J..Y..H	4) Q..1..E	4) A..A..C
5) L..S..R	5) T..V..P	5) B..W..L	5) K..Z..J	5) R..2..F	5) B..B..D
6) M..T..S	6) U..W..Q	6) C..X..M	6) L..1..K	6) S..3..G	6) C..C..E
7) N..U..T	7) V..X..R	7) D..Y..N	7) M..2..L	7) T..A..H	7) D..D..F
8) O..V..U	8) W..Y..S	8) E..Z..O	8) N..3..M	8) U..B..J	8) E..E..G
9) P..W..V	9) X..Z..T	9) F..1..P	9) O..A..N	9) V..C..K	9) F..F..H
10) Q..X..W	10) A..1..U	10) G..2..Q	10) P..B..O	10) W..D..L	10) G..G..J
11) R..Y..X	11) B..2..V	11) H..3..R	11) Q..C..P	11) X..E..M	11) H..H..K
12) S..Z..Y	12) C..3..W	12) J..A..S	12) R..D..Q	12) A..F..N	12) J..J..L
13) T..1..Z	13) D..A..X	13) K..B..T	13) S..E..R	13) B..G..O	13) K..K..M
14) U..2..1	14) E..B..Y	14) L..C..U	14) T..F..S	14) C..H..P	14) L..L..N
15) V..3..2	15) F..C..Z	15) M..D..V	15) U..G..T	15) D..J..Q	15) M..M..O
16) W..A..3	16) G..D..1	16) N..E..W	16) V..H..U	16) E..K..R	16) N..N..P
17) X..B..4	17) H..E..2	17) O..F..X	17) W..J..V	17) F..L..S	17) O..O..Q
18) A..C..5	18) J..F..3	18) P..G..Y	18) X..K..W	18) G..M..T	18) P..P..R
19) B..D..6	19) K..G..4	19) Q..H..Z	19) A..L..X	19) H..N..U	19) Q..Q..S
20) C..E..7	20) L..H..5	20) R..J..1	20) B..M..Y	20) J..O..V	20) R..R..T
21) D..F..8	21) M..J..6	21) S..K..2	21) C..N..Z	21) K..P..W	21) S..S..U
22) E..G..A	22) N..K..7	22) T..L..3	22) D..O..1	22) L..Q..X	22) T..T..V
23) F..H..B	23) O..L..8	23) U..M..4	23) E..P..2	23) M..R..Y	23) U..U..W
24) G..J..C	24) P..M..A	24) V..N..5	24) F..Q..3	24) N..S..Z	24) V..V..X
25) H..K..D	25) Q..N..B	25) W..O..6	25) G..R..4	25) O..T..1	25) W..W..Y
26) J..L..E	26) R..O..C	26) X..P..7	26) H..S..5	26) P..U..2	26) X..X..Z
27) K..M..F	27) S..P..D	27) A..Q..8	27) J..T..6	27) Q..V..3	27) A..Y..1
28) L..N..G	28) T..Q..E	28) B..R..A	28) K..U..7	28) R..W..4	28) B..Z..2
29) M..O..H	29) U..R..F	29) C..S..B	29) L..V..8	29) S..X..5	29) C..1..3
30) N..P..J		30) D..T..C	30) M..W..A	30) T..Y..6	30) D..2..4
31) O..Q..K		31) E..U..D		31) U..Z..7	

....JULY....	...AUGUST...	..SEPTEMBER.	..OCTOBER...	..NOVEMBER..	..DECEMBER..
P--E--I	P--E--I	P--E--I	P--E--I	P--E--I	P--E--I
1) E..3..5	1) N..C..3	1) V..F..1	1) E..H..X	1) N..L..V	1) U..N..S
2) F..A..6	2) O..D..4	2) W..G..2	2) F..J..Y	2) O..M..W	2) V..O..T
3) G..B..7	3) P..E..5	3) X..H..3	3) G..K..Z	3) P..N..X	3) W..P..U
4) H..C..8	4) Q..F..6	4) A..J..4	4) H..L..1	4) Q..O..Y	4) X..Q..V
5) J..D..A	5) R..G..7	5) B..K..5	5) J..M..2	5) R..P..Z	5) A..R..W
6) K..E..B	6) S..H..8	6) C..L..6	6) K..N..3	6) S..Q..1	6) B..S..X
7) L..F..C	7) T..J..A	7) D..M..7	7) L..O..4	7) T..R..2	7) C..T..Y
8) M..G..D	8) U..K..B	8) E..N..8	8) M..P..5	8) U..S..3	8) D..U..Z
9) N..H..E	9) V..L..C	9) F..O..A	9) N..Q..6	9) V..T..4	9) E..V..1
10) O..J..F	10) W..M..D	10) G..P..B	10) O..R..7	10) W..U..5	10) F..W..2
11) P..K..G	11) X..N..E	11) H..Q..C	11) P..S..8	11) X..V..6	11) G..X..3
12) Q..L..H	12) A..O..F	12) J..R..D	12) Q..T..A	12) A..W..7	12) H..Y..4
13) R..M..J	13) B..P..G	13) K..S..E	13) R..U..B	13) B..X..8	13) J..Z..5
14) S..N..K	14) C..Q..H	14) L..T..F	14) S..V..C	14) C..Y..A	14) K..1..6
15) T..O..L	15) D..R..J	15) M..U..G	15) T..W..D	15) D..Z..B	15) L..2..7
16) U..P..M	16) E..S..K	16) N..V..H	16) U..X..E	16) E..1..C	16) M..3..8
17) V..Q..N	17) F..T..L	17) O..W..J	17) V..Y..F	17) F..2..D	17) N..A..A
18) W..R..O	18) G..U..M	18) P..X..K	18) W..Z..G	18) G..3..E	18) O..B..B
19) X..S..P	19) H..V..N	19) Q..Y..L	19) X..1..H	19) H..A..F	19) P..C..C
20) A..T..Q	20) J..W..O	20) R..Z..M	20) A..2..J	20) J..B..G	20) Q..D..D
21) B..U..R	21) K..X..P	21) S..1..N	21) B..3..K	21) K..C..H	21) R..E..E
22) C..V..S	22) L..Y..Q	22) T..2..O	22) C..A..L	22) L..D..J	22) S..F..F
23) D..W..T	23) M..Z..R	23) U..3..P	23) D..B..M	23) M..E..K	23) T..G..G
24) E..X..U	24) N..1..S	24) V..A..Q	24) E..C..N	24) N..F..L	24) U..H..H
25) F..Y..V	25) O..2..T	25) W..B..R	25) F..D..O	25) O..G..M	25) V..J..J
26) G..Z..W	26) P..3..U	26) X..C..S	26) G..E..P	26) P..H..N	26) W..K..K
27) H..1..X	27) Q..A..V	27) A..D..T	27) H..F..Q	27) Q..J..O	27) X..L..L
28) J..2..Y	28) R..B..W	28) B..E..U	28) J..G..R	28) R..K..P	28) A..M..M
29) K..3..Z	29) S..C..X	29) C..F..V	29) K..H..S	29) S..L..Q	29) B..N..N
30) L..A..1	30) T..D..Y	30) D..G..W	30) L..J..T	30) T..M..R	30) C..O..O
31) M..B..2	31) U..E..Z		31) M..K..U		31) D..P..P

CODES: P-PHYSICAL BIORHYTHM CURVE,E-EMOTIONAL BIORHYTHM CURVE,I-INTELLECTUAL BIORHYTHM CURVE

	...JANUARY.. P--E--I	.FEBRUARY.. P--E--I	...MARCH... P--E--I	...APRIL... P--E--I	....MAY.... P--E--I	...JUNE.... P--E--I
1)	E..Q..Q	N..T..O	S..T..J	C..W..G	K..Y..D	S..2..B
2)	F..R..R	O..U..P	T..U..K	D..X..H	L..Z..E	T..3..C
3)	G..S..S	P..V..Q	U..V..L	E..Y..J	M..1..F	U..A..D
4)	H..T..T	Q..W..R	V..W..M	F..Z..K	N..2..G	V..B..E
5)	J..U..U	R..X..S	W..X..N	G..1..L	O..3..H	W..C..F
6)	K..V..V	S..Y..T	X..Y..O	H..2..M	P..A..J	X..D..G
7)	L..W..W	T..Z..U	A..Z..P	J..3..N	Q..B..K	A..E..H
8)	M..X..X	U..1..V	B..1..Q	K..A..O	R..C..L	B..F..J
9)	N..Y..Y	V..2..W	C..2..R	L..B..P	S..D..M	C..G..K
10)	O..Z..Z	W..3..X	D..3..S	M..C..Q	T..E..N	D..H..L
11)	P..1..1	X..A..Y	E..A..T	N..D..R	U..F..O	E..J..M
12)	Q..2..2	A..B..Z	F..B..U	O..E..S	V..G..P	F..K..N
13)	R..3..3	B..C..1	G..C..V	P..F..T	W..H..Q	G..L..O
14)	S..A..4	C..D..2	H..D..W	Q..G..U	X..J..R	H..M..P
15)	T..B..5	D..E..3	J..E..X	R..H..V	A..K..S	J..N..Q
16)	U..C..6	E..F..4	K..F..Y	S..J..W	B..L..T	K..O..R
17)	V..D..7	F..G..5	L..G..Z	T..K..X	C..M..U	L..P..S
18)	W..E..8	G..H..6	M..H..1	U..L..Y	D..N..V	M..Q..T
19)	X..F..A	H..J..7	N..J..2	V..M..Z	E..O..W	N..R..U
20)	A..G..B	J..K..8	O..K..3	W..N..1	F..P..X	O..S..V
21)	B..H..C	K..L..A	P..L..4	X..O..2	G..Q..Y	P..T..W
22)	C..J..D	L..M..B	Q..M..5	A..P..3	H..R..Z	Q..U..X
23)	D..K..E	M..N..C	R..N..6	B..Q..4	J..S..1	R..V..Y
24)	E..L..F	N..O..D	S..O..7	C..R..5	K..T..2	S..W..Z
25)	F..M..G	O..P..E	T..P..8	D..S..6	L..U..3	T..X..1
26)	G..N..H	P..Q..F	U..Q..A	E..T..7	M..V..4	U..Y..2
27)	H..O..J	Q..R..G	V..R..B	F..U..8	N..W..5	V..Z..3
28)	J..P..K	R..S..H	W..S..C	G..V..A	O..X..6	W..1..4
29)	K..Q..L		X..T..D	H..W..B	P..Y..7	X..2..5
30)	L..R..M		A..U..E	J..X..C	Q..Z..8	A..3..6
31)	M..S..N		B..V..F		R..1..A	

	....JULY.... P--E--I	...AUGUST... P--E--I	.SEPTEMBER. P--E--I	..OCTOBER... P--E--I	.NOVEMBER.. P--E--I	.DECEMBER.. P--E--I
1)	B..A..7	K..D..5	S..G..3	B..J..Z	K..M..X	R..O..U
2)	C..B..8	L..E..6	T..H..4	C..K..1	L..N..Y	S..P..V
3)	D..C..A	M..F..7	U..J..5	D..L..2	M..O..Z	T..Q..W
4)	E..D..B	N..G..8	V..K..6	E..M..3	N..P..1	U..R..X
5)	F..E..C	O..H..A	W..L..7	F..N..4	O..Q..2	V..S..Y
6)	G..F..D	P..J..B	X..M..8	G..O..5	P..R..3	W..T..Z
7)	H..G..E	Q..K..C	A..N..A	H..P..6	Q..S..4	X..U..1
8)	J..H..F	R..L..D	B..O..B	J..Q..7	R..T..5	A..V..2
9)	K..J..G	S..M..E	C..P..C	K..R..8	S..U..6	B..W..3
10)	L..K..H	T..N..F	D..Q..D	L..S..A	T..V..7	C..X..4
11)	M..L..J	U..O..G	E..R..E	M..T..B	U..W..8	D..Y..5
12)	N..M..K	V..P..H	F..S..F	N..U..C	V..X..A	E..Z..6
13)	O..N..L	W..Q..J	G..T..G	O..V..D	W..Y..B	F..1..7
14)	P..O..M	X..R..K	H..U..H	P..W..E	X..Z..C	G..2..8
15)	Q..P..N	A..S..L	J..V..J	Q..X..F	A..1..D	H..3..A
16)	R..Q..O	B..T..M	K..W..K	R..Y..G	B..2..E	J..A..B
17)	S..R..P	C..U..N	L..X..L	S..Z..H	C..3..F	K..B..C
18)	T..S..Q	D..V..O	M..Y..M	T..1..J	D..A..G	L..C..D
19)	U..T..R	E..W..P	N..Z..N	U..2..K	E..B..H	M..D..E
20)	V..U..S	F..X..Q	O..1..O	V..3..L	F..C..J	N..E..F
21)	W..V..T	G..Y..R	P..2..P	W..A..M	G..D..K	O..F..G
22)	X..W..U	H..Z..S	Q..3..Q	X..B..N	H..E..L	P..G..H
23)	A..X..V	J..1..T	R..A..R	A..C..O	J..F..M	Q..H..J
24)	B..Y..W	K..2..U	S..B..S	B..D..P	K..G..N	R..J..K
25)	C..Z..X	L..3..V	T..C..T	C..E..Q	L..H..O	S..K..L
26)	D..1..Y	M..A..W	U..D..U	D..F..R	M..J..P	T..L..M
27)	E..2..Z	N..B..X	V..E..V	E..G..S	N..K..Q	U..M..N
28)	F..3..1	O..C..Y	W..F..W	F..H..T	O..L..R	V..N..O
29)	G..A..2	P..D..Z	X..G..X	G..J..U	P..M..S	W..O..P
30)	H..B..3	Q..E..1	A..H..Y	H..K..V	Q..N..T	X..P..Q
31)	J..C..4	R..F..2		J..L..W		A..Q..R

CODES: P-PHYSICAL BIORHYTHM CURVE,E-EMOTIONAL BIORHYTHM CURVE,I-INTELLECTUAL BIORHYTHM CURVE

	...JANUARY..	..FEBRUARY..	...MARCH...	...APRIL...	....MAY....	...JUNE....
	P--E--I	P--E--I	P--E--I	P--E--I	P--E--I	P--E--I
1)	B..R..S	K..U..Q	P..U..L	X..X..J	G..Z..F	P..3..D
2)	C..S..T	L..V..R	Q..V..M	A..Y..K	H..1..G	Q..A..E
3)	D..T..U	M..W..S	R..W..N	B..Z..L	J..2..H	R..B..F
4)	E..U..V	N..X..T	S..X..O	C..1..M	K..3..J	S..C..G
5)	F..V..W	O..Y..U	T..Y..P	D..2..N	L..A..K	T..D..H
6)	G..W..X	P..Z..V	U..Z..Q	E..3..O	M..B..L	U..E..J
7)	H..X..Y	Q..1..W	V..1..R	F..A..P	N..C..M	V..F..K
8)	J..Y..Z	R..2..X	W..2..S	G..B..Q	O..D..N	W..G..L
9)	K..Z..1	S..3..Y	X..3..T	H..C..R	P..E..O	X..H..M
10)	L..1..2	T..A..Z	A..A..U	J..D..S	Q..F..P	A..J..N
11)	M..2..3	U..B..1	B..B..V	K..E..T	R..G..Q	B..K..O
12)	N..3..4	V..C..2	C..C..W	L..F..U	S..H..R	C..L..P
13)	O..A..5	W..D..3	D..D..X	M..G..V	T..J..S	D..M..Q
14)	P..B..6	X..E..4	E..E..Y	N..H..W	U..K..T	E..N..R
15)	Q..C..7	A..F..5	F..F..Z	O..J..X	V..L..U	F..O..S
16)	R..D..8	B..G..6	G..G..1	P..K..Y	W..M..V	G..P..T
17)	S..E..A	C..H..7	H..H..2	Q..L..Z	X..N..W	H..Q..U
18)	T..F..B	D..J..8	J..J..3	R..M..1	A..O..X	J..R..V
19)	U..G..C	E..K..A	K..K..4	S..N..2	B..P..Y	K..S..W
20)	V..H..D	F..L..B	L..L..5	T..O..3	C..Q..Z	L..T..X
21)	W..J..E	G..M..C	M..M..6	U..P..4	D..R..1	M..U..Y
22)	X..K..F	H..N..D	N..N..7	V..Q..5	E..S..2	N..V..Z
23)	A..L..G	J..O..E	O..O..8	W..R..6	F..T..3	O..W..1
24)	B..M..H	K..P..F	P..P..A	X..S..7	G..U..4	P..X..2
25)	C..N..J	L..Q..G	Q..Q..B	A..T..8	H..V..5	Q..Y..3
26)	D..O..K	M..R..H	R..R..C	B..U..A	J..W..6	R..Z..4
27)	E..P..L	N..S..J	S..S..D	C..V..B	K..X..7	S..1..5
28)	F..Q..M	O..T..K	T..T..E	D..W..C	L..Y..8	T..2..6
29)	G..R..N		U..U..F	E..X..D	M..Z..A	U..3..7
30)	H..S..O		V..V..G	F..Y..E	N..1..B	V..A..8
31)	J..T..P		W..W..H		O..2..C	

	....JULY....	...AUGUST...	..SEPTEMBER.	..OCTOBER...	..NOVEMBER..	..DECEMBER..
	P--E--I	P--E--I	P--E--I	P--E--I	P--E--I	P--E--I
1)	W..B..A	G..E..7	P..H..5	W..K..2	G..N..Z	O..P..W
2)	X..C..B	H..F..8	Q..J..6	X..L..3	H..O..1	P..Q..X
3)	A..D..C	J..G..A	R..K..7	A..M..4	J..P..2	Q..R..Y
4)	B..E..D	K..H..B	S..L..8	B..N..5	K..Q..3	R..S..Z
5)	C..F..E	L..J..C	T..M..A	C..O..6	L..R..4	S..T..1
6)	D..G..F	M..K..D	U..N..B	D..P..7	M..S..5	T..U..2
7)	E..H..G	N..L..E	V..O..C	E..Q..8	N..T..6	U..V..3
8)	F..J..H	O..M..F	W..P..D	F..R..A	O..U..7	V..W..4
9)	G..K..J	P..N..G	X..Q..E	G..S..B	P..V..8	W..X..5
10)	H..L..K	Q..O..H	A..R..F	H..T..C	Q..W..A	X..Y..6
11)	J..M..L	R..P..J	B..S..G	J..U..D	R..X..B	A..Z..7
12)	K..N..M	S..Q..K	C..T..H	K..V..E	S..Y..C	B..1..8
13)	L..O..N	T..R..L	D..U..J	L..W..F	T..Z..D	C..2..A
14)	M..P..O	U..S..M	E..V..K	M..X..G	U..1..E	D..3..B
15)	N..Q..P	V..T..N	F..W..L	N..Y..H	V..2..F	E..A..C
16)	O..R..Q	W..U..O	G..X..M	O..Z..J	W..3..G	F..B..D
17)	P..S..R	X..V..P	H..Y..N	P..1..K	X..A..H	G..C..E
18)	Q..T..S	A..W..Q	J..Z..O	Q..2..L	A..B..J	H..D..F
19)	R..U..T	B..X..R	K..1..P	R..3..M	B..C..K	J..E..G
20)	S..V..U	C..Y..S	L..2..Q	S..A..N	C..D..L	K..F..H
21)	T..W..V	D..Z..T	M..3..R	T..B..O	D..E..M	L..G..J
22)	U..X..W	E..1..U	N..A..S	U..C..P	E..F..N	M..H..K
23)	V..Y..X	F..2..V	O..B..T	V..D..Q	F..G..O	N..J..L
24)	W..Z..Y	G..3..W	P..C..U	W..E..R	G..H..P	O..K..M
25)	X..1..Z	H..A..X	Q..D..V	X..F..S	H..J..Q	P..L..N
26)	A..2..1	J..B..Y	R..E..W	A..G..T	J..K..R	Q..M..O
27)	B..3..2	K..C..Z	S..F..X	B..H..U	K..L..S	R..N..P
28)	C..A..3	L..D..1	T..G..Y	C..J..V	L..M..T	S..O..Q
29)	D..B..4	M..E..2	U..H..Z	D..K..W	M..N..U	T..P..R
30)	E..C..5	N..F..3	V..J..1	E..L..X	N..O..V	U..Q..S
31)	F..D..6	O..G..4		F..M..Y		V..R..T

CODES: P-PHYSICAL BIORHYTHM CURVE,E-EMOTIONAL BIORHYTHM CURVE,I-INTELLECTUAL BIORHYTHM CURVE

...JANUARY..

```
     P--E--I
 1)  W..S..U
 2)  X..T..V
 3)  A..U..W
 4)  B..V..X
 5)  C..W..Y
 6)  D..X..Z
 7)  E..Y..1
 8)  F..Z..2
 9)  G..1..3
10)  H..2..4
11)  J..3..5
12)  K..A..6
13)  L..B..7
14)  M..C..8
15)  N..D..A
16)  O..E..B
17)  P..F..C
18)  Q..G..D
19)  R..H..E
20)  S..J..F
21)  T..K..G
22)  U..L..H
23)  V..M..J
24)  W..N..K
25)  X..O..L
26)  A..P..M
27)  B..Q..N
28)  C..R..O
29)  D..S..P
30)  E..T..Q
31)  F..U..R
```

..FEBRUARY..

```
     P--E--I
 1)  G..V..S
 2)  H..W..T
 3)  J..X..U
 4)  K..Y..V
 5)  L..Z..W
 6)  M..1..X
 7)  N..2..Y
 8)  O..3..Z
 9)  P..A..1
10)  Q..B..2
11)  R..C..3
12)  S..D..4
13)  T..E..5
14)  U..F..6
15)  V..G..7
16)  W..H..8
17)  X..J..A
18)  A..K..B
19)  B..L..C
20)  C..M..D
21)  D..N..E
22)  E..O..F
23)  F..P..G
24)  G..Q..H
25)  H..R..J
26)  J..S..K
27)  K..T..L
28)  L..U..M
```

...MARCH...

```
     P--E--I
 1)  M..V..N
 2)  N..W..O
 3)  O..X..P
 4)  P..Y..Q
 5)  Q..Z..R
 6)  R..1..S
 7)  S..2..T
 8)  T..3..U
 9)  U..A..V
10)  V..B..W
11)  W..C..X
12)  X..D..Y
13)  A..E..Z
14)  B..F..1
15)  C..G..2
16)  D..H..3
17)  E..J..4
18)  F..K..5
19)  G..L..6
20)  H..M..7
21)  J..N..8
22)  K..O..A
23)  L..P..B
24)  M..Q..C
25)  N..R..D
26)  O..S..E
27)  P..T..F
28)  Q..U..G
29)  R..V..H
30)  S..W..J
31)  T..X..K
```

...APRIL...

```
     P--E--I
 1)  U..Y..L
 2)  V..Z..M
 3)  W..1..N
 4)  X..2..O
 5)  A..3..P
 6)  B..A..Q
 7)  C..B..R
 8)  D..C..S
 9)  E..D..T
10)  F..E..U
11)  G..F..V
12)  H..G..W
13)  J..H..X
14)  K..J..Y
15)  L..K..Z
16)  M..L..1
17)  N..M..2
18)  O..N..3
19)  P..O..4
20)  Q..P..5
21)  R..Q..6
22)  S..R..7
23)  T..S..8
24)  U..T..A
25)  V..U..B
26)  W..V..C
27)  X..W..D
28)  A..X..E
29)  B..Y..F
30)  C..Z..G
```

....MAY....

```
     P--E--I
 1)  D..1..H
 2)  E..2..J
 3)  F..3..K
 4)  G..A..L
 5)  H..B..M
 6)  J..C..N
 7)  K..D..O
 8)  L..E..P
 9)  M..F..Q
10)  N..G..R
11)  O..H..S
12)  P..J..T
13)  Q..K..U
14)  R..L..V
15)  S..M..W
16)  T..N..X
17)  U..O..Y
18)  V..P..Z
19)  W..Q..1
20)  X..R..2
21)  A..S..3
22)  B..T..4
23)  C..U..5
24)  D..V..6
25)  E..W..7
26)  F..X..8
27)  G..Y..A
28)  H..Z..B
29)  J..1..C
30)  K..2..D
31)  L..3..E
```

...JUNE....

```
     P--E--I
 1)  M..A..F
 2)  N..B..G
 3)  O..C..H
 4)  P..D..J
 5)  Q..E..K
 6)  R..F..L
 7)  S..G..M
 8)  T..H..N
 9)  U..J..O
10)  V..K..P
11)  W..L..Q
12)  X..M..R
13)  A..N..S
14)  B..O..T
15)  C..P..U
16)  D..Q..V
17)  E..R..W
18)  F..S..X
19)  G..T..Y
20)  H..U..Z
21)  J..V..1
22)  K..W..2
23)  L..X..3
24)  M..Y..4
25)  N..Z..5
26)  O..1..6
27)  P..2..7
28)  Q..3..8
29)  R..A..A
30)  S..B..B
```

....JULY....

```
     P--E--I
 1)  T..C..C
 2)  U..D..D
 3)  V..E..E
 4)  W..F..F
 5)  X..G..G
 6)  A..H..H
 7)  B..J..J
 8)  C..K..K
 9)  D..L..L
10)  E..M..M
11)  F..N..N
12)  G..O..O
13)  H..P..P
14)  J..Q..Q
15)  K..R..R
16)  L..S..S
17)  M..T..T
18)  N..U..U
19)  O..V..V
20)  P..W..W
21)  Q..X..X
22)  R..Y..Y
23)  S..Z..Z
24)  T..1..1
25)  U..2..2
26)  V..3..3
27)  W..A..4
28)  X..B..5
29)  A..C..6
30)  B..D..7
31)  C..E..8
```

...AUGUST...

```
     P--E--I
 1)  D..F..A
 2)  E..G..B
 3)  F..H..C
 4)  G..J..D
 5)  H..K..E
 6)  J..L..F
 7)  K..M..G
 8)  L..N..H
 9)  M..O..J
10)  N..P..K
11)  O..Q..L
12)  P..R..M
13)  Q..S..N
14)  R..T..O
15)  S..U..P
16)  T..V..Q
17)  U..W..R
18)  V..X..S
19)  W..Y..T
20)  X..Z..U
21)  A..1..V
22)  B..2..W
23)  C..3..X
24)  D..A..Y
25)  E..B..Z
26)  F..C..1
27)  G..D..2
28)  H..E..3
29)  J..F..4
30)  K..G..5
31)  L..H..6
```

..SEPTEMBER.

```
     P--E--I
 1)  M..J..7
 2)  N..K..8
 3)  O..L..A
 4)  P..M..B
 5)  Q..N..C
 6)  R..O..D
 7)  S..P..E
 8)  T..Q..F
 9)  U..R..G
10)  V..S..H
11)  W..T..J
12)  X..U..K
13)  A..V..L
14)  B..W..M
15)  C..X..N
16)  D..Y..O
17)  E..Z..P
18)  F..1..Q
19)  G..2..R
20)  H..3..S
21)  J..A..T
22)  K..B..U
23)  L..C..V
24)  M..D..W
25)  N..E..X
26)  O..F..Y
27)  P..G..Z
28)  Q..H..1
29)  R..J..2
30)  S..K..3
```

..OCTOBER...

```
     P--E--I
 1)  T..L..4
 2)  U..M..5
 3)  V..N..6
 4)  W..O..7
 5)  X..P..8
 6)  A..Q..A
 7)  B..R..B
 8)  C..S..C
 9)  D..T..D
10)  E..U..E
11)  F..V..F
12)  G..W..G
13)  H..X..H
14)  J..Y..J
15)  K..Z..K
16)  L..1..L
17)  M..2..M
18)  N..3..N
19)  O..A..O
20)  P..B..P
21)  Q..C..Q
22)  R..D..R
23)  S..E..S
24)  T..F..T
25)  U..G..U
26)  V..H..V
27)  W..J..W
28)  X..K..X
29)  A..L..Y
30)  B..M..Z
31)  C..N..1
```

..NOVEMBER..

```
     P--E--I
 1)  D..O..2
 2)  E..P..3
 3)  F..Q..4
 4)  G..R..5
 5)  H..S..6
 6)  J..T..7
 7)  K..U..8
 8)  L..V..A
 9)  M..W..B
10)  N..X..C
11)  O..Y..D
12)  P..Z..E
13)  Q..1..F
14)  R..2..G
15)  S..3..H
16)  T..A..J
17)  U..B..K
18)  V..C..L
19)  W..D..M
20)  X..E..N
21)  A..F..O
22)  B..G..P
23)  C..H..Q
24)  D..J..R
25)  E..K..S
26)  F..L..T
27)  G..M..U
28)  H..N..V
29)  J..O..W
30)  K..P..X
```

..DECEMBER..

```
     P--E--I
 1)  L..Q..Y
 2)  M..R..Z
 3)  N..S..1
 4)  O..T..2
 5)  P..U..3
 6)  Q..V..4
 7)  R..W..5
 8)  S..X..6
 9)  T..Y..7
10)  U..Z..8
11)  V..1..A
12)  W..2..B
13)  X..3..C
14)  A..A..D
15)  B..B..E
16)  C..C..F
17)  D..D..G
18)  E..E..H
19)  F..F..J
20)  G..G..K
21)  H..H..L
22)  J..J..M
23)  K..K..N
24)  L..L..O
25)  M..M..P
26)  N..N..Q
27)  O..O..R
28)  P..P..S
29)  Q..Q..T
30)  R..R..U
31)  S..S..V
```

CODES: P-PHYSICAL BIORHYTHM CURVE, E-EMOTIONAL BIORHYTHM CURVE, I-INTELLECTUAL BIORHYTHM CURVE

	...JANUARY..		..FEBRUARY..		...MARCH...		...APRIL...		....MAY....		...JUNE....
	P--E--I		P--E--I		P--E--I		P--E--I		P--E--I		P--E--I
1)	T..T..W	1)	D..W..U	1)	K..X..Q	1)	S..1..O	1)	B..3..L	1)	K..C..J
2)	U..U..X	2)	E..X..V	2)	L..Y..R	2)	T..2..P	2)	C..A..M	2)	L..D..K
3)	V..V..Y	3)	F..Y..W	3)	M..Z..S	3)	U..3..Q	3)	D..B..N	3)	M..E..L
4)	W..W..Z	4)	G..Z..X	4)	N..1..T	4)	V..A..R	4)	E..C..O	4)	N..F..M
5)	X..X..1	5)	H..1..Y	5)	O..2..U	5)	W..B..S	5)	F..D..P	5)	O..G..N
6)	A..Y..2	6)	J..2..Z	6)	P..3..V	6)	X..C..T	6)	G..E..Q	6)	P..H..O
7)	B..Z..3	7)	K..3..1	7)	Q..A..W	7)	A..D..U	7)	H..F..R	7)	Q..J..P
8)	C..1..4	8)	L..A..2	8)	R..B..X	8)	B..E..V	8)	J..G..S	8)	R..K..Q
9)	D..2..5	9)	M..B..3	9)	S..C..Y	9)	C..F..W	9)	K..H..T	9)	S..L..R
10)	E..3..6	10)	N..C..4	10)	T..D..Z	10)	D..G..X	10)	L..J..U	10)	T..M..S
11)	F..A..7	11)	O..D..5	11)	U..E..1	11)	E..H..Y	11)	M..K..V	11)	U..N..T
12)	G..B..8	12)	P..E..6	12)	V..F..2	12)	F..J..Z	12)	N..L..W	12)	V..O..U
13)	H..C..A	13)	Q..F..7	13)	W..G..3	13)	G..K..1	13)	O..M..X	13)	W..P..V
14)	J..D..B	14)	R..G..8	14)	X..H..4	14)	H..L..2	14)	P..N..Y	14)	X..Q..W
15)	K..E..C	15)	S..H..A	15)	A..J..5	15)	J..M..3	15)	Q..O..Z	15)	A..R..X
16)	L..F..D	16)	T..J..B	16)	B..K..6	16)	K..N..4	16)	R..P..1	16)	B..S..Y
17)	M..G..E	17)	U..K..C	17)	C..L..7	17)	L..O..5	17)	S..Q..2	17)	C..T..Z
18)	N..H..F	18)	V..L..D	18)	D..M..8	18)	M..P..6	18)	T..R..3	18)	D..U..1
19)	O..J..G	19)	W..M..E	19)	E..N..A	19)	N..Q..7	19)	U..S..4	19)	E..V..2
20)	P..K..H	20)	X..N..F	20)	F..O..B	20)	O..R..8	20)	V..T..5	20)	F..W..3
21)	Q..L..J	21)	A..O..G	21)	G..P..C	21)	P..S..A	21)	W..U..6	21)	G..X..4
22)	R..M..K	22)	B..P..H	22)	H..Q..D	22)	Q..T..B	22)	X..V..7	22)	H..Y..5
23)	S..N..L	23)	C..Q..J	23)	J..R..E	23)	R..U..C	23)	A..W..8	23)	J..Z..6
24)	T..O..M	24)	D..R..K	24)	K..S..F	24)	S..V..D	24)	B..X..A	24)	K..1..7
25)	U..P..N	25)	E..S..L	25)	L..T..G	25)	T..W..E	25)	C..Y..B	25)	L..2..8
26)	V..Q..O	26)	F..T..M	26)	M..U..H	26)	U..X..F	26)	D..Z..C	26)	M..3..A
27)	W..R..P	27)	G..U..N	27)	N..V..J	27)	V..Y..G	27)	E..1..D	27)	N..A..B
28)	X..S..Q	28)	H..V..O	28)	O..W..K	28)	W..Z..H	28)	F..2..E	28)	O..B..C
29)	A..T..R	29)	J..W..P	29)	P..X..L	29)	X..1..J	29)	G..3..F	29)	P..C..D
30)	B..U..S			30)	Q..Y..M	30)	A..2..K	30)	H..A..G	30)	Q..D..E
31)	C..V..T			31)	R..Z..N			31)	J..B..H		

	....JULY....		...AUGUST...		.SEPTEMBER.		..OCTOBER...		..NOVEMBER..		..DECEMBER..
	P--E--I		P--E--I		P--E--I		P--E--I		P--E--I		P--E--I
1)	R..E..F	1)	B..H..D	1)	K..L..B	1)	R..N..7	1)	B..Q..5	1)	J..S..2
2)	S..F..G	2)	C..J..E	2)	L..M..C	2)	S..O..8	2)	C..R..6	2)	K..T..3
3)	T..G..H	3)	D..K..F	3)	M..N..D	3)	T..P..A	3)	D..S..7	3)	L..U..4
4)	U..H..J	4)	E..L..G	4)	N..O..E	4)	U..Q..B	4)	E..T..8	4)	M..V..5
5)	V..J..K	5)	F..M..H	5)	O..P..F	5)	V..R..C	5)	F..U..A	5)	N..W..6
6)	W..K..L	6)	G..N..J	6)	P..Q..G	6)	W..S..D	6)	G..V..B	6)	O..X..7
7)	X..L..M	7)	H..O..K	7)	Q..R..H	7)	X..T..E	7)	H..W..C	7)	P..Y..8
8)	A..M..N	8)	J..P..L	8)	R..S..J	8)	A..U..F	8)	J..X..D	8)	Q..Z..A
9)	B..N..O	9)	K..Q..M	9)	S..T..K	9)	B..V..G	9)	K..Y..E	9)	R..1..B
10)	C..O..P	10)	L..R..N	10)	T..U..L	10)	C..W..H	10)	L..Z..F	10)	S..2..C
11)	D..P..Q	11)	M..S..O	11)	U..V..M	11)	D..X..J	11)	M..1..G	11)	T..3..D
12)	E..Q..R	12)	N..T..P	12)	V..W..N	12)	E..Y..K	12)	N..2..H	12)	U..A..E
13)	F..R..S	13)	O..U..Q	13)	W..X..O	13)	F..Z..L	13)	O..3..J	13)	V..B..F
14)	G..S..T	14)	P..V..R	14)	X..Y..P	14)	G..1..M	14)	P..A..K	14)	W..C..G
15)	H..T..U	15)	Q..W..S	15)	A..Z..Q	15)	H..2..N	15)	Q..B..L	15)	X..D..H
16)	J..U..V	16)	R..X..T	16)	B..1..R	16)	J..3..O	16)	R..C..M	16)	A..E..J
17)	K..V..W	17)	S..Y..U	17)	C..2..S	17)	K..A..P	17)	S..D..N	17)	B..F..K
18)	L..W..X	18)	T..Z..V	18)	D..3..T	18)	L..B..Q	18)	T..E..O	18)	C..G..L
19)	M..X..Y	19)	U..1..W	19)	E..A..U	19)	M..C..R	19)	U..F..P	19)	D..H..M
20)	N..Y..Z	20)	V..2..X	20)	F..B..V	20)	N..D..S	20)	V..G..Q	20)	E..J..N
21)	O..Z..1	21)	W..3..Y	21)	G..C..W	21)	O..E..T	21)	W..H..R	21)	F..K..O
22)	P..1..2	22)	X..A..Z	22)	H..D..X	22)	P..F..U	22)	X..J..S	22)	G..L..P
23)	Q..2..3	23)	A..B..1	23)	J..E..Y	23)	Q..G..V	23)	A..K..T	23)	H..M..Q
24)	R..3..4	24)	B..C..2	24)	K..F..Z	24)	R..H..W	24)	B..L..U	24)	J..N..R
25)	S..A..5	25)	C..D..3	25)	L..G..1	25)	S..J..X	25)	C..M..V	25)	K..O..S
26)	T..B..6	26)	D..E..4	26)	M..H..2	26)	T..K..Y	26)	D..N..W	26)	L..P..T
27)	U..C..7	27)	E..F..5	27)	N..J..3	27)	U..L..Z	27)	E..O..X	27)	M..Q..U
28)	V..D..8	28)	F..G..6	28)	O..K..4	28)	V..M..1	28)	F..P..Y	28)	N..R..V
29)	W..E..A	29)	G..H..7	29)	P..L..5	29)	W..N..2	29)	G..Q..Z	29)	O..S..W
30)	X..F..B	30)	H..J..8	30)	Q..M..6	30)	X..O..3	30)	H..R..1	30)	P..T..X
31)	A..G..C	31)	J..K..A			31)	A..P..4			31)	Q..U..Y

CODES: P-PHYSICAL BIORHYTHM CURVE,E-EMOTIONAL BIORHYTHM CURVE,I-INTELLECTUAL BIORHYTHM CURVE

	...JANUARY..		..FEBRUARY..		....MARCH...		....APRIL...		....MAY....		....JUNE....
	P--E--I		P--E--I		P--E--I		P--E--I		P--E--I		P--E--I
1)	R..V..Z	1)	B..Y..X	1)	G..Y..S	1)	P..2..Q	1)	W..A..N	1)	G..D..L
2)	S..W..1	2)	C..Z..Y	2)	H..Z..T	2)	Q..3..R	2)	X..B..O	2)	H..E..M
3)	T..X..2	3)	D..1..Z	3)	J..1..U	3)	R..A..S	3)	A..C..P	3)	J..F..N
4)	U..Y..3	4)	E..2..1	4)	K..2..V	4)	S..B..T	4)	B..D..Q	4)	K..G..O
5)	V..Z..4	5)	F..3..2	5)	L..3..W	5)	T..C..U	5)	C..E..R	5)	L..H..P
6)	W..1..5	6)	G..A..3	6)	M..A..X	6)	U..D..V	6)	D..F..S	6)	M..J..Q
7)	X..2..6	7)	H..B..4	7)	N..B..Y	7)	V..E..W	7)	E..G..T	7)	N..K..R
8)	A..3..7	8)	J..C..5	8)	O..C..Z	8)	W..F..X	8)	F..H..U	8)	O..L..S
9)	B..A..8	9)	K..D..6	9)	P..D..1	9)	X..G..Y	9)	G..J..V	9)	P..M..T
10)	C..B..A	10)	L..E..7	10)	Q..E..2	10)	A..H..Z	10)	H..K..W	10)	Q..N..U
11)	D..C..B	11)	M..F..8	11)	R..F..3	11)	B..J..1	11)	J..L..X	11)	R..O..V
12)	E..D..C	12)	N..G..A	12)	S..G..4	12)	C..K..2	12)	K..M..Y	12)	S..P..W
13)	F..E..D	13)	O..H..B	13)	T..H..5	13)	D..L..3	13)	L..N..Z	13)	T..Q..X
14)	G..F..E	14)	P..J..C	14)	U..J..6	14)	E..M..4	14)	M..O..1	14)	U..R..Y
15)	H..G..F	15)	Q..K..D	15)	V..K..7	15)	F..N..5	15)	N..P..2	15)	V..S..Z
16)	J..H..G	16)	R..L..E	16)	W..L..8	16)	G..O..6	16)	O..Q..3	16)	W..T..1
17)	K..J..H	17)	S..M..F	17)	X..M..A	17)	H..P..7	17)	P..R..4	17)	X..U..2
18)	L..K..J	18)	T..N..G	18)	A..N..B	18)	J..Q..8	18)	Q..S..5	18)	A..V..3
19)	M..L..K	19)	U..O..H	19)	B..O..C	19)	K..R..A	19)	R..T..6	19)	B..W..4
20)	N..M..L	20)	V..P..J	20)	C..P..D	20)	L..S..B	20)	S..U..7	20)	C..X..5
21)	O..N..M	21)	W..Q..K	21)	D..Q..E	21)	M..T..C	21)	T..V..8	21)	D..Y..6
22)	P..O..N	22)	X..R..L	22)	E..R..F	22)	N..U..D	22)	U..W..A	22)	E..Z..7
23)	Q..P..O	23)	A..S..M	23)	F..S..G	23)	O..V..E	23)	V..X..B	23)	F..1..8
24)	R..Q..P	24)	B..T..N	24)	G..T..H	24)	P..W..F	24)	W..Y..C	24)	G..2..A
25)	S..R..Q	25)	C..U..O	25)	H..U..J	25)	Q..X..G	25)	X..Z..D	25)	H..3..B
26)	T..S..R	26)	D..V..P	26)	J..V..K	26)	R..Y..H	26)	A..1..E	26)	J..A..C
27)	U..T..S	27)	E..W..Q	27)	K..W..L	27)	S..Z..J	27)	B..2..F	27)	K..B..D
28)	V..U..T	28)	F..X..R	28)	L..X..M	28)	T..1..K	28)	C..3..G	28)	L..C..E
29)	W..V..U			29)	M..Y..N	29)	U..2..L	29)	D..A..H	29)	M..D..F
30)	X..W..V			30)	N..Z..O	30)	V..3..M	30)	E..B..J	30)	N..E..G
31)	A..X..W			31)	O..1..P			31)	F..C..K		

	....JULY....		...AUGUST...		.SEPTEMBER.		..OCTOBER...		..NOVEMBER..		..DECEMBER..
	P--E--I		P--E--I		P--E--I		P--E--I		P--E--I		P--E--I
1)	O..F..H	1)	W..J..F	1)	G..M..D	1)	O..O..A	1)	W..R..7	1)	F..T..4
2)	P..G..J	2)	X..K..G	2)	H..N..E	2)	P..P..B	2)	X..S..8	2)	G..U..5
3)	Q..H..K	3)	A..L..H	3)	J..O..F	3)	Q..Q..C	3)	A..T..A	3)	H..V..6
4)	R..J..L	4)	B..M..J	4)	K..P..G	4)	R..R..D	4)	B..U..B	4)	J..W..7
5)	S..K..M	5)	C..N..K	5)	L..Q..H	5)	S..S..E	5)	C..V..C	5)	K..X..8
6)	T..L..N	6)	D..O..L	6)	M..R..J	6)	T..T..F	6)	D..W..D	6)	L..Y..A
7)	U..M..O	7)	E..P..M	7)	N..S..K	7)	U..U..G	7)	E..X..E	7)	M..Z..B
8)	V..N..P	8)	F..Q..N	8)	O..T..L	8)	V..V..H	8)	F..Y..F	8)	N..1..C
9)	W..O..Q	9)	G..R..O	9)	P..U..M	9)	W..W..J	9)	G..Z..G	9)	O..2..D
10)	X..P..R	10)	H..S..P	10)	Q..V..N	10)	X..X..K	10)	H..1..H	10)	P..3..E
11)	A..Q..S	11)	J..T..Q	11)	R..W..O	11)	A..Y..L	11)	J..2..J	11)	Q..A..F
12)	B..R..T	12)	K..U..R	12)	S..X..P	12)	B..Z..M	12)	K..3..K	12)	R..B..G
13)	C..S..U	13)	L..V..S	13)	T..Y..Q	13)	C..1..N	13)	L..A..L	13)	S..C..H
14)	D..T..V	14)	M..W..T	14)	U..Z..R	14)	D..2..O	14)	M..B..M	14)	T..D..J
15)	E..U..W	15)	N..X..U	15)	V..1..S	15)	E..3..P	15)	N..C..N	15)	U..E..K
16)	F..V..X	16)	O..Y..V	16)	W..2..T	16)	F..A..Q	16)	O..D..O	16)	V..F..L
17)	G..W..Y	17)	P..Z..W	17)	X..3..U	17)	G..B..R	17)	P..E..P	17)	W..G..M
18)	H..X..Z	18)	Q..1..X	18)	A..A..V	18)	H..C..S	18)	Q..F..Q	18)	X..H..N
19)	J..Y..1	19)	R..2..Y	19)	B..B..W	19)	J..D..T	19)	R..G..R	19)	A..J..O
20)	K..Z..2	20)	S..3..Z	20)	C..C..X	20)	K..E..U	20)	S..H..S	20)	B..K..P
21)	L..1..3	21)	T..A..1	21)	D..D..Y	21)	L..F..V	21)	T..J..T	21)	C..L..Q
22)	M..2..4	22)	U..B..2	22)	E..E..Z	22)	M..G..W	22)	U..K..U	22)	D..M..R
23)	N..3..5	23)	V..C..3	23)	F..F..1	23)	N..H..X	23)	V..L..V	23)	E..N..S
24)	O..A..6	24)	W..D..4	24)	G..G..2	24)	O..J..Y	24)	W..M..W	24)	F..O..T
25)	P..B..7	25)	X..E..5	25)	H..H..3	25)	P..K..Z	25)	X..N..X	25)	G..P..U
26)	Q..C..8	26)	A..F..6	26)	J..J..4	26)	Q..L..1	26)	A..O..Y	26)	H..Q..V
27)	R..D..A	27)	B..G..7	27)	K..K..5	27)	R..M..2	27)	B..P..Z	27)	J..R..W
28)	S..E..B	28)	C..H..8	28)	L..L..6	28)	S..N..3	28)	C..Q..1	28)	K..S..X
29)	T..F..C	29)	D..J..A	29)	M..M..7	29)	T..O..4	29)	D..R..2	29)	L..T..Y
30)	U..G..D	30)	E..K..B	30)	N..N..8	30)	U..P..5	30)	E..S..3	30)	M..U..Z
31)	V..H..E	31)	F..L..C			31)	V..Q..6			31)	N..V..1

CODES: P-PHYSICAL BIORHYTHM CURVE,E-EMOTIONAL BIORHYTHM CURVE,I-INTELLECTUAL BIORHYTHM CURVE

| ...JANUARY.. | ..FEBRUARY.. | ...MARCH... | ...APRIL... | ....MAY.... | ...JUNE.... |
P--E--I	P--E--I	P--E--I	P--E--I	P--E--I	P--E--I
1) O..W..2	1) W..Z..Z	1) D..Z..U	1) M..3..S	1) T..B..P	1) D..E..N
2) P..X..3	2) X..1..1	2) E..1..V	2) N..A..T	2) U..C..Q	2) E..F..O
3) Q..Y..4	3) A..2..2	3) F..2..W	3) O..B..U	3) V..D..R	3) F..G..P
4) R..Z..5	4) B..3..3	4) G..3..X	4) P..C..V	4) W..E..S	4) G..H..Q
5) S..1..6	5) C..A..4	5) H..A..Y	5) Q..D..W	5) X..F..T	5) H..J..R
6) T..2..7	6) D..B..5	6) J..B..Z	6) R..E..X	6) A..G..U	6) J..K..S
7) U..3..8	7) E..C..6	7) K..C..1	7) S..F..Y	7) B..H..V	7) K..L..T
8) V..A..A	8) F..D..7	8) L..D..2	8) T..G..Z	8) C..J..W	8) L..M..U
9) W..B..B	9) G..E..8	9) M..E..3	9) U..H..1	9) D..K..X	9) M..N..V
10) X..C..C	10) H..F..A	10) N..F..4	10) V..J..2	10) E..L..Y	10) N..O..W
11) A..D..D	11) J..G..B	11) O..G..5	11) W..K..3	11) F..M..Z	11) O..P..X
12) B..E..E	12) K..H..C	12) P..H..6	12) X..L..4	12) G..N..1	12) P..Q..Y
13) C..F..F	13) L..J..D	13) Q..J..7	13) A..M..5	13) H..O..2	13) Q..R..Z
14) D..G..G	14) M..K..E	14) R..K..8	14) B..N..6	14) J..P..3	14) R..S..1
15) E..H..H	15) N..L..F	15) S..L..A	15) C..O..7	15) K..Q..4	15) S..T..2
16) F..J..J	16) O..M..G	16) T..M..B	16) D..P..8	16) L..R..5	16) T..U..3
17) G..K..K	17) P..N..H	17) U..N..C	17) E..Q..A	17) M..S..6	17) U..V..4
18) H..L..L	18) Q..O..J	18) V..O..D	18) F..R..B	18) N..T..7	18) V..W..5
19) J..M..M	19) R..P..K	19) W..P..E	19) G..S..C	19) O..U..8	19) W..X..6
20) K..N..N	20) S..Q..L	20) X..Q..F	20) H..T..D	20) P..V..A	20) X..Y..7
21) L..O..O	21) T..R..M	21) A..R..G	21) J..U..E	21) Q..W..B	21) A..Z..8
22) M..P..P	22) U..S..N	22) B..S..H	22) K..V..F	22) R..X..C	22) B..1..A
23) N..Q..Q	23) V..T..O	23) C..T..J	23) L..W..G	23) S..Y..D	23) C..2..B
24) O..R..R	24) W..U..P	24) D..U..K	24) M..X..H	24) T..Z..E	24) D..3..C
25) P..S..S	25) X..V..Q	25) E..V..L	25) N..Y..J	25) U..1..F	25) E..A..D
26) Q..T..T	26) A..W..R	26) F..W..M	26) O..Z..K	26) V..2..G	26) F..B..E
27) R..U..U	27) B..X..S	27) G..X..N	27) P..1..L	27) W..3..H	27) G..C..F
28) S..V..V	28) C..Y..T	28) H..Y..O	28) Q..2..M	28) X..A..J	28) H..D..G
29) T..W..W		29) J..Z..P	29) R..3..N	29) A..B..K	29) J..E..H
30) U..X..X		30) K..1..Q	30) S..A..O	30) B..C..L	30) K..F..J
31) V..Y..Y		31) L..2..R		31) C..D..M	

| ....JULY.... | ...AUGUST... | .SEPTEMBER. | .OCTOBER... | .NOVEMBER.. | .DECEMBER.. |
P--E--I	P--E--I	P--E--I	P--E--I	P--E--I	P--E--I
1) L..G..K	1) T..K..H	1) D..N..F	1) L..P..C	1) T..S..A	1) C..U..6
2) M..H..L	2) U..L..J	2) E..O..G	2) M..Q..D	2) U..T..B	2) D..V..7
3) N..J..M	3) V..M..K	3) F..P..H	3) N..R..E	3) V..U..C	3) E..W..8
4) O..K..N	4) W..N..L	4) G..Q..J	4) O..S..F	4) W..V..D	4) F..X..A
5) P..L..O	5) X..O..M	5) H..R..K	5) P..T..G	5) X..W..E	5) G..Y..B
6) Q..M..P	6) A..P..N	6) J..S..L	6) Q..U..H	6) A..X..F	6) H..Z..C
7) R..N..Q	7) B..Q..O	7) K..T..M	7) R..V..J	7) B..Y..G	7) J..1..D
8) S..O..R	8) C..R..P	8) L..U..N	8) S..W..K	8) C..Z..H	8) K..2..E
9) T..P..S	9) D..S..Q	9) M..V..O	9) T..X..L	9) D..1..J	9) L..3..F
10) U..Q..T	10) E..T..R	10) N..W..P	10) U..Y..M	10) E..2..K	10) M..A..G
11) V..R..U	11) F..U..S	11) O..X..Q	11) V..Z..N	11) F..3..L	11) N..B..H
12) W..S..V	12) G..V..T	12) P..Y..R	12) W..1..O	12) G..A..M	12) O..C..J
13) X..T..W	13) H..W..U	13) Q..Z..S	13) X..2..P	13) H..B..N	13) P..D..K
14) A..U..X	14) J..X..V	14) R..1..T	14) A..3..Q	14) J..C..O	14) Q..E..L
15) B..V..Y	15) K..Y..W	15) S..2..U	15) B..A..R	15) K..D..P	15) R..F..M
16) C..W..Z	16) L..Z..X	16) T..3..V	16) C..B..S	16) L..E..Q	16) S..G..N
17) D..X..1	17) M..1..Y	17) U..A..W	17) D..C..T	17) M..F..R	17) T..H..O
18) E..Y..2	18) N..2..Z	18) V..B..X	18) E..D..U	18) N..G..S	18) U..J..P
19) F..Z..3	19) O..3..1	19) W..C..Y	19) F..E..V	19) O..H..T	19) V..K..Q
20) G..1..4	20) P..A..2	20) X..D..Z	20) G..F..W	20) P..J..U	20) W..L..R
21) H..2..5	21) Q..B..3	21) A..E..1	21) H..G..X	21) Q..K..V	21) X..M..S
22) J..3..6	22) R..C..4	22) B..F..2	22) J..H..Y	22) R..L..W	22) A..N..T
23) K..A..7	23) S..D..5	23) C..G..3	23) K..J..Z	23) S..M..X	23) B..O..U
24) L..B..8	24) T..E..6	24) D..H..4	24) L..K..1	24) T..N..Y	24) C..P..V
25) M..C..A	25) U..F..7	25) E..J..5	25) M..L..2	25) U..O..Z	25) D..Q..W
26) N..D..B	26) V..G..8	26) F..K..6	26) N..M..3	26) V..P..1	26) E..R..X
27) O..E..C	27) W..H..A	27) G..L..7	27) O..N..4	27) W..Q..2	27) F..S..Y
28) P..F..D	28) X..J..B	28) H..M..8	28) P..O..5	28) X..R..3	28) G..T..Z
29) Q..G..E	29) A..K..C	29) J..N..A	29) Q..P..6	29) A..S..4	29) H..U..1
30) R..H..F	30) B..L..D	30) K..O..B	30) R..Q..7	30) B..T..5	30) J..V..2
31) S..J..G	31) C..M..E		31) S..R..8		31) K..W..3

CODES: P-PHYSICAL BIORHYTHM CURVE,E-EMOTIONAL BIORHYTHM CURVE,I-INTELLECTUAL BIORHYTHM CURVE

	...JANUARY..	..FEBRUARY..	....MARCH...	....APRIL...	.....MAY....	....JUNE....
	P--E--I	P--E--I	P--E--I	P--E--I	P--E--I	P--E--I
1)	L..X..4	T..1..2	A..1..W	J..A..U	Q..C..R	A..F..P
2)	M..Y..5	U..2..3	B..2..X	K..B..V	R..D..S	B..G..Q
3)	N..Z..6	V..3..4	C..3..Y	L..C..W	S..E..T	C..H..R
4)	O..1..7	W..A..5	D..A..Z	M..D..X	T..F..U	D..J..S
5)	P..2..8	X..B..6	E..B..1	N..E..Y	U..G..V	E..K..T
6)	Q..3..A	A..C..7	F..C..2	O..F..Z	V..H..W	F..L..U
7)	R..A..B	B..D..8	G..D..3	P..G..1	W..J..X	G..M..V
8)	S..B..C	C..E..A	H..E..4	Q..H..2	X..K..Y	H..N..W
9)	T..C..D	D..F..B	J..F..5	R..J..3	A..L..Z	J..O..X
10)	U..D..E	E..G..C	K..G..6	S..K..4	B..M..1	K..P..Y
11)	V..E..F	F..H..D	L..H..7	T..L..5	C..N..2	L..Q..Z
12)	W..F..G	G..J..E	M..J..8	U..M..6	D..O..3	M..R..1
13)	X..G..H	H..K..F	N..K..A	V..N..7	E..P..4	N..S..2
14)	A..H..J	J..L..G	O..L..B	W..O..8	F..Q..5	O..T..3
15)	B..J..K	K..M..H	P..M..C	X..P..A	G..R..6	P..U..4
16)	C..K..L	L..N..J	Q..N..D	A..Q..B	H..S..7	Q..V..5
17)	D..L..M	M..O..K	R..O..E	B..R..C	J..T..8	R..W..6
18)	E..M..N	N..P..L	S..P..F	C..S..D	K..U..A	S..X..7
19)	F..N..O	O..Q..M	T..Q..G	D..T..E	L..V..B	T..Y..8
20)	G..O..P	P..R..N	U..R..H	E..U..F	M..W..C	U..Z..A
21)	H..P..Q	Q..S..O	V..S..J	F..V..G	N..X..D	V..1..B
22)	J..Q..R	R..T..P	W..T..K	G..W..H	O..Y..E	W..2..C
23)	K..R..S	S..U..Q	X..U..L	H..X..J	P..Z..F	X..3..D
24)	L..S..T	T..V..R	A..V..M	J..Y..K	Q..1..G	A..A..E
25)	M..T..U	U..W..S	B..W..N	K..Z..L	R..2..H	B..B..F
26)	N..U..V	V..X..T	C..X..O	L..1..M	S..3..J	C..C..G
27)	O..V..W	W..Y..U	D..Y..P	M..2..N	T..A..K	D..D..H
28)	P..W..X	X..Z..V	E..Z..Q	N..3..O	U..B..L	E..E..J
29)	Q..X..Y		F..1..R	O..A..P	V..C..M	F..F..K
30)	R..Y..Z		G..2..S	P..B..Q	W..D..N	G..G..L
31)	S..Z..1		H..3..T		X..E..O	

	....JULY....	..AUGUST...	.SEPTEMBER.	.OCTOBER...	.NOVEMBER..	.DECEMBER..
	P--E--I	P--E--I	P--E--I	P--E--I	P--E--I	P--E--I
1)	H..H..M	Q..L..K	A..O..H	H..Q..E	Q..T..C	X..V..8
2)	J..J..N	R..M..L	B..P..J	J..R..F	R..U..D	A..W..A
3)	K..K..O	S..N..M	C..Q..K	K..S..G	S..V..E	B..X..B
4)	L..L..P	T..O..N	D..R..L	L..T..H	T..W..F	C..Y..C
5)	M..M..Q	U..P..O	E..S..M	M..U..J	U..X..G	D..Z..D
6)	N..N..R	V..Q..P	F..T..N	N..V..K	V..Y..H	E..1..E
7)	O..O..S	W..R..Q	G..U..O	O..W..L	W..Z..J	F..2..F
8)	P..P..T	X..S..R	H..V..P	P..X..M	X..1..K	G..3..G
9)	Q..Q..U	A..T..S	J..W..Q	Q..Y..N	A..2..L	H..A..H
10)	R..R..V	B..U..T	K..X..R	R..Z..O	B..3..M	J..B..J
11)	S..S..W	C..V..U	L..Y..S	S..1..P	C..A..N	K..C..K
12)	T..T..X	D..W..V	M..Z..T	T..2..Q	D..B..O	L..D..L
13)	U..U..Y	E..X..W	N..1..U	U..3..R	E..C..P	M..E..M
14)	V..V..Z	F..Y..X	O..2..V	V..A..S	F..D..Q	N..F..N
15)	W..W..1	G..Z..Y	P..3..W	W..B..T	G..E..R	O..G..O
16)	X..X..2	H..1..Z	Q..A..X	X..C..U	H..F..S	P..H..P
17)	A..Y..3	J..2..1	R..B..Y	A..D..V	J..G..T	Q..J..Q
18)	B..Z..4	K..3..2	S..C..Z	B..E..W	K..H..U	R..K..R
19)	C..1..5	L..A..3	T..D..1	C..F..X	L..J..V	S..L..S
20)	D..2..6	M..B..4	U..E..2	D..G..Y	M..K..W	T..M..T
21)	E..3..7	N..C..5	V..F..3	E..H..Z	N..L..X	U..N..U
22)	F..A..8	O..D..6	W..G..4	F..J..1	O..M..Y	V..O..V
23)	G..B..A	P..E..7	X..H..5	G..K..2	P..N..Z	W..P..W
24)	H..C..B	Q..F..8	A..J..6	H..L..3	Q..O..1	X..Q..X
25)	J..D..C	R..G..A	B..K..7	J..M..4	R..P..2	A..R..Y
26)	K..E..D	S..H..B	C..L..8	K..N..5	S..Q..3	B..S..Z
27)	L..F..E	T..J..C	D..M..A	L..O..6	T..R..4	C..T..1
28)	M..G..F	U..K..D	E..N..B	M..P..7	U..S..5	D..U..2
29)	N..H..G	V..L..E	F..O..C	N..Q..8	V..T..6	E..V..3
30)	O..J..H	W..M..F	G..P..D	O..R..A	W..U..7	F..W..4
31)	P..K..J	X..N..G		P..S..B		G..X..5

CODES: P-PHYSICAL BIORHYTHM CURVE,E-EMOTIONAL BIORHYTHM CURVE,I-INTELLECTUAL BIORHYTHM CURVE

...JANUARY..	..FEBRUARY..	...MARCH...	...APRIL...	....MAY....	...JUNE....
P--E--I	P--E--I	P--E--I	P--E--I	P--E--I	P--E--I
1) H..Y..6	1) Q..2..4	1) W..3..Z	1) G..C..X	1) O..E..U	1) W..H..S
2) J..Z..7	2) R..3..5	2) X..A..1	2) H..D..Y	2) P..F..V	2) X..J..T
3) K..1..8	3) S..A..6	3) A..B..2	3) J..E..Z	3) Q..G..W	3) A..K..U
4) L..2..A	4) T..B..7	4) B..C..3	4) K..F..1	4) R..H..X	4) B..L..V
5) M..3..B	5) U..C..8	5) C..D..4	5) L..G..2	5) S..J..Y	5) C..M..W
6) N..A..C	6) V..D..A	6) D..E..5	6) M..H..3	6) T..K..Z	6) D..N..X
7) O..B..D	7) W..E..B	7) E..F..6	7) N..J..4	7) U..L..1	7) E..O..Y
8) P..C..E	8) X..F..C	8) F..G..7	8) O..K..5	8) V..M..2	8) F..P..Z
9) Q..D..F	9) A..G..D	9) G..H..8	9) P..L..6	9) W..N..3	9) G..Q..1
10) R..E..G	10) B..H..E	10) H..J..A	10) Q..M..7	10) X..O..4	10) H..R..2
11) S..F..H	11) C..J..F	11) J..K..B	11) R..N..8	11) A..P..5	11) J..S..3
12) T..G..J	12) D..K..G	12) K..L..C	12) S..O..A	12) B..Q..6	12) K..T..4
13) U..H..K	13) E..L..H	13) L..M..D	13) T..P..B	13) C..R..7	13) L..U..5
14) V..J..L	14) F..M..J	14) M..N..E	14) U..Q..C	14) D..S..8	14) M..V..6
15) W..K..M	15) G..N..K	15) N..O..F	15) V..R..D	15) E..T..A	15) N..W..7
16) X..L..N	16) H..O..L	16) O..P..G	16) W..S..E	16) F..U..B	16) O..X..8
17) A..M..O	17) J..P..M	17) P..Q..H	17) X..T..F	17) G..V..C	17) P..Y..A
18) B..N..P	18) K..Q..N	18) Q..R..J	18) A..U..G	18) H..W..D	18) Q..Z..B
19) C..O..Q	19) L..R..O	19) R..S..K	19) B..V..H	19) J..X..E	19) R..1..C
20) D..P..R	20) M..S..P	20) S..T..L	20) C..W..J	20) K..Y..F	20) S..2..D
21) E..Q..S	21) N..T..Q	21) T..U..M	21) D..X..K	21) L..Z..G	21) T..3..E
22) F..R..T	22) O..U..R	22) U..V..N	22) E..Y..L	22) M..1..H	22) U..A..F
23) G..S..U	23) P..V..S	23) V..W..O	23) F..Z..M	23) N..2..J	23) V..B..G
24) H..T..V	24) Q..W..T	24) W..X..P	24) G..1..N	24) O..3..K	24) W..C..H
25) J..U..W	25) R..X..U	25) X..Y..Q	25) H..2..O	25) P..A..L	25) X..D..J
26) K..V..X	26) S..Y..V	26) A..Z..R	26) J..3..P	26) Q..B..M	26) A..E..K
27) L..W..Y	27) T..Z..W	27) B..1..S	27) K..A..Q	27) R..C..N	27) B..F..L
28) M..X..Z	28) U..1..X	28) C..2..T	28) L..B..R	28) S..D..O	28) C..G..M
29) N..Y..1	29) V..2..Y	29) D..3..U	29) M..C..S	29) T..E..P	29) D..H..N
30) O..Z..2		30) E..A..V	30) N..D..T	30) U..F..Q	30) E..J..O
31) P..1..3		31) F..B..W		31) V..G..R	

....JULY....	...AUGUST...	..SEPTEMBER.	..OCTOBER...	..NOVEMBER..	..DECEMBER..
P--E--I	P--E--I	P--E--I	P--E--I	P--E--I	P--E--I
1) F..K..P	1) O..N..N	1) W..Q..L	1) F..S..H	1) O..V..F	1) V..X..C
2) G..L..Q	2) P..O..O	2) X..R..M	2) G..T..J	2) P..W..G	2) W..Y..D
3) H..M..R	3) Q..P..P	3) A..S..N	3) H..U..K	3) Q..X..H	3) X..Z..E
4) J..N..S	4) R..Q..Q	4) B..T..O	4) J..V..L	4) R..Y..J	4) A..1..F
5) K..O..T	5) S..R..R	5) C..U..P	5) K..W..M	5) S..Z..K	5) B..2..G
6) L..P..U	6) T..S..S	6) D..V..Q	6) L..X..N	6) T..1..L	6) C..3..H
7) M..Q..V	7) U..T..T	7) E..W..R	7) M..Y..O	7) U..2..M	7) D..A..J
8) N..R..W	8) V..U..U	8) F..X..S	8) N..Z..P	8) V..3..N	8) E..B..K
9) O..S..X	9) W..V..V	9) G..Y..T	9) O..1..Q	9) W..A..O	9) F..C..L
10) P..T..Y	10) X..W..W	10) H..Z..U	10) P..2..R	10) X..B..P	10) G..D..M
11) Q..U..Z	11) A..X..X	11) J..1..V	11) Q..3..S	11) A..C..Q	11) H..E..N
12) R..V..1	12) B..Y..Y	12) K..2..W	12) R..A..T	12) B..D..R	12) J..F..O
13) S..W..2	13) C..Z..Z	13) L..3..X	13) S..B..U	13) C..E..S	13) K..G..P
14) T..X..3	14) D..1..1	14) M..A..Y	14) T..C..V	14) D..F..T	14) L..H..Q
15) U..Y..4	15) E..2..2	15) N..B..Z	15) U..D..W	15) E..G..U	15) M..J..R
16) V..Z..5	16) F..3..3	16) O..C..1	16) V..E..X	16) F..H..V	16) N..K..S
17) W..1..6	17) G..A..4	17) P..D..2	17) W..F..Y	17) G..J..W	17) O..L..T
18) X..2..7	18) H..B..5	18) Q..E..3	18) X..G..Z	18) H..K..X	18) P..M..U
19) A..3..8	19) J..C..6	19) R..F..4	19) A..H..1	19) J..L..Y	19) Q..N..V
20) B..A..A	20) K..D..7	20) S..G..5	20) B..J..2	20) K..M..Z	20) R..O..W
21) C..B..B	21) L..E..8	21) T..H..6	21) C..K..3	21) L..N..1	21) S..P..X
22) D..C..C	22) M..F..A	22) U..J..7	22) D..L..4	22) M..O..2	22) T..Q..Y
23) E..D..D	23) N..G..B	23) V..K..8	23) E..M..5	23) N..P..3	23) U..R..Z
24) F..E..E	24) O..H..C	24) W..L..A	24) F..N..6	24) O..Q..4	24) V..S..1
25) G..F..F	25) P..J..D	25) X..M..B	25) G..O..7	25) P..R..5	25) W..T..2
26) H..G..G	26) Q..K..E	26) A..N..C	26) H..P..8	26) Q..S..6	26) X..U..3
27) J..H..H	27) R..L..F	27) B..O..D	27) J..Q..A	27) R..T..7	27) A..V..4
28) K..J..J	28) S..M..G	28) C..P..E	28) K..R..B	28) S..U..8	28) B..W..5
29) L..K..K	29) T..N..H	29) D..Q..F	29) L..S..C	29) T..V..A	29) C..X..6
30) M..L..L	30) U..O..J	30) E..R..G	30) M..T..D	30) U..W..B	30) D..Y..7
31) N..M..M	31) V..P..K		31) N..U..E		31) E..Z..8

CODES: P-PHYSICAL BIORHYTHM CURVE,E-EMOTIONAL BIORHYTHM CURVE,I-INTELLECTUAL BIORHYTHM CURVE

	...JANUARY..	..FEBRUARY..	....MARCH...	...APRIL...	.....MAY....	....JUNE....
	P--E--I	P--E--I	P--E--I	P--E--I	P--E--I	P--E--I
1)	F..1..A	O..A..7	T..A..2	D..D..Z	L..F..W	T..J..U
2)	G..2..B	P..B..8	U..B..3	E..E..1	M..G..X	U..K..V
3)	H..3..C	Q..C..A	V..C..4	F..F..2	N..H..Y	V..L..W
4)	J..A..D	R..D..B	W..D..5	G..G..3	O..J..Z	W..M..X
5)	K..B..E	S..E..C	X..E..6	H..H..4	P..K..1	X..N..Y
6)	L..C..F	T..F..D	A..F..7	J..J..5	Q..L..2	A..O..Z
7)	M..D..G	U..G..E	B..G..8	K..K..6	R..M..3	B..P..1
8)	N..E..H	V..H..F	C..H..A	L..L..7	S..N..4	C..Q..2
9)	O..F..J	W..J..G	D..J..B	M..M..8	T..O..5	D..R..3
10)	P..G..K	X..K..H	E..K..C	N..N..A	U..P..6	E..S..4
11)	Q..H..L	A..L..J	F..L..D	O..O..B	V..Q..7	F..T..5
12)	R..J..M	B..M..K	G..M..E	P..P..C	W..R..8	G..U..6
13)	S..K..N	C..N..L	H..N..F	Q..Q..D	X..S..A	H..V..7
14)	T..L..O	D..O..M	J..O..G	R..R..E	A..T..B	J..W..8
15)	U..M..P	E..P..N	K..P..H	S..S..F	B..U..C	K..X..A
16)	V..N..Q	F..Q..O	L..Q..J	T..T..G	C..V..D	L..Y..B
17)	W..O..R	G..R..P	M..R..K	U..U..H	D..W..E	M..Z..C
18)	X..P..S	H..S..Q	N..S..L	V..V..J	E..X..F	N..1..D
19)	A..Q..T	J..T..R	O..T..M	W..W..K	F..Y..G	O..2..E
20)	B..R..U	K..U..S	P..U..N	X..X..L	G..Z..H	P..3..F
21)	C..S..V	L..V..T	Q..V..O	A..Y..M	H..1..J	Q..A..G
22)	D..T..W	M..W..U	R..W..P	B..Z..N	J..2..K	R..B..H
23)	E..U..X	N..X..V	S..X..Q	C..1..O	K..3..L	S..C..J
24)	F..V..Y	O..Y..W	T..Y..R	D..2..P	L..A..M	T..D..K
25)	G..W..Z	P..Z..X	U..Z..S	E..3..Q	M..B..N	U..E..L
26)	H..X..1	Q..1..Y	V..1..T	F..A..R	N..C..O	V..F..M
27)	J..Y..2	R..2..Z	W..2..U	G..B..S	O..D..P	W..G..N
28)	K..Z..3	S..3..1	X..3..V	H..C..T	P..E..Q	X..H..O
29)	L..1..4		A..A..W	J..D..U	Q..F..R	A..J..P
30)	M..2..5		B..B..X	K..E..V	R..G..S	B..K..Q
31)	N..3..6		C..C..Y		S..H..T	

	....JULY....	...AUGUST...	..SEPTEMBER.	..OCTOBER...	..NOVEMBER..	..DECEMBER..
	P--E--I	P--E--I	P--E--I	P--E--I	P--E--I	P--E--I
1)	C..L..R	L..O..P	T..R..N	C..T..K	L..W..H	S..Y..E
2)	D..M..S	M..P..Q	U..S..O	D..U..L	M..X..J	T..Z..F
3)	E..N..T	N..Q..R	V..T..P	E..V..M	N..Y..K	U..1..G
4)	F..O..U	O..R..S	W..U..Q	F..W..N	O..Z..L	V..2..H
5)	G..P..V	P..S..T	X..V..R	G..X..O	P..1..M	W..3..J
6)	H..Q..W	Q..T..U	A..W..S	H..Y..P	Q..2..N	X..A..K
7)	J..R..X	R..U..V	B..X..T	J..Z..Q	R..3..O	A..B..L
8)	K..S..Y	S..V..W	C..Y..U	K..1..R	S..A..P	B..C..M
9)	L..T..Z	T..W..X	D..Z..V	L..2..S	T..B..Q	C..D..N
10)	M..U..1	U..X..Y	E..1..W	M..3..T	U..C..R	D..E..O
11)	N..V..2	V..Y..Z	F..2..X	N..A..U	V..D..S	E..F..P
12)	O..W..3	W..Z..1	G..3..Y	O..B..V	W..E..T	F..G..Q
13)	P..X..4	X..1..2	H..A..Z	P..C..W	X..F..U	G..H..R
14)	Q..Y..5	A..2..3	J..B..1	Q..D..X	A..G..V	H..J..S
15)	R..Z..6	B..3..4	K..C..2	R..E..Y	B..H..W	J..K..T
16)	S..1..7	C..A..5	L..D..3	S..F..Z	C..J..X	K..L..U
17)	T..2..8	D..B..6	M..E..4	T..G..1	D..K..Y	L..M..V
18)	U..3..A	E..C..7	N..F..5	U..H..2	E..L..Z	M..N..W
19)	V..A..B	F..D..8	O..G..6	V..J..3	F..M..1	N..O..X
20)	W..B..C	G..E..A	P..H..7	W..K..4	G..N..2	O..P..Y
21)	X..C..D	H..F..B	Q..J..8	X..L..5	H..O..3	P..Q..Z
22)	A..D..E	J..G..C	R..K..A	A..M..6	J..P..4	Q..R..1
23)	B..E..F	K..H..D	S..L..B	B..N..7	K..Q..5	R..S..2
24)	C..F..G	L..J..E	T..M..C	C..O..8	L..R..6	S..T..3
25)	D..G..H	M..K..F	U..N..D	D..P..A	M..S..7	T..U..4
26)	E..H..J	N..L..G	V..O..E	E..Q..B	N..T..8	U..V..5
27)	F..J..K	O..M..H	W..P..F	F..R..C	O..U..A	V..W..6
28)	G..K..L	P..N..J	X..Q..G	G..S..D	P..V..B	W..X..7
29)	H..L..M	Q..O..K	A..R..H	H..T..E	Q..W..C	X..Y..8
30)	J..M..N	R..P..L	B..S..J	J..U..F	R..X..D	A..Z..A
31)	K..N..O	S..Q..M		K..V..G		B..1..B

CODES: P-PHYSICAL BIORHYTHM CURVE,E-EMOTIONAL BIORHYTHM CURVE,I-INTELLECTUAL BIORHYTHM CURVE

...JANUARY..	..FEBRUARY..	...MARCH...	...APRIL...	...MAY...	...JUNE....
P--E--I	P--E--I	P--E--I	P--E--I	P--E--I	P--E--I
1) C..2..C	1) L..B..A	1) Q..B..4	1) A..E..2	1) H..G..Y	1) Q..K..W
2) D..3..D	2) M..C..B	2) R..C..5	2) B..F..3	2) J..H..Z	2) R..L..X
3) E..A..E	3) N..D..C	3) S..D..6	3) C..G..4	3) K..J..1	3) S..M..Y
4) F..B..F	4) O..E..D	4) T..E..7	4) D..H..5	4) L..K..2	4) T..N..Z
5) G..C..G	5) P..F..E	5) U..F..8	5) E..J..6	5) M..L..3	5) U..O..1
6) H..D..H	6) Q..G..F	6) V..G..A	6) F..K..7	6) N..M..4	6) V..P..2
7) J..E..J	7) R..H..G	7) W..H..B	7) G..L..8	7) O..N..5	7) W..Q..3
8) K..F..K	8) S..J..H	8) X..J..C	8) H..M..A	8) P..O..6	8) X..R..4
9) L..G..L	9) T..K..J	9) A..K..D	9) J..N..B	9) Q..P..7	9) A..S..5
10) M..H..M	10) U..L..K	10) B..L..E	10) K..O..C	10) R..Q..8	10) B..T..6
11) N..J..N	11) V..M..L	11) C..M..F	11) L..P..D	11) S..R..A	11) C..U..7
12) O..K..O	12) W..N..M	12) D..N..G	12) M..Q..E	12) T..S..B	12) D..V..8
13) P..L..P	13) X..O..N	13) E..O..H	13) N..R..F	13) U..T..C	13) E..W..A
14) Q..M..Q	14) A..P..O	14) F..P..J	14) O..S..G	14) V..U..D	14) F..X..B
15) R..N..R	15) B..Q..P	15) G..Q..K	15) P..T..H	15) W..V..E	15) G..Y..C
16) S..O..S	16) C..R..Q	16) H..R..L	16) Q..U..J	16) X..W..F	16) H..Z..D
17) T..P..T	17) D..S..R	17) J..S..M	17) R..V..K	17) A..X..G	17) J..1..E
18) U..Q..U	18) E..T..S	18) K..T..N	18) S..W..L	18) B..Y..H	18) K..2..F
19) V..R..V	19) F..U..T	19) L..U..O	19) T..X..M	19) C..Z..J	19) L..3..G
20) W..S..W	20) G..V..U	20) M..V..P	20) U..Y..N	20) D..1..K	20) M..A..H
21) X..T..X	21) H..W..V	21) N..W..Q	21) V..Z..O	21) E..2..L	21) N..B..J
22) A..U..Y	22) J..X..W	22) O..X..R	22) W..1..P	22) F..3..M	22) O..C..K
23) B..V..Z	23) K..Y..X	23) P..Y..S	23) X..2..Q	23) G..A..N	23) P..D..L
24) C..W..1	24) L..Z..Y	24) Q..Z..T	24) A..3..R	24) H..B..O	24) Q..E..M
25) D..X..2	25) M..1..Z	25) R..1..U	25) B..A..S	25) J..C..P	25) R..F..N
26) E..Y..3	26) N..2..1	26) S..2..V	26) C..B..T	26) K..D..Q	26) S..G..O
27) F..Z..4	27) O..3..2	27) T..3..W	27) D..C..U	27) L..E..R	27) T..H..P
28) G..1..5	28) P..A..3	28) U..A..X	28) E..D..V	28) M..F..S	28) U..J..Q
29) H..2..6		29) V..B..Y	29) F..E..W	29) N..G..T	29) V..K..R
30) J..3..7		30) W..C..Z	30) G..F..X	30) O..H..U	30) W..L..S
31) K..A..8		31) X..D..1		31) P..J..V	

....JULY....	...AUGUST...	.SEPTEMBER.	..OCTOBER...	..NOVEMBER..	..DECEMBER..
P--E--I	P--E--I	P--E--I	P--E--I	P--E--I	P--E--I
1) X..M..T	1) H..P..R	1) Q..S..P	1) X..U..M	1) H..X..K	1) P..Z..G
2) A..N..U	2) J..Q..S	2) R..T..Q	2) A..V..N	2) J..Y:.L	2) Q..1..H
3) B..O..V	3) K..R..T	3) S..U..R	3) B..W..O	3) K..Z..M	3) R..2..J
4) C..P..W	4) L..S..U	4) T..V..S	4) C..X..P	4) L..1..N	4) S..3..K
5) D..Q..X	5) M..T..V	5) U..W..T	5) D..Y..Q	5) M..2..O	5) T..A..L
6) E..R..Y	6) N..U..W	6) V..X..U	6) E..Z..R	6) N..3..P	6) U..B..M
7) F..S..Z	7) O..V..X	7) W..Y..V	7) F..1..S	7) O..A..Q	7) V..C..N
8) G..T..1	8) P..W..Y	8) X..Z..W	8) G..2..T	8) P..B..R	8) W..D..O
9) H..U..2	9) Q..X..Z	9) A..1..X	9) H..3..U	9) Q..C..S	9) X..E..P
10) J..V..3	10) R..Y..1	10) B..2..Y	10) J..A..V	10) R..D..T	10) A..F..Q
11) K..W..4	11) S..Z..2	11) C..3..Z	11) K..B..W	11) S..E..U	11) B..G..R
12) L..X..5	12) T..1..3	12) D..A..1	12) L..C..X	12) T..F..V	12) C..H..S
13) M..Y..6	13) U..2..4	13) E..B..2	13) M..D..Y	13) U..G..W	13) D..J..T
14) N..Z..7	14) V..3..5	14) F..C..3	14) N..E..Z	14) V..H..X	14) E..K..U
15) O..1..8	15) W..A..6	15) G..D..4	15) O..F..1	15) W..J..Y	15) F..L..V
16) P..2..A	16) X..B..7	16) H..E..5	16) P..G..2	16) X..K..Z	16) G..M..W
17) Q..3..B	17) A..C..8	17) J..F..6	17) Q..H..3	17) A..L..1	17) H..N..X
18) R..A..C	18) B..D..A	18) K..G..7	18) R..J..4	18) B..M..2	18) J..O..Y
19) S..B..D	19) C..E..B	19) L..H..8	19) S..K..5	19) C..N..3	19) K..P..Z
20) T..C..E	20) D..F..C	20) M..J..A	20) T..L..6	20) D..O..4	20) L..Q..1
21) U..D..F	21) E..G..D	21) N..K..B	21) U..M..7	21) E..P..5	21) M..R..2
22) V..E..G	22) F..H..E	22) O..L..C	22) V..N..8	22) F..Q..6	22) N..S..3
23) W..F..H	23) G..J..F	23) P..M..D	23) W..O..A	23) G..R..7	23) O..T..4
24) X..G..J	24) H..K..G	24) Q..N..E	24) X..P..B	24) H..S..8	24) P..U..5
25) A..H..K	25) J..L..H	25) R..O..F	25) A..Q..C	25) J..T..A	25) Q..V..6
26) B..J..L	26) K..M..J	26) S..P..G	26) B..R..D	26) K..U..B	26) R..W..7
27) C..K..M	27) L..N..K	27) T..Q..H	27) C..S..E	27) L..V..C	27) S..X..8
28) D..L..N	28) M..O..L	28) U..R..J	28) D..T..F	28) M..W..D	28) T..Y..A
29) E..M..O	29) N..P..M	29) V..S..K	29) E..U..G	29) N..X..E	29) U..Z..B
30) F..N..P	30) O..Q..N	30) W..T..L	30) F..V..H	30) O..Y..F	30) V..1..C
31) G..O..Q	31) P..R..O		31) G..W..J		31) W..2..D

CODES: P-PHYSICAL BIORHYTHM CURVE, E-EMOTIONAL BIORHYTHM CURVE, I-INTELLECTUAL BIORHYTHM CURVE

	...JANUARY.. P--E--I	..FEBRUARY.. P--E--I	....MARCH... P--E--I	...APRIL... P--E--I	.....MAY.... P--E--I	....JUNE.... P--E--I
1)	X..3..E	H..C..C	N..C..6	V..F..4	E..H..1	N..L..Y
2)	A..A..F	J..D..D	O..D..7	W..G..5	F..J..2	O..M..Z
3)	B..B..G	K..E..E	P..E..8	X..H..6	G..K..3	P..N..1
4)	C..C..H	L..F..F	Q..F..A	A..J..7	H..L..4	Q..O..2
5)	D..D..J	M..G..G	R..G..B	B..K..8	J..M..5	R..P..3
6)	E..E..K	N..H..H	S..H..C	C..L..A	K..N..6	S..Q..4
7)	F..F..L	O..J..J	T..J..D	D..M..B	L..O..7	T..R..5
8)	G..G..M	P..K..K	U..K..E	E..N..C	M..P..8	U..S..6
9)	H..H..N	Q..L..L	V..L..F	F..O..D	N..Q..A	V..T..7
10)	J..J..O	R..M..M	W..M..G	G..P..E	O..R..B	W..U..8
11)	K..K..P	S..N..N	X..N..H	H..Q..F	P..S..C	X..V..A
12)	L..L..Q	T..O..O	A..O..J	J..R..G	Q..T..D	A..W..B
13)	M..M..R	U..P..P	B..P..K	K..S..H	R..U..E	B..X..C
14)	N..N..S	V..Q..Q	C..Q..L	L..T..J	S..V..F	C..Y..D
15)	O..O..T	W..R..R	D..R..M	M..U..K	T..W..G	D..Z..E
16)	P..P..U	X..S..S	E..S..N	N..V..L	U..X..H	E..1..F
17)	Q..Q..V	A..T..T	F..T..O	O..W..M	V..Y..J	F..2..G
18)	R..R..W	B..U..U	G..U..P	P..X..N	W..Z..K	G..3..H
19)	S..S..X	C..V..V	H..V..Q	Q..Y..O	X..1..L	H..A..J
20)	T..T..Y	D..W..W	J..W..R	R..Z..P	A..2..M	J..B..K
21)	U..U..Z	E..X..X	K..X..S	S..1..Q	B..3..N	K..C..L
22)	V..V..1	F..Y..Y	L..Y..T	T..2..R	C..A..O	L..D..M
23)	W..W..2	G..Z..Z	M..Z..U	U..3..S	D..B..P	M..E..N
24)	X..X..3	H..1..1	N..1..V	V..A..T	E..C..Q	N..F..O
25)	A..Y..4	J..2..2	O..2..W	W..B..U	F..D..R	O..G..P
26)	B..Z..5	K..3..3	P..3..X	X..C..V	G..E..S	P..H..Q
27)	C..1..6	L..A..4	Q..A..Y	A..D..W	H..F..T	Q..J..R
28)	D..2..7	M..B..5	R..B..Z	B..E..X	J..G..U	R..K..S
29)	E..3..8		S..C..1	C..F..Y	K..H..V	S..L..T
30)	F..A..A		T..D..2	D..G..Z	L..J..W	T..M..U
31)	G..B..B		U..E..3		M..K..X	

	....JULY.... P--E--I	...AUGUST... P--E--I	..SEPTEMBER. P--E--I	..OCTOBER... P--E--I	..NOVEMBER.. P--E--I	..DECEMBER.. P--E--I
1)	U..N..V	E..Q..T	N..T..R	U..V..O	E..Y..M	M..1..J
2)	V..O..W	F..R..U	O..U..S	V..W..P	F..Z..N	N..2..K
3)	W..P..X	G..S..V	P..V..T	W..X..Q	G..1..O	O..3..L
4)	X..Q..Y	H..T..W	Q..W..U	X..Y..R	H..2..P	P..A..M
5)	A..R..Z	J..U..X	R..X..V	A..Z..S	J..3..Q	Q..B..N
6)	B..S..1	K..V..Y	S..Y..W	B..1..T	K..A..R	R..C..O
7)	C..T..2	L..W..Z	T..Z..X	C..2..U	L..B..S	S..D..P
8)	D..U..3	M..X..1	U..1..Y	D..3..V	M..C..T	T..E..Q
9)	E..V..4	N..Y..2	V..2..Z	E..A..W	N..D..U	U..F..R
10)	F..W..5	O..Z..3	W..3..1	F..B..X	O..E..V	V..G..S
11)	G..X..6	P..1..4	X..A..2	G..C..Y	P..F..W	W..H..T
12)	H..Y..7	Q..2..5	A..B..3	H..D..Z	Q..G..X	X..J..U
13)	J..Z..8	R..3..6	B..C..4	J..E..1	R..H..Y	A..K..V
14)	K..1..A	S..A..7	C..D..5	K..F..2	S..J..Z	B..L..W
15)	L..2..B	T..B..8	D..E..6	L..G..3	T..K..1	C..M..X
16)	M..3..C	U..C..A	E..F..7	M..H..4	U..L..2	D..N..Y
17)	N..A..D	V..D..B	F..G..8	N..J..5	V..M..3	E..O..Z
18)	O..B..E	W..E..C	G..H..A	O..K..6	W..N..4	F..P..1
19)	P..C..F	X..F..D	H..J..B	P..L..7	X..O..5	G..Q..2
20)	Q..D..G	A..G..E	J..K..C	Q..M..8	A..P..6	H..R..3
21)	R..E..H	B..H..F	K..L..D	R..N..A	B..Q..7	J..S..4
22)	S..F..J	C..J..G	L..M..E	S..O..B	C..R..8	K..T..5
23)	T..G..K	D..K..H	M..N..F	T..P..C	D..S..A	L..U..6
24)	U..H..L	E..L..J	N..O..G	U..Q..D	E..T..B	M..V..7
25)	V..J..M	F..M..K	O..P..H	V..R..E	F..U..C	N..W..8
26)	W..K..N	G..N..L	P..Q..J	W..S..F	G..V..D	O..X..A
27)	X..L..O	H..O..M	Q..R..K	X..T..G	H..W..E	P..Y..B
28)	A..M..P	J..P..N	R..S..L	A..U..H	J..X..F	Q..Z..C
29)	B..N..Q	K..Q..O	S..T..M	B..V..J	K..Y..G	R..1..D
30)	C..O..R	L..R..P	T..U..N	C..W..K	L..Z..H	S..2..E
31)	D..P..S	M..S..Q		D..X..L		T..3..F

CODES: P-PHYSICAL BIORHYTHM CURVE,E-EMOTIONAL BIORHYTHM CURVE,I-INTELLECTUAL BIORHYTHM CURVE

	...JANUARY..	..FEBRUARY..	...MARCH...	...APRIL...	....MAY....	...JUNE....
	P--E--I	P--E--I	P--E--I	P--E--I	P--E--I	P--E--I
1)	U..A..G	E..D..E	L..E..A	T..H..7	C..K..4	L..N..2
2)	V..B..H	F..E..F	M..F..B	U..J..8	D..L..5	M..O..3
3)	W..C..J	G..F..G	N..G..C	V..K..A	E..M..6	N..P..4
4)	X..D..K	H..G..H	O..H..D	W..L..B	F..N..7	O..Q..5
5)	A..E..L	J..H..J	P..J..E	X..M..C	G..O..8	P..R..6
6)	B..F..M	K..J..K	Q..K..F	A..N..D	H..P..A	Q..S..7
7)	C..G..N	L..K..L	R..L..G	B..O..E	J..Q..B	R..T..8
8)	D..H..O	M..L..M	S..M..H	C..P..F	K..R..C	S..U..A
9)	E..J..P	N..M..N	T..N..J	D..Q..G	L..S..D	T..V..B
10)	F..K..Q	O..N..O	U..O..K	E..R..H	M..T..E	U..W..C
11)	G..L..R	P..O..P	V..P..L	F..S..J	N..U..F	V..X..D
12)	H..M..S	Q..P..Q	W..Q..M	G..T..K	O..V..G	W..Y..E
13)	J..N..T	R..Q..R	X..R..N	H..U..L	P..W..H	X..Z..F
14)	K..O..U	S..R..S	A..S..O	J..V..M	Q..X..J	A..1..G
15)	L..P..V	T..S..T	B..T..P	K..W..N	R..Y..K	B..2..H
16)	M..Q..W	U..T..U	C..U..Q	L..X..O	S..Z..L	C..3..J
17)	N..R..X	V..U..V	D..V..R	M..Y..P	T..1..M	D..A..K
18)	O..S..Y	W..V..W	E..W..S	N..Z..Q	U..2..N	E..B..L
19)	P..T..Z	X..W..X	F..X..T	O..1..R	V..3..O	F..C..M
20)	Q..U..1	A..X..Y	G..Y..U	P..2..S	W..A..P	G..D..N
21)	R..V..2	B..Y..Z	H..Z..V	Q..3..T	X..B..Q	H..E..O
22)	S..W..3	C..Z..1	J..1..W	R..A..U	A..C..R	J..F..P
23)	T..X..4	D..1..2	K..2..X	S..B..V	B..D..S	K..G..Q
24)	U..Y..5	E..2..3	L..3..Y	T..C..W	C..E..T	L..H..R
25)	V..Z..6	F..3..4	M..A..Z	U..D..X	D..F..U	M..J..S
26)	W..1..7	G..A..5	N..B..1	V..E..Y	E..G..V	N..K..T
27)	X..2..8	H..B..6	O..C..2	W..F..Z	F..H..W	O..L..U
28)	A..3..A	J..C..7	P..D..3	X..G..1	G..J..X	P..M..V
29)	B..A..B	K..D..8	Q..E..4	A..H..2	H..K..Y	Q..N..W
30)	C..B..C		R..F..5	B..J..3	J..L..Z	R..O..X
31)	D..C..D		S..G..6		K..M..1	

	....JULY....	...AUGUST...	.SEPTEMBER.	..OCTOBER...	..NOVEMBER..	..DECEMBER..
	P--E--I	P--E--I	P--E--I	P--E--I	P--E--I	P--E--I
1)	S..P..Y	C..S..W	L..V..U	S..X..R	C..1..P	K..3..M
2)	T..Q..Z	D..T..X	M..W..V	T..Y..S	D..2..Q	L..A..N
3)	U..R..1	E..U..Y	N..X..W	U..Z..T	E..3..R	M..B..O
4)	V..S..2	F..V..Z	O..Y..X	V..1..U	F..A..S	N..C..P
5)	W..T..3	G..W..1	P..Z..Y	W..2..V	G..B..T	O..D..Q
6)	X..U..4	H..X..2	Q..1..Z	X..3..W	H..C..U	P..E..R
7)	A..V..5	J..Y..3	R..2..1	A..A..X	J..D..V	Q..F..S
8)	B..W..6	K..Z..4	S..3..2	B..B..Y	K..E..W	R..G..T
9)	C..X..7	L..1..5	T..A..3	C..C..Z	L..F..X	S..H..U
10)	D..Y..8	M..2..6	U..B..4	D..D..1	M..G..Y	T..J..V
11)	E..Z..A	N..3..7	V..C..5	E..E..2	N..H..Z	U..K..W
12)	F..1..B	O..A..8	W..D..6	F..F..3	O..J..1	V..L..X
13)	G..2..C	P..B..A	X..E..7	G..G..4	P..K..2	W..M..Y
14)	H..3..D	Q..C..B	A..F..8	H..H..5	Q..L..3	X..N..Z
15)	J..A..E	R..D..C	B..G..A	J..J..6	R..M..4	A..O..1
16)	K..B..F	S..E..D	C..H..B	K..K..7	S..N..5	B..P..2
17)	L..C..G	T..F..E	D..J..C	L..L..8	T..O..6	C..Q..3
18)	M..D..H	U..G..F	E..K..D	M..M..A	U..P..7	D..R..4
19)	N..E..J	V..H..G	F..L..E	N..N..B	V..Q..8	E..S..5
20)	O..F..K	W..J..H	G..M..F	O..O..C	W..R..A	F..T..6
21)	P..G..L	X..K..J	H..N..G	P..P..D	X..S..B	G..U..7
22)	Q..H..M	A..L..K	J..O..H	Q..Q..E	A..T..C	H..V..8
23)	R..J..N	B..M..L	K..P..J	R..R..F	B..U..D	J..W..A
24)	S..K..O	C..N..M	L..Q..K	S..S..G	C..V..E	K..X..B
25)	T..L..P	D..O..N	M..R..L	T..T..H	D..W..F	L..Y..C
26)	U..M..Q	E..P..O	N..S..M	U..U..J	E..X..G	M..Z..D
27)	V..N..R	F..Q..P	O..T..N	V..V..K	F..Y..H	N..1..E
28)	W..O..S	G..R..Q	P..U..O	W..W..L	G..Z..J	O..2..F
29)	X..P..T	H..S..R	Q..V..P	X..X..M	H..1..K	P..3..G
30)	A..Q..U	J..T..S	R..W..Q	A..Y..N	J..2..L	Q..A..H
31)	B..R..V	K..U..T		B..Z..O		R..B..J

CODES: P-PHYSICAL BIORHYTHM CURVE,E-EMOTIONAL BIORHYTHM CURVE,I-INTELLECTUAL BIORHYTHM CURVE

JANUARY — FEBRUARY — MARCH — APRIL — MAY — JUNE

Day	JAN P	E	I	FEB P	E	I	MAR P	E	I	APR P	E	I	MAY P	E	I	JUN P	E	I
1	S	C	K	C	F	H	H	F	C	Q	J	A	X	L	6	H	O	4
2	T	D	L	D	G	J	J	G	D	R	K	B	A	M	7	J	P	5
3	U	E	M	E	H	K	K	H	E	S	L	C	B	N	8	K	Q	6
4	V	F	N	F	J	L	L	J	F	T	M	D	C	O	A	L	R	7
5	W	G	O	G	K	M	M	K	G	U	N	E	D	P	B	M	S	8
6	X	H	P	H	L	N	N	L	H	V	O	F	E	Q	C	N	T	A
7	A	J	Q	J	M	O	O	M	J	W	P	G	F	R	D	O	U	B
8	B	K	R	K	N	P	P	N	K	X	Q	H	G	S	E	P	V	C
9	C	L	S	L	O	Q	Q	O	L	A	R	J	H	T	F	Q	W	D
10	D	M	T	M	P	R	R	P	M	B	S	K	J	U	G	R	X	E
11	E	N	U	N	Q	S	S	Q	N	C	T	L	K	V	H	S	Y	F
12	F	O	V	O	R	T	T	R	O	D	U	M	L	W	J	T	Z	G
13	G	P	W	P	S	U	U	S	P	E	V	N	M	X	K	U	1	H
14	H	Q	X	Q	T	V	V	T	Q	F	W	O	N	Y	L	V	2	J
15	J	R	Y	R	U	W	W	U	R	G	X	P	O	Z	M	W	3	K
16	K	S	Z	S	V	X	X	V	S	H	Y	Q	P	1	N	X	A	L
17	L	T	1	T	W	Y	A	W	T	J	Z	R	Q	2	O	A	B	M
18	M	U	2	U	X	Z	B	X	U	K	1	S	R	3	P	B	C	N
19	N	V	3	V	Y	1	C	Y	V	L	2	T	S	A	Q	C	D	O
20	O	W	4	W	Z	2	D	Z	W	M	3	U	T	B	R	D	E	P
21	P	X	5	X	1	3	E	1	X	N	A	V	U	C	S	E	F	Q
22	Q	Y	6	A	2	4	F	2	Y	O	B	W	V	D	T	F	G	R
23	R	Z	7	B	3	5	G	3	Z	P	C	X	W	E	U	G	H	S
24	S	1	8	C	A	6	H	A	1	Q	D	Y	X	F	V	H	J	T
25	T	2	A	D	B	7	J	B	2	R	E	Z	A	G	W	J	K	U
26	U	3	B	E	C	8	K	C	3	S	F	1	B	H	X	K	L	V
27	V	A	C	F	D	A	L	D	4	T	G	2	C	J	Y	L	M	W
28	W	B	D	G	E	B	M	E	5	U	H	3	D	K	Z	M	N	X
29	X	C	E				N	F	6	V	J	4	E	L	1	N	O	Y
30	A	D	F				O	G	7	W	K	5	F	M	2	O	P	Z
31	B	E	G				P	H	8				G	N	3			

JULY — AUGUST — SEPTEMBER — OCTOBER — NOVEMBER — DECEMBER

Day	JUL P	E	I	AUG P	E	I	SEP P	E	I	OCT P	E	I	NOV P	E	I	DEC P	E	I
1	P	Q	1	X	T	Y	H	W	W	P	Y	T	X	2	R	G	A	O
2	Q	R	2	A	U	Z	J	X	X	Q	Z	U	A	3	S	H	B	P
3	R	S	3	B	V	1	K	Y	Y	R	1	V	B	A	T	J	C	Q
4	S	T	4	C	W	2	L	Z	Z	S	2	W	C	B	U	K	D	R
5	T	U	5	D	X	3	M	1	1	T	3	X	D	C	V	L	E	S
6	U	V	6	E	Y	4	N	2	2	U	A	Y	E	D	W	M	F	T
7	V	W	7	F	Z	5	O	3	3	V	B	Z	F	E	X	N	G	U
8	W	X	8	G	1	6	P	A	4	W	C	1	G	F	Y	O	H	V
9	X	Y	A	H	2	7	Q	B	5	X	D	2	H	G	Z	P	J	W
10	A	Z	B	J	3	8	R	C	6	A	E	3	J	H	1	Q	K	X
11	B	1	C	K	A	A	S	D	7	B	F	4	K	J	2	R	L	Y
12	C	2	D	L	B	B	T	E	8	C	G	5	L	K	3	S	M	Z
13	D	3	E	M	C	C	U	F	A	D	H	6	M	L	4	T	N	1
14	E	A	F	N	D	D	V	G	B	E	J	7	N	M	5	U	O	2
15	F	B	G	O	E	E	W	H	C	F	K	8	O	N	6	V	P	3
16	G	C	H	P	F	F	X	J	D	G	L	A	P	O	7	W	Q	4
17	H	D	J	Q	G	G	A	K	E	H	M	B	Q	P	8	X	R	5
18	J	E	K	R	H	H	B	L	F	J	N	C	R	Q	A	A	S	6
19	K	F	L	S	J	J	C	M	G	K	O	D	S	R	B	B	T	7
20	L	G	M	T	K	K	D	N	H	L	P	E	T	S	C	C	U	8
21	M	H	N	U	L	L	E	O	J	M	Q	F	U	T	D	D	V	A
22	N	J	O	V	M	M	F	P	K	N	R	G	V	U	E	E	W	B
23	O	K	P	W	N	N	G	Q	L	O	S	H	W	V	F	F	X	C
24	P	L	Q	X	O	O	H	R	M	P	T	J	X	W	G	G	Y	D
25	Q	M	R	A	P	P	J	S	N	Q	U	K	A	X	H	H	Z	E
26	R	N	S	B	Q	Q	K	T	O	R	V	L	B	Y	J	J	1	F
27	S	O	T	C	R	R	L	U	P	S	W	M	C	Z	K	K	2	G
28	T	P	U	D	S	S	M	V	Q	T	X	N	D	1	L	L	3	H
29	U	Q	V	E	T	T	N	W	R	U	Y	O	E	2	M	M	A	J
30	V	R	W	F	U	U	O	X	S	V	Z	P	F	3	N	N	B	K
31	W	S	X	G	V	V				W	1	Q				O	C	L

CODES: P-PHYSICAL BIORHYTHM CURVE, E-EMOTIONAL BIORHYTHM CURVE, I-INTELLECTUAL BIORHYTHM CURVE

...JANUARY.. | ..FEBRUARY.. | ....MARCH... | ....APRIL... | ....MAY.... | ....JUNE....

	JANUARY P--E--I	FEBRUARY P--E--I	MARCH P--E--I	APRIL P--E--I	MAY P--E--I	JUNE P--E--I
1)	P..D..M	X..G..K	E..G..E	N..K..C	U..M..8	E..P..6
2)	Q..E..N	A..H..L	F..H..F	O..L..D	V..N..A	F..Q..7
3)	R..F..O	B..J..M	G..J..G	P..M..E	W..O..B	G..R..8
4)	S..G..P	C..K..N	H..K..H	Q..N..F	X..P..C	H..S..A
5)	T..H..Q	D..L..O	J..L..J	R..O..G	A..Q..D	J..T..B
6)	U..J..R	E..M..P	K..M..K	S..P..H	B..R..E	K..U..C
7)	V..K..S	F..N..Q	L..N..L	T..Q..J	C..S..F	L..V..D
8)	W..L..T	G..O..R	M..O..M	U..R..K	D..T..G	M..W..E
9)	X..M..U	H..P..S	N..P..N	V..S..L	E..U..H	N..X..F
10)	A..N..V	J..Q..T	O..Q..O	W..T..M	F..V..J	O..Y..G
11)	B..O..W	K..R..U	P..R..P	X..U..N	G..W..K	P..Z..H
12)	C..P..X	L..S..V	Q..S..Q	A..V..O	H..X..L	Q..1..J
13)	D..Q..Y	M..T..W	R..T..R	B..W..P	J..Y..M	R..2..K
14)	E..R..Z	N..U..X	S..U..S	C..X..Q	K..Z..N	S..3..L
15)	F..S..1	O..V..Y	T..V..T	D..Y..R	L..1..O	T..A..M
16)	G..T..2	P..W..Z	U..W..U	E..Z..S	M..2..P	U..B..N
17)	H..U..3	Q..X..1	V..X..V	F..1..T	N..3..Q	V..C..O
18)	J..V..4	R..Y..2	W..Y..W	G..2..U	O..A..R	W..D..P
19)	K..W..5	S..Z..3	X..Z..X	H..3..V	P..B..S	X..E..Q
20)	L..X..6	T..1..4	A..1..Y	J..A..W	Q..C..T	A..F..R
21)	M..Y..7	U..2..5	B..2..Z	K..B..X	R..D..U	B..G..S
22)	N..Z..8	V..3..6	C..3..1	L..C..Y	S..E..V	C..H..T
23)	O..1..A	W..A..7	D..A..2	M..D..Z	T..F..W	D..J..U
24)	P..2..B	X..B..8	E..B..3	N..E..1	U..G..X	E..K..V
25)	Q..3..C	A..C..A	F..C..4	O..F..2	V..H..Y	F..L..W
26)	R..A..D	B..D..B	G..D..5	P..G..3	W..J..Z	G..M..X
27)	S..B..E	C..E..C	H..E..6	Q..H..4	X..K..1	H..N..Y
28)	T..C..F	D..F..D	J..F..7	R..J..5	A..L..2	J..O..Z
29)	U..D..G		K..G..8	S..K..6	B..M..3	K..P..1
30)	V..E..H		L..H..A	T..L..7	C..N..4	L..Q..2
31)	W..F..J		M..J..B		D..O..5	

....JULY.... | ...AUGUST... | .SEPTEMBER. | ..OCTOBER... | ..NOVEMBER.. | ..DECEMBER..

	JULY P--E--I	AUGUST P--E--I	SEPTEMBER P--E--I	OCTOBER P--E--I	NOVEMBER P--E--I	DECEMBER P--E--I
1)	M..R..3	U..U..1	E..X..Y	M..Z..V	U..3..T	D..B..Q
2)	N..S..4	V..V..2	F..Y..Z	N..1..W	V..A..U	E..C..R
3)	O..T..5	W..W..3	G..Z..1	O..2..X	W..B..V	F..D..S
4)	P..U..6	X..X..4	H..1..2	P..3..Y	X..C..W	G..E..T
5)	Q..V..7	A..Y..5	J..2..3	Q..A..Z	A..D..X	H..F..U
6)	R..W..8	B..Z..6	K..3..4	R..B..1	B..E..Y	J..G..V
7)	S..X..A	C..1..7	L..A..5	S..C..2	C..F..Z	K..H..W
8)	T..Y..B	D..2..8	M..B..6	T..D..3	D..G..1	L..J..X
9)	U..Z..C	E..3..A	N..C..7	U..E..4	E..H..2	M..K..Y
10)	V..1..D	F..A..B	O..D..8	V..F..5	F..J..3	N..L..Z
11)	W..2..E	G..B..C	P..E..A	W..G..6	G..K..4	O..M..1
12)	X..3..F	H..C..D	Q..F..B	X..H..7	H..L..5	P..N..2
13)	A..A..G	J..D..E	R..G..C	A..J..8	J..M..6	Q..O..3
14)	B..B..H	K..E..F	S..H..D	B..K..A	K..N..7	R..P..4
15)	C..C..J	L..F..G	T..J..E	C..L..B	L..O..8	S..Q..5
16)	D..D..K	M..G..H	U..K..F	D..M..C	M..P..A	T..R..6
17)	E..E..L	N..H..J	V..L..G	E..N..D	N..Q..B	U..S..7
18)	F..F..M	O..J..K	W..M..H	F..O..E	O..R..C	V..T..8
19)	G..G..N	P..K..L	X..N..J	G..P..F	P..S..D	W..U..A
20)	H..H..O	Q..L..M	A..O..K	H..Q..G	Q..T..E	X..V..B
21)	J..J..P	R..M..N	B..P..L	J..R..H	R..U..F	A..W..C
22)	K..K..Q	S..N..O	C..Q..M	K..S..J	S..V..G	B..X..D
23)	L..L..R	T..O..P	D..R..N	L..T..K	T..W..H	C..Y..E
24)	M..M..S	U..P..Q	E..S..O	M..U..L	U..X..J	D..Z..F
25)	N..N..T	V..Q..R	F..T..P	N..V..M	V..Y..K	E..1..G
26)	O..O..U	W..R..S	G..U..Q	O..W..N	W..Z..L	F..2..H
27)	P..P..V	X..S..T	H..V..R	P..X..O	X..1..M	G..3..J
28)	Q..Q..W	A..T..U	J..W..S	Q..Y..P	A..2..N	H..A..K
29)	R..R..X	B..U..V	K..X..T	R..Z..Q	B..3..O	J..B..L
30)	S..S..Y	C..V..W	L..Y..U	S..1..R	C..A..P	K..C..M
31)	T..T..Z	D..W..X		T..2..S		L..D..N

CODES: P-PHYSICAL BIORHYTHM CURVE,E-EMOTIONAL BIORHYTHM CURVE,I-INTELLECTUAL BIORHYTHM CURVE

...JANUARY..	..FEBRUARY..	...MARCH...	...APRIL...	....MAY....	....JUNE....
P--E--I	P--E--I	P--E--I	P--E--I	P--E--I	P--E--I
1) M..E..O	1) U..H..M	1) B..H..G	1) K..L..E	1) R..N..B	1) B..Q..8
2) N..F..P	2) V..J..N	2) C..J..H	2) L..M..F	2) S..O..C	2) C..R..A
3) O..G..Q	3) W..K..O	3) D..K..J	3) M..N..G	3) T..P..D	3) D..S..B
4) P..H..R	4) X..L..P	4) E..L..K	4) N..O..H	4) U..Q..E	4) E..T..C
5) Q..J..S	5) A..M..Q	5) F..M..L	5) O..P..J	5) V..R..F	5) F..U..D
6) R..K..T	6) B..N..R	6) G..N..M	6) P..Q..K	6) W..S..G	6) G..V..E
7) S..L..U	7) C..O..S	7) H..O..N	7) Q..R..L	7) X..T..H	7) H..W..F
8) T..M..V	8) D..P..T	8) J..P..O	8) R..S..M	8) A..U..J	8) J..X..G
9) U..N..W	9) E..Q..U	9) K..Q..P	9) S..T..N	9) B..V..K	9) K..Y..H
10) V..O..X	10) F..R..V	10) L..R..Q	10) T..U..O	10) C..W..L	10) L..Z..J
11) W..P..Y	11) G..S..W	11) M..S..R	11) U..V..P	11) D..X..M	11) M..1..K
12) X..Q..Z	12) H..T..X	12) N..T..S	12) V..W..Q	12) E..Y..N	12) N..2..L
13) A..R..1	13) J..U..Y	13) O..U..T	13) W..X..R	13) F..Z..O	13) O..3..M
14) B..S..2	14) K..V..Z	14) P..V..U	14) X..Y..S	14) G..1..P	14) P..A..N
15) C..T..3	15) L..W..1	15) Q..W..V	15) A..Z..T	15) H..2..Q	15) Q..B..O
16) D..U..4	16) M..X..2	16) R..X..W	16) B..1..U	16) J..3..R	16) R..C..P
17) E..V..5	17) N..Y..3	17) S..Y..X	17) C..2..V	17) K..A..S	17) S..D..Q
18) F..W..6	18) O..Z..4	18) T..Z..Y	18) D..3..W	18) L..B..T	18) T..E..R
19) G..X..7	19) P..1..5	19) U..1..Z	19) E..A..X	19) M..C..U	19) U..F..S
20) H..Y..8	20) Q..2..6	20) V..2..1	20) F..B..Y	20) N..D..V	20) V..G..T
21) J..Z..A	21) R..3..7	21) W..3..2	21) G..C..Z	21) O..E..W	21) W..H..U
22) K..1..B	22) S..A..8	22) X..A..3	22) H..D..1	22) P..F..X	22) X..J..V
23) L..2..C	23) T..B..A	23) A..B..4	23) J..E..2	23) Q..G..Y	23) A..K..W
24) M..3..D	24) U..C..B	24) B..C..5	24) K..F..3	24) R..H..Z	24) B..L..X
25) N..A..E	25) V..D..C	25) C..D..6	25) L..G..4	25) S..J..1	25) C..M..Y
26) O..B..F	26) W..E..D	26) D..E..7	26) M..H..5	26) T..K..2	26) D..N..Z
27) P..C..G	27) X..F..E	27) E..F..8	27) N..J..6	27) U..L..3	27) E..O..1
28) Q..D..H	28) A..G..F	28) F..G..A	28) O..K..7	28) V..M..4	28) F..P..2
29) R..E..J		29) G..H..B	29) P..L..8	29) W..N..5	29) G..Q..3
30) S..F..K		30) H..J..C	30) Q..M..A	30) X..O..6	30) H..R..4
31) T..G..L		31) J..K..D		31) A..P..7	

....JULY....	...AUGUST...	..SEPTEMBER.	..OCTOBER...	..NOVEMBER..	.DECEMBER..
P--E--I	P--E--I	P--E--I	P--E--I	P--E--I	P--E--I
1) J..S..5	1) R..V..3	1) B..Y..1	1) J..1..X	1) R..A..V	1) A..C..S
2) K..T..6	2) S..W..4	2) C..Z..2	2) K..2..Y	2) S..B..W	2) B..D..T
3) L..U..7	3) T..X..5	3) D..1..3	3) L..3..Z	3) T..C..X	3) C..E..U
4) M..V..8	4) U..Y..6	4) E..2..4	4) M..A..1	4) U..D..Y	4) D..F..V
5) N..W..A	5) V..Z..7	5) F..3..5	5) N..B..2	5) V..E..Z	5) E..G..W
6) O..X..B	6) W..1..8	6) G..A..6	6) O..C..3	6) W..F..1	6) F..H..X
7) P..Y..C	7) X..2..A	7) H..B..7	7) P..D..4	7) X..G..2	7) G..J..Y
8) Q..Z..D	8) A..3..B	8) J..C..8	8) Q..E..5	8) A..H..3	8) H..K..Z
9) R..1..E	9) B..A..C	9) K..D..A	9) R..F..6	9) B..J..4	9) J..L..1
10) S..2..F	10) C..B..D	10) L..E..B	10) S..G..7	10) C..K..5	10) K..M..2
11) T..3..G	11) D..C..E	11) M..F..C	11) T..H..8	11) D..L..6	11) L..N..3
12) U..A..H	12) E..D..F	12) N..G..D	12) U..J..A	12) E..M..7	12) M..O..4
13) V..B..J	13) F..E..G	13) O..H..E	13) V..K..B	13) F..N..8	13) N..P..5
14) W..C..K	14) G..F..H	14) P..J..F	14) W..L..C	14) G..O..A	14) O..Q..6
15) X..D..L	15) H..G..J	15) Q..K..G	15) X..M..D	15) H..P..B	15) P..R..7
16) A..E..M	16) J..H..K	16) R..L..H	16) A..N..E	16) J..Q..C	16) Q..S..8
17) B..F..N	17) K..J..L	17) S..M..J	17) B..O..F	17) K..R..D	17) R..T..A
18) C..G..O	18) L..K..M	18) T..N..K	18) C..P..G	18) L..S..E	18) S..U..B
19) D..H..P	19) M..L..N	19) U..O..L	19) D..Q..H	19) M..T..F	19) T..V..C
20) E..J..Q	20) N..M..O	20) V..P..M	20) E..R..J	20) N..U..G	20) U..W..D
21) F..K..R	21) O..N..P	21) W..Q..N	21) F..S..K	21) O..V..H	21) V..X..E
22) G..L..S	22) P..O..Q	22) X..R..O	22) G..T..L	22) P..W..J	22) W..Y..F
23) H..M..T	23) Q..P..R	23) A..S..P	23) H..U..M	23) Q..X..K	23) X..Z..G
24) J..N..U	24) R..Q..S	24) B..T..Q	24) J..V..N	24) R..Y..L	24) A..1..H
25) K..O..V	25) S..R..T	25) C..U..R	25) K..W..O	25) S..Z..M	25) B..2..J
26) L..P..W	26) T..S..U	26) D..V..S	26) L..X..P	26) T..1..N	26) C..3..K
27) M..Q..X	27) U..T..V	27) E..W..T	27) M..Y..Q	27) U..2..O	27) D..A..L
28) N..R..Y	28) V..U..W	28) F..X..U	28) N..Z..R	28) V..3..P	28) E..B..M
29) O..S..Z	29) W..V..X	29) G..Y..V	29) O..1..S	29) W..A..Q	29) F..C..N
30) P..T..1	30) X..W..Y	30) H..Z..W	30) P..2..T	30) X..B..R	30) G..D..O
31) Q..U..2	31) A..X..Z		31) Q..3..U		31) H..E..P

CODES: P-PHYSICAL BIORHYTHM CURVE, E-EMOTIONAL BIORHYTHM CURVE, I-INTELLECTUAL BIORHYTHM CURVE

```
...JANUARY..      ..FEBRUARY..      ...MARCH...       ...APRIL...       ....MAY....       ....JUNE....

    P--E--I           P--E--I           P--E--I           P--E--I           P--E--I           P--E--I

 1)   J..F..Q      1)   R..J..O      1)   X..K..K      1)   H..N..H      1)   P..P..E      1)   X..S..C
 2)   K..G..R      2)   S..K..P      2)   A..L..L      2)   J..O..J      2)   Q..Q..F      2)   A..T..D
 3)   L..H..S      3)   T..L..Q      3)   B..M..M      3)   K..P..K      3)   R..R..G      3)   B..U..E
 4)   M..J..T      4)   U..M..R      4)   C..N..N      4)   L..Q..L      4)   S..S..H      4)   C..V..F
 5)   N..K..U      5)   V..N..S      5)   D..O..O      5)   M..R..M      5)   T..T..J      5)   D..W..G
 6)   O..L..V      6)   W..O..T      6)   E..P..P      6)   N..S..N      6)   U..U..K      6)   E..X..H
 7)   P..M..W      7)   X..P..U      7)   F..Q..Q      7)   O..T..O      7)   V..V..L      7)   F..Y..J
 8)   Q..N..X      8)   A..Q..V      8)   G..R..R      8)   P..U..P      8)   W..W..M      8)   G..Z..K
 9)   R..O..Y      9)   B..R..W      9)   H..S..S      9)   Q..V..Q      9)   X..X..N      9)   H..1..L
10)   S..P..Z     10)   C..S..X     10)   J..T..T     10)   R..W..R     10)   A..Y..O     10)   J..2..M
11)   T..Q..1     11)   D..T..Y     11)   K..U..U     11)   S..X..S     11)   B..Z..P     11)   K..3..N
12)   U..R..2     12)   E..U..Z     12)   L..V..V     12)   T..Y..T     12)   C..1..Q     12)   L..A..O
13)   V..S..3     13)   F..V..1     13)   M..W..W     13)   U..Z..U     13)   D..2..R     13)   M..B..P
14)   W..T..4     14)   G..W..2     14)   N..X..X     14)   V..1..V     14)   E..3..S     14)   N..C..Q
15)   X..U..5     15)   H..X..3     15)   O..Y..Y     15)   W..2..W     15)   F..A..T     15)   O..D..R
16)   A..V..6     16)   J..Y..4     16)   P..Z..Z     16)   X..3..X     16)   G..B..U     16)   P..E..S
17)   B..W..7     17)   K..Z..5     17)   Q..1..1     17)   A..A..Y     17)   H..C..V     17)   Q..F..T
18)   C..X..8     18)   L..1..6     18)   R..2..2     18)   B..B..Z     18)   J..D..W     18)   R..G..U
19)   D..Y..A     19)   M..2..7     19)   S..3..3     19)   C..C..1     19)   K..E..X     19)   S..H..V
20)   E..Z..B     20)   N..3..8     20)   T..A..4     20)   D..D..2     20)   L..F..Y     20)   T..J..W
21)   F..1..C     21)   O..A..A     21)   U..B..5     21)   E..E..3     21)   M..G..Z     21)   U..K..X
22)   G..2..D     22)   P..B..B     22)   V..C..6     22)   F..F..4     22)   N..H..1     22)   V..L..Y
23)   H..3..E     23)   Q..C..C     23)   W..D..7     23)   G..G..5     23)   O..J..2     23)   W..M..Z
24)   J..A..F     24)   R..D..D     24)   X..E..8     24)   H..H..6     24)   P..K..3     24)   X..N..1
25)   K..B..G     25)   S..E..E     25)   A..F..A     25)   J..J..7     25)   Q..L..4     25)   A..O..2
26)   L..C..H     26)   T..F..F     26)   B..G..B     26)   K..K..8     26)   R..M..5     26)   B..P..3
27)   M..D..J     27)   U..G..G     27)   C..H..C     27)   L..L..A     27)   S..N..6     27)   C..Q..4
28)   N..E..K     28)   V..H..H     28)   D..J..D     28)   M..M..B     28)   T..O..7     28)   D..R..5
29)   O..F..L     29)   W..J..J     29)   E..K..E     29)   N..N..C     29)   U..P..8     29)   E..S..6
30)   P..G..M                       30)   F..L..F     30)   O..O..D     30)   V..Q..A     30)   F..T..7
31)   Q..H..N                       31)   G..M..G                       31)   W..R..B
```

```
....JULY....      ...AUGUST...      ..SEPTEMBER.      ..OCTOBER...      ..NOVEMBER..      ..DECEMBER..

    P--E--I           P--E--I           P--E--I           P--E--I           P--E--I           P--E--I

 1)   G..U..8      1)   P..X..6      1)   X..1..4      1)   G..3..1      1)   P..C..Y      1)   W..E..V
 2)   H..V..A      2)   Q..Y..7      2)   A..2..5      2)   H..A..2      2)   Q..D..Z      2)   X..F..W
 3)   J..W..B      3)   R..Z..8      3)   B..3..6      3)   J..B..3      3)   R..E..1      3)   A..G..X
 4)   K..X..C      4)   S..1..A      4)   C..A..7      4)   K..C..4      4)   S..F..2      4)   B..H..Y
 5)   L..Y..D      5)   T..2..B      5)   D..B..8      5)   L..D..5      5)   T..G..3      5)   C..J..Z
 6)   M..Z..E      6)   U..3..C      6)   E..C..A      6)   M..E..6      6)   U..H..4      6)   D..K..1
 7)   N..1..F      7)   V..A..D      7)   F..D..B      7)   N..F..7      7)   V..J..5      7)   E..L..2
 8)   O..2..G      8)   W..B..E      8)   G..E..C      8)   O..G..8      8)   W..K..6      8)   F..M..3
 9)   P..3..H      9)   X..C..F      9)   H..F..D      9)   P..H..A      9)   X..L..7      9)   G..N..4
10)   Q..A..J     10)   A..D..G     10)   J..G..E     10)   Q..J..B     10)   A..M..8     10)   H..O..5
11)   R..B..K     11)   B..E..H     11)   K..H..F     11)   R..K..C     11)   B..N..A     11)   J..P..6
12)   S..C..L     12)   C..F..J     12)   L..J..G     12)   S..L..D     12)   C..O..B     12)   K..Q..7
13)   T..D..M     13)   D..G..K     13)   M..K..H     13)   T..M..E     13)   D..P..C     13)   L..R..8
14)   U..E..N     14)   E..H..L     14)   N..L..J     14)   U..N..F     14)   E..Q..D     14)   M..S..A
15)   V..F..O     15)   F..J..M     15)   O..M..K     15)   V..O..G     15)   F..R..E     15)   N..T..B
16)   W..G..P     16)   G..K..N     16)   P..N..L     16)   W..P..H     16)   G..S..F     16)   O..U..C
17)   X..H..Q     17)   H..L..O     17)   Q..O..M     17)   X..Q..J     17)   H..T..G     17)   P..V..D
18)   A..J..R     18)   J..M..P     18)   R..P..N     18)   A..R..K     18)   J..U..H     18)   Q..W..E
19)   B..K..S     19)   K..N..Q     19)   S..Q..O     19)   B..S..L     19)   K..V..J     19)   R..X..F
20)   C..L..T     20)   L..O..R     20)   T..R..P     20)   C..T..M     20)   L..W..K     20)   S..Y..G
21)   D..M..U     21)   M..P..S     21)   U..S..Q     21)   D..U..N     21)   M..X..L     21)   T..Z..H
22)   E..N..V     22)   N..Q..T     22)   V..T..R     22)   E..V..O     22)   N..Y..M     22)   U..1..J
23)   F..O..W     23)   O..R..U     23)   W..U..S     23)   F..W..P     23)   O..Z..N     23)   V..2..K
24)   G..P..X     24)   P..S..V     24)   X..V..T     24)   G..X..Q     24)   P..1..O     24)   W..3..L
25)   H..Q..Y     25)   Q..T..W     25)   A..W..U     25)   H..Y..R     25)   Q..2..P     25)   X..A..M
26)   J..R..Z     26)   R..U..X     26)   B..X..V     26)   J..Z..S     26)   R..3..Q     26)   A..B..N
27)   K..S..1     27)   S..V..Y     27)   C..Y..W     27)   K..1..T     27)   S..A..R     27)   B..C..O
28)   L..T..2     28)   T..W..Z     28)   D..Z..X     28)   L..2..U     28)   T..B..S     28)   C..D..P
29)   M..U..3     29)   U..X..1     29)   E..1..Y     29)   M..3..V     29)   U..C..T     29)   D..E..Q
30)   N..V..4     30)   V..Y..2     30)   F..2..Z     30)   N..A..W     30)   V..D..U     30)   E..F..R
31)   O..W..5     31)   W..Z..3                       31)   O..B..X                       31)   F..G..S
```

CODES: P-PHYSICAL BIORHYTHM CURVE,E-EMOTIONAL BIORHYTHM CURVE,I-INTELLECTUAL BIORHYTHM CURVE

	...JANUARY..	..FEBRUARY..	...MARCH...	...APRIL...	....MAY....	...JUNE....
	P--E--I	P--E--I	P--E--I	P--E--I	P--E--I	P--E--I
1)	G..H..T	P..L..R	U..L..M	E..O..K	M..Q..G	U..T..E
2)	H..J..U	Q..M..S	V..M..N	F..P..L	N..R..H	V..U..F
3)	J..K..V	R..N..T	W..N..O	G..Q..M	O..S..J	W..V..G
4)	K..L..W	S..O..U	X..O..P	H..R..N	P..T..K	X..W..H
5)	L..M..X	T..P..V	A..P..Q	J..S..O	Q..U..L	A..X..J
6)	M..N..Y	U..Q..W	B..Q..R	K..T..P	R..V..M	B..Y..K
7)	N..O..Z	V..R..X	C..R..S	L..U..Q	S..W..N	C..Z..L
8)	O..P..1	W..S..Y	D..S..T	M..V..R	T..X..O	D..1..M
9)	P..Q..2	X..T..Z	E..T..U	N..W..S	U..Y..P	E..2..N
10)	Q..R..3	A..U..1	F..U..V	O..X..T	V..Z..Q	F..3..O
11)	R..S..4	B..V..2	G..V..W	P..Y..U	W..1..R	G..A..P
12)	S..T..5	C..W..3	H..W..X	Q..Z..V	X..2..S	H..B..Q
13)	T..U..6	D..X..4	J..X..Y	R..1..W	A..3..T	J..C..R
14)	U..V..7	E..Y..5	K..Y..Z	S..2..X	B..A..U	K..D..S
15)	V..W..8	F..Z..6	L..Z..1	T..3..Y	C..B..V	L..E..T
16)	W..X..A	G..1..7	M..1..2	U..A..Z	D..C..W	M..F..U
17)	X..Y..B	H..2..8	N..2..3	V..B..1	E..D..X	N..G..V
18)	A..Z..C	J..3..A	O..3..4	W..C..2	F..E..Y	O..H..W
19)	B..1..D	K..A..B	P..A..5	X..D..3	G..F..Z	P..J..X
20)	C..2..E	L..B..C	Q..B..6	A..E..4	H..G..1	Q..K..Y
21)	D..3..F	M..C..D	R..C..7	B..F..5	J..H..2	R..L..Z
22)	E..A..G	N..D..E	S..D..8	C..G..6	K..J..3	S..M..1
23)	F..B..H	O..E..F	T..E..A	D..H..7	L..K..4	T..N..2
24)	G..C..J	P..F..G	U..F..B	E..J..8	M..L..5	U..O..3
25)	H..D..K	Q..G..H	V..G..C	F..K..A	N..M..6	V..P..4
26)	J..E..L	R..H..J	W..H..D	G..L..B	O..N..7	W..Q..5
27)	K..F..M	S..J..K	X..J..E	H..M..C	P..O..8	X..R..6
28)	L..G..N	T..K..L	A..K..F	J..N..D	Q..P..A	A..S..7
29)	M..H..O		B..L..G	K..O..E	R..Q..B	B..T..8
30)	N..J..P		C..M..H	L..P..F	S..R..C	C..U..A
31)	O..K..Q		D..N..J		T..S..D	

	....JULY....	...AUGUST...	..SEPTEMBER.	.OCTOBER...	.NOVEMBER..	.DECEMBER..
	P--E--I	P--E--I	P--E--I	P--E--I	P--E--I	P--E--I
1)	D..V..B	M..Y..8	U..2..6	D..A..3	M..D..1	T..F..X
2)	E..W..C	N..Z..A	V..3..7	E..B..4	N..E..2	U..G..Y
3)	F..X..D	O..1..B	W..A..8	F..C..5	O..F..3	V..H..Z
4)	G..Y..E	P..2..C	X..B..A	G..D..6	P..G..4	W..J..1
5)	H..Z..F	Q..3..D	A..C..B	H..E..7	Q..H..5	X..K..2
6)	J..1..G	R..A..E	B..D..C	J..F..8	R..J..6	A..L..3
7)	K..2..H	S..B..F	C..E..D	K..G..A	S..K..7	B..M..4
8)	L..3..J	T..C..G	D..F..E	L..H..B	T..L..8	C..N..5
9)	M..A..K	U..D..H	E..G..F	M..J..C	U..M..A	D..O..6
10)	N..B..L	V..E..J	F..H..G	N..K..D	V..N..B	E..P..7
11)	O..C..M	W..F..K	G..J..H	O..L..E	W..O..C	F..Q..8
12)	P..D..N	X..G..L	H..K..J	P..M..F	X..P..D	G..R..A
13)	Q..E..O	A..H..M	J..L..K	Q..N..G	A..Q..E	H..S..B
14)	R..F..P	B..J..N	K..M..L	R..O..H	B..R..F	J..T..C
15)	S..G..Q	C..K..O	L..N..M	S..P..J	C..S..G	K..U..D
16)	T..H..R	D..L..P	M..O..N	T..Q..K	D..T..H	L..V..E
17)	U..J..S	E..M..Q	N..P..O	U..R..L	E..U..J	M..W..F
18)	V..K..T	F..N..R	O..Q..P	V..S..M	F..V..K	N..X..G
19)	W..L..U	G..O..S	P..R..Q	W..T..N	G..W..L	O..Y..H
20)	X..M..V	H..P..T	Q..S..R	X..U..O	H..X..M	P..Z..J
21)	A..N..W	J..Q..U	R..T..S	A..V..P	J..Y..N	Q..1..K
22)	B..O..X	K..R..V	S..U..T	B..W..Q	K..Z..O	R..2..L
23)	C..P..Y	L..S..W	T..V..U	C..X..R	L..1..P	S..3..M
24)	D..Q..Z	M..T..X	U..W..V	D..Y..S	M..2..Q	T..A..N
25)	E..R..1	N..U..Y	V..X..W	E..Z..T	N..3..R	U..B..O
26)	F..S..2	O..V..Z	W..Y..X	F..1..U	O..A..S	V..C..P
27)	G..T..3	P..W..1	X..Z..Y	G..2..V	P..B..T	W..D..Q
28)	H..U..4	Q..X..2	A..1..Z	H..3..W	Q..C..U	X..E..R
29)	J..V..5	R..Y..3	B..2..1	J..A..X	R..D..V	A..F..S
30)	K..W..6	S..Z..4	C..3..2	K..B..Y	S..E..W	B..G..T
31)	L..X..7	T..1..5		L..C..Z		C..H..U

CODES: P-PHYSICAL BIORHYTHM CURVE,E-EMOTIONAL BIORHYTHM CURVE,I-INTELLECTUAL BIORHYTHM CURVE

	...JANUARY..		..FEBRUARY..		...MARCH...		...APRIL...		...MAY....		...JUNE....
	P--E--I		P--E--I		P--E--I		P--E--I		P--E--I		P--E--I
1)	D..J..V	1)	M..M..T	1)	R..M..O	1)	B..P..M	1)	J..R..J	1)	R..U..G
2)	E..K..W	2)	N..N..U	2)	S..N..P	2)	C..Q..N	2)	K..S..K	2)	S..V..H
3)	F..L..X	3)	O..O..V	3)	T..O..Q	3)	D..R..O	3)	L..T..L	3)	T..W..J
4)	G..M..Y	4)	P..P..W	4)	U..P..R	4)	E..S..P	4)	M..U..M	4)	U..X..K
5)	H..N..Z	5)	Q..Q..X	5)	V..Q..S	5)	F..T..Q	5)	N..V..N	5)	V..Y..L
6)	J..O..1	6)	R..R..Y	6)	W..R..T	6)	G..U..R	6)	O..W..O	6)	W..Z..M
7)	K..P..2	7)	S..S..Z	7)	X..S..U	7)	H..V..S	7)	P..X..P	7)	X..1..N
8)	L..Q..3	8)	T..T..1	8)	A..T..V	8)	J..W..T	8)	Q..Y..Q	8)	A..2..O
9)	M..R..4	9)	U..U..2	9)	B..U..W	9)	K..X..U	9)	R..Z..R	9)	B..3..P
10)	N..S..5	10)	V..V..3	10)	C..V..X	10)	L..Y..V	10)	S..1..S	10)	C..A..Q
11)	O..T..6	11)	W..W..4	11)	D..W..Y	11)	M..Z..W	11)	T..2..T	11)	D..B..R
12)	P..U..7	12)	X..X..5	12)	E..X..Z	12)	N..1..X	12)	U..3..U	12)	E..C..S
13)	Q..V..8	13)	A..Y..6	13)	F..Y..1	13)	O..2..Y	13)	V..A..V	13)	F..D..T
14)	R..W..A	14)	B..Z..7	14)	G..Z..2	14)	P..3..Z	14)	W..B..W	14)	G..E..U
15)	S..X..B	15)	C..1..8	15)	H..1..3	15)	Q..A..1	15)	X..C..X	15)	H..F..V
16)	T..Y..C	16)	D..2..A	16)	J..2..4	16)	R..B..2	16)	A..D..Y	16)	J..G..W
17)	U..Z..D	17)	E..3..B	17)	K..3..5	17)	S..C..3	17)	B..E..Z	17)	K..H..X
18)	V..1..E	18)	F..A..C	18)	L..A..6	18)	T..D..4	18)	C..F..1	18)	L..J..Y
19)	W..2..F	19)	G..B..D	19)	M..B..7	19)	U..E..5	19)	D..G..2	19)	M..K..Z
20)	X..3..G	20)	H..C..E	20)	N..C..8	20)	V..F..6	20)	E..H..3	20)	N..L..1
21)	A..A..H	21)	J..D..F	21)	O..D..A	21)	W..G..7	21)	F..J..4	21)	O..M..2
22)	B..B..J	22)	K..E..G	22)	P..E..B	22)	X..H..8	22)	G..K..5	22)	P..N..3
23)	C..C..K	23)	L..F..H	23)	Q..F..C	23)	A..J..A	23)	H..L..6	23)	Q..O..4
24)	D..D..L	24)	M..G..J	24)	R..G..D	24)	B..K..B	24)	J..M..7	24)	R..P..5
25)	E..E..M	25)	N..H..K	25)	S..H..E	25)	C..L..C	25)	K..N..8	25)	S..Q..6
26)	F..F..N	26)	O..J..L	26)	T..J..F	26)	D..M..D	26)	L..O..A	26)	T..R..7
27)	G..G..O	27)	P..K..M	27)	U..K..G	27)	E..N..E	27)	M..P..B	27)	U..S..8
28)	H..H..P	28)	Q..L..N	28)	V..L..H	28)	F..O..F	28)	N..Q..C	28)	V..T..A
29)	J..J..Q			29)	W..M..J	29)	G..P..G	29)	O..R..D	29)	W..U..B
30)	K..K..R			30)	X..N..K	30)	H..Q..H	30)	P..S..E	30)	X..V..C
31)	L..L..S			31)	A..O..L			31)	Q..T..F		

	...JULY....		...AUGUST...		.SEPTEMBER.		..OCTOBER...		..NOVEMBER..		..DECEMBER..
	P--E--I		P--E--I		P--E--I		P--E--I		P--E--I		P--E--I
1)	A..W..D	1)	J..Z..B	1)	R..3..8	1)	A..B..5	1)	J..E..3	1)	Q..G..Z
2)	B..X..E	2)	K..1..C	2)	S..A..A	2)	B..C..6	2)	K..F..4	2)	R..H..1
3)	C..Y..F	3)	L..2..D	3)	T..B..B	3)	C..D..7	3)	L..G..5	3)	S..J..2
4)	D..Z..G	4)	M..3..E	4)	U..C..C	4)	D..E..8	4)	M..H..6	4)	T..K..3
5)	E..1..H	5)	N..A..F	5)	V..D..D	5)	E..F..A	5)	N..J..7	5)	U..L..4
6)	F..2..J	6)	O..B..G	6)	W..E..E	6)	F..G..B	6)	O..K..8	6)	V..M..5
7)	G..3..K	7)	P..C..H	7)	X..F..F	7)	G..H..C	7)	P..L..A	7)	W..N..6
8)	H..A..L	8)	Q..D..J	8)	A..G..G	8)	H..J..D	8)	Q..M..B	8)	X..O..7
9)	J..B..M	9)	R..E..K	9)	B..H..H	9)	J..K..E	9)	R..N..C	9)	A..P..8
10)	K..C..N	10)	S..F..L	10)	C..J..J	10)	K..L..F	10)	S..O..D	10)	B..Q..A
11)	L..D..O	11)	T..G..M	11)	D..K..K	11)	L..M..G	11)	T..P..E	11)	C..R..B
12)	M..E..P	12)	U..H..N	12)	E..L..L	12)	M..N..H	12)	U..Q..F	12)	D..S..C
13)	N..F..Q	13)	V..J..O	13)	F..M..M	13)	N..O..J	13)	V..R..G	13)	E..T..D
14)	O..G..R	14)	W..K..P	14)	G..N..N	14)	O..P..K	14)	W..S..H	14)	F..U..E
15)	P..H..S	15)	X..L..Q	15)	H..O..O	15)	P..Q..L	15)	X..T..J	15)	G..V..F
16)	Q..J..T	16)	A..M..R	16)	J..P..P	16)	Q..R..M	16)	A..U..K	16)	H..W..G
17)	R..K..U	17)	B..N..S	17)	K..Q..Q	17)	R..S..N	17)	B..V..L	17)	J..X..H
18)	S..L..V	18)	C..O..T	18)	L..R..R	18)	S..T..O	18)	C..W..M	18)	K..Y..J
19)	T..M..W	19)	D..P..U	19)	M..S..S	19)	T..U..P	19)	D..X..N	19)	L..Z..K
20)	U..N..X	20)	E..Q..V	20)	N..T..T	20)	U..V..Q	20)	E..Y..O	20)	M..1..L
21)	V..O..Y	21)	F..R..W	21)	O..U..U	21)	V..W..R	21)	F..Z..P	21)	N..2..M
22)	W..P..Z	22)	G..S..X	22)	P..V..V	22)	W..X..S	22)	G..1..Q	22)	O..3..N
23)	X..Q..1	23)	H..T..Y	23)	Q..W..W	23)	X..Y..T	23)	H..2..R	23)	P..A..O
24)	A..R..2	24)	J..U..Z	24)	R..X..X	24)	A..Z..U	24)	J..3..S	24)	Q..B..P
25)	B..S..3	25)	K..V..1	25)	S..Y..Y	25)	B..1..V	25)	K..A..T	25)	R..C..Q
26)	C..T..4	26)	L..W..2	26)	T..Z..Z	26)	C..2..W	26)	L..B..U	26)	S..D..R
27)	D..U..5	27)	M..X..3	27)	U..1..1	27)	D..3..X	27)	M..C..V	27)	T..E..S
28)	E..V..6	28)	N..Y..4	28)	V..2..2	28)	E..A..Y	28)	N..D..W	28)	U..F..T
29)	F..W..7	29)	O..Z..5	29)	W..3..3	29)	F..B..Z	29)	O..E..X	29)	V..G..U
30)	G..X..8	30)	P..1..6	30)	X..A..4	30)	G..C..1	30)	P..F..Y	30)	W..H..V
31)	H..Y..A	31)	Q..2..7			31)	H..D..2			31)	X..J..W

CODES: P-PHYSICAL BIORHYTHM CURVE, E-EMOTIONAL BIORHYTHM CURVE, I-INTELLECTUAL BIORHYTHM CURVE

```
...JANUARY..    ..FEBRUARY..    ...MARCH...    ...APRIL...    ....MAY....    ...JUNE....

   P--E--I         P--E--I         P--E--I        P--E--I        P--E--I        P--E--I

 1)  A..K..X    1)  J..N..V    1)  O..N..Q    1)  W..Q..O    1)  F..S..L    1)  O..V..J
 2)  B..L..Y    2)  K..O..W    2)  P..O..R    2)  X..R..P    2)  G..T..M    2)  P..W..K
 3)  C..M..Z    3)  L..P..X    3)  Q..P..S    3)  A..S..Q    3)  H..U..N    3)  Q..X..L
 4)  D..N..1    4)  M..Q..Y    4)  R..Q..T    4)  B..T..R    4)  J..V..O    4)  R..Y..M
 5)  E..O..2    5)  N..R..Z    5)  S..R..U    5)  C..U..S    5)  K..W..P    5)  S..Z..N
 6)  F..P..3    6)  O..S..1    6)  T..S..V    6)  D..V..T    6)  L..X..Q    6)  T..1..O
 7)  G..Q..4    7)  P..T..2    7)  U..T..W    7)  E..W..U    7)  M..Y..R    7)  U..2..P
 8)  H..R..5    8)  Q..U..3    8)  V..U..X    8)  F..X..V    8)  N..Z..S    8)  V..3..Q
 9)  J..S..6    9)  R..V..4    9)  W..V..Y    9)  G..Y..W    9)  O..1..T    9)  W..A..R
10)  K..T..7   10)  S..W..5   10)  X..W..Z   10)  H..Z..X   10)  P..2..U   10)  X..B..S
11)  L..U..8   11)  T..X..6   11)  A..X..1   11)  J..1..Y   11)  Q..3..V   11)  A..C..T
12)  M..V..A   12)  U..Y..7   12)  B..Y..2   12)  K..2..Z   12)  R..A..W   12)  B..D..U
13)  N..W..B   13)  V..Z..8   13)  C..Z..3   13)  L..3..1   13)  S..B..X   13)  C..E..V
14)  O..X..C   14)  W..1..A   14)  D..1..4   14)  M..A..2   14)  T..C..Y   14)  D..F..W
15)  P..Y..D   15)  X..2..B   15)  E..2..5   15)  N..B..3   15)  U..D..Z   15)  E..G..X
16)  Q..Z..E   16)  A..3..C   16)  F..3..6   16)  O..C..4   16)  V..E..1   16)  F..H..Y
17)  R..1..F   17)  B..A..D   17)  G..A..7   17)  P..D..5   17)  W..F..2   17)  G..J..Z
18)  S..2..G   18)  C..B..E   18)  H..B..8   18)  Q..E..6   18)  X..G..3   18)  H..K..1
19)  T..3..H   19)  D..C..F   19)  J..C..A   19)  R..F..7   19)  A..H..4   19)  J..L..2
20)  U..A..J   20)  E..D..G   20)  K..D..B   20)  S..G..8   20)  B..J..5   20)  K..M..3
21)  V..B..K   21)  F..E..H   21)  L..E..C   21)  T..H..A   21)  C..K..6   21)  L..N..4
22)  W..C..L   22)  G..F..J   22)  M..F..D   22)  U..J..B   22)  D..L..7   22)  M..O..5
23)  X..D..M   23)  H..G..K   23)  N..G..E   23)  V..K..C   23)  E..M..8   23)  N..P..6
24)  A..E..N   24)  J..H..L   24)  O..H..F   24)  W..L..D   24)  F..N..A   24)  O..Q..7
25)  B..F..O   25)  K..J..M   25)  P..J..G   25)  X..M..E   25)  G..O..B   25)  P..R..8
26)  C..G..P   26)  L..K..N   26)  Q..K..H   26)  A..N..F   26)  H..P..C   26)  Q..S..A
27)  D..H..Q   27)  M..L..O   27)  R..L..J   27)  B..O..G   27)  J..Q..D   27)  R..T..B
28)  E..J..R   28)  N..M..P   28)  S..M..K   28)  C..P..H   28)  K..R..E   28)  S..U..C
29)  F..K..S                  29)  T..N..L   29)  D..Q..J   29)  L..S..F   29)  T..V..D
30)  G..L..T                  30)  U..O..M   30)  E..R..K   30)  M..T..G   30)  U..W..E
31)  H..M..U                  31)  V..P..N                  31)  N..U..H
```

```
....JULY....    ...AUGUST...    ..SEPTEMBER.    ..OCTOBER...    ..NOVEMBER..    ..DECEMBER..

   P--E--I         P--E--I         P--E--I         P--E--I         P--E--I         P--E--I

 1)  V..X..F    1)  F..1..D    1)  O..A..B    1)  V..C..7    1)  F..F..5    1)  N..H..2
 2)  W..Y..G    2)  G..2..E    2)  P..B..C    2)  W..D..8    2)  G..G..6    2)  O..J..3
 3)  X..Z..H    3)  H..3..F    3)  Q..C..D    3)  X..E..A    3)  H..H..7    3)  P..K..4
 4)  A..1..J    4)  J..A..G    4)  R..D..E    4)  A..F..B    4)  J..J..8    4)  Q..L..5
 5)  B..2..K    5)  K..B..H    5)  S..E..F    5)  B..G..C    5)  K..K..A    5)  R..M..6
 6)  C..3..L    6)  L..C..J    6)  T..F..G    6)  C..H..D    6)  L..L..B    6)  S..N..7
 7)  D..A..M    7)  M..D..K    7)  U..G..H    7)  D..J..E    7)  M..M..C    7)  T..O..8
 8)  E..B..N    8)  N..E..L    8)  V..H..J    8)  E..K..F    8)  N..N..D    8)  U..P..A
 9)  F..C..O    9)  O..F..M    9)  W..J..K    9)  F..L..G    9)  O..O..E    9)  V..Q..B
10)  G..D..P   10)  P..G..N   10)  X..K..L   10)  G..M..H   10)  P..P..F   10)  W..R..C
11)  H..E..Q   11)  Q..H..O   11)  A..L..M   11)  H..N..J   11)  Q..Q..G   11)  X..S..D
12)  J..F..R   12)  R..J..P   12)  B..M..N   12)  J..O..K   12)  R..R..H   12)  A..T..E
13)  K..G..S   13)  S..K..Q   13)  C..N..O   13)  K..P..L   13)  S..S..J   13)  B..U..F
14)  L..H..T   14)  T..L..R   14)  D..O..P   14)  L..Q..M   14)  T..T..K   14)  C..V..G
15)  M..J..U   15)  U..M..S   15)  E..P..Q   15)  M..R..N   15)  U..U..L   15)  D..W..H
16)  N..K..V   16)  V..N..T   16)  F..Q..R   16)  N..S..O   16)  V..V..M   16)  E..X..J
17)  O..L..W   17)  W..O..U   17)  G..R..S   17)  O..T..P   17)  W..W..N   17)  F..Y..K
18)  P..M..X   18)  X..P..V   18)  H..S..T   18)  P..U..Q   18)  X..X..O   18)  G..Z..L
19)  Q..N..Y   19)  A..Q..W   19)  J..T..U   19)  Q..V..R   19)  A..Y..P   19)  H..1..M
20)  R..O..Z   20)  B..R..X   20)  K..U..V   20)  R..W..S   20)  B..Z..Q   20)  J..2..N
21)  S..P..1   21)  C..S..Y   21)  L..V..W   21)  S..X..T   21)  C..1..R   21)  K..3..O
22)  T..Q..2   22)  D..T..Z   22)  M..W..X   22)  T..Y..U   22)  D..2..S   22)  L..A..P
23)  U..R..3   23)  E..U..1   23)  N..X..Y   23)  U..Z..V   23)  E..3..T   23)  M..B..Q
24)  V..S..4   24)  F..V..2   24)  O..Y..Z   24)  V..1..W   24)  F..A..U   24)  N..C..R
25)  W..T..5   25)  G..W..3   25)  P..Z..1   25)  W..2..X   25)  G..B..V   25)  O..D..S
26)  X..U..6   26)  H..X..4   26)  Q..1..2   26)  X..3..Y   26)  H..C..W   26)  P..E..T
27)  A..V..7   27)  J..Y..5   27)  R..2..3   27)  A..A..Z   27)  J..D..X   27)  Q..F..U
28)  B..W..8   28)  K..Z..6   28)  S..3..4   28)  B..B..1   28)  K..E..Y   28)  R..G..V
29)  C..X..A   29)  L..1..7   29)  T..A..5   29)  C..C..2   29)  L..F..Z   29)  S..H..W
30)  D..Y..B   30)  M..2..8   30)  U..B..6   30)  D..D..3   30)  M..G..1   30)  T..J..X
31)  E..Z..C   31)  N..3..A                  31)  E..E..4                  31)  U..K..Y
```

CODES: P-PHYSICAL BIORHYTHM CURVE,E-EMOTIONAL BIORHYTHM CURVE,I-INTELLECTUAL BIORHYTHM CURVE

...JANUARY..	..FEBRUARY..	...MARCH...	...APRIL...	....MAY....	...JUNE....
P--E--I	P--E--I	P--E--I	P--E--I	P--E--I	P--E--I
1) V..L..Z	1) F..O..X	1) M..P..T	1) U..S..R	1) D..U..O	1) M..X..M
2) W..M..1	2) G..P..Y	2) N..Q..U	2) V..T..S	2) E..V..P	2) N..Y..N
3) X..N..2	3) H..Q..Z	3) O..R..V	3) W..U..T	3) F..W..Q	3) O..Z..O
4) A..O..3	4) J..R..1	4) P..S..W	4) X..V..U	4) G..X..R	4) P..1..P
5) B..P..4	5) K..S..2	5) Q..T..X	5) A..W..V	5) H..Y..S	5) Q..2..Q
6) C..Q..5	6) L..T..3	6) R..U..Y	6) B..X..W	6) J..Z..T	6) R..3..R
7) D..R..6	7) M..U..4	7) S..V..Z	7) C..Y..X	7) K..1..U	7) S..A..S
8) E..S..7	8) N..V..5	8) T..W..1	8) D..Z..Y	8) L..2..V	8) T..B..T
9) F..T..8	9) O..W..6	9) U..X..2	9) E..1..Z	9) M..3..W	9) U..C..U
10) G..U..A	10) P..X..7	10) V..Y..3	10) F..2..1	10) N..A..X	10) V..D..V
11) H..V..B	11) Q..Y..8	11) W..Z..4	11) G..3..2	11) O..B..Y	11) W..E..W
12) J..W..C	12) R..Z..A	12) X..1..5	12) H..A..3	12) P..C..Z	12) X..F..X
13) K..X..D	13) S..1..B	13) A..2..6	13) J..B..4	13) Q..D..1	13) A..G..Y
14) L..Y..E	14) T..2..C	14) B..3..7	14) K..C..5	14) R..E..2	14) B..H..Z
15) M..Z..F	15) U..3..D	15) C..A..8	15) L..D..6	15) S..F..3	15) C..J..1
16) N..1..G	16) V..A..E	16) D..B..A	16) M..E..7	16) T..G..4	16) D..K..2
17) O..2..H	17) W..B..F	17) E..C..B	17) N..F..8	17) U..H..5	17) E..L..3
18) P..3..J	18) X..C..G	18) F..D..C	18) O..G..A	18) V..J..6	18) F..M..4
19) Q..A..K	19) A..D..H	19) G..E..D	19) P..H..B	19) W..K..7	19) G..N..5
20) R..B..L	20) B..E..J	20) H..F..E	20) Q..J..C	20) X..L..8	20) H..O..6
21) S..C..M	21) C..F..K	21) J..G..F	21) R..K..D	21) A..M..A	21) J..P..7
22) T..D..N	22) D..G..L	22) K..H..G	22) S..L..E	22) B..N..B	22) K..Q..8
23) U..E..O	23) E..H..M	23) L..J..H	23) T..M..F	23) C..O..C	23) L..R..A
24) V..F..P	24) F..J..N	24) M..K..J	24) U..N..G	24) D..P..D	24) M..S..B
25) W..G..Q	25) G..K..O	25) N..L..K	25) V..O..H	25) E..Q..E	25) N..T..C
26) X..H..R	26) H..L..P	26) O..M..L	26) W..P..J	26) F..R..F	26) O..U..D
27) A..J..S	27) J..M..Q	27) P..N..M	27) X..Q..K	27) G..S..G	27) P..V..E
28) B..K..T	28) K..N..R	28) Q..O..N	28) A..R..L	28) H..T..H	28) Q..W..F
29) C..L..U	29) L..O..S	29) R..P..O	29) B..S..M	29) J..U..J	29) R..X..G
30) D..M..V		30) S..Q..P	30) C..T..N	30) K..V..K	30) S..Y..H
31) E..N..W		31) T..R..Q		31) L..W..L	

....JULY....	...AUGUST...	..SEPTEMBER.	..OCTOBER...	..NOVEMBER..	..DECEMBER..
P--E--I	P--E--I	P--E--I	P--E--I	P--E--I	P--E--I
1) T..Z..J	1) D..3..G	1) M..C..E	1) T..E..B	1) D..H..8	1) L..K..5
2) U..1..K	2) E..A..H	2) N..D..F	2) U..F..C	2) E..J..A	2) M..L..6
3) V..2..L	3) F..B..J	3) O..E..G	3) V..G..D	3) F..K..B	3) N..M..7
4) W..3..M	4) G..C..K	4) P..F..H	4) W..H..E	4) G..L..C	4) O..N..8
5) X..A..N	5) H..D..L	5) Q..G..J	5) X..J..F	5) H..M..D	5) P..O..A
6) A..B..O	6) J..E..M	6) R..H..K	6) A..K..G	6) J..N..E	6) Q..P..B
7) B..C..P	7) K..F..N	7) S..J..L	7) B..L..H	7) K..O..F	7) R..Q..C
8) C..D..Q	8) L..G..O	8) T..K..M	8) C..M..J	8) L..P..G	8) S..R..D
9) D..E..R	9) M..H..P	9) U..L..N	9) D..N..K	9) M..Q..H	9) T..S..E
10) E..F..S	10) N..J..Q	10) V..M..O	10) E..O..L	10) N..R..J	10) U..T..F
11) F..G..T	11) O..K..R	11) W..N..P	11) F..P..M	11) O..S..K	11) V..U..G
12) G..H..U	12) P..L..S	12) X..O..Q	12) G..Q..N	12) P..T..L	12) W..V..H
13) H..J..V	13) Q..M..T	13) A..P..R	13) H..R..O	13) Q..U..M	13) X..W..J
14) J..K..W	14) R..N..U	14) B..Q..S	14) J..S..P	14) R..V..N	14) A..X..K
15) K..L..X	15) S..O..V	15) C..R..T	15) K..T..Q	15) S..W..O	15) B..Y..L
16) L..M..Y	16) T..P..W	16) D..S..U	16) L..U..R	16) T..X..P	16) C..Z..M
17) M..N..Z	17) U..Q..X	17) E..T..V	17) M..V..S	17) U..Y..Q	17) D..1..N
18) N..O..1	18) V..R..Y	18) F..U..W	18) N..W..T	18) V..Z..R	18) E..2..O
19) O..P..2	19) W..S..Z	19) G..V..X	19) O..X..U	19) W..1..S	19) F..3..P
20) P..Q..3	20) X..T..1	20) H..W..Y	20) P..Y..V	20) X..2..T	20) G..A..Q
21) Q..R..4	21) A..U..2	21) J..X..Z	21) Q..Z..W	21) A..3..U	21) H..B..R
22) R..S..5	22) B..V..3	22) K..Y..1	22) R..1..X	22) B..A..V	22) J..C..S
23) S..T..6	23) C..W..4	23) L..Z..2	23) S..2..Y	23) C..B..W	23) K..D..T
24) T..U..7	24) D..X..5	24) M..1..3	24) T..3..Z	24) D..C..X	24) L..E..U
25) U..V..8	25) E..Y..6	25) N..2..4	25) U..A..1	25) E..D..Y	25) M..F..V
26) V..W..A	26) F..Z..7	26) O..3..5	26) V..B..2	26) F..E..Z	26) N..G..W
27) W..X..B	27) G..1..8	27) P..A..6	27) W..C..3	27) G..F..1	27) O..H..X
28) X..Y..C	28) H..2..A	28) Q..B..7	28) X..D..4	28) H..G..2	28) P..J..Y
29) A..Z..D	29) J..3..B	29) R..C..8	29) A..E..5	29) J..H..3	29) Q..K..Z
30) B..1..E	30) K..A..C	30) S..D..A	30) B..F..6	30) K..J..4	30) R..L..1
31) C..2..F	31) L..B..D		31) C..G..7		31) S..M..2

CODES: P-PHYSICAL BIORHYTHM CURVE, E-EMOTIONAL BIORHYTHM CURVE, I-INTELLECTUAL BIORHYTHM CURVE

...JANUARY..

```
        P--E--I
 1)    T..N..3
 2)    U..O..4
 3)    V..P..5
 4)    W..Q..6
 5)    X..R..7
 6)    A..S..8
 7)    B..T..A
 8)    C..U..B
 9)    D..V..C
10)    E..W..D
11)    F..X..E
12)    G..Y..F
13)    H..Z..G
14)    J..1..H
15)    K..2..J
16)    L..3..K
17)    M..A..L
18)    N..B..M
19)    O..C..N
20)    P..D..O
21)    Q..E..P
22)    R..F..Q
23)    S..G..R
24)    T..H..S
25)    U..J..T
26)    V..K..U
27)    W..L..V
28)    X..M..W
29)    A..N..X
30)    B..O..Y
31)    C..P..Z
```

..FEBRUARY..

```
        P--E--I
 1)    D..Q..1
 2)    E..R..2
 3)    F..S..3
 4)    G..T..4
 5)    H..U..5
 6)    J..V..6
 7)    K..W..7
 8)    L..X..8
 9)    M..Y..A
10)    N..Z..B
11)    O..1..C
12)    P..2..D
13)    Q..3..E
14)    R..A..F
15)    S..B..G
16)    T..C..H
17)    U..D..J
18)    V..E..K
19)    W..F..L
20)    X..G..M
21)    A..H..N
22)    B..J..O
23)    C..K..P
24)    D..L..Q
25)    E..M..R
26)    F..N..S
27)    G..O..T
28)    H..P..U
```

...MARCH...

```
        P--E--I
 1)    J..Q..V
 2)    K..R..W
 3)    L..S..X
 4)    M..T..Y
 5)    N..U..Z
 6)    O..V..1
 7)    P..W..2
 8)    Q..X..3
 9)    R..Y..4
10)    S..Z..5
11)    T..1..6
12)    U..2..7
13)    V..3..8
14)    W..A..A
15)    X..B..B
16)    A..C..C
17)    B..D..D
18)    C..E..E
19)    D..F..F
20)    E..G..G
21)    F..H..H
22)    G..J..J
23)    H..K..K
24)    J..L..L
25)    K..M..M
26)    L..N..N
27)    M..O..O
28)    N..P..P
29)    O..Q..Q
30)    P..R..R
31)    Q..S..S
```

...APRIL...

```
        P--E--I
 1)    R..T..T
 2)    S..U..U
 3)    T..V..V
 4)    U..W..W
 5)    V..X..X
 6)    W..Y..Y
 7)    X..Z..Z
 8)    A..1..1
 9)    B..2..2
10)    C..3..3
11)    D..A..4
12)    E..B..5
13)    F..C..6
14)    G..D..7
15)    H..E..8
16)    J..F..A
17)    K..G..B
18)    L..H..C
19)    M..J..D
20)    N..K..E
21)    O..L..F
22)    P..M..G
23)    Q..N..H
24)    R..O..J
25)    S..P..K
26)    T..Q..L
27)    U..R..M
28)    V..S..N
29)    W..T..O
30)    X..U..P
```

....MAY....

```
        P--E--I
 1)    A..V..Q
 2)    B..W..R
 3)    C..X..S
 4)    D..Y..T
 5)    E..Z..U
 6)    F..1..V
 7)    G..2..W
 8)    H..3..X
 9)    J..A..Y
10)    K..B..Z
11)    L..C..1
12)    M..D..2
13)    N..E..3
14)    O..F..4
15)    P..G..5
16)    Q..H..6
17)    R..J..7
18)    S..K..8
19)    T..L..A
20)    U..M..B
21)    V..N..C
22)    W..O..D
23)    X..P..E
24)    A..Q..F
25)    B..R..G
26)    C..S..H
27)    D..T..J
28)    E..U..K
29)    F..V..L
30)    G..W..M
31)    H..X..N
```

....JUNE....

```
        P--E--I
 1)    J..Y..O
 2)    K..Z..P
 3)    L..1..Q
 4)    M..2..R
 5)    N..3..S
 6)    O..A..T
 7)    P..B..U
 8)    Q..C..V
 9)    R..D..W
10)    S..E..X
11)    T..F..Y
12)    U..G..Z
13)    V..H..1
14)    W..J..2
15)    X..K..3
16)    A..L..4
17)    B..M..5
18)    C..N..6
19)    D..O..7
20)    E..P..8
21)    F..Q..A
22)    G..R..B
23)    H..S..C
24)    J..T..D
25)    K..U..E
26)    L..V..F
27)    M..W..G
28)    N..X..H
29)    O..Y..J
30)    P..Z..K
```

....JULY....

```
        P--E--I
 1)    Q..1..L
 2)    R..2..M
 3)    S..3..N
 4)    T..A..O
 5)    U..B..P
 6)    V..C..Q
 7)    W..D..R
 8)    X..E..S
 9)    A..F..T
10)    B..G..U
11)    C..H..V
12)    D..J..W
13)    E..K..X
14)    F..L..Y
15)    G..M..Z
16)    H..N..1
17)    J..O..2
18)    K..P..3
19)    L..Q..4
20)    M..R..5
21)    N..S..6
22)    O..T..7
23)    P..U..8
24)    Q..V..A
25)    R..W..B
26)    S..X..C
27)    T..Y..D
28)    U..Z..E
29)    V..1..F
30)    W..2..G
31)    X..3..H
```

...AUGUST...

```
        P--E--I
 1)    A..A..J
 2)    B..B..K
 3)    C..C..L
 4)    D..D..M
 5)    E..E..N
 6)    F..F..O
 7)    G..G..P
 8)    H..H..Q
 9)    J..J..R
10)    K..K..S
11)    L..L..T
12)    M..M..U
13)    N..N..V
14)    O..O..W
15)    P..P..X
16)    Q..Q..Y
17)    R..R..Z
18)    S..S..1
19)    T..T..2
20)    U..U..3
21)    V..V..4
22)    W..W..5
23)    X..X..6
24)    A..Y..7
25)    B..Z..8
26)    C..1..A
27)    D..2..B
28)    E..3..C
29)    F..A..D
30)    G..B..E
31)    H..C..F
```

..SEPTEMBER.

```
        P--E--I
 1)    J..D..G
 2)    K..E..H
 3)    L..F..J
 4)    M..G..K
 5)    N..H..L
 6)    O..J..M
 7)    P..K..N
 8)    Q..L..O
 9)    R..M..P
10)    S..N..Q
11)    T..O..R
12)    U..P..S
13)    V..Q..T
14)    W..R..U
15)    X..S..V
16)    A..T..W
17)    B..U..X
18)    C..V..Y
19)    D..W..Z
20)    E..X..1
21)    F..Y..2
22)    G..Z..3
23)    H..1..4
24)    J..2..5
25)    K..3..6
26)    L..A..7
27)    M..B..8
28)    N..C..A
29)    O..D..B
30)    P..E..C
```

..OCTOBER...

```
        P--E--I
 1)    Q..F..D
 2)    R..G..E
 3)    S..H..F
 4)    T..J..G
 5)    U..K..H
 6)    V..L..J
 7)    W..M..K
 8)    X..N..L
 9)    A..O..M
10)    B..P..N
11)    C..Q..O
12)    D..R..P
13)    E..S..Q
14)    F..T..R
15)    G..U..S
16)    H..V..T
17)    J..W..U
18)    K..X..V
19)    L..Y..W
20)    M..Z..X
21)    N..1..Y
22)    O..2..Z
23)    P..3..1
24)    Q..A..2
25)    R..B..3
26)    S..C..4
27)    T..D..5
28)    U..E..6
29)    V..F..7
30)    W..G..8
31)    X..H..A
```

..NOVEMBER..

```
        P--E--I
 1)    A..J..B
 2)    B..K..C
 3)    C..L..D
 4)    D..M..E
 5)    E..N..F
 6)    F..O..G
 7)    G..P..H
 8)    H..Q..J
 9)    J..R..K
10)    K..S..L
11)    L..T..M
12)    M..U..N
13)    N..V..O
14)    O..W..P
15)    P..X..Q
16)    Q..Y..R
17)    R..Z..S
18)    S..1..T
19)    T..2..U
20)    U..3..V
21)    V..A..W
22)    W..B..X
23)    X..C..Y
24)    A..D..Z
25)    B..E..1
26)    C..F..2
27)    D..G..3
28)    E..H..4
29)    F..J..5
30)    G..K..6
```

..DECEMBER..

```
        P--E--I
 1)    H..L..7
 2)    J..M..8
 3)    K..N..A
 4)    L..O..B
 5)    M..P..C
 6)    N..Q..D
 7)    O..R..E
 8)    P..S..F
 9)    Q..T..G
10)    R..U..H
11)    S..V..J
12)    T..W..K
13)    U..X..L
14)    V..Y..M
15)    W..Z..N
16)    X..1..O
17)    A..2..P
18)    B..3..Q
19)    C..A..R
20)    D..B..S
21)    E..C..T
22)    F..D..U
23)    G..E..V
24)    H..F..W
25)    J..G..X
26)    K..H..Y
27)    L..J..Z
28)    M..K..1
29)    N..L..2
30)    O..M..3
31)    P..N..4
```

CODES: P-PHYSICAL BIORHYTHM CURVE,E-EMOTIONAL BIORHYTHM CURVE,I-INTELLECTUAL BIORHYTHM CURVE

...JANUARY..	..FEBRUARY..	...MARCH...	...APRIL...	....MAY....	....JUNE....
P--E--I	P--E--I	P--E--I	P--E--I	P--E--I	P--E--I
1) Q..O..5	1) A..R..3	1) F..R..X	1) O..U..V	1) V..W..S	1) F..Z..Q
2) R..P..6	2) B..S..4	2) G..S..Y	2) P..V..W	2) W..X..T	2) G..1..R
3) S..Q..7	3) C..T..5	3) H..T..Z	3) Q..W..X	3) X..Y..U	3) H..2..S
4) T..R..8	4) D..U..6	4) J..U..1	4) R..X..Y	4) A..Z..V	4) J..3..T
5) U..S..A	5) E..V..7	5) K..V..2	5) S..Y..Z	5) B..1..W	5) K..A..U
6) V..T..B	6) F..W..8	6) L..W..3	6) T..Z..1	6) C..2..X	6) L..B..V
7) W..U..C	7) G..X..A	7) M..X..4	7) U..1..2	7) D..3..Y	7) M..C..W
8) X..V..D	8) H..Y..B	8) N..Y..5	8) V..2..3	8) E..A..Z	8) N..D..X
9) A..W..E	9) J..Z..C	9) O..Z..6	9) W..3..4	9) F..B..1	9) O..E..Y
10) B..X..F	10) K..1..D	10) P..1..7	10) X..A..5	10) G..C..2	10) P..F..Z
11) C..Y..G	11) L..2..E	11) Q..2..8	11) A..B..6	11) H..D..3	11) Q..G..1
12) D..Z..H	12) M..3..F	12) R..3..A	12) B..C..7	12) J..E..4	12) R..H..2
13) E..1..J	13) N..A..G	13) S..A..B	13) C..D..8	13) K..F..5	13) S..J..3
14) F..2..K	14) O..B..H	14) T..B..C	14) D..E..A	14) L..G..6	14) T..K..4
15) G..3..L	15) P..C..J	15) U..C..D	15) E..F..B	15) M..H..7	15) U..L..5
16) H..A..M	16) Q..D..K	16) V..D..E	16) F..G..C	16) N..J..8	16) V..M..6
17) J..B..N	17) R..E..L	17) W..E..F	17) G..H..D	17) O..K..A	17) W..N..7
18) K..C..O	18) S..F..M	18) X..F..G	18) H..J..E	18) P..L..B	18) X..O..8
19) L..D..P	19) T..G..N	19) A..G..H	19) J..K..F	19) Q..M..C	19) A..P..A
20) M..E..Q	20) U..H..O	20) B..H..J	20) K..L..G	20) R..N..D	20) B..Q..B
21) N..F..R	21) V..J..P	21) C..J..K	21) L..M..H	21) S..O..E	21) C..R..C
22) O..G..S	22) W..K..Q	22) D..K..L	22) M..N..J	22) T..P..F	22) D..S..D
23) P..H..T	23) X..L..R	23) E..L..M	23) N..O..K	23) U..Q..G	23) E..T..E
24) Q..J..U	24) A..M..S	24) F..M..N	24) O..P..L	24) V..R..H	24) F..U..F
25) R..K..V	25) B..N..T	25) G..N..O	25) P..Q..M	25) W..S..J	25) G..V..G
26) S..L..W	26) C..O..U	26) H..O..P	26) Q..R..N	26) X..T..K	26) H..W..H
27) T..M..X	27) D..P..V	27) J..P..Q	27) R..S..O	27) A..U..L	27) J..X..J
28) U..N..Y	28) E..Q..W	28) K..Q..R	28) S..T..P	28) B..V..M	28) K..Y..K
29) V..O..Z		29) L..R..S	29) T..U..Q	29) C..W..N	29) L..Z..L
30) W..P..1		30) M..S..T	30) U..V..R	30) D..X..O	30) M..1..M
31) X..Q..2		31) N..T..U		31) E..Y..P	

....JULY....	...AUGUST...	.SEPTEMBER.	..OCTOBER...	..NOVEMBER..	..DECEMBER..
P--E--I	P--E--I	P--E--I	P--E--I	P--E--I	P--E--I
1) N..2..N	1) V..B..L	1) F..E..J	1) N..G..F	1) V..K..D	1) E..M..A
2) O..3..O	2) W..C..M	2) G..F..K	2) O..H..G	2) W..L..E	2) F..N..B
3) P..A..P	3) X..D..N	3) H..G..L	3) P..J..H	3) X..M..F	3) G..O..C
4) Q..B..Q	4) A..E..O	4) J..H..M	4) Q..K..J	4) A..N..G	4) H..P..D
5) R..C..R	5) B..F..P	5) K..J..N	5) R..L..K	5) B..O..H	5) J..Q..E
6) S..D..S	6) C..G..Q	6) L..K..O	6) S..M..L	6) C..P..J	6) K..R..F
7) T..E..T	7) D..H..R	7) M..L..P	7) T..N..M	7) D..Q..K	7) L..S..G
8) U..F..U	8) E..J..S	8) N..M..Q	8) U..O..N	8) E..R..L	8) M..T..H
9) V..G..V	9) F..K..T	9) O..N..R	9) V..P..O	9) F..S..M	9) N..U..J
10) W..H..W	10) G..L..U	10) P..O..S	10) W..Q..P	10) G..T..N	10) O..V..K
11) X..J..X	11) H..M..V	11) Q..P..T	11) X..R..Q	11) H..U..O	11) P..W..L
12) A..K..Y	12) J..N..W	12) R..Q..U	12) A..S..R	12) J..V..P	12) Q..X..M
13) B..L..Z	13) K..O..X	13) S..R..V	13) B..T..S	13) K..W..Q	13) R..Y..N
14) C..M..1	14) L..P..Y	14) T..S..W	14) C..U..T	14) L..X..R	14) S..Z..O
15) D..N..2	15) M..Q..Z	15) U..T..X	15) D..V..U	15) M..Y..S	15) T..1..P
16) E..O..3	16) N..R..1	16) V..U..Y	16) E..W..V	16) N..Z..T	16) U..2..Q
17) F..P..4	17) O..S..2	17) W..V..Z	17) F..X..W	17) O..1..U	17) V..3..R
18) G..Q..5	18) P..T..3	18) X..W..1	18) G..Y..X	18) P..2..V	18) W..A..S
19) H..R..6	19) Q..U..4	19) A..X..2	19) H..Z..Y	19) Q..3..W	19) X..B..T
20) J..S..7	20) R..V..5	20) B..Y..3	20) J..1..Z	20) R..A..X	20) A..C..U
21) K..T..8	21) S..W..6	21) C..Z..4	21) K..2..1	21) S..B..Y	21) B..D..V
22) L..U..A	22) T..X..7	22) D..1..5	22) L..3..2	22) T..C..Z	22) C..E..W
23) M..V..B	23) U..Y..8	23) E..2..6	23) M..A..3	23) U..D..1	23) D..F..X
24) N..W..C	24) V..Z..A	24) F..3..7	24) N..B..4	24) V..E..2	24) E..G..Y
25) O..X..D	25) W..1..B	25) G..A..8	25) O..C..5	25) W..F..3	25) F..H..Z
26) P..Y..E	26) X..2..C	26) H..B..A	26) P..D..6	26) X..G..4	26) G..J..1
27) Q..Z..F	27) A..3..D	27) J..C..B	27) Q..E..7	27) A..H..5	27) H..K..2
28) R..1..G	28) B..A..E	28) K..D..C	28) R..F..8	28) B..J..6	28) J..L..3
29) S..2..H	29) C..B..F	29) L..E..D	29) S..G..A	29) C..K..7	29) K..M..4
30) T..3..J	30) D..C..G	30) M..F..E	30) T..H..B	30) D..L..8	30) L..N..5
31) U..A..K	31) E..D..H		31) U..J..C		31) M..O..6

CODES: P-PHYSICAL BIORHYTHM CURVE,E-EMOTIONAL BIORHYTHM CURVE,I-INTELLECTUAL BIORHYTHM CURVE

```
...JANUARY..      ..FEBRUARY..      ....MARCH...      ....APRIL...      ....MAY....      ....JUNE....

   P--E--I           P--E--I           P--E--I           P--E--I           P--E--I           P--E--I

 1) N..P..7       1) V..S..5       1) C..S..Z       1) L..V..X       1) S..X..U       1) C..1..S
 2) O..Q..8       2) W..T..6       2) D..T..1       2) M..W..Y       2) T..Y..V       2) D..2..T
 3) P..R..A       3) X..U..7       3) E..U..2       3) N..X..Z       3) U..Z..W       3) E..3..U
 4) Q..S..B       4) A..V..8       4) F..V..3       4) O..Y..1       4) V..1..X       4) F..A..V
 5) R..T..C       5) B..W..A       5) G..W..4       5) P..Z..2       5) W..2..Y       5) G..B..W
 6) S..U..D       6) C..X..B       6) H..X..5       6) Q..1..3       6) X..3..Z       6) H..C..X
 7) T..V..E       7) D..Y..C       7) J..Y..6       7) R..2..4       7) A..A..1       7) J..D..Y
 8) U..W..F       8) E..Z..D       8) K..Z..7       8) S..3..5       8) B..B..2       8) K..E..Z
 9) V..X..G       9) F..1..E       9) L..1..8       9) T..A..6       9) C..C..3       9) L..F..1
10) W..Y..H      10) G..2..F      10) M..2..A      10) U..B..7      10) D..D..4      10) M..G..2
11) X..Z..J      11) H..3..G      11) N..3..B      11) V..C..8      11) E..E..5      11) N..H..3
12) A..1..K      12) J..A..H      12) O..A..C      12) W..D..A      12) F..F..6      12) O..J..4
13) B..2..L      13) K..B..J      13) P..B..D      13) X..E..B      13) G..G..7      13) P..K..5
14) C..3..M      14) L..C..K      14) Q..C..E      14) A..F..C      14) H..H..8      14) Q..L..6
15) D..A..N      15) M..D..L      15) R..D..F      15) B..G..D      15) J..J..A      15) R..M..7
16) E..B..O      16) N..E..M      16) S..E..G      16) C..H..E      16) K..K..B      16) S..N..8
17) F..C..P      17) O..F..N      17) T..F..H      17) D..J..F      17) L..L..C      17) T..O..A
18) G..D..Q      18) P..G..O      18) U..G..J      18) E..K..G      18) M..M..D      18) U..P..B
19) H..E..R      19) Q..H..P      19) V..H..K      19) F..L..H      19) N..N..E      19) V..Q..C
20) J..F..S      20) R..J..Q      20) W..J..L      20) G..M..J      20) O..O..F      20) W..R..D
21) K..G..T      21) S..K..R      21) X..K..M      21) H..N..K      21) P..P..G      21) X..S..E
22) L..H..U      22) T..L..S      22) A..L..N      22) J..O..L      22) Q..Q..H      22) A..T..F
23) M..J..V      23) U..M..T      23) B..M..O      23) K..P..M      23) R..R..J      23) B..U..G
24) N..K..W      24) V..N..U      24) C..N..P      24) L..Q..N      24) S..S..K      24) C..V..H
25) O..L..X      25) W..O..V      25) D..O..Q      25) M..R..O      25) T..T..L      25) D..W..J
26) P..M..Y      26) X..P..W      26) E..P..R      26) N..S..P      26) U..U..M      26) E..X..K
27) Q..N..Z      27) A..Q..X      27) F..Q..S      27) O..T..Q      27) V..V..N      27) F..Y..L
28) R..O..1      28) B..R..Y      28) G..R..T      28) P..U..R      28) W..W..O      28) G..Z..M
29) S..P..2                       29) H..S..U      29) Q..V..S      29) X..X..P      29) H..1..N
30) T..Q..3                       30) J..T..V      30) R..W..T      30) A..Y..Q      30) J..2..O
31) U..R..4                       31) K..U..W                       31) B..Z..R
```

```
....JULY....      ...AUGUST...      ..SEPTEMBER.      ..OCTOBER...      ..NOVEMBER..      ..DECEMBER..

   P--E--I           P--E--I           P--E--I           P--E--I           P--E--I           P--E--I

 1) K..3..P       1) S..C..N       1) C..F..L       1) K..H..H       1) S..L..F       1) B..N..C
 2) L..A..Q       2) T..D..O       2) D..G..M       2) L..J..J       2) T..M..G       2) C..O..D
 3) M..B..R       3) U..E..P       3) E..H..N       3) M..K..K       3) U..N..H       3) D..P..E
 4) N..C..S       4) V..F..Q       4) F..J..O       4) N..L..L       4) V..O..J       4) E..Q..F
 5) O..D..T       5) W..G..R       5) G..K..P       5) O..M..M       5) W..P..K       5) F..R..G
 6) P..E..U       6) X..H..S       6) H..L..Q       6) P..N..N       6) X..Q..L       6) G..S..H
 7) Q..F..V       7) A..J..T       7) J..M..R       7) Q..O..O       7) A..R..M       7) H..T..J
 8) R..G..W       8) B..K..U       8) K..N..S       8) R..P..P       8) B..S..N       8) J..U..K
 9) S..H..X       9) C..L..V       9) L..O..T       9) S..Q..Q       9) C..T..O       9) K..V..L
10) T..J..Y      10) D..M..W      10) M..P..U      10) T..R..R      10) D..U..P      10) L..W..M
11) U..K..Z      11) E..N..X      11) N..Q..V      11) U..S..S      11) E..V..Q      11) M..X..N
12) V..L..1      12) F..O..Y      12) O..R..W      12) V..T..T      12) F..W..R      12) N..Y..O
13) W..M..2      13) G..P..Z      13) P..S..X      13) W..U..U      13) G..X..S      13) O..Z..P
14) X..N..3      14) H..Q..1      14) Q..T..Y      14) X..V..V      14) H..Y..T      14) P..1..Q
15) A..O..4      15) J..R..2      15) R..U..Z      15) A..W..W      15) J..Z..U      15) Q..2..R
16) B..P..5      16) K..S..3      16) S..V..1      16) B..X..X      16) K..1..V      16) R..3..S
17) C..Q..6      17) L..T..4      17) T..W..2      17) C..Y..Y      17) L..2..W      17) S..A..T
18) D..R..7      18) M..U..5      18) U..X..3      18) D..Z..Z      18) M..3..X      18) T..B..U
19) E..S..8      19) N..V..6      19) V..Y..4      19) E..1..1      19) N..A..Y      19) U..C..V
20) F..T..A      20) O..W..7      20) W..Z..5      20) F..2..2      20) O..B..Z      20) V..D..W
21) G..U..B      21) P..X..8      21) X..1..6      21) G..3..3      21) P..C..1      21) W..E..X
22) H..V..C      22) Q..Y..A      22) A..2..7      22) H..A..4      22) Q..D..2      22) X..F..Y
23) J..W..D      23) R..Z..B      23) B..3..8      23) J..B..5      23) R..E..3      23) A..G..Z
24) K..X..E      24) S..1..C      24) C..A..A      24) K..C..6      24) S..F..4      24) B..H..1
25) L..Y..F      25) T..2..D      25) D..B..B      25) L..D..7      25) T..G..5      25) C..J..2
26) M..Z..G      26) U..3..E      26) E..C..C      26) M..E..8      26) U..H..6      26) D..K..3
27) N..1..H      27) V..A..F      27) F..D..D      27) N..F..A      27) V..J..7      27) E..L..4
28) O..2..J      28) W..B..G      28) G..E..E      28) O..G..B      28) W..K..8      28) F..M..5
29) P..3..K      29) X..C..H      29) H..F..F      29) P..H..C      29) X..L..A      29) G..N..6
30) Q..A..L      30) A..D..J      30) J..G..G      30) Q..J..D      30) A..M..B      30) H..O..7
31) R..B..M      31) B..E..K                       31) R..K..E                       31) J..P..8
```

CODES: P-PHYSICAL BIORHYTHM CURVE,E-EMOTIONAL BIORHYTHM CURVE,I-INTELLECTUAL BIORHYTHM CURVE

	...JANUARY..	..FEBRUARY..	...MARCH...	...APRIL...	....MAY....	....JUNE....
	P--E--I	P--E--I	P--E--I	P--E--I	P--E--I	P--E--I
1)	K..Q..A	S..T..7	A..U..3	J..X..1	Q..Z..X	A..3..V
2)	L..R..B	T..U..8	B..V..4	K..Y..2	R..1..Y	B..A..W
3)	M..S..C	U..V..A	C..W..5	L..Z..3	S..2..Z	C..B..X
4)	N..T..D	V..W..B	D..X..6	M..1..4	T..3..1	D..C..Y
5)	O..U..E	W..X..C	E..Y..7	N..2..5	U..A..2	E..D..Z
6)	P..V..F	X..Y..D	F..Z..8	O..3..6	V..B..3	F..E..1
7)	Q..W..G	A..Z..E	G..1..A	P..A..7	W..C..4	G..F..2
8)	R..X..H	B..1..F	H..2..B	Q..B..8	X..D..5	H..G..3
9)	S..Y..J	C..2..G	J..3..C	R..C..A	A..E..6	J..H..4
10)	T..Z..K	D..3..H	K..A..D	S..D..B	B..F..7	K..J..5
11)	U..1..L	E..A..J	L..B..E	T..E..C	C..G..8	L..K..6
12)	V..2..M	F..B..K	M..C..F	U..F..D	D..H..A	M..L..7
13)	W..3..N	G..C..L	N..D..G	V..G..E	E..J..B	N..M..8
14)	X..A..O	H..D..M	O..E..H	W..H..F	F..K..C	O..N..A
15)	A..B..P	J..E..N	P..F..J	X..J..G	G..L..D	P..O..B
16)	B..C..Q	K..F..O	Q..G..K	A..K..H	H..M..E	Q..P..C
17)	C..D..R	L..G..P	R..H..L	B..L..J	J..N..F	R..Q..D
18)	D..E..S	M..H..Q	S..J..M	C..M..K	K..O..G	S..R..E
19)	E..F..T	N..J..R	T..K..N	D..N..L	L..P..H	T..S..F
20)	F..G..U	O..K..S	U..L..O	E..O..M	M..Q..J	U..T..G
21)	G..H..V	P..L..T	V..M..P	F..P..N	N..R..K	V..U..H
22)	H..J..W	Q..M..U	W..N..Q	G..Q..O	O..S..L	W..V..J
23)	J..K..X	R..N..V	X..O..R	H..R..P	P..T..M	X..W..K
24)	K..L..Y	S..O..W	A..P..S	J..S..Q	Q..U..N	A..X..L
25)	L..M..Z	T..P..X	B..Q..T	K..T..R	R..V..O	B..Y..M
26)	M..N..1	U..Q..Y	C..R..U	L..U..S	S..W..P	C..Z..N
27)	N..O..2	V..R..Z	D..S..V	M..V..T	T..X..Q	D..1..O
28)	O..P..3	W..S..1	E..T..W	N..W..U	U..Y..R	E..2..P
29)	P..Q..4	X..T..2	F..U..X	O..X..V	V..Z..S	F..3..Q
30)	Q..R..5		G..V..Y	P..Y..W	W..1..T	G..A..R
31)	R..S..6		H..W..Z		X..2..U	

	....JULY....	...AUGUST...	..SEPTEMBER.	..OCTOBER...	..NOVEMBER..	..DECEMBER..
	P--E--I	P--E--I	P--E--I	P--E--I	P--E--I	P--E--I
1)	H..B..S	Q..E..Q	A..H..O	H..K..L	Q..N..J	X..P..F
2)	J..C..T	R..F..R	B..J..P	J..L..M	R..O..K	A..Q..G
3)	K..D..U	S..G..S	C..K..Q	K..M..N	S..P..L	B..R..H
4)	L..E..V	T..H..T	D..L..R	L..N..O	T..Q..M	C..S..J
5)	M..F..W	U..J..U	E..M..S	M..O..P	U..R..N	D..T..K
6)	N..G..X	V..K..V	F..N..T	N..P..Q	V..S..O	E..U..L
7)	O..H..Y	W..L..W	G..O..U	O..Q..R	W..T..P	F..V..M
8)	P..J..Z	X..M..X	H..P..V	P..R..S	X..U..Q	G..W..N
9)	Q..K..1	A..N..Y	J..Q..W	Q..S..T	A..V..R	H..X..O
10)	R..L..2	B..O..Z	K..R..X	R..T..U	B..W..S	J..Y..P
11)	S..M..3	C..P..1	L..S..Y	S..U..V	C..X..T	K..Z..Q
12)	T..N..4	D..Q..2	M..T..Z	T..V..W	D..Y..U	L..1..R
13)	U..O..5	E..R..3	N..U..1	U..W..X	E..Z..V	M..2..S
14)	V..P..6	F..S..4	O..V..2	V..X..Y	F..1..W	N..3..T
15)	W..Q..7	G..T..5	P..W..3	W..Y..Z	G..2..X	O..A..U
16)	X..R..8	H..U..6	Q..X..4	X..Z..1	H..3..Y	P..B..V
17)	A..S..A	J..V..7	R..Y..5	A..1..2	J..A..Z	Q..C..W
18)	B..T..B	K..W..8	S..Z..6	B..2..3	K..B..1	R..D..X
19)	C..U..C	L..X..A	T..1..7	C..3..4	L..C..2	S..E..Y
20)	D..V..D	M..Y..B	U..2..8	D..A..5	M..D..3	T..F..Z
21)	E..W..E	N..Z..C	V..3..A	E..B..6	N..E..4	U..G..1
22)	F..X..F	O..1..D	W..A..B	F..C..7	O..F..5	V..H..2
23)	G..Y..G	P..2..E	X..B..C	G..D..8	P..G..6	W..J..3
24)	H..Z..H	Q..3..F	A..C..D	H..E..A	Q..H..7	X..K..4
25)	J..1..J	R..A..G	B..D..E	J..F..B	R..J..8	A..L..5
26)	K..2..K	S..B..H	C..E..F	K..G..C	S..K..A	B..M..6
27)	L..3..L	T..C..J	D..F..G	L..H..D	T..L..B	C..N..7
28)	M..A..M	U..D..K	E..G..H	M..J..E	U..M..C	D..O..8
29)	N..B..N	V..E..L	F..H..J	N..K..F	V..N..D	E..P..A
30)	O..C..O	W..F..M	G..J..K	O..L..G	W..O..E	F..Q..B
31)	P..D..P	X..G..N		P..M..H		G..R..C

CODES: P-PHYSICAL BIORHYTHM CURVE, E-EMOTIONAL BIORHYTHM CURVE, I-INTELLECTUAL BIORHYTHM CURVE

...JANUARY..

Day	P	E	I
1)	H	S	D
2)	J	T	E
3)	K	U	F
4)	L	V	G
5)	M	W	H
6)	N	X	J
7)	O	Y	K
8)	P	Z	L
9)	Q	1	M
10)	R	2	N
11)	S	3	O
12)	T	A	P
13)	U	B	Q
14)	V	C	R
15)	W	D	S
16)	X	E	T
17)	A	F	U
18)	B	G	V
19)	C	H	W
20)	D	J	X
21)	E	K	Y
22)	F	L	Z
23)	G	M	1
24)	H	N	2
25)	J	O	3
26)	K	P	4
27)	L	Q	5
28)	M	R	6
29)	N	S	7
30)	O	T	8
31)	P	U	A

..FEBRUARY..

Day	P	E	I
1)	Q	V	B
2)	R	W	C
3)	S	X	D
4)	T	Y	E
5)	U	Z	F
6)	V	1	G
7)	W	2	H
8)	X	3	J
9)	A	A	K
10)	B	B	L
11)	C	C	M
12)	D	D	N
13)	E	E	O
14)	F	F	P
15)	G	G	Q
16)	H	H	R
17)	J	J	S
18)	K	K	T
19)	L	L	U
20)	M	M	V
21)	N	N	W
22)	O	O	X
23)	P	P	Y
24)	Q	Q	Z
25)	R	R	1
26)	S	S	2
27)	T	T	3
28)	U	U	4

...MARCH...

Day	P	E	I
1)	V	V	5
2)	W	W	6
3)	X	X	7
4)	A	Y	8
5)	B	Z	A
6)	C	1	B
7)	D	2	C
8)	E	3	D
9)	F	A	E
10)	G	B	F
11)	H	C	G
12)	J	D	H
13)	K	E	J
14)	L	F	K
15)	M	G	L
16)	N	H	M
17)	O	J	N
18)	P	K	O
19)	Q	L	P
20)	R	M	Q
21)	S	N	R
22)	T	O	S
23)	U	P	T
24)	V	Q	U
25)	W	R	V
26)	X	S	W
27)	A	T	X
28)	B	U	Y
29)	C	V	Z
30)	D	W	1
31)	E	X	2

...APRIL...

Day	P	E	I
1)	F	Y	3
2)	G	Z	4
3)	H	1	5
4)	J	2	6
5)	K	3	7
6)	L	A	8
7)	M	B	A
8)	N	C	B
9)	O	D	C
10)	P	E	D
11)	Q	F	E
12)	R	G	F
13)	S	H	G
14)	T	J	H
15)	U	K	J
16)	V	L	K
17)	W	M	L
18)	X	N	M
19)	A	O	N
20)	B	P	O
21)	C	Q	P
22)	D	R	Q
23)	E	S	R
24)	F	T	S
25)	G	U	T
26)	H	V	U
27)	J	W	V
28)	K	X	W
29)	L	Y	X
30)	M	Z	Y

....MAY....

Day	P	E	I
1)	N	1	Z
2)	O	2	1
3)	P	3	2
4)	Q	A	3
5)	R	B	4
6)	S	C	5
7)	T	D	6
8)	U	E	7
9)	V	F	8
10)	W	G	A
11)	X	H	B
12)	A	J	C
13)	B	K	D
14)	C	L	E
15)	D	M	F
16)	E	N	G
17)	F	O	H
18)	G	P	J
19)	H	Q	K
20)	J	R	L
21)	K	S	M
22)	L	T	N
23)	M	U	O
24)	N	V	P
25)	O	W	Q
26)	P	X	R
27)	Q	Y	S
28)	R	Z	T
29)	S	1	U
30)	T	2	V
31)	U	3	W

...JUNE....

Day	P	E	I
1)	V	A	X
2)	W	B	Y
3)	X	C	Z
4)	A	D	1
5)	B	E	2
6)	C	F	3
7)	D	G	4
8)	E	H	5
9)	F	J	6
10)	G	K	7
11)	H	L	8
12)	J	M	A
13)	K	N	B
14)	L	O	C
15)	M	P	D
16)	N	Q	E
17)	O	R	F
18)	P	S	G
19)	Q	T	H
20)	R	U	J
21)	S	V	K
22)	T	W	L
23)	U	X	M
24)	V	Y	N
25)	W	Z	O
26)	X	1	P
27)	A	2	Q
28)	B	3	R
29)	C	A	S
30)	D	B	T

....JULY....

Day	P	E	I
1)	E	C	U
2)	F	D	V
3)	G	E	W
4)	H	F	X
5)	J	G	Y
6)	K	H	Z
7)	L	J	1
8)	M	K	2
9)	N	L	3
10)	O	M	4
11)	P	N	5
12)	Q	O	6
13)	R	P	7
14)	S	Q	8
15)	T	R	A
16)	U	S	B
17)	V	T	C
18)	W	U	D
19)	X	V	E
20)	A	W	F
21)	B	X	G
22)	C	Y	H
23)	D	Z	J
24)	E	1	K
25)	F	2	L
26)	G	3	M
27)	H	A	N
28)	J	B	O
29)	K	C	P
30)	L	D	Q
31)	M	E	R

...AUGUST...

Day	P	E	I
1)	N	F	S
2)	O	G	T
3)	P	H	U
4)	Q	J	V
5)	R	K	W
6)	S	L	X
7)	T	M	Y
8)	U	N	Z
9)	V	O	1
10)	W	P	2
11)	X	Q	3
12)	A	R	4
13)	B	S	5
14)	C	T	6
15)	D	U	7
16)	E	V	8
17)	F	W	A
18)	G	X	B
19)	H	Y	C
20)	J	Z	D
21)	K	1	E
22)	L	2	F
23)	M	3	G
24)	N	A	H
25)	O	B	J
26)	P	C	K
27)	Q	D	L
28)	R	E	M
29)	S	F	N
30)	T	G	O
31)	U	H	P

.SEPTEMBER.

Day	P	E	I
1)	V	J	Q
2)	W	K	R
3)	X	L	S
4)	A	M	T
5)	B	N	U
6)	C	O	V
7)	D	P	W
8)	E	Q	X
9)	F	R	Y
10)	G	S	Z
11)	H	T	1
12)	J	U	2
13)	K	V	3
14)	L	W	4
15)	M	X	5
16)	N	Y	6
17)	O	Z	7
18)	P	1	8
19)	Q	2	A
20)	R	3	B
21)	S	A	C
22)	T	B	D
23)	U	C	E
24)	V	D	F
25)	W	E	G
26)	X	F	H
27)	A	G	J
28)	B	H	K
29)	C	J	L
30)	D	K	M

..OCTOBER...

Day	P	E	I
1)	E	L	N
2)	F	M	O
3)	G	N	P
4)	H	O	Q
5)	J	P	R
6)	K	Q	S
7)	L	R	T
8)	M	S	U
9)	N	T	V
10)	O	U	W
11)	P	V	X
12)	Q	W	Y
13)	R	X	Z
14)	S	Y	1
15)	T	Z	2
16)	U	1	3
17)	V	2	4
18)	W	3	5
19)	X	A	6
20)	A	B	7
21)	B	C	8
22)	C	D	A
23)	D	E	B
24)	E	F	C
25)	F	G	D
26)	G	H	E
27)	H	J	F
28)	J	K	G
29)	K	L	H
30)	L	M	J
31)	M	N	K

..NOVEMBER..

Day	P	E	I
1)	N	O	L
2)	O	P	M
3)	P	Q	N
4)	Q	R	O
5)	R	S	P
6)	S	T	Q
7)	T	U	R
8)	U	V	S
9)	V	W	T
10)	W	X	U
11)	X	Y	V
12)	A	Z	W
13)	B	1	X
14)	C	2	Y
15)	D	3	Z
16)	E	A	1
17)	F	B	2
18)	G	C	3
19)	H	D	4
20)	J	E	5
21)	K	F	6
22)	L	G	7
23)	M	H	8
24)	N	J	A
25)	O	K	B
26)	P	L	C
27)	Q	M	D
28)	R	N	E
29)	S	O	F
30)	T	P	G

..DECEMBER..

Day	P	E	I
1)	U	Q	H
2)	V	R	J
3)	W	S	K
4)	X	T	L
5)	A	U	M
6)	B	V	N
7)	C	W	O
8)	D	X	P
9)	E	Y	Q
10)	F	Z	R
11)	G	1	S
12)	H	2	T
13)	J	3	U
14)	K	A	V
15)	L	B	W
16)	M	C	X
17)	N	D	Y
18)	O	E	Z
19)	P	F	1
20)	Q	G	2
21)	R	H	3
22)	S	J	4
23)	T	K	5
24)	U	L	6
25)	V	M	7
26)	W	N	8
27)	X	O	A
28)	A	P	B
29)	B	Q	C
30)	C	R	D
31)	D	S	E

CODES: P-PHYSICAL BIORHYTHM CURVE, E-EMOTIONAL BIORHYTHM CURVE, I-INTELLECTUAL BIORHYTHM CURVE

...JANUARY..	.FEBRUARY..	...MARCH...	...APRIL...	....MAY....	...JUNE....
P--E--I	P--E--I	P--E--I	P--E--I	P--E--I	P--E--I
1) E..T..F	1) N..W..D	1) S..W..7	1) C..Z..5	1) K..2..2	1) S..B..Z
2) F..U..G	2) O..X..E	2) T..X..8	2) D..1..6	2) L..3..3	2) T..C..1
3) G..V..H	3) P..Y..F	3) U..Y..A	3) E..2..7	3) M..A..4	3) U..D..2
4) H..W..J	4) Q..Z..G	4) V..Z..B	4) F..3..8	4) N..B..5	4) V..E..3
5) J..X..K	5) R..1..H	5) W..1..C	5) G..A..A	5) O..C..6	5) W..F..4
6) K..Y..L	6) S..2..J	6) X..2..D	6) H..B..B	6) P..D..7	6) X..G..5
7) L..Z..M	7) T..3..K	7) A..3..E	7) J..C..C	7) Q..E..8	7) A..H..6
8) M..1..N	8) U..A..L	8) B..A..F	8) K..D..D	8) R..F..A	8) B..J..7
9) N..2..O	9) V..B..M	9) C..B..G	9) L..E..E	9) S..G..B	9) C..K..8
10) O..3..P	10) W..C..N	10) D..C..H	10) M..F..F	10) T..H..C	10) D..L..A
11) P..A..Q	11) X..D..O	11) E..D..J	11) N..G..G	11) U..J..D	11) E..M..B
12) Q..B..R	12) A..E..P	12) F..E..K	12) O..H..H	12) V..K..E	12) F..N..C
13) R..C..S	13) B..F..Q	13) G..F..L	13) P..J..J	13) W..L..F	13) G..O..D
14) S..D..T	14) C..G..R	14) H..G..M	14) Q..K..K	14) X..M..G	14) H..P..E
15) T..E..U	15) D..H..S	15) J..H..N	15) R..L..L	15) A..N..H	15) J..Q..F
16) U..F..V	16) E..J..T	16) K..J..O	16) S..M..M	16) B..O..J	16) K..R..G
17) V..G..W	17) F..K..U	17) L..K..P	17) T..N..N	17) C..P..K	17) L..S..H
18) W..H..X	18) G..L..V	18) M..L..Q	18) U..O..O	18) D..Q..L	18) M..T..J
19) X..J..Y	19) H..M..W	19) N..M..R	19) V..P..P	19) E..R..M	19) N..U..K
20) A..K..Z	20) J..N..X	20) O..N..S	20) W..Q..Q	20) F..S..N	20) O..V..L
21) B..L..1	21) K..O..Y	21) P..O..T	21) X..R..R	21) G..T..O	21) P..W..M
22) C..M..2	22) L..P..Z	22) Q..P..U	22) A..S..S	22) H..U..P	22) Q..X..N
23) D..N..3	23) M..Q..1	23) R..Q..V	23) B..T..T	23) J..V..Q	23) R..Y..O
24) E..O..4	24) N..R..2	24) S..R..W	24) C..U..U	24) K..W..R	24) S..Z..P
25) F..P..5	25) O..S..3	25) T..S..X	25) D..V..V	25) L..X..S	25) T..1..Q
26) G..Q..6	26) P..T..4	26) U..T..Y	26) E..W..W	26) M..Y..T	26) U..2..R
27) H..R..7	27) Q..U..5	27) V..U..Z	27) F..X..X	27) N..Z..U	27) V..3..S
28) J..S..8	28) R..V..6	28) W..V..1	28) G..Y..Y	28) O..1..V	28) W..A..T
29) K..T..A		29) X..W..2	29) H..Z..Z	29) P..2..W	29) X..B..U
30) L..U..B		30) A..X..3	30) J..1..1	30) Q..3..X	30) A..C..V
31) M..V..C		31) B..Y..4		31) R..A..Y	

....JULY....	...AUGUST...	.SEPTEMBER.	.OCTOBER...	.NOVEMBER..	.DECEMBER..
P--E--I	P--E--I	P--E--I	P--E--I	P--E--I	P--E--I
1) B..D..W	1) K..G..U	1) S..K..S	1) B..M..P	1) K..P..N	1) R..R..K
2) C..E..X	2) L..H..V	2) T..L..T	2) C..N..Q	2) L..Q..O	2) S..S..L
3) D..F..Y	3) M..J..W	3) U..M..U	3) D..O..R	3) M..R..P	3) T..T..M
4) E..G..Z	4) N..K..X	4) V..N..V	4) E..P..S	4) N..S..Q	4) U..U..N
5) F..H..1	5) O..L..Y	5) W..O..W	5) F..Q..T	5) O..T..R	5) V..V..O
6) G..J..2	6) P..M..Z	6) X..P..X	6) G..R..U	6) P..U..S	6) W..W..P
7) H..K..3	7) Q..N..1	7) A..Q..Y	7) H..S..V	7) Q..V..T	7) X..X..Q
8) J..L..4	8) R..O..2	8) B..R..Z	8) J..T..W	8) R..W..U	8) A..Y..R
9) K..M..5	9) S..P..3	9) C..S..1	9) K..U..X	9) S..X..V	9) B..Z..S
10) L..N..6	10) T..Q..4	10) D..T..2	10) L..V..Y	10) T..Y..W	10) C..1..T
11) M..O..7	11) U..R..5	11) E..U..3	11) M..W..Z	11) U..Z..X	11) D..2..U
12) N..P..8	12) V..S..6	12) F..V..4	12) N..X..1	12) V..1..Y	12) E..3..V
13) O..Q..A	13) W..T..7	13) G..W..5	13) O..Y..2	13) W..2..Z	13) F..A..W
14) P..R..B	14) X..U..8	14) H..X..6	14) P..Z..3	14) X..3..1	14) G..B..X
15) Q..S..C	15) A..V..A	15) J..Y..7	15) Q..1..4	15) A..A..2	15) H..C..Y
16) R..T..D	16) B..W..B	16) K..Z..8	16) R..2..5	16) B..B..3	16) J..D..Z
17) S..U..E	17) C..X..C	17) L..1..A	17) S..3..6	17) C..C..4	17) K..E..1
18) T..V..F	18) D..Y..D	18) M..2..B	18) T..A..7	18) D..D..5	18) L..F..2
19) U..W..G	19) E..Z..E	19) N..3..C	19) U..B..8	19) E..E..6	19) M..G..3
20) V..X..H	20) F..1..F	20) O..A..D	20) V..C..A	20) F..F..7	20) N..H..4
21) W..Y..J	21) G..2..G	21) P..B..E	21) W..D..B	21) G..G..8	21) O..J..5
22) X..Z..K	22) H..3..H	22) Q..C..F	22) X..E..C	22) H..H..A	22) P..K..6
23) A..1..L	23) J..A..J	23) R..D..G	23) A..F..D	23) J..J..B	23) Q..L..7
24) B..2..M	24) K..B..K	24) S..E..H	24) B..G..E	24) K..K..C	24) R..M..8
25) C..3..N	25) L..C..L	25) T..F..J	25) C..H..F	25) L..L..D	25) S..N..A
26) D..A..O	26) M..D..M	26) U..G..K	26) D..J..G	26) M..M..E	26) T..O..B
27) E..B..P	27) N..E..N	27) V..H..L	27) E..K..H	27) N..N..F	27) U..P..C
28) F..C..Q	28) O..F..O	28) W..J..M	28) F..L..J	28) O..O..G	28) V..Q..D
29) G..D..R	29) P..G..P	29) X..K..N	29) G..M..K	29) P..P..H	29) W..R..E
30) H..E..S	30) Q..H..Q	30) A..L..O	30) H..N..L	30) Q..Q..J	30) X..S..F
31) J..F..T	31) R..J..R		31) J..O..M		31) A..T..G

CODES: P-PHYSICAL BIORHYTHM CURVE, E-EMOTIONAL BIORHYTHM CURVE, I-INTELLECTUAL BIORHYTHM CURVE

```
...JANUARY..      ..FEBRUARY..      ...MARCH...       ...APRIL...       .....MAY....      ....JUNE....

     P--E--I           P--E--I           P--E--I           P--E--I           P--E--I           P--E--I

 1)  B..U..H       1)  K..X..F       1)  P..X..A       1)  X..1..7       1)  G..3..4       1)  P..C..2
 2)  C..V..J       2)  L..Y..G       2)  Q..Y..B       2)  A..2..8       2)  H..A..5       2)  Q..D..3
 3)  D..W..K       3)  M..Z..H       3)  R..Z..C       3)  B..3..A       3)  J..B..6       3)  R..E..4
 4)  E..X..L       4)  N..1..J       4)  S..1..D       4)  C..A..B       4)  K..C..7       4)  S..F..5
 5)  F..Y..M       5)  O..2..K       5)  T..2..E       5)  D..B..C       5)  L..D..8       5)  T..G..6
 6)  G..Z..N       6)  P..3..L       6)  U..3..F       6)  E..C..D       6)  M..E..A       6)  U..H..7
 7)  H..1..O       7)  Q..A..M       7)  V..A..G       7)  F..D..E       7)  N..F..B       7)  V..J..8
 8)  J..2..P       8)  R..B..N       8)  W..B..H       8)  G..E..F       8)  O..G..C       8)  W..K..A
 9)  K..3..Q       9)  S..C..O       9)  X..C..J       9)  H..F..G       9)  P..H..D       9)  X..L..B
10)  L..A..R      10)  T..D..P      10)  A..D..K      10)  J..G..H      10)  Q..J..E      10)  A..M..C
11)  M..B..S      11)  U..E..Q      11)  B..E..L      11)  K..H..J      11)  R..K..F      11)  B..N..D
12)  N..C..T      12)  V..F..R      12)  C..F..M      12)  L..J..K      12)  S..L..G      12)  C..O..E
13)  O..D..U      13)  W..G..S      13)  D..G..N      13)  M..K..L      13)  T..M..H      13)  D..P..F
14)  P..E..V      14)  X..H..T      14)  E..H..O      14)  N..L..M      14)  U..N..J      14)  E..Q..G
15)  Q..F..W      15)  A..J..U      15)  F..J..P      15)  O..M..N      15)  V..O..K      15)  F..R..H
16)  R..G..X      16)  B..K..V      16)  G..K..Q      16)  P..N..O      16)  W..P..L      16)  G..S..J
17)  S..H..Y      17)  C..L..W      17)  H..L..R      17)  Q..O..P      17)  X..Q..M      17)  H..T..K
18)  T..J..Z      18)  D..M..X      18)  J..M..S      18)  R..P..Q      18)  A..R..N      18)  J..U..L
19)  U..K..1      19)  E..N..Y      19)  K..N..T      19)  S..Q..R      19)  B..S..O      19)  K..V..M
20)  V..L..2      20)  F..O..Z      20)  L..O..U      20)  T..R..S      20)  C..T..P      20)  L..W..N
21)  W..M..3      21)  G..P..1      21)  M..P..V      21)  U..S..T      21)  D..U..Q      21)  M..X..O
22)  X..N..4      22)  H..Q..2      22)  N..Q..W      22)  V..T..U      22)  E..V..R      22)  N..Y..P
23)  A..O..5      23)  J..R..3      23)  O..R..X      23)  W..U..V      23)  F..W..S      23)  O..Z..Q
24)  B..P..6      24)  K..S..4      24)  P..S..Y      24)  X..V..W      24)  G..X..T      24)  P..1..R
25)  C..Q..7      25)  L..T..5      25)  Q..T..Z      25)  A..W..X      25)  H..Y..U      25)  Q..2..S
26)  D..R..8      26)  M..U..6      26)  R..U..1      26)  B..X..Y      26)  J..Z..V      26)  R..3..T
27)  E..S..A      27)  N..V..7      27)  S..V..2      27)  C..Y..Z      27)  K..1..W      27)  S..A..U
28)  F..T..B      28)  O..W..8      28)  T..W..3      28)  D..Z..1      28)  L..2..X      28)  T..B..V
29)  G..U..C                        29)  U..X..4      29)  E..1..2      29)  M..3..Y      29)  U..C..W
30)  H..V..D                        30)  V..Y..5      30)  F..2..3      30)  N..A..Z      30)  V..D..X
31)  J..W..E                        31)  W..Z..6                        31)  O..B..1
```

```
....JULY....      ...AUGUST...      ..SEPTEMBER.      ..OCTOBER...      ..NOVEMBER..      ..DECEMBER..

     P--E--I           P--E--I           P--E--I           P--E--I           P--E--I           P--E--I

 1)  W..E..Y       1)  G..H..W       1)  P..L..U       1)  W..N..R       1)  G..Q..P       1)  O..S..M
 2)  X..F..Z       2)  H..J..X       2)  Q..M..V       2)  X..O..S       2)  H..R..Q       2)  P..T..N
 3)  A..G..1       3)  J..K..Y       3)  R..N..W       3)  A..P..T       3)  J..S..R       3)  Q..U..O
 4)  B..H..2       4)  K..L..Z       4)  S..O..X       4)  B..Q..U       4)  K..T..S       4)  R..V..P
 5)  C..J..3       5)  L..M..1       5)  T..P..Y       5)  C..R..V       5)  L..U..T       5)  S..W..Q
 6)  D..K..4       6)  M..N..2       6)  U..Q..Z       6)  D..S..W       6)  M..V..U       6)  T..X..R
 7)  E..L..5       7)  N..O..3       7)  V..R..1       7)  E..T..X       7)  N..W..V       7)  U..Y..S
 8)  F..M..6       8)  O..P..4       8)  W..S..2       8)  F..U..Y       8)  O..X..W       8)  V..Z..T
 9)  G..N..7       9)  P..Q..5       9)  X..T..3       9)  G..V..Z       9)  P..Y..X       9)  W..1..U
10)  H..O..8      10)  Q..R..6      10)  A..U..4      10)  H..W..1      10)  Q..Z..Y      10)  X..2..V
11)  J..P..A      11)  R..S..7      11)  B..V..5      11)  J..X..2      11)  R..1..Z      11)  A..3..W
12)  K..Q..B      12)  S..T..8      12)  C..W..6      12)  K..Y..3      12)  S..2..1      12)  B..A..X
13)  L..R..C      13)  T..U..A      13)  D..X..7      13)  L..Z..4      13)  T..3..2      13)  C..B..Y
14)  M..S..D      14)  U..V..B      14)  E..Y..8      14)  M..1..5      14)  U..A..3      14)  D..C..Z
15)  N..T..E      15)  V..W..C      15)  F..Z..A      15)  N..2..6      15)  V..B..4      15)  E..D..1
16)  O..U..F      16)  W..X..D      16)  G..1..B      16)  O..3..7      16)  W..C..5      16)  F..E..2
17)  P..V..G      17)  X..Y..E      17)  H..2..C      17)  P..A..8      17)  X..D..6      17)  G..F..3
18)  Q..W..H      18)  A..Z..F      18)  J..3..D      18)  Q..B..A      18)  A..E..7      18)  H..G..4
19)  R..X..J      19)  B..1..G      19)  K..A..E      19)  R..C..B      19)  B..F..8      19)  J..H..5
20)  S..Y..K      20)  C..2..H      20)  L..B..F      20)  S..D..C      20)  C..G..A      20)  K..J..6
21)  T..Z..L      21)  D..3..J      21)  M..C..G      21)  T..E..D      21)  D..H..B      21)  L..K..7
22)  U..1..M      22)  E..A..K      22)  N..D..H      22)  U..F..E      22)  E..J..C      22)  M..L..8
23)  V..2..N      23)  F..B..L      23)  O..E..J      23)  V..G..F      23)  F..K..D      23)  N..M..A
24)  W..3..O      24)  G..C..M      24)  P..F..K      24)  W..H..G      24)  G..L..E      24)  O..N..B
25)  X..A..P      25)  H..D..N      25)  Q..G..L      25)  X..J..H      25)  H..M..F      25)  P..O..C
26)  A..B..Q      26)  J..E..O      26)  R..H..M      26)  A..K..J      26)  J..N..G      26)  Q..P..D
27)  B..C..R      27)  K..F..P      27)  S..J..N      27)  B..L..K      27)  K..O..H      27)  R..Q..E
28)  C..D..S      28)  L..G..Q      28)  T..K..O      28)  C..M..L      28)  L..P..J      28)  S..R..F
29)  D..E..T      29)  M..H..R      29)  U..L..P      29)  D..N..M      29)  M..Q..K      29)  T..S..G
30)  E..F..U      30)  N..J..S      30)  V..M..Q      30)  E..O..N      30)  N..R..L      30)  U..T..H
31)  F..G..V      31)  O..K..T                        31)  F..P..O                        31)  V..U..J
```

CODES: P-PHYSICAL BIORHYTHM CURVE,E-EMOTIONAL BIORHYTHM CURVE,I-INTELLECTUAL BIORHYTHM CURVE

	JANUARY P--E--I	FEBRUARY P--E--I	MARCH P--E--I	APRIL P--E--I	MAY P--E--I	JUNE P--E--I
1)	W..V..K	G..Y..H	N..Z..D	V..3..B	E..B..7	N..E..5
2)	X..W..L	H..Z..J	O..1..E	W..A..C	F..C..8	O..F..6
3)	A..X..M	J..1..K	P..2..F	X..B..D	G..D..A	P..G..7
4)	B..Y..N	K..2..L	Q..3..G	A..C..E	H..E..B	Q..H..8
5)	C..Z..O	L..3..M	R..A..H	B..D..F	J..F..C	R..J..A
6)	D..1..P	M..A..N	S..B..J	C..E..G	K..G..D	S..K..B
7)	E..2..Q	N..B..O	T..C..K	D..F..H	L..H..E	T..L..C
8)	F..3..R	O..C..P	U..D..L	E..G..J	M..J..F	U..M..D
9)	G..A..S	P..D..Q	V..E..M	F..H..K	N..K..G	V..N..E
10)	H..B..T	Q..E..R	W..F..N	G..J..L	O..L..H	W..O..F
11)	J..C..U	R..F..S	X..G..O	H..K..M	P..M..J	X..P..G
12)	K..D..V	S..G..T	A..H..P	J..L..N	Q..N..K	A..Q..H
13)	L..E..W	T..H..U	B..J..Q	K..M..O	R..O..L	B..R..J
14)	M..F..X	U..J..V	C..K..R	L..N..P	S..P..M	C..S..K
15)	N..G..Y	V..K..W	D..L..S	M..O..Q	T..Q..N	D..T..L
16)	O..H..Z	W..L..X	E..M..T	N..P..R	U..R..O	E..U..M
17)	P..J..1	X..M..Y	F..N..U	O..Q..S	V..S..P	F..V..N
18)	Q..K..2	A..N..Z	G..O..V	P..R..T	W..T..Q	G..W..O
19)	R..L..3	B..O..1	H..P..W	Q..S..U	X..U..R	H..X..P
20)	S..M..4	C..P..2	J..Q..X	R..T..V	A..V..S	J..Y..Q
21)	T..N..5	D..Q..3	K..R..Y	S..U..W	B..W..T	K..Z..R
22)	U..O..6	E..R..4	L..S..Z	T..V..X	C..X..U	L..1..S
23)	V..P..7	F..S..5	M..T..1	U..W..Y	D..Y..V	M..2..T
24)	W..Q..8	G..T..6	N..U..2	V..X..Z	E..Z..W	N..3..U
25)	X..R..A	H..U..7	O..V..3	W..Y..1	F..1..X	O..A..V
26)	A..S..B	J..V..8	P..W..4	X..Z..2	G..2..Y	P..B..W
27)	B..T..C	K..W..A	Q..X..5	A..1..3	H..3..Z	Q..C..X
28)	C..U..D	L..X..B	R..Y..6	B..2..4	J..A..1	R..D..Y
29)	D..V..E	M..Y..C	S..Z..7	C..3..5	K..B..2	S..E..Z
30)	E..W..F		T..1..8	D..A..6	L..C..3	T..F..1
31)	F..X..G		U..2..A		M..D..4	

	JULY P--E--I	AUGUST P--E--I	SEPTEMBER P--E--I	OCTOBER P--E--I	NOVEMBER P--E--I	DECEMBER P--E--I
1)	U..G..2	E..K..Z	N..N..X	U..P..U	E..S..S	M..U..P
2)	V..H..3	F..L..1	O..O..Y	V..Q..V	F..T..T	N..V..Q
3)	W..J..4	G..M..2	P..P..Z	W..R..W	G..U..U	O..W..R
4)	X..K..5	H..N..3	Q..Q..1	X..S..X	H..V..V	P..X..S
5)	A..L..6	J..O..4	R..R..2	A..T..Y	J..W..W	Q..Y..T
6)	B..M..7	K..P..5	S..S..3	B..U..Z	K..X..X	R..Z..U
7)	C..N..8	L..Q..6	T..T..4	C..V..1	L..Y..Y	S..1..V
8)	D..O..A	M..R..7	U..U..5	D..W..2	M..Z..Z	T..2..W
9)	E..P..B	N..S..8	V..V..6	E..X..3	N..1..1	U..3..X
10)	F..Q..C	O..T..A	W..W..7	F..Y..4	O..2..2	V..A..Y
11)	G..R..D	P..U..B	X..X..8	G..Z..5	P..3..3	W..B..Z
12)	H..S..E	Q..V..C	A..Y..A	H..1..6	Q..A..4	X..C..1
13)	J..T..F	R..W..D	B..Z..B	J..2..7	R..B..5	A..D..2
14)	K..U..G	S..X..E	C..1..C	K..3..8	S..C..6	B..E..3
15)	L..V..H	T..Y..F	D..2..D	L..A..A	T..D..7	C..F..4
16)	M..W..J	U..Z..G	E..3..E	M..B..B	U..E..8	D..G..5
17)	N..X..K	V..1..H	F..A..F	N..C..C	V..F..A	E..H..6
18)	O..Y..L	W..2..J	G..B..G	O..D..D	W..G..B	F..J..7
19)	P..Z..M	X..3..K	H..C..H	P..E..E	X..H..C	G..K..8
20)	Q..1..N	A..A..L	J..D..J	Q..F..F	A..J..D	H..L..A
21)	R..2..O	B..B..M	K..E..K	R..G..G	B..K..E	J..M..B
22)	S..3..P	C..C..N	L..F..L	S..H..H	C..L..F	K..N..C
23)	T..A..Q	D..D..O	M..G..M	T..J..J	D..M..G	L..O..D
24)	U..B..R	E..E..P	N..H..N	U..K..K	E..N..H	M..P..E
25)	V..C..S	F..F..Q	O..J..O	V..L..L	F..O..J	N..Q..F
26)	W..D..T	G..G..R	P..K..P	W..M..M	G..P..K	O..R..G
27)	X..E..U	H..H..S	Q..L..Q	X..N..N	H..Q..L	P..S..H
28)	A..F..V	J..J..T	R..M..R	A..O..O	J..R..M	Q..T..J
29)	B..G..W	K..K..U	S..N..S	B..P..P	K..S..N	R..U..K
30)	C..H..X	L..L..V	T..O..T	C..Q..Q	L..T..O	S..V..L
31)	D..J..Y	M..M..W		D..R..R		T..W..M

CODES: P-PHYSICAL BIORHYTHM CURVE, E-EMOTIONAL BIORHYTHM CURVE, I-INTELLECTUAL BIORHYTHM CURVE

	...JANUARY..	..FEBRUARY..	...MARCH...	...APRIL...	....MAY....	...JUNE....
	P--E--I	P--E--I	P--E--I	P--E--I	P--E--I	P--E--I
1)	U..X..N	E..1..L	K..1..F	S..A..D	B..C..A	K..F..7
2)	V..Y..O	F..2..M	L..2..G	T..B..E	C..D..B	L..G..8
3)	W..Z..P	G..3..N	M..3..H	U..C..F	D..E..C	M..H..A
4)	X..1..Q	H..A..O	N..A..J	V..D..G	E..F..D	N..J..B
5)	A..2..R	J..B..P	O..B..K	W..E..H	F..G..E	O..K..C
6)	B..3..S	K..C..Q	P..C..L	X..F..J	G..H..F	P..L..D
7)	C..A..T	L..D..R	Q..D..M	A..G..K	H..J..G	Q..M..E
8)	D..B..U	M..E..S	R..E..N	B..H..L	J..K..H	R..N..F
9)	E..C..V	N..F..T	S..F..O	C..J..M	K..L..J	S..O..G
10)	F..D..W	O..G..U	T..G..P	D..K..N	L..M..K	T..P..H
11)	G..E..X	P..H..V	U..H..Q	E..L..O	M..N..L	U..Q..J
12)	H..F..Y	Q..J..W	V..J..R	F..M..P	N..O..M	V..R..K
13)	J..G..Z	R..K..X	W..K..S	G..N..Q	O..P..N	W..S..L
14)	K..H..1	S..L..Y	X..L..T	H..O..R	P..Q..O	X..T..M
15)	L..J..2	T..M..Z	A..M..U	J..P..S	Q..R..P	A..U..N
16)	M..K..3	U..N..1	B..N..V	K..Q..T	R..S..Q	B..V..O
17)	N..L..4	V..O..2	C..O..W	L..R..U	S..T..R	C..W..P
18)	O..M..5	W..P..3	D..P..X	M..S..V	T..U..S	D..X..Q
19)	P..N..6	X..Q..4	E..Q..Y	N..T..W	U..V..T	E..Y..R
20)	Q..O..7	A..R..5	F..R..Z	O..U..X	V..W..U	F..Z..S
21)	R..P..8	B..S..6	G..S..1	P..V..Y	W..X..V	G..1..T
22)	S..Q..A	C..T..7	H..T..2	Q..W..Z	X..Y..W	H..2..U
23)	T..R..B	D..U..8	J..U..3	R..X..1	A..Z..X	J..3..V
24)	U..S..C	E..V..A	K..V..4	S..Y..2	B..1..Y	K..A..W
25)	V..T..D	F..W..B	L..W..5	T..Z..3	C..2..Z	L..B..X
26)	W..U..E	G..X..C	M..X..6	U..1..4	D..3..1	M..C..Y
27)	X..V..F	H..Y..D	N..Y..7	V..2..5	E..A..2	N..D..Z
28)	A..W..G	J..Z..E	O..Z..8	W..3..6	F..B..3	O..E..1
29)	B..X..H		P..1..A	X..A..7	G..C..4	P..F..2
30)	C..Y..J		Q..2..B	A..B..8	H..D..5	Q..G..3
31)	D..Z..K		R..3..C		J..E..6	

	....JULY....	...AUGUST...	..SEPTEMBER.	..OCTOBER...	.NOVEMBER..	.DECEMBER..
	P--E--I	P--E--I	P--E--I	P--E--I	P--E--I	P--E--I
1)	R..H..4	B..L..2	K..O..Z	R..Q..W	B..T..U	J..V..R
2)	S..J..5	C..M..3	L..P..1	S..R..X	C..U..V	K..W..S
3)	T..K..6	D..N..4	M..Q..2	T..S..Y	D..V..W	L..X..T
4)	U..L..7	E..O..5	N..R..3	U..T..Z	E..W..X	M..Y..U
5)	V..M..8	F..P..6	O..S..4	V..U..1	F..X..Y	N..Z..V
6)	W..N..A	G..Q..7	P..T..5	W..V..2	G..Y..Z	O..1..W
7)	X..O..B	H..R..8	Q..U..6	X..W..3	H..Z..1	P..2..X
8)	A..P..C	J..S..A	R..V..7	A..X..4	J..1..2	Q..3..Y
9)	B..Q..D	K..T..B	S..W..8	B..Y..5	K..2..3	R..A..Z
10)	C..R..E	L..U..C	T..X..A	C..Z..6	L..3..4	S..B..1
11)	D..S..F	M..V..D	U..Y..B	D..1..7	M..A..5	T..C..2
12)	E..T..G	N..W..E	V..Z..C	E..2..8	N..B..6	U..D..3
13)	F..U..H	O..X..F	W..1..D	F..3..A	O..C..7	V..E..4
14)	G..V..J	P..Y..G	X..2..E	G..A..B	P..D..8	W..F..5
15)	H..W..K	Q..Z..H	A..3..F	H..B..C	Q..E..A	X..G..6
16)	J..X..L	R..1..J	B..A..G	J..C..D	R..F..B	A..H..7
17)	K..Y..M	S..2..K	C..B..H	K..D..E	S..G..C	B..J..8
18)	L..Z..N	T..3..L	D..C..J	L..E..F	T..H..D	C..K..A
19)	M..1..O	U..A..M	E..D..K	M..F..G	U..J..E	D..L..B
20)	N..2..P	V..B..N	F..E..L	N..G..H	V..K..F	E..M..C
21)	O..3..Q	W..C..O	G..F..M	O..H..J	W..L..G	F..N..D
22)	P..A..R	X..D..P	H..G..N	P..J..K	X..M..H	G..O..E
23)	Q..B..S	A..E..Q	J..H..O	Q..K..L	A..N..J	H..P..F
24)	R..C..T	B..F..R	K..J..P	R..L..M	B..O..K	J..Q..G
25)	S..D..U	C..G..S	L..K..Q	S..M..N	C..P..L	K..R..H
26)	T..E..V	D..H..T	M..L..R	T..N..O	D..Q..M	L..S..J
27)	U..F..W	E..J..U	N..M..S	U..O..P	E..R..N	M..T..K
28)	V..G..X	F..K..V	O..N..T	V..P..Q	F..S..O	N..U..L
29)	W..H..Y	G..L..W	P..O..U	W..Q..R	G..T..P	O..V..M
30)	X..J..Z	H..M..X	Q..P..V	X..R..S	H..U..Q	P..W..N
31)	A..K..1	J..N..Y		A..S..T		Q..X..O

CODES: P-PHYSICAL BIORHYTHM CURVE,E-EMOTIONAL BIORHYTHM CURVE,I-INTELLECTUAL BIORHYTHM CURVE

	...JANUARY..	..FEBRUARY..	...MARCH...	...APRIL...	....MAY....	...JUNE....
	P--E--I	P--E--I	P--E--I	P--E--I	P--E--I	P--E--I
1)	R..Y..P	B..2..N	G..2..H	P..B..F	W..D..C	G..G..A
2)	S..Z..Q	C..3..O	H..3..J	Q..C..G	X..E..D	H..H..B
3)	T..1..R	D..A..P	J..A..K	R..D..H	A..F..E	J..J..C
4)	U..2..S	E..B..Q	K..B..L	S..E..J	B..G..F	K..K..D
5)	V..3..T	F..C..R	L..C..M	T..F..K	C..H..G	L..L..E
6)	W..A..U	G..D..S	M..D..N	U..G..L	D..J..H	M..M..F
7)	X..B..V	H..E..T	N..E..O	V..H..M	E..K..J	N..N..G
8)	A..C..W	J..F..U	O..F..P	W..J..N	F..L..K	O..O..H
9)	B..D..X	K..G..V	P..G..Q	X..K..O	G..M..L	P..P..J
10)	C..E..Y	L..H..W	Q..H..R	A..L..P	H..N..M	Q..Q..K
11)	D..F..Z	M..J..X	R..J..S	B..M..Q	J..O..N	R..R..L
12)	E..G..1	N..K..Y	S..K..T	C..N..R	K..P..O	S..S..M
13)	F..H..2	O..L..Z	T..L..U	D..O..S	L..Q..P	T..T..N
14)	G..J..3	P..M..1	U..M..V	E..P..T	M..R..Q	U..U..O
15)	H..K..4	Q..N..2	V..N..W	F..Q..U	N..S..R	V..V..P
16)	J..L..5	R..O..3	W..O..X	G..R..V	O..T..S	W..W..Q
17)	K..M..6	S..P..4	X..P..Y	H..S..W	P..U..T	X..X..R
18)	L..N..7	T..Q..5	A..Q..Z	J..T..X	Q..V..U	A..Y..S
19)	M..O..8	U..R..6	B..R..1	K..U..Y	R..W..V	B..Z..T
20)	N..P..A	V..S..7	C..S..2	L..V..Z	S..X..W	C..1..U
21)	O..Q..B	W..T..8	D..T..3	M..W..1	T..Y..X	D..2..V
22)	P..R..C	X..U..A	E..U..4	N..X..2	U..Z..Y	E..3..W
23)	Q..S..D	A..V..B	F..V..5	O..Y..3	V..1..Z	F..A..X
24)	R..T..E	B..W..C	G..W..6	P..Z..4	W..2..1	G..B..Y
25)	S..U..F	C..X..D	H..X..7	Q..1..5	X..3..2	H..C..Z
26)	T..V..G	D..Y..E	J..Y..8	R..2..6	A..A..3	J..D..1
27)	U..W..H	E..Z..F	K..Z..A	S..3..7	B..B..4	K..E..2
28)	V..X..J	F..1..G	L..1..B	T..A..8	C..C..5	L..F..3
29)	W..Y..K		M..2..C	U..B..A	D..D..6	M..G..4
30)	X..Z..L		N..3..D	V..C..B	E..E..7	N..H..5
31)	A..1..M		O..A..E		F..F..8	

	....JULY....	...AUGUST...	..SEPTEMBER.	..OCTOBER...	.NOVEMBER..	.DECEMBER..
	P--E--I	P--E--I	P--E--I	P--E--I	P--E--I	P--E--I
1)	O..J..6	W..M..4	G..P..2	O..R..Y	W..U..W	F..W..T
2)	P..K..7	X..N..5	H..Q..3	P..S..Z	X..V..X	G..X..U
3)	Q..L..8	A..O..6	J..R..4	Q..T..1	A..W..Y	H..Y..V
4)	R..M..A	B..P..7	K..S..5	R..U..2	B..X..Z	J..Z..W
5)	S..N..B	C..Q..8	L..T..6	S..V..3	C..Y..1	K..1..X
6)	T..O..C	D..R..A	M..U..7	T..W..4	D..Z..2	L..2..Y
7)	U..P..D	E..S..B	N..V..8	U..X..5	E..1..3	M..3..Z
8)	V..Q..E	F..T..C	O..W..A	V..Y..6	F..2..4	N..A..1
9)	W..R..F	G..U..D	P..X..B	W..Z..7	G..3..5	O..B..2
10)	X..S..G	H..V..E	Q..Y..C	X..1..8	H..A..6	P..C..3
11)	A..T..H	J..W..F	R..Z..D	A..2..A	J..B..7	Q..D..4
12)	B..U..J	K..X..G	S..1..E	B..3..B	K..C..8	R..E..5
13)	C..V..K	L..Y..H	T..2..F	C..A..C	L..D..A	S..F..6
14)	D..W..L	M..Z..J	U..3..G	D..B..D	M..E..B	T..G..7
15)	E..X..M	N..1..K	V..A..H	E..C..E	N..F..C	U..H..8
16)	F..Y..N	O..2..L	W..B..J	F..D..F	O..G..D	V..J..A
17)	G..Z..O	P..3..M	X..C..K	G..E..G	P..H..E	W..K..B
18)	H..1..P	Q..A..N	A..D..L	H..F..H	Q..J..F	X..L..C
19)	J..2..Q	R..B..O	B..E..M	J..G..J	R..K..G	A..M..D
20)	K..3..R	S..C..P	C..F..N	K..H..K	S..L..H	B..N..E
21)	L..A..S	T..D..Q	D..G..O	L..J..L	T..M..J	C..O..F
22)	M..B..T	U..E..R	E..H..P	M..K..M	U..N..K	D..P..G
23)	N..C..U	V..F..S	F..J..Q	N..L..N	V..O..L	E..Q..H
24)	O..D..V	W..G..T	G..K..R	O..M..O	W..P..M	F..R..J
25)	P..E..W	X..H..U	H..L..S	P..N..P	X..Q..N	G..S..K
26)	Q..F..X	A..J..V	J..M..T	Q..O..Q	A..R..O	H..T..L
27)	R..G..Y	B..K..W	K..N..U	R..P..R	B..S..P	J..U..M
28)	S..H..Z	C..L..X	L..O..V	S..Q..S	C..T..Q	K..V..N
29)	T..J..1	D..M..Y	M..P..W	T..R..T	D..U..R	L..W..O
30)	U..K..2	E..N..Z	N..Q..X	U..S..U	E..V..S	M..X..P
31)	V..L..3	F..O..1		V..T..V		N..Y..Q

CODES: P-PHYSICAL BIORHYTHM CURVE,E-EMOTIONAL BIORHYTHM CURVE,I-INTELLECTUAL BIORHYTHM CURVE

...JANUARY.. ..FEBRUARY.. ...MARCH... ...APRIL... ....MAY.... ...JUNE....

Day	JANUARY P--E--I	FEBRUARY P--E--I	MARCH P--E--I	APRIL P--E--I	MAY P--E--I	JUNE P--E--I
1)	O..Z..R	W..3..P	D..3..K	M..C..H	T..E..E	D..H..C
2)	P..1..S	X..A..Q	E..A..L	N..D..J	U..F..F	E..J..D
3)	Q..2..T	A..B..R	F..B..M	O..E..K	V..G..G	F..K..E
4)	R..3..U	B..C..S	G..C..N	P..F..L	W..H..H	G..L..F
5)	S..A..V	C..D..T	H..D..O	Q..G..M	X..J..J	H..M..G
6)	T..B..W	D..E..U	J..E..P	R..H..N	A..K..K	J..N..H
7)	U..C..X	E..F..V	K..F..Q	S..J..O	B..L..L	K..O..J
8)	V..D..Y	F..G..W	L..G..R	T..K..P	C..M..M	L..P..K
9)	W..E..Z	G..H..X	M..H..S	U..L..Q	D..N..N	M..Q..L
10)	X..F..1	H..J..Y	N..J..T	V..M..R	E..O..O	N..R..M
11)	A..G..2	J..K..Z	O..K..U	W..N..S	F..P..P	O..S..N
12)	B..H..3	K..L..1	P..L..V	X..O..T	G..Q..Q	P..T..O
13)	C..J..4	L..M..2	Q..M..W	A..P..U	H..R..R	Q..U..P
14)	D..K..5	M..N..3	R..N..X	B..Q..V	J..S..S	R..V..Q
15)	E..L..6	N..O..4	S..O..Y	C..R..W	K..T..T	S..W..R
16)	F..M..7	O..P..5	T..P..Z	D..S..X	L..U..U	T..X..S
17)	G..N..8	P..Q..6	U..Q..1	E..T..Y	M..V..V	U..Y..T
18)	H..O..A	Q..R..7	V..R..2	F..U..Z	N..W..W	V..Z..U
19)	J..P..B	R..S..8	W..S..3	G..V..1	O..X..X	W..1..V
20)	K..Q..C	S..T..A	X..T..4	H..W..2	P..Y..Y	X..2..W
21)	L..R..D	T..U..B	A..U..5	J..X..3	Q..Z..Z	A..3..X
22)	M..S..E	U..V..C	B..V..6	K..Y..4	R..1..1	B..A..Y
23)	N..T..F	V..W..D	C..W..7	L..Z..5	S..2..2	C..B..Z
24)	O..U..G	W..X..E	D..X..8	M..1..6	T..3..3	D..C..1
25)	P..V..H	X..Y..F	E..Y..A	N..2..7	U..A..4	E..D..2
26)	Q..W..J	A..Z..G	F..Z..B	O..3..8	V..B..5	F..E..3
27)	R..X..K	B..1..H	G..1..C	P..A..A	W..C..6	G..F..4
28)	S..Y..L	C..2..J	H..2..D	Q..B..B	X..D..7	H..G..5
29)	T..Z..M		J..3..E	R..C..C	A..E..8	J..H..6
30)	U..1..N		K..A..F	S..D..D	B..F..A	K..J..7
31)	V..2..O		L..B..G		C..G..B	

....JULY.... ...AUGUST... ..SEPTEMBER. ..OCTOBER... .NOVEMBER.. ..DECEMBER..

Day	JULY P--E--I	AUGUST P--E--I	SEPTEMBER P--E--I	OCTOBER P--E--I	NOVEMBER P--E--I	DECEMBER P--E--I
1)	L..K..8	T..N..6	D..Q..4	L..S..1	T..V..Y	C..X..V
2)	M..L..A	U..O..7	E..R..5	M..T..2	U..W..Z	D..Y..W
3)	N..M..B	V..P..8	F..S..6	N..U..3	V..X..1	E..Z..X
4)	O..N..C	W..Q..A	G..T..7	O..V..4	W..Y..2	F..1..Y
5)	P..O..D	X..R..B	H..U..8	P..W..5	X..Z..3	G..2..Z
6)	Q..P..E	A..S..C	J..V..A	Q..X..6	A..1..4	H..3..1
7)	R..Q..F	B..T..D	K..W..B	R..Y..7	B..2..5	J..A..2
8)	S..R..G	C..U..E	L..X..C	S..Z..8	C..3..6	K..B..3
9)	T..S..H	D..V..F	M..Y..D	T..1..A	D..A..7	L..C..4
10)	U..T..J	E..W..G	N..Z..E	U..2..B	E..B..8	M..D..5
11)	V..U..K	F..X..H	O..1..F	V..3..C	F..C..A	N..E..6
12)	W..V..L	G..Y..J	P..2..G	W..A..D	G..D..B	O..F..7
13)	X..W..M	H..Z..K	Q..3..H	X..B..E	H..E..C	P..G..8
14)	A..X..N	J..1..L	R..A..J	A..C..F	J..F..D	Q..H..A
15)	B..Y..O	K..2..M	S..B..K	B..D..G	K..G..E	R..J..B
16)	C..Z..P	L..3..N	T..C..L	C..E..H	L..H..F	S..K..C
17)	D..1..Q	M..A..O	U..D..M	D..F..J	M..J..G	T..L..D
18)	E..2..R	N..B..P	V..E..N	E..G..K	N..K..H	U..M..E
19)	F..3..S	O..C..Q	W..F..O	F..H..L	O..L..J	V..N..F
20)	G..A..T	P..D..R	X..G..P	G..J..M	P..M..K	W..O..G
21)	H..B..U	Q..E..S	A..H..Q	H..K..N	Q..N..L	X..P..H
22)	J..C..V	R..F..T	B..J..R	J..L..O	R..O..M	A..Q..J
23)	K..D..W	S..G..U	C..K..S	K..M..P	S..P..N	B..R..K
24)	L..E..X	T..H..V	D..L..T	L..N..Q	T..Q..O	C..S..L
25)	M..F..Y	U..J..W	E..M..U	M..O..R	U..R..P	D..T..M
26)	N..G..Z	V..K..X	F..N..V	N..P..S	V..S..Q	E..U..N
27)	O..H..1	W..L..Y	G..O..W	O..Q..T	W..T..R	F..V..O
28)	P..J..2	X..M..Z	H..P..X	P..R..U	X..U..S	G..W..P
29)	Q..K..3	A..N..1	J..Q..Y	Q..S..V	A..V..T	H..X..Q
30)	R..L..4	B..O..2	K..R..Z	R..T..W	B..W..U	J..Y..R
31)	S..M..5	C..P..3		S..U..X		K..Z..S

CODES: P-PHYSICAL BIORHYTHM CURVE, E-EMOTIONAL BIORHYTHM CURVE, I-INTELLECTUAL BIORHYTHM CURVE

PHYSICAL

JANUARY 1977 JANUARY 1977

1 SA	2 SU	3 M	4 TU	5 W	6 TH	7 F	8 SA	9 SU	10 M	11 TU	12 W	13 TH	14 F	15 SA	16 SU	17 M	18 TU	19 W	20 TH	21 F	22 SA	23 SU	24 M	25 TU	26 W	27 TH	28 F	29 SA	30 SU	31 M	
DC	ED	FE	GF	HG	JH	KJ	LK	ML	NM	ON	PO	QP	RQ	SR	TS	UT	VU	WV	XW	AX	BA	CB	DC	ED	FE	GF	HG	JH	KJ	LK	
EB	FC	GD	HE	JF	KG	LH	MJ	NK	OL	PM	QN	RO	SP	TQ	UR	VS	WT	XU	AV	BW	CX	DA	EB	FC	GD	HE	JF	KG	LH	MJ	
FA	GB	HC	JD	KE	LF	MG	NH	OJ	PK	QL	RM	SN	TO	UP	VQ	WR	XS	AT	BU	CV	DW	EX	FA	GB	HC	JD	KE	LF	MG	NH	+
GX	HA	JB	KC	LD	ME	NF	OG	PH	QJ	RK	SL	TM	UN	VO	WP	XQ	AR	BS	CT	DU	EV	FW	GX	HA	JB	KC	LD	ME	NF	OG	
HW	JX	KA	LB	MC	ND	OE	PF	QG	RH	SJ	TK	UL	VM	WN	XO	AP	BQ	CR	DS	ET	FU	GV	HW	JX	KA	LB	MC	ND	OE	PF	
JV	KW	LX	MA	NB	OC	PD	QE	RF	SG	TH	UJ	VK	WL	XM	AN	BO	CP	DQ	ER	FS	GT	HU	JV	KW	LX	MA	NB	OC	PD	QE	0
KU	LV	MW	NX	OA	PB	QC	RD	SE	TF	UG	VH	WJ	XK	AL	BM	CN	DO	EP	FQ	GR	HS	JT	KU	LV	MW	NX	OA	PB	QC	RD	
LT	MU	NV	OW	PX	QA	RB	SC	TD	UE	VF	WG	XH	AJ	BK	CL	DM	EN	FO	GP	HQ	JR	KS	LT	MU	NV	OW	PX	QA	RB	SC	
MS	NT	OU	PV	QW	RX	SA	TB	UC	VD	WE	XF	AG	BH	CJ	DK	EL	FM	GN	HO	JP	KQ	LR	MS	NT	OU	PV	QW	RX	SA	TB	−
NR	OS	PT	QU	RV	SW	TX	UA	VB	WC	XD	AE	BF	CG	DH	EJ	FK	GL	HM	JN	KO	LP	MQ	NR	OS	PT	QU	RV	SW	TX	UA	
OQ	PR	QS	RT	SU	TV	UW	VX	WA	XB	AC	BD	CE	DF	EG	FH	GJ	HK	JL	KM	LN	MO	NP	OQ	PR	QS	RT	SU	TV	UW	VX	
P	Q	R	S	T	U	V	W	X	A	B	C	D	E	F	G	H	J	K	L	M	N	O	P	Q	R	S	T	U	V	W	

EMOTIONAL

JANUARY 1977 JANUARY 1977

1 SA	2 SU	3 M	4 TU	5 W	6 TH	7 F	8 SA	9 SU	10 M	11 TU	12 W	13 TH	14 F	15 SA	16 SU	17 M	18 TU	19 W	20 TH	21 F	22 SA	23 SU	24 M	25 TU	26 W	27 TH	28 F	29 SA	30 SU	31 M	
V	W	X	Y	Z	1	2	3	A	B	C	D	E	F	G	H	J	K	L	M	N	O	P	Q	R	S	T	U	V	W	X	
WU	XV	YW	ZX	1Y	2Z	31	A2	B3	CA	DB	EC	FD	GE	HF	JG	KH	LJ	MK	NL	OM	PN	QO	RP	SQ	TR	US	VT	WU	XV	YW	
XT	YU	ZV	1W	2X	3Y	AZ	B1	C2	D3	EA	FB	GC	HD	JE	KF	LG	MH	NJ	OK	PL	QM	RN	SO	TP	UQ	VR	WS	XT	YU	ZV	
YS	ZT	1U	2V	3W	AX	BY	CZ	D1	E2	F3	GA	HB	JC	KD	LE	MF	NG	OH	PJ	QK	RL	SM	TN	UO	VP	WQ	XR	YS	ZT	1U	
ZR	1S	2T	3U	AV	BW	CX	DY	EZ	F1	G2	H3	JA	KB	LC	MD	NE	OF	PG	QH	RJ	SK	TL	UM	VN	WO	XP	YQ	ZR	1S	2T	+
1Q	2R	3S	AT	BU	CV	DW	EX	FY	GZ	H1	J2	K3	LA	MB	NC	OD	PE	QF	RG	SH	TJ	UK	VL	WM	XN	YO	ZP	1Q	2R	3S	
2P	3Q	AR	BS	CT	DU	EV	FW	GX	HY	JZ	K1	L2	M3	NA	OB	PC	QD	RE	SF	TG	UH	VJ	WK	XL	YM	ZN	1O	2P	3Q	AR	
3O	AP	BQ	CR	DS	ET	FU	GV	HW	JX	KY	LZ	M1	N2	O3	PA	QB	RC	SD	TE	UF	VG	WH	XJ	YK	ZL	1M	2N	3O	AP	BQ	0
AN	BO	CP	DQ	ER	FS	GT	HU	JV	KW	LX	MY	NZ	O1	P2	Q3	RA	SB	TC	UD	VE	WF	XG	YH	ZJ	1K	2L	3M	AN	BO	CP	
BM	CN	DO	EP	FQ	GR	HS	JT	KU	LV	MW	NX	OY	PZ	Q1	R2	S3	TA	UB	VC	WD	XE	YF	ZG	1H	2J	3K	AL	BM	CN	DO	
CL	DM	EN	FO	GP	HQ	JR	KS	LT	MU	NV	OW	PX	QY	RZ	S1	T2	U3	VA	WB	XC	YD	ZE	1F	2G	3H	AJ	BK	CL	DM	EN	−
DK	EL	FM	GN	HO	JP	KQ	LR	MS	NT	OU	PV	QW	RX	SY	TZ	U1	V2	W3	XA	YB	ZC	1D	2E	3F	AG	BH	CJ	DK	EL	FM	
EJ	FK	GL	HM	JN	KO	LP	MQ	NR	OS	PT	QU	RV	SW	TX	UY	VZ	W1	X2	Y3	ZA	1B	2C	3D	AE	BF	CG	DH	EJ	FK	GL	
FH	GJ	HK	JL	KM	LN	MO	NP	OQ	PR	QS	RT	SU	TV	UW	VX	WY	XZ	Y1	Z2	13	2A	3B	AC	BD	CE	DF	EG	FH	GJ	HK	
G	H	J	K	L	M	N	O	P	Q	R	S	T	U	V	W	X	Y	Z	1	2	3	A	B	C	D	E	F	G	H	J	

INTELLECTUAL

JANUARY 1977 JANUARY 1977

1 SA	2 SU	3 M	4 TU	5 W	6 TH	7 F	8 SA	9 SU	10 M	11 TU	12 W	13 TH	14 F	15 SA	16 SU	17 M	18 TU	19 W	20 TH	21 F	22 SA	23 SU	24 M	25 TU	26 W	27 TH	28 F	29 SA	30 SU	31 M	
O	P	Q	R	S	T	U	V	W	X	Y	Z	1	2	3	4	5	6	7	8	A	B	C	D	E	F	G	H	J	K	L	
PN	QO	RP	SQ	TR	US	VT	WU	XV	YW	ZX	1Y	2Z	31	42	53	64	75	86	A7	B8	CA	DB	EC	FD	GE	HF	JG	KH	LJ	MK	
QM	RN	SO	TP	UQ	VR	WS	XT	YU	ZV	1W	2X	3Y	4Z	51	62	73	84	A5	B6	C7	D8	EA	FB	GC	HD	JE	KF	LG	MH	NJ	
RL	SM	TN	UO	VP	WQ	XR	YS	ZT	1U	2V	3W	4X	5Y	6Z	71	82	A3	B4	C5	D6	E7	F8	GA	HB	JC	KD	LE	MF	NG	OH	
SK	TL	UM	VN	WO	XP	YQ	ZR	1S	2T	3U	4V	5W	6X	7Y	8Z	A1	B2	C3	D4	E5	F6	G7	H8	JA	KB	LC	MD	NE	OF	PG	
TJ	UK	VL	WM	XN	YO	ZP	1Q	2R	3S	4T	5U	6V	7W	8X	AY	BZ	C1	D2	E3	F4	G5	H6	J7	K8	LA	MB	NC	OD	PE	QF	
UH	VJ	WK	XL	YM	ZN	1O	2P	3Q	4R	5S	6T	7U	8V	AW	BX	CY	DZ	E1	F2	G3	H4	J5	K6	L7	M8	NA	OB	PC	QD	RE	+
VG	WH	XJ	YK	ZL	1M	2N	3O	4P	5Q	6R	7S	8T	AU	BV	CW	DX	EY	FZ	G1	H2	J3	K4	L5	M6	N7	O8	PA	QB	RC	SD	
WF	XG	YH	ZJ	1K	2L	3M	4N	5O	6P	7Q	8R	AS	BT	CU	DV	EW	FX	GY	HZ	J1	K2	L3	M4	N5	O6	P7	Q8	RA	SB	TC	0
XE	YF	ZG	1H	2J	3K	4L	5M	6N	7O	8P	AQ	BR	CS	DT	EU	FV	GW	HX	JY	KZ	L1	M2	N3	O4	P5	Q6	R7	S8	TA	UB	
YD	ZE	1F	2G	3H	4J	5K	6L	7M	8N	AO	BP	CQ	DR	ES	FT	GU	HV	JW	KX	LY	MZ	N1	O2	P3	Q4	R5	S6	T7	U8	VA	−
ZC	1D	2E	3F	4G	5H	6J	7K	8L	AM	BN	CO	DP	EQ	FR	GS	HT	JU	KV	LW	MX	NY	OZ	P1	Q2	R3	S4	T5	U6	V7	W8	
1B	2C	3D	4E	5F	6G	7H	8J	AK	BL	CM	DN	EO	FP	GQ	HR	JS	KT	LU	MV	NW	OX	PY	QZ	R1	S2	T3	U4	V5	W6	X7	
2A	3B	4C	5D	6E	7F	8G	AH	BJ	CK	DL	EM	FN	GO	HP	JQ	KR	LS	MT	NU	OV	PW	QX	RY	SZ	T1	U2	V3	W4	X5	Y6	
38	4A	5B	6C	7D	8E	AF	BG	CH	DJ	EK	FL	GM	HN	JO	KP	LQ	MR	NS	OT	PU	QV	RW	SX	TY	UZ	V1	W2	X3	Y4	Z5	
47	58	6A	7B	8C	AD	BE	CF	DG	EH	FJ	GK	HL	JM	KN	LO	MP	NQ	OR	PS	QT	RU	SV	TW	UX	VY	WZ	X1	Y2	Z3	14	
56	67	78	8A	AB	BC	CD	DE	EF	FG	GH	HJ	JK	KL	LM	MN	NO	OP	PQ	QR	RS	ST	TU	UV	VW	WX	XY	YZ	Z1	12	23	

1 TU	2 W	3 TH	4 F	5 SA	6 SU	7 M	8 TU	9 W	10 TH	11 F	12 SA	13 SU	14 M	15 TU	16 W	17 TH	18 F	19 SA	20 SU	21 M	22 TU	23 W	24 TH	25 F	26 SA	27 SU	28 M
ML	NM	ON	PO	QP	RQ	SR	TS	UT	VU	WV	XW	AX	BA	CB	DC	ED	FE	GF	HG	JH	KJ	LK	ML	NM	ON	PO	QP
NK	OL	PM	QN	RO	SP	TQ	UR	VS	WT	XU	AV	BW	CX	DA	EB	FC	GD	HE	JF	KG	LH	MJ	NK	OL	PM	QN	RO
OJ	PK	QL	RM	SN	TO	UP	VQ	WR	XS	AT	BU	CV	DW	EX	FA	GB	HC	JD	KE	LF	MG	NH	OJ	PK	QL	RM	SN
PH	QJ	RK	SL	TM	UN	VO	WP	XQ	AR	BS	CT	DU	EV	FW	GX	HA	JB	KC	LD	ME	NF	OG	PH	QJ	RK	SL	TM
QG	RH	SJ	TK	UL	VM	WN	XO	AP	BQ	CR	DS	ET	FU	GV	HW	JX	KA	LB	MC	ND	OE	PF	QG	RH	SJ	TK	UL
RF	**SG**	**TH**	**UJ**	**VK**	**WL**	**XM**	**AN**	**BO**	**CP**	**DQ**	**ER**	**FS**	**GT**	**HU**	**JV**	**KW**	**LX**	**MA**	**NB**	**OC**	**PD**	**QE**	**RF**	**SG**	**TH**	**UJ**	**VK**
SE	TF	UG	VH	WJ	XK	AL	BM	CN	DO	EP	FQ	GR	HS	JT	KU	LV	MW	NX	OA	PB	QC	RD	SE	TF	UG	VH	WJ
TD	UE	VF	WG	XH	AJ	BK	CL	DM	EN	FO	GP	HQ	JR	KS	LT	MU	NV	OW	PX	QA	RB	SC	TD	UE	VF	WG	XH
UC	VD	WE	XF	AG	BH	CJ	DK	EL	FM	GN	HO	JP	KQ	LR	MS	NT	OU	PV	QW	RX	SA	TB	UC	VD	WE	XF	AG
VB	WC	XD	AE	BF	CG	DH	EJ	FK	GL	HM	JN	KO	LP	MQ	NR	OS	PT	QU	RV	SW	TX	UA	VB	WC	XD	AE	BF
WA	XB	AC	BD	CE	DF	EG	FH	GJ	HK	JL	KM	LN	MO	NP	OQ	PR	QS	RT	SU	TV	UW	VX	WA	XB	AC	BD	CE
X	A	B	C	D	E	F	G	H	J	K	L	M	N	O	P	Q	R	S	T	U	V	W	X	A	B	C	D

1 TU	2 W	3 TH	4 F	5 SA	6 SU	7 M	8 TU	9 W	10 TH	11 F	12 SA	13 SU	14 M	15 TU	16 W	17 TH	18 F	19 SA	20 SU	21 M	22 TU	23 W	24 TH	25 F	26 SA	27 SU	28 M	
Y	Z	1	2	3	A	B	C	D	E	F	G	H	J	K	L	M	N	O	P	Q	R	S	T	U	V	W	X	
ZX	1Y	2Z	31	A2	B3	CA	DB	EC	FD	GE	HF	JG	KH	LJ	MK	NL	OM	PN	QO	RP	SQ	TR	US	VT	WU	XV	YW	
1W	2X	3Y	AZ	B1	C2	D3	EA	FB	GC	HD	JE	KF	LG	MH	NJ	OK	PL	QM	RN	SO	TP	UQ	VR	WS	XT	YU	ZV	
2V	3W	AX	BY	CZ	D1	E2	F3	GA	HB	JC	KD	LE	MF	NG	OH	PJ	QK	RL	SM	TN	UO	VP	WQ	XR	YS	ZT	1U	
3U	AV	BW	CX	DY	EZ	F1	G2	H3	JA	KB	LC	MD	NE	OF	PG	QH	RJ	SK	TL	UM	VN	WO	XP	YQ	ZR	1S	2T	+
AT	BU	CV	DW	EX	FY	GZ	H1	J2	K3	LA	MB	NC	OD	PE	QF	RG	SH	TJ	UK	VL	WM	XN	YO	ZP	1Q	2R	3S	
BS	CT	DU	EV	FW	GX	HY	JZ	K1	L2	M3	NA	OB	PC	QD	RE	SF	TG	UH	VJ	WK	XL	YM	ZN	1O	2P	3Q	AR	
CR	DS	ET	FU	GV	HW	JX	KY	LZ	M1	N2	O3	PA	QB	RC	SD	TE	UF	VG	WH	XJ	YK	ZL	1M	2N	3O	AP	BQ	0
DQ	ER	FS	GT	HU	JV	KW	LX	MY	NZ	O1	P2	Q3	RA	SB	TC	UD	VE	WF	XG	YH	ZJ	1K	2L	3M	AN	BO	CP	
EP	FQ	GR	HS	JT	KU	LV	MW	NX	OY	PZ	Q1	R2	S3	TA	UB	VC	WD	XE	YF	ZG	1H	2J	3K	AL	BM	CN	DO	—
FO	GP	HQ	JR	KS	LT	MU	NV	OW	PX	QY	RZ	S1	T2	U3	VA	WB	XC	YD	ZE	1F	2G	3H	AJ	BK	CL	DM	EN	
GN	HO	JP	KQ	LR	MS	NT	OU	PV	QW	RX	SY	TZ	U1	V2	W3	XA	YB	ZC	1D	2E	3F	AG	BH	CJ	DK	EL	FM	
HM	JN	KO	LP	MQ	NR	OS	PT	QU	RV	SW	TX	UY	VZ	W1	X2	Y3	ZA	1B	2C	3D	AE	BF	CG	DH	EJ	FK	GL	
JL	KM	LN	MO	NP	OQ	PR	QS	RT	SU	TV	UW	VX	WY	XZ	Y1	Z2	13	2A	3B	AC	BD	CE	DF	EG	FH	GJ	HK	
K	L	M	N	O	P	Q	R	S	T	U	V	W	X	Y	Z	1	2	3	A	B	C	D	E	F	G	H	J	

1 TU	2 W	3 TH	4 F	5 SA	6 SU	7 M	8 TU	9 W	10 TH	11 F	12 SA	13 SU	14 M	15 TU	16 W	17 TH	18 F	19 SA	20 SU	21 M	22 TU	23 W	24 TH	25 F	26 SA	27 SU	28 M
M	N	O	P	Q	R	S	T	U	V	W	X	Y	Z	1	2	3	4	5	6	7	8	A	B	C	D	E	F
NL	OM	PN	QO	RP	SQ	TR	US	VT	WU	XV	YW	ZX	1Y	2Z	31	42	53	64	75	86	A7	B8	CA	DB	EC	FD	GE
OK	PL	QM	RN	SO	TP	UQ	VR	WS	XT	YU	ZV	1W	2X	3Y	4Z	51	62	73	84	A5	B6	C7	D8	EA	FB	GC	HD
PJ	QK	RL	SM	TN	UO	VP	WQ	XR	YS	ZT	1U	2V	3W	4X	5Y	6Z	71	82	A3	B4	C5	D6	E7	F8	GA	HB	JC
QH	RJ	SK	TL	UM	VN	WO	XP	YQ	ZR	1S	2T	3U	4V	5W	6X	7Y	8Z	A1	B2	C3	D4	E5	F6	G7	H8	JA	KB
RG	SH	TJ	UK	VL	WM	XN	YO	ZP	1Q	2R	3S	4T	5U	6V	7W	8X	AY	BZ	C1	D2	E3	F4	G5	H6	J7	K8	LA
SF	TG	UH	VJ	WK	XL	YM	ZN	1O	2P	3Q	4R	5S	6T	7U	8V	AW	BX	CY	DZ	E1	F2	G3	H4	J5	K6	L7	M8
TE	UF	VG	WH	XJ	YK	ZL	1M	2N	3O	4P	5Q	6R	7S	8T	AU	BV	CW	DX	EY	FZ	G1	H2	J3	K4	L5	M6	N7
UD	VE	WF	XG	YH	ZJ	1K	2L	3M	4N	5O	6P	7Q	8R	AS	BT	CU	DV	EW	FX	GY	HZ	J1	K2	L3	M4	N5	O6
VC	WD	XE	YF	ZG	1H	2J	3K	4L	5M	6N	7O	8P	AQ	BR	CS	DT	EU	FV	GW	HX	JY	KZ	L1	M2	N3	O4	P5
WB	XC	YD	ZE	1F	2G	3H	4J	5K	6L	7M	8N	AO	BP	CQ	DR	ES	FT	GU	HV	JW	KX	LY	MZ	N1	O2	P3	Q4
XA	YB	ZC	1D	2E	3F	4G	5H	6J	7K	8L	AM	BN	CO	DP	EQ	FR	GS	HT	JU	KV	LW	MX	NY	OZ	P1	Q2	R3
Y8	ZA	1B	2C	3D	4E	5F	6G	7H	8J	AK	BL	CM	DN	EO	FP	GQ	HR	JS	KT	LU	MV	NW	OX	PY	QZ	R1	S2
Z7	18	2A	3B	4C	5D	6E	7F	8G	AH	BJ	CK	DL	EM	FN	GO	HP	JQ	KR	LS	MT	NU	OV	PW	QX	RY	SZ	T1
16	27	38	4A	5B	6C	7D	8E	AF	BG	CH	DJ	EK	FL	GM	HN	JO	KP	LQ	MR	NS	OT	PU	QV	RW	SX	TY	UZ
25	36	47	58	6A	7B	8C	AD	BE	CF	DG	EH	FJ	GK	HL	JM	KN	LO	MP	NQ	OR	PS	QT	RU	SV	TW	UX	VY
34	45	56	67	78	8A	AB	BC	CD	DE	EF	FG	GH	HJ	JK	KL	LM	MN	NO	OP	PQ	QR	RS	ST	TU	UV	VW	WX

1 TU	2 W	3 TH	4 F	5 SA	6 SU	7 M	8 TU	9 W	10 TH	11 F	12 SA	13 SU	14 M	15 TU	16 W	17 TH	18 F	19 SA	20 SU	21 M	22 TU	23 W	24 TH	25 F	26 SA	27 SU	28 M	29 TU	30 W	31 TH	
RQ	SR	TS	UT	VU	WV	XW	AX	BA	CB	DC	ED	FE	GF	HG	JH	KJ	LK	ML	NM	ON	PO	QP	RQ	SR	TS	UT	VU	WV	XW	AX	
SP	TQ	UR	VS	WT	XU	AV	BW	CX	DA	EB	FC	GD	HE	JF	KG	LH	MJ	NK	OL	PM	QN	RO	SP	TQ	UR	VS	WT	XU	AV	BW	
TO	UP	VQ	WR	XS	AT	BU	CV	DW	EX	FA	GB	HC	JD	KE	LF	MG	NH	OJ	PK	QL	RM	SN	TO	UP	VQ	WR	XS	AT	BU	CV	+
UN	VO	WP	XQ	AR	BS	CT	DU	EV	FW	GX	HA	JB	KC	LD	ME	NF	OG	PH	QJ	RK	SL	TM	UN	VO	WP	XQ	AR	BS	CT	DU	
VM	WN	XO	AP	BQ	CR	DS	ET	FU	GV	HW	JX	KA	LB	MC	ND	OE	PF	QG	RH	SJ	TK	UL	VM	WN	XO	AP	BQ	CR	DS	ET	
WL	XM	AN	BO	CP	DQ	ER	FS	GT	HU	JV	KW	LX	MA	NB	OC	PD	QE	RF	SG	TH	UJ	VK	WL	XM	AN	BO	CP	DQ	ER	FS	0
XK	AL	BM	CN	DO	EP	FQ	GR	HS	JT	KU	LV	MW	NX	OA	PB	QC	RD	SE	TF	UG	VH	WJ	XK	AL	BM	CN	DO	EP	FQ	GR	
AJ	BK	CL	DM	EN	FO	GP	HQ	JR	KS	LT	MU	NV	OW	PX	QA	RB	SC	TD	UE	VF	WG	XH	AJ	BK	CL	DM	EN	FO	GP	HQ	
BH	CJ	DK	EL	FM	GN	HO	JP	KQ	LR	MS	NT	OU	PV	QW	RX	SA	TB	UC	VD	WE	XF	AG	BH	CJ	DK	EL	FM	GN	HO	JP	−
CG	DH	EJ	FK	GL	HM	JN	KO	LP	MQ	NR	OS	PT	QU	RV	SW	TX	UA	VB	WC	XD	AE	BF	CG	DH	EJ	FK	GL	HM	JN	KO	
DF	EG	FH	GJ	HK	JL	KM	LN	MO	NP	OQ	PR	QS	RT	SU	TV	UW	VX	WA	XB	AC	BD	CE	DF	EG	FH	GJ	HK	JL	KM	LN	
E	F	G	H	J	K	L	M	N	O	P	Q	R	S	T	U	V	W	X	A	B	C	D	E	F	G	H	J	K	L	M	

1 TU	2 W	3 TH	4 F	5 SA	6 SU	7 M	8 TU	9 W	10 TH	11 F	12 SA	13 SU	14 M	15 TU	16 W	17 TH	18 F	19 SA	20 SU	21 M	22 TU	23 W	24 TH	25 F	26 SA	27 SU	28 M	29 TU	30 W	31 TH	
Y	Z	1	2	3	A	B	C	D	E	F	G	H	J	K	L	M	N	O	P	Q	R	S	T	U	V	W	X	Y	Z	1	
ZX	1Y	2Z	31	A2	B3	CA	DB	EC	FD	GE	HF	JG	KH	LJ	MK	NL	OM	PN	QO	RP	SQ	TR	US	VT	WU	XV	YW	ZX	1Y	2Z	
1W	2X	3Y	AZ	B1	C2	D3	EA	FB	GC	HD	JE	KF	LG	MH	NJ	OK	PL	QM	RN	SO	TP	UQ	VR	WS	XT	YU	ZV	1W	2X	3Y	+
2V	3W	AX	BY	CZ	D1	E2	F3	GA	HB	JC	KD	LE	MF	NG	OH	PJ	QK	RL	SM	TN	UO	VP	WQ	XR	YS	ZT	1U	2V	3W	AX	
3U	AV	BW	CX	DY	EZ	F1	G2	H3	JA	KB	LC	MD	NE	OF	PG	QH	RJ	SK	TL	UM	VN	WO	XP	YQ	ZR	1S	2T	3U	AV	BW	
AT	BU	CV	DW	EX	FY	GZ	H1	J2	K3	LA	MB	NC	OD	PE	QF	RG	SH	TJ	UK	VL	WM	XN	YO	ZP	1Q	2R	3S	AT	BU	CV	
BS	CT	DU	EV	FW	GX	HY	JZ	K1	L2	M3	NA	OB	PC	QD	RE	SF	TG	UH	VJ	WK	XL	YM	ZN	1O	2P	3Q	AR	BS	CT	DU	
CR	DS	ET	FU	GV	HW	JX	KY	LZ	M1	N2	O3	PA	QB	RC	SD	TE	UF	VG	WH	XJ	YK	ZL	1M	2N	3O	AP	BQ	CR	DS	ET	0
DQ	ER	FS	GT	HU	JV	KW	LX	MY	NZ	O1	P2	Q3	RA	SB	TC	UD	VE	WF	XG	YH	ZJ	1K	2L	3M	AN	BO	CP	DQ	ER	FS	
EP	FQ	GR	HS	JT	KU	LV	MW	NX	OY	PZ	Q1	R2	S3	TA	UB	VC	WD	XE	YF	ZG	1H	2J	3K	AL	BM	CN	DO	EP	FQ	GR	
FO	GP	HQ	JR	KS	LT	MU	NV	OW	PX	QY	RZ	S1	T2	U3	VA	WB	XC	YD	ZE	1F	2G	3H	AJ	BK	CL	DM	EN	FO	GP	HQ	−
GN	HO	JP	KQ	LR	MS	NT	OU	PV	QW	RX	SY	TZ	U1	V2	W3	XA	YB	ZC	1D	2E	3F	AG	BH	CJ	DK	EL	FM	GN	HO	JP	
HM	JN	KO	LP	MQ	NR	OS	PT	QU	RV	SW	TX	UY	VZ	W1	X2	Y3	ZA	1B	2C	3D	AE	BF	CG	DH	EJ	FK	GL	HM	JN	KO	
JL	KM	LN	MO	NP	OQ	PR	QS	RT	SU	TV	UW	VX	WY	XZ	Y1	Z2	13	2A	3B	AC	BD	CE	DF	EG	FH	GJ	HK	JL	KM	LN	
K	L	M	N	O	P	Q	R	S	T	U	V	W	X	Y	Z	1	2	3	A	B	C	D	E	F	G	H	J	K	L	M	

1 TU	2 W	3 TH	4 F	5 SA	6 SU	7 M	8 TU	9 W	10 TH	11 F	12 SA	13 SU	14 M	15 TU	16 W	17 TH	18 F	19 SA	20 SU	21 M	22 TU	23 W	24 TH	25 F	26 SA	27 SU	28 M	29 TU	30 W	31 TH	
G	H	J	K	L	M	N	O	P	Q	R	S	T	U	V	W	X	Y	Z	1	2	3	4	5	6	7	8	A	B	C	D	
HF	JG	KH	LJ	MK	NL	OM	PN	QO	RP	SQ	TR	US	VT	WU	XV	YW	ZX	1Y	2Z	31	42	53	64	75	86	A7	B8	CA	DB	EC	
JE	KF	LG	MH	NJ	OK	PL	QM	RN	SO	TP	UQ	VR	WS	XT	YU	ZV	1W	2X	3Y	4Z	51	62	73	84	A5	B6	C7	D8	EA	FB	
KD	LE	MF	NG	OH	PJ	QK	RL	SM	TN	UO	VP	WQ	XR	YS	ZT	1U	2V	3W	4X	5Y	6Z	71	82	A3	B4	C5	D6	E7	F8	GA	
LC	MD	NE	OF	PG	QH	RJ	SK	TL	UM	VN	WO	XP	YQ	ZR	1S	2T	3U	4V	5W	6X	7Y	8Z	A1	B2	C3	D4	E5	F6	G7	H8	
MB	NC	OD	PE	QF	RG	SH	TJ	UK	VL	WM	XN	YO	ZP	1Q	2R	3S	4T	5U	6V	7W	8X	AY	BZ	C1	D2	E3	F4	G5	H6	J7	+
NA	OB	PC	QD	RE	SF	TG	UH	VJ	WK	XL	YM	ZN	1M	2N	3O	4P	5Q	6R	7S	8T	AU	BV	CW	DX	EY	FZ	G1	H2	J3	K4	
O8	PA	QB	RC	SD	TE	UF	VG	WH	XJ	YK	ZL	1M	2N	3O	4P	5Q	6R	7S	8T	AU	BV	CW	DX	EY	FZ	G1	H2	J3	K4	L5	
P7	Q8	RA	SB	TC	UD	VE	WF	XG	YH	ZJ	1K	2L	3M	4N	5O	6P	7Q	8R	AS	BT	CU	DV	EW	FX	GY	HZ	J1	K2	L3	M4	0
Q6	R7	S8	TA	UB	VC	WD	XE	YF	ZG	1H	2J	3K	4L	5M	6N	7O	8P	AQ	BR	CS	DT	EU	FV	GW	HX	JY	KZ	L1	M2	N3	
R5	S6	T7	U8	VA	WB	XC	YD	ZE	1F	2G	3H	4J	5K	6L	7M	8N	AO	BP	CQ	DR	ES	FT	GU	HV	JW	KX	LY	MZ	N1	O2	
S4	T5	U6	V7	W8	XA	YB	ZC	1D	2E	3F	4G	5H	6J	7K	8L	AM	BN	CO	DP	EQ	FR	GS	HT	JU	KV	LW	MX	NY	OZ	P1	−
T3	U4	V5	W6	X7	Y8	ZA	1B	2C	3D	4E	5F	6G	7H	8J	AK	BL	CM	DN	EO	FP	GQ	HR	JS	KT	LU	MV	NW	OX	PY	QZ	
U2	V3	W4	X5	Y6	Z7	18	2A	3B	4C	5D	6E	7F	8G	AH	BJ	CK	DL	EM	FN	GO	HP	JQ	KR	LS	MT	NU	OV	PW	QX	RY	
V1	W2	X3	Y4	Z5	16	27	38	4A	5B	6C	7D	8E	AF	BG	CH	DJ	EK	FL	GM	HN	JO	KP	LQ	MR	NS	OT	PU	QV	RW	SX	
WZ	X1	Y2	Z3	14	25	36	47	58	6A	7B	8C	AD	BE	CF	DG	EH	FJ	GK	HL	JM	KN	LO	MP	NQ	OR	PS	QT	RU	SV	TW	
XY	YZ	Z1	12	23	34	45	56	67	78	8A	AB	BC	CD	DE	EF	FG	GH	HJ	JK	KL	LM	MN	NO	OP	PQ	QR	RS	ST	TU	UV	

1 F	2 SA	3 SU	4 M	5 TU	6 W	7 TH	8 F	9 SA	10 SU	11 M	12 TU	13 W	14 TH	15 F	16 SA	17 SU	18 M	19 TU	20 W	21 TH	22 F	23 SA	24 SU	25 M	26 TU	27 W	28 TH	29 F	30 SA	
BA	CB	DC	ED	FE	GF	HG	JH	KJ	LK	ML	NM	ON	PO	QP	RQ	SR	TS	UT	VU	WV	XW	AX	BA	CB	DC	ED	FE	GF	HG	
CX	DA	EB	FC	GD	HE	JF	KG	LH	MJ	NK	OL	PM	QN	RO	SP	TQ	UR	VS	WT	XU	AV	BW	CX	DA	EB	FC	GD	HE	JF	
DW	EX	FA	GB	HC	JD	KE	LF	MG	NH	OJ	PK	QL	RM	SN	TO	UP	VQ	WR	XS	AT	BU	CV	DW	EX	FA	GB	HC	JD	KE	+
EV	FW	GX	HA	JB	KC	LD	ME	NF	OG	PH	QJ	RK	SL	TM	UN	VO	WP	XQ	AR	BS	CT	DU	EV	FW	GX	HA	JB	KC	LD	
FU	GV	HW	JX	KA	LB	MC	ND	OE	PF	QG	RH	SJ	TK	UL	VM	WN	XO	AP	BQ	CR	DS	ET	FU	GV	HW	JX	KA	LB	MC	
GT	HU	JV	KW	LX	MA	NB	OC	PD	QE	RF	SG	TH	UJ	VK	WL	XM	AN	BO	CP	DQ	ER	FS	GT	HU	JV	KW	LX	MA	NB	0
HS	JT	KU	LV	MW	NX	OA	PB	QC	RD	SE	TF	UG	VH	WJ	XK	AL	BM	CN	DO	EP	FQ	GR	HS	JT	KU	LV	MW	NX	OA	
JR	KS	LT	MU	NV	OW	PX	QA	RB	SC	TD	UE	VF	WG	XH	AJ	BK	CL	DM	EN	FO	GP	HQ	JR	KS	LT	MU	NV	OW	PX	
KQ	LR	MS	NT	OU	PV	QW	RX	SA	TB	UC	VD	WE	XF	AG	BH	CJ	DK	EL	FM	GN	HO	JP	KQ	LR	MS	NT	OU	PV	QW	−
LP	MQ	NR	OS	PT	QU	RV	SW	TX	UA	VB	WC	XD	AE	BF	CG	DH	EJ	FK	GL	HM	JN	KO	LP	MQ	NR	OS	PT	QU	RV	
MO	NP	OQ	PR	QS	RT	SU	TV	UW	VX	WA	XB	AC	BD	CE	DF	EG	FH	GJ	HK	JL	KM	LN	MO	NP	OQ	PR	QS	RT	SU	
N	O	P	Q	R	S	T	U	V	W	X	A	B	C	D	E	F	G	H	J	K	L	M	N	O	P	Q	R	S	T	

1 F	2 SA	3 SU	4 M	5 TU	6 W	7 TH	8 F	9 SA	10 SU	11 M	12 TU	13 W	14 TH	15 F	16 SA	17 SU	18 M	19 TU	20 W	21 TH	22 F	23 SA	24 SU	25 M	26 TU	27 W	28 TH	29 F	30 SA	
2	3	A	B	C	D	E	F	G	H	J	K	L	M	N	O	P	Q	R	S	T	U	V	W	X	Y	Z	1	2	3	
31	A2	B3	CA	DB	EC	FD	GE	HF	JG	KH	LJ	MK	NL	OM	PN	QO	RP	SQ	TR	US	VT	WU	XV	YW	ZX	1Y	2Z	31	A2	
AZ	B1	C2	D3	EA	FB	GC	HD	JE	KF	LG	MH	NJ	OK	PL	QM	RN	SO	TP	UQ	VR	WS	XT	YU	ZV	1W	2X	3Y	AZ	B1	
BY	CZ	D1	E2	F3	GA	HB	JC	KD	LE	MF	NG	OH	PJ	QK	RL	SM	TN	UO	VP	WQ	XR	YS	ZT	1U	2V	3W	AX	BY	CZ	
CX	DY	EZ	F1	G2	H3	JA	KB	LC	MD	NE	OF	PG	QH	RJ	SK	TL	UM	VN	WO	XP	YQ	ZR	1S	2T	3U	AV	BW	CX	DY	+
DW	EX	FY	GZ	H1	J2	K3	LA	MB	NC	OD	PE	QF	RG	SH	TJ	UK	VL	WM	XN	YO	ZP	1Q	2R	3S	AT	BU	CV	DW	EX	
EV	FW	GX	HY	JZ	K1	L2	M3	NA	OB	PC	QD	RE	SF	TG	UH	VJ	WK	XL	YM	ZN	1O	2P	3Q	AR	BS	CT	DU	EV	FW	
FU	GV	HW	JX	KY	LZ	M1	N2	O3	PA	QB	RC	SD	TE	UF	VG	WH	XJ	YK	ZL	1M	2N	3O	AP	BQ	CR	DS	ET	FU	GV	0
GT	HU	JV	KW	LX	MY	NZ	O1	P2	Q3	RA	SB	TC	UD	VE	WF	XG	YH	ZJ	1K	2L	3M	AN	BO	CP	DQ	ER	FS	GT	HU	
HS	JT	KU	LV	MW	NX	OY	PZ	Q1	R2	S3	TA	UB	VC	WD	XE	YF	ZG	1H	2J	3K	AL	BM	CN	DO	EP	FQ	GR	HS	JT	
JR	KS	LT	MU	NV	OW	PX	QY	RZ	S1	T2	U3	VA	WB	XC	YD	ZE	1F	2G	3H	AJ	BK	CL	DM	EN	FO	GP	HQ	JR	KS	−
KQ	LR	MS	NT	OU	PV	QW	RX	SY	TZ	U1	V2	W3	XA	YB	ZC	1D	2E	3F	AG	BH	CJ	DK	EL	FM	GN	HO	JP	KQ	LR	
LP	MQ	NR	OS	PT	QU	RV	SW	TX	UY	VZ	W1	X2	Y3	ZA	1B	2C	3D	AE	BF	CG	DH	EJ	FK	GL	HM	JN	KO	LP	MQ	
MO	NP	OQ	PR	QS	RT	SU	TV	UW	VX	WY	XZ	Y1	Z2	13	2A	3B	AC	BD	CE	DF	EG	FH	GJ	HK	JL	KM	LN	MO	NP	
N	O	P	Q	R	S	T	U	V	W	X	Y	Z	1	2	3	A	B	C	D	E	F	G	H	J	K	L	M	N	O	

1 F	2 SA	3 SU	4 M	5 TU	6 W	7 TH	8 F	9 SA	10 SU	11 M	12 TU	13 W	14 TH	15 F	16 SA	17 SU	18 M	19 TU	20 W	21 TH	22 F	23 SA	24 SU	25 M	26 TU	27 W	28 TH	29 F	30 SA	
E	F	G	H	J	K	L	M	N	O	P	Q	R	S	T	U	V	W	X	Y	Z	1	2	3	4	5	6	7	8	A	
FD	GE	HF	JG	KH	LJ	MK	NL	OM	PN	QO	RP	SQ	TR	US	VT	WU	XV	YW	ZX	1Y	2Z	31	42	53	64	75	86	A7	B8	
GC	HD	JE	KF	LG	MH	NJ	OK	PL	QM	RN	SO	TP	UQ	VR	WS	XT	YU	ZV	1W	2X	3Y	4Z	51	62	73	84	A5	B6	C7	
HB	JC	KD	LE	MF	NG	OH	PJ	QK	RL	SM	TN	UO	VP	WQ	XR	YS	ZT	1U	2V	3W	4X	5Y	6Z	71	82	A3	B4	C5	D6	
JA	KB	LC	MD	NE	OF	PG	QH	RJ	SK	TL	UM	VN	WO	XP	YQ	ZR	1S	2T	3U	4V	5W	6X	7Y	8Z	A1	B2	C3	D4	E5	
K8	LA	MB	NC	OD	PE	QF	RG	SH	TJ	UK	VL	WM	XN	YO	ZP	1Q	2R	3S	4T	5U	6V	7W	8X	AY	BZ	C1	D2	E3	F4	+
L7	M8	NA	OB	PC	QD	RE	SF	TG	UH	VJ	WK	XL	YM	ZN	1O	2P	3Q	4R	5S	6T	7U	8V	AW	BX	CY	DZ	E1	F2	G3	
M6	N7	O8	PA	QB	RC	SD	TE	UF	VG	WH	XJ	YK	ZL	1M	2N	3O	4P	5Q	6R	7S	8T	AU	BV	CW	DX	EY	FZ	G1	H2	
N5	O6	P7	Q8	RA	SB	TC	UD	VE	WF	XG	YH	ZJ	1K	2L	3M	4N	5O	6P	7Q	8R	AS	BT	CU	DV	EW	FX	GY	HZ	J1	0
O4	P5	Q6	R7	S8	TA	UB	VC	WD	XE	YF	ZG	1H	2J	3K	4L	5M	6N	7O	8P	AQ	BR	CS	DT	EU	FV	GW	HX	JY	KZ	
P3	Q4	R5	S6	T7	U8	VA	WB	XC	YD	ZE	1F	2G	3H	4J	5K	6L	7M	8N	AO	BP	CQ	DR	ES	FT	GU	HV	JW	KX	LY	
Q2	R3	S4	T5	U6	V7	W8	XA	YB	ZC	1D	2E	3F	4G	5H	6J	7K	8L	AM	BN	CO	DP	EQ	FR	GS	HT	JU	KV	LW	MX	−
R1	S2	T3	U4	V5	W6	X7	Y8	ZA	1B	2C	3D	4E	5F	6G	7H	8J	AK	BL	CM	DN	EO	FP	GQ	HR	JS	KT	LU	MV	NW	
SZ	T1	U2	V3	W4	X5	Y6	Z7	18	2A	3B	4C	5D	6E	7F	8G	AH	BJ	CK	DL	EM	FN	GO	HP	JQ	KR	LS	MT	NU	OV	
TY	UZ	V1	W2	X3	Y4	Z5	16	27	38	4A	5B	6C	7D	8E	AF	BG	CH	DJ	EK	FL	GM	HN	JO	KP	LQ	MR	NS	OT	PU	
UX	VY	WZ	X1	Y2	Z3	14	25	36	47	58	6A	7B	8C	AD	BE	CF	DG	EH	FJ	GK	HL	JM	KN	LO	MP	NQ	OR	PS	QT	
VW	WX	XY	YZ	Z1	12	23	34	45	56	67	78	8A	AB	BC	CD	DE	EF	FG	GH	HJ	JK	KL	LM	MN	NO	OP	PQ	QR	RS	

PHYSICAL

1 SU	2 M	3 TU	4 W	5 TH	6 F	7 SA	8 SU	9 M	10 TU	11 W	12 TH	13 F	14 SA	15 SU	16 M	17 TU	18 W	19 TH	20 F	21 SA	22 SU	23 M	24 TU	25 W	26 TH	27 F	28 SA	29 SU	30 M	31 TU	
JH	KJ	LK	ML	NM	ON	PO	QP	RQ	SR	TS	UT	VU	WV	XW	AX	BA	CB	DC	ED	FE	GF	HG	JH	KJ	LK	ML	NM	ON	PO	QP	
KG	LH	MJ	NK	OL	PM	QN	RO	SP	TQ	UR	VS	WT	XU	AV	BW	CX	DA	EB	FC	GD	HE	JF	KG	LH	MJ	NK	OL	PM	QN	RO	
LF	MG	NH	OJ	PK	QL	RM	SN	TO	UP	VQ	WR	XS	AT	BU	CV	DW	EX	FA	GB	HC	JD	KE	LF	MG	NH	OJ	PK	QL	RM	SN	
ME	NF	OG	PH	QJ	RK	SL	TM	UN	VO	WP	XQ	AR	BS	CT	DU	EV	FW	GX	HA	JB	KC	LD	ME	NF	OG	PH	QJ	RK	SL	TM	+
ND	OE	PF	QG	RH	SJ	TK	UL	VM	WN	XO	AP	BQ	CR	DS	ET	FU	GV	HW	JX	KA	LB	MC	ND	OE	PF	QG	RH	SJ	TK	UL	
OC	PD	QE	RF	SG	TH	UJ	VK	WL	XM	AN	BO	CP	DQ	ER	FS	GT	HU	JV	KW	LX	MA	NB	OC	PD	QE	RF	SG	TH	UJ	VK	0
PB	QC	RD	SE	TF	UG	VH	WJ	XK	AL	BM	CN	DO	EP	FQ	GR	HS	JT	KU	LV	MW	NX	OA	PB	QC	RD	SE	TF	UG	VH	WJ	
QA	RB	SC	TD	UE	VF	WG	XH	AJ	BK	CL	DM	EN	FO	GP	HQ	JR	KS	LT	MU	NV	OW	PX	QA	RB	SC	TD	UE	VF	WG	XH	
RX	SA	TB	UC	VD	WE	XF	AG	BH	CJ	DK	EL	FM	GN	HO	JP	KQ	LR	MS	NT	OU	PV	QW	RX	SA	TB	UC	VD	WE	XF	AG	−
SW	TX	UA	VB	WC	XD	AE	BF	CG	DH	EJ	FK	GL	HM	JN	KO	LP	MQ	NR	OS	PT	QU	RV	SW	TX	UA	VB	WC	XD	AE	BF	
TV	UW	VX	WA	XB	AC	BD	CE	DF	EG	FH	GJ	HK	JL	KM	LN	MO	NP	OQ	PR	QS	RT	SU	TV	UW	VX	WA	XB	AC	BD	CE	
U	V	W	X	A	B	C	D	E	F	G	H	J	K	L	M	N	O	P	Q	R	S	T	U	V	W	X	A	B	C	D	

EMOTIONAL

1 SU	2 M	3 TU	4 W	5 TH	6 F	7 SA	8 SU	9 M	10 TU	11 W	12 TH	13 F	14 SA	15 SU	16 M	17 TU	18 W	19 TH	20 F	21 SA	22 SU	23 M	24 TU	25 W	26 TH	27 F	28 SA	29 SU	30 M	31 TU	
A	B	C	D	E	F	G	H	J	K	L	M	N	O	P	Q	R	S	T	U	V	W	X	Y	Z	1	2	3	A	B	C	
B3	CA	DB	EC	FD	GE	HF	JG	KH	LJ	MK	NL	OM	PN	QO	RP	SQ	TR	US	VT	WU	XV	YW	ZX	1Y	2Z	31	A2	B3	CA	DB	
C2	D3	EA	FB	GC	HD	JE	KF	LG	MH	NJ	OK	PL	QM	RN	SO	TP	UQ	VR	WS	XT	YU	ZV	1W	2X	3Y	AZ	B1	C2	D3	EA	
D1	E2	F3	GA	HB	JC	KD	LE	MF	NG	OH	PJ	QK	RL	SM	TN	UO	VP	WQ	XR	YS	ZT	1U	2V	3W	AX	BY	CZ	D1	E2	F3	
EZ	F1	G2	H3	JA	KB	LC	MD	NE	OF	PG	QH	RJ	SK	TL	UM	VN	WO	XP	YQ	ZR	1S	2T	3U	AV	BW	CX	DY	EZ	F1	G2	+
FY	GZ	H1	J2	K3	LA	MB	NC	OD	PE	QF	RG	SH	TJ	UK	VL	WM	XN	YO	ZP	1Q	2R	3S	AT	BU	CV	DW	EX	FY	GZ	H1	
GX	HY	JZ	K1	L2	M3	NA	OB	PC	QD	RE	SF	TG	UH	VJ	WK	XL	YM	ZN	1O	2P	3Q	AR	BS	CT	DU	EV	FW	GX	HY	JZ	
HW	JX	KY	LZ	M1	N2	O3	PA	QB	RC	SD	TE	UF	VG	WH	XJ	YK	ZL	1M	2N	3O	AP	BQ	CR	DS	ET	FU	GV	HW	JX	KY	0
JV	KW	LX	MY	NZ	O1	P2	Q3	RA	SB	TC	UD	VE	WF	XG	YH	ZJ	1K	2L	3M	AN	BO	CP	DQ	ER	FS	GT	HU	JV	KW	LX	
KU	LV	MW	NX	OY	PZ	Q1	R2	S3	TA	UB	VC	WD	XE	YF	ZG	1H	2J	3K	AL	BM	CN	DO	EP	FQ	GR	HS	JT	KU	LV	MW	
LT	MU	NV	OW	PX	QY	RZ	S1	T2	U3	VA	WB	XC	YD	ZE	1F	2G	3H	AJ	BK	CL	DM	EN	FO	GP	HQ	JR	KS	LT	MU	NV	−
MS	NT	OU	PV	QW	RX	SY	TZ	U1	V2	W3	XA	YB	ZC	1D	2E	3F	AG	BH	CJ	DK	EL	FM	GN	HO	JP	KQ	LR	MS	NT	OU	
NR	OS	PT	QU	RV	SW	TX	UY	VZ	W1	X2	Y3	ZA	1B	2C	3D	AE	BF	CG	DH	EJ	FK	GL	HM	JN	KO	LP	MQ	NR	OS	PT	
OQ	PR	QS	RT	SU	TV	UW	VX	WY	XZ	Y1	Z2	13	2A	3B	AC	BD	CE	DF	EG	FH	GJ	HK	JL	KM	LN	MO	NP	OQ	PR	QS	
P	Q	R	S	T	U	V	W	X	Y	Z	1	2	3	A	B	C	D	E	F	G	H	J	K	L	M	N	O	P	Q	R	

INTELLECTUAL

1 SU	2 M	3 TU	4 W	5 TH	6 F	7 SA	8 SU	9 M	10 TU	11 W	12 TH	13 F	14 SA	15 SU	16 M	17 TU	18 W	19 TH	20 F	21 SA	22 SU	23 M	24 TU	25 W	26 TH	27 F	28 SA	29 SU	30 M	31 TU	
B	C	D	E	F	G	H	J	K	L	M	N	O	P	Q	R	S	T	U	V	W	X	Y	Z	1	2	3	4	5	6	7	
CA	DB	EC	FD	GE	HF	JG	KH	LJ	MK	NL	OM	PN	QO	RP	SQ	TR	US	VT	WU	XV	YW	ZX	1Y	2Z	31	42	53	64	75	86	
D8	EA	FB	GC	HD	JE	KF	LG	MH	NJ	OK	PL	QM	RN	SO	TP	UQ	VR	WS	XT	YU	ZV	1W	2X	3Y	4Z	51	62	73	84	A5	
E7	F8	GA	HB	JC	KD	LE	MF	NG	OH	PJ	QK	RL	SM	TN	UO	VP	WQ	XR	YS	ZT	1U	2V	3W	4X	5Y	6Z	71	82	A3	B4	
F6	G7	H8	JA	KB	LC	MD	NE	OF	PG	QH	RJ	SK	TL	UM	VN	WO	XP	YQ	ZR	1S	2T	3U	4V	5W	6X	7Y	8Z	A1	B2	C3	
G5	H6	J7	K8	LA	MB	NC	OD	PE	QF	RG	SH	TJ	UK	VL	WM	XN	YO	ZP	1Q	2R	3S	4T	5U	6V	7W	8X	AY	BZ	C1	D2	
H4	J5	K6	L7	M8	NA	OB	PC	QD	RE	SF	TG	UH	VJ	WK	XL	YM	ZN	1O	2P	3Q	4R	5S	6T	7U	8V	AW	BX	CY	DZ	E1	+
J3	K4	L5	M6	N7	O8	PA	QB	RC	SD	TE	UF	VG	WH	XJ	YK	ZL	1M	2N	3O	4P	5Q	6R	7S	8T	AU	BV	CW	DX	EY	FZ	
K2	L3	M4	N5	O6	P7	Q8	RA	SB	TC	UD	VE	WF	XG	YH	ZJ	1K	2L	3M	4N	5O	6P	7Q	8R	AS	BT	CU	DV	EW	FX	GY	0
L1	M2	N3	O4	P5	Q6	R7	S8	TA	UB	VC	WD	XE	YF	ZG	1H	2J	3K	4L	5M	6N	7O	8P	AQ	BR	CS	DT	EU	FV	GW	HX	
MZ	N1	O2	P3	Q4	R5	S6	T7	U8	VA	WB	XC	YD	ZE	1F	2G	3H	4J	5K	6L	7M	8N	AO	BP	CQ	DR	ES	FT	GU	HV	JW	
NY	OZ	P1	Q2	R3	S4	T5	U6	V7	W8	XA	YB	ZC	1D	2E	3F	4G	5H	6J	7K	8L	AM	BN	CO	DP	EQ	FR	GS	HT	JU	KV	−
OX	PY	QZ	R1	S2	T3	U4	V5	W6	X7	Y8	ZA	1B	2C	3D	4E	5F	6G	7H	8J	AK	BL	CM	DN	EO	FP	GQ	HR	JS	KT	LU	
PW	QX	RY	SZ	T1	U2	V3	W4	X5	Y6	Z7	18	2A	3B	4C	5D	6E	7F	8G	AH	BJ	CK	DL	EM	FN	GO	HP	JQ	KR	LS	MT	
QV	RW	SX	TY	UZ	V1	W2	X3	Y4	Z5	16	27	38	4A	5B	6C	7D	8E	AF	BG	CH	DJ	EK	FL	GM	HN	JO	KP	LQ	MR	NS	
RU	SV	TW	UX	VY	WZ	X1	Y2	Z3	14	25	36	47	58	6A	7B	8C	AD	BE	CF	DG	EH	FJ	GK	HL	JM	KN	LO	MP	NQ	OR	
ST	TU	UV	VW	WX	XY	YZ	Z1	12	23	34	45	56	67	78	8A	AB	BC	CD	DE	EF	FG	GH	HJ	JK	KL	LM	MN	NO	OP	PQ	

207

	1 W	2 TH	3 F	4 SA	5 SU	6 M	7 TU	8 W	9 TH	10 F	11 SA	12 SU	13 M	14 TU	15 W	16 TH	17 F	18 SA	19 SU	20 M	21 TU	22 W	23 TH	24 F	25 SA	26 SU	27 M	28 TU	29 W	30 TH
	RQ	SR	TS	UT	VU	WV	XW	AX	BA	CB	DC	ED	FE	GF	HG	JH	KJ	LK	ML	NM	ON	PO	QP	RQ	SR	TS	UT	VU	WV	XW
	SP	TQ	UR	VS	WT	XU	AV	BW	CX	DA	EB	FC	GD	HE	JF	KG	LH	MJ	NK	OL	PM	QN	RO	SP	TQ	UR	VS	WT	XU	AV
	TO	UP	VQ	WR	XS	AT	BU	CV	DW	EX	FA	GB	HC	JD	KE	LF	MG	NH	OJ	PK	QL	RM	SN	TO	UP	VQ	WR	XS	AT	BU
	UN	VO	WP	XQ	AR	BS	CT	DU	EV	FW	GX	HA	JB	KC	LD	ME	NF	OG	PH	QJ	RK	SL	TM	UN	VO	WP	XQ	AR	BS	CT
	VM	WN	XO	AP	BQ	CR	DS	ET	FU	GV	HW	JX	KA	LB	MC	ND	OE	PF	QG	RH	SJ	TK	UL	VM	WN	XO	AP	BQ	CR	DS
	WL	XM	AN	BO	CP	DQ	ER	FS	GT	HU	JV	KW	LX	MA	NB	OC	PD	QE	RF	SG	TH	UJ	VK	WL	XM	AN	BO	CP	DQ	ER
	XK	AL	BM	CN	DO	EP	FQ	GR	HS	JT	KU	LV	MW	NX	OA	PB	QC	RD	SE	TF	UG	VH	WJ	XK	AL	BM	CN	DO	EP	FQ
	AJ	BK	CL	DM	EN	FO	GP	HQ	JR	KS	LT	MU	NV	OW	PX	QA	RB	SC	TD	UE	VF	WG	XH	AJ	BK	CL	DM	EN	FO	GP
	BH	CJ	DK	EL	FM	GN	HO	JP	KQ	LR	MS	NT	OU	PV	QW	RX	SA	TB	UC	VD	WE	XF	AG	BH	CJ	DK	EL	FM	GN	HO
	CG	DH	EJ	FK	GL	HM	JN	KO	LP	MQ	NR	OS	PT	QU	RV	SW	TX	UA	VB	WC	XD	AE	BF	CG	DH	EJ	FK	GL	HM	JN
	DF	EG	FH	GJ	HK	JL	KM	LN	MO	NP	OQ	PR	QS	RT	SU	TV	UW	VX	WA	XB	AC	BD	CE	DF	EG	FH	GJ	HK	JL	KM
	E	F	G	H	J	K	L	M	N	O	P	Q	R	S	T	U	V	W	X	A	B	C	D	E	F	G	H	J	K	L

	1 W	2 TH	3 F	4 SA	5 SU	6 M	7 TU	8 W	9 TH	10 F	11 SA	12 SU	13 M	14 TU	15 W	16 TH	17 F	18 SA	19 SU	20 M	21 TU	22 W	23 TH	24 F	25 SA	26 SU	27 M	28 TU	29 W	30 TH	
	D	E	F	G	H	J	K	L	M	N	O	P	Q	R	S	T	U	V	W	X	Y	Z	1	2	3	A	B	C	D	E	
	EC	FD	GE	HF	JG	KH	LJ	MK	NL	OM	PN	QO	RP	SQ	TR	US	VT	WU	XV	YW	ZX	1Y	2Z	31	A2	B3	CA	DB	EC	FD	
	FB	GC	HD	JE	KF	LG	MH	NJ	OK	PL	QM	RN	SO	TP	UQ	VR	WS	XT	YU	ZV	1W	2X	3Y	AZ	B1	C2	D3	EA	FB	GC	
	GA	HB	JC	KD	LE	MF	NG	OH	PJ	QK	RL	SM	TN	UO	VP	WQ	XR	YS	ZT	1U	2V	3W	AX	BY	CZ	D1	E2	F3	GA	HB	
	H3	JA	KB	LC	MD	NE	OF	PG	QH	RJ	SK	TL	UM	VN	WO	XP	YQ	ZR	1S	2T	3U	AV	BW	CX	DY	EZ	F1	G2	H3	JA	+
	J2	K3	LA	MB	NC	OD	PE	QF	RG	SH	TJ	UK	VL	WM	XN	YO	ZP	1Q	2R	3S	AT	BU	CV	DW	EX	FY	GZ	H1	J2	K3	
	K1	L2	M3	NA	OB	PC	QD	RE	SF	TG	UH	VJ	WK	XL	YM	ZN	1O	2P	3Q	AR	BS	CT	DU	EV	FW	GX	HY	JZ	K1	L2	
	LZ	M1	N2	O3	PA	QB	RC	SD	TE	UF	VG	WH	XJ	YK	ZL	1M	2N	3O	AP	BQ	CR	DS	ET	FU	GV	HW	JX	KY	LZ	M1	0
	MY	NZ	O1	P2	Q3	RA	SB	TC	UD	VE	WF	XG	YH	ZJ	1K	2L	3M	AN	BO	CP	DQ	ER	FS	GT	HU	JV	KW	LX	MY	NZ	
	NX	OY	PZ	Q1	R2	S3	TA	UB	VC	WD	XE	YF	ZG	1H	2J	3K	AL	BM	CN	DO	EP	FQ	GR	HS	JT	KU	LV	MW	NX	OY	
	OW	PX	QY	RZ	S1	T2	U3	VA	WB	XC	YD	ZE	1F	2G	3H	AJ	BK	CL	DM	EN	FO	GP	HQ	JR	KS	LT	MU	NV	OW	PX	—
	PV	QW	RX	SY	TZ	U1	V2	W3	XA	YB	ZC	1D	2E	3F	AG	BH	CJ	DK	EL	FM	GN	HO	JP	KQ	LR	MS	NT	OU	PV	QW	
	QU	RV	SW	TX	UY	VZ	W1	X2	Y3	ZA	1B	2C	3D	AE	BF	CG	DH	EJ	FK	GL	HM	JN	KO	LP	MQ	NR	OS	PT	QU	RV	
	RT	SU	TV	UW	VX	WY	XZ	Y1	Z2	13	2A	3B	AC	BD	CE	DF	EG	FH	GJ	HK	JL	KM	LN	MO	NP	OQ	PR	QS	RT	SU	
	S	T	U	V	W	X	Y	Z	1	2	3	A	B	C	D	E	F	G	H	J	K	L	M	N	O	P	Q	R	S	T	

	1 W	2 TH	3 F	4 SA	5 SU	6 M	7 TU	8 W	9 TH	10 F	11 SA	12 SU	13 M	14 TU	15 W	16 TH	17 F	18 SA	19 SU	20 M	21 TU	22 W	23 TH	24 F	25 SA	26 SU	27 M	28 TU	29 W	30 TH
	8	A	B	C	D	E	F	G	H	J	K	L	M	N	O	P	Q	R	S	T	U	V	W	X	Y	Z	1	2	3	4
	A7	B8	CA	DB	EC	FD	GE	HF	JG	KH	LJ	MK	NL	OM	PN	QO	RP	SQ	TR	US	VT	WU	XV	YW	ZX	1Y	2Z	31	42	53
	B6	C7	D8	EA	FB	GC	HD	JE	KF	LG	MH	NJ	OK	PL	QM	RN	SO	TP	UQ	VR	WS	XT	YU	ZV	1W	2X	3Y	4Z	51	62
	C5	D6	E7	F8	GA	HB	JC	KD	LE	MF	NG	OH	PJ	QK	RL	SM	TN	UO	VP	WQ	XR	YS	ZT	1U	2V	3W	4X	5Y	6Z	71
	D4	E5	F6	G7	H8	JA	KB	LC	MD	NE	OF	PG	QH	RJ	SK	TL	UM	VN	WO	XP	YQ	ZR	1S	2T	3U	4V	5W	6X	7Y	8Z
	E3	F4	G5	H6	J7	K8	LA	MB	NC	OD	PE	QF	RG	SH	TJ	UK	VL	WM	XN	YO	ZP	1Q	2R	3S	4T	5U	6V	7W	8X	AY
	F2	G3	H4	J5	K6	L7	M8	NA	OB	PC	QD	RE	SF	TG	UH	VJ	WK	XL	YM	ZN	1O	2P	3Q	4R	5S	6T	7U	8V	AW	BX
	G1	H2	J3	K4	L5	M6	N7	O8	PA	QB	RC	SD	TE	UF	VG	WH	XJ	YK	ZL	1M	2N	3O	4P	5Q	6R	7S	8T	AU	BV	CW
	HZ	J1	K2	L3	M4	N5	O6	P7	Q8	RA	SB	TC	UD	VE	WF	XG	YH	ZJ	1K	2L	3M	4N	5O	6P	7Q	8R	AS	BT	CU	DV
	JY	KZ	L1	M2	N3	O4	P5	Q6	R7	S8	TA	UB	VC	WD	XE	YF	ZG	1H	2J	3K	4L	5M	6N	7O	8P	AQ	BR	CS	DT	EU
	KX	LY	MZ	N1	O2	P3	Q4	R5	S6	T7	U8	VA	WB	XC	YD	ZE	1F	2G	3H	4J	5K	6L	7M	8N	AO	BP	CQ	DR	ES	FT
	LW	MX	NY	OZ	P1	Q2	R3	S4	T5	U6	V7	W8	XA	YB	ZC	1D	2E	3F	4G	5H	6J	7K	8L	AM	BN	CO	DP	EQ	FR	GS
	MV	NW	OX	PY	QZ	R1	S2	T3	U4	V5	W6	X7	Y8	ZA	1B	2C	3D	4E	5F	6G	7H	8J	AK	BL	CM	DN	EO	FP	GQ	HR
	NU	OV	PW	QX	RY	SZ	T1	U2	V3	W4	X5	Y6	Z7	18	2A	3B	4C	5D	6E	7F	8G	AH	BJ	CK	DL	EM	FN	GO	HP	JQ
	OT	PU	QV	RW	SX	TY	UZ	V1	W2	X3	Y4	Z5	16	27	38	4A	5B	6C	7D	8E	AF	BG	CH	DJ	EK	FL	GM	HN	JO	KP
	PS	QT	RU	SV	TW	UX	VY	WZ	X1	Y2	Z3	14	25	36	47	58	6A	7B	8C	AD	BE	CF	DG	EH	FJ	GK	HL	JM	KN	LO
	QR	RS	ST	TU	UV	VW	WX	XY	YZ	Z1	12	23	34	45	56	67	78	8A	AB	BC	CD	DE	EF	FG	GH	HJ	JK	KL	LM	MN

1 F	2 SA	3 SU	4 M	5 TU	6 W	7 TH	8 F	9 SA	10 SU	11 M	12 TU	13 W	14 TH	15 F	16 SA	17 SU	18 M	19 TU	20 W	21 TH	22 F	23 SA	24 SU	25 M	26 TU	27 W	28 TH	29 F	30 SA	31 SU	
AX	BA	CB	DC	ED	FE	GF	HG	JH	KJ	LK	ML	NM	ON	PO	QP	RQ	SR	TS	UT	VU	WV	XW	AX	BA	CB	DC	ED	FE	GF	HG	
BW	CX	DA	EB	FC	GD	HE	JF	KG	LH	MJ	NK	OL	PM	QN	RO	SP	TQ	UR	VS	WT	XU	AV	BW	CX	DA	EB	FC	GD	HE	JF	
CV	DW	EX	FA	GB	HC	JD	KE	LF	MG	NH	OJ	PK	QL	RM	SN	TO	UP	VQ	WR	XS	AT	BU	CV	DW	EX	FA	GB	HC	JD	KE	+
DU	EV	FW	GX	HA	JB	KC	LD	ME	NF	OG	PH	QJ	RK	SL	TM	UN	VO	WP	XQ	AR	BS	CT	DU	EV	FW	GX	HA	JB	KC	LD	
ET	FU	GV	HW	JX	KA	LB	MC	ND	OE	PF	QG	RH	SJ	TK	UL	VM	WN	XO	AP	BQ	CR	DS	ET	FU	GV	HW	JX	KA	LB	MC	
FS	GT	HU	JV	KW	LX	MA	NB	OC	PD	QE	RF	SG	TH	UJ	VK	WL	XM	AN	BO	CP	DQ	ER	FS	GT	HU	JV	KW	LX	MA	NB	0
GR	HS	JT	KU	LV	MW	NX	OA	PB	QC	RD	SE	TF	UG	VH	WJ	XK	AL	BM	CN	DO	EP	FQ	GR	HS	JT	KU	LV	MW	NX	OA	
HQ	JR	KS	LT	MU	NV	OW	PX	QA	RB	SC	TD	UE	VF	WG	XH	AJ	BK	CL	DM	EN	FO	GP	HQ	JR	KS	LT	MU	NV	OW	PX	
JP	KQ	LR	MS	NT	OU	PV	QW	RX	SA	TB	UC	VD	WE	XF	AG	BH	CJ	DK	EL	FM	GN	HO	JP	KQ	LR	MS	NT	OU	PV	QW	—
KO	LP	MQ	NR	OS	PT	QU	RV	SW	TX	UA	VB	WC	XD	AE	BF	CG	DH	EJ	FK	GL	HM	JN	KO	LP	MQ	NR	OS	PT	QU	RV	
LN	MO	NP	OQ	PR	QS	RT	SU	TV	UW	VX	WA	XB	AC	BD	CE	DF	EG	FH	GJ	HK	JL	KM	LN	MO	NP	OQ	PR	QS	RT.	SU	
M	N	O	P	Q	R	S	T	U	V	W	X	A	B	C	D	E	F	G	H	J	K	L	M	N	O	P	Q	R	S	T	

1 F	2 SA	3 SU	4 M	5 TU	6 W	7 TH	8 F	9 SA	10 SU	11 M	12 TU	13 W	14 TH	15 F	16 SA	17 SU	18 M	19 TU	20 W	21 TH	22 F	23 SA	24 SU	25 M	26 TU	27 W	28 TH	29 F	30 SA	31 SU	
F	G	H	J	K	L	M	N	O	P	Q	R	S	T	U	V	W	X	Y	Z	1	2	3	A	B	C	D	E	F	G	H	
GE	HF	JG	KH	LJ	MK	NL	OM	PN	QO	RP	SQ	TR	US	VT	WU	XV	YW	ZX	1Y	2Z	31	A2	B3	CA	DB	EC	FD	GE	HF	JG	
HD	JE	KF	LG	MH	NJ	OK	PL	QM	RN	SO	TP	UQ	VR	WS	XT	YU	ZV	1W	2X	3Y	AZ	B1	C2	D3	EA	FB	GC	HD	JE	KF	
JC	KD	LE	MF	NG	OH	PJ	QK	RL	SM	TN	UO	VP	WQ	XR	YS	ZT	1U	2V	3W	AX	BY	CZ	D1	E2	F3	GA	HB	JC	KD	LE	
KB	LC	MD	NE	OF	PG	QH	RJ	SK	TL	UM	VN	WO	XP	YQ	ZR	1S	2T	3U	AV	BW	CX	DY	EZ	F1	G2	H3	JA	KB	LC	MD	+
LA	MB	NC	OD	PE	QF	RG	SH	TJ	UK	VL	WM	XN	YO	ZP	1Q	2R	3S	AT	BU	CV	DW	EX	FY	GZ	H1	J2	K3	LA	MB	NC	
M3	NA	OB	PC	QD	RE	SF	TG	UH	VJ	WK	XL	YM	ZN	1O	2P	3Q	AR	BS	CT	DU	EV	FW	GX	HY	JZ	K1	L2	M3	NA	OB	
N2	O3	PA	QB	RC	SD	TE	UF	VG	WH	XJ	YK	ZL	1M	2N	3O	AP	BQ	CR	DS	ET	FU	GV	HW	JX	KY	LZ	M1	N2	O3	PA	0
O1	P2	Q3	RA	SB	TC	UD	VE	WF	XG	YH	ZJ	1K	2L	3M	AN	BO	CP	DQ	ER	FS	GT	HU	JV	KW	LX	MY	NZ	O1	P2	Q3	
PZ	Q1	R2	S3	TA	UB	VC	WD	XE	YF	ZG	1H	2J	3K	AL	BM	CN	DO	EP	FQ	GR	HS	JT	KU	LV	MW	NX	OY	PZ	Q1	R2	
QY	RZ	S1	T2	U3	VA	WB	XC	YD	ZE	1F	2G	3H	AJ	BK	CL	DM	EN	FO	GP	HQ	JR	KS	LT	MU	NV	OW	PX	QY	RZ	S1	—
RX	SY	TZ	U1	V2	W3	XA	YB	ZC	1D	2E	3F	AG	BH	CJ	DK	EL	FM	GN	HO	JP	KQ	LR	MS	NT	OU	PV	QW	RX	SY	TZ	
SW	TX	UY	VZ	W1	X2	Y3	ZA	1B	2C	3D	AE	BF	CG	DH	EJ	FK	GL	HM	JN	KO	LP	MQ	NR	OS	PT	QU	RV	SW	TX	UY	
TV	UW	VX	WY	XZ	Y1	Z2	13	2A	3B	AC	BD	CE	DF	EG	FH	GJ	HK	JL	KM	LN	MO	NP	OQ	PR	QS	RT	SU	TV	UW	VX	
U	V	W	X	Y	Z	1	2	3	A	B	C	D	E	F	G	H	J	K	L	M	N	O	P	Q	R	S	T	U	V	W	

1 F	2 SA	3 SU	4 M	5 TU	6 W	7 TH	8 F	9 SA	10 SU	11 M	12 TU	13 W	14 TH	15 F	16 SA	17 SU	18 M	19 TU	20 W	21 TH	22 F	23 SA	24 SU	25 M	26 TU	27 W	28 TH	29 F	30 SA	31 SU	
5	6	7	8	A	B	C	D	E	F	G	H	J	K	L	M	N	O	P	Q	R	S	T	U	V	W	X	Y	Z	1	2	
64	75	86	A7	B8	CA	DB	EC	FD	GE	HF	JG	KH	LJ	MK	NL	OM	PN	QO	RP	SQ	TR	US	VT	WU	XV	YW	ZX	1Y	2Z	31	
73	84	A5	B6	C7	D8	EA	FB	GC	HD	JE	KF	LG	MH	NJ	OK	PL	QM	RN	SO	TP	UQ	VR	WS	XT	YU	ZV	1W	2X	3Y	4Z	
82	A3	B4	C5	D6	E7	F8	GA	HB	JC	KD	LE	MF	NG	OH	PJ	QK	RL	SM	TN	UO	VP	WQ	XR	YS	ZT	1U	2V	3W	4X	5Y	
A1	B2	C3	D4	E5	F6	G7	H8	JA	KB	LC	MD	NE	OF	PG	QH	RJ	SK	TL	UM	VN	WO	XP	YQ	ZR	1S	2T	3U	4V	5W	6X	
BZ	C1	D2	E3	F4	G5	H6	J7	K8	LA	MB	NC	OD	PE	QF	RG	SH	TJ	UK	VL	WM	XN	YO	ZP	1Q	2R	3S	4T	5U	6V	7W	+
CY	DZ	E1	F2	G3	H4	J5	K6	L7	M8	NA	OB	PC	QD	RE	SF	TG	UH	VJ	WK	XL	YM	ZN	1O	2P	3Q	4R	5S	6T	7U	8V	
DX	EY	FZ	G1	H2	J3	K4	L5	M6	N7	O8	PA	QB	RC	SD	TE	UF	VG	WH	XJ	YK	ZL	1M	2N	3O	4P	5Q	6R	7S	8T	AU	
EW	FX	GY	HZ	J1	K2	L3	M4	N5	O6	P7	Q8	RA	SB	TC	UD	VE	WF	XG	YH	ZJ	1K	2L	3M	4N	5O	6P	7Q	8R	AS	BT	0
FV	GW	HX	JY	KZ	L1	M2	N3	O4	P5	Q6	R7	S8	TA	UB	VC	WD	XE	YF	ZG	1H	2J	3K	4L	5M	6N	7O	8P	AQ	BR	CS	
GU	HV	JW	KX	LY	MZ	N1	O2	P3	Q4	R5	S6	T7	U8	VA	WB	XC	YD	ZE	1F	2G	3H	4J	5K	6L	7M	8N	AO	BP	CQ	DR	
HT	JU	KV	LW	MX	NY	OZ	P1	Q2	R3	S4	T5	U6	V7	W8	XA	YB	ZC	1D	2E	3F	4G	5H	6J	7K	8L	AM	BN	CO	DP	EQ	—
JS	KT	LU	MV	NW	OX	PY	QZ	R1	S2	T3	U4	V5	W6	X7	Y8	ZA	1B	2C	3D	4E	5F	6G	7H	8J	AK	BL	CM	DN	EO	FP	
KR	LS	MT	NU	OV	PW	QX	RY	SZ	T1	U2	V3	W4	X5	Y6	Z7	18	2A	3B	4C	5D	6E	7F	8G	AH	BJ	CK	DL	EM	FN	GO	
LQ	MR	NS	OT	PU	QV	RW	SX	TY	UZ	V1	W2	X3	Y4	Z5	16	27	38	4A	5B	6C	7D	8E	AF	BG	CH	DJ	EK	FL	GM	HN	
MP	NQ	OR	PS	QT	RU	SV	TW	UX	VY	WZ	X1	Y2	Z3	14	25	36	47	58	6A	7B	8C	AD	BE	CF	DG	EH	FJ	GK	HL	JM	
NO	OP	PQ	QR	RS	ST	TU	UV	VW	WX	XY	YZ	Z1	12	23	34	45	56	67	78	8A	AB	BC	CD	DE	EF	FG	GH	HJ	JK	KL	

PHYSICAL

1 M	2 TU	3 W	4 TH	5 F	6 SA	7 SU	8 M	9 TU	10 W	11 TH	12 F	13 SA	14 SU	15 M	16 TU	17 W	18 TH	19 F	20 SA	21 SU	22 M	23 TU	24 W	25 TH	26 F	27 SA	28 SU	29 M	30 TU	31 W
JH	KJ	LK	ML	NM	ON	PO	QP	RQ	SR	TS	UT	VU	WV	XW	AX	BA	CB	DC	ED	FE	GF	HG	JH	KJ	LK	ML	NM	ON	PO	QP
KG	LH	MJ	NK	OL	PM	QN	RO	SP	TQ	UR	VS	WT	XU	AV	BW	CX	DA	EB	FC	GD	HE	JF	KG	LH	MJ	NK	OL	PM	QN	RO
LF	MG	NH	OJ	PK	QL	RM	SN	TO	UP	VQ	WR	XS	AT	BU	CV	DW	EX	FA	GB	HC	JD	KE	LF	MG	NH	OJ	PK	QL	RM	SN
ME	NF	OG	PH	QJ	RK	SL	TM	UN	VO	WP	XQ	AR	BS	CT	DU	EV	FW	GX	HA	JB	KC	LD	ME	NF	OG	PH	QJ	RK	SL	TM
ND	OE	PF	QG	RH	SJ	TK	UL	VM	WN	XO	AP	BQ	CR	DS	ET	FU	GV	HW	JX	KA	LB	MC	ND	OE	PF	QG	RH	SJ	TK	UL
OC	PD	QE	RF	SG	TH	UJ	VK	WL	XM	AN	BO	CP	DQ	ER	FS	GT	HU	JV	KW	LX	MA	NB	OC	PD	QE	RF	SG	TH	UJ	VK
PB	QC	RD	SE	TF	UG	VH	WJ	XK	AL	BM	CN	DO	EP	FQ	GR	HS	JT	KU	LV	MW	NX	OA	PB	QC	RD	SE	TF	UG	VH	WJ
QA	RB	SC	TD	UE	VF	WG	XH	AJ	BK	CL	DM	EN	FO	GP	HQ	JR	KS	LT	MU	NV	OW	PX	QA	RB	SC	TD	UE	VF	WG	XH
RX	SA	TB	UC	VD	WE	XF	AG	BH	CJ	DK	EL	FM	GN	HO	JP	KQ	LR	MS	NT	OU	PV	QW	RX	SA	TB	UC	VD	WE	XF	AG
SW	TX	UA	VB	WC	XD	AE	BF	CG	DH	EJ	FK	GL	HM	JN	KO	LP	MQ	NR	OS	PT	QU	RV	SW	TX	UA	VB	WC	XD	AE	BF
TV	UW	VX	WA	XB	AC	BD	CE	DF	EG	FH	GJ	HK	JL	KM	LN	MO	NP	OQ	PR	QS	RT	SU	TV	UW	VX	WA	XB	AC	BD	CE
U	V	W	X	A	B	C	D	E	F	G	H	J	K	L	M	N	O	P	Q	R	S	T	U	V	W	X	A	B	C	D

EMOTIONAL

1 M	2 TU	3 W	4 TH	5 F	6 SA	7 SU	8 M	9 TU	10 W	11 TH	12 F	13 SA	14 SU	15 M	16 TU	17 W	18 TH	19 F	20 SA	21 SU	22 M	23 TU	24 W	25 TH	26 F	27 SA	28 SU	29 M	30 TU	31 W	
J	K	L	M	N	O	P	Q	R	S	T	U	V	W	X	Y	Z	1	2	3	A	B	C	D	E	F	G	H	J	K	L	
KH	LJ	MK	NL	OM	PN	QO	RP	SQ	TR	US	VT	WU	XV	YW	ZX	1Y	2Z	31	A2	B3	CA	DB	EC	FD	GE	HF	JG	KH	LJ	MK	
LG	MH	NJ	OK	PL	QM	RN	SO	TP	UQ	VR	WS	XT	YU	ZV	1W	2X	3Y	AZ	B1	C2	D3	EA	FB	GC	HD	JE	KF	LG	MH	NJ	
MF	NG	OH	PJ	QK	RL	SM	TN	UO	VP	WQ	XR	YS	ZT	1U	2V	3W	AX	BY	CZ	D1	E2	F3	GA	HB	JC	KD	LE	MF	NG	OH	
NE	OF	PG	QH	RJ	SK	TL	UM	VN	WO	XP	YQ	ZR	1S	2T	3U	AV	BW	CX	DY	EZ	F1	G2	H3	JA	KB	LC	MD	NE	OF	PG	
OD	PE	QF	RG	SH	TJ	UK	VL	WM	XN	YO	ZP	1Q	2R	3S	AT	BU	CV	DW	EX	FY	GZ	H1	J2	K3	LA	MB	NC	OD	PE	QF	
PC	QD	RE	SF	TG	UH	VJ	WK	XL	YM	ZN	1O	2P	3Q	AR	BS	CT	DU	EV	FW	GX	HY	JZ	K1	L2	M3	NA	OB	PC	QD	RE	+
QB	RC	SD	TE	UF	VG	WH	XJ	YK	ZL	1M	2N	3O	AP	BQ	CR	DS	ET	FU	GV	HW	JX	KY	LZ	M1	N2	O3	PA	QB	RC	SD	0
RA	SB	TC	UD	VE	WF	XG	YH	ZJ	1K	2L	3M	AN	BO	CP	DQ	ER	FS	GT	HU	JV	KW	LX	MY	NZ	O1	P2	Q3	RA	SB	TC	
S3	TA	UB	VC	WD	XE	YF	ZG	1H	2J	3K	AL	BM	CN	DO	EP	FQ	GR	HS	JT	KU	LV	MW	NX	OY	PZ	Q1	R2	S3	TA	UB	−
T2	U3	VA	WB	XC	YD	ZE	1F	2G	3H	AJ	BK	CL	DM	EN	FO	GP	HQ	JR	KS	LT	MU	NV	OW	PX	QY	RZ	S1	T2	U3	VA	
U1	V2	W3	XA	YB	ZC	1D	2E	3F	AG	BH	CJ	DK	EL	FM	GN	HO	JP	KQ	LR	MS	NT	OU	PV	QW	RX	SY	TZ	U1	V2	W3	
VZ	W1	X2	Y3	ZA	1B	2C	3D	AE	BF	CG	DH	EJ	FK	GL	HM	JN	KO	LP	MQ	NR	OS	PT	QU	RV	SW	TX	UY	VZ	W1	X2	
WY	XZ	Y1	Z2	13	2A	3B	AC	BD	CE	DF	EG	FH	GJ	HK	JL	KM	LN	MO	NP	OQ	PR	QS	RT	SU	TV	UW	VX	WY	XZ	Y1	
X	Y	Z	1	2	3	A	B	C	D	E	F	G	H	J	K	L	M	N	O	P	Q	R	S	T	U	V	W	X	Y	Z	

INTELLECTUAL

1 M	2 TU	3 W	4 TH	5 F	6 SA	7 SU	8 M	9 TU	10 W	11 TH	12 F	13 SA	14 SU	15 M	16 TU	17 W	18 TH	19 F	20 SA	21 SU	22 M	23 TU	24 W	25 TH	26 F	27 SA	28 SU	29 M	30 TU	31 W
3	4	5	6	7	8	A	B	C	D	E	F	G	H	J	K	L	M	N	O	P	Q	R	S	T	U	V	W	X	Y	Z
42	53	64	75	86	A7	B8	CA	DB	EC	FD	GE	HF	JG	KH	LJ	MK	NL	OM	PN	QO	RP	SQ	TR	US	VT	WU	XV	YW	ZX	1Y
51	62	73	84	A5	B6	C7	D8	EA	FB	GC	HD	JE	KF	LG	MH	NJ	OK	PL	QM	RN	SO	TP	UQ	VR	WS	XT	YU	ZV	1W	2X
6Z	71	82	A3	B4	C5	D6	E7	F8	GA	HB	JC	KD	LE	MF	NG	OH	PJ	QK	RL	SM	TN	UO	VP	WQ	XR	YS	ZT	1U	2V	3W
7Y	8Z	A1	B2	C3	D4	E5	F6	G7	H8	JA	KB	LC	MD	NE	OF	PG	QH	RJ	SK	TL	UM	VN	WO	XP	YQ	ZR	1S	2T	3U	4V
8X	AY	BZ	C1	D2	E3	F4	G5	H6	J7	K8	LA	MB	NC	OD	PE	QF	RG	SH	TJ	UK	VL	WM	XN	YO	ZP	1Q	2R	3S	4T	5U
AW	BX	CY	DZ	E1	F2	G3	H4	J5	K6	L7	M8	NA	OB	PC	QD	RE	SF	TG	UH	VJ	WK	XL	YM	ZN	1O	2P	3Q	4R	5S	6T
BV	CW	DX	EY	FZ	G1	H2	J3	K4	L5	M6	N7	O8	PA	QB	RC	SD	TE	UF	VG	WH	XJ	YK	ZL	1M	2N	3O	4P	5Q	6R	7S
CU	DV	EW	FX	GY	HZ	J1	K2	L3	M4	N5	O6	P7	Q8	RA	SB	TC	UD	VE	WF	XG	YH	ZJ	1K	2L	3M	4N	5O	6P	7Q	8R
DT	EU	FV	GW	HX	JY	KZ	L1	M2	N3	O4	P5	Q6	R7	S8	TA	UB	VC	WD	XE	YF	ZG	1H	2J	3K	4L	5M	6N	7O	8P	AQ
ES	FT	GU	HV	JW	KX	LY	MZ	N1	O2	P3	Q4	R5	S6	T7	U8	VA	WB	XC	YD	ZE	1F	2G	3H	4J	5K	6L	7M	8N	AO	BP
FR	GS	HT	JU	KV	LW	MX	NY	OZ	P1	Q2	R3	S4	T5	U6	V7	W8	XA	YB	ZC	1D	2E	3F	4G	5H	6J	7K	8L	AM	BN	CO
GQ	HR	JS	KT	LU	MV	NW	OX	PY	QZ	R1	S2	T3	U4	V5	W6	X7	Y8	ZA	1B	2C	3D	4E	5F	6G	7H	8J	AK	BL	CM	DN
HP	JQ	KR	LS	MT	NU	OV	PW	QX	RY	SZ	T1	U2	V3	W4	X5	Y6	Z7	18	2A	3B	4C	5D	6E	7F	8G	AH	BJ	CK	DL	EM
JO	KP	LQ	MR	NS	OT	PU	QV	RW	SX	TY	UZ	V1	W2	X3	Y4	Z5	16	27	38	4A	5B	6C	7D	8E	AF	BG	CH	DJ	EK	FL
KN	LO	MP	NQ	OR	PS	QT	RU	SV	TW	UX	VY	WZ	X1	Y2	Z3	14	25	36	47	58	6A	7B	8C	AD	BE	CF	DG	EH	FJ	GK
LM	MN	NO	OP	PQ	QR	RS	ST	TU	UV	VW	WX	XY	YZ	Z1	12	23	34	45	56	67	78	8A	AB	BC	CD	DE	EF	FG	GH	HJ

1 TH	2 F	3 SA	4 SU	5 M	6 TU	7 W	8 TH	9 F	10 SA	11 SU	12 M	13 TU	14 W	15 TH	16 F	17 SA	18 SU	19 M	20 TU	21 W	22 TH	23 F	24 SA	25 SU	26 M	27 TU	28 W	29 TH	30 F	
RQ	SR	TS	UT	VU	WV	XW	AX	BA	CB	DC	ED	FE	GF	HG	JH	KJ	LK	ML	NM	ON	PO	QP	RQ	SR	TS	UT	VU	WV	XW	
SP	TQ	UR	VS	WT	XU	AV	BW	CX	DA	EB	FC	GD	HE	JF	KG	LH	MJ	NK	OL	PM	QN	RO	SP	TQ	UR	VS	WT	XU	AV	
TO	UP	VQ	WR	XS	AT	BU	CV	DW	EX	FA	GB	HC	JD	KE	LF	MG	NH	OJ	PK	QL	RM	SN	TO	UP	VQ	WR	XS	AT	BU	
UN	VO	WP	XQ	AR	BS	CT	DU	EV	FW	GX	HA	JB	KC	LD	ME	NF	OG	PH	QJ	RK	SL	TM	UN	VO	WP	XQ	AR	BS	CT	+
VM	WN	XO	AP	BQ	CR	DS	ET	FU	GV	HW	JX	KA	LB	MC	ND	OE	PF	QG	RH	SJ	TK	UL	VM	WN	XO	AP	BQ	CR	DS	
WL	XM	AN	BO	CP	DQ	ER	FS	GT	HU	JV	KW	LX	MA	NB	OC	PD	QE	RF	SG	TH	UJ	VK	WL	XM	AN	BO	CP	DQ	ER	0
XK	AL	BM	CN	DO	EP	FQ	GR	HS	JT	KU	LV	MW	NX	OA	PB	QC	RD	SE	TF	UG	VH	WJ	XK	AL	BM	CN	DO	EP	FQ	
AJ	BK	CL	DM	EN	FO	GP	HQ	JR	KS	LT	MU	NV	OW	PX	QA	RB	SC	TD	UE	VF	WG	XH	AJ	BK	CL	DM	EN	FO	GP	
BH	CJ	DK	EL	FM	GN	HO	JP	KQ	LR	MS	NT	OU	PV	QW	RX	SA	TB	UC	VD	WE	XF	AG	BH	CJ	DK	EL	FM	GN	HO	
CG	DH	EJ	FK	GL	HM	JN	KO	LP	MQ	NR	OS	PT	QU	RV	SW	TX	UA	VB	WC	XD	AE	BF	CG	DH	EJ	FK	GL	HM	JN	−
DF	EG	FH	GJ	HK	JL	KM	LN	MO	NP	OQ	PR	QS	RT	SU	TV	UW	VX	WA	XB	AC	BD	CE	DF	EG	FH	GJ	HK	JL	KM	
E	F	G	H	J	K	L	M	N	O	P	Q	R	S	T	U	V	W	X	A	B	C	D	E	F	G	H	J	K	L	

1 TH	2 F	3 SA	4 SU	5 M	6 TU	7 W	8 TH	9 F	10 SA	11 SU	12 M	13 TU	14 W	15 TH	16 F	17 SA	18 SU	19 M	20 TU	21 W	22 TH	23 F	24 SA	25 SU	26 M	27 TU	28 W	29 TH	30 F	
M	N	O	P	Q	R	S	T	U	V	W	X	Y	Z	1	2	3	A	B	C	D	E	F	G	H	J	K	L	M	N	
NL	OM	PN	QO	RP	SQ	TR	US	VT	WU	XV	YW	ZX	1Y	2Z	31	A2	B3	CA	DB	EC	FD	GE	HF	JG	KH	LJ	MK	NL	OM	
OK	PL	QM	RN	SO	TP	UQ	VR	WS	XT	YU	ZV	1W	2X	3Y	AZ	B1	C2	D3	EA	FB	GC	HD	JE	KF	LG	MH	NJ	OK	PL	
PJ	QK	RL	SM	TN	UO	VP	WQ	XR	YS	ZT	1U	2V	3W	AX	BY	CZ	D1	E2	F3	GA	HB	JC	KD	LE	MF	NG	OH	PJ	QK	
QH	RJ	SK	TL	UM	VN	WO	XP	YQ	ZR	1S	2T	3U	AV	BW	CX	DY	EZ	F1	G2	H3	JA	KB	LC	MD	NE	OF	PG	QH	RJ	
RG	SH	TJ	UK	VL	WM	XN	YO	ZP	1Q	2R	3S	AT	BU	CV	DW	EX	FY	GZ	H1	J2	K3	LA	MB	NC	OD	PE	QF	RG	SH	+
SF	TG	UH	VJ	WK	XL	YM	ZN	1O	2P	3Q	AR	BS	CT	DU	EV	FW	GX	HY	JZ	K1	L2	M3	NA	OB	PC	QD	RE	SF	TG	
TE	UF	VG	WH	XJ	YK	ZL	1M	2N	3O	AP	BQ	CR	DS	ET	FU	GV	HW	JX	KY	LZ	M1	N2	O3	PA	QB	RC	SD	TE	UF	0
UD	VE	WF	XG	YH	ZJ	1K	2L	3M	AN	BO	CP	DQ	ER	FS	GT	HU	JV	KW	LX	MY	NZ	O1	P2	Q3	RA	SB	TC	UD	VE	
VC	WD	XE	YF	ZG	1H	2J	3K	AL	BM	CN	DO	EP	FQ	GR	HS	JT	KU	LV	MW	NX	OY	PZ	Q1	R2	S3	TA	UB	VC	WD	
WB	XC	YD	ZE	1F	2G	3H	AJ	BK	CL	DM	EN	FO	GP	HQ	JR	KS	LT	MU	NV	OW	PX	QY	RZ	S1	T2	U3	VA	WB	XC	−
XA	YB	ZC	1D	2E	3F	AG	BH	CJ	DK	EL	FM	GN	HO	JP	KQ	LR	MS	NT	OU	PV	QW	RX	SY	TZ	U1	V2	W3	XA	YB	
Y3	ZA	1B	2C	3D	AE	BF	CG	DH	EJ	FK	GL	HM	JN	KO	LP	MQ	NR	OS	PT	QU	RV	SW	TX	UY	VZ	W1	X2	Y3	ZA	
Z2	13	2A	3B	AC	BD	CE	DF	EG	FH	GJ	HK	JL	KM	LN	MO	NP	OQ	PR	QS	RT	SU	TV	UW	VX	WY	XZ	Y1	Z2	13	
1	2	3	A	B	C	D	E	F	G	H	J	K	L	M	N	O	P	Q	R	S	T	U	V	W	X	Y	Z	1	2	

1 TH	2 F	3 SA	4 SU	5 M	6 TU	7 W	8 TH	9 F	10 SA	11 SU	12 M	13 TU	14 W	15 TH	16 F	17 SA	18 SU	19 M	20 TU	21 W	22 TH	23 F	24 SA	25 SU	26 M	27 TU	28 W	29 TH	30 F	
1	2	3	4	5	6	7	8	A	B	C	D	E	F	G	H	J	K	L	M	N	O	P	Q	R	S	T	U	V	W	
2Z	31	42	53	64	75	86	A7	B8	CA	DB	EC	FD	GE	HF	JG	KH	LJ	MK	NL	OM	PN	QO	RP	SQ	TR	US	VT	WU	XV	
3Y	4Z	51	62	73	84	A5	B6	C7	D8	EA	FB	GC	HD	JE	KF	LG	MH	NJ	OK	PL	QM	RN	SO	TP	UQ	VR	WS	XT	YU	
4X	5Y	6Z	71	82	A3	B4	C5	D6	E7	F8	GA	HB	JC	KD	LE	MF	NG	OH	PJ	QK	RL	SM	TN	UO	VP	WQ	XR	YS	ZT	
5W	6X	7Y	8Z	A1	B2	C3	D4	E5	F6	G7	H8	JA	KB	LC	MD	NE	OF	PG	QH	RJ	SK	TL	UM	VN	WO	XP	YQ	ZR	1S	
6V	7W	8X	AY	BZ	C1	D2	E3	F4	G5	H6	J7	K8	LA	MB	NC	OD	PE	QF	RG	SH	TJ	UK	VL	WM	XN	YO	ZP	1Q	2R	+
7U	8V	AW	BX	CY	DZ	E1	F2	G3	H4	J5	K6	L7	M8	NA	OB	PC	QD	RE	SF	TG	UH	VJ	WK	XL	YM	ZN	1O	2P	3Q	
8T	AU	BV	CW	DX	EY	FZ	G1	H2	J3	K4	L5	M6	N7	O8	PA	QB	RC	SD	TE	UF	VG	WH	XJ	YK	ZL	1M	2N	3O	4P	
AS	BT	CU	DV	EW	FX	GY	HZ	J1	K2	L3	M4	N5	O6	P7	Q8	RA	SB	TC	UD	VE	WF	XG	YH	ZJ	1K	2L	3M	4N	5O	0
BR	CS	DT	EU	FV	GW	HX	JY	KZ	L1	M2	N3	O4	P5	Q6	R7	S8	TA	UB	VC	WD	XE	YF	ZG	1H	2J	3K	4L	5M	6N	
CQ	DR	ES	FT	GU	HV	JW	KX	LY	MZ	N1	O2	P3	Q4	R5	S6	T7	U8	VA	WB	XC	YD	ZE	1F	2G	3H	4J	5K	6L	7M	
DP	EQ	FR	GS	HT	JU	KV	LW	MX	NY	OZ	P1	Q2	R3	S4	T5	U6	V7	W8	XA	YB	ZC	1D	2E	3F	4G	5H	6J	7K	8L	−
EO	FP	GQ	HR	JS	KT	LU	MV	NW	OX	PY	QZ	R1	S2	T3	U4	V5	W6	X7	Y8	ZA	1B	2C	3D	4E	5F	6G	7H	8J	AK	
FN	GO	HP	JQ	KR	LS	MT	NU	OV	PW	QX	RY	SZ	T1	U2	V3	W4	X5	Y6	Z7	18	2A	3B	4C	5D	6E	7F	8G	AH	BJ	
GM	HN	JO	KP	LQ	MR	NS	OT	PU	QV	RW	SX	TY	UZ	V1	W2	X3	Y4	Z5	16	27	38	4A	5B	6C	7D	8E	AF	BG	CH	
HL	JM	KN	LO	MP	NQ	OR	PS	QT	RU	SV	TW	UX	VY	WZ	X1	Y2	Z3	14	25	36	47	58	6A	7B	8C	AD	BE	CF	DG	
JK	KL	LM	MN	NO	OP	PQ	QR	RS	ST	TU	UV	VW	WX	XY	YZ	Z1	12	23	34	45	56	67	78	8A	AB	BC	CD	DE	EF	

```
 1   2   3   4   5   6   7   8   9  10  11  12  13  14  15  16  17  18  19  20  21  22  23  24  25  26  27  28  29  30  31
SA  SU   M  TU   W  TH   F  SA  SU   M  TU   W  TH   F  SA  SU   M  TU   W  TH   F  SA  SU   M  TU   W  TH   F  SA  SU   M

AX  BA  CB  DC  ED  FE  GF  HG  JH  KJ  LK  ML  NM  ON  PO  QP  RQ  SR  TS  UT  VU  WV  XW  AX  BA  CB  DC  ED  FE  GF  HG
BW  CX  DA  EB  FC  GD  HE  JF  KG  LH  MJ  NK  OL  PM  QN  RO  SP  TQ  UR  VS  WT  XU  AV  BW  CX  DA  EB  FC  GD  HE  JF
CV  DW  EX  FA  GB  HC  JD  KE  LF  MG  NH  OJ  PK  QL  RM  SN  TO  UP  VQ  WR  XS  AT  BU  CV  DW  EX  FA  GB  HC  JD  KE   +
DU  EV  FW  GX  HA  JB  KC  LD  ME  NF  OG  PH  QJ  RK  SL  TM  UN  VO  WP  XQ  AR  BS  CT  DU  EV  FW  GX  HA  JB  KC  LD
ET  FU  GV  HW  JX  KA  LB  MC  ND  OE  PF  QG  RH  SJ  TK  UL  VM  WN  XO  AP  BQ  CR  DS  ET  FU  GV  HW  JX  KA  LB  MC
FS  GT  HU  JV  KW  LX  MA  NB  OC  PD  QE  RF  SG  TH  UJ  VK  WL  XM  AN  BO  CP  DQ  ER  FS  GT  HU  JV  KW  LX  MA  NB   0
GR  HS  JT  KU  LV  MW  NX  OA  PB  QC  RD  SE  TF  UG  VH  WJ  XK  AL  BM  CN  DO  EP  FQ  GR  HS  JT  KU  LV  MW  NX  OA
HQ  JR  KS  LT  MU  NV  OW  PX  QA  RB  SC  TD  UE  VF  WG  XH  AJ  BK  CL  DM  EN  FO  GP  HQ  JR  KS  LT  MU  NV  OW  PX
JP  KQ  LR  MS  NT  OU  PV  QW  RX  SA  TB  UC  VD  WE  XF  AG  BH  CJ  DK  EL  FM  GN  HO  JP  KQ  LR  MS  NT  OU  PV  QW   −
KO  LP  MQ  NR  OS  PT  QU  RV  SW  TX  UA  VB  WC  XD  AE  BF  CG  DH  EJ  FK  GL  HM  JN  KO  LP  MQ  NR  OS  PT  QU  RV
LN  MO  NP  OQ  PR  QS  RT  SU  TV  UW  VX  WA  XB  AC  BD  CE  DF  EG  FH  GJ  HK  JL  KM  LN  MO  NP  OQ  PR  QS  RT  SU
 M   N   O   P   Q   R   S   T   U   V   W   X   A   B   C   D   E   F   G   H   J   K   L   M   N   O   P   Q   R   S   T
```

```
 1   2   3   4   5   6   7   8   9  10  11  12  13  14  15  16  17  18  19  20  21  22  23  24  25  26  27  28  29  30  31
SA  SU   M  TU   W  TH   F  SA  SU   M  TU   W  TH   F  SA  SU   M  TU   W  TH   F  SA  SU   M  TU   W  TH   F  SA  SU   M

 O   P   Q   R   S   T   U   V   W   X   Y   Z   1   2   3   A   B   C   D   E   F   G   H   J   K   L   M   N   O   P   Q
PN  QO  RP  SQ  TR  US  VT  WU  XV  YW  ZX  1Y  2Z  31  A2  B3  CA  DB  EC  FD  GE  HF  JG  KH  LJ  MK  NL  OM  PN  QO  RP
QM  RN  SO  TP  UQ  VR  WS  XT  YU  ZV  1W  2X  3Y  AZ  B1  C2  D3  EA  FB  GC  HD  JE  KF  LG  MH  NJ  OK  PL  QM  RN  SO
RL  SM  TN  UO  VP  WQ  XR  YS  ZT  1U  2V  3W  AX  BY  CZ  D1  E2  F3  GA  HB  JC  KD  LE  MF  NG  OH  PJ  QK  RL  SM  TN
SK  TL  UM  VN  WO  XP  YQ  ZR  1S  2T  3U  AV  BW  CX  DY  EZ  F1  G2  H3  JA  KB  LC  MD  NE  OF  PG  QH  RJ  SK  TL  UM   +
TJ  UK  VL  WM  XN  YO  ZP  1Q  2R  3S  AT  BU  CV  DW  EX  FY  GZ  H1  J2  K3  LA  MB  NC  OD  PE  QF  RG  SH  TJ  UK  VL
UH  VJ  WK  XL  YM  ZN  1O  2P  3Q  AR  BS  CT  DU  EV  FW  GX  HY  JZ  K1  L2  M3  NA  OB  PC  QD  RE  SF  TG  UH  VJ  WK
VG  WH  XJ  YK  ZL  1M  2N  3O  AP  BQ  CR  DS  ET  FU  GV  HW  JX  KY  LZ  M1  N2  O3  PA  QB  RC  SD  TE  UF  VG  WH  XJ   0
WF  XG  YH  ZJ  1K  2L  3M  AN  BO  CP  DQ  ER  FS  GT  HU  JV  KW  LX  MY  NZ  O1  P2  Q3  RA  SB  TC  UD  VE  WF  XG  YH
XE  YF  ZG  1H  2J  3K  AL  BM  CN  DO  EP  FQ  GR  HS  JT  KU  LV  MW  NX  OY  PZ  Q1  R2  S3  TA  UB  VC  WD  XE  YF  ZG
YD  ZE  1F  2G  3H  AJ  BK  CL  DM  EN  FO  GP  HQ  JR  KS  LT  MU  NV  OW  PX  QY  RZ  S1  T2  U3  VA  WB  XC  YD  ZE  1F   −
ZC  1D  2E  3F  AG  BH  CJ  DK  EL  FM  GN  HO  JP  KQ  LR  MS  NT  OU  PV  QW  RX  SY  TZ  U1  V2  W3  XA  YB  ZC  1D  2E
1B  2C  3D  AE  BF  CG  DH  EJ  FK  GL  HM  JN  KO  LP  MQ  NR  OS  PT  QU  RV  SW  TX  UY  VZ  W1  X2  Y3  ZA  1B  2C  3D
2A  3B  AC  BD  CE  DF  EG  FH  GJ  HK  JL  KM  LN  MO  NP  OQ  PR  QS  RT  SU  TV  UW  VX  WY  XZ  Y1  Z2  13  2A  3B  AC
 3   A   B   C   D   E   F   G   H   J   K   L   M   N   O   P   Q   R   S   T   U   V   W   X   Y   Z   1   2   3   A   B
```

```
 1   2   3   4   5   6   7   8   9  10  11  12  13  14  15  16  17  18  19  20  21  22  23  24  25  26  27  28  29  30  31
SA  SU   M  TU   W  TH   F  SA  SU   M  TU   W  TH   F  SA  SU   M  TU   W  TH   F  SA  SU   M  TU   W  TH   F  SA  SU   M

 X   Y   Z   1   2   3   4   5   6   7   8   A   B   C   D   E   F   G   H   J   K   L   M   N   O   P   Q   R   S   T   U
YW  ZX  1Y  2Z  31  42  53  64  75  86  A7  B8  CA  DB  EC  FD  GE  HF  JG  KH  LJ  MK  NL  OM  PN  QO  RP  SQ  TR  US  VT
ZV  1W  2X  3Y  4Z  51  62  73  84  A5  B6  C7  D8  EA  FB  GC  HD  JE  KF  LG  MH  NJ  OK  PL  QM  RN  SO  TP  UQ  VR  WS
1U  2V  3W  4X  5Y  6Z  71  82  A3  B4  C5  D6  E7  F8  GA  HB  JC  KD  LE  MF  NG  OH  PJ  QK  RL  SM  TN  UO  VP  WQ  XR
2T  3U  4V  5W  6X  7Y  8Z  A1  B2  C3  D4  E5  F6  G7  H8  JA  KB  LC  MD  NE  OF  PG  QH  RJ  SK  TL  UM  VN  WO  XP  YQ
3S  4T  5U  6V  7W  8X  AY  BZ  C1  D2  E3  F4  G5  H6  J7  K8  LA  MB  NC  OD  PE  QF  RG  SH  TJ  UK  VL  WM  XN  YO  ZP   +
4R  5S  6T  7U  8V  AW  BX  CY  DZ  E1  F2  G3  H4  J5  K6  L7  M8  NA  OB  PC  QD  RE  SF  TG  UH  VJ  WK  XL  YM  ZN  1O
5Q  6R  7S  8T  AU  BV  CW  DX  EY  FZ  G1  H2  J3  K4  L5  M6  N7  O8  PA  QB  RC  SD  TE  UF  VG  WH  XJ  YK  ZL  1M  2N
6P  7Q  8R  AS  BT  CU  DV  EW  FX  GY  HZ  J1  K2  L3  M4  N5  O6  P7  Q8  RA  SB  TC  UD  VE  WF  XG  YH  ZJ  1K  2L  3M   0
7O  8P  AQ  BR  CS  DT  EU  FV  GW  HX  JY  KZ  L1  M2  N3  O4  P5  Q6  R7  S8  TA  UB  VC  WD  XE  YF  ZG  1H  2J  3K  4L
8N  AO  BP  CQ  DR  ES  FT  GU  HV  JW  KX  LY  MZ  N1  O2  P3  Q4  R5  S6  T7  U8  VA  WB  XC  YD  ZE  1F  2G  3H  4J  5K   −
AM  BN  CO  DP  EQ  FR  GS  HT  JU  KV  LW  MX  NY  OZ  P1  Q2  R3  S4  T5  U6  V7  W8  XA  YB  ZC  1D  2E  3F  4G  5H  6J
BL  CM  DN  EO  FP  GQ  HR  JS  KT  LU  MV  NW  OX  PY  QZ  R1  S2  T3  U4  V5  W6  X7  Y8  ZA  1B  2C  3D  4E  5F  6G  7H
CK  DL  EM  FN  GO  HP  JQ  KR  LS  MT  NU  OV  PW  QX  RY  SZ  T1  U2  V3  W4  X5  Y6  Z7  18  2A  3B  4C  5D  6E  7F  8G
DJ  EK  FL  GM  HN  JO  KP  LQ  MR  NS  OT  PU  QV  RW  SX  TY  UZ  V1  W2  X3  Y4  Z5  16  27  38  4A  5B  6C  7D  8E  AF
EH  FJ  GK  HL  JM  KN  LO  MP  NQ  OR  PS  QT  RU  SV  TW  UX  VY  WZ  X1  Y2  Z3  14  25  36  47  58  6A  7B  8C  AD  BE
FG  GH  HJ  JK  KL  LM  MN  NO  OP  PQ  QR  RS  ST  TU  UV  VW  WX  XY  YZ  Z1  12  23  34  45  56  67  78  8A  AB  BC  CD
```

212

PHYSICAL

1 TU	2 W	3 TH	4 F	5 SA	6 SU	7 M	8 TU	9 W	10 TH	11 F	12 SA	13 SU	14 M	15 TU	16 W	17 TH	18 F	19 SA	20 SU	21 M	22 TU	23 TH	24 F	25 SA	26 SU	27 M	28 TU	29 TU	30 W	
JH	KJ	LK	ML	NM	ON	PO	QP	RQ	SR	TS	UT	VU	WV	XW	AX	BA	CB	DC	ED	FE	GF	HG	JH	KJ	LK	ML	NM	ON	PO	
KG	LH	MJ	NK	OL	PM	QN	RO	SP	TQ	UR	VS	WT	XU	AV	BW	CX	DA	EB	FC	GD	HE	JF	KG	LH	MJ	NK	OL	PM	QN	
LF	MG	NH	OJ	PK	QL	RM	SN	TO	UP	VQ	WR	XS	AT	BU	CV	DW	EX	FA	GB	HC	JD	KE	LF	MG	NH	OJ	PK	QL	RM	+
ME	NF	OG	PH	QJ	RK	SL	TM	UN	VO	WP	XQ	AR	BS	CT	DU	EV	FW	GX	HA	JB	KC	LD	ME	NF	OG	PH	QJ	RK	SL	
ND	OE	PF	QG	RH	SJ	TK	UL	VM	WN	XO	AP	BQ	CR	DS	ET	FU	GV	HW	JX	KA	LB	MC	ND	OE	PF	QG	RH	SJ	TK	
OC	PD	QE	RF	SG	TH	UJ	VK	WL	XM	AN	BO	CP	DQ	ER	FS	GT	HU	JV	KW	LX	MA	NB	OC	PD	QE	RF	SG	TH	UJ	0
PB	QC	RD	SE	TF	UG	VH	WJ	XK	AL	BM	CN	DO	EP	FQ	GR	HS	JT	KU	LV	MW	NX	OA	PB	QC	RD	SE	TF	UG	VH	
QA	RB	SC	TD	UE	VF	WG	XH	AJ	BK	CL	DM	EN	FO	GP	HQ	JR	KS	LT	MU	NV	OW	PX	QA	RB	SC	TD	UE	VF	WG	
RX	SA	TB	UC	VD	WE	XF	AG	BH	CJ	DK	EL	FM	GN	HO	JP	KQ	LR	MS	NT	OU	PV	QW	RX	SA	TB	UC	VD	WE	XF	−
SW	TX	UA	VB	WC	XD	AE	BF	CG	DH	EJ	FK	GL	HM	JN	KO	LP	MQ	NR	OS	PT	QU	RV	SW	TX	UA	VB	WC	XD	AE	
TV	UW	VX	WA	XB	AC	BD	CE	DF	EG	FH	GJ	HK	JL	KM	LN	MO	NP	OQ	PR	QS	RT	SU	TV	UW	VX	WA	XB	AC	BD	
U	V	W	X	A	B	C	D	E	F	G	H	J	K	L	M	N	O	P	Q	R	S	T	U	V	W	X	A	B	C	

EMOTIONAL

1 TU	2 W	3 TH	4 F	5 SA	6 SU	7 M	8 TU	9 W	10 TH	11 F	12 SA	13 SU	14 M	15 TU	16 W	17 TH	18 F	19 SA	20 SU	21 M	22 TU	23 TH	24 F	25 SA	26 SU	27 M	28 TU	29 TU	30 W	
R	S	T	U	V	W	X	Y	Z	1	2	3	A	B	C	D	E	F	G	H	J	K	L	M	N	O	P	Q	R	S	
SQ	TR	US	VT	WU	XV	YW	ZX	1Y	2Z	31	A2	B3	CA	DB	EC	FD	GE	HF	JG	KH	LJ	MK	NL	OM	PN	QO	RP	SQ	TR	
TP	UQ	VR	WS	XT	YU	ZV	1W	2X	3Y	AZ	B1	C2	D3	EA	FB	GC	HD	JE	KF	LG	MH	NJ	OK	PL	QM	RN	SO	TP	UQ	
UO	VP	WQ	XR	YS	ZT	1U	2V	3W	AX	BY	CZ	D1	E2	F3	GA	HB	JC	KD	LE	MF	NG	OH	PJ	QK	RL	SM	TN	UO	VP	+
VN	WO	XP	YQ	ZR	1S	2T	3U	AV	BW	CX	DY	EZ	F1	G2	H3	JA	KB	LC	MD	NE	OF	PG	QH	RJ	SK	TL	UM	VN	WO	
WM	XN	YO	ZP	1Q	2R	3S	AT	BU	CV	DW	EX	FY	GZ	H1	J2	K3	LA	MB	NC	OD	PE	QF	RG	SH	TJ	UK	VL	WM	XN	
XL	YM	ZN	1O	2P	3Q	AR	BS	CT	DU	EV	FW	GX	HY	JZ	K1	L2	M3	NA	OB	PC	QD	RE	SF	TG	UH	VJ	WK	XL	YM	
YK	ZL	1M	2N	3O	AP	BQ	CR	DS	ET	FU	GV	HW	JX	KY	LZ	M1	N2	O3	PA	QB	RC	SD	TE	UF	VG	WH	XJ	YK	ZL	0
ZJ	1K	2L	3M	AN	BO	CP	DQ	ER	FS	GT	HU	JV	KW	LX	MY	NZ	O1	P2	Q3	RA	SB	TC	UD	VE	WF	XG	YH	ZJ	1K	
1H	2J	3K	AL	BM	CN	DO	EP	FQ	GR	HS	JT	KU	LV	MW	NX	OY	PZ	Q1	R2	S3	TA	UB	VC	WD	XE	YF	ZG	1H	2J	
2G	3H	AJ	BK	CL	DM	EN	FO	GP	HQ	JR	KS	LT	MU	NV	OW	PX	QY	RZ	S1	T2	U3	VA	WB	XC	YD	ZE	1F	2G	3H	−
3F	AG	BH	CG	DK	EL	FM	GN	HO	JP	KQ	LR	MS	NT	OU	PV	QW	RX	SY	TZ	U1	V2	W3	XA	YB	ZC	1D	2E	3F	AG	
AE	BF	CG	DH	EJ	FK	GL	HM	JN	KO	LP	MQ	NR	OS	PT	QU	RV	SW	TX	UY	VZ	W1	X2	Y3	ZA	1B	2C	3D	AE	BF	
BD	CE	DF	EG	FH	GJ	HK	JL	KM	LN	MO	NP	OQ	PR	QS	RT	SU	TV	UW	VX	WY	XZ	Y1	Z2	13	2A	3B	AC	BD	CE	
C	D	E	F	G	H	J	K	L	M	N	O	P	Q	R	S	T	U	V	W	X	Y	Z	1	2	3	A	B	C	D	

INTELLECTUAL

1 TU	2 W	3 TH	4 F	5 SA	6 SU	7 M	8 TU	9 W	10 TH	11 F	12 SA	13 SU	14 M	15 TU	16 W	17 TH	18 F	19 SA	20 SU	21 M	22 TU	23 TH	24 F	25 SA	26 SU	27 M	28 TU	29 TU	30 W	
V	W	X	Y	Z	1	2	3	4	5	6	7	8	A	B	C	D	E	F	G	H	J	K	L	M	N	O	P	Q	R	
WU	XV	YW	ZX	1Y	2Z	31	42	53	64	75	86	A7	B8	CA	DB	EC	FD	GE	HF	JG	KH	LJ	MK	NL	OM	PN	QO	RP	SQ	
XT	YU	ZV	1W	2X	3Y	4Z	51	62	73	84	A5	B6	C7	D8	EA	FB	GC	HD	JE	KF	LG	MH	NJ	OK	PL	QM	RN	SO	TP	
YS	ZT	1U	2V	3W	4X	5Y	6Z	71	82	A3	B4	C5	D6	E7	F8	GA	HB	JC	KD	LE	MF	NG	OH	PJ	QK	RL	SM	TN	UO	
ZR	1S	2T	3U	4V	5W	6X	7Y	8Z	A1	B2	C3	D4	E5	F6	G7	H8	JA	KB	LC	MD	NE	OF	PG	QH	RJ	SK	TL	UM	VN	
1Q	2R	3S	4T	5U	6V	7W	8X	AY	BZ	C1	D2	E3	F4	G5	H6	J7	K8	LA	MB	NC	OD	PE	QF	RG	SH	TJ	UK	VL	WM	+
2P	3Q	4R	5S	6T	7U	8V	AW	BX	CY	DZ	E1	F2	G3	H4	J5	K6	L7	M8	NA	OB	PC	QD	RE	SF	TG	UH	VJ	WK	XL	
3O	4P	5Q	6R	7S	8T	AU	BV	CW	DX	EY	FZ	G1	H2	J3	K4	L5	M6	N7	O8	PA	QB	RC	SD	TE	UF	VG	WH	XJ	YK	
4N	5O	6P	7Q	8R	AS	BT	CU	DV	EW	FX	GY	HZ	J1	K2	L3	M4	N5	O6	P7	Q8	RA	SB	TC	UD	VE	WF	XG	YH	ZJ	0
5M	6N	7O	8P	AQ	BR	CS	DT	EU	FV	GW	HX	JY	KZ	L1	M2	N3	O4	P5	Q6	R7	S8	TA	UB	VC	WD	XE	YF	ZG	1H	
6L	7M	8N	AO	BP	CQ	DR	ES	FT	GU	HV	JW	KX	LY	MZ	N1	O2	P3	Q4	R5	S6	T7	U8	VA	WB	XC	YD	ZE	1F	2G	−
7K	8L	AM	BN	CO	DP	EQ	FR	GS	HT	JU	KV	LW	MX	NY	OZ	P1	Q2	R3	S4	T5	U6	V7	W8	XA	YB	ZC	1D	2E	3F	
8J	AK	BL	CM	DN	EO	FP	GQ	HR	JS	KT	LU	MV	NW	OX	PY	QZ	R1	S2	T3	U4	V5	W6	X7	Y8	ZA	1B	2C	3D	4E	
AH	BJ	CK	DL	EM	FN	GO	HP	JQ	KR	LS	MT	NU	OV	PW	QX	RY	SZ	T1	U2	V3	W4	X5	Y6	Z7	18	2A	3B	4C	5D	
BG	CH	DJ	EK	FL	GM	HN	JO	KP	LQ	MR	NS	OT	PU	QV	RW	SX	TY	UZ	V1	W2	X3	Y4	Z5	16	27	38	4A	5B	6C	
CF	DG	EH	FJ	GK	HL	JM	KN	LO	MP	NQ	OR	PS	QT	RU	SV	TW	UX	VY	WZ	X1	Y2	Z3	14	25	36	47	58	6A	7B	
DE	EF	FG	GH	HJ	JK	KL	LM	MN	NO	OP	PQ	QR	RS	ST	TU	UV	VW	WX	XY	YZ	Z1	12	23	34	45	56	67	78	8A	

1 TH	2 F	3 SA	4 SU	5 M	6 TU	7 W	8 TH	9 F	10 SA	11 SU	12 M	13 TU	14 W	15 TH	16 F	17 SA	18 SU	19 M	20 TU	21 W	22 TH	23 F	24 SA	25 SU	26 M	27 TU	28 W	29 TH	30 F	31 SA	
QP	RQ	SR	TS	UT	VU	WV	XW	AX	BA	CB	DC	ED	FE	GF	HG	JH	KJ	LK	ML	NM	ON	PO	QP	RQ	SR	TS	UT	VU	WV	XW	
RO	SP	TQ	UR	VS	WT	XU	AV	BW	CX	DA	EB	FC	GD	HE	JF	KG	LH	MJ	NK	OL	PM	QN	RO	SP	TQ	UR	VS	WT	XU	AV	+
SN	TO	UP	VQ	WR	XS	AT	BU	CV	DW	EX	FA	GB	HC	JD	KE	LF	MG	NH	OJ	PK	QL	RM	SN	TO	UP	VQ	WR	XS	AT	BU	
TM	UN	VO	WP	XQ	AR	BS	CT	DU	EV	FW	GX	HA	JB	KC	LD	ME	NF	OG	PH	QJ	RK	SL	TM	UN	VO	WP	XQ	AR	BS	CT	
UL	VM	WN	XO	AP	BQ	CR	DS	ET	FU	GV	HW	JX	KA	LB	MC	ND	OE	PF	QG	RH	SJ	TK	UL	VM	WN	XO	AP	BQ	CR	DS	
VK	WL	XM	AN	BO	CP	DQ	ER	FS	GT	HU	JV	KW	LX	MA	NB	OC	PD	QE	RF	SG	TH	UJ	VK	WL	XM	AN	BO	CP	DQ	ER	0
WJ	XK	AL	BM	CN	DO	EP	FQ	GR	HS	JT	KU	LV	MW	NX	OA	PB	QC	RD	SE	TF	UG	VH	WJ	XK	AL	BM	CN	DO	EP	FQ	
XH	AJ	BK	CL	DM	EN	FO	GP	HQ	JR	KS	LT	MU	NV	OW	PX	QA	RB	SC	TD	UE	VF	WG	XH	AJ	BK	CL	DM	EN	FO	GP	
AG	BH	CJ	DK	EL	FM	GN	HO	JP	KQ	LR	MS	NT	OU	PV	QW	RX	SA	TB	UC	VD	WE	XF	AG	BH	CJ	DK	EL	FM	GN	HO	—
BF	CG	DH	EJ	FK	GL	HM	JN	KO	LP	MQ	NR	OS	PT	QU	RV	SW	TX	UA	VB	WC	XD	AE	BF	CG	DH	EJ	FK	GL	HM	JN	
CE	DF	EG	FH	GJ	HK	JL	KM	LN	MO	NP	OQ	PR	QS	RT	SU	TV	UW	VX	WA	XB	AC	BD	CE	DF	EG	FH	GJ	HK	JL	KM	
D	E	F	G	H	J	K	L	M	N	O	P	Q	R	S	T	U	V	W	X	A	B	C	D	E	F	G	H	J	K	L	

1 TH	2 F	3 SA	4 SU	5 M	6 TU	7 W	8 TH	9 F	10 SA	11 SU	12 M	13 TU	14 W	15 TH	16 F	17 SA	18 SU	19 M	20 TU	21 W	22 TH	23 F	24 SA	25 SU	26 M	27 TU	28 W	29 TH	30 F	31 SA	
T	U	V	W	X	Y	Z	1	2	3	A	B	C	D	E	F	G	H	J	K	L	M	N	O	P	Q	R	S	T	U	V	
US	VT	WU	XV	YW	ZX	1Y	2Z	31	A2	B3	CA	DB	EC	FD	GE	HF	JG	KH	LJ	MK	NL	OM	PN	QO	RP	SQ	TR	US	VT	WU	
VR	WS	XT	YU	ZV	1W	2X	3Y	AZ	B1	C2	D3	EA	FB	GC	HD	JE	KF	LG	MH	NJ	OK	PL	QM	RN	SO	TP	UQ	VR	WS	XT	
WQ	XR	YS	ZT	1U	2V	3W	AX	BY	CZ	D1	E2	F3	GA	HB	JC	KD	LE	MF	NG	OH	PJ	QK	RL	SM	TN	UO	VP	WQ	XR	YS	+
XP	YQ	ZR	1S	2T	3U	AV	BW	CX	DY	EZ	F1	G2	H3	JA	KB	LC	MD	NE	OF	PG	QH	RJ	SK	TL	UM	VN	WO	XP	YQ	ZR	
YO	ZP	1Q	2R	3S	AT	BU	CV	DW	EX	FY	GZ	H1	J2	K3	LA	MB	NC	OD	PE	QF	RG	SH	TJ	UK	VL	WM	XN	YO	ZP	1Q	
ZN	1O	2P	3Q	AR	BS	CT	DU	EV	FW	GX	HY	JZ	K1	L2	M3	NA	OB	PC	QD	RE	SF	TG	UH	VJ	WK	XL	YM	ZN	1O	2P	
1M	2N	3O	AP	BQ	CR	DS	ET	FU	GV	HW	JX	KY	LZ	M1	N2	O3	PA	QB	RC	SD	TE	UF	VG	WH	XJ	YK	ZL	1M	2N	3O	0
2L	3M	AN	BO	CP	DQ	ER	FS	GT	HU	JV	KW	LX	MY	NZ	O1	P2	Q3	RA	SB	TC	UD	VE	WF	XG	YH	ZJ	1K	2L	3M	AN	
3K	AL	BM	CN	DO	EP	FQ	GR	HS	JT	KU	LV	MW	NX	OY	PZ	Q1	R2	S3	TA	UB	VC	WD	XE	YF	ZG	1H	2J	3K	AL	BM	
AJ	BK	CL	DM	EN	FO	GP	HQ	JR	KS	LT	MU	NV	OW	PX	QY	RZ	S1	T2	U3	VA	WB	XC	YD	ZE	1F	2G	3H	AJ	BK	CL	—
BH	CJ	DK	EL	FM	GN	HO	JP	KQ	LR	MS	NT	OU	PV	QW	RX	SY	TZ	U1	V2	W3	XA	YB	ZC	1D	2E	3F	AG	BH	CJ	DK	
CG	DH	EJ	FK	GL	HM	JN	KO	LP	MQ	NR	OS	PT	QU	RV	SW	TX	UY	VZ	W1	X2	Y3	ZA	1B	2C	3D	AE	BF	CG	DH	EJ	
DF	EG	FH	GJ	HK	JL	KM	LN	MO	NP	OQ	PR	QS	RT	SU	TV	UW	VX	WY	XZ	Y1	Z2	13	2A	3B	AC	BD	CE	DF	EG	FH	
E	F	G	H	J	K	L	M	N	O	P	Q	R	S	T	U	V	W	X	Y	Z	1	2	3	A	B	C	D	E	F	G	

1 TH	2 F	3 SA	4 SU	5 M	6 TU	7 W	8 TH	9 F	10 SA	11 SU	12 M	13 TU	14 W	15 TH	16 F	17 SA	18 SU	19 M	20 TU	21 W	22 TH	23 F	24 SA	25 SU	26 M	27 TU	28 W	29 TH	30 F	31 SA	
S	T	U	V	W	X	Y	Z	1	2	3	4	5	6	7	8	A	B	C	D	E	F	G	H	J	K	L	M	N	O	P	
TR	US	VT	WU	XV	YW	ZX	1Y	2Z	31	42	53	64	75	86	A7	B8	CA	DB	EC	FD	GE	HF	JG	KH	LJ	MK	NL	OM	PN	QO	
UQ	VR	WS	XT	YU	ZV	1W	2X	3Y	4Z	51	62	73	84	A5	B6	C7	D8	EA	FB	GC	HD	JE	KF	LG	MH	NJ	OK	PL	QM	RN	
VP	WQ	XR	YS	ZT	1U	2V	3W	4X	5Y	6Z	71	82	A3	B4	C5	D6	E7	F8	GA	HB	JC	KD	LE	MF	NG	OH	PJ	QK	RL	SM	
WO	XP	YQ	ZR	1S	2T	3U	4V	5W	6X	7Y	8Z	A1	B2	C3	D4	E5	F6	G7	H8	JA	KB	LC	MD	NE	OF	PG	QH	RJ	SK	TL	+
XN	YO	ZP	1Q	2R	3S	4T	5U	6V	7W	8X	AY	BZ	C1	D2	E3	F4	G5	H6	J7	K8	LA	MB	NC	OD	PE	QF	RG	SH	TJ	UK	
YM	ZN	1O	2P	3Q	4R	5S	6T	7U	8V	AW	BX	CY	DZ	E1	F2	G3	H4	J5	K6	L7	M8	NA	OB	PC	QD	RE	SF	TG	UH	VJ	
ZL	1M	2N	3O	4P	5Q	6R	7S	8T	AU	BV	CW	DX	EY	FZ	G1	H2	J3	K4	L5	M6	N7	O8	PA	QB	RC	SD	TE	UF	VG	WH	
1K	2L	3M	4N	5O	6P	7Q	8R	AS	BT	CU	DV	EW	FX	GY	HZ	J1	K2	L3	M4	N5	O6	P7	Q8	RA	SB	TC	UD	VE	WF	XG	0
2J	3K	4L	5M	6N	7O	8P	AQ	BR	CS	DT	EU	FV	GW	HX	JY	KZ	L1	M2	N3	O4	P5	Q6	R7	S8	TA	UB	VC	WD	XE	YF	
3H	4J	5K	6L	7M	8N	AO	BP	CQ	DR	ES	FT	GU	HV	JW	KX	LY	MZ	N1	O2	P3	Q4	R5	S6	T7	U8	VA	WB	XC	YD	ZE	
4G	5H	6J	7K	8L	AM	BN	CO	DP	EQ	FR	GS	HT	JU	KV	LW	MX	NY	OZ	P1	Q2	R3	S4	T5	U6	V7	W8	XA	YB	ZC	1D	—
5F	6G	7H	8J	AK	BL	CM	DN	EO	FP	GQ	HR	JS	KT	LU	MV	NW	OX	PY	QZ	R1	S2	T3	U4	V5	W6	X7	Y8	ZA	1B	2C	
6E	7F	8G	AH	BJ	CK	DL	EM	FN	GO	HP	JQ	KR	LS	MT	NU	OV	PW	QX	RY	SZ	T1	U2	V3	W4	X5	Y6	Z7	18	2A	3B	
7D	8E	AF	BG	CH	DJ	EK	FL	GM	HN	JO	KP	LQ	MR	NS	OT	PU	QV	RW	SX	TY	UZ	V1	W2	X3	Y4	Z5	16	27	38	4A	
8C	AD	BE	CF	DG	EH	FJ	GK	HL	JM	KN	LO	MP	NQ	OR	PS	QT	RU	SV	TW	UX	VY	WZ	X1	Y2	Z3	14	25	36	47	58	
AB	BC	CD	DE	EF	FG	GH	HJ	JK	KL	LM	MN	NO	OP	PQ	QR	RS	ST	TU	UV	VW	WX	XY	YZ	Z1	12	23	34	45	56	67	

JANUARY 1978 — PHYSICAL — JANUARY 1978

| 1 | 2 | 3 | 4 | 5 | 6 | 7 | 8 | 9 | 10 | 11 | 12 | 13 | 14 | 15 | 16 | 17 | 18 | 19 | 20 | 21 | 22 | 23 | 24 | 25 | 26 | 27 | 28 | 29 | 30 | 31 | |
SU	M	TU	W	TH	F	SA	SU	M	TU	W	TH	F	SA	SU	M	TU	W	TH	F	SA	SU	M	TU	W	TH	F	SA	SU	M	TU	
AX	BA	CB	DC	ED	FE	GF	HG	JH	KJ	LK	ML	NM	ON	PO	QP	RQ	SR	TS	UT	VU	WV	XW	AX	BA	CB	DC	ED	FE	GF	HG	
BW	CX	DA	EB	FC	GD	HE	JF	KG	LH	MJ	NK	OL	PM	QN	RO	SP	TQ	UR	VS	WT	XU	AV	BW	CX	DA	EB	FC	GD	HE	JF	
CV	DW	EX	FA	GB	HC	JD	KE	LF	MG	NH	OJ	PK	QL	RM	SN	TO	UP	VQ	WR	XS	AT	BU	CV	DW	EX	FA	GB	HC	JD	KE	
DU	EV	FW	GX	HA	JB	KC	LD	ME	NF	OG	PH	QJ	RK	SL	TM	UN	VO	WP	XQ	AR	BS	CT	DU	EV	FW	GX	HA	JB	KC	LD	+
ET	FU	GV	HW	JX	KA	LB	MC	ND	OE	PF	QG	RH	SJ	TK	UL	VM	WN	XO	AP	BQ	CR	DS	ET	FU	GV	HW	JX	KA	LB	MC	
FS	GT	HU	JV	KW	LX	MA	NB	OC	PD	QE	RF	SG	TH	UJ	VK	WL	XM	AN	BO	CP	DQ	ER	FS	GT	HU	JV	KW	LX	MA	NB	0
GR	HS	JT	KU	LV	MW	NX	OA	PB	QC	RD	SE	TF	UG	VH	WJ	XK	AL	BM	CN	DO	EP	FQ	GR	HS	JT	KU	LV	MW	NX	OA	
HQ	JR	KS	LT	MU	NV	OW	PX	QA	RB	SC	TD	UE	VF	WG	XH	AJ	BK	CL	DM	EN	FO	GP	HQ	JR	KS	LT	MU	NV	OW	PX	
JP	KQ	LR	MS	NT	OU	PV	QW	RX	SA	TB	UC	VD	WE	XF	AG	BH	CJ	DK	EL	FM	GN	HO	JP	KQ	LR	MS	NT	OU	PV	QW	−
KO	LP	MQ	NR	OS	PT	QU	RV	SW	TX	UA	VB	WC	XD	AE	BF	CG	DH	EJ	FK	GL	HM	JN	KO	LP	MQ	NR	OS	PT	QU	RV	
LN	MO	NP	OQ	PR	QS	RT	SU	TV	UW	VX	WA	XB	AC	BD	CE	DF	EG	FH	GJ	HK	JL	KM	LN	MO	NP	OQ	PR	QS	RT	SU	
M	N	O	P	Q	R	S	T	U	V	W	X	A	B	C	D	E	F	G	H	J	K	L	M	N	O	P	Q	R	S	T	

JANUARY 1978 — EMOTIONAL — JANUARY 1978

| 1 | 2 | 3 | 4 | 5 | 6 | 7 | 8 | 9 | 10 | 11 | 12 | 13 | 14 | 15 | 16 | 17 | 18 | 19 | 20 | 21 | 22 | 23 | 24 | 25 | 26 | 27 | 28 | 29 | 30 | 31 | |
SU	M	TU	W	TH	F	SA	SU	M	TU	W	TH	F	SA	SU	M	TU	W	TH	F	SA	SU	M	TU	W	TH	F	SA	SU	M	TU	
W	X	Y	Z	1	2	3	A	B	C	D	E	F	G	H	J	K	L	M	N	O	P	Q	R	S	T	U	V	W	X	Y	
XV	YW	ZX	1Y	2Z	31	A2	B3	CA	DB	EC	FD	GE	HF	JG	KH	LJ	MK	NL	OM	PN	QO	RP	SQ	TR	US	VT	WU	XV	YW	ZX	
YU	ZV	1W	2X	3Y	AZ	B1	C2	D3	EA	FB	GC	HD	JE	KF	LG	MH	NJ	OK	PL	QM	RN	SO	TP	UQ	VR	WS	XT	YU	ZV	1W	
ZT	1U	2V	3W	AX	BY	CZ	D1	E2	F3	GA	HB	JC	KD	LE	MF	NG	OH	PJ	QK	RL	SM	TN	UO	VP	WQ	XR	YS	ZT	1U	2V	
1S	2T	3U	AV	BW	CX	DY	EZ	F1	G2	H3	JA	KB	LC	MD	NE	OF	PG	QH	RJ	SK	TL	UM	VN	WO	XP	YQ	ZR	1S	2T	3U	
2R	3S	AT	BU	CV	DW	EX	FY	GZ	H1	J2	K3	LA	MB	NC	OD	PE	QF	RG	SH	TJ	UK	VL	WM	XN	YO	ZP	1Q	2R	3S	AT	+
3Q	AR	BS	CT	DU	EV	FW	GX	HY	JZ	K1	L2	M3	NA	OB	PC	QD	RE	SF	TG	UH	VJ	WK	XL	YM	ZN	1O	2P	3Q	AR	BS	
AP	BQ	CR	DS	ET	FU	GV	HW	JX	KY	LZ	M1	N2	O3	PA	QB	RC	SD	TE	UF	VG	WH	XJ	YK	ZL	1M	2N	3O	AP	BQ	CR	0
BO	CP	DQ	ER	FS	GT	HU	JV	KW	LX	MY	NZ	O1	P2	Q3	RA	SB	TC	UD	VE	WF	XG	YH	ZJ	1K	2L	3M	AN	BO	CP	DQ	
CN	DO	EP	FQ	GR	HS	JT	KU	LV	MW	NX	OY	PZ	Q1	R2	S3	TA	UB	VC	WD	XE	YF	ZG	1H	2J	3K	AL	BM	CN	DO	EP	
DM	EN	FO	GP	HQ	JR	KS	LT	MU	NV	OW	PX	QY	RZ	S1	T2	U3	VA	WB	XC	YD	ZE	1F	2G	3H	AJ	BK	CL	DM	EN	FO	−
EL	FM	GN	HO	JP	KQ	LR	MS	NT	OU	PV	QW	RX	SY	TZ	U1	V2	W3	XA	YB	ZC	1D	2E	3F	AG	BH	CJ	DK	EL	FM	GN	
FK	GL	HM	JN	KO	LP	MQ	NR	OS	PT	QU	RV	SW	TX	UY	VZ	W1	X2	Y3	ZA	1B	2C	3D	AE	BF	CG	DH	EJ	FK	GL	HM	
GJ	HK	JL	KM	LN	MO	NP	OQ	PR	QS	RT	SU	TV	UW	VX	WY	XZ	Y1	Z2	13	2A	3B	AC	BD	CE	DF	EG	FH	GJ	HK	JL	
H	J	K	L	M	N	O	P	Q	R	S	T	U	V	W	X	Y	Z	1	2	3	A	B	C	D	E	F	G	H	J	K	

JANUARY 1978 — INTELLECTUAL — JANUARY 1978

| 1 | 2 | 3 | 4 | 5 | 6 | 7 | 8 | 9 | 10 | 11 | 12 | 13 | 14 | 15 | 16 | 17 | 18 | 19 | 20 | 21 | 22 | 23 | 24 | 25 | 26 | 27 | 28 | 29 | 30 | 31 | |
SU	M	TU	W	TH	F	SA	SU	M	TU	W	TH	F	SA	SU	M	TU	W	TH	F	SA	SU	M	TU	W	TH	F	SA	SU	M	TU	
Q	R	S	T	U	V	W	X	Y	Z	1	2	3	4	5	6	7	8	A	B	C	D	E	F	G	H	J	K	L	M	N	
RP	SQ	TR	US	VT	WU	XV	YW	ZX	1Y	2Z	31	42	53	64	75	86	A7	B8	CA	DB	EC	FD	GE	HF	JG	KH	LJ	MK	NL	OM	
SO	TP	UQ	VR	WS	XT	YU	ZV	1W	2X	3Y	4Z	51	62	73	84	A5	B6	C7	D8	EA	FB	GC	HD	JE	KF	LG	MH	NJ	OK	PL	
TN	UO	VP	WQ	XR	YS	ZT	1U	2V	3W	4X	5Y	6Z	71	82	A3	B4	C5	D6	E7	F8	GA	HB	JC	KD	LE	MF	NG	OH	PJ	QK	
UM	VN	WO	XP	YQ	ZR	1S	2T	3U	4V	5W	6X	7Y	8Z	A1	B2	C3	D4	E5	F6	G7	H8	JA	KB	LC	MD	NE	OF	PG	QH	RJ	
VL	WM	XN	YO	ZP	1Q	2R	3S	4T	5U	6V	7W	8X	AY	BZ	C1	D2	E3	F4	G5	H6	J7	K8	LA	MB	NC	OD	PE	QF	RG	SH	+
WK	XL	YM	ZN	1O	2P	3Q	4R	5S	6T	7U	8V	AW	BX	CY	DZ	E1	F2	G3	H4	J5	K6	L7	M8	NA	OB	PC	QD	RE	SF	TG	
XJ	YK	ZL	1M	2N	3O	4P	5Q	6R	7S	8T	AU	BV	CW	DX	EY	FZ	G1	H2	J3	K4	L5	M6	N7	O8	PA	QB	RC	SD	TE	UF	
YH	ZJ	1K	2L	3M	4N	5O	6P	7Q	8R	AS	BT	CU	DV	EW	FX	GY	HZ	J1	K2	L3	M4	N5	O6	P7	Q8	RA	SB	TC	UD	VE	0
ZG	1H	2J	3K	4L	5M	6N	7O	8P	AQ	BR	CS	DT	EU	FV	GW	HX	JY	KZ	L1	M2	N3	O4	P5	Q6	R7	S8	TA	UB	VC	WD	
1F	2G	3H	4J	5K	6L	7M	8N	AO	BP	CQ	DR	ES	FT	GU	HV	JW	KX	LY	MZ	N1	O2	P3	Q4	R5	S6	T7	U8	VA	WB	XC	
2E	3F	4G	5H	6J	7K	8L	AM	BN	CO	DP	EQ	FR	GS	HT	JU	KV	LW	MX	NY	OZ	P1	Q2	R3	S4	T5	U6	V7	W8	XA	YB	−
3D	4E	5F	6G	7H	8J	AK	BL	CM	DN	EO	FP	GQ	HR	JS	KT	LU	MV	NW	OX	PY	QZ	R1	S2	T3	U4	V5	W6	X7	Y8	ZA	
4C	5D	6E	7F	8G	AH	BJ	CK	DL	EM	FN	GO	HP	JQ	KR	LS	MT	NU	OV	PW	QX	RY	SZ	T1	U2	V3	W4	X5	Y6	Z7	18	
5B	6C	7D	8E	AF	BG	CH	DJ	EK	FL	GM	HN	JO	KP	LQ	MR	NS	OT	PU	QV	RW	SX	TY	UZ	V1	W2	X3	Y4	Z5	16	27	
6A	7B	8C	AD	BE	CF	DG	EH	FJ	GK	HL	JM	KN	LO	MP	NQ	OR	PS	QT	RU	SV	TW	UX	VY	WZ	X1	Y2	Z3	14	25	36	
78	8A	AB	BC	CD	DE	EF	FG	GH	HJ	JK	KL	LM	MN	NO	OP	PQ	QR	RS	ST	TU	UV	VW	WX	XY	YZ	Z1	12	23	34	45	

215

1 W	2 TH	3 F	4 SA	5 SU	6 M	7 TU	8 W	9 TH	10 F	11 SA	12 SU	13 M	14 TU	15 W	16 TH	17 F	18 SA	19 SU	20 M	21 TU	22 W	23 TH	24 F	25 SA	26 SU	27 M	28 TU	
JH	KJ	LK	ML	NM	ON	PO	QP	RQ	SR	TS	UT	VU	WV	XW	AX	BA	CB	DC	ED	FE	GF	HG	JH	KJ	LK	ML	NM	
KG	LH	MJ	NK	OL	PM	QN	RO	SP	TQ	UR	VS	WT	XU	AV	BW	CX	DA	EB	FC	GD	HE	JF	KG	LH	MJ	NK	OL	
LF	MG	NH	OJ	PK	QL	RM	SN	TO	UP	VQ	WR	XS	AT	BU	CV	DW	EX	FA	GB	HC	JD	KE	LF	MG	NH	OJ	PK	
ME	NF	OG	PH	QJ	RK	SL	TM	UN	VO	WP	XQ	AR	BS	CT	DU	EV	FW	GX	HA	JB	KC	LD	ME	NF	OG	PH	QJ	+
ND	OE	PF	QG	RH	SJ	TK	UL	VM	WN	XO	AP	BQ	CR	DS	ET	FU	GV	HW	JX	KA	LB	MC	ND	OE	PF	QG	RH	
OC	PD	QE	RF	SG	TH	UJ	VK	WL	XM	AN	BO	CP	DQ	ER	FS	GT	HU	JV	KW	LX	MA	NB	OC	PD	QE	RF	SG	0
PB	QC	RD	SE	TF	UG	VH	WJ	XK	AL	BM	CN	DO	EP	FQ	GR	HS	JT	KU	LV	MW	NX	OA	PB	QC	RD	SE	TF	
QA	RB	SC	TD	UE	VF	WG	XH	AJ	BK	CL	DM	EN	FO	GP	HQ	JR	KS	LT	MU	NV	OW	PX	QA	RB	SC	TD	UE	
RX	SA	TB	UC	VD	WE	XF	AG	BH	CJ	DK	EL	FM	GN	HO	JP	KQ	LR	MS	NT	OU	PV	QW	RX	SA	TB	UC	VD	−
SW	TX	UA	VB	WC	XD	AE	BF	CG	DH	EJ	FK	GL	HM	JN	KO	LP	MQ	NR	OS	PT	QU	RV	SW	TX	UA	VB	WC	
TV	UW	VX	WA	XB	AC	BD	CE	DF	EG	FH	GJ	HK	JL	KM	LN	MO	NP	OQ	PR	QS	RT	SU	TV	UW	VX	WA	XB	
U	V	W	X	A	B	C	D	E	F	G	H	J	K	L	M	N	O	P	Q	R	S	T	U	V	W	X	A	

1 W	2 TH	3 F	4 SA	5 SU	6 M	7 TU	8 W	9 TH	10 F	11 SA	12 SU	13 M	14 TU	15 W	16 TH	17 F	18 SA	19 SU	20 M	21 TU	22 W	23 TH	24 F	25 SA	26 SU	27 M	28 TU	
Z	1	2	3	A	B	C	D	E	F	G	H	J	K	L	M	N	O	P	Q	R	S	T	U	V	W	X	Y	
1Y	2Z	31	A2	B3	CA	DB	EC	FD	GE	HF	JG	KH	LJ	MK	NL	OM	PN	QO	RP	SQ	TR	US	VT	WU	XV	YW	ZX	
2X	3Y	AZ	B1	C2	D3	EA	FB	GC	HD	JE	KF	LG	MH	NJ	OK	PL	QM	RN	SO	TP	UQ	VR	WS	XT	YU	ZV	1W	
3W	AX	BY	CZ	D1	E2	F3	GA	HB	JC	KD	LE	MF	NG	OH	PJ	QK	RL	SM	TN	UO	VP	WQ	XR	YS	ZT	1U	2V	
AV	BW	CX	DY	EZ	F1	G2	H3	JA	KB	LC	MD	NE	OF	PG	QH	RJ	SK	TL	UM	VN	WO	XP	YQ	ZR	1S	2T	3U	+
BU	CV	DW	EX	FY	GZ	H1	J2	K3	LA	MB	NC	OD	PE	QF	RG	SH	TJ	UK	VL	WM	XN	YO	ZP	1Q	2R	3S	AT	
CT	DU	EV	FW	GX	HY	JZ	K1	L2	M3	NA	OB	PC	QD	RE	SF	TG	UH	VJ	WK	XL	YM	ZN	1O	2P	3Q	AR	BS	
DS	ET	FU	GV	HW	JX	KY	LZ	M1	N2	O3	PA	QB	RC	SD	TE	UF	VG	WH	XJ	YK	ZL	1M	2N	3O	AP	BQ	CR	0
ER	FS	GT	HU	JV	KW	LX	MY	NZ	O1	P2	Q3	RA	SB	TC	UD	VE	WF	XG	YH	ZJ	1K	2L	3M	AN	BO	CP	DQ	
FQ	GR	HS	JT	KU	LV	MW	NX	OY	PZ	Q1	R2	S3	TA	UB	VC	WD	XE	YF	ZG	1H	2J	3K	AL	BM	CN	DO	EP	
GP	HQ	JR	KS	LT	MU	NV	OW	PX	QY	RZ	S1	T2	U3	VA	WB	XC	YD	ZE	1F	2G	3H	AJ	BK	CL	DM	EN	FO	−
HO	JP	KQ	LR	MS	NT	OU	PV	QW	RX	SY	TZ	U1	V2	W3	XA	YB	ZC	1D	2E	3F	AG	BH	CJ	DK	EL	FM	GN	
JN	KO	LP	MQ	NR	OS	PT	QU	RV	SW	TX	UY	VZ	W1	X2	Y3	ZA	1B	2C	3D	AE	BF	CG	DH	EJ	FK	GL	HM	
KM	LN	MO	NP	OQ	PR	QS	RT	SU	TV	UW	VX	WY	XZ	Y1	Z2	13	2A	3B	AC	BD	CE	DF	EG	FH	GJ	HK	JL	
L	M	N	O	P	Q	R	S	T	U	V	W	X	Y	Z	1	2	3	A	B	C	D	E	F	G	H	J	K	

1 W	2 TH	3 F	4 SA	5 SU	6 M	7 TU	8 W	9 TH	10 F	11 SA	12 SU	13 M	14 TU	15 W	16 TH	17 F	18 SA	19 SU	20 M	21 TU	22 W	23 TH	24 F	25 SA	26 SU	27 M	28 TU	
O	P	Q	R	S	T	U	V	W	X	Y	Z	1	2	3	4	5	6	7	8	A	B	C	D	E	F	G	H	
PN	QO	RP	SQ	TR	US	VT	WU	XV	YW	ZX	1Y	2Z	31	42	53	64	75	86	A7	B8	CA	DB	EC	FD	GE	HF	JG	
QM	RN	SO	TP	UQ	VR	WS	XT	YU	ZV	1W	2X	3Y	4Z	51	62	73	84	A5	B6	C7	D8	EA	FB	GC	HD	JE	KF	
RL	SM	TN	UO	VP	WQ	XR	YS	ZT	1U	2V	3W	4X	5Y	6Z	71	82	A3	B4	C5	D6	E7	F8	GA	HB	JC	KD	LE	
SK	TL	UM	VN	WO	XP	YQ	ZR	1S	2T	3U	4V	5W	6X	7Y	8Z	A1	B2	C3	D4	E5	F6	G7	H8	JA	KB	LC	MD	
TJ	UK	VL	WM	XN	YO	ZP	1Q	2R	3S	4T	5U	6V	7W	8X	AY	BZ	C1	D2	E3	F4	G5	H6	J7	K8	LA	MB	NC	+
UH	VJ	WK	XL	YM	ZN	1O	2P	3Q	4R	5S	6T	7U	8V	AW	BX	CY	DZ	E1	F2	G3	H4	J5	K6	L7	M8	NA	OB	
VG	WH	XJ	YK	ZL	1M	2N	3O	4P	5Q	6R	7S	8T	AU	BV	CW	DX	EY	FZ	G1	H2	J3	K4	L5	M6	N7	O8	PA	
WF	XG	YH	ZJ	1K	2L	3M	4N	5O	6P	7Q	8R	AS	BT	CU	DV	EW	FX	GY	HZ	J1	K2	L3	M4	N5	O6	P7	Q8	0
XE	YF	ZG	1H	2J	3K	4L	5M	6N	7O	8P	AQ	BR	CS	DT	EU	FV	GW	HX	JY	KZ	L1	M2	N3	O4	P5	Q6	R7	
YD	ZE	1F	2G	3H	4J	5K	6L	7M	8N	AO	BP	CQ	DR	ES	FT	GU	HV	JW	KX	LY	MZ	N1	O2	P3	Q4	R5	S6	−
ZC	1D	2E	3F	4G	5H	6J	7K	8L	AM	BN	CO	DP	EQ	FR	GS	HT	JU	KV	LW	MX	NY	OZ	P1	Q2	R3	S4	T5	
1B	2C	3D	4E	5F	6G	7H	8J	AK	BL	CM	DN	EO	FP	GQ	HR	JS	KT	LU	MV	NW	OX	PY	QZ	R1	S2	T3	U4	
2A	3B	4C	5D	6E	7F	8G	AH	BJ	CK	DL	EM	FN	GO	HP	JQ	KR	LS	MT	NU	OV	PW	QX	RY	SZ	T1	U2	V3	
38	4A	5B	6C	7D	8E	AF	BG	CH	DJ	EK	FL	GM	HN	JO	KP	LQ	MR	NS	OT	PU	QV	RW	SX	TY	UZ	V1	W2	
47	58	6A	7B	8C	AD	BE	CF	DG	EH	FJ	GK	HL	JM	KN	LO	MP	NQ	OR	PS	QT	RU	SV	TW	UX	VY	WZ	X1	
56	67	78	8A	AB	BC	CD	DE	EF	FG	GH	HJ	JK	KL	LM	MN	NO	OP	PQ	QR	RS	ST	TU	UV	VW	WX	XY	YZ	

1 W	2 TH	3 F	4 SA	5 SU	6 M	7 TU	8 W	9 TH	10 F	11 SA	12 SU	13 M	14 TU	15 W	16 TH	17 F	18 SA	19 SU	20 M	21 TU	22 W	23 TH	24 F	25 SA	26 SU	27 M	28 TU	29 W	30 TH	31 F	
ON	PO	QP	RQ	SR	TS	UT	VU	WV	XW	AX	BA	CB	DC	ED	FE	GF	HG	JH	KJ	LK	ML	NM	ON	PO	QP	RQ	SR	TS	UT	VU	
PM	QN	RO	SP	TQ	UR	VS	WT	XU	AV	BW	CX	DA	EB	FC	GD	HE	JF	KG	LH	MJ	NK	OL	PM	QN	RO	SP	TQ	UR	VS	WT	
QL	RM	SN	TO	UP	VQ	WR	XS	AT	BU	CV	DW	EX	FA	GB	HC	JD	KE	LF	MG	NH	OJ	PK	QL	RM	SN	TO	UP	VQ	WR	XS	
RK	SL	TM	UN	VO	WP	XQ	AR	BS	CT	DU	EV	FW	GX	HA	JB	KC	LD	ME	NF	OG	PH	QJ	RK	SL	TM	UN	VO	WP	XQ	AR	+
SJ	TK	UL	VM	WN	XO	AP	BQ	CR	DS	ET	FU	GV	HW	JX	KA	LB	MC	ND	OE	PF	QG	RH	SJ	TK	UL	VM	WN	XO	AP	BQ	
TH	UJ	VK	WL	XM	AN	BO	CP	DQ	ER	FS	GT	HU	JV	KW	LX	MA	NB	OC	PD	QE	RF	SG	TH	UJ	VK	WL	XM	AN	BO	CP	0
UG	VH	WJ	XK	AL	BM	CN	DO	EP	FQ	GR	HS	JT	KU	LV	MW	NX	OA	PB	QC	RD	SE	TF	UG	VH	WJ	XK	AL	BM	CN	DO	
VF	WG	XH	AJ	BK	CL	DM	EN	FO	GP	HQ	JR	KS	LT	MU	NV	OW	PX	QA	RB	SC	TD	UE	VF	WG	XH	AJ	BK	CL	DM	EN	
WE	XF	AG	BH	CJ	DK	EL	FM	GN	HO	JP	KQ	LR	MS	NT	OU	PV	QW	RX	SA	TB	UC	VD	WE	XF	AG	BH	CJ	DK	EL	FM	−
XD	AE	BF	CG	DH	EJ	FK	GL	HM	JN	KO	LP	MQ	NR	OS	PT	QU	RV	SW	TX	UA	VB	WC	XD	AE	BF	CG	DH	EJ	FK	GL	
AC	BD	CE	DF	EG	FH	GJ	HK	JL	KM	LN	MO	NP	OQ	PR	QS	RT	SU	TV	UW	VX	WA	XB	AC	BD	CE	DF	EG	FH	GJ	HK	
B	C	D	E	F	G	H	J	K	L	M	N	O	P	Q	R	S	T	U	V	W	X	A	B	C	D	E	F	G	H	J	

1 W	2 TH	3 F	4 SA	5 SU	6 M	7 TU	8 W	9 TH	10 F	11 SA	12 SU	13 M	14 TU	15 W	16 TH	17 F	18 SA	19 SU	20 M	21 TU	22 W	23 TH	24 F	25 SA	26 SU	27 M	28 TU	29 W	30 TH	31 F	
Z	1	2	3	A	B	C	D	E	F	G	H	J	K	L	M	N	O	P	Q	R	S	T	U	V	W	X	Y	Z	1	2	
1Y	2Z	31	A2	B3	CA	DB	EC	FD	GE	HF	JG	KH	LJ	MK	NL	OM	PN	QO	RP	SQ	TR	US	VT	WU	XV	YW	ZX	1Y	2Z	31	
2X	3Y	AZ	B1	C2	D3	EA	FB	GC	HD	JE	KF	LG	MH	NJ	OK	PL	QM	RN	SO	TP	UQ	VR	WS	XT	YU	ZV	1W	2X	3Y	AZ	
3W	AX	BY	CZ	D1	E2	F3	GA	HB	JC	KD	LE	MF	NG	OH	PJ	QK	RL	SM	TN	UO	VP	WQ	XR	YS	ZT	1U	2V	3W	AX	BY	
AV	BW	CX	DY	EZ	F1	G2	H3	JA	KB	LC	MD	NE	OF	PG	QH	RJ	SK	TL	UM	VN	WO	XP	YQ	ZR	1S	2T	3U	AV	BW	CX	+
BU	CV	DW	EX	FY	GZ	H1	J2	K3	LA	MB	NC	OD	PE	QF	RG	SH	TJ	UK	VL	WM	XN	YO	ZP	1Q	2R	3S	AT	BU	CV	DW	
CT	DU	EV	FW	GX	HY	JZ	K1	L2	M3	NA	OB	PC	QD	RE	SF	TG	UH	VJ	WK	XL	YM	ZN	1O	2P	3Q	AR	BS	CT	DU	EV	
DS	ET	FU	GV	HW	JX	KY	LZ	M1	N2	O3	PA	QB	RC	SD	TE	UF	VG	WH	XJ	YK	ZL	1M	2N	3O	AP	BQ	CR	DS	ET	FU	0
ER	FS	GT	HU	JV	KW	LX	MY	NZ	O1	P2	Q3	RA	SB	TC	UD	VE	WF	XG	YH	ZJ	1K	2L	3M	AN	BO	CP	DQ	ER	FS	GT	
FQ	GR	HS	JT	KU	LV	MW	NX	OY	PZ	Q1	R2	S3	TA	UB	VC	WD	XE	YF	ZG	1H	2J	3K	AL	BM	CN	DO	EP	FQ	GR	HS	
GP	HQ	JR	KS	LT	MU	NV	OW	PX	QY	RZ	S1	T2	U3	VA	WB	XC	YD	ZE	1F	2G	3H	AJ	BK	CL	DM	EN	FO	GP	HQ	JR	−
HO	JP	KQ	LR	MS	NT	OU	PV	QW	RX	SY	TZ	U1	V2	W3	XA	YB	ZC	1D	2E	3F	AG	BH	CJ	DK	EL	FM	GN	HO	JP	KQ	
JN	KO	LP	MQ	NR	OS	PT	QU	RV	SW	TX	UY	VZ	W1	X2	Y3	ZA	1B	2C	3D	AE	BF	CG	DH	EJ	FK	GL	HM	JN	KO	LP	
KM	LN	MO	NP	OQ	PR	QS	RT	SU	TV	UW	VX	WY	XZ	Y1	Z2	13	2A	3B	AC	BD	CE	DF	EG	FH	GJ	HK	JL	KM	LN	MO	
L	M	N	O	P	Q	R	S	T	U	V	W	X	Y	Z	1	2	3	A	B	C	D	E	F	G	H	J	K	L	M	N	

1 W	2 TH	3 F	4 SA	5 SU	6 M	7 TU	8 W	9 TH	10 F	11 SA	12 SU	13 M	14 TU	15 W	16 TH	17 F	18 SA	19 SU	20 M	21 TU	22 W	23 TH	24 F	25 SA	26 SU	27 M	28 TU	29 W	30 TH	31 F	
J	K	L	M	N	O	P	Q	R	S	T	U	V	W	X	Y	Z	1	2	3	4	5	6	7	8	A	B	C	D	E	F	
KH	LJ	MK	NL	OM	PN	QO	RP	SQ	TR	US	VT	WU	XV	YW	ZX	1Y	2Z	31	42	53	64	75	86	A7	B8	CA	DB	EC	FD	GE	
LG	MH	NJ	OK	PL	QM	RN	SO	TP	UQ	VR	WS	XT	YU	ZV	1W	2X	3Y	4Z	51	62	73	84	A5	B6	C7	D8	EA	FB	GC	HD	
MF	NG	OH	PJ	QK	RL	SM	TN	UO	VP	WQ	XR	YS	ZT	1U	2V	3W	4X	5Y	6Z	71	82	A3	B4	C5	D6	E7	F8	GA	HB	JC	
NE	OF	PG	QH	RJ	SK	TL	UM	VN	WO	XP	YQ	ZR	1S	2T	3U	4V	5W	6X	7Y	8Z	A1	B2	C3	D4	E5	F6	G7	H8	JA	KB	
OD	PE	QF	RG	SH	TJ	UK	VL	WM	XN	YO	ZP	1Q	2R	3S	4T	5U	6V	7W	8X	AY	BZ	C1	D2	E3	F4	G5	H6	J7	K8	LA	+
PC	QD	RE	SF	TG	UH	VJ	WK	XL	YM	ZN	1O	2P	3Q	4R	5S	6T	7U	8V	AW	BX	CY	DZ	E1	F2	G3	H4	J5	K6	L7	M8	
QB	RC	SD	TE	UF	VG	WH	XJ	YK	ZL	1M	2N	3O	4P	5Q	6R	7S	8T	AU	BV	CW	DX	EY	FZ	G1	H2	J3	K4	L5	M6	N7	
RA	SB	TC	UD	VE	WF	XG	YH	ZJ	1K	2L	3M	4N	5O	6P	7Q	8R	AS	BT	CU	DV	EW	FX	GY	HZ	J1	K2	L3	M4	N5	O6	0
S8	TA	UB	VC	WD	XE	YF	ZG	1H	2J	3K	4L	5M	6N	7O	8P	AQ	BR	CS	DT	EU	FV	GW	HX	JY	KZ	L1	M2	N3	O4	P5	
T7	U8	VA	WB	XC	YD	ZE	1F	2G	3H	4J	5K	6L	7M	8N	AO	BP	CQ	DR	ES	FT	GU	HV	JW	KX	LY	MZ	N1	O2	P3	Q4	
U6	V7	W8	XA	YB	ZC	1D	2E	3F	4G	5H	6J	7K	8L	AM	BN	CO	DP	EQ	FR	GS	HT	JU	KV	LW	MX	NY	OZ	P1	Q2	R3	
V5	W6	X7	Y8	ZA	1B	2C	3D	4E	5F	6G	7H	8J	AK	BL	CM	DN	EO	FP	GQ	HR	JS	KT	LU	MV	NW	OX	PY	QZ	R1	S2	−
W4	X5	Y6	Z7	18	2A	3B	4C	5D	6E	7F	8G	AH	BJ	CK	DL	EM	FN	GO	HP	JQ	KR	LS	MT	NU	OV	PW	QX	RY	SZ	T1	
X3	Y4	Z5	16	27	38	4A	5B	6C	7D	8E	AF	BG	CH	DJ	EK	FL	GM	HN	JO	KP	LQ	MR	NS	OT	PU	QV	RW	SX	TY	UZ	
Y2	Z3	14	25	36	47	58	6A	7B	8C	AD	BE	CF	DG	EH	FJ	GK	HL	JM	KN	LO	MP	NQ	OR	PS	QT	RU	SV	TW	UX	VY	
Z1	12	23	34	45	56	67	78	8A	AB	BC	CD	DE	EF	FG	GH	HJ	JK	KL	LM	MN	NO	OP	PQ	QR	RS	ST	TU	UV	VW	WX	

PHYSICAL

1 SA	2 SU	3 M	4 TU	5 W	6 TH	7 F	8 SA	9 SU	10 M	11 TU	12 W	13 TH	14 F	15 SA	16 SU	17 M	18 TU	19 W	20 TH	21 F	22 SA	23 SU	24 M	25 TU	26 W	27 TH	28 F	29 SA	30 SU	
WV	XW	AX	BA	CB	DC	ED	FE	GF	HG	JH	KJ	LK	ML	NM	ON	PO	QP	RQ	SR	TS	UT	VU	WV	XW	AX	BA	CB	DC	ED	
XU	AV	BW	CX	DA	EB	FC	GD	HE	JF	KG	LH	MJ	NK	OL	PM	QN	RO	SP	TQ	UR	VS	WT	XU	AV	BW	CX	DA	EB	FC	
AT	BU	CV	DW	EX	FA	GB	HC	JD	KE	LF	MG	NH	OJ	PK	QL	RM	SN	TO	UP	VQ	WR	XS	AT	BU	CV	DW	EX	FA	GB	
BS	CT	DU	EV	FW	GX	HA	JB	KC	LD	ME	NF	OG	PH	QJ	RK	SL	TM	UN	VO	WP	XQ	AR	BS	CT	DU	EV	FW	GX	HA	
CR	DS	ET	FU	GV	HW	JX	KA	LB	MC	ND	OE	PF	QG	RH	SJ	TK	UL	VM	WN	XO	AP	BQ	CR	DS	ET	FU	GV	HW	JX	+
DQ	ER	FS	GT	HU	JV	KW	LX	MA	NB	OC	PD	QE	RF	SG	TH	UJ	VK	WL	XM	AN	BO	CP	DQ	ER	FS	GT	HU	JV	KW	0
EP	FQ	GR	HS	JT	KU	LV	MW	NX	OA	PB	QC	RD	SE	TF	UG	VH	WJ	XK	AL	BM	CN	DO	EP	FQ	GR	HS	JT	KU	LV	
FO	GP	HQ	JR	KS	LT	MU	NV	OW	PX	QA	RB	SC	TD	UE	VF	WG	XH	AJ	BK	CL	DM	EN	FO	GP	HQ	JR	KS	LT	MU	
GN	HO	JP	KQ	LR	MS	NT	OU	PV	QW	RX	SA	TB	UC	VD	WE	XF	AG	BH	CJ	DK	EL	FM	GN	HO	JP	KQ	LR	MS	NT	−
HM	JN	KO	LP	MQ	NR	OS	PT	QU	RV	SW	TX	UA	VB	WC	XD	AE	BF	CG	DH	EJ	FK	GL	HM	JN	KO	LP	MQ	NR	OS	
JL	KM	LN	MO	NP	OQ	PR	QS	RT	SU	TV	UW	VX	WA	XB	AC	BD	CE	DF	EG	FH	GJ	HK	JL	KM	LN	MO	NP	OQ	PR	
K	L	M	N	O	P	Q	R	S	T	U	V	W	X	A	B	C	D	E	F	G	H	J	K	L	M	N	O	P	Q	

EMOTIONAL

1 SA	2 SU	3 M	4 TU	5 W	6 TH	7 F	8 SA	9 SU	10 M	11 TU	12 W	13 TH	14 F	15 SA	16 SU	17 M	18 TU	19 W	20 TH	21 F	22 SA	23 SU	24 M	25 TU	26 W	27 TH	28 F	29 SA	30 SU	
3	A	B	C	D	E	F	G	H	J	K	L	M	N	O	P	Q	R	S	T	U	V	W	X	Y	Z	1	2	3	A	
A2	B3	CA	DB	EC	FD	GE	HF	JG	KH	LJ	MK	NL	OM	PN	QO	RP	SQ	TR	US	VT	WU	XV	YW	ZX	1Y	2Z	31	A2	B3	
B1	C2	D3	EA	FB	GC	HD	JE	KF	LG	MH	NJ	OK	PL	QM	RN	SO	TP	UQ	VR	WS	XT	YU	ZV	1W	2X	3Y	AZ	B1	C2	
CZ	D1	E2	F3	GA	HB	JC	KD	LE	MF	NG	OH	PJ	QK	RL	SM	TN	UO	VP	WQ	XR	YS	ZT	1U	2V	3W	AX	BY	CZ	D1	
DY	EZ	F1	G2	H3	JA	KB	LC	MD	NE	OF	PG	QH	RJ	SK	TL	UM	VN	WO	XP	YQ	ZR	1S	2T	3U	AV	BW	CX	DY	EZ	+
EX	FY	GZ	H1	J2	K3	LA	MB	NC	OD	PE	QF	RG	SH	TJ	UK	VL	WM	XN	YO	ZP	1Q	2R	3S	AT	BU	CV	DW	EX	FY	
FW	GX	HY	JZ	K1	L2	M3	NA	OB	PC	QD	RE	SF	TG	UH	VJ	WK	XL	YM	ZN	1O	2P	3Q	AR	BS	CT	DU	EV	FW	GX	
GV	HW	JX	KY	LZ	M1	N2	O3	PA	QB	RC	SD	TE	UF	VG	WH	XJ	YK	ZL	1M	2N	3O	AP	BQ	CR	DS	ET	FU	GV	HW	0
HU	JV	KW	LX	MY	NZ	O1	P2	Q3	RA	SB	TC	UD	VE	WF	XG	YH	ZJ	1K	2L	3M	AN	BO	CP	DQ	ER	FS	GT	HU	JV	
JT	KU	LV	MW	NX	OY	PZ	Q1	R2	S3	TA	UB	VC	WD	XE	YF	ZG	1H	2J	3K	AL	BM	CN	DO	EP	FQ	GR	HS	JT	KU	
KS	LT	MU	NV	OW	PX	QY	RZ	S1	T2	U3	VA	WB	XC	YD	ZE	1F	2G	3H	AJ	BK	CL	DM	EN	FO	GP	HQ	JR	KS	LT	−
LR	MS	NT	OU	PV	QW	RX	SY	TZ	U1	V2	W3	XA	YB	ZC	1D	2E	3F	AG	BH	CJ	DK	EL	FM	GN	HO	JP	KQ	LR	MS	
MQ	NR	OS	PT	QU	RV	SW	TX	UY	VZ	W1	X2	Y3	ZA	1B	2C	3D	AE	BF	CG	DH	EJ	FK	GL	HM	JN	KO	LP	MQ	NR	
NP	OQ	PR	QS	RT	SU	TV	UW	VX	WY	XZ	Y1	Z2	13	2A	3B	AC	BD	CE	DF	EG	FH	GJ	HK	JL	KM	LN	MO	NP	OQ	
O	P	Q	R	S	T	U	V	W	X	Y	Z	1	2	3	A	B	C	D	E	F	G	H	J	K	L	M	N	O	P	

INTELLECTUAL

1 SA	2 SU	3 M	4 TU	5 W	6 TH	7 F	8 SA	9 SU	10 M	11 TU	12 W	13 TH	14 F	15 SA	16 SU	17 M	18 TU	19 W	20 TH	21 F	22 SA	23 SU	24 M	25 TU	26 W	27 TH	28 F	29 SA	30 SU	
G	H	J	K	L	M	N	O	P	Q	R	S	T	U	V	W	X	Y	Z	1	2	3	4	5	6	7	8	A	B	C	
HF	JG	KH	LJ	MK	NL	OM	PN	QO	RP	SQ	TR	US	VT	WU	XV	YW	ZX	1Y	2Z	31	42	53	64	75	86	A7	B8	CA	DB	
JE	KF	LG	MH	NJ	OK	PL	QM	RN	SO	TP	UQ	VR	WS	XT	YU	ZV	1W	2X	3Y	4Z	51	62	73	84	A5	B6	C7	D8	EA	
KD	LE	MF	NG	OH	PJ	QK	RL	SM	TN	UO	VP	WQ	XR	YS	ZT	1U	2V	3W	4X	5Y	6Z	71	82	A3	B4	C5	D6	E7	F8	
LC	MD	NE	OF	PG	QH	RJ	SK	TL	UM	VN	WO	XP	YQ	ZR	1S	2T	3U	4V	5W	6X	7Y	8Z	A1	B2	C3	D4	E5	F6	G7	
MB	NC	OD	PE	QF	RG	SH	TJ	UK	VL	WM	XN	YO	ZP	1Q	2R	3S	4T	5U	6V	7W	8X	AY	BZ	C1	D2	E3	F4	G5	H6	+
NA	OB	PC	QD	RE	SF	TG	UH	VJ	WK	XL	YM	ZN	1O	2P	3Q	4R	5S	6T	7U	8V	AW	BX	CY	DZ	E1	F2	G3	H4	J5	
O8	PA	QB	RC	SD	TE	UF	VG	WH	XJ	YK	ZL	1M	2N	3O	4P	5Q	6R	7S	8T	AU	BV	CW	DX	EY	FZ	G1	H2	J3	K4	
P7	Q8	RA	SB	TC	UD	VE	WF	XG	YH	ZJ	1K	2L	3M	4N	5O	6P	7Q	8R	AS	BT	CU	DV	EW	FX	GY	HZ	J1	K2	L3	0
Q6	R7	S8	TA	UB	VC	WD	XE	YF	ZG	1H	2J	3K	4L	5M	6N	7O	8P	AQ	BR	CS	DT	EU	FV	GW	HX	JY	KZ	L1	M2	
R5	S6	T7	U8	VA	WB	XC	YD	ZE	1F	2G	3H	4J	5K	6L	7M	8N	AO	BP	CQ	DR	ES	FT	GU	HV	JW	KX	LY	MZ	N1	
S4	T5	U6	V7	W8	XA	YB	ZC	1D	2E	3F	4G	5H	6J	7K	8L	AM	BN	CO	DP	EQ	FR	GS	HT	JU	KV	LW	MX	NY	OZ	−
T3	U4	V5	W6	X7	Y8	ZA	1B	2C	3D	4E	5F	6G	7H	8J	AK	BL	CM	DN	EO	FP	GQ	HR	JS	KT	LU	MV	NW	OX	PY	
U2	V3	W4	X5	Y6	Z7	18	2A	3B	4C	5D	6E	7F	8G	AH	BJ	CK	DL	EM	FN	GO	HP	JQ	KR	LS	MT	NU	OV	PW	QX	
V1	W2	X3	Y4	Z5	16	27	38	4A	5B	6C	7D	8E	AF	BG	CH	DJ	EK	FL	GM	HN	JO	KP	LQ	MR	NS	OT	PU	QV	RW	
WZ	X1	Y2	Z3	14	25	36	47	58	6A	7B	8C	AD	BE	CF	DG	EH	FJ	GK	HL	JM	KN	LO	MP	NQ	OR	PS	QT	RU	SV	
XY	YZ	Z1	12	23	34	45	56	67	78	8A	AB	BC	CD	DE	EF	FG	GH	HJ	JK	KL	LM	MN	NO	OP	PQ	QR	RS	ST	TU	

1	2	3	4	5	6	7	8	9	10	11	12	13	14	15	16	17	18	19	20	21	22	23	24	25	26	27	28	29	30	31	
M	TU	W	TH	F	SA	SU	M	TU	W	TH	F	SA	SU	M	TU	W	TH	F	SA	SU	M	TU	W	TH	F	SA	SU	M	TU	W	
FE	GF	HG	JH	KJ	LK	ML	NM	ON	PO	QP	RQ	SR	TS	UT	VU	WV	XW	AX	BA	CB	DC	ED	FE	GF	HG	JH	KJ	LK	ML	NM	
GD	HE	JF	KG	LH	MJ	NK	OL	PM	QN	RO	SP	TQ	UR	VS	WT	XU	AV	BW	CX	DA	EB	FC	GD	HE	JF	KG	LH	MJ	NK	OL	
HC	JD	KE	LF	MG	NH	OJ	PK	QL	RM	SN	TO	UP	VQ	WR	XS	AT	BU	CV	DW	EX	FA	GB	HC	JD	KE	LF	MG	NH	OJ	PK	+
JB	KC	LD	ME	NF	OG	PH	QJ	RK	SL	TM	UN	VO	WP	XQ	AR	BS	CT	DU	EV	FW	GX	HA	JB	KC	LD	ME	NF	OG	PH	QJ	
KA	LB	MC	ND	OE	PF	QG	RH	SJ	TK	UL	VM	WN	XO	AP	BQ	CR	DS	ET	FU	GV	HW	JX	KA	LB	MC	ND	OE	PF	QG	RH	
LX	MA	NB	OC	PD	QE	RF	SG	TH	UJ	VK	WL	XM	AN	BO	CP	DQ	ER	FS	GT	HU	JV	KW	LX	MA	NB	OC	PD	QE	RF	SG	0
MW	NX	OA	PB	QC	RD	SE	TF	UG	VH	WJ	XK	AL	BM	CN	DO	EP	FQ	GR	HS	JT	KU	LV	MW	NX	OA	PB	QC	RD	SE	TF	
NV	OW	PX	QA	RB	SC	TD	UE	VF	WG	XH	AJ	BK	CL	DM	EN	FO	GP	HQ	JR	KS	LT	MU	NV	OW	PX	QA	RB	SC	TD	UE	
OU	PV	QW	RX	SA	TB	UC	VD	WE	XF	AG	BH	CJ	DK	EL	FM	GN	HO	JP	KQ	LR	MS	NT	OU	PV	QW	RX	SA	TB	UC	VD	−
PT	QU	RV	SW	TX	UA	VB	WC	XD	AE	BF	CG	DH	EJ	FK	GL	HM	JN	KO	LP	MQ	NR	OS	PT	QU	RV	SW	TX	UA	VB	WC	
QS	RT	SU	TV	UW	VX	WA	XB	AC	BD	CE	DF	EG	FH	GJ	HK	JL	KM	LN	MO	NP	OQ	PR	QS	RT	SU	TV	UW	VX	WA	XB	
R	S	T	U	V	W	X	A	B	C	D	E	F	G	H	J	K	L	M	N	O	P	Q	R	S	T	U	V	W	X	A	

1	2	3	4	5	6	7	8	9	10	11	12	13	14	15	16	17	18	19	20	21	22	23	24	25	26	27	28	29	30	31	
M	TU	W	TH	F	SA	SU	M	TU	W	TH	F	SA	SU	M	TU	W	TH	F	SA	SU	M	TU	W	TH	F	SA	SU	M	TU	W	
B	C	D	E	F	G	H	J	K	L	M	N	O	P	Q	R	S	T	U	V	W	X	Y	Z	1	2	3	A	B	C	D	
CA	DB	EC	FD	GE	HF	JG	KH	LJ	MK	NL	OM	PN	QO	RP	SQ	TR	US	VT	WU	XV	YW	ZX	1Y	2Z	31	A2	B3	CA	DB	EC	
D3	EA	FB	GC	HD	JE	KF	LG	MH	NJ	OK	PL	QM	RN	SO	TP	UQ	VR	WS	XT	YU	ZV	1W	2X	3Y	AZ	B1	C2	D3	EA	FB	
E2	F3	GA	HB	JC	KD	LE	MF	NG	OH	PJ	QK	RL	SM	TN	UO	VP	WQ	XR	YS	ZT	1U	2V	3W	AX	BY	CZ	D1	E2	F3	GA	+
F1	G2	H3	JA	KB	LC	MD	NE	OF	PG	QH	RJ	SK	TL	UM	VN	WO	XP	YQ	ZR	1S	2T	3U	AV	BW	CX	DY	EZ	F1	G2	H3	
GZ	H1	J2	K3	LA	MB	NC	OD	PE	QF	RG	SH	TJ	UK	VL	WM	XN	YM	ZN	1O	2P	3Q	AR	BS	CT	DU	EV	FW	GX	HY	JZ	K1	
HY	JZ	K1	L2	M3	NA	OB	PC	QD	RE	SF	TG	UH	VJ	WK	XL	YM	ZN	1O	2P	3Q	AR	BS	CT	DU	EV	FW	GX	HY	JZ	K1	
JX	KY	LZ	M1	N2	O3	PA	QB	RC	SD	TE	UF	VG	WH	XJ	YK	ZL	1M	2N	3O	AP	BQ	CR	DS	ET	FU	GV	HW	JX	KY	LZ	0
KW	LX	MY	NZ	O1	P2	Q3	RA	SB	TC	UD	VE	WF	XG	YH	ZJ	1K	2L	3M	AN	BO	CP	DQ	ER	FS	GT	HU	JV	KW	LX	MY	
LV	MW	NX	OY	PZ	Q1	R2	S3	TA	UB	VC	WD	XE	YF	ZG	1H	2J	3K	AL	BM	CN	DO	EP	FQ	GR	HS	JT	KU	LV	MW	NX	
MU	NV	OW	PX	QY	RZ	S1	T2	U3	VA	WB	XC	YD	ZE	1F	2G	3H	AJ	BK	CL	DM	EN	FO	GP	HQ	JR	KS	LT	MU	NV	OW	−
NT	OU	PV	QW	RX	SY	TZ	U1	V2	W3	XA	YB	ZC	1D	2E	3F	AG	BH	CJ	DK	EL	FM	GN	HO	JP	KQ	LR	MS	NT	OU	PV	
OS	PT	QU	RV	SW	TX	UY	VZ	W1	X2	Y3	ZA	1B	2C	3D	AE	BF	CG	DH	EJ	FK	GL	HM	JN	KO	LP	MQ	NR	OS	PT	QU	
PR	QS	RT	SU	TV	UW	VX	WY	XZ	Y1	Z2	13	2A	3B	AC	BD	CE	DF	EG	FH	GJ	HK	JL	KM	LN	MO	NP	OQ	PR	QS	RT	
Q	R	S	T	U	V	W	X	Y	Z	1	2	3	A	B	C	D	E	F	G	H	J	K	L	M	N	O	P	Q	R	S	

1	2	3	4	5	6	7	8	9	10	11	12	13	14	15	16	17	18	19	20	21	22	23	24	25	26	27	28	29	30	31	
M	TU	W	TH	F	SA	SU	M	TU	W	TH	F	SA	SU	M	TU	W	TH	F	SA	SU	M	TU	W	TH	F	SA	SU	M	TU	W	
D	E	F	G	H	J	K	L	M	N	O	P	Q	R	S	T	U	V	W	X	Y	Z	1	2	3	4	5	6	7	8	A	
EC	FD	GE	HF	JG	KH	LJ	MK	NL	OM	PN	QO	RP	SQ	TR	US	VT	WU	XV	YW	ZX	1Y	2Z	31	42	53	64	75	86	A7	B8	
FB	GC	HD	JE	KF	LG	MH	NJ	OK	PL	QM	RN	SO	TP	UQ	VR	WS	XT	YU	ZV	1W	2X	3Y	4Z	51	62	73	84	A5	B6	C7	
GA	HB	JC	KD	LE	MF	NG	OH	PJ	QK	RL	SM	TN	UO	VP	WQ	XR	YS	ZT	1U	2V	3W	4X	5Y	6Z	71	82	A3	B4	C5	D6	
H8	JA	KB	LC	MD	NE	OF	PG	QH	RJ	SK	TL	UM	VN	WO	XP	YQ	ZR	1S	2T	3U	4V	5W	6X	7Y	8Z	A1	B2	C3	D4	E5	
J7	K8	LA	MB	NC	OD	PE	QF	RG	SH	TJ	UK	VL	WM	XN	YO	ZP	1Q	2R	3S	4T	5U	6V	7W	8X	AY	BZ	C1	D2	E3	F4	+
K6	L7	M8	NA	OB	PC	QD	RE	SF	TG	UH	VJ	WK	XL	YM	ZN	1O	2P	3Q	4R	5S	6T	7U	8V	AW	BX	CY	DZ	E1	F2	G3	
L5	M6	N7	O8	PA	QB	RC	SD	TE	UF	VG	WH	XJ	YK	ZL	1M	2N	3O	4P	5Q	6R	7S	8T	AU	BV	CW	DX	EY	FZ	G1	H2	
M4	N5	O6	P7	Q8	RA	SB	TC	UD	VE	WF	XG	YH	ZJ	1K	2L	3M	4N	5O	6P	7Q	8R	AS	BT	CU	DV	EW	FX	GY	HZ	J1	0
N3	O4	P5	Q6	R7	S8	TA	UB	VC	WD	XE	YF	ZG	1H	2J	3K	4L	5M	6N	7O	8P	AQ	BR	CS	DT	EU	FV	GW	HX	JY	KZ	
O2	P3	Q4	R5	S6	T7	U8	VA	WB	XC	YD	ZE	1F	2G	3H	4J	5K	6L	7M	8N	AO	BP	CQ	DR	ES	FT	GU	HV	JW	KX	LY	
P1	Q2	R3	S4	T5	U6	V7	W8	XA	YB	ZC	1D	2E	3F	4G	5H	6J	7K	8L	AM	BN	CO	DP	EQ	FR	GS	HT	JU	KV	LW	MX	−
QZ	R1	S2	T3	U4	V5	W6	X7	Y8	ZA	1B	2C	3D	4E	5F	6G	7H	8J	AK	BL	CM	DN	EO	FP	GQ	HR	JS	KT	LU	MV	NW	
RY	SZ	T1	U2	V3	W4	X5	Y6	Z7	18	2A	3B	4C	5D	6E	7F	8G	AH	BJ	CK	DL	EM	FN	GO	HP	JQ	KR	LS	MT	NU	OV	
SX	TY	UZ	V1	W2	X3	Y4	Z5	16	27	38	4A	5B	6C	7D	8E	AF	BG	CH	DJ	EK	FL	GM	HN	JO	KP	LQ	MR	NS	OT	PU	
TW	UX	VY	WZ	X1	Y2	Z3	14	25	36	47	58	6A	7B	8C	AD	BE	CF	DG	EH	FJ	GK	HL	JM	KN	LO	MP	NQ	OR	PS	QT	
UV	VW	WX	XY	YZ	Z1	12	23	34	45	56	67	78	8A	AB	BC	CD	DE	EF	FG	GH	HJ	JK	KL	LM	MN	NO	OP	PQ	QR	RS	

JUNE 1978 — PHYSICAL — JUNE 1978

1 TH	2 F	3 SA	4 SU	5 M	6 TU	7 W	8 TH	9 F	10 SA	11 SU	12 M	13 TU	14 W	15 TH	16 F	17 SA	18 SU	19 M	20 TU	21 W	22 TH	23 F	24 SA	25 SU	26 M	27 TU	28 W	29 TH	30 F
ON	PO	QP	RQ	SR	TS	UT	VU	WV	XW	AX	BA	CB	DC	ED	FE	GF	HG	JH	KJ	LK	ML	NM	ON	PO	QP	RQ	SR	TS	UT
PM	QN	RO	SP	TQ	UR	VS	WT	XU	AV	BW	CX	DA	EB	FC	GD	HE	JF	KG	LH	MJ	NK	OL	PM	QN	RO	SP	TQ	UR	VS
QL	RM	SN	TO	UP	VQ	WR	XS	AT	BU	CV	DW	EX	FA	GB	HC	JD	KE	LF	MG	NH	OJ	PK	QL	RM	SN	TO	UP	VQ	WR
RK	SL	TM	UN	VO	WP	XQ	AR	BS	CT	DU	EV	FW	GX	HA	JB	KC	LD	ME	NF	OG	PH	QJ	RK	SL	TM	UN	VO	WP	XQ
SJ	TK	UL	VM	WN	XO	AP	BQ	CR	DS	ET	FU	GV	HW	JX	KA	LB	MC	ND	OE	PF	QG	RH	SJ	TK	UL	VM	WN	XO	AP
TH	UJ	VK	WL	XM	AN	BO	CP	DQ	ER	FS	GT	HU	JV	KW	LX	MA	NB	OC	PD	QE	RF	SG	TH	UJ	VK	WL	XM	AN	BO
UG	VH	WJ	XK	AL	BM	CN	DO	EP	FQ	GR	HS	JT	KU	LV	MW	NX	OA	PB	QC	RD	SE	TF	UG	VH	WJ	XK	AL	BM	CN
VF	WG	XH	AJ	BK	CL	DM	EN	FO	GP	HQ	JR	KS	LT	MU	NV	OW	PX	QA	RB	SC	TD	UE	VF	WG	XH	AJ	BK	CL	DM
WE	XF	AG	BH	CJ	DK	EL	FM	GN	HO	JP	KQ	LR	MS	NT	OU	PV	QW	RX	SA	TB	UC	VD	WE	XF	AG	BH	CJ	DK	EL
XD	AE	BF	CG	DH	EJ	FK	GL	HM	JN	KO	LP	MQ	NR	OS	PT	QU	RV	SW	TX	UA	VB	WC	XD	AE	BF	CG	DH	EJ	FK
AC	BD	CE	DF	EG	FH	GJ	HK	JL	KM	LN	MO	NP	OQ	PR	QS	RT	SU	TV	UW	VX	WA	XB	AC	BD	CE	DF	EG	FH	GJ
B	C	D	E	F	G	H	J	K	L	M	N	O	P	Q	R	S	T	U	V	W	X	A	B	C	D	E	F	G	H

JUNE 1978 — EMOTIONAL — JUNE 1978

1 TH	2 F	3 SA	4 SU	5 M	6 TU	7 W	8 TH	9 F	10 SA	11 SU	12 M	13 TU	14 W	15 TH	16 F	17 SA	18 SU	19 M	20 TU	21 W	22 TH	23 F	24 SA	25 SU	26 M	27 TU	28 W	29 TH	30 F
E	F	G	H	J	K	L	M	N	O	P	Q	R	S	T	U	V	W	X	Y	Z	1	2	3	A	B	C	D	E	F
FD	GE	HF	JG	KH	LJ	MK	NL	OM	PN	QO	RP	SQ	TR	US	VT	WU	XV	YW	ZX	1Y	2Z	31	A2	B3	CA	DB	EC	FD	GE
GC	HD	JE	KF	LG	MH	NJ	OK	PL	QM	RN	SO	TP	UQ	VR	WS	XT	YU	ZV	1W	2X	3Y	AZ	B1	C2	D3	EA	FB	GC	HD
HB	JC	KD	LE	MF	NG	OH	PJ	QK	RL	SM	TN	UO	VP	WQ	XR	YS	ZT	1U	2V	3W	AX	BY	CZ	D1	E2	F3	GA	HB	JC
JA	KB	LC	MD	NE	OF	PG	QH	RJ	SK	TL	UM	VN	WO	XP	YQ	ZR	1S	2T	3U	AV	BW	CX	DY	EZ	F1	G2	H3	JA	KB
K3	LA	MB	NC	OD	PE	QF	RG	SH	TJ	UK	VL	WM	XN	YO	ZP	1Q	2R	3S	AT	BU	CV	DW	EX	FY	GZ	H1	J2	K3	LA
L2	M3	NA	OB	PC	QD	RE	SF	TG	UH	VJ	WK	XL	YM	ZN	1O	2P	3Q	AR	BS	CT	DU	EV	FW	GX	HY	JZ	K1	L2	M3
M1	N2	O3	PA	QB	RC	SD	TE	UF	VG	WH	XJ	YK	ZL	1M	2N	3O	AP	BQ	CR	DS	ET	FU	GV	HW	JX	KY	LZ	M1	N2
NZ	O1	P2	Q3	RA	SB	TC	UD	VE	WF	XG	YH	ZJ	1K	2L	3M	AN	BO	CP	DQ	ER	FS	GT	HU	JV	KW	LX	MY	NZ	O1
OY	PZ	Q1	R2	S3	TA	UB	VC	WD	XE	YF	ZG	1H	2J	3K	AL	BM	CN	DO	EP	FQ	GR	HS	JT	KU	LV	MW	NX	OY	PZ
PX	QY	RZ	S1	T2	U3	VA	WB	XC	YD	ZE	1F	2G	3H	AJ	BK	CL	DM	EN	FO	GP	HQ	JR	KS	LT	MU	NV	OW	PX	QY
QW	RX	SY	TZ	U1	V2	W3	XA	YB	ZC	1D	2E	3F	AG	BH	CJ	DK	EL	FM	GN	HO	JP	KQ	LR	MS	NT	OU	PV	QW	RX
RV	SW	TX	UY	VZ	W1	X2	Y3	ZA	1B	2C	3D	AE	BF	CG	DH	EJ	FK	GL	HM	JN	KO	LP	MQ	NR	OS	PT	QU	RV	SW
SU	TV	UW	VX	WY	XZ	Y1	Z2	13	2A	3B	AC	BD	CE	DF	EG	FH	GJ	HK	JL	KM	LN	MO	NP	OQ	PR	QS	RT	SU	TV
T	U	V	W	X	Y	Z	1	2	3	A	B	C	D	E	F	G	H	J	K	L	M	N	O	P	Q	R	S	T	U

Right-hand markers: **+** (upper section), **0** (centre line, at the "M1 N2…" row), **—** (lower section).

JUNE 1978 — INTELLECTUAL — JUNE 1978

1 TH	2 F	3 SA	4 SU	5 M	6 TU	7 W	8 TH	9 F	10 SA	11 SU	12 M	13 TU	14 W	15 TH	16 F	17 SA	18 SU	19 M	20 TU	21 W	22 TH	23 F	24 SA	25 SU	26 M	27 TU	28 W	29 TH	30 F
B	C	D	E	F	G	H	J	K	L	M	N	O	P	Q	R	S	T	U	V	W	X	Y	Z	1	2	3	4	5	6
CA	DB	EC	FD	GE	HF	JG	KH	LJ	MK	NL	OM	PN	QO	RP	SQ	TR	US	VT	WU	XV	YW	ZX	1Y	2Z	31	42	53	64	75
D8	EA	FB	GC	HD	JE	KF	LG	MH	NJ	OK	PL	QM	RN	SO	TP	UQ	VR	WS	XT	YU	ZV	1W	2X	3Y	4Z	51	62	73	84
E7	F8	GA	HB	JC	KD	LE	MF	NG	OH	PJ	QK	RL	SM	TN	UO	VP	WQ	XR	YS	ZT	1U	2V	3W	4X	5Y	6Z	71	82	A3
F6	G7	H8	JA	KB	LC	MD	NE	OF	PG	QH	RJ	SK	TL	UM	VN	WO	XP	YQ	ZR	1S	2T	3U	4V	5W	6X	7Y	8Z	A1	B2
G5	H6	J7	K8	LA	MB	NC	OD	PE	QF	RG	SH	TJ	UK	VL	WM	XN	YO	ZP	1Q	2R	3S	4T	5U	6V	7W	8X	AY	BZ	C1
H4	J5	K6	L7	M8	NA	OB	PC	QD	RE	SF	TG	UH	VJ	WK	XL	YM	ZN	1O	2P	3Q	4R	5S	6T	7U	8V	AW	BX	CY	DZ
J3	K4	L5	M6	N7	O8	PA	QB	RC	SD	TE	UF	VG	WH	XJ	YK	ZL	1M	2N	3O	4P	5Q	6R	7S	8T	AU	BV	CW	DX	EY
K2	L3	M4	N5	O6	P7	Q8	RA	SB	TC	UD	VE	WF	XG	YH	ZJ	1K	2L	3M	4N	5O	6P	7Q	8R	AS	BT	CU	DV	EW	FX
L1	M2	N3	O4	P5	Q6	R7	S8	TA	UB	VC	WD	XE	YF	ZG	1H	2J	3K	4L	5M	6N	7O	8P	AQ	BR	CS	DT	EU	FV	GW
MZ	N1	O2	P3	Q4	R5	S6	T7	U8	VA	WB	XC	YD	ZE	1F	2G	3H	4J	5K	6L	7M	8N	AO	BP	CQ	DR	ES	FT	GU	HV
NY	OZ	P1	Q2	R3	S4	T5	U6	V7	W8	XA	YB	ZC	1D	2E	3F	4G	5H	6J	7K	8L	AM	BN	CO	DP	EQ	FR	GS	HT	JU
OX	PY	QZ	R1	S2	T3	U4	V5	W6	X7	Y8	ZA	1B	2C	3D	4E	5F	6G	7H	8J	AK	BL	CM	DN	EO	FP	GQ	HR	JS	KT
PW	QX	RY	SZ	T1	U2	V3	W4	X5	Y6	Z7	18	2A	3B	4C	5D	6E	7F	8G	AH	BJ	CK	DL	EM	FN	GO	HP	JQ	KR	LS
QV	RW	SX	TY	UZ	V1	W2	X3	Y4	Z5	16	27	38	4A	5B	6C	7D	8E	AF	BG	CH	DJ	EK	FL	GM	HN	JO	KP	LQ	MR
RU	SV	TW	UX	VY	WZ	X1	Y2	Z3	14	25	36	47	58	6A	7B	8C	AD	BE	CF	DG	EH	FJ	GK	HL	JM	KN	LO	MP	NQ
ST	TU	UV	VW	WX	XY	YZ	Z1	12	23	34	45	56	67	78	8A	AB	BC	CD	DE	EF	FG	GH	HJ	JK	KL	LM	MN	NO	OP

PHYSICAL

1 SA	2 SU	3 M	4 TU	5 W	6 TH	7 F	8 SA	9 SU	10 M	11 TU	12 W	13 TH	14 F	15 SA	16 SU	17 M	18 TU	19 W	20 TH	21 F	22 SA	23 SU	24 M	25 TU	26 W	27 TH	28 F	29 SA	30 SU	31 M	
VU	WV	XW	AX	BA	CB	DC	ED	FE	GF	HG	JH	KJ	LK	ML	NM	ON	PO	QP	RQ	SR	TS	UT	VU	WV	XW	AX	BA	CB	DC	ED	
WT	XU	AV	BW	CX	DA	EB	FC	GD	HE	JF	KG	LH	MJ	NK	OL	PM	QN	RO	SP	TQ	UR	VS	WT	XU	AV	BW	CX	DA	EB	FC	
XS	AT	BU	CV	DW	EX	FA	GB	HC	JD	KE	LF	MG	NH	OJ	PK	QL	RM	SN	TO	UP	VQ	WR	XS	AT	BU	CV	DW	EX	FA	GB	+
AR	BS	CT	DU	EV	FW	GX	HA	JB	KC	LD	ME	NF	OG	PH	QJ	RK	SL	TM	UN	VO	WP	XQ	AR	BS	CT	DU	EV	FW	GX	HA	
BQ	CR	DS	ET	FU	GV	HW	JX	KA	LB	MC	ND	OE	PF	QG	RH	SJ	TK	UL	VM	WN	XO	AP	BQ	CR	DS	ET	FU	GV	HW	JX	
CP	DQ	ER	FS	GT	HU	JV	KW	LX	MA	NB	OC	PD	QE	RF	SG	TH	UJ	VK	WL	XM	AN	BO	CP	DQ	ER	FS	GT	HU	JV	KW	0
DO	EP	FQ	GR	HS	JT	KU	LV	MW	NX	OA	PB	QC	RD	SE	TF	UG	VH	WJ	XK	AL	BM	CN	DO	EP	FQ	GR	HS	JT	KU	LV	
EN	FO	GP	HQ	JR	KS	LT	MU	NV	OW	PX	QA	RB	SC	TD	UE	VF	WG	XH	AJ	BK	CL	DM	EN	FO	GP	HQ	JR	KS	LT	MU	
FM	GN	HO	JP	KQ	LR	MS	NT	OU	PV	QW	RX	SA	TB	UC	VD	WE	XF	AG	BH	CJ	DK	EL	FM	GN	HO	JP	KQ	LR	MS	NT	−
GL	HM	JN	KO	LP	MQ	NR	OS	PT	QU	RV	SW	TX	UA	VB	WC	XD	AE	BF	CG	DH	EJ	FK	GL	HM	JN	KO	LP	MQ	NR	OS	
HK	JL	KM	LN	MO	NP	OQ	PR	QS	RT	SU	TV	UW	VX	WA	XB	AC	BD	CE	DF	EG	FH	GJ	HK	JL	KM	LN	MO	NP	OQ	PR	
J	K	L	M	N	O	P	Q	R	S	T	U	V	W	X	A	B	C	D	E	F	G	H	J	K	L	M	N	O	P	Q	

EMOTIONAL

1 SA	2 SU	3 M	4 TU	5 W	6 TH	7 F	8 SA	9 SU	10 M	11 TU	12 W	13 TH	14 F	15 SA	16 SU	17 M	18 TU	19 W	20 TH	21 F	22 SA	23 SU	24 M	25 TU	26 W	27 TH	28 F	29 SA	30 SU	31 M	
G	H	J	K	L	M	N	O	P	Q	R	S	T	U	V	W	X	Y	Z	1	2	3	A	B	C	D	E	F	G	H	J	
HF	JG	KH	LJ	MK	NL	OM	PN	QO	RP	SQ	TR	US	VT	WU	XV	YW	ZX	1Y	2Z	31	A2	B3	CA	DB	EC	FD	GE	HF	JG	KH	
JE	KF	LG	MH	NJ	OK	PL	QM	RN	SO	TP	UQ	VR	WS	XT	YU	ZV	1W	2X	3Y	AZ	B1	C2	D3	EA	FB	GC	HD	JE	KF	LG	
KD	LE	MF	NG	OH	PJ	QK	RL	SM	TN	UO	VP	WQ	XR	YS	ZT	1U	2V	3W	AX	BY	CZ	D1	E2	F3	GA	HB	JC	KD	LE	MF	+
LC	MD	NE	OF	PG	QH	RJ	SK	TL	UM	VN	WO	XP	YQ	ZR	1S	2T	3U	AV	BW	CX	DY	EZ	F1	G2	H3	JA	KB	LC	MD	NE	
MB	NC	OD	PE	QF	RG	SH	TJ	UK	VL	WM	XN	YO	ZP	1Q	2R	3S	AT	BU	CV	DW	EX	FY	GZ	H1	J2	K3	LA	MB	NC	OD	
NA	OB	PC	QD	RE	SF	TG	UH	VJ	WK	XL	YM	ZN	1O	2P	3Q	AR	BS	CT	DU	EV	FW	GX	HY	JZ	K1	L2	M3	NA	OB	PC	
O3	PA	QB	RC	SD	TE	UF	VG	WH	XJ	YK	ZL	1M	2N	3O	AP	BQ	CR	DS	ET	FU	GV	HW	JX	KY	LZ	M1	N2	O3	PA	QB	0
P2	Q3	RA	SB	TC	UD	VE	WF	XG	YH	ZJ	1K	2L	3M	AN	BO	CP	DQ	ER	FS	GT	HU	JV	KW	LX	MY	NZ	O1	P2	Q3	RA	
Q1	R2	S3	TA	UB	VC	WD	XE	YF	ZG	1H	2J	3K	AL	BM	CN	DO	EP	FQ	GR	HS	JT	KU	LV	MW	NX	OY	PZ	Q1	R2	S3	
RZ	S1	T2	U3	VA	WB	XC	YD	ZE	1F	2G	3H	AJ	BK	CL	DM	EN	FO	GP	HQ	JR	KS	LT	MU	NV	OW	PX	QY	RZ	S1	T2	
SY	TZ	U1	V2	W3	XA	YB	ZC	1D	2E	3F	AG	BH	CJ	DK	EL	FM	GN	HO	JP	KQ	LR	MS	NT	OU	PV	QW	RX	SY	TZ	U1	−
TX	UY	VZ	W1	X2	Y3	ZA	1B	2C	3D	AE	BF	CG	DH	EJ	FK	GL	HM	JN	KO	LP	MQ	NR	OS	PT	QU	RV	SW	TX	UY	VZ	
UW	VX	WY	XZ	Y1	Z2	13	2A	3B	AC	BD	CE	DF	EG	FH	GJ	HK	JL	KM	LN	MO	NP	OQ	PR	QS	RT	SU	TV	UW	VX	WY	
V	W	X	Y	Z	1	2	3	A	B	C	D	E	F	G	H	J	K	L	M	N	O	P	Q	R	S	T	U	V	W	X	

INTELLECTUAL

1 SA	2 SU	3 M	4 TU	5 W	6 TH	7 F	8 SA	9 SU	10 M	11 TU	12 W	13 TH	14 F	15 SA	16 SU	17 M	18 TU	19 W	20 TH	21 F	22 SA	23 SU	24 M	25 TU	26 W	27 TH	28 F	29 SA	30 SU	31 M	
7	8	A	B	C	D	E	F	G	H	J	K	L	M	N	O	P	Q	R	S	T	U	V	W	X	Y	Z	1	2	3	4	
86	A7	B8	CA	DB	EC	FD	GE	HF	JG	KH	LJ	MK	NL	OM	PN	QO	RP	SQ	TR	US	VT	WU	XV	YW	ZX	1Y	2Z	31	42	53	
A5	B6	C7	D8	EA	FB	GC	HD	JE	KF	LG	MH	NJ	OK	PL	QM	RN	SO	TP	UQ	VR	WS	XT	YU	ZV	1W	2X	3Y	4Z	51	62	
B4	C5	D6	E7	F8	GA	HB	JC	KD	LE	MF	NG	OH	PJ	QK	RL	SM	TN	UO	VP	WQ	XR	YS	ZT	1U	2V	3W	4X	5Y	6Z	71	
C3	D4	E5	F6	G7	H8	JA	KB	LC	MD	NE	OF	PG	QH	RJ	SK	TL	UM	VN	WO	XP	YQ	ZR	1S	2T	3U	4V	5W	6X	7Y	8Z	+
D2	E3	F4	G5	H6	J7	K8	LA	MB	NC	OD	PE	QF	RG	SH	TJ	UK	VL	WM	XN	YO	ZP	1Q	2R	3S	4T	5U	6V	7W	8X	AY	
E1	F2	G3	H4	J5	K6	L7	M8	NA	OB	PC	QD	RE	SF	TG	UH	VJ	WK	XL	YM	ZN	1O	2P	3Q	4R	5S	6T	7U	8V	AW	BX	
FZ	G1	H2	J3	K4	L5	M6	N7	O8	PA	QB	RC	SD	TE	UF	VG	WH	XJ	YK	ZL	1M	2N	3O	4P	5Q	6R	7S	8T	AU	BV	CW	
GY	HZ	J1	K2	L3	M4	N5	O6	P7	Q8	RA	SB	TC	UD	VE	WF	XG	YH	ZJ	1K	2L	3M	4N	5O	6P	7Q	8R	AS	BT	CU	DV	0
HX	JY	KZ	L1	M2	N3	O4	P5	Q6	R7	S8	TA	UB	VC	WD	XE	YF	ZG	1H	2J	3K	4L	5M	6N	7O	8P	AQ	BR	CS	DT	EU	
JW	KX	LY	MZ	N1	O2	P3	Q4	R5	S6	T7	U8	VA	WB	XC	YD	ZE	1F	2G	3H	4J	5K	6L	7M	8N	AO	BP	CQ	DR	ES	FT	
KV	LW	MX	NY	OZ	P1	Q2	R3	S4	T5	U6	V7	W8	XA	YB	ZC	1D	2E	3F	4G	5H	6J	7K	8L	AM	BN	CO	DP	EQ	FR	GS	
LU	MV	NW	OX	PY	QZ	R1	S2	T3	U4	V5	W6	X7	Y8	ZA	1B	2C	3D	4E	5F	6G	7H	8J	AK	BL	CM	DN	EO	FP	GQ	HR	−
MT	NU	OV	PW	QX	RY	SZ	T1	U2	V3	W4	X5	Y6	Z7	18	2A	3B	4C	5D	6E	7F	8G	AH	BJ	CK	DL	EM	FN	GO	HP	JQ	
NS	OT	PU	QV	RW	SX	TY	UZ	V1	W2	X3	Y4	Z5	16	27	38	4A	5B	6C	7D	8E	AF	BG	CH	DJ	EK	FL	GM	HN	JO	KP	
OR	PS	QT	RU	SV	TW	UX	VY	WZ	X1	Y2	Z3	14	25	36	47	58	6A	7B	8C	AD	BE	CF	DG	EH	FJ	GK	HL	JM	KN	LO	
PQ	QR	RS	ST	TU	UV	VW	WX	XY	YZ	Z1	12	23	34	45	56	67	78	8A	AB	BC	CD	DE	EF	FG	GH	HJ	JK	KL	LM	MN	

1 TU	2 W	3 TH	4 F	5 SA	6 SU	7 M	8 TU	9 W	10 TH	11 F	12 SA	13 SU	14 M	15 TU	16 W	17 TH	18 F	19 SA	20 SU	21 M	22 TU	23 W	24 TH	25 F	26 SA	27 SU	28 M	29 TU	30 W	31 TH	
FE	GF	HG	JH	KJ	LK	ML	NM	ON	PO	QP	RQ	SR	TS	UT	VU	WV	XW	AX	BA	CB	DC	ED	FE	GF	HG	JH	KJ	LK	ML	NM	
GD	HE	JF	KG	LH	MJ	NK	OL	PM	QN	RO	SP	TQ	UR	VS	WT	XU	AV	BW	CX	DA	EB	FC	GD	HE	JF	KG	LH	MJ	NK	OL	
HC	JD	KE	LF	MG	NH	OJ	PK	QL	RM	SN	TO	UP	VQ	WR	XS	AT	BU	CV	DW	EX	FA	GB	HC	JD	KE	LF	MG	NH	OJ	PK	
JB	KC	LD	ME	NF	OG	PH	QJ	RK	SL	TM	UN	VO	WP	XQ	AR	BS	CT	DU	EV	FW	GX	HA	JB	KC	LD	ME	NF	OG	PH	QJ	
KA	LB	MC	ND	OE	PF	QG	RH	SJ	TK	UL	VM	WN	XO	AP	BQ	CR	DS	ET	FU	GV	HW	JX	KA	LB	MC	ND	OE	PF	QG	RH	+
LX	MA	NB	OC	PD	QE	RF	SG	TH	UJ	VK	WL	XM	AN	BO	CP	DQ	ER	FS	GT	HU	JV	KW	LX	MA	NB	OC	PD	QE	RF	SG	0
MW	NX	OA	PB	QC	RD	SE	TF	UG	VH	WJ	XK	AL	BM	CN	DO	EP	FQ	GR	HS	JT	KU	LV	MW	NX	OA	PB	QC	RD	SE	TF	
NV	OW	PX	QA	RB	SC	TD	UE	VF	WG	XH	AJ	BK	CL	DM	EN	FO	GP	HQ	JR	KS	LT	MU	NV	OW	PX	QA	RB	SC	TD	UE	−
OU	PV	QW	RX	SA	TB	UC	VD	WE	XF	AG	BH	CJ	DK	EL	FM	GN	HO	JP	KQ	LR	MS	NT	OU	PV	QW	RX	SA	TB	UC	VD	
PT	QU	RV	SW	TX	UA	VB	WC	XD	AE	BF	CG	DH	EJ	FK	GL	HM	JN	KO	LP	MQ	NR	OS	PT	QU	RV	SW	TX	UA	VB	WC	
QS	RT	SU	TV	UW	VX	WA	XB	AC	BD	CE	DF	EG	FH	GJ	HK	JL	KM	LN	MO	NP	OQ	PR	QS	RT	SU	TV	UW	VX	WA	XB	
R	S	T	U	V	W	X	A	B	C	D	E	F	G	H	J	K	L	M	N	O	P	Q	R	S	T	U	V	W	X	A	

1 TU	2 W	3 TH	4 F	5 SA	6 SU	7 M	8 TU	9 W	10 TH	11 F	12 SA	13 SU	14 M	15 TU	16 W	17 TH	18 F	19 SA	20 SU	21 M	22 TU	23 W	24 TH	25 F	26 SA	27 SU	28 M	29 TU	30 W	31 TH	
K	L	M	N	O	P	Q	R	S	T	U	V	W	X	Y	Z	1	2	3	A	B	C	D	E	F	G	H	J	K	L	M	
LJ	MK	NL	OM	PN	QO	RP	SQ	TR	US	VT	WU	XV	YW	ZX	1Y	2Z	31	A2	B3	CA	DB	EC	FD	GE	HF	JG	KH	LJ	MK	NL	
MH	NJ	OK	PL	QM	RN	SO	TP	UQ	VR	WS	XT	YU	ZV	1W	2X	3Y	AZ	B1	C2	D3	EA	FB	GC	HD	JE	KF	LG	MH	NJ	OK	
NG	OH	PJ	QK	RL	SM	TN	UO	VP	WQ	XR	YS	ZT	1U	2V	3W	AX	BY	CZ	D1	E2	F3	GA	HB	JC	KD	LE	MF	NG	OH	PJ	
OF	PG	QH	RJ	SK	TL	UM	VN	WO	XP	YQ	ZR	1S	2T	3U	AV	BW	CX	DY	EZ	F1	G2	H3	JA	KB	LC	MD	NE	OF	PG	QH	+
PE	QF	RG	SH	TJ	UK	VL	WM	XN	YO	ZP	1Q	2R	3S	AT	BU	CV	DW	EX	FY	GZ	H1	J2	K3	LA	MB	NC	OD	PE	QF	RG	
QD	RE	SF	TG	UH	VJ	WK	XL	YM	ZN	1O	2P	3Q	AR	BS	CT	DU	EV	FW	GX	HY	JZ	K1	L2	M3	NA	OB	PC	QD	RE	SF	
RC	SD	TE	UF	VG	WH	XJ	YK	ZL	1M	2N	3O	AP	BQ	CR	DS	ET	FU	GV	HW	JX	KY	LZ	M1	N2	O3	PA	QB	RC	SD	TE	0
SB	TC	UD	VE	WF	XG	YH	ZJ	1K	2L	3M	AN	BO	CP	DQ	ER	FS	GT	HU	JV	KW	LX	MY	NZ	O1	P2	Q3	RA	SB	TC	UD	
TA	UB	VC	WD	XE	YF	ZG	1H	2J	3K	AL	BM	CN	DO	EP	FQ	GR	HS	JT	KU	LV	MW	NX	OY	PZ	Q1	R2	S3	TA	UB	VC	−
U3	VA	WB	XC	YD	ZE	1F	2G	3H	AJ	BK	CL	DM	EN	FO	GP	HQ	JR	KS	LT	MU	NV	OW	PX	QY	RZ	S1	T2	U3	VA	WB	
V2	W3	XA	YB	ZC	1D	2E	3F	AG	BH	CJ	DK	EL	FM	GN	HO	JP	KQ	LR	MS	NT	OU	PV	QW	RX	SY	TZ	U1	V2	W3	XA	
W1	X2	Y3	ZA	1B	2C	3D	AE	BF	CG	DH	EJ	FK	GL	HM	JN	KO	LP	MQ	NR	OS	PT	QU	RV	SW	TX	UY	VZ	W1	X2	Y3	
XZ	Y1	Z2	13	2A	3B	AC	BD	CE	DF	EG	FH	GJ	HK	JL	KM	LN	MO	NP	OQ	PR	QS	RT	SU	TV	UW	VX	WY	XZ	Y1	Z2	
Y	Z	1	2	3	A	B	C	D	E	F	G	H	J	K	L	M	N	O	P	Q	R	S	T	U	V	W	X	Y	Z	1	

1 TU	2 W	3 TH	4 F	5 SA	6 SU	7 M	8 TU	9 W	10 TH	11 F	12 SA	13 SU	14 M	15 TU	16 W	17 TH	18 F	19 SA	20 SU	21 M	22 TU	23 W	24 TH	25 F	26 SA	27 SU	28 M	29 TU	30 W	31 TH	
5	6	7	8	A	B	C	D	E	F	G	H	J	K	L	M	N	O	P	Q	R	S	T	U	V	W	X	Y	Z	1	2	
64	75	86	A7	B8	CA	DB	EC	FD	GE	HF	JG	KH	LJ	MK	NL	OM	PN	QO	RP	SQ	TR	US	VT	WU	XV	YW	ZX	1Y	2Z	31	
73	84	A5	B6	C7	D8	EA	FB	GC	HD	JE	KF	LG	MH	NJ	OK	PL	QM	RN	SO	TP	UQ	VR	WS	XT	YU	ZV	1W	2X	3Y	4Z	
82	A3	B4	C5	D6	E7	F8	GA	HB	JC	KD	LE	MF	NG	OH	PJ	QK	RL	SM	TN	UO	VP	WQ	XR	YS	ZT	1U	2V	3W	4X	5Y	
A1	B2	C3	D4	E5	F6	G7	H8	JA	KB	LC	MD	NE	OF	PG	QH	RJ	SK	TL	UM	VN	WO	XP	YQ	ZR	1S	2T	3U	4V	5W	6X	
BZ	C1	D2	E3	F4	G5	H6	J7	K8	LA	MB	NC	OD	PE	QF	RG	SH	TJ	UK	VL	WM	XN	YO	ZP	1Q	2R	3S	4T	5U	6V	7W	
CY	DZ	E1	F2	G3	H4	J5	K6	L7	M8	NA	OB	PC	QD	RE	SF	TG	UH	VJ	WK	XL	YM	ZN	1O	2P	3Q	4R	5S	6T	7U	8V	+
DX	EY	FZ	G1	H2	J3	K4	L5	M6	N7	O8	PA	QB	RC	SD	TE	UF	VG	WH	XJ	YK	ZL	1M	2N	3O	4P	5Q	6R	7S	8T	AU	
EW	FX	GY	HZ	J1	K2	L3	M4	N5	O6	P7	Q8	RA	SB	TC	UD	VE	WF	XG	YH	ZJ	1K	2L	3M	4N	5O	6P	7Q	8R	AS	BT	0
FV	GW	HX	JY	KZ	L1	M2	N3	O4	P5	Q6	R7	S8	TA	UB	VC	WD	XE	YF	ZG	1H	2J	3K	4L	5M	6N	7O	8P	AQ	BR	CS	
GU	HV	JW	KX	LY	MZ	N1	O2	P3	Q4	R5	S6	T7	U8	VA	WB	XC	YD	ZE	1F	2G	3H	4J	5K	6L	7M	8N	AO	BP	CQ	DR	−
HT	JU	KV	LW	MX	NY	OZ	P1	Q2	R3	S4	T5	U6	V7	W8	XA	YB	ZC	1D	2E	3F	4G	5H	6J	7K	8L	AM	BN	CO	DP	EQ	
JS	KT	LU	MV	NW	OX	PY	QZ	R1	S2	T3	U4	V5	W6	X7	Y8	ZA	1B	2C	3D	4E	5F	6G	7H	8J	AK	BL	CM	DN	EO	FP	
KR	LS	MT	NU	OV	PW	QX	RY	SZ	T1	U2	V3	W4	X5	Y6	Z7	18	2A	3B	4C	5D	6E	7F	8G	AH	BJ	CK	DL	EM	FN	GO	
LQ	MR	NS	OT	PU	QV	RW	SX	TY	UZ	V1	W2	X3	Y4	Z5	16	27	38	4A	5B	6C	7D	8E	AF	BG	CH	DJ	EK	FL	GM	HN	
MP	NQ	OR	PS	QT	RU	SV	TW	UX	VY	WZ	X1	Y2	Z3	14	25	36	47	58	6A	7B	8C	AD	BE	CF	DG	EH	FJ	GK	HL	JM	
NO	OP	PQ	QR	RS	ST	TU	UV	VW	WX	XY	YZ	Z1	12	23	34	45	56	67	78	8A	AB	BC	CD	DE	EF	FG	GH	HJ	JK	KL	

1 F	2 SA	3 SU	4 M	5 TU	6 W	7 TH	8 F	9 SA	10 SU	11 M	12 TU	13 W	14 TH	15 F	16 SA	17 SU	18 M	19 TU	20 W	21 TH	22 F	23 SA	24 SU	25 M	26 TU	27 W	28 TH	29 F	30 SA	
ON	PO	QP	RQ	SR	TS	UT	VU	WV	XW	AX	BA	CB	DC	ED	FE	GF	HG	JH	KJ	LK	ML	NM	ON	PO	QP	RQ	SR	TS	UT	
PM	QN	RO	SP	TQ	UR	VS	WT	XU	AV	BW	CX	DA	EB	FC	GD	HE	JF	KG	LH	MJ	NK	OL	PM	QN	RO	SP	TQ	UR	VS	
QL	RM	SN	TO	UP	VQ	WR	XS	AT	BU	CV	DW	EX	FA	GB	HC	JD	KE	LF	MG	NH	OJ	PK	QL	RM	SN	TO	UP	VQ	WR	+
RK	SL	TM	UN	VO	WP	XQ	AR	BS	CT	DU	EV	FW	GX	HA	JB	KC	LD	ME	NF	OG	PH	QJ	RK	SL	TM	UN	VO	WP	XQ	
SJ	TK	UL	VM	WN	XO	AP	BQ	CR	DS	ET	FU	GV	HW	JX	KA	LB	MC	ND	OE	PF	QG	RH	SJ	TK	UL	VM	WN	XO	AP	
TH	UJ	VK	WL	XM	AN	BO	CP	DQ	ER	FS	GT	HU	JV	KW	LX	MA	NB	OC	PD	QE	RF	SG	TH	UJ	VK	WL	XM	AN	BO	0
UG	VH	WJ	XK	AL	BM	CN	DO	EP	FQ	GR	HS	JT	KU	LV	MW	NX	OA	PB	QC	RD	SE	TF	UG	VH	WJ	XK	AL	BM	CN	
VF	WG	XH	AJ	BK	CL	DM	EN	FO	GP	HQ	JR	KS	LT	MU	NV	OW	PX	QA	RB	SC	TD	UE	VF	WG	XH	AJ	BK	CL	DM	
WE	XF	AG	BH	CJ	DK	EL	FM	GN	HO	JP	KQ	LR	MS	NT	OU	PV	QW	RX	SA	TB	UC	VD	WE	XF	AG	BH	CJ	DK	EL	—
XD	AE	BF	CG	DH	EJ	FK	GL	HM	JN	KO	LP	MQ	NR	OS	PT	QU	RV	SW	TX	UA	VB	WC	XD	AE	BF	CG	DH	EJ	FK	
AC	BD	CE	DF	EG	FH	GJ	HK	JL	KM	LN	MO	NP	OQ	PR	QS	RT	SU	TV	UW	VX	WA	XB	AC	BD	CE	DF	EG	FH	GJ	
B	C	D	E	F	G	H	J	K	L	M	N	O	P	Q	R	S	T	U	V	W	X	A	B	C	D	E	F	G	H	

1 F	2 SA	3 SU	4 M	5 TU	6 W	7 TH	8 F	9 SA	10 SU	11 M	12 TU	13 W	14 TH	15 F	16 SA	17 SU	18 M	19 TU	20 W	21 TH	22 F	23 SA	24 SU	25 M	26 TU	27 W	28 TH	29 F	30 SA	
N	O	P	Q	R	S	T	U	V	W	X	Y	Z	1	2	3	A	B	C	D	E	F	G	H	J	K	L	M	N	O	
OM	PN	QO	RP	SQ	TR	US	VT	WU	XV	YW	ZX	1Y	2Z	31	A2	B3	CA	DB	EC	FD	GE	HF	JG	KH	LJ	MK	NL	OM	PN	
PL	QM	RN	SO	TP	UQ	VR	WS	XT	YU	ZV	1W	2X	3Y	AZ	B1	C2	D3	EA	FB	GC	HD	JE	KF	LG	MH	NJ	OK	PL	QM	
QK	RL	SM	TN	UO	VP	WQ	XR	YS	ZT	1U	2V	3W	AX	BY	CZ	D1	E2	F3	GA	HB	JC	KD	LE	MF	NG	OH	PJ	QK	RL	+
RJ	SK	TL	UM	VN	WO	XP	YQ	ZR	1S	2T	3U	AV	BW	CX	DY	EZ	F1	G2	H3	JA	KB	LC	MD	NE	OF	PG	QH	RJ	SK	
SH	TJ	UK	VL	WM	XN	YO	ZP	1Q	2R	3S	AT	BU	CV	DW	EX	FY	GZ	H1	J2	K3	LA	MB	NC	OD	PE	QF	RG	SH	TJ	
TG	UH	VJ	WK	XL	YM	ZN	1O	2P	3Q	AR	BS	CT	DU	EV	FW	GX	HY	JZ	K1	L2	M3	NA	OB	PC	QD	RE	SF	TG	UH	
UF	VG	WH	XJ	YK	ZL	1M	2N	3O	AP	BQ	CR	DS	ET	FU	GV	HW	JX	KY	LZ	M1	N2	O3	PA	QB	RC	SD	TE	UF	VG	0
VE	WF	XG	YH	ZJ	1K	2L	3M	AN	BO	CP	DQ	ER	FS	GT	HU	JV	KW	LX	MY	NZ	O1	P2	Q3	RA	SB	TC	UD	VE	WF	
WD	XE	YF	ZG	1H	2J	3K	AL	BM	CN	DO	EP	FQ	GR	HS	JT	KU	LV	MW	NX	OY	PZ	Q1	R2	S3	TA	UB	VC	WD	XE	
XC	YD	ZE	1F	2G	3H	AJ	BK	CL	DM	EN	FO	GP	HQ	JR	KS	LT	MU	NV	OW	PX	QY	RZ	S1	T2	U3	VA	WB	XC	YD	—
YB	ZC	1D	2E	3F	AG	BH	CJ	DK	EL	FM	GN	HO	JP	KQ	LR	MS	NT	OU	PV	QW	RX	SY	TZ	U1	V2	W3	XA	YB	ZC	
ZA	1B	2C	3D	AE	BF	CG	DH	EJ	FK	GL	HM	JN	KO	LP	MQ	NR	OS	PT	QU	RV	SW	TX	UY	VZ	W1	X2	Y3	ZA	1B	
13	2A	3B	AC	BD	CE	DF	EG	FH	GJ	HK	JL	KM	LN	MO	NP	OQ	PR	QS	RT	SU	TV	UW	VX	WY	XZ	Y1	Z2	13	2A	
2	3	A	B	C	D	E	F	G	H	J	K	L	M	N	O	P	Q	R	S	T	U	V	W	X	Y	Z	1	2	3	

1 F	2 SA	3 SU	4 M	5 TU	6 W	7 TH	8 F	9 SA	10 SU	11 M	12 TU	13 W	14 TH	15 F	16 SA	17 SU	18 M	19 TU	20 W	21 TH	22 F	23 SA	24 SU	25 M	26 TU	27 W	28 TH	29 F	30 SA	
3	4	5	6	7	8	A	B	C	D	E	F	G	H	J	K	L	M	N	O	P	Q	R	S	T	U	V	W	X	Y	
42	53	64	75	86	A7	B8	CA	DB	EC	FD	GE	HF	JG	KH	LJ	MK	NL	OM	PN	QO	RP	SQ	TR	US	VT	WU	XV	YW	ZX	
51	62	73	84	A5	B6	C7	D8	EA	FB	GC	HD	JE	KF	LG	MH	NJ	OK	PL	QM	RN	SO	TP	UQ	VR	WS	XT	YU	ZV	1W	
6Z	71	82	A3	B4	C5	D6	E7	F8	GA	HB	JC	KD	LE	MF	NG	OH	PJ	QK	RL	SM	TN	UO	VP	WQ	XR	YS	ZT	1U	2V	
7Y	8Z	A1	B2	C3	D4	E5	F6	G7	H8	JA	KB	LC	MD	NE	OF	PG	QH	RJ	SK	TL	UM	VN	WO	XP	YQ	ZR	1S	2T	3U	
8X	AY	BZ	C1	D2	E3	F4	G5	H6	J7	K8	LA	MB	NC	OD	PE	QF	RG	SH	TJ	UK	VL	WM	XN	YO	ZP	1Q	2R	3S	4T	+
AW	BX	CY	DZ	E1	F2	G3	H4	J5	K6	L7	M8	NA	OB	PC	QD	RE	SF	TG	UH	VJ	WK	XL	YM	ZN	1O	2P	3Q	4R	5S	
BV	CW	DX	EY	FZ	G1	H2	J3	K4	L5	M6	N7	O8	PA	QB	RC	SD	TE	UF	VG	WH	XJ	YK	ZL	1M	2N	3O	4P	5Q	6R	
CU	DV	EW	FX	GY	HZ	J1	K2	L3	M4	N5	O6	P7	Q8	RA	SB	TC	UD	VE	WF	XG	YH	ZJ	1K	2L	3M	4N	5O	6P	7Q	0
DT	EU	FV	GW	HX	JY	KZ	L1	M2	N3	O4	P5	Q6	R7	S8	TA	UB	VC	WD	XE	YF	ZG	1H	2J	3K	4L	5M	6N	7O	8P	
ES	FT	GU	HV	JW	KX	LY	MZ	N1	O2	P3	Q4	R5	S6	T7	U8	VA	WB	XC	YD	ZE	1F	2G	3H	4J	5K	6L	7M	8N	AO	
FR	GS	HT	JU	KV	LW	MX	NY	OZ	P1	Q2	R3	S4	T5	U6	V7	W8	XA	YB	ZC	1D	2E	3F	4G	5H	6J	7K	8L	AM	BN	—
GQ	HR	JS	KT	LU	MV	NW	OX	PY	QZ	R1	S2	T3	U4	V5	W6	X7	Y8	ZA	1B	2C	3D	4E	5F	6G	7H	8J	AK	BL	CM	
HP	JQ	KR	LS	MT	NU	OV	PW	QX	RY	SZ	T1	U2	V3	W4	X5	Y6	Z7	18	2A	3B	4C	5D	6E	7F	8G	AH	BJ	CK	DL	
JO	KP	LQ	MR	NS	OT	PU	QV	RW	SX	TY	UZ	V1	W2	X3	Y4	Z5	16	27	38	4A	5B	6C	7D	8E	AF	BG	CH	DJ	EK	
KN	LO	MP	NQ	OR	PS	QT	RU	SV	TW	UX	VY	WZ	X1	Y2	Z3	14	25	36	47	58	6A	7B	8C	AD	BE	CF	DG	EH	FJ	
LM	MN	NO	OP	PQ	QR	RS	ST	TU	UV	VW	WX	XY	YZ	Z1	12	23	34	45	56	67	78	8A	AB	BC	CD	DE	EF	FG	GH	

PHYSICAL

1	2	3	4	5	6	7	8	9	10	11	12	13	14	15	16	17	18	19	20	21	22	23	24	25	26	27	28	29	30	31	
SU	M	TU	W	TH	F	SA	SU	M	TU	W	TH	F	SA	SU	M	TU	W	TH	F	SA	SU	M	TU	W	TH	F	SA	SU	M	TU	
VU	WV	XW	AX	BA	CB	DC	ED	FE	GF	HG	JH	KJ	LK	ML	NM	ON	PO	QP	RQ	SR	TS	UT	VU	WV	XW	AX	BA	CB	DC	ED	
WT	XU	AV	BW	CX	DA	EB	FC	GD	HE	JF	KG	LH	MJ	NK	OL	PM	QN	RO	SP	TQ	UR	VS	WT	XU	AV	BW	CX	DA	EB	FC	
XS	AT	BU	CV	DW	EX	FA	GB	HC	JD	KE	LF	MG	NH	OJ	PK	QL	RM	SN	TO	UP	VQ	WR	XS	AT	BU	CV	DW	EX	FA	GB	+
AR	BS	CT	DU	EV	FW	GX	HA	JB	KC	LD	ME	NF	OG	PH	QJ	RK	SL	TM	UN	VO	WP	XQ	AR	BS	CT	DU	EV	FW	GX	HA	
BQ	CR	DS	ET	FU	GV	HW	JX	KA	LB	MC	ND	OE	PF	QG	RH	SJ	TK	UL	VM	WN	XO	AP	BQ	CR	DS	ET	FU	GV	HW	JX	
CP	DQ	ER	FS	GT	HU	JV	KW	LX	MA	NB	OC	PD	QE	RF	SG	TH	UJ	VK	WL	XM	AN	BO	CP	DQ	ER	FS	GT	HU	JV	KW	0
DO	EP	FQ	GR	HS	JT	KU	LV	MW	NX	OA	PB	QC	RD	SE	TF	UG	VH	WJ	XK	AL	BM	CN	DO	EP	FQ	GR	HS	JT	KU	LV	
EN	FO	GP	HQ	JR	KS	LT	MU	NV	OW	PX	QA	RB	SC	TD	UE	VF	WG	XH	AJ	BK	CL	DM	EN	FO	GP	HQ	JR	KS	LT	MU	
FM	GN	HO	JP	KQ	LR	MS	NT	OU	PV	QW	RX	SA	TB	UC	VD	WE	XF	AG	BH	CJ	DK	EL	FM	GN	HO	JP	KQ	LR	MS	NT	−
GL	HM	JN	KO	LP	MQ	NR	OS	PT	QU	RV	SW	TX	UA	VB	WC	XD	AE	BF	CG	DH	EJ	FK	GL	HM	JN	KO	LP	MQ	NR	OS	
HK	JL	KM	LN	MO	NP	OQ	PR	QS	RT	SU	TV	UW	VX	WA	XB	AC	BD	CE	DF	EG	FH	GJ	HK	JL	KM	LN	MO	NP	OQ	PR	
J	K	L	M	N	O	P	Q	R	S	T	U	V	W	X	A	B	C	D	E	F	G	H	J	K	L	M	N	O	P	Q	

EMOTIONAL

1	2	3	4	5	6	7	8	9	10	11	12	13	14	15	16	17	18	19	20	21	22	23	24	25	26	27	28	29	30	31	
SU	M	TU	W	TH	F	SA	SU	M	TU	W	TH	F	SA	SU	M	TU	W	TH	F	SA	SU	M	TU	W	TH	F	SA	SU	M	TU	
P	Q	R	S	T	U	V	W	X	Y	Z	1	2	3	A	B	C	D	E	F	G	H	J	K	L	M	N	O	P	Q	R	
QO	RP	SQ	TR	US	VT	WU	XV	YW	ZX	1Y	2Z	31	A2	B3	CA	DB	EC	FD	GE	HF	JG	KH	LJ	MK	NL	OM	PN	QO	RP	SQ	
RN	SO	TP	UQ	VR	WS	XT	YU	ZV	1W	2X	3Y	AZ	B1	C2	D3	EA	FB	GC	HD	JE	KF	LG	MH	NJ	OK	PL	QM	RN	SO	TP	
SM	TN	UO	VP	WQ	XR	YS	ZT	1U	2V	3W	AX	BY	CZ	D1	E2	F3	GA	HB	JC	KD	LE	MF	NG	OH	PJ	QK	RL	SM	TN	UO	
TL	UM	VN	WO	XP	YQ	ZR	1S	2T	3U	AV	BW	CX	DY	EZ	F1	G2	H3	JA	KB	LC	MD	NE	OF	PG	QH	RJ	SK	TL	UM	VN	+
UK	VL	WM	XN	YO	ZP	1Q	2R	3S	AT	BU	CV	DW	EX	FY	GZ	H1	J2	K3	LA	MB	NC	OD	PE	QF	RG	SH	TJ	UK	VL	WM	
VJ	WK	XL	YM	ZN	1O	2P	3Q	AR	BS	CT	DU	EV	FW	GX	HY	JZ	K1	L2	M3	NA	OB	PC	QD	RE	SF	TG	UH	VJ	WK	XL	
WH	XJ	YK	ZL	1M	2N	3O	AP	BQ	CR	DS	ET	FU	GV	HW	JX	KY	LZ	M1	N2	O3	PA	QB	RC	SD	TE	UF	VG	WH	XJ	YK	0
XG	YH	ZJ	1K	2L	3M	AN	BO	CP	DQ	ER	FS	GT	HU	JV	KW	LX	MY	NZ	O1	P2	Q3	RA	SB	TC	UD	VE	WF	XG	YH	ZJ	
YF	ZG	1H	2J	3K	AL	BM	CN	DO	EP	FQ	GR	HS	JT	KU	LV	MW	NX	OY	PZ	Q1	R2	S3	TA	UB	VC	WD	XE	YF	ZG	1H	
ZE	1F	2G	3H	AJ	BK	CL	DM	EN	FO	GP	HQ	JR	KS	LT	MU	NV	OW	PX	QY	RZ	S1	T2	U3	VA	WB	XC	YD	ZE	1F	2G	−
1D	2E	3F	AG	BH	CJ	DK	EL	FM	GN	HO	JP	KQ	LR	MS	NT	OU	PV	QW	RX	SY	TZ	U1	V2	W3	XA	YB	ZC	1D	2E	3F	
2C	3D	AE	BF	CG	DH	EJ	FK	GL	HM	JN	KO	LP	MQ	NR	OS	PT	QU	RV	SW	TX	UY	VZ	W1	X2	Y3	ZA	1B	2C	3D	AE	
3B	AC	BD	CE	DF	EG	FH	GJ	HK	JL	KM	LN	MO	NP	OQ	PR	QS	RT	SU	TV	UW	VX	WY	XZ	Y1	Z2	13	2A	3B	AC	BD	
A	B	C	D	E	F	G	H	J	K	L	M	N	O	P	Q	R	S	T	U	V	W	X	Y	Z	1	2	3	A	B	C	

INTELLECTUAL

1	2	3	4	5	6	7	8	9	10	11	12	13	14	15	16	17	18	19	20	21	22	23	24	25	26	27	28	29	30	31	
SU	M	TU	W	TH	F	SA	SU	M	TU	W	TH	F	SA	SU	M	TU	W	TH	F	SA	SU	M	TU	W	TH	F	SA	SU	M	TU	
Z	1	2	3	4	5	6	7	8	A	B	C	D	E	F	G	H	J	K	L	M	N	O	P	Q	R	S	T	U	V	W	
1Y	2Z	31	42	53	64	75	86	A7	B8	CA	DB	EC	FD	GE	HF	JG	KH	LJ	MK	NL	OM	PN	QO	RP	SQ	TR	US	VT	WU	XV	
2X	3Y	4Z	51	62	73	84	A5	B6	C7	D8	EA	FB	GC	HD	JE	KF	LG	MH	NJ	OK	PL	QM	RN	SO	TP	UQ	VR	WS	XT	YU	
3W	4X	5Y	6Z	71	82	A3	B4	C5	D6	E7	F8	GA	HB	JC	KD	LE	MF	NG	OH	PJ	QK	RL	SM	TN	UO	VP	WQ	XR	YS	ZT	
4V	5W	6X	7Y	8Z	A1	B2	C3	D4	E5	F6	G7	H8	JA	KB	LC	MD	NE	OF	PG	QH	RJ	SK	TL	UM	VN	WO	XP	YQ	ZR	1S	
5U	6V	7W	8X	AY	BZ	C1	D2	E3	F4	G5	H6	J7	K8	LA	MB	NC	OD	PE	QF	RG	SH	TJ	UK	VL	WM	XN	YO	ZP	1Q	2R	+
6T	7U	8V	AW	BX	CY	DZ	E1	F2	G3	H4	J5	K6	L7	M8	NA	OB	PC	QD	RE	SF	TG	UH	VJ	WK	XL	YM	ZN	1O	2P	3Q	
7S	8T	AU	BV	CW	DX	EY	FZ	G1	H2	J3	K4	L5	M6	N7	O8	PA	QB	RC	SD	TE	UF	VG	WH	XJ	YK	ZL	1M	2N	3O	4P	
8R	AS	BT	CU	DV	EW	FX	GY	HZ	J1	K2	L3	M4	N5	O6	P7	Q8	RA	SB	TC	UD	VE	WF	XG	YH	ZJ	1K	2L	3M	4N	5O	0
AQ	BR	CS	DT	EU	FV	GW	HX	JY	KZ	L1	M2	N3	O4	P5	Q6	R7	S8	TA	UB	VC	WD	XE	YF	ZG	1H	2J	3K	4L	5M	6N	
BP	CQ	DR	ES	FT	GU	HV	JW	KX	LY	MZ	N1	O2	P3	Q4	R5	S6	T7	U8	VA	WB	XC	YD	ZE	1F	2G	3H	4J	5K	6L	7M	
CO	DP	EQ	FR	GS	HT	JU	KV	LW	MX	NY	OZ	P1	Q2	R3	S4	T5	U6	V7	W8	XA	YB	ZC	1D	2E	3F	4G	5H	6J	7K	8L	−
DN	EO	FP	GQ	HR	JS	KT	LU	MV	NW	OX	PY	QZ	R1	S2	T3	U4	V5	W6	X7	Y8	ZA	1B	2C	3D	4E	5F	6G	7H	8J	AK	
EM	FN	GO	HP	JQ	KR	LS	MT	NU	OV	PW	QX	RY	SZ	T1	U2	V3	W4	X5	Y6	Z7	18	2A	3B	4C	5D	6E	7F	8G	AH	BJ	
FL	GM	HN	JO	KP	LQ	MR	NS	OT	PU	QV	RW	SX	TY	UZ	V1	W2	X3	Y4	Z5	16	27	38	4A	5B	6C	7D	8E	AF	BG	CH	
GK	HL	JM	KN	LO	MP	NQ	OR	PS	QT	RU	SV	TW	UX	VY	WZ	X1	Y2	Z3	14	25	36	47	58	6A	7B	8C	AD	BE	CF	DG	
HJ	JK	KL	LM	MN	NO	OP	PQ	QR	RS	ST	TU	UV	VW	WX	XY	YZ	Z1	12	23	34	45	56	67	78	8A	AB	BC	CD	DE	EF	

224

PHYSICAL — NOVEMBER 1978

1 W	2 TH	3 F	4 SA	5 SU	6 M	7 TU	8 W	9 TH	10 F	11 SA	12 SU	13 M	14 TU	15 W	16 TH	17 F	18 SA	19 SU	20 M	21 TU	22 W	23 TH	24 F	25 SA	26 SU	27 M	28 TU	29 W	30 TH	
FE	GF	HG	JH	KJ	LK	ML	NM	ON	PO	QP	RQ	SR	TS	UT	VU	WV	XW	AX	BA	CB	DC	ED	FE	GF	HG	JH	KJ	LK	ML	
GD	HE	JF	KG	LH	MJ	NK	OL	PM	QN	RO	SP	TQ	UR	VS	WT	XU	AV	BW	CX	DA	EB	FC	GD	HE	JF	KG	LH	MJ	NK	
HC	JD	KE	LF	MG	NH	OJ	PK	QL	RM	SN	TO	UP	VQ	WR	XS	AT	BU	CV	DW	EX	FA	GB	HC	JD	KE	LF	MG	NH	OJ	
JB	KC	LD	ME	NF	OG	PH	QJ	RK	SL	TM	UN	VO	WP	XQ	AR	BS	CT	DU	EV	FW	GX	HA	JB	KC	LD	ME	NF	OG	PH	+
KA	LB	MC	ND	OE	PF	QG	RH	SJ	TK	UL	VM	WN	XO	AP	BQ	CR	DS	ET	FU	GV	HW	JX	KA	LB	MC	ND	OE	PF	QG	
LX	MA	NB	OC	PD	QE	RF	SG	TH	UJ	VK	WL	XM	AN	BO	CP	DQ	ER	FS	GT	HU	JV	KW	LX	MA	NB	OC	PD	QE	RF	0
MW	NX	OA	PB	QC	RD	SE	TF	UG	VH	WJ	XK	AL	BM	CN	DO	EP	FQ	GR	HS	JT	KU	LV	MW	NX	OA	PB	QC	RD	SE	
NV	OW	PX	QA	RB	SC	TD	UE	VF	WG	XH	AJ	BK	CL	DM	EN	FO	GP	HQ	JR	KS	LT	MU	NV	OW	PX	QA	RB	SC	TD	−
OU	PV	QW	RX	SA	TB	UC	VD	WE	XF	AG	BH	CJ	DK	EL	FM	GN	HO	JP	KQ	LR	MS	NT	OU	PV	QW	RX	SA	TB	UC	
PT	QU	RV	SW	TX	UA	VB	WC	XD	AE	BF	CG	DH	EJ	FK	GL	HM	JN	KO	LP	MQ	NR	OS	PT	QU	RV	SW	TX	UA	VB	
QS	RT	SU	TV	UW	VX	WA	XB	AC	BD	CE	DF	EG	FH	GJ	HK	JL	KM	LN	MO	NP	OQ	PR	QS	RT	SU	TV	UW	VX	WA	
R	S	T	U	V	W	X	A	B	C	D	E	F	G	H	J	K	L	M	N	O	P	Q	R	S	T	U	V	W	X	

EMOTIONAL — NOVEMBER 1978

1 W	2 TH	3 F	4 SA	5 SU	6 M	7 TU	8 W	9 TH	10 F	11 SA	12 SU	13 M	14 TU	15 W	16 TH	17 F	18 SA	19 SU	20 M	21 TU	22 W	23 TH	24 F	25 SA	26 SU	27 M	28 TU	29 W	30 TH	
S	T	U	V	W	X	Y	Z	1	2	3	A	B	C	D	E	F	G	H	J	K	L	M	N	O	P	Q	R	S	T	
TR	US	VT	WU	XV	YW	ZX	1Y	2Z	31	A2	B3	CA	DB	EC	FD	GE	HF	JG	KH	LJ	MK	NL	OM	PN	QO	RP	SQ	TR	US	
UQ	VR	WS	XT	YU	ZV	1W	2X	3Y	AZ	B1	C2	D3	EA	FB	GC	HD	JE	KF	LG	MH	NJ	OK	PL	QM	RN	SO	TP	UQ	VR	
VP	WQ	XR	YS	ZT	1U	2V	3W	AX	BY	CZ	D1	E2	F3	GA	HB	JC	KD	LE	MF	NG	OH	PJ	QK	RL	SM	TN	UO	VP	WQ	
WO	XP	YQ	ZR	1S	2T	3U	AV	BW	CX	DY	EZ	F1	G2	H3	JA	KB	LC	MD	NE	OF	PG	QH	RJ	SK	TL	UM	VN	WO	XP	+
XN	YO	ZP	1Q	2R	3S	AT	BU	CV	DW	EX	FY	GZ	H1	J2	K3	LA	MB	NC	OD	PE	QF	RG	SH	TJ	UK	VL	WM	XN	YO	
YM	ZN	1O	2P	3Q	AR	BS	CT	DU	EV	FW	GX	HY	JZ	K1	L2	M3	NA	OB	PC	QD	RE	SF	TG	UH	VJ	WK	XL	YM	ZN	
ZL	1M	2N	3O	AP	BQ	CR	DS	ET	FU	GV	HW	JX	KY	LZ	M1	N2	O3	PA	QB	RC	SD	TE	UF	VG	WH	XJ	YK	ZL	1M	0
1K	2L	3M	AN	BO	CP	DQ	ER	FS	GT	HU	JV	KW	LX	MY	NZ	O1	P2	Q3	RA	SB	TC	UD	VE	WF	XG	YH	ZJ	1K	2L	
2J	3K	AL	BM	CN	DO	EP	FQ	GR	HS	JT	KU	LV	MW	NX	OY	PZ	Q1	R2	S3	TA	UB	VC	WD	XE	YF	ZG	1H	2J	3K	−
3H	AJ	BK	CL	DM	EN	FO	GP	HQ	JR	KS	LT	MU	NV	OW	PX	QY	RZ	S1	T2	U3	VA	WB	XC	YD	ZE	1F	2G	3H	AJ	
AG	BH	CJ	DK	EL	FM	GN	HO	JP	KQ	LR	MS	NT	OU	PV	QW	RX	SY	TZ	U1	V2	W3	XA	YB	ZC	1D	2E	3F	AG	BH	
BF	CG	DH	EJ	FK	GL	HM	JN	KO	LP	MQ	NR	OS	PT	QU	RV	SW	TX	UY	VZ	W1	X2	Y3	ZA	1B	2C	3D	AE	BF	CG	
CE	DF	EG	FH	GJ	HK	JL	KM	LN	MO	NP	OQ	PR	QS	RT	SU	TV	UW	VX	WY	XZ	Y1	Z2	13	2A	3B	AC	BD	CE	DF	
D	E	F	G	H	J	K	L	M	N	O	P	Q	R	S	T	U	V	W	X	Y	Z	1	2	3	A	B	C	D	E	

INTELLECTUAL — NOVEMBER 1978

1 W	2 TH	3 F	4 SA	5 SU	6 M	7 TU	8 W	9 TH	10 F	11 SA	12 SU	13 M	14 TU	15 W	16 TH	17 F	18 SA	19 SU	20 M	21 TU	22 W	23 TH	24 F	25 SA	26 SU	27 M	28 TU	29 W	30 TH	
X	Y	Z	1	2	3	4	5	6	7	8	A	B	C	D	E	F	G	H	J	K	L	M	N	O	P	Q	R	S	T	
YW	ZX	1Y	2Z	31	42	53	64	75	86	A7	B8	CA	DB	EC	FD	GE	HF	JG	KH	LJ	MK	NL	OM	PN	QO	RP	SQ	TR	US	
ZV	1W	2X	3Y	4Z	51	62	73	84	A5	B6	C7	D8	EA	FB	GC	HD	JE	KF	LG	MH	NJ	OK	PL	QM	RN	SO	TP	UQ	VR	
1U	2V	3W	4X	5Y	6Z	71	82	A3	B4	C5	D6	E7	F8	GA	HB	JC	KD	LE	MF	NG	OH	PJ	QK	RL	SM	TN	UO	VP	WQ	
2T	3U	4V	5W	6X	7Y	8Z	A1	B2	C3	D4	E5	F6	G7	H8	JA	KB	LC	MD	NE	OF	PG	QH	RJ	SK	TL	UM	VN	WO	XP	+
3S	4T	5U	6V	7W	8X	AY	BZ	C1	D2	E3	F4	G5	H6	J7	K8	LA	MB	NC	OD	PE	QF	RG	SH	TJ	UK	VL	WM	XN	YO	
4R	5S	6T	7U	8V	AW	BX	CY	DZ	E1	F2	G3	H4	J5	K6	L7	M8	NA	OB	PC	QD	RE	SF	TG	UH	VJ	WK	XL	YM	ZN	
5Q	6R	7S	8T	AU	BV	CW	DX	EY	FZ	G1	H2	J3	K4	L5	M6	N7	O8	PA	QB	RC	SD	TE	UF	VG	WH	XJ	YK	ZL	1M	
6P	7Q	8R	AS	BT	CU	DV	EW	FX	GY	HZ	J1	K2	L3	M4	N5	O6	P7	Q8	RA	SB	TC	UD	VE	WF	XG	YH	ZJ	1K	2L	0
7O	8P	AQ	BR	CS	DT	EU	FV	GW	HX	JY	KZ	L1	M2	N3	O4	P5	Q6	R7	S8	TA	UB	VC	WD	XE	YF	ZG	1H	2J	3K	
8N	AO	BP	CQ	DR	ES	FT	GU	HV	JW	KX	LY	MZ	N1	O2	P3	Q4	R5	S6	T7	U8	VA	WB	XC	YD	ZE	1F	2G	3H	4J	−
AM	BN	CO	DP	EQ	FR	GS	HT	JU	KV	LW	MX	NY	OZ	P1	Q2	R3	S4	T5	U6	V7	W8	XA	YB	ZC	1D	2E	3F	4G	5H	
BL	CM	DN	EO	FP	GQ	HR	JS	KT	LU	MV	NW	OX	PY	QZ	R1	S2	T3	U4	V5	W6	X7	Y8	ZA	1B	2C	3D	4E	5F	6G	
CK	DL	EM	FN	GO	HP	JQ	KR	LS	MT	NU	OV	PW	QX	RY	SZ	T1	U2	V3	W4	X5	Y6	Z7	18	2A	3B	4C	5D	6E	7F	
DJ	EK	FL	GM	HN	JO	KP	LQ	MR	NS	OT	PU	QV	RW	SX	TY	UZ	V1	W2	X3	Y4	Z5	16	27	38	4A	5B	6C	7D	8E	
EH	FJ	GK	HL	JM	KN	LO	MP	NQ	OR	PS	QT	RU	SV	TW	UX	VY	WZ	X1	Y2	Z3	14	25	36	47	58	6A	7B	8C	AD	
FG	GH	HJ	JK	KL	LM	MN	NO	OP	PQ	QR	RS	ST	TU	UV	VW	WX	XY	YZ	Z1	12	23	34	45	56	67	78	8A	AB	BC	

PHYSICAL

1 F	2 SA	3 SU	4 M	5 TU	6 W	7 TH	8 F	9 SA	10 SU	11 M	12 TU	13 W	14 TH	15 F	16 SA	17 SU	18 M	19 TU	20 W	21 TH	22 F	23 SA	24 SU	25 M	26 TU	27 W	28 TH	29 F	30 SA	31 SU	
NM	ON	PO	QP	RQ	SR	TS	UT	VU	WV	XW	AX	BA	CB	DC	ED	FE	GF	HG	JH	KJ	LK	ML	NM	ON	PO	QP	RQ	SR	TS	UT	
OL	PM	QN	RO	SP	TQ	UR	VS	WT	XU	AV	BW	CX	DA	EB	FC	GD	HE	JF	KG	LH	MJ	NK	OL	PM	QN	RO	SP	TQ	UR	VS	
PK	QL	RM	SN	TO	UP	VQ	WR	XS	AT	BU	CV	DW	EX	FA	GB	HC	JD	KE	LF	MG	NH	OJ	PK	QL	RM	SN	TO	UP	VQ	WR	+
QJ	RK	SL	TM	UN	VO	WP	XQ	AR	BS	CT	DU	EV	FW	GX	HA	JX	KC	LD	ME	ND	OE	PF	QG	RH	SJ	TK	UL	VM	WN	XO	AP	
RH	SJ	TK	UL	VM	WN	XO	AP	BQ	CR	DS	ET	FU	GV	HW	JX	KA	LB	MC	ND	OE	PF	QG	RH	SJ	TK	UL	VM	WN	XO	
SG	TH	UJ	VK	WL	XM	AN	BO	CP	DQ	ER	FS	GT	HU	JV	KW	LX	MA	NB	OC	PD	QE	RF	SG	TH	UJ	VK	WL	XM	AN	BO	0
TF	UG	VH	WJ	XK	AL	BM	CN	DO	EP	FQ	GR	HS	JT	KU	LV	MW	NX	OA	PB	QC	RD	SE	TF	UG	VH	WJ	XK	AL	BM	CN	
UE	VF	WG	XH	AJ	BK	CL	DM	EN	FO	GP	HQ	JR	KS	LT	MU	NV	OW	PX	QA	RB	SC	TD	UE	VF	WG	XH	AJ	BK	CL	DM	
VD	WE	XF	AG	BH	CJ	DK	EL	FM	GN	HO	JP	KQ	LR	MS	NT	OU	PV	QW	RX	SA	TB	UC	VD	WE	XF	AG	BH	CJ	DK	EL	—
WC	XD	AE	BF	CG	DH	EJ	FK	GL	HM	JN	KO	LP	MQ	NR	OS	PT	QU	RV	SW	TX	UA	VB	WC	XD	AE	BF	CG	DH	EJ	FK	
XB	AC	BD	CE	DF	EG	FH	GJ	HK	JL	KM	LN	MO	NP	OQ	PR	QS	RT	SU	TV	UW	VX	WA	XB	AC	BD	CE	DF	EG	FH	GJ	
A	B	C	D	E	F	G	H	J	K	L	M	N	O	P	Q	R	S	T	U	V	W	X	A	B	C	D	E	F	G	H	

EMOTIONAL

1 F	2 SA	3 SU	4 M	5 TU	6 W	7 TH	8 F	9 SA	10 SU	11 M	12 TU	13 W	14 TH	15 F	16 SA	17 SU	18 M	19 TU	20 W	21 TH	22 F	23 SA	24 SU	25 M	26 TU	27 W	28 TH	29 F	30 SA	31 SU	
U	V	W	X	Y	Z	1	2	3	A	B	C	D	E	F	G	H	J	K	L	M	N	O	P	Q	R	S	T	U	V	W	
VT	WU	XV	YW	ZX	1Y	2Z	31	A2	B3	CA	DB	EC	FD	GE	HF	JG	KH	LJ	MK	NL	OM	PN	QO	RP	SQ	TR	US	VT	WU	XV	
WS	XT	YU	ZV	1W	2X	3Y	AZ	B1	C2	D3	EA	FB	GC	HD	JE	KF	LG	MH	NJ	OK	PL	QM	RN	SO	TP	UQ	VR	WS	XT	YU	
XR	YS	ZT	1U	2V	3W	AX	BY	CZ	D1	E2	F3	GA	HB	JC	KD	LE	MF	NG	OH	PJ	QK	RL	SM	TN	UO	VP	WQ	XR	YS	ZT	+
YQ	ZR	1S	2T	3U	AV	BW	CX	DY	EZ	F1	G2	H3	JA	KB	LC	MD	NE	OF	PG	QH	RJ	SK	TL	UM	VN	WO	XP	YQ	ZR	1S	
ZP	1Q	2R	3S	AT	BU	CV	DW	EX	FY	GZ	H1	J2	K3	LA	MB	NC	OD	PE	QF	RG	SH	TJ	UK	VL	WM	XN	YO	ZP	1Q	2R	
1O	2P	3Q	AR	BS	CT	DU	EV	FW	GX	HY	JZ	K1	L2	M3	NA	OB	PC	QD	RE	SF	TG	UH	VJ	WK	XL	YM	ZN	1O	2P	3Q	
2N	3O	AP	BQ	CR	DS	ET	FU	GV	HW	JX	KY	LZ	M1	N2	O3	PA	QB	RC	SD	TE	UF	VG	WH	XJ	YK	ZL	1M	2N	3O	AP	0
3M	AN	BO	CP	DQ	ER	FS	GT	HU	JV	KW	LX	MY	NZ	O1	P2	Q3	RA	SB	TC	UD	VE	WF	XG	YH	ZJ	1K	2L	3M	AN	BO	
AL	BM	CN	DO	EP	FQ	GR	HS	JT	KU	LV	MW	NX	OY	PZ	Q1	R2	S3	TA	UB	VC	WD	XE	YF	ZG	1H	2J	3K	AL	BM	CN	
BK	CL	DM	EN	FO	GP	HQ	JR	KS	LT	MU	NV	OW	PX	QY	RZ	S1	T2	U3	VA	WB	XC	YD	ZE	1F	2G	3H	AJ	BK	CL	DM	—
CJ	DK	EL	FM	GN	HO	JP	KQ	LR	MS	NT	OU	PV	QW	RX	SY	TZ	U1	V2	W3	XA	YB	ZC	1D	2E	3F	AG	BH	CJ	DK	EL	
DH	EJ	FK	GL	HM	JN	KO	LP	MQ	NR	OS	PT	QU	RV	SW	TX	UY	VZ	W1	X2	Y3	ZA	1B	2C	3D	AE	BF	CG	DH	EJ	FK	
EG	FH	GJ	HK	JL	KM	LN	MO	NP	OQ	PR	QS	RT	SU	TV	UW	VX	WY	XZ	Y1	Z2	13	2A	3B	AC	BD	CE	DF	EG	FH	GJ	
F	G	H	J	K	L	M	N	O	P	Q	R	S	T	U	V	W	X	Y	Z	1	2	3	A	B	C	D	E	F	G	H	

INTELLECTUAL

1 F	2 SA	3 SU	4 M	5 TU	6 W	7 TH	8 F	9 SA	10 SU	11 M	12 TU	13 W	14 TH	15 F	16 SA	17 SU	18 M	19 TU	20 W	21 TH	22 F	23 SA	24 SU	25 M	26 TU	27 W	28 TH	29 F	30 SA	31 SU	
U	V	W	X	Y	Z	1	2	3	4	5	6	7	8	A	B	C	D	E	F	G	H	J	K	L	M	N	O	P	Q	R	
VT	WU	XV	YW	ZX	1Y	2Z	31	42	53	64	75	86	A7	B8	CA	DB	EC	FD	GE	HF	JG	KH	LJ	MK	NL	OM	PN	QO	RP	SQ	
WS	XT	YU	ZV	1W	2X	3Y	4Z	51	62	73	84	A5	B6	C7	D8	EA	FB	GC	HD	JE	KF	LG	MH	NJ	OK	PL	QM	RN	SO	TP	
XR	YS	ZT	1U	2V	3W	4X	5Y	6Z	71	82	A3	B4	C5	D6	E7	F8	GA	HB	JC	KD	LE	MF	NG	OH	PJ	QK	RL	SM	TN	UO	
YQ	ZR	1S	2T	3U	4V	5W	6X	7Y	8Z	A1	B2	C3	D4	E5	F6	G7	H8	JA	KB	LC	MD	NE	OF	PG	QH	RJ	SK	TL	UM	VN	
ZP	1Q	2R	3S	4T	5U	6V	7W	8X	AY	BZ	C1	D2	E3	F4	G5	H6	J7	K8	LA	MB	NC	OD	PE	QF	RG	SH	TJ	UK	VL	WM	+
1O	2P	3Q	4R	5S	6T	7U	8V	AW	BX	CY	DZ	E1	F2	G3	H4	J5	K6	L7	M8	NA	OB	PC	QD	RE	SF	TG	UH	VJ	WK	XL	
2N	3O	4P	5Q	6R	7S	8T	AU	BV	CW	DX	EY	FZ	G1	H2	J3	K4	L5	M6	N7	O8	PA	QB	RC	SD	TE	UF	VG	WH	XJ	YK	
3M	4N	5O	6P	7Q	8R	AS	BT	CU	DV	EW	FX	GY	HZ	J1	K2	L3	M4	N5	O6	P7	Q8	RA	SB	TC	UD	VE	WF	XG	YH	ZJ	0
4L	5M	6N	7O	8P	AQ	BR	CS	DT	EU	FV	GW	HX	JY	KZ	L1	M2	N3	O4	P5	Q6	R7	S8	TA	UB	VC	WD	XE	YF	ZG	1H	
5K	6L	7M	8N	AO	BP	CQ	DR	ES	FT	GU	HV	JW	KX	LY	MZ	N1	O2	P3	Q4	R5	S6	T7	U8	VA	WB	XC	YD	ZE	1F	2G	
6J	7K	8L	AM	BN	CO	DP	EQ	FR	GS	HT	JU	KV	LW	MX	NY	OZ	P1	Q2	R3	S4	T5	U6	V7	W8	XA	YB	ZC	1D	2E	3F	—
7H	8J	AK	BL	CM	DN	EO	FP	GQ	HR	JS	KT	LU	MV	NW	OX	PY	QZ	R1	S2	T3	U4	V5	W6	X7	Y8	ZA	1B	2C	3D	4E	
8G	AH	BJ	CK	DL	EM	FN	GO	HP	JQ	KR	LS	MT	NU	OV	PW	QX	RY	SZ	T1	U2	V3	W4	X5	Y6	Z7	18	2A	3B	4C	5D	
AF	BG	CH	DJ	EK	FL	GM	HN	JO	KP	LQ	MR	NS	OT	PU	QV	RW	SX	TY	UZ	V1	W2	X3	Y4	Z5	16	27	38	4A	5B	6C	
BE	CF	DG	EH	FJ	GK	HL	JM	KN	LO	MP	NQ	OR	PS	QT	RU	SV	TW	UX	VY	WZ	X1	Y2	Z3	14	25	36	47	58	6A	7B	
CD	DE	EF	FG	GH	HJ	JK	KL	LM	MN	NO	OP	PQ	QR	RS	ST	TU	UV	VW	WX	XY	YZ	Z1	12	23	34	45	56	67	78	8A	

PHYSICAL — JANUARY 1979

	1 M	2 TU	3 W	4 TH	5 F	6 SA	7 SU	8 M	9 TU	10 W	11 TH	12 F	13 SA	14 SU	15 M	16 TU	17 W	18 TH	19 F	20 SA	21 SU	22 M	23 TU	24 W	25 TH	26 F	27 SA	28 SU	29 M	30 TU	31 W	
	VU	WV	XW	AX	BA	CB	DC	ED	FE	GF	HG	JH	KJ	LK	ML	NM	ON	PO	QP	RQ	SR	TS	UT	VU	WV	XW	AX	BA	CB	DC	ED	
	WT	XU	AV	BW	CX	DA	EB	FC	GD	HE	JF	KG	LH	MJ	NK	OL	PM	QN	RO	SP	TQ	UR	VS	WT	XU	AV	BW	CX	DA	EB	FC	
	XS	AT	BU	CV	DW	EX	FA	GB	HC	JD	KE	LF	MG	NH	OJ	PK	QL	RM	SN	TO	UP	VQ	WR	XS	AT	BU	CV	DW	EX	FA	GB	+
	AR	BS	CT	DU	EV	FW	GX	HA	JB	KC	LD	ME	NF	OG	PH	QJ	RK	SL	TM	UN	VO	WP	XQ	AR	BS	CT	DU	EV	FW	GX	HA	
	BQ	CR	DS	ET	FU	GV	HW	JX	KA	LB	MC	ND	OE	PF	QG	RH	SJ	TK	UL	VM	WN	XO	AP	BQ	CR	DS	ET	FU	GV	HW	JX	
	CP	DQ	ER	FS	GT	HU	JV	KW	LX	MA	NB	OC	PD	QE	RF	SG	TH	UJ	VK	WL	XM	AN	BO	CP	DQ	ER	FS	GT	HU	JV	KW	0
	DO	EP	FQ	GR	HS	JT	KU	LV	MW	NX	OA	PB	QC	RD	SE	TF	UG	VH	WJ	XK	AL	BM	CN	DO	EP	FQ	GR	HS	JT	KU	LV	
	EN	FO	GP	HQ	JR	KS	LT	MU	NV	OW	PX	QA	RB	SC	TD	UE	VF	WG	XH	AJ	BK	CL	DM	EN	FO	GP	HQ	JR	KS	LT	MU	
	FM	GN	HO	JP	KQ	LR	MS	NT	OU	PV	QW	RX	SA	TB	UC	VD	WE	XF	AG	BH	CJ	DK	EL	FM	GN	HO	JP	KQ	LR	MS	NT	—
	GL	HM	JN	KO	LP	MQ	NR	OS	PT	QU	RV	SW	TX	UA	VB	WC	XD	AE	BF	CG	DH	EJ	FK	GL	HM	JN	KO	LP	MQ	NR	OS	
	HK	JL	KM	LN	MO	NP	OQ	PR	QS	RT	SU	TV	UW	VX	WA	XB	AC	BD	CE	DF	EG	FH	GJ	HK	JL	KM	LN	MO	NP	OQ		
	J	K	L	M	N	O	P	Q	R	S	T	U	V	W	X	A	B	C	D	E	F	G	H	J	K	L	M	N	O	P	Q	

EMOTIONAL — JANUARY 1979

	1 M	2 TU	3 W	4 TH	5 F	6 SA	7 SU	8 M	9 TU	10 W	11 TH	12 F	13 SA	14 SU	15 M	16 TU	17 W	18 TH	19 F	20 SA	21 SU	22 M	23 TU	24 W	25 TH	26 F	27 SA	28 SU	29 M	30 TU	31 W	
	X	Y	Z	1	2	3	A	B	C	D	E	F	G	H	J	K	L	M	N	O	P	Q	R	S	T	U	V	W	X	Y	Z	
	YW	ZX	1Y	2Z	31	A2	B3	CA	DB	EC	FD	GE	HF	JG	KH	LJ	MK	NL	OM	PN	QO	RP	SQ	TR	US	VT	WU	XV	YW	ZX	1Y	
	ZV	1W	2X	3Y	AZ	B1	C2	D3	EA	FB	GC	HD	JE	KF	LG	MH	NJ	OK	PL	QM	RN	SO	TP	UQ	VR	WS	XT	YU	ZV	1W	2X	
	1U	2V	3W	AX	BY	CZ	D1	E2	F3	GA	HB	JC	KD	LE	MF	NG	OH	PJ	QK	RL	SM	TN	UO	VP	WQ	XR	YS	ZT	1U	2V	3W	
	2T	3U	AV	BW	CX	DY	EZ	F1	G2	H3	JA	KB	LC	MD	NE	OF	PG	QH	RJ	SK	TL	UM	VN	WO	XP	YQ	ZR	1S	2T	3U	AV	+
	3S	AT	BU	CV	DW	EX	FY	GZ	H1	J2	K3	LA	MB	NC	OD	PE	QF	RG	SH	TJ	UK	VL	WM	XN	YO	ZP	1Q	2R	3S	AT	BU	
	AR	BS	CT	DU	EV	FW	GX	HY	JZ	K1	L2	M3	NA	OB	PC	QD	RE	SF	TG	UH	VJ	WK	XL	YM	ZN	1O	2P	3Q	AR	BS	CT	
	BQ	CR	DS	ET	FU	GV	HW	JX	KY	LZ	M1	N2	O3	PA	QB	RC	SD	TE	UF	VG	WH	XJ	YK	ZL	1M	2N	3O	AP	BQ	CR	DS	0
	CP	DQ	ER	FS	GT	HU	JV	KW	LX	MY	NZ	O1	P2	Q3	RA	SB	TC	UD	VE	WF	XG	YH	ZJ	1K	2L	3M	AN	BO	CP	DQ	ER	
	DO	EP	FQ	GR	HS	JT	KU	LV	MW	NX	OY	PZ	Q1	R2	S3	TA	UB	VC	WD	XE	YF	ZG	1H	2J	3K	AL	BM	CN	DO	EP	FQ	
	EN	FO	GP	HQ	JR	KS	LT	MU	NV	OW	PX	QY	RZ	S1	T2	U3	VA	WB	XC	YD	ZE	1F	2G	3H	AJ	BK	CL	DM	EN	FO	GP	—
	FM	GN	HO	JP	KQ	LR	MS	NT	OU	PV	QW	RX	SY	TZ	U1	V2	W3	XA	YB	ZC	1D	2E	3F	AG	BH	CJ	DK	EL	FM	GN	HO	
	GL	HM	JN	KO	LP	MQ	NR	OS	PT	QU	RV	SW	TX	UY	VZ	W1	X2	Y3	ZA	1B	2C	3D	AE	BF	CG	DH	EJ	FK	GL	HM	JN	
	HK	JL	KM	LN	MO	NP	OQ	PR	QS	RT	SU	TV	UW	VX	WY	XZ	Y1	Z2	13	2A	3B	AC	BD	CE	DF	EG	FH	GJ	HK	JL	KM	
	J	K	L	M	N	O	P	Q	R	S	T	U	V	W	X	Y	Z	1	2	3	A	B	C	D	E	F	G	H	J	K	L	

INTELLECTUAL — JANUARY 1979

	1 M	2 TU	3 W	4 TH	5 F	6 SA	7 SU	8 M	9 TU	10 W	11 TH	12 F	13 SA	14 SU	15 M	16 TU	17 W	18 TH	19 F	20 SA	21 SU	22 M	23 TU	24 W	25 TH	26 F	27 SA	28 SU	29 M	30 TU	31 W	
	S	T	U	V	W	X	Y	Z	1	2	3	4	5	6	7	8	A	B	C	D	E	F	G	H	J	K	L	M	N	O	P	
	TR	US	VT	WU	XV	YW	ZX	1Y	2Z	31	42	53	64	75	86	A7	B8	CA	DB	EC	FD	GE	HF	JG	KH	LJ	MK	NL	OM	PN	QO	
	UQ	VR	WS	XT	YU	ZV	1W	2X	3Y	4Z	51	62	73	84	A5	B6	C7	D8	EA	FB	GC	HD	JE	KF	LG	MH	NJ	OK	PL	QM	RN	
	VP	WQ	XR	YS	ZT	1U	2V	3W	4X	5Y	6Z	71	82	A3	B4	C5	D6	E7	F8	GA	HB	JC	KD	LE	MF	NG	OH	PJ	QK	RL	SM	
	WO	XP	YQ	ZR	1S	2T	3U	4V	5W	6X	7Y	8Z	A1	B2	C3	D4	E5	F6	G7	H8	JA	KB	LC	MD	NE	OF	PG	QH	RJ	SK	TL	
	XN	YO	ZP	1Q	2R	3S	4T	5U	6V	7W	8X	AY	BZ	C1	D2	E3	F4	G5	H6	J7	K8	LA	MB	NC	OD	PE	QF	RG	SH	TJ	UK	
	YM	ZN	1O	2P	3Q	4R	5S	6T	7U	8V	AW	BX	CY	DZ	E1	F2	G3	H4	J5	K6	L7	M8	NA	OB	PC	QD	RE	SF	TG	UH	VJ	+
	ZL	1M	2N	3O	4P	5Q	6R	7S	8T	AU	BV	CW	DX	EY	FZ	G1	H2	J3	K4	L5	M6	N7	O8	PA	QB	RC	SD	TE	UF	VG	WH	
	1K	2L	3M	4N	5O	6P	7Q	8R	AS	BT	CU	DV	EW	FX	GY	HZ	J1	K2	L3	M4	N5	O6	P7	Q8	RA	SB	TC	UD	VE	WF	XG	0
	2J	3K	4L	5M	6N	7O	8P	AQ	BR	CS	DT	EU	FV	GW	HX	JY	KZ	L1	M2	N3	O4	P5	Q6	R7	S8	TA	UB	VC	WD	XE	YF	
	3H	4J	5K	6L	7M	8N	AO	BP	CQ	DR	ES	FT	GU	HV	JW	KX	LY	MZ	N1	O2	P3	Q4	R5	S6	T7	U8	VA	WB	XC	YD	ZE	—
	4G	5H	6J	7K	8L	AM	BN	CO	DP	EQ	FR	GS	HT	JU	KV	LW	MX	NY	OZ	P1	Q2	R3	S4	T5	U6	V7	W8	XA	YB	ZC	1D	
	5F	6G	7H	8J	AK	BL	CM	DN	EO	FP	GQ	HR	JS	KT	LU	MV	NW	OX	PY	QZ	R1	S2	T3	U4	V5	W6	X7	Y8	ZA	1B	2C	
	6E	7F	8G	AH	BJ	CK	DL	EM	FN	GO	HP	JQ	KR	LS	MT	NU	OV	PW	QX	RY	SZ	T1	U2	V3	W4	X5	Y6	Z7	18	2A	3B	
	7D	8E	AF	BG	CH	DJ	EK	FL	GM	HN	JO	KP	LQ	MR	NS	OT	PU	QV	RW	SX	TY	UZ	V1	W2	X3	Y4	Z5	16	27	38	4A	
	8C	AD	BE	CF	DG	EH	FJ	GK	HL	JM	KN	LO	MP	NQ	OR	PS	QT	RU	SV	TW	UX	VY	WZ	X1	Y2	Z3	14	25	36	47	58	
	AB	BC	CD	DE	EF	FG	GH	HJ	JK	KL	LM	MN	NO	OP	PQ	QR	RS	ST	TU	UV	VW	WX	XY	YZ	Z1	12	23	34	45	56	67	

1 TH	2 F	3 SA	4 SU	5 M	6 TU	7 W	8 TH	9 F	10 SA	11 SU	12 M	13 TU	14 W	15 TH	16 F	17 SA	18 SU	19 M	20 TU	21 W	22 TH	23 F	24 SA	25 SU	26 M	27 TU	28 W	
FE	GF	HG	JH	KJ	LK	ML	NM	ON	PO	QP	RQ	SR	TS	UT	VU	WV	XW	AX	BA	CB	DC	ED	FE	GF	HG	JH	KJ	
GD	HE	JF	KG	LH	MJ	NK	OL	PM	QN	RO	SP	TQ	UR	VS	WT	XU	AV	BW	CX	DA	EB	FC	GD	HE	JF	KG	LH	
HC	JD	KE	LF	MG	NH	OJ	PK	QL	RM	SN	TO	UP	VQ	WR	XS	AT	BU	CV	DW	EX	FA	GB	HC	JD	KE	LF	MG	+
JB	KC	LD	ME	NF	OG	PH	QJ	RK	SL	TM	UN	VO	WP	XQ	AR	BS	CT	DU	EV	FW	GX	HA	JB	KC	LD	ME	NF	
KA	LB	MC	ND	OE	PF	QG	RH	SJ	TK	UL	VM	WN	XO	AP	BQ	CR	DS	ET	FU	GV	HW	JX	KA	LB	MC	ND	OE	
LX	MA	NB	OC	PD	QE	RF	SG	TH	UJ	VK	WL	XM	AN	BO	CP	DQ	ER	FS	GT	HU	JV	KW	LX	MA	NB	OC	PD	0
MW	NX	OA	PB	QC	RD	SE	TF	UG	VH	WJ	XK	AL	BM	CN	DO	EP	FQ	GR	HS	JT	KU	LV	MW	NX	OA	PB	QC	
NV	OW	PX	QA	RB	SC	TD	UE	VF	WG	XH	AJ	BK	CL	DM	EN	FO	GP	HQ	JR	KS	LT	MU	NV	OW	PX	QA	RB	−
OU	PV	QW	RX	SA	TB	UC	VD	WE	XF	AG	BH	CJ	DK	EL	FM	GN	HO	JP	KQ	LR	MS	NT	OU	PV	QW	RX	SA	
PT	QU	RV	SW	TX	UA	VB	WC	XD	AE	BF	CG	DH	EJ	FK	GL	HM	JN	KO	LP	MQ	NR	OS	PT	QU	RV	SW	TX	
QS	RT	SU	TV	UW	VX	WA	XB	AC	BD	CE	DF	EG	FH	GJ	HK	JL	KM	LN	MO	NP	OQ	PR	QS	RT	SU	TV	UW	
R	S	T	U	V	W	X	A	B	C	D	E	F	G	H	J	K	L	M	N	O	P	Q	R	S	T	U	V	

1 TH	2 F	3 SA	4 SU	5 M	6 TU	7 W	8 TH	9 F	10 SA	11 SU	12 M	13 TU	14 W	15 TH	16 F	17 SA	18 SU	19 M	20 TU	21 W	22 TH	23 F	24 SA	25 SU	26 M	27 TU	28 W	
1	2	3	A	B	C	D	E	F	G	H	J	K	L	M	N	O	P	Q	R	S	T	U	V	W	X	Y	Z	
2Z	31	A2	B3	CA	DB	EC	FD	GE	HF	JG	KH	LJ	MK	NL	OM	PN	QO	RP	SQ	TR	US	VT	WU	XV	YW	ZX	1Y	
3Y	AZ	B1	C2	D3	EA	FB	GC	HD	JE	KF	LG	MH	NJ	OK	PL	QM	RN	SO	TP	UQ	VR	WS	XT	YU	ZV	1W	2X	
AX	BY	CZ	D1	E2	F3	GA	HB	JC	KD	LE	MF	NG	OH	PJ	QK	RL	SM	TN	UO	VP	WQ	XR	YS	ZT	1U	2V	3W	+
BW	CX	DY	EZ	F1	G2	H3	JA	KB	LC	MD	NE	OF	PG	QH	RJ	SK	TL	UM	VN	WO	XP	YQ	ZR	1S	2T	3U	AV	
CV	DW	EX	FY	GZ	H1	J2	K3	LA	MB	NC	OD	PE	QF	RG	SH	TJ	UK	VL	WM	XN	YO	ZP	1Q	2R	3S	AT	BU	
DU	EV	FW	GX	HY	JZ	K1	L2	M3	NA	OB	PC	QD	RE	SF	TG	UH	VJ	WK	XL	YM	ZN	1O	2P	3Q	AR	BS	CT	
ET	FU	GV	HW	JX	KY	LZ	M1	N2	O3	PA	QB	RC	SD	TE	UF	VG	WH	XJ	YK	ZL	1M	2N	3O	AP	BQ	CR	DS	0
FS	GT	HU	JV	KW	LX	MY	NZ	O1	P2	Q3	RA	SB	TC	UD	VE	WF	XG	YH	ZJ	1K	2L	3M	AN	BO	CP	DQ	ER	
GR	HS	JT	KU	LV	MW	NX	OY	PZ	Q1	R2	S3	TA	UB	VC	WD	XE	YF	ZG	1H	2J	3K	AL	BM	CN	DO	EP	FQ	
HQ	JR	KS	LT	MU	NV	OW	PX	QY	RZ	S1	T2	U3	VA	WB	XC	YD	ZE	1F	2G	3H	AJ	BK	CL	DM	EN	FO	GP	
JP	KQ	LR	MS	NT	OU	PV	QW	RX	SY	TZ	U1	V2	W3	XA	YB	ZC	1D	2E	3F	AG	BH	CJ	DK	EL	FM	GN	HO	−
KO	LP	MQ	NR	OS	PT	QU	RV	SW	TX	UY	VZ	W1	X2	Y3	ZA	1B	2C	3D	AE	BF	CG	DH	EJ	FK	GL	HM	JN	
LN	MO	NP	OQ	PR	QS	RT	SU	TV	UW	VX	WY	XZ	Y1	Z2	13	2A	3B	AC	BD	CE	DF	EG	FH	GJ	HK	JL	KM	
M	N	O	P	Q	R	S	T	U	V	W	X	Y	Z	1	2	3	A	B	C	D	E	F	G	H	J	K	L	

1 TH	2 F	3 SA	4 SU	5 M	6 TU	7 W	8 TH	9 F	10 SA	11 SU	12 M	13 TU	14 W	15 TH	16 F	17 SA	18 SU	19 M	20 TU	21 W	22 TH	23 F	24 SA	25 SU	26 M	27 TU	28 W	
Q	R	S	T	U	V	W	X	Y	Z	1	2	3	4	5	6	7	8	A	B	C	D	E	F	G	H	J	K	
RP	SQ	TR	US	VT	WU	XV	YW	ZX	1Y	2Z	31	42	53	64	75	86	A7	B8	CA	DB	EC	FD	GE	HF	JG	KH	LJ	
SO	TP	UQ	VR	WS	XT	YU	ZV	1W	2X	3Y	4Z	51	62	73	84	A5	B6	C7	D8	EA	FB	GC	HD	JE	KF	LG	MH	
TN	UO	VP	WQ	XR	YS	ZT	1U	2V	3W	4X	5Y	6Z	71	82	A3	B4	C5	D6	E7	F8	GA	HB	JC	KD	LE	MF	NG	
UM	VN	WO	XP	YQ	ZR	1S	2T	3U	4V	5W	6X	7Y	8Z	A1	B2	C3	D4	E5	F6	G7	H8	JA	KB	LC	MD	NE	OF	+
VL	WM	XN	YO	ZP	1Q	2R	3S	4T	5U	6V	7W	8X	AY	BZ	C1	D2	E3	F4	G5	H6	J7	K8	LA	MB	NC	OD	PE	
WK	XL	YM	ZN	1O	2P	3Q	4R	5S	6T	7U	8V	AW	BX	CY	DZ	E1	F2	G3	H4	J5	K6	L7	M8	NA	OB	PC	QD	
XJ	YK	ZL	1M	2N	3O	4P	5Q	6R	7S	8T	AU	BV	CW	DX	EY	FZ	G1	H2	J3	K4	L5	M6	N7	O8	PA	QB	RC	
YH	ZJ	1K	2L	3M	4N	5O	6P	7Q	8R	AS	BT	CU	DV	EW	FX	GY	HZ	J1	K2	L3	M4	N5	O6	P7	Q8	RA	SB	0
ZG	1H	2J	3K	4L	5M	6N	7O	8P	AQ	BR	CS	DT	EU	FV	GW	HX	JY	KZ	L1	M2	N3	O4	P5	Q6	R7	S8	TA	
1F	2G	3H	4J	5K	6L	7M	8N	AO	BP	CQ	DR	ES	FT	GU	HV	JW	KX	LY	MZ	N1	O2	P3	Q4	R5	S6	T7	U8	
2E	3F	4G	5H	6J	7K	8L	AM	BN	CO	DP	EQ	FR	GS	HT	JU	KV	LW	MX	NY	OZ	P1	Q2	R3	S4	T5	U6	V7	
3D	4E	5F	6G	7H	8J	AK	BL	CM	DN	EO	FP	GQ	HR	JS	KT	LU	MV	NW	OX	PY	QZ	R1	S2	T3	U4	V5	W6	−
4C	5D	6E	7F	8G	AH	BJ	CK	DL	EM	FN	GO	HP	JQ	KR	LS	MT	NU	OV	PW	QX	RY	SZ	T1	U2	V3	W4	X5	
5B	6C	7D	8E	AF	BG	CH	DJ	EK	FL	GM	HN	JO	KP	LQ	MR	NS	OT	PU	QV	RW	SX	TY	UZ	V1	W2	X3	Y4	
6A	7B	8C	AD	BE	CF	DG	EH	FJ	GK	HL	JM	KN	LO	MP	NQ	OR	PS	QT	RU	SV	TW	UX	VY	WZ	X1	Y2	Z3	
78	8A	AB	BC	CD	DE	EF	FG	GH	HJ	JK	KL	LM	MN	NO	OP	PQ	QR	RS	ST	TU	UV	VW	WX	XY	YZ	Z1	12	

PHYSICAL

1	2	3	4	5	6	7	8	9	10	11	12	13	14	15	16	17	18	19	20	21	22	23	24	25	26	27	28	29	30	31	
TH	F	SA	SU	M	TU	W	TH	F	SA	SU	M	TU	W	TH	F	SA	SU	M	TU	W	TH	F	SA	SU	M	TU	W	TH	F	SA	
LK	ML	NM	ON	PO	QP	RQ	SR	TS	UT	VU	WV	XW	AX	BA	CB	DC	ED	FE	GF	HG	JH	KJ	LK	ML	NM	ON	PO	QP	RQ	SR	
MJ	NK	OL	PM	QN	RO	SP	TQ	UR	VS	WT	XU	AV	BW	CX	DA	EB	FC	GD	HE	JF	KG	LH	MJ	NK	OL	PM	QN	RO	SP	TQ	
NH	OJ	PK	QL	RM	SN	TO	UP	VQ	WR	XS	AT	BU	CV	DW	EX	FA	GB	HC	JD	KE	LF	MG	NH	OJ	PK	QL	RM	SN	TO	UP	+
OG	PH	QJ	RK	SL	TM	UN	VO	WP	XQ	AR	BS	CT	DU	EV	FW	GX	HA	JB	KC	LD	ME	NF	OG	PH	QJ	RK	SL	TM	UN	VO	
PF	QG	RH	SJ	TK	UL	VM	WN	XO	AP	BQ	CR	DS	ET	FU	GV	HW	JX	KA	LB	MC	ND	OE	PF	QG	RH	SJ	TK	UL	VM	WN	
QE	RF	SG	TH	UJ	VK	WL	XM	AN	BO	CP	DQ	ER	FS	GT	HU	JV	KW	LX	MA	NB	OC	PD	QE	RF	SG	TH	UJ	VK	WL	XM	0
RD	SE	TF	UG	VH	WJ	XK	AL	BM	CN	DO	EP	FQ	GR	HS	JT	KU	LV	MW	NX	OA	PB	QC	RD	SE	TF	UG	VH	WJ	XK	AL	
SC	TD	UE	VF	WG	XH	AJ	BK	CL	DM	EN	FO	GP	HQ	JR	KS	LT	MU	NV	OW	PX	QA	RB	SC	TD	UE	VF	WG	XH	AJ	BK	
TB	UC	VD	WE	XF	AG	BH	CJ	DK	EL	FM	GN	HO	JP	KQ	LR	MS	NT	OU	PV	QW	RX	SA	TB	UC	VD	WE	XF	AG	BH	CJ	−
UA	VB	WC	XD	AE	BF	CG	DH	EJ	FK	GL	HM	JN	KO	LP	MQ	NR	OS	PT	QU	RV	SW	TX	UA	VB	WC	XD	AE	BF	CG	DH	
VX	WA	XB	AC	BD	CE	DF	EG	FH	GJ	HK	JL	KM	LN	MO	NP	OQ	PR	QS	RT	SU	TV	UW	VX	WA	XB	AC	BD	CE	DF	EG	
W	X	A	B	C	D	E	F	G	H	J	K	L	M	N	O	P	Q	R	S	T	U	V	W	X	A	B	C	D	E	F	

EMOTIONAL

1	2	3	4	5	6	7	8	9	10	11	12	13	14	15	16	17	18	19	20	21	22	23	24	25	26	27	28	29	30	31	
TH	F	SA	SU	M	TU	W	TH	F	SA	SU	M	TU	W	TH	F	SA	SU	M	TU	W	TH	F	SA	SU	M	TU	W	TH	F	SA	
1	2	3	A	B	C	D	E	F	G	H	J	K	L	M	N	O	P	Q	R	S	T	U	V	W	X	Y	Z	1	2	3	
2Z	31	A2	B3	CA	DB	EC	FD	GE	HF	JG	KH	LJ	MK	NL	OM	PN	QO	RP	SQ	TR	US	VT	WU	XV	YW	ZX	1Y	2Z	31	A2	
3Y	AZ	B1	C2	D3	EA	FB	GC	HD	JE	KF	LG	MH	NJ	OK	PL	QM	RN	SO	TP	UQ	VR	WS	XT	YU	ZV	1W	2X	3Y	AZ	B1	
AX	BY	CZ	D1	E2	F3	GA	HB	JC	KD	LE	MF	NG	OH	PJ	QK	RL	SM	TN	UO	VP	WQ	XR	YS	ZT	1U	2V	3W	AX	BY	CZ	
BW	CX	DY	EZ	F1	G2	H3	JA	KB	LC	MD	NE	OF	PG	QH	RJ	SK	TL	UM	VN	WO	XP	YQ	ZR	1S	2T	3U	AV	BW	CX	DY	+
CV	DW	EX	FY	GZ	H1	J2	K3	LA	MB	NC	OD	PE	QF	RG	SH	TJ	UK	VL	WM	XN	YO	ZP	1Q	2R	3S	AT	BU	CV	DW	EX	
DU	EV	FW	GX	HY	JZ	K1	L2	M3	NA	OB	PC	QD	RE	SF	TG	UH	VJ	WK	XL	YM	ZN	1O	2P	3Q	AR	BS	CT	DU	EV	FW	
ET	FU	GV	HW	JX	KY	LZ	M1	N2	O3	PA	QB	RC	SD	TE	UF	VG	WH	XJ	YK	ZL	1M	2N	3O	AP	BQ	CR	DS	ET	FU	GV	0
FS	GT	HU	JV	KW	LX	MY	NZ	O1	P2	Q3	RA	SB	TC	UD	VE	WF	XG	YH	ZJ	1K	2L	3M	AN	BO	CP	DQ	ER	FS	GT	HU	
GR	HS	JT	KU	LV	MW	NX	OY	PZ	Q1	R2	S3	TA	UB	VC	WD	XE	YF	ZG	1H	2J	3K	AL	BM	CN	DO	EP	FQ	GR	HS	JT	
HQ	JR	KS	LT	MU	NV	OW	PX	QY	RZ	S1	T2	U3	VA	WB	XC	YD	ZE	1F	2G	3H	AJ	BK	CL	DM	EN	FO	GP	HQ	JR	KS	−
JP	KQ	LR	MS	NT	OU	PV	QW	RX	SY	TZ	U1	V2	W3	XA	YB	ZC	1D	2E	3F	AG	BH	CJ	DK	EL	FM	GN	HO	JP	KQ	LR	
KO	LP	MQ	NR	OS	PT	QU	RV	SW	TX	UY	VZ	W1	X2	Y3	ZA	1B	2C	3D	AE	BF	CG	DH	EJ	FK	GL	HM	JN	KO	LP	MQ	
LN	MO	NP	OQ	PR	QS	RT	SU	TV	UW	VX	WY	XZ	Y1	Z2	13	2A	3B	AC	BD	CE	DF	EG	FH	GJ	HK	JL	KM	LN	MO	NP	
M	N	O	P	Q	R	S	T	U	V	W	X	Y	Z	1	2	3	A	B	C	D	E	F	G	H	J	K	L	M	N	O	

INTELLECTUAL

1	2	3	4	5	6	7	8	9	10	11	12	13	14	15	16	17	18	19	20	21	22	23	24	25	26	27	28	29	30	31	
TH	F	SA	SU	M	TU	W	TH	F	SA	SU	M	TU	W	TH	F	SA	SU	M	TU	W	TH	F	SA	SU	M	TU	W	TH	F	SA	
L	M	N	O	P	Q	R	S	T	U	V	W	X	Y	Z	1	2	3	4	5	6	7	8	A	B	C	D	E	F	G	H	
MK	NL	OM	PN	QO	RP	SQ	TR	US	VT	WU	XV	YW	ZX	1Y	2Z	31	42	53	64	75	86	A7	B8	CA	DB	EC	FD	GE	HF	JG	
NJ	OK	PL	QM	RN	SO	TP	UQ	VR	WS	XT	YU	ZV	1W	2X	3Y	4Z	51	62	73	84	A5	B6	C7	D8	EA	FB	GC	HD	JE	KF	
OH	PJ	QK	RL	SM	TN	UO	VP	WQ	XR	YS	ZT	1U	2V	3W	4X	5Y	6Z	71	82	A3	B4	C5	D6	E7	F8	GA	HB	JC	KD	LE	
PG	QH	RJ	SK	TL	UM	VN	WO	XP	YQ	ZR	1S	2T	3U	4V	5W	6X	7Y	8Z	A1	B2	C3	D4	E5	F6	G7	H8	JA	KB	LC	MD	
QF	RG	SH	TJ	UK	VL	WM	XN	YO	ZP	1Q	2R	3S	4T	5U	6V	7W	8X	AY	BZ	C1	D2	E3	F4	G5	H6	J7	K8	LA	MB	NC	
RE	SF	TG	UH	VJ	WK	XL	YM	ZN	1O	2P	3Q	4R	5S	6T	7U	8V	AW	BX	CY	DZ	E1	F2	G3	H4	J5	K6	L7	M8	NA	OB	+
SD	TE	UF	VG	WH	XJ	YK	ZL	1M	2N	3O	4P	5Q	6R	7S	8T	AU	BV	CW	DX	EY	FZ	G1	H2	J3	K4	L5	M6	N7	O8	PA	
TC	UD	VE	WF	XG	YH	ZJ	1K	2L	3M	4N	5O	6P	7Q	8R	AS	BT	CU	DV	EW	FX	GY	HZ	J1	K2	L3	M4	N5	O6	P7	Q8	0
UB	VC	WD	XE	YF	ZG	1H	2J	3K	4L	5M	6N	7O	8P	AQ	BR	CS	DT	EU	FV	GW	HX	JY	KZ	L1	M2	N3	O4	P5	Q6	R7	
VA	WB	XC	YD	ZE	1F	2G	3H	4J	5K	6L	7M	8N	AO	BP	CQ	DR	ES	FT	GU	HV	JW	KX	LY	MZ	N1	O2	P3	Q4	R5	S6	
W8	XA	YB	ZC	1D	2E	3F	4G	5H	6J	7K	8L	AM	BN	CO	DP	EQ	FR	GS	HT	JU	KV	LW	MX	NY	OZ	P1	Q2	R3	S4	T5	−
X7	Y8	ZA	1B	2C	3D	4E	5F	6G	7H	8J	AK	BL	CM	DN	EO	FP	GQ	HR	JS	KT	LU	MV	NW	OX	PY	QZ	R1	S2	T3	U4	
Y6	Z7	18	2A	3B	4C	5D	6E	7F	8G	AH	BJ	CK	DL	EM	FN	GO	HP	JQ	KR	LS	MT	NU	OV	PW	QX	RY	SZ	T1	U2	V3	
Z5	16	27	38	4A	5B	6C	7D	8E	AF	BG	CH	DJ	EK	FL	GM	HN	JO	KP	LQ	MR	NS	OT	PU	QV	RW	SX	TY	UZ	V1	W2	
14	25	36	47	58	6A	7B	8C	AD	BE	CF	DG	EH	FJ	GK	HL	JM	KN	LO	MP	NQ	OR	PS	QT	RU	SV	TW	UX	VY	WZ	X1	
23	34	45	56	67	78	8A	AB	BC	CD	DE	EF	FG	GH	HJ	JK	KL	LM	MN	NO	OP	PQ	QR	RS	ST	TU	UV	VW	WX	XY	YZ	

1 SU	2 M	3 TU	4 W	5 TH	6 F	7 SA	8 SU	9 M	10 TU	11 W	12 TH	13 F	14 SA	15 SU	16 M	17 TU	18 W	19 TH	20 F	21 SA	22 SU	23 M	24 TU	25 W	26 TH	27 F	28 SA	29 SU	30 M	
TS	UT	VU	WV	XW	AX	BA	CB	DC	ED	FE	GF	HG	JH	KJ	LK	ML	NM	ON	PO	QP	RQ	SR	TS	UT	VU	WV	XW	AX	BA	
UR	VS	WT	XU	AV	BW	CX	DA	EB	FC	GD	HE	JF	KG	LH	MJ	NK	OL	PM	QN	RO	SP	TQ	UR	VS	WT	XU	AV	BW	CX	
VQ	WR	XS	AT	BU	CV	DW	EX	FA	GB	HC	JD	KE	LF	MG	NH	OJ	PK	QL	RM	SN	TO	UP	VQ	WR	XS	AT	BU	CV	DW	
WP	XQ	AR	BS	CT	DU	EV	FW	GX	HA	JB	KC	LD	ME	NF	OG	PH	QJ	RK	SL	TM	UN	VO	WP	XQ	AR	BS	CT	DU	EV	+
XO	AP	BQ	CR	DS	ET	FU	GV	HW	JX	KA	LB	MC	ND	OE	PF	QG	RH	SJ	TK	UL	VM	WN	XO	AP	BQ	CR	DS	ET	FU	
AN	BO	CP	DQ	ER	FS	GT	HU	JV	KW	LX	MA	NB	OC	PD	QE	RF	SG	TH	UJ	VK	WL	XM	AN	BO	CP	DQ	ER	FS	GT	0
BM	CN	DO	EP	FQ	GR	HS	JT	KU	LV	MW	NX	OA	PB	QC	RD	SE	TF	UG	VH	WJ	XK	AL	BM	CN	DO	EP	FQ	GR	HS	
CL	DM	EN	FO	GP	HQ	JR	KS	LT	MU	NV	OW	PX	QA	RB	SC	TD	UE	VF	WG	XH	AJ	BK	CL	DM	EN	FO	GP	HQ	JR	−
DK	EL	FM	GN	HO	JP	KQ	LR	MS	NT	OU	PV	QW	RX	SA	TB	UC	VD	WE	XF	AG	BH	CJ	DK	EL	FM	GN	HO	JP	KQ	
EJ	FK	GL	HM	JN	KO	LP	MQ	NR	OS	PT	QU	RV	SW	TX	UA	VB	WC	XD	AE	BF	CG	DH	EJ	FK	GL	HM	JN	KO	LP	
FH	GJ	HK	JL	KM	LN	MO	NP	OQ	PR	QS	RT	SU	TV	UW	VX	WA	XB	AC	BD	CE	DF	EG	FH	GJ	HK	JL	KM	LN	MO	
G	H	J	K	L	M	N	O	P	Q	R	S	T	U	V	W	X	A	B	C	D	E	F	G	H	J	K	L	M	N	

1 SU	2 M	3 TU	4 W	5 TH	6 F	7 SA	8 SU	9 M	10 TU	11 W	12 TH	13 F	14 SA	15 SU	16 M	17 TU	18 W	19 TH	20 F	21 SA	22 SU	23 M	24 TU	25 W	26 TH	27 F	28 SA	29 SU	30 M	
A	B	C	D	E	F	G	H	J	K	L	M	N	O	P	Q	R	S	T	U	V	W	X	Y	Z	1	2	3	A	B	
B3	CA	DB	EC	FD	GE	HF	JG	KH	LJ	MK	NL	OM	PN	QO	RP	SQ	TR	US	VT	WU	XV	YW	ZX	1Y	2Z	31	A2	B3	CA	
C2	D3	EA	FB	GC	HD	JE	KF	LG	MH	NJ	OK	PL	QM	RN	SO	TP	UQ	VR	WS	XT	YU	ZV	1W	2X	3Y	AZ	B1	C2	D3	
D1	E2	F3	GA	HB	JC	KD	LE	MF	NG	OH	PJ	QK	RL	SM	TN	UO	VP	WQ	XR	YS	ZT	1U	2V	3W	AX	BY	CZ	D1	E2	
EZ	F1	G2	H3	JA	KB	LC	MD	NE	OF	PG	QH	RJ	SK	TL	UM	VN	WO	XP	YQ	ZR	1S	2T	3U	AV	BW	CX	DY	EZ	F1	
FY	GZ	H1	J2	K3	LA	MB	NC	OD	PE	QF	RG	SH	TJ	UK	VL	WM	XN	YO	ZP	1Q	2R	3S	AT	BU	CV	DW	EX	FY	GZ	+
GX	HY	JZ	K1	L2	M3	NA	OB	PC	QD	RE	SF	TG	UH	VJ	WK	XL	YM	ZN	1O	2P	3Q	AR	BS	CT	DU	EV	FW	GX	HY	
HW	JX	KY	LZ	M1	N2	O3	PA	QB	RC	SD	TE	UF	VG	WH	XJ	YK	ZL	1M	2N	3O	AP	BQ	CR	DS	ET	FU	GV	HW	JX	0
JV	KW	LX	MY	NZ	O1	P2	Q3	RA	SB	TC	UD	VE	WF	XG	YH	ZJ	1K	2L	3M	AN	BO	CP	DQ	ER	FS	GT	HU	JV	KW	
KU	LV	MW	NX	OY	PZ	Q1	R2	S3	TA	UB	VC	WD	XE	YF	ZG	1H	2J	3K	AL	BM	CN	DO	EP	FQ	GR	HS	JT	KU	LV	−
LT	MU	NV	OW	PX	QY	RZ	S1	T2	U3	VA	WB	XC	YD	ZE	1F	2G	3H	AJ	BK	CL	DM	EN	FO	GP	HQ	JR	KS	LT	MU	
MS	NT	OU	PV	QW	RX	SY	TZ	U1	V2	W3	XA	YB	ZC	1D	2E	3F	AG	BH	CJ	DK	EL	FM	GN	HO	JP	KQ	LR	MS	NT	
NR	OS	PT	QU	RV	SW	TX	UY	VZ	W1	X2	Y3	ZA	1B	2C	3D	AE	BF	CG	DH	EJ	FK	GL	HM	JN	KO	LP	MQ	NR	OS	
OQ	PR	QS	RT	SU	TV	UW	VX	WY	XZ	Y1	Z2	13	2A	3B	AC	BD	CE	DF	EG	FH	GJ	HK	JL	KM	LN	MO	NP	OQ	PR	
P	Q	R	S	T	U	V	W	X	Y	Z	1	2	3	A	B	C	D	E	F	G	H	J	K	L	M	N	O	P	Q	

1 SU	2 M	3 TU	4 W	5 TH	6 F	7 SA	8 SU	9 M	10 TU	11 W	12 TH	13 F	14 SA	15 SU	16 M	17 TU	18 W	19 TH	20 F	21 SA	22 SU	23 M	24 TU	25 W	26 TH	27 F	28 SA	29 SU	30 M	
J	K	L	M	N	O	P	Q	R	S	T	U	V	W	X	Y	Z	1	2	3	4	5	6	7	8	A	B	C	D	E	
KH	LJ	MK	NL	OM	PN	QO	RP	SQ	TR	US	VT	WU	XV	YW	ZX	1Y	2Z	31	42	53	64	75	86	A7	B8	CA	DB	EC	FD	
LG	MH	NJ	OK	PL	QM	RN	SO	TP	UQ	VR	WS	XT	YU	ZV	1W	2X	3Y	4Z	51	62	73	84	A5	B6	C7	D8	EA	FB	GC	
MF	NG	OH	PJ	QK	RL	SM	TN	UO	VP	WQ	XR	YS	ZT	1U	2V	3W	4X	5Y	6Z	71	82	A3	B4	C5	D6	E7	F8	GA	HB	
NE	OF	PG	QH	RJ	SK	TL	UM	VN	WO	XP	YQ	ZR	1S	2T	3U	4V	5W	6X	7Y	8Z	A1	B2	C3	D4	E5	F6	G7	H8	JA	
OD	PE	QF	RG	SH	TJ	UK	VL	WM	XN	YO	ZP	1Q	2R	3S	4T	5U	6V	7W	8X	AY	BZ	C1	D2	E3	F4	G5	H6	J7	K8	
PC	QD	RE	SF	TG	UH	VJ	WK	XL	YM	ZN	1O	2P	3Q	4R	5S	6T	7U	8V	AW	BX	CY	DZ	E1	F2	G3	H4	J5	K6	L7	+
QB	RC	SD	TE	UF	VG	WH	XJ	YK	ZL	1M	2N	3O	4P	5Q	6R	7S	8T	AU	BV	CW	DX	EY	FZ	G1	H2	J3	K4	L5	M6	
RA	SB	TC	UD	VE	WF	XG	YH	ZJ	1K	2L	3M	4N	5O	6P	7Q	8R	AS	BT	CU	DV	EW	FX	GY	HZ	J1	K2	L3	M4	N5	0
S8	TA	UB	VC	WD	XE	YF	ZG	1H	2J	3K	4L	5M	6N	7O	8P	AQ	BR	CS	DT	EU	FV	GW	HX	JY	KZ	L1	M2	N3	O4	
T7	U8	VA	WB	XC	YD	ZE	1F	2G	3H	4J	5K	6L	7M	8N	AO	BP	CQ	DR	ES	FT	GU	HV	JW	KX	LY	MZ	N1	O2	P3	−
U6	V7	W8	XA	YB	ZC	1D	2E	3F	4G	5H	6J	7K	8L	AM	BN	CO	DP	EQ	FR	GS	HT	JU	KV	LW	MX	NY	OZ	P1	Q2	
V5	W6	X7	Y8	ZA	1B	2C	3D	4E	5F	6G	7H	8J	AK	BL	CM	DN	EO	FP	GQ	HR	JS	KT	LU	MV	NW	OX	PY	QZ	R1	
W4	X5	Y6	Z7	18	2A	3B	4C	5D	6E	7F	8G	AH	BJ	CK	DL	EM	FN	GO	HP	JQ	KR	LS	MT	NU	OV	PW	QX	RY	SZ	
X3	Y4	Z5	16	27	38	4A	5B	6C	7D	8E	AF	BG	CH	DJ	EK	FL	GM	HN	JO	KP	LQ	MR	NS	OT	PU	QV	RW	SX	TY	
Y2	Z3	14	25	36	47	58	6A	7B	8C	AD	BE	CF	DG	EH	FJ	GK	HL	JM	KN	LO	MP	NQ	OR	PS	QT	RU	SV	TW	UX	
Z1	12	23	34	45	56	67	78	8A	AB	BC	CD	DE	EF	FG	GH	HJ	JK	KL	LM	MN	NO	OP	PQ	QR	RS	ST	TU	UV	VW	

PHYSICAL

1 TU	2 W	3 TH	4 F	5 SA	6 SU	7 M	8 TU	9 W	10 TH	11 F	12 SA	13 SU	14 M	15 TU	16 W	17 TH	18 F	19 SA	20 SU	21 M	22 TU	23 W	24 TH	25 F	26 SA	27 SU	28 M	29 TU	30 W	31 TH	
CB	DC	ED	FE	GF	HG	JH	KJ	LK	ML	NM	ON	PO	QP	RQ	SR	TS	UT	VU	WV	XW	AX	BA	CB	DC	ED	FE	GF	HG	JH	KJ	
DA	EB	FC	GD	HE	JF	KG	LH	MJ	NK	OL	PM	QN	RO	SP	TQ	UR	VS	WT	XU	AV	BW	CX	DA	EB	FC	GD	HE	JF	KG	LH	
EX	FA	GB	HC	JD	KE	LF	MG	NH	OJ	PK	QL	RM	SN	TO	UP	VQ	WR	XS	AT	BU	CV	DW	EX	FA	GB	HC	JD	KE	LF	MG	+
FW	GX	HA	JB	KC	LD	ME	NF	OG	PH	QJ	RK	SL	TM	UN	VO	WP	XQ	AR	BS	CT	DU	EV	FW	GX	HA	JB	KC	LD	ME	NF	
GV	HW	JX	KA	LB	MC	ND	OE	PF	QG	RH	SJ	TK	UL	VM	WN	XO	AP	BQ	CR	DS	ET	FU	GV	HW	JX	KA	LB	MC	ND	OE	
HU	JV	KW	LX	MA	NB	OC	PD	QE	RF	SG	TH	UJ	VK	WL	XM	AN	BO	CP	DQ	ER	FS	GT	HU	JV	KW	LX	MA	NB	OC	PD	0
JT	KU	LV	MW	NX	OA	PB	QC	RD	SE	TF	UG	VH	WJ	XK	AL	BM	CN	DO	EP	FQ	GR	HS	JT	KU	LV	MW	NX	OA	PB	QC	
KS	LT	MU	NV	OW	PX	QA	RB	SC	TD	UE	VF	WG	XH	AJ	BK	CL	DM	EN	FO	GP	HQ	JR	KS	LT	MU	NV	OW	PX	QA	RB	
LR	MS	NT	OU	PV	QW	RX	SA	TB	UC	VD	WE	XF	AG	BH	CJ	DK	EL	FM	GN	HM	JN	KM	LR	MS	NT	OU	PV	QW	RX	SA	−
MQ	NR	OS	PT	QU	RV	SW	TX	UA	VB	WC	XD	AE	BF	CG	DH	EJ	FK	GL	HM	JN	KO	LP	MQ	NR	OS	PT	QU	RV	SW	TX	
NP	OQ	PR	QS	RT	SU	TV	UW	VX	WA	XB	AC	BD	CE	DF	EG	FH	GJ	HK	JL	KM	LN	MO	NP	OQ	PR	QS	RT	SU	TV	UW	
O	P	Q	R	S	T	U	V	W	X	A	B	C	D	E	F	G	H	J	K	L	M	N	O	P	Q	R	S	T	U		

EMOTIONAL

1 TU	2 W	3 TH	4 F	5 SA	6 SU	7 M	8 TU	9 W	10 TH	11 F	12 SA	13 SU	14 M	15 TU	16 W	17 TH	18 F	19 SA	20 SU	21 M	22 TU	23 W	24 TH	25 F	26 SA	27 SU	28 M	29 TU	30 W	31 TH	
C	D	E	F	G	H	J	K	L	M	N	O	P	Q	R	S	T	U	V	W	X	Y	Z	1	2	3	A	B	C	D	E	
DB	EC	FD	GE	HF	JG	KH	LJ	MK	NL	OM	PN	QO	RP	SQ	TR	US	VT	WU	XV	YW	ZX	1Y	2Z	31	A2	B3	CA	DB	EC	FD	
EA	FB	GC	HD	JE	KF	LG	MH	NJ	OK	PL	QM	RN	SO	TP	UQ	VR	WS	XT	YU	ZV	1W	2X	3Y	AZ	B1	C2	D3	EA	FB	GC	
F3	GA	HB	JC	KD	LE	MF	NG	OH	PJ	QK	RL	SM	TN	UO	VP	WQ	XR	YS	ZT	1U	2V	3W	AX	BY	CZ	D1	E2	F3	GA	HB	+
G2	H3	JA	KB	LC	MD	NE	OF	PG	QH	RJ	SK	TL	UM	VN	WO	XP	YQ	ZR	1S	2T	3U	AV	BW	CX	DY	EZ	F1	G2	H3	JA	
H1	J2	K3	LA	MB	NC	OD	PE	QF	RG	SH	TJ	UK	VL	WM	XN	YO	ZP	1Q	2R	3S	AT	BU	CV	DW	EX	FY	GZ	H1	J2	K3	
JZ	K1	L2	M3	NA	OB	PC	QD	RE	SF	TG	UH	VJ	WK	XL	YM	ZN	1O	2P	3Q	AR	BS	CT	DU	EV	FW	GX	HY	JZ	K1	L2	
KY	LZ	M1	N2	O3	PA	QB	RC	SD	TE	UF	VG	WH	XJ	YK	ZL	1M	2N	3O	AP	BQ	CR	DS	ET	FU	GV	HW	JX	KY	LZ	M1	0
LX	MY	NZ	O1	P2	Q3	RA	SB	TC	UD	VE	WF	XG	YH	ZJ	1K	2L	3M	AN	BO	CP	DQ	ER	FS	GT	HU	JV	KW	LX	MY	NZ	
MW	NX	OY	PZ	Q1	R2	S3	TA	UB	VC	WD	XE	YF	ZG	1H	2J	3K	AL	BM	CN	DO	EP	FQ	GR	HS	JT	KU	LV	MW	NX	OY	−
NV	OW	PX	QY	RZ	S1	T2	U3	VA	WB	XC	YD	ZE	1F	2G	3H	AJ	BK	CL	DM	EN	FO	GP	HQ	JR	KS	LT	MU	NV	OW	PX	
OU	PV	QW	RX	SY	TZ	U1	V2	W3	XA	YB	ZC	1D	2E	3F	AG	BH	CJ	DK	EL	FM	GN	HO	JP	KQ	LR	MS	NT	OU	PV	QW	
PT	QU	RV	SW	TX	UY	VZ	W1	X2	Y3	ZA	1B	2C	3D	AE	BF	CG	DH	EJ	FK	GL	HM	JN	KO	LP	MQ	NR	OS	PT	QU	RV	
QS	RT	SU	TV	UW	VX	WY	XZ	Y1	Z2	13	2A	3B	AC	BD	CE	DF	EG	FH	GJ	HK	JL	KM	LN	MO	NP	OQ	PR	QS	RT	SU	
R	S	T	U	V	W	X	Y	Z	1	2	3	A	B	C	D	E	F	G	H	J	K	L	M	N	O	P	Q	R	S	T	

INTELLECTUAL

1 TU	2 W	3 TH	4 F	5 SA	6 SU	7 M	8 TU	9 W	10 TH	11 F	12 SA	13 SU	14 M	15 TU	16 W	17 TH	18 F	19 SA	20 SU	21 M	22 TU	23 W	24 TH	25 F	26 SA	27 SU	28 M	29 TU	30 W	31 TH	
F	G	H	J	K	L	M	N	O	P	Q	R	S	T	U	V	W	X	Y	Z	1	2	3	4	5	6	7	8	A	B	C	
GE	HF	JG	KH	LJ	MK	NL	OM	PN	QO	RP	SQ	TR	US	VT	WU	XV	YW	ZX	1Y	2Z	31	42	53	64	75	86	A7	B8	CA	DB	
HD	JE	KF	LG	MH	NJ	OK	PL	QM	RN	SO	TP	UQ	VR	WS	XT	YU	ZV	1W	2X	3Y	4Z	51	62	73	84	A5	B6	C7	D8	EA	
JC	KD	LE	MF	NG	OH	PJ	QK	RL	SM	TN	UO	VP	WQ	XR	YS	ZT	1U	2V	3W	4X	5Y	6Z	71	82	A3	B4	C5	D6	E7	F8	
KB	LC	MD	NE	OF	PG	QH	RJ	SK	TL	UM	VN	WO	XP	YQ	ZR	1S	2T	3U	4V	5W	6X	7Y	8Z	A1	B2	C3	D4	E5	F6	G7	
LA	MB	NC	OD	PE	QF	RG	SH	TJ	UK	VL	WM	XN	YO	ZP	1Q	2R	3S	4T	5U	6V	7W	8X	AY	BZ	C1	D2	E3	F4	G5	H6	+
M8	NA	OB	PC	QD	RE	SF	TG	UH	VJ	WK	XL	YM	ZN	1O	2P	3Q	4R	5S	6T	7U	8V	AW	BX	CY	DZ	E1	F2	G3	H4	J5	
N7	O8	PA	QB	RC	SD	TE	UF	VG	WH	XJ	YK	ZL	1M	2N	3O	4P	5Q	6R	7S	8T	AU	BV	CW	DX	EY	FZ	G1	H2	J3	K4	
O6	P7	Q8	RA	SB	TC	UD	VE	WF	XG	YH	ZJ	1K	2L	3M	4N	5O	6P	7Q	8R	AS	BT	CU	DV	EW	FX	GY	HZ	J1	K2	L3	0
P5	Q6	R7	S8	TA	UB	VC	WD	XE	YF	ZG	1H	2J	3K	4L	5M	6N	7O	8P	AQ	BR	CS	DT	EU	FV	GW	HX	JY	KZ	L1	M2	
Q4	R5	S6	T7	U8	VA	WB	XC	YD	ZE	1F	2G	3H	4J	5K	6L	7M	8N	AO	BP	CQ	DR	ES	FT	GU	HV	JW	KX	LY	MZ	N1	
R3	S4	T5	U6	V7	W8	XA	YB	ZC	1D	2E	3F	4G	5H	6J	7K	8L	AM	BN	CO	DP	EQ	FR	GS	HT	JU	KV	LW	MX	NY	OZ	−
S2	T3	U4	V5	W6	X7	Y8	ZA	1B	2C	3D	4E	5F	6G	7H	8J	AK	BL	CM	DN	EO	FP	GQ	HR	JS	KT	LU	MV	NW	OX	PY	
T1	U2	V3	W4	X5	Y6	Z7	18	2A	3B	4C	5D	6E	7F	8G	AH	BJ	CK	DL	EM	FN	GO	HP	JQ	KR	LS	MT	NU	OV	PW	QX	
UZ	V1	W2	X3	Y4	Z5	16	27	38	4A	5B	6C	7D	8E	AF	BG	CH	DJ	EK	FL	GM	HN	JO	KP	LQ	MR	NS	OT	PU	QV	RW	
VY	WZ	X1	Y2	Z3	14	25	36	47	58	6A	7B	8C	AD	BE	CF	DG	EH	FJ	GK	HL	JM	KN	LO	MP	NQ	OR	PS	QT	RU	SV	
WX	XY	YZ	Z1	12	23	34	45	56	67	78	8A	AB	BC	CD	DE	EF	FG	GH	HJ	JK	KL	LM	MN	NO	OP	PQ	QR	RS	ST	TU	

PHYSICAL

1 F	2 SA	3 SU	4 M	5 TU	6 W	7 TH	8 F	9 SA	10 SU	11 M	12 TU	13 W	14 TH	15 F	16 SA	17 SU	18 M	19 TU	20 W	21 TH	22 F	23 SA	24 SU	25 M	26 TU	27 W	28 TH	29 F	30 SA	
LK	ML	NM	ON	PO	QP	RQ	SR	TS	UT	VU	WV	XW	AX	BA	CB	DC	ED	FE	GF	HG	JH	KJ	LK	ML	NM	ON	PO	QP	RQ	
MJ	NK	OL	PM	QN	RO	SP	TQ	UR	VS	WT	XU	AV	BW	CX	DA	EB	FC	GD	HE	JF	KG	LH	MJ	NK	OL	PM	QN	RO	SP	
NH	OJ	PK	QL	RM	SN	TO	UP	VQ	WR	XS	AT	BU	CV	DW	EX	FA	GB	HC	JD	KE	LF	MG	NH	OJ	PK	QL	RM	SN	TO	+
OG	PH	QJ	RK	SL	TM	UN	VO	WP	XQ	AR	BS	CT	DU	EV	FW	GX	HA	JB	KC	LD	ME	NF	OG	PH	QJ	RK	SL	TM	UN	
PF	QG	RH	SJ	TK	UL	VM	WN	XO	AP	BQ	CR	DS	ET	FU	GV	HW	JX	KA	LB	MC	ND	OE	PF	QG	RH	SJ	TK	UL	VM	
QE	RF	SG	TH	UJ	VK	WL	XM	AN	BO	CP	DQ	ER	FS	GT	HU	JV	KW	LX	MA	NB	OC	PD	QE	RF	SG	TH	UJ	VK	WL	0
RD	SE	TF	UG	VH	WJ	XK	AL	BM	CN	DO	EP	FQ	GR	HS	JT	KU	LV	MW	NX	OA	PB	QC	RD	SE	TF	UG	VH	WJ	XK	
SC	TD	UE	VF	WG	XH	AJ	BK	CL	DM	EN	FO	GP	HQ	JR	KS	LT	MU	NV	OW	PX	QA	RB	SC	TD	UE	VF	WG	XH	AJ	−
TB	UC	VD	WE	XF	AG	BH	CJ	DK	EL	FM	GN	HO	JP	KQ	LR	MS	NT	OU	PV	QW	RX	SA	TB	UC	VD	WE	XF	AG	BH	
UA	VB	WC	XD	AE	BF	CG	DH	EJ	FK	GL	HM	JN	KO	LP	MQ	NR	OS	PT	QU	RV	SW	TX	UA	VB	WC	XD	AE	BF	CG	
VX	WA	XB	AC	BD	CE	DF	EG	FH	GJ	HK	JL	KM	LN	MO	NP	OQ	PR	QS	RT	SU	TV	UW	VX	WA	XB	AC	BD	CE	DF	
W	X	A	B	C	D	E	F	G	H	J	K	L	M	N	O	P	Q	R	S	T	U	V	W	X	A	B	C	D	E	

EMOTIONAL

1 F	2 SA	3 SU	4 M	5 TU	6 W	7 TH	8 F	9 SA	10 SU	11 M	12 TU	13 W	14 TH	15 F	16 SA	17 SU	18 M	19 TU	20 W	21 TH	22 F	23 SA	24 SU	25 M	26 TU	27 W	28 TH	29 F	30 SA	
F	G	H	J	K	L	M	N	O	P	Q	R	S	T	U	V	W	X	Y	Z	1	2	3	A	B	C	D	E	F	G	
GE	HF	JG	KH	LJ	MK	NL	OM	PN	QO	RP	SQ	TR	US	VT	WU	XV	YW	ZX	1Y	2Z	31	A2	B3	CA	DB	EC	FD	GE	HF	
HD	JE	KF	LG	MH	NJ	OK	PL	QM	RN	SO	TP	UQ	VR	WS	XT	YU	ZV	1W	2X	3Y	AZ	B1	C2	D3	EA	FB	GC	HD	JE	
JC	KD	LE	MF	NG	OH	PJ	QK	RL	SM	TN	UO	VP	WQ	XR	YS	ZT	1U	2V	3W	AX	BY	CZ	D1	E2	F3	GA	HB	JC	KD	
KB	LC	MD	NE	OF	PG	QH	RJ	SK	TL	UM	VN	WO	XP	YQ	ZR	1S	2T	3U	AV	BW	CX	DY	EZ	F1	G2	H3	JA	KB	LC	+
LA	MB	NC	OD	PE	QF	RG	SH	TJ	UK	VL	WM	XN	YO	ZP	1Q	2R	3S	AT	BU	CV	DW	EX	FY	GZ	H1	J2	K3	LA	MB	
M3	NA	OB	PC	QD	RE	SF	TG	UH	VJ	WK	XL	YM	ZN	1O	2P	3Q	AR	BS	CT	DU	EV	FW	GX	HY	JZ	K1	L2	M3	NA	
N2	O3	PA	QB	RC	SD	TE	UF	VG	WH	XJ	YK	ZL	1M	2N	30	AP	BQ	CR	DS	ET	FU	GV	HW	JX	KY	LZ	M1	N2	O3	0
O1	P2	Q3	RA	SB	TC	UD	VE	WF	XG	YH	ZJ	1K	2L	3M	AN	BO	CP	DQ	ER	FS	GT	HU	JV	KW	LX	MY	NZ	O1	P2	
PZ	Q1	R2	S3	TA	UB	VC	WD	XE	YF	ZG	1H	2J	3K	AL	BM	CN	DO	EP	FQ	GR	HS	JT	KU	LV	MW	NX	OY	PZ	Q1	−
QY	RZ	S1	T2	U3	VA	WB	XC	YD	ZE	1F	2G	3H	AJ	BK	CL	DM	EN	FO	GP	HQ	JR	KS	LT	MU	NV	OW	PX	QY	RZ	
RX	SY	TZ	U1	V2	W3	XA	YB	ZC	1D	2E	3F	AG	BH	CJ	DK	EL	FM	GN	HO	JP	KQ	LR	MS	NT	OU	PV	QW	RX	SY	
SW	TX	UY	VZ	W1	X2	Y3	ZA	1B	2C	3D	AE	BF	CG	DH	EJ	FK	GL	HM	JN	KO	LP	MQ	NR	OS	PT	QU	RV	SW	TX	
TV	UW	VX	WY	XZ	Y1	Z2	13	2A	3B	AC	BD	CE	DF	EG	FH	GJ	HK	JL	KM	LN	MO	NP	OQ	PR	QS	RT	SU	TV	UW	
U	V	W	X	Y	Z	1	2	3	A	B	C	D	E	F	G	H	J	K	L	M	N	O	P	Q	R	S	T	U	V	

INTELLECTUAL

1 F	2 SA	3 SU	4 M	5 TU	6 W	7 TH	8 F	9 SA	10 SU	11 M	12 TU	13 W	14 TH	15 F	16 SA	17 SU	18 M	19 TU	20 W	21 TH	22 F	23 SA	24 SU	25 M	26 TU	27 W	28 TH	29 F	30 SA	
D	E	F	G	H	J	K	L	M	N	O	P	Q	R	S	T	U	V	W	X	Y	Z	1	2	3	4	5	6	7	8	
EC	FD	GE	HF	JG	KH	LJ	MK	NL	OM	PN	QO	RP	SQ	TR	US	VT	WU	XV	YW	ZX	1Y	2Z	31	42	53	64	75	86	A7	
FB	GC	HD	JE	KF	LG	MH	NJ	OK	PL	QM	RN	SO	TP	UQ	VR	WS	XT	YU	ZV	1W	2X	3Y	4Z	51	62	73	84	A5	B6	
GA	HB	JC	KD	LE	MF	NG	OH	PJ	QK	RL	SM	TN	UO	VP	WQ	XR	YS	ZT	1U	2V	3W	4X	5Y	6Z	71	82	A3	B4	C5	
H8	JA	KB	LC	MD	NE	OF	PG	QH	RJ	SK	TL	UM	VN	WO	XP	YQ	ZR	1S	2T	3U	4V	5W	6X	7Y	8Z	A1	B2	C3	D4	+
J7	K8	LA	MB	NC	OD	PE	QF	RG	SH	TJ	UK	VL	WM	XN	YO	ZP	1Q	2R	3S	4T	5U	6V	7W	8X	AY	BZ	C1	D2	E3	
K6	L7	M8	NA	OB	PC	QD	RE	SF	TG	UH	VJ	WK	XL	YM	ZN	1O	2P	3Q	4R	5S	6T	7U	8V	AW	BX	CY	DZ	E1	F2	
L5	M6	N7	O8	PA	QB	RC	SD	TE	UF	VG	WH	XJ	YK	ZL	1M	2N	3O	4P	5Q	6R	7S	8T	AU	BV	CW	DX	EY	FZ	G1	
M4	N5	O6	P7	Q8	RA	SB	TC	UD	VE	WF	XG	YH	ZJ	1K	2L	3M	4N	5O	6P	7Q	8R	AS	BT	CU	DV	EW	FX	GY	HZ	0
N3	O4	P5	Q6	R7	S8	TA	UB	VC	WD	XE	YF	ZG	1H	2J	3K	4L	5M	6N	7O	8P	AQ	BR	CS	DT	EU	FV	GW	HX	JY	
O2	P3	Q4	R5	S6	T7	U8	VA	WB	XC	YD	ZE	1F	2G	3H	4J	5K	6L	7M	8N	AO	BP	CQ	DR	ES	FT	GU	HV	JW	KX	−
P1	Q2	R3	S4	T5	U6	V7	W8	XA	YB	ZC	1D	2E	3F	4G	5H	6J	7K	8L	AM	BN	CO	DP	EQ	FR	GS	HT	JU	KV	LW	
QZ	R1	S2	T3	U4	V5	W6	X7	Y8	ZA	1B	2C	3D	4E	5F	6G	7H	8J	AK	BL	CM	DN	EO	FP	GQ	HR	JS	KT	LU	MV	
RY	SZ	T1	U2	V3	W4	X5	Y6	Z7	18	2A	3B	4C	5D	6E	7F	8G	AH	BJ	CK	DL	EM	FN	GO	HP	JQ	KR	LS	MT	NU	
SX	TY	UZ	V1	W2	X3	Y4	Z5	16	27	38	4A	5B	6C	7D	8E	AF	BG	CH	DJ	EK	FL	GM	HN	JO	KP	LQ	MR	NS	OT	
TW	UX	VY	WZ	X1	Y2	Z3	14	25	36	47	58	6A	7B	8C	AD	BE	CF	DG	EH	FJ	GK	HL	JM	KN	LO	MP	NQ	OR	PS	
UV	VW	WX	XY	YZ	Z1	12	23	34	45	56	67	78	8A	AB	BC	CD	DE	EF	FG	GH	HJ	JK	KL	LM	MN	NO	OP	PQ	QR	
V	W	X	Y	Z	1	2	3	4	5	6	7	8	A	B	C	D	E	F	G	H	J	K	L	M	N	O	P	Q	R	

1 SU	2 M	3 TU	4 W	5 TH	6 F	7 SA	8 SU	9 M	10 TU	11 W	12 TH	13 F	14 SA	15 SU	16 M	17 TU	18 W	19 TH	20 F	21 SA	22 SU	23 M	24 TU	25 W	26 TH	27 F	28 SA	29 SU	30 M	31 TU	
SR	TS	UT	VU	WV	XW	AX	BA	CB	DC	ED	FE	GF	HG	JH	KJ	LK	ML	NM	ON	PO	QP	RQ	SR	TS	UT	VU	WV	XW	AX	BA	
TQ	UR	VS	WT	XU	AV	BW	CX	DA	EB	FC	GD	HE	JF	KG	LH	MJ	NK	OL	PM	QN	RO	SP	TQ	UR	VS	WT	XU	AV	BW	CX	
UP	VQ	WR	XS	AT	BU	CV	DW	EX	FA	GB	HC	JD	KE	LF	MG	NH	OJ	PK	QL	RM	SN	TO	UP	VQ	WR	XS	AT	BU	CV	DW	
VO	WP	XQ	AR	BS	CT	DU	EV	FW	GX	HA	JB	KC	LD	ME	NF	OG	PH	QJ	RK	SL	TM	UN	VO	WP	XQ	AR	BS	CT	DU	EV	
WN	XO	AP	BQ	CR	DS	ET	FU	GV	HW	JX	KA	LB	MC	ND	OE	PF	QG	RH	SJ	TK	UL	VM	WN	XO	AP	BQ	CR	DS	ET	FU	+
XM	AN	BO	CP	DQ	ER	FS	GT	HU	JV	KW	LX	MA	NB	OC	PD	QE	RF	SG	TH	UJ	VK	WL	XM	AN	BO	CP	DQ	ER	FS	GT	0
AL	BM	CN	DO	EP	FQ	GR	HS	JT	KU	LV	MW	NX	OA	PB	QC	RD	SE	TF	UG	VH	WJ	XK	AL	BM	CN	DO	EP	FQ	GR	HS	
BK	CL	DM	EN	FO	GP	HQ	JR	KS	LT	MU	NV	OW	PX	QA	RB	SC	TD	UE	VF	WG	XH	AJ	BK	CL	DM	EN	FO	GP	HQ	JR	
CJ	DK	EL	FM	GN	HO	JP	KQ	LR	MS	NT	OU	PV	QW	RX	SA	TB	UC	VD	WE	XF	AG	BH	CJ	DK	EL	FM	GN	HO	JP	KQ	−
DH	EJ	FK	GL	HM	JN	KO	LP	MQ	NR	OS	PT	QU	RV	SW	TX	UA	VB	WC	XD	AE	BF	CG	DH	EJ	FK	GL	HM	JN	KO	LP	
EG	FH	GJ	HK	JL	KM	LN	MO	NP	OQ	PR	QS	RT	SU	TV	UW	VX	WA	XB	AC	BD	CE	DF	EG	FH	GJ	HK	JL	KM	LN	MO	
F	G	H	J	K	L	M	N	O	P	Q	R	S	T	U	V	W	X	A	B	C	D	E	F	G	H	J	K	L	M	N	

1 SU	2 M	3 TU	4 W	5 TH	6 F	7 SA	8 SU	9 M	10 TU	11 W	12 TH	13 F	14 SA	15 SU	16 M	17 TU	18 W	19 TH	20 F	21 SA	22 SU	23 M	24 TU	25 W	26 TH	27 F	28 SA	29 SU	30 M	31 TU	
H	J	K	L	M	N	O	P	Q	R	S	T	U	V	W	X	Y	Z	1	2	3	A	B	C	D	E	F	G	H	J	K	
JG	KH	LJ	MK	NL	OM	PN	QO	RP	SQ	TR	US	VT	WU	XV	YW	ZX	1Y	2Z	31	A2	B3	CA	DB	EC	FD	GE	HF	JG	KH	LJ	
KF	LG	MH	NJ	OK	PL	QM	RN	SO	TP	UQ	VR	WS	XT	YU	ZV	1W	2X	3Y	AZ	B1	C2	D3	EA	FB	GC	HD	JE	KF	LG	MH	
LE	MF	NG	OH	PJ	QK	RL	SM	TN	UO	VP	WQ	XR	YS	ZT	1U	2V	3W	AX	BY	CZ	D1	E2	F3	GA	HB	JC	KD	LE	MF	NG	+
MD	NE	OF	PG	QH	RJ	SK	TL	UM	VN	WO	XP	YQ	ZR	1S	2T	3U	AV	BW	CX	DY	EZ	F1	G2	H3	JA	KB	LC	MD	NE	OF	
NC	OD	PE	QF	RG	SH	TJ	UK	VL	WM	XN	YO	ZP	1Q	2R	3S	AT	BU	CV	DW	EX	FY	GZ	H1	J2	K3	LA	MB	NC	OD	PE	
OB	PC	QD	RE	SF	TG	UH	VJ	WK	XL	YM	ZN	1O	2P	3Q	AR	BS	CT	DU	EV	FW	GX	HY	JZ	K1	L2	M3	NA	OB	PC	QD	
PA	QB	RC	SD	TE	UF	VG	WH	XJ	YK	ZL	1M	2N	3O	AP	BQ	CR	DS	ET	FU	GV	HW	JX	KY	LZ	M1	N2	O3	PA	QB	RC	0
Q3	RA	SB	TC	UD	VE	WF	XG	YH	ZJ	1K	2L	3M	AN	BO	CP	DQ	ER	FS	GT	HU	JV	KW	LX	MY	NZ	O1	P2	Q3	RA	SB	
R2	S3	TA	UB	VC	WD	XE	YF	ZG	1H	2J	3K	AL	BM	CN	DO	EP	FQ	GR	HS	JT	KU	LV	MW	NX	OY	PZ	Q1	R2	S3	TA	
S1	T2	U3	VA	WB	XC	YD	ZE	1F	2G	3H	AJ	BK	CL	DM	EN	FO	GP	HQ	JR	KS	LT	MU	NV	OW	PX	QY	RZ	S1	T2	U3	−
TZ	U1	V2	W3	XA	YB	ZC	1D	2E	3F	AG	BH	CJ	DK	EL	FM	GN	HO	JP	KQ	LR	MS	NT	OU	PV	QW	RX	SY	TZ	U1	V2	
UY	VZ	W1	X2	Y3	ZA	1B	2C	3D	AE	BF	CG	DH	EJ	FK	GL	HM	JN	KO	LP	MQ	NR	OS	PT	QU	RV	SW	TX	UY	VZ	W1	
VX	WY	XZ	Y1	Z2	13	2A	3B	AC	BD	CE	DF	EG	FH	GJ	HK	JL	KM	LN	MO	NP	OQ	PR	QS	RT	SU	TV	UW	VX	WY	XZ	
W	X	Y	Z	1	2	3	A	B	C	D	E	F	G	H	J	K	L	M	N	O	P	Q	R	S	T	U	V	W	X	Y	

1 SU	2 M	3 TU	4 W	5 TH	6 F	7 SA	8 SU	9 M	10 TU	11 W	12 TH	13 F	14 SA	15 SU	16 M	17 TU	18 W	19 TH	20 F	21 SA	22 SU	23 M	24 TU	25 W	26 TH	27 F	28 SA	29 SU	30 M	31 TU	
A	B	C	D	E	F	G	H	J	K	L	M	N	O	P	Q	R	S	T	U	V	W	X	Y	Z	1	2	3	4	5	6	
B8	CA	DB	EC	FD	GE	HF	JG	KH	LJ	MK	NL	OM	PN	QO	RP	SQ	TR	US	VT	WU	XV	YW	ZX	1Y	2Z	31	42	53	64	75	
C7	D8	EA	FB	GC	HD	JE	KF	LG	MH	NJ	OK	PL	QM	RN	SO	TP	UQ	VR	WS	XT	YU	ZV	1W	2X	3Y	4Z	51	62	73	84	
D6	E7	F8	GA	HB	JC	KD	LE	MF	NG	OH	PJ	QK	RL	SM	TN	UO	VP	WQ	XR	YS	ZT	1U	2V	3W	4X	5Y	6Z	71	82	A3	
E5	F6	G7	H8	JA	KB	LC	MD	NE	OF	PG	QH	RJ	SK	TL	UM	VN	WO	XP	YQ	ZR	1S	2T	3U	4V	5W	6X	7Y	8Z	A1	B2	
F4	G5	H6	J7	K8	LA	MB	NC	OD	PE	QF	RG	SH	TJ	UK	VL	WM	XN	YO	ZP	1Q	2R	3S	4T	5U	6V	7W	8X	AY	BZ	C1	+
G3	H4	J5	K6	L7	M8	NA	OB	PC	QD	RE	SF	TG	UH	VJ	WK	XL	YM	ZN	1O	2P	3Q	4R	5S	6T	7U	8V	AW	BX	CY	DZ	
H2	J3	K4	L5	M6	N7	O8	PA	QB	RC	SD	TE	UF	VG	WH	XJ	YK	ZL	1M	2N	3O	4P	5Q	6R	7S	8T	AU	BV	CW	DX	EY	
J1	K2	L3	M4	N5	O6	P7	Q8	RA	SB	TC	UD	VE	WF	XG	YH	ZJ	1K	2L	3M	4N	5O	6P	7Q	8R	AS	BT	CU	DV	EW	FX	0
KZ	L1	M2	N3	O4	P5	Q6	R7	S8	TA	UB	VC	WD	XE	YF	ZG	1H	2J	3K	4L	5M	6N	7O	8P	AQ	BR	CS	DT	EU	FV	GW	
LY	MZ	N1	O2	P3	Q4	R5	S6	T7	U8	VA	WB	XC	YD	ZE	1F	2G	3H	4J	5K	6L	7M	8N	AO	BP	CQ	DR	ES	FT	GU	HV	
MX	NY	OZ	P1	Q2	R3	S4	T5	U6	V7	W8	XA	YB	ZC	1D	2E	3F	4G	5H	6J	7K	8L	AM	BN	CO	DP	EQ	FR	GS	HT	JU	−
NW	OX	PY	QZ	R1	S2	T3	U4	V5	W6	X7	Y8	ZA	1B	2C	3D	4E	5F	6G	7H	8J	AK	BL	CM	DN	EO	FP	GQ	HR	JS	KT	
OV	PW	QX	RY	SZ	T1	U2	V3	W4	X5	Y6	Z7	18	2A	3B	4C	5D	6E	7F	8G	AH	BJ	CK	DL	EM	FN	GO	HP	JQ	KR	LS	
PU	QV	RW	SX	TY	UZ	V1	W2	X3	Y4	Z5	16	27	38	4A	5B	6C	7D	8E	AF	BG	CH	DJ	EK	FL	GM	HN	JO	KP	LQ	MR	
QT	RU	SV	TW	UX	VY	WZ	X1	Y2	Z3	14	25	36	47	58	6A	7B	8C	AD	BE	CF	DG	EH	FJ	GK	HL	JM	KN	LO	MP	NQ	
RS	ST	TU	UV	VW	WX	XY	YZ	Z1	12	23	34	45	56	67	78	8A	AB	BC	CD	DE	EF	FG	GH	HJ	JK	KL	LM	MN	NO	OP	

233

PHYSICAL

1	2	3	4	5	6	7	8	9	10	11	12	13	14	15	16	17	18	19	20	21	22	23	24	25	26	27	28	29	30	31	
W	TH	F	SA	SU	M	TU	W	TH	F	SA	SU	M	TU	W	TH	F	SA	SU	M	TU	W	TH	F	SA	SU	M	TU	W	TH	F	
CB	DC	ED	FE	GF	HG	JH	KJ	LK	ML	NM	ON	PO	QP	RQ	SR	TS	UT	VU	WV	XW	AX	BA	CB	DC	ED	FE	GF	HG	JH	KJ	
DA	EB	FC	GD	HE	JF	KG	LH	MJ	NK	OL	PM	QN	RO	SP	TQ	UR	VS	WT	XU	AV	BW	CX	DA	EB	FC	GD	HE	JF	KG	LH	
EX	FA	GB	HC	JD	KE	LF	MG	NH	OJ	PK	QL	RM	SN	TO	UP	VQ	WR	XS	AT	BU	CV	DW	EX	FA	GB	HC	JD	KE	LF	MG	+
FW	GX	HA	JB	KC	LD	ME	NF	OG	PH	QJ	RK	SL	TM	UN	VO	WP	XQ	AR	BS	CT	DU	EV	FW	GX	HA	JB	KC	LD	ME	NF	
GV	HW	JX	KA	LB	MC	ND	OE	PF	QG	RH	SJ	TK	UL	VM	WN	XO	AP	BQ	CR	DS	ET	FU	GV	HW	JX	KA	LB	MC	ND	OE	
HU	JV	KW	LX	MA	NB	OC	PD	QE	RF	SG	TH	UJ	VK	WL	XM	AN	BO	CP	DQ	ER	FS	GT	HU	JV	KW	LX	MA	NB	OC	PD	0
JT	KU	LV	MW	NX	OA	PB	QC	RD	SE	TF	UG	VH	WJ	XK	AL	BM	CN	DO	EP	FQ	GR	HS	JT	KU	LV	MW	NX	OA	PB	QC	
KS	LT	MU	NV	OW	PX	QA	RB	SC	TD	UE	VF	WG	XH	AJ	BK	CL	DM	EN	FO	GP	HQ	JR	KS	LT	MU	NV	OW	PX	QA	RB	
LR	MS	NT	OU	PV	QW	RX	SA	TB	UC	VD	WE	XF	AG	BH	CJ	DK	EL	FM	GN	HO	JP	KQ	LR	MS	NT	OU	PV	QW	RX	SA	−
MQ	NR	OS	PT	QU	RV	SW	TX	UA	VB	WC	XD	AE	BF	CG	DH	EJ	FK	GL	HM	JN	KO	LP	MQ	NR	OS	PT	QU	RV	SW	TX	
NP	OQ	PR	QS	RT	SU	TV	UW	VX	WA	XB	AC	BD	CE	DF	EG	FH	GJ	HK	JL	KM	LN	MO	NP	OQ	PR	QS	RT	SU	TV	UW	
O	P	Q	R	S	T	U	V	W	X	A	B	C	D	E	F	G	H	J	K	L	M	N	O	P	Q	R	S	T	U	V	

EMOTIONAL

1	2	3	4	5	6	7	8	9	10	11	12	13	14	15	16	17	18	19	20	21	22	23	24	25	26	27	28	29	30	31	
W	TH	F	SA	SU	M	TU	W	TH	F	SA	SU	M	TU	W	TH	F	SA	SU	M	TU	W	TH	F	SA	SU	M	TU	W	TH	F	
L	M	N	O	P	Q	R	S	T	U	V	W	X	Y	Z	1	2	3	A	B	C	D	E	F	G	H	J	K	L	M	N	
MK	NL	OM	PN	QO	RP	SQ	TR	US	VT	WU	XV	YW	ZX	1Y	2Z	31	A2	B3	CA	DB	EC	FD	GE	HF	JG	KH	LJ	MK	NL	OM	
NJ	OK	PL	QM	RN	SO	TP	UQ	VR	WS	XT	YU	ZV	1W	2X	3Y	AZ	B1	C2	D3	EA	FB	GC	HD	JE	KF	LG	MH	NJ	OK	PL	
OH	PJ	QK	RL	SM	TN	UO	VP	WQ	XR	YS	ZT	1U	2V	3W	AX	BY	CZ	D1	E2	F3	GA	HB	JC	KD	LE	MF	NG	OH	PJ	QK	
PG	QH	RJ	SK	TL	UM	VN	WO	XP	YQ	ZR	1S	2T	3U	AV	BW	CX	DY	EZ	F1	G2	H3	JA	KB	LC	MD	NE	OF	PG	QH	RJ	+
QF	RG	SH	TJ	UK	VL	WM	XN	YO	ZP	1Q	2R	3S	AT	BU	CV	DW	EX	FY	GZ	H1	J2	K3	LA	MB	NC	OD	PE	QF	RG	SH	
RE	SF	TG	UH	VJ	WK	XL	YM	ZN	1O	2P	3Q	AR	BS	CT	DU	EV	FW	GX	HY	JZ	K1	L2	M3	NA	OB	PC	QD	RE	SF	TG	
SD	TE	UF	VG	WH	XJ	YK	ZL	1M	2N	3O	AP	BQ	CR	DS	ET	FU	GV	HW	JX	KY	LZ	M1	N2	O3	PA	QB	RC	SD	TE	UF	0
TC	UD	VE	WF	XG	YH	ZJ	1K	2L	3M	AN	BO	CP	DQ	ER	FS	GT	HU	JV	KW	LX	MY	NZ	O1	P2	Q3	RA	SB	TC	UD	VE	
UB	VC	WD	XE	YF	ZG	1H	2J	3K	AL	BM	CN	DO	EP	FQ	GR	HS	JT	KU	LV	MW	NX	OY	PZ	Q1	R2	S3	TA	UB	VC	WD	
VA	WB	XC	YD	ZE	1F	2G	3H	AJ	BK	CL	DM	EN	FO	GP	HQ	JR	KS	LT	MU	NV	OW	PX	QY	RZ	S1	T2	U3	VA	WB	XC	−
W3	XA	YB	ZC	1D	2E	3F	AG	BH	CJ	DK	EL	FM	GN	HO	JP	KQ	LR	MS	NT	OU	PV	QW	RX	SY	TZ	U1	V2	W3	XA	YB	
X2	Y3	ZA	1B	2C	3D	AE	BF	CG	DH	EJ	FK	GL	HM	JN	KO	LP	MQ	NR	OS	PT	QU	RV	SW	TX	UY	VZ	W1	X2	Y3	ZA	
Y1	Z2	13	2A	3B	AC	BD	CE	DF	EG	FH	GJ	HK	JL	KM	LN	MO	NP	OQ	PR	QS	RT	SU	TV	UW	VX	WY	XZ	Y1	Z2	13	
Z	1	2	3	A	B	C	D	E	F	G	H	J	K	L	M	N	O	P	Q	R	S	T	U	V	W	X	Y	Z	1	2	

INTELLECTUAL

1	2	3	4	5	6	7	8	9	10	11	12	13	14	15	16	17	18	19	20	21	22	23	24	25	26	27	28	29	30	31	
W	TH	F	SA	SU	M	TU	W	TH	F	SA	SU	M	TU	W	TH	F	SA	SU	M	TU	W	TH	F	SA	SU	M	TU	W	TH	F	
7	8	A	B	C	D	E	F	G	H	J	K	L	M	N	O	P	Q	R	S	T	U	V	W	X	Y	Z	1	2	3	4	
86	A7	B8	CA	DB	EC	FD	GE	HF	JG	KH	LJ	MK	NL	OM	PN	QO	RP	SQ	TR	US	VT	WU	XV	YW	ZX	1Y	2Z	31	42	53	
A5	B6	C7	D8	EA	FB	GC	HD	JE	KF	LG	MH	NJ	OK	PL	QM	RN	SO	TP	UQ	VR	WS	XT	YU	ZV	1W	2X	3Y	4Z	51	62	
B4	C5	D6	E7	F8	GA	HB	JC	KD	LE	MF	NG	OH	PJ	QK	RL	SM	TN	UO	VP	WQ	XR	YS	ZT	1U	2V	3W	4X	5Y	6Z	71	
C3	D4	E5	F6	G7	H8	JA	KB	LC	MD	NE	OF	PG	QH	RJ	SK	TL	UM	VN	WO	XP	YQ	ZR	1S	2T	3U	4V	5W	6X	7Y	8Z	+
D2	E3	F4	G5	H6	J7	K8	LA	MB	NC	OD	PE	QF	RG	SH	TJ	UK	VL	WM	XN	YO	ZP	1Q	2R	3S	4T	5U	6V	7W	8X	AY	
E1	F2	G3	H4	J5	K6	L7	M8	NA	OB	PC	QD	RE	SF	TG	UH	VJ	WK	XL	YM	ZN	1O	2P	3Q	4R	5S	6T	7U	8V	AW	BX	
FZ	G1	H2	J3	K4	L5	M6	N7	O8	PA	QB	RC	SD	TE	UF	VG	WH	XJ	YK	ZL	1M	2N	3O	4P	5Q	6R	7S	8T	AU	BV	CW	
GY	HZ	J1	K2	L3	M4	N5	O6	P7	Q8	RA	SB	TC	UD	VE	WF	XG	YH	ZJ	1K	2L	3M	4N	5O	6P	7Q	8R	AS	BT	CU	DV	0
HX	JY	KZ	L1	M2	N3	O4	P5	Q6	R7	S8	TA	UB	VC	WD	XE	YF	ZG	1H	2J	3K	4L	5M	6N	7O	8P	AQ	BR	CS	DT	EU	
JW	KX	LY	MZ	N1	O2	P3	Q4	R5	S6	T7	U8	VA	WB	XC	YD	ZE	1F	2G	3H	4J	5K	6L	7M	8N	AO	BP	CQ	DR	ES	FT	
KV	LW	MX	NY	OZ	P1	Q2	R3	S4	T5	U6	V7	W8	XA	YB	ZC	1D	2E	3F	4G	5H	6J	7K	8L	AM	BN	CO	DP	EQ	FR	GS	
LU	MV	NW	OX	PY	QZ	R1	S2	T3	U4	V5	W6	X7	Y8	ZA	1B	2C	3D	4E	5F	6G	7H	8J	AK	BL	CM	DN	EO	FP	GQ	HR	−
MT	NU	OV	PW	QX	RY	SZ	T1	U2	V3	W4	X5	Y6	Z7	18	2A	3B	4C	5D	6E	7F	8G	AH	BJ	CK	DL	EM	FN	GO	HP	JQ	
NS	OT	PU	QV	RW	SX	TY	UZ	V1	W2	X3	Y4	Z5	16	27	38	4A	5B	6C	7D	8E	AF	BG	CH	DJ	EK	FL	GM	HN	JO	KP	
OR	PS	QT	RU	SV	TW	UX	VY	WZ	X1	Y2	Z3	14	25	36	47	58	6A	7B	8C	AD	BE	CF	DG	EH	FJ	GK	HL	JM	KN	LO	
PQ	QR	RS	ST	TU	UV	VW	WX	XY	YZ	Z1	12	23	34	45	56	67	78	8A	AB	BC	CD	DE	EF	FG	GH	HJ	JK	KL	LM	MN	

1 SA	2 SU	3 M	4 TU	5 W	6 TH	7 F	8 SA	9 SU	10 M	11 TU	12 W	13 TH	14 F	15 SA	16 SU	17 M	18 TU	19 W	20 TH	21 F	22 SA	23 SU	24 M	25 TU	26 W	27 TH	28 F	29 SA	30 SU	
LK	ML	NM	ON	PO	QP	RQ	SR	TS	UT	VU	WV	XW	AX	BA	CB	DC	ED	FE	GF	HG	JH	KJ	LK	ML	NM	ON	PO	QP	RQ	
MJ	NK	OL	PM	QN	RO	SP	TQ	UR	VS	WT	XU	AV	BW	CX	DA	EB	FC	GD	HE	JF	KG	LH	MJ	NK	OL	PM	QN	RO	SP	
NH	OJ	PK	QL	RM	SN	TO	UP	VQ	WR	XS	AT	BU	CV	DW	EX	FA	GB	HC	JD	KE	LF	MG	NH	OJ	PK	QL	RM	SN	TO	
OG	PH	QJ	RK	SL	TM	UN	VO	WP	XQ	AR	BS	CT	DU	EV	FW	GX	HA	JB	KC	LD	ME	NF	OG	PH	QJ	RK	SL	TM	UN	+
PF	QG	RH	SJ	TK	UL	VM	WN	XO	AP	BQ	CR	DS	ET	FU	GV	HW	JX	KA	LB	MC	ND	OE	PF	QG	RH	SJ	TK	UL	VM	
QE	RF	SG	TH	UJ	VK	WL	XM	AN	BO	CP	DQ	ER	FS	GT	HU	JV	KW	LX	MA	NB	OC	PD	QE	RF	SG	TH	UJ	VK	WL	0
RD	SE	TF	UG	VH	WJ	XK	AL	BM	CN	DO	EP	FQ	GR	HS	JT	KU	LV	MW	NX	OA	PB	QC	RD	SE	TF	UG	VH	WJ	XK	
SC	TD	UE	VF	WG	XH	AJ	BK	CL	DM	EN	FO	GP	HQ	JR	KS	LT	MU	NV	OW	PX	QA	RB	SC	TD	UE	VF	WG	XH	AJ	
TB	UC	VD	WE	XF	AG	BH	CJ	DK	EL	FM	GN	HO	JP	KQ	LR	MS	NT	OU	PV	QW	RX	SA	TB	UC	VD	WE	XF	AG	BH	−
UA	VB	WC	XD	AE	BF	CG	DH	EJ	FK	GL	HM	JN	KO	LP	MQ	NR	OS	PT	QU	RV	SW	TX	UA	VB	WC	XD	AE	BF	CG	
VX	WA	XB	AC	BD	CE	DF	EG	FH	GJ	HK	JL	KM	LN	MO	NP	OQ	PR	QS	RT	SU	TV	UW	VX	WA	XB	AC	BD	CE	DF	
W	X	A	B	C	D	E	F	G	H	J	K	L	M	N	O	P	Q	R	S	T	U	V	W	X	A	B	C	D	E	

1 SA	2 SU	3 M	4 TU	5 W	6 TH	7 F	8 SA	9 SU	10 M	11 TU	12 W	13 TH	14 F	15 SA	16 SU	17 M	18 TU	19 W	20 TH	21 F	22 SA	23 SU	24 M	25 TU	26 W	27 TH	28 F	29 SA	30 SU	
O	P	Q	R	S	T	U	V	W	X	Y	Z	1	2	3	A	B	C	D	E	F	G	H	J	K	L	M	N	O	P	
PN	QO	RP	SQ	TR	US	VT	WU	XV	YW	ZX	1Y	2Z	31	A2	B3	CA	DB	EC	FD	GE	HF	JG	KH	LJ	MK	NL	OM	PN	QO	
QM	RN	SO	TP	UQ	VR	WS	XT	YU	ZV	1W	2X	3Y	AZ	B1	C2	D3	EA	FB	GC	HD	JE	KF	LG	MH	NJ	OK	PL	QM	RN	
RL	SM	TN	UO	VP	WQ	XR	YS	ZT	1U	2V	3W	AX	BY	CZ	D1	E2	F3	GA	HB	JC	KD	LE	MF	NG	OH	PJ	QK	RL	SM	
SK	TL	UM	VN	WO	XP	YQ	ZR	1S	2T	3U	AV	BW	CX	DY	EZ	F1	G2	H3	JA	KB	LC	MD	NE	OF	PG	QH	RJ	SK	TL	+
TJ	UK	VL	WM	XN	YO	ZP	1Q	2R	3S	AT	BU	CV	DW	EX	FY	GZ	H1	J2	K3	LA	MB	NC	OD	PE	QF	RG	SF	TJ	UK	
UH	VJ	WK	XL	YM	ZN	1O	2P	3Q	AR	BS	CT	DU	EV	FW	GX	HY	JZ	K1	L2	M3	NA	OB	PC	QD	RE	SF	TG	UH	VJ	
VG	WH	XJ	YK	ZL	1M	2N	3O	AP	BQ	CR	DS	ET	FU	GV	HW	JX	KY	LZ	M1	N2	O3	PA	QB	RC	SD	TE	UF	VG	WH	0
WF	XG	YH	ZJ	1K	2L	3M	AN	BO	CP	DQ	ER	FS	GT	HU	JV	KW	LX	MY	NZ	O1	P2	Q3	RA	SB	TC	UD	VE	WF	XG	
XE	YF	ZG	1H	2J	3K	AL	BM	CN	DO	EP	FQ	GR	HS	JT	KU	LV	MW	NX	OY	PZ	Q1	R2	S3	TA	UB	VC	WD	XE	YF	
YD	ZE	1F	2G	3H	AJ	BK	CL	DM	EN	FO	GP	HQ	JR	KS	LT	MU	NV	OW	PX	QY	RZ	S1	T2	U3	VA	WB	XC	YD	ZE	−
ZC	1D	2E	3F	AG	BH	CJ	DK	EL	FM	GN	HO	JP	KQ	LR	MS	NT	OU	PV	QW	RX	SY	TZ	U1	V2	W3	XA	YB	ZC	1D	
1B	2C	3D	AE	BF	CG	DH	EJ	FK	GL	HM	JN	KO	LP	MQ	NR	OS	PT	QU	RV	SW	TX	UY	VZ	W1	X2	Y3	ZA	1B	2C	
2A	3B	AC	BD	CE	DF	EG	FH	GJ	HK	JL	KM	LN	MO	NP	OQ	PR	QS	RT	SU	TV	UW	VX	WY	XZ	Y1	Z2	13	2A	3B	
3	A	B	C	D	E	F	G	H	J	K	L	M	N	O	P	Q	R	S	T	U	V	W	X	Y	Z	1	2	3	A	

1 SA	2 SU	3 M	4 TU	5 W	6 TH	7 F	8 SA	9 SU	10 M	11 TU	12 W	13 TH	14 F	15 SA	16 SU	17 M	18 TU	19 W	20 TH	21 F	22 SA	23 SU	24 M	25 TU	26 W	27 TH	28 F	29 SA	30 SU	
5	6	7	8	A	B	C	D	E	F	G	H	J	K	L	M	N	O	P	Q	R	S	T	U	V	W	X	Y	Z	1	
64	75	86	A7	B8	CA	DB	EC	FD	GE	HF	JG	KH	LJ	MK	NL	OM	PN	QO	RP	SQ	TR	US	VT	WU	XV	YW	ZX	1Y	2Z	
73	84	A5	B6	C7	D8	EA	FB	GC	HD	JE	KF	LG	MH	NJ	OK	PL	QM	RN	SO	TP	UQ	VR	WS	XT	YU	ZV	1W	2X	3Y	
82	A3	B4	C5	D6	E7	F8	GA	HB	JC	KD	LE	MF	NG	OH	PJ	QK	RL	SM	TN	UO	VP	WQ	XR	YS	ZT	1U	2V	3W	4X	
A1	B2	C3	D4	E5	F6	G7	H8	JA	KB	LC	MD	NE	OF	PG	QH	RJ	SK	TL	UM	VN	WO	XP	YQ	ZR	1S	2T	3U	4V	5W	
BZ	C1	D2	E3	F4	G5	H6	J7	K8	LA	MB	NC	OD	PE	QF	RG	SH	TJ	UK	VL	WM	XN	YO	ZP	1Q	2R	3S	4T	5U	6V	+
CY	DZ	E1	F2	G3	H4	J5	K6	L7	M8	NA	OB	PC	QD	RE	SF	TG	UH	VJ	WK	XL	YM	ZN	1O	2P	3Q	4R	5S	6T	7U	
DX	EY	FZ	G1	H2	J3	K4	L5	M6	N7	O8	PA	QB	RC	SD	TE	UF	VG	WH	XJ	YK	ZL	1M	2N	3O	4P	5Q	6R	7S	8T	
EW	FX	GY	HZ	J1	K2	L3	M4	N5	O6	P7	Q8	RA	SB	TC	UD	VE	WF	XG	YH	ZJ	1K	2L	3M	4N	5O	6P	7Q	8R	AS	0
FV	GW	HX	JY	KZ	L1	M2	N3	O4	P5	Q6	R7	S8	TA	UB	VC	WD	XE	YF	ZG	1H	2J	3K	4L	5M	6N	7O	8P	AQ	BR	
GU	HV	JW	KX	LY	MZ	N1	O2	P3	Q4	R5	S6	T7	U8	VA	WB	XC	YD	ZE	1F	2G	3H	4J	5K	6L	7M	8N	AO	BP	CQ	
HT	JU	KV	LW	MX	NY	OZ	P1	Q2	R3	S4	T5	U6	V7	W8	XA	YB	ZC	1D	2E	3F	4G	5H	6J	7K	8L	AM	BN	CO	DP	−
JS	KT	LU	MV	NW	OX	PY	QZ	R1	S2	T3	U4	V5	W6	X7	Y8	ZA	1B	2C	3D	4E	5F	6G	7H	8J	AK	BL	CM	DN	EO	
KR	LS	MT	NU	OV	PW	QX	RY	SZ	T1	U2	V3	W4	X5	Y6	Z7	18	2A	3B	4C	5D	6E	7F	8G	AH	BJ	CK	DL	EM	FN	
LQ	MR	NS	OT	PU	QV	RW	SX	TY	UZ	V1	W2	X3	Y4	Z5	16	27	38	4A	5B	6C	7D	8E	AF	BG	CH	DJ	EK	FL	GM	
MP	NQ	OR	PS	QT	RU	SV	TW	UX	VY	WZ	X1	Y2	Z3	14	25	36	47	58	6A	7B	8C	AD	BE	CF	DG	EH	FJ	GK	HL	
NO	OP	PQ	QR	RS	ST	TU	UV	VW	WX	XY	YZ	Z1	12	23	34	45	56	67	78	8A	AB	BC	CD	DE	EF	FG	GH	HJ	JK	

1 M	2 TU	3 W	4 TH	5 F	6 SA	7 SU	8 M	9 TU	10 W	11 TH	12 F	13 SA	14 SU	15 M	16 TU	17 W	18 TH	19 F	20 SA	21 SU	22 M	23 TU	24 W	25 TH	26 F	27 SA	28 SU	29 M	30 TU	31 W	
SR	TS	UT	VU	WV	XW	AX	BA	CB	DC	ED	FE	GF	HG	JH	KJ	LK	ML	NM	ON	PO	QP	RQ	SR	TS	UT	VU	WV	XW	AX	BA	
TQ	UR	VS	WT	XU	AV	BW	CX	DA	EB	FC	GD	HE	JF	KG	LH	MJ	NK	OL	PM	QN	RO	SP	TQ	UR	VS	WT	XU	AV	BW	CX	
UP	VQ	WR	XS	AT	BU	CV	DW	EX	FA	GB	HC	JD	KE	LF	MG	NH	OJ	PK	QL	RM	SN	TO	UP	VQ	WR	XS	AT	BU	CV	DW	+
VO	WP	XQ	AR	BS	CT	DU	EV	FW	GX	HA	JB	KC	LD	ME	NF	OG	PH	QJ	RK	SL	TM	UN	VO	WP	XQ	AR	BS	CT	DU	EV	
WN	XO	AP	BQ	CR	DS	ET	FU	GV	HW	JX	KA	LB	MC	ND	OE	PF	QG	RH	SJ	TK	UL	VM	WN	XO	AP	BQ	CR	DS	ET	FU	
XM	AN	BO	CP	DQ	ER	FS	GT	HU	JV	KW	LX	MA	NB	OC	PD	QE	RF	SG	TH	UJ	VK	WL	XM	AN	BO	CP	DQ	ER	FS	GT	0
AL	BM	CN	DO	EP	FQ	GR	HS	JT	KU	LV	MW	NX	OA	PB	QC	RD	SE	TF	UG	VH	WJ	XK	AL	BM	CN	DO	EP	FQ	GR	HS	
BK	CL	DM	EN	FO	GP	HQ	JR	KS	LT	MU	NV	OW	PX	QA	RB	SC	TD	UE	VF	WG	XH	AJ	BK	CL	DM	EN	FO	GP	HQ	JR	
CJ	DK	EL	FM	GN	HO	JP	KQ	LR	MS	NT	OU	PV	QW	RX	SA	TB	UC	VD	WE	XF	AG	BH	CJ	DK	EL	FM	GN	HO	JP	KQ	−
DH	EJ	FK	GL	HM	JN	KO	LP	MQ	NR	OS	PT	QU	RV	SW	TX	UA	VB	WC	XD	AE	BF	CG	DH	EJ	FK	GL	HM	JN	KO	LP	
EG	FH	GJ	HK	JL	KM	LN	MO	NP	OQ	PR	QS	RT	SU	TV	UW	VX	WA	XB	AC	BD	CE	DF	EG	FH	GJ	HK	JL	KM	LN	MO	
F	G	H	J	K	L	M	N	O	P	Q	R	S	T	U	V	W	X	A	B	C	D	E	F	G	H	J	K	L	M	N	

1 M	2 TU	3 W	4 TH	5 F	6 SA	7 SU	8 M	9 TU	10 W	11 TH	12 F	13 SA	14 SU	15 M	16 TU	17 W	18 TH	19 F	20 SA	21 SU	22 M	23 TU	24 W	25 TH	26 F	27 SA	28 SU	29 M	30 TU	31 W	
Q	R	S	T	U	V	W	X	Y	Z	1	2	3	A	B	C	D	E	F	G	H	J	K	L	M	N	O	P	Q	R	S	
RP	SQ	TR	US	VT	WU	XV	YW	ZX	1Y	2Z	31	A2	B3	CA	DB	EC	FD	GE	HF	JG	KH	LJ	MK	NL	OM	PN	QO	RP	SQ	TR	
SO	TP	UQ	VR	WS	XT	YU	ZV	1W	2X	3Y	AZ	B1	C2	D3	EA	FB	GC	HD	JE	KF	LG	MH	NJ	OK	PL	QM	RN	SO	TP	UQ	
TN	UO	VP	WQ	XR	YS	ZT	1U	2V	3W	AX	BY	CZ	D1	E2	F3	GA	HB	JC	KD	LE	MF	NG	OH	PJ	QK	RL	SM	TN	UO	VP	+
UM	VN	WO	XP	YQ	ZR	1S	2T	3U	AV	BW	CX	DY	EZ	F1	G2	H3	JA	KB	LC	MD	NE	OF	PG	QH	RJ	SK	TL	UM	VN	WO	
VL	WM	XN	YO	ZP	1Q	2R	3S	AT	BU	CV	DW	EX	FY	GZ	H1	J2	K3	LA	MB	NC	OD	PE	QF	RG	SH	TJ	UK	VL	WM	XN	
WK	XL	YM	ZN	1O	2P	3Q	AR	BS	CT	DU	EV	FW	GX	HY	JZ	K1	L2	M3	NA	OB	PC	QD	RE	SF	TG	UH	VJ	WK	XL	YM	
XJ	YK	ZL	1M	2N	3O	AP	BQ	CR	DS	ET	FU	GV	HW	JX	KY	LZ	M1	N2	O3	PA	QB	RC	SD	TE	UF	VG	WH	XJ	YK	ZL	0
YH	ZJ	1K	2L	3M	AN	BO	CP	DQ	ER	FS	GT	HU	JV	KW	LX	MY	NZ	O1	P2	Q3	RA	SB	TC	UD	VE	WF	XG	YH	ZJ	1K	
ZG	1H	2J	3K	AL	BM	CN	DO	EP	FQ	GR	HS	JT	KU	LV	MW	NX	OY	PZ	Q1	R2	S3	TA	UB	VC	WD	XE	YF	ZG	1H	2J	
1F	2G	3H	AJ	BK	CL	DM	EN	FO	GP	HQ	JR	KS	LT	MU	NV	OW	PX	QY	RZ	S1	T2	U3	VA	WB	XC	YD	ZE	1F	2G	3H	−
2E	3F	AG	BH	CJ	DK	EL	FM	GN	HO	JP	KQ	LR	MS	NT	OU	PV	QW	RX	SY	TZ	U1	V2	W3	XA	YB	ZC	1D	2E	3F	AG	
3D	AE	BF	CG	DH	EJ	FK	GL	HM	JN	KO	LP	MQ	NR	OS	PT	QU	RV	SW	TX	UY	VZ	W1	X2	Y3	ZA	1B	2C	3D	AE	BF	
AC	BD	CE	DF	EG	FH	GJ	HK	JL	KM	LN	MO	NP	OQ	PR	QS	RT	SU	TV	UW	VX	WY	XZ	Y1	Z2	13	2A	3B	AC	BD	CE	
B	C	D	E	F	G	H	J	K	L	M	N	O	P	Q	R	S	T	U	V	W	X	Y	Z	1	2	3	A	B	C	D	

1 M	2 TU	3 W	4 TH	5 F	6 SA	7 SU	8 M	9 TU	10 W	11 TH	12 F	13 SA	14 SU	15 M	16 TU	17 W	18 TH	19 F	20 SA	21 SU	22 M	23 TU	24 W	25 TH	26 F	27 SA	28 SU	29 M	30 TU	31 W	
2	3	4	5	6	7	8	A	B	C	D	E	F	G	H	J	K	L	M	N	O	P	Q	R	S	T	U	V	W	X	Y	
31	42	53	64	75	86	A7	B8	CA	DB	EC	FD	GE	HF	JG	KH	LJ	MK	NL	OM	PN	QO	RP	SQ	TR	US	VT	WU	XV	YW	ZX	
4Z	51	62	73	84	A5	B6	C7	D8	EA	FB	GC	HD	JE	KF	LG	MH	NJ	OK	PL	QM	RN	SO	TP	UQ	VR	WS	XT	YU	ZV	1W	
5Y	6Z	71	82	A3	B4	C5	D6	E7	F8	GA	HB	JC	KD	LE	MF	NG	OH	PJ	QK	RL	SM	TN	UO	VP	WQ	XR	YS	ZT	1U	2V	
6X	7Y	8Z	A1	B2	C3	D4	E5	F6	G7	H8	JA	KB	LC	MD	NE	OF	PG	QH	RJ	SK	TL	UM	VN	WO	XP	YQ	ZR	1S	2T	3U	
7W	8X	AY	BZ	C1	D2	E3	F4	G5	H6	J7	K8	LA	MB	NC	OD	PE	QF	RG	SH	TJ	UK	VL	WM	XN	YO	ZP	1Q	2R	3S	4T	+
8V	AW	BX	CY	DZ	E1	F2	G3	H4	J5	K6	L7	M8	NA	OB	PC	QD	RE	SF	TG	UH	VJ	WK	XL	YM	ZN	1O	2P	3Q	4R	5S	
AU	BV	CW	DX	EY	FZ	G1	H2	J3	K4	L5	M6	N7	O8	PA	QB	RC	SD	TE	UF	VG	WH	XJ	YK	ZL	1M	2N	3O	4P	5Q	6R	
BT	CU	DV	EW	FX	GY	HZ	J1	K2	L3	M4	N5	O6	P7	Q8	RA	SB	TC	UD	VE	WF	XG	YH	ZJ	1K	2L	3M	4N	5O	6P	7Q	0
CS	DT	EU	FV	GW	HX	JY	KZ	L1	M2	N3	O4	P5	Q6	R7	S8	TA	UB	VC	WD	XE	YF	ZG	1H	2J	3K	4L	5M	6N	7O	8P	
DR	ES	FT	GU	HV	JW	KX	LY	MZ	N1	O2	P3	Q4	R5	S6	T7	U8	VA	WB	XC	YD	ZE	1F	2G	3H	4J	5K	6L	7M	8N	AO	−
EQ	FR	GS	HT	JU	KV	LW	MX	NY	OZ	P1	Q2	R3	S4	T5	U6	V7	W8	XA	YB	ZC	1D	2E	3F	4G	5H	6J	7K	8L	AM	BN	
FP	GQ	HR	JS	KT	LU	MV	NW	OX	PY	QZ	R1	S2	T3	U4	V5	W6	X7	Y8	ZA	1B	2C	3D	4E	5F	6G	7H	8J	AK	BL	CM	
GO	HP	JQ	KR	LS	MT	NU	OV	PW	QX	RY	SZ	T1	U2	V3	W4	X5	Y6	Z7	18	2A	3B	4C	5D	6E	7F	8G	AH	BJ	CK	DL	
HN	JO	KP	LQ	MR	NS	OT	PU	QV	RW	SX	TY	UZ	V1	W2	X3	Y4	Z5	16	27	38	4A	5B	6C	7D	8E	AF	BG	CH	DJ	EK	
JM	KN	LO	MP	NQ	OR	PS	QT	RU	SV	TW	UX	VY	WZ	X1	Y2	Z3	14	25	36	47	58	6A	7B	8C	AD	BE	CF	DG	EH	FJ	
KL	LM	MN	NO	OP	PQ	QR	RS	ST	TU	UV	VW	WX	XY	YZ	Z1	12	23	34	45	56	67	78	8A	AB	BC	CD	DE	EF	FG	GH	

PHYSICAL — NOVEMBER 1979

1 TH	2 F	3 SA	4 SU	5 M	6 TU	7 W	8 TH	9 F	10 SA	11 SU	12 M	13 TU	14 W	15 TH	16 F	17 SA	18 SU	19 M	20 TU	21 W	22 TH	23 F	24 SA	25 SU	26 M	27 TU	28 W	29 TH	30 F	
CB	DC	ED	FE	GF	HG	JH	KJ	LK	ML	NM	ON	PO	QP	RQ	SR	TS	UT	VU	WV	XW	AX	BA	CB	DC	ED	FE	GF	HG	JH	
DA	EB	FC	GD	HE	JF	KG	LH	MJ	NK	OL	PM	QN	RO	SP	TQ	UR	VS	WT	XU	AV	BW	CX	DA	EB	FC	GD	HE	JF	KG	
EX	FA	GB	HC	JD	KE	LF	MG	NH	OJ	PK	QL	RM	SN	TO	UP	VQ	WR	XS	AT	BU	CV	DW	EX	FA	GB	HC	JD	KE	LF	+
FW	GX	HA	JB	KC	LD	ME	NF	OG	PH	QJ	RK	SL	TM	UN	VO	WP	XQ	AR	BS	CT	DU	EV	FW	GX	HA	JB	KC	LD	ME	
GV	HW	JX	KA	LB	MC	ND	OE	PF	QG	RH	SJ	TK	UL	VM	WN	XO	AP	BQ	CR	DS	ET	FU	GV	HW	JX	KA	LB	MC	ND	
HU	JV	KW	LX	MA	NB	OC	PD	QE	RF	SG	TH	UJ	VK	WL	XM	AN	BO	CP	DQ	ER	FS	GT	HU	JV	KW	LX	MA	NB	OC	0
JT	KU	LV	MW	NX	OA	PB	QC	RD	SE	TF	UG	VH	WJ	XK	AL	BM	CN	DO	EP	FQ	GR	HS	JT	KU	LV	MW	NX	OA	PB	
KS	LT	MU	NV	OW	PX	QA	RB	SC	TD	UE	VF	WG	XH	AJ	BK	CL	DM	EN	FO	GP	HQ	JR	KS	LT	MU	NV	OW	PX	QA	
LR	MS	NT	OU	PV	QW	RX	SA	TB	UC	VD	WE	XF	AG	BH	CJ	DK	EL	FM	GN	HO	JP	KQ	LR	MS	NT	OU	PV	QW	RX	−
MQ	NR	OS	PT	QU	RV	SW	TX	UA	VB	WC	XD	AE	BF	CG	DH	EJ	FK	GL	HM	JN	KO	LP	MQ	NR	OS	PT	QU	RV	SW	
NP	OQ	PR	QS	RT	SU	TV	UW	VX	WA	XB	AC	BD	CE	DF	EG	FH	GJ	HK	JL	KM	LN	MO	NP	OQ	PR	QS	RT	SU	TV	
O	P	Q	R	S	T	U	V	W	X	A	B	C	D	E	F	G	H	J	K	L	M	N	O	P	Q	R	S	T	U	

EMOTIONAL — NOVEMBER 1979

1 TH	2 F	3 SA	4 SU	5 M	6 TU	7 W	8 TH	9 F	10 SA	11 SU	12 M	13 TU	14 W	15 TH	16 F	17 SA	18 SU	19 M	20 TU	21 W	22 TH	23 F	24 SA	25 SU	26 M	27 TU	28 W	29 TH	30 F	
T	U	V	W	X	Y	Z	1	2	3	A	B	C	D	E	F	G	H	J	K	L	M	N	O	P	Q	R	S	T	U	
US	VT	WU	XV	YW	ZX	1Y	2Z	31	A2	B3	CA	DB	EC	FD	GE	HF	JG	KH	LJ	MK	NL	OM	PN	QO	RP	SQ	TR	US	VT	
VR	WS	XT	YU	ZV	1W	2X	3Y	AZ	B1	C2	D3	EA	FB	GC	HD	JE	KF	LG	MH	NJ	OK	PL	QM	RN	SO	TP	UQ	VR	WS	
WQ	XR	YS	ZT	1U	2V	3W	AX	BY	CZ	D1	E2	F3	GA	HB	JC	KD	LE	MF	NG	OH	PJ	QK	RL	SM	TN	UO	VP	WQ	XR	
XP	YQ	ZR	1S	2T	3U	AV	BW	CX	DY	EZ	F1	G2	H3	JA	KB	LC	MD	NE	OF	PG	QH	RJ	SK	TL	UM	VN	WO	XP	YQ	+
YO	ZP	1Q	2R	3S	AT	BU	CV	DW	EX	FY	GZ	H1	J2	K3	LA	MB	NC	OD	PE	QF	RG	SH	TJ	UK	VL	WM	XN	YO	ZP	
ZN	1O	2P	3Q	AR	BS	CT	DU	EV	FW	GX	HY	JZ	K1	L2	M3	NA	OB	PC	QD	RE	SF	TG	UH	VJ	WK	XL	YM	ZN	1O	
1M	2N	3O	AP	BQ	CR	DS	ET	FU	GV	HW	JX	KY	LZ	M1	N2	O3	PA	QB	RC	SD	TE	UF	VG	WH	XJ	YK	ZL	1M	2N	0
2L	3M	AN	BO	CP	DQ	ER	FS	GT	HU	JV	KW	LX	MY	NZ	O1	P2	Q3	RA	SB	TC	UD	VE	WF	XG	YH	ZJ	1K	2L	3M	
3K	AL	BM	CN	DO	EP	FQ	GR	HS	JT	KU	LV	MW	NX	OY	PZ	Q1	R2	S3	TA	UB	VC	WD	XE	YF	ZG	1H	2J	3K	AL	
AJ	BK	CL	DM	EN	FO	GP	HQ	JR	KS	LT	MU	NV	OW	PX	QY	RZ	S1	T2	U3	VA	WB	XC	YD	ZE	1F	2G	3H	AJ	BK	−
BH	CJ	DK	EL	FM	GN	HO	JP	KQ	LR	MS	NT	OU	PV	QW	RX	SY	TZ	U1	V2	W3	XA	YB	ZC	1D	2E	3F	AG	BH	CJ	
CG	DH	EJ	FK	GL	HM	JN	KO	LP	MQ	NR	OS	PT	QU	RV	SW	TX	UY	VZ	W1	X2	Y3	ZA	1B	2C	3D	AE	BF	CG	DH	
DF	EG	FH	GJ	HK	JL	KM	LN	MO	NP	OQ	PR	QS	RT	SU	TV	UW	VX	WY	XZ	Y1	Z2	13	2A	3B	AC	BD	CE	DF	EG	
E	F	G	H	J	K	L	M	N	O	P	Q	R	S	T	U	V	W	X	Y	Z	1	2	3	A	B	C	D	E	F	

INTELLECTUAL — NOVEMBER 1979

1 TH	2 F	3 SA	4 SU	5 M	6 TU	7 W	8 TH	9 F	10 SA	11 SU	12 M	13 TU	14 W	15 TH	16 F	17 SA	18 SU	19 M	20 TU	21 W	22 TH	23 F	24 SA	25 SU	26 M	27 TU	28 W	9 TH	30 F	
Z	1	2	3	4	5	6	7	8	A	B	C	D	E	F	G	H	J	K	L	M	N	O	P	Q	R	S	T	U	V	
1Y	2Z	31	42	53	64	75	86	A7	B8	CA	DB	EC	FD	GE	HF	JG	KH	LJ	MK	NL	OM	PN	QO	RP	SQ	TR	US	VT	WU	
2X	3Y	4Z	51	62	73	84	A5	B6	C7	D8	EA	FB	GC	HD	JE	KF	LG	MH	NJ	OK	PL	QM	RN	SO	TP	UQ	VR	WS	XT	
3W	4X	5Y	6Z	71	82	A3	B4	C5	D6	E7	F8	GA	HB	JC	KD	LE	MF	NG	OH	PJ	QK	RL	SM	TN	UO	VP	WQ	XR	YS	
4V	5W	6X	7Y	8Z	A1	B2	C3	D4	E5	F6	G7	H8	JA	KB	LC	MD	NE	OF	PG	QH	RJ	SK	TL	UM	VN	WO	XP	YQ	ZR	+
5U	6V	7W	8X	AY	BZ	C1	D2	E3	F4	G5	H6	J7	K8	LA	MB	NC	OD	PE	QF	RG	SH	TJ	UK	VL	WM	XN	YO	ZP	1Q	
6T	7U	8V	AW	BX	CY	DZ	E1	F2	G3	H4	J5	K6	L7	M8	NA	OB	PC	QD	RE	SF	TG	UH	VJ	WK	XL	YM	ZN	1O	2P	
7S	8T	AU	BV	CW	DX	EY	FZ	G1	H2	J3	K4	L5	M6	N7	O8	PA	QB	RC	SD	TE	UF	VG	WH	XJ	YK	ZL	1M	2N	3O	
8R	AS	BT	CU	DV	EW	FX	GY	HZ	J1	K2	L3	M4	N5	O6	P7	Q8	RA	SB	TC	UD	VE	WF	XG	YH	ZJ	1K	2L	3M	4N	0
AQ	BR	CS	DT	EU	FV	GW	HX	JY	KZ	L1	M2	N3	O4	P5	Q6	R7	S8	TA	UB	VC	WD	XE	YF	ZG	1H	2J	3K	4L	5M	
BP	CQ	DR	ES	FT	GU	HV	JW	KX	LY	MZ	N1	O2	P3	Q4	R5	S6	T7	U8	VA	WB	XC	YD	ZE	1F	2G	3H	4J	5K	6L	
CO	DP	EQ	FR	GS	HT	JU	KV	LW	MX	NY	OZ	P1	Q2	R3	S4	T5	U6	V7	W8	XA	YB	ZC	1D	2E	3F	4G	5H	6J	7K	−
DN	EO	FP	GQ	HR	JS	KT	LU	MV	NW	OX	PY	QZ	R1	S2	T3	U4	V5	W6	X7	Y8	ZA	1B	2C	3D	4E	5F	6G	7H	8J	
EM	FN	GO	HP	JQ	KR	LS	MT	NU	OV	PW	QX	RY	SZ	T1	U2	V3	W4	X5	Y6	Z7	18	2A	3B	4C	5D	6E	7F	8G	AH	
FL	GM	HN	JO	KP	LQ	MR	NS	OT	PU	QV	RW	SX	TY	UZ	V1	W2	X3	Y4	Z5	16	27	38	4A	5B	6C	7D	8E	AF	BG	
GK	HL	JM	KN	LO	MP	NQ	OR	PS	QT	RU	SV	TW	UX	VY	WZ	X1	Y2	Z3	14	25	36	47	58	6A	7B	8C	AD	BE	CF	
HJ	JK	KL	LM	MN	NO	OP	PQ	QR	RS	ST	TU	UV	VW	WX	XY	YZ	Z1	12	23	34	45	56	67	78	8A	AB	BC	CD	DE	

237

PHYSICAL

1 SA	2 SU	3 M	4 TU	5 W	6 TH	7 F	8 SA	9 SU	10 M	11 TU	12 W	13 TH	14 F	15 SA	16 SU	17 M	18 TU	19 W	20 TH	21 F	22 SA	23 SU	24 M	25 TU	26 W	27 TH	28 F	29 SA	30 SU	31 M	
KJ	LK	ML	NM	ON	PO	QP	RQ	SR	TS	UT	VU	WV	XW	AX	BA	CB	DC	ED	FE	GF	HG	JH	KJ	LK	ML	NM	ON	PO	QP	RQ	
LH	MJ	NK	OL	PM	QN	RO	SP	TQ	UR	VS	WT	XU	AV	BW	CX	DA	EB	FC	GD	HE	JF	KG	LH	MJ	NK	OL	PM	QN	RO	SP	
MG	NH	OJ	PK	QL	RM	SN	TO	UP	VQ	WR	XS	AT	BU	CV	DW	EX	FA	GB	HC	JD	KE	LF	MG	NH	OJ	PK	QL	RM	SN	TO	
NF	OG	PH	QJ	RK	SL	TM	UN	VO	WP	XQ	AR	BS	CT	DU	EV	FW	GX	HA	JB	KC	LD	ME	NF	OG	PH	QJ	RK	SL	TM	UN	+
OE	PF	QG	RH	SJ	TK	UL	VM	WN	XO	AP	BQ	CR	DS	ET	FU	GV	HW	JX	KA	LB	MC	ND	OE	PF	QG	RH	SJ	TK	UL	VM	
PD	QE	RF	SG	TH	UJ	VK	WL	XM	AN	BO	CP	DQ	ER	FS	GT	HU	JV	KW	LX	MA	NB	OC	PD	QE	RF	SG	TH	UJ	VK	WL	0
QC	RD	SE	TF	UG	VH	WJ	XK	AL	BM	CN	DO	EP	FQ	GR	HS	JT	KU	LV	MW	NX	OA	PB	QC	RD	SE	TF	UG	VH	WJ	XK	
RB	SC	TD	UE	VF	WG	XH	AJ	BK	CL	DM	EN	FO	GP	HQ	JR	KS	LT	MU	NV	OW	PX	QA	RB	SC	TD	UE	VF	WG	XH	AJ	
SA	TB	UC	VD	WE	XF	AG	BH	CJ	DK	EL	FM	GN	HO	JP	KQ	LR	MS	NT	OU	PV	QW	RX	SA	TB	UC	VD	WE	XF	AG	BH	−
TX	UA	VB	WC	XD	AE	BF	CG	DH	EJ	FK	GL	HM	JN	KO	LP	MQ	NR	OS	PT	QU	RV	SW	TX	UA	VB	WC	XD	AE	BF	CG	
UW	VX	WA	XB	AC	BD	CE	DF	EG	FH	GJ	HK	JL	KM	LN	MO	NP	OQ	PR	QS	RT	SU	TV	UW	VX	WA	XB	AC	BD	CE	DF	
V	W	X	A	B	C	D	E	F	G	H	J	K	L	M	N	O	P	Q	R	S	T	U	V	W	X	A	B	C	D	E	

EMOTIONAL

1 SA	2 SU	3 M	4 TU	5 W	6 TH	7 F	8 SA	9 SU	10 M	11 TU	12 W	13 TH	14 F	15 SA	16 SU	17 M	18 TU	19 W	20 TH	21 F	22 SA	23 SU	24 M	25 TU	26 W	27 TH	28 F	29 SA	30 SU	31 M	
V	W	X	Y	Z	1	2	3	A	B	C	D	E	F	G	H	J	K	L	M	N	O	P	Q	R	S	T	U	V	W	X	
WU	XV	YW	ZX	1Y	2Z	31	A2	B3	CA	DB	EC	FD	GE	HF	JG	KH	LJ	MK	NL	OM	PN	QO	RP	SQ	TR	US	VT	WU	XV	YW	
XT	YU	ZV	1W	2X	3Y	AZ	B1	C2	D3	EA	FB	GC	HD	JE	KF	LG	MH	NJ	OK	PL	QM	RN	SO	TP	UQ	VR	WS	XT	YU	ZV	
YS	ZT	1U	2V	3W	AX	BY	CZ	D1	E2	F3	GA	HB	JC	KD	LE	MF	NG	OH	PJ	QK	RL	SM	TN	UO	VP	WQ	XR	YS	ZT	1U	+
ZR	1S	2T	3U	AV	BW	CX	DY	EZ	F1	G2	H3	JA	KB	LC	MD	NE	OF	PG	QH	RJ	SK	TL	UM	VN	WO	XP	YQ	ZR	1S	2T	
1Q	2R	3S	AT	BU	CV	DW	EX	FY	GZ	H1	J2	K3	LA	MB	NC	OD	PE	QF	RG	SH	TJ	UK	VL	WM	XN	YO	ZP	1Q	2R	3S	
2P	3Q	AR	BS	CT	DU	EV	FW	GX	HY	JZ	K1	L2	M3	NA	OB	PC	QD	RE	SF	TG	UH	VJ	WK	XL	YM	ZN	1O	2P	3Q	AR	
3O	AP	BQ	CR	DS	ET	FU	GV	HW	JX	KY	LZ	M1	N2	O3	PA	QB	RC	SD	TE	UF	VG	WH	XJ	YK	ZL	1M	2N	3O	AP	BQ	0
AN	BO	CP	DQ	ER	FS	GT	HU	JV	KW	LX	MY	NZ	O1	P2	Q3	RA	SB	TC	UD	VE	WF	XG	YH	ZJ	1K	2L	3M	AN	BO	CP	
BM	CN	DO	EP	FQ	GR	HS	JT	KU	LV	MW	NX	OY	PZ	Q1	R2	S3	TA	UB	VC	WD	XE	YF	ZG	1H	2J	3K	AL	BM	CN	DO	
CL	DM	EN	FO	GP	HQ	JR	KS	LT	MU	NV	OW	PX	QY	RZ	S1	T2	U3	VA	WB	XC	YD	ZE	1F	2G	3H	AJ	BK	CL	DM	EN	
DK	EL	FM	GN	HO	JP	KQ	LR	MS	NT	OU	PV	QW	RX	SY	TZ	U1	V2	W3	XA	YB	ZC	1D	2E	3F	AG	BH	CJ	DK	EL	FM	−
EJ	FK	GL	HM	JN	KO	LP	MQ	NR	OS	PT	QU	RV	SW	TX	UY	VZ	W1	X2	Y3	ZA	1B	2C	3D	AE	BF	CG	DH	EJ	FK	GL	
FH	GJ	HK	JL	KM	LN	MO	NP	OQ	PR	QS	RT	SU	TV	UW	VX	WY	XZ	Y1	Z2	13	2A	3B	AC	BD	CE	DF	EG	FH	GJ	HK	
G	H	J	K	L	M	N	O	P	Q	R	S	T	U	V	W	X	Y	Z	1	2	3	A	B	C	D	E	F	G	H	J	

INTELLECTUAL

1 SA	2 SU	3 M	4 TU	5 W	6 TH	7 F	8 SA	9 SU	10 M	11 TU	12 W	13 TH	14 F	15 SA	16 SU	17 M	18 TU	19 W	20 TH	21 F	22 SA	23 SU	24 M	25 TU	26 W	27 TH	28 F	29 SA	30 SU	31 M	
W	X	Y	Z	1	2	3	4	5	6	7	8	A	B	C	D	E	F	G	H	J	K	L	M	N	O	P	Q	R	S	T	
XV	YW	ZX	1Y	2Z	31	42	53	64	75	86	A7	B8	CA	DB	EC	FD	GE	HF	JG	KH	LJ	MK	NL	OM	PN	QO	RP	SQ	TR	US	
YU	ZV	1W	2X	3Y	4Z	51	62	73	84	A5	B6	C7	D8	EA	FB	GC	HD	JE	KF	LG	MH	NJ	OK	PL	QM	RN	SO	TP	UQ	VR	
ZT	1U	2V	3W	4X	5Y	6Z	71	82	A3	B4	C5	D6	E7	F8	GA	HB	JC	KD	LE	MF	NG	OH	PJ	QK	RL	SM	TN	UO	VP	WQ	
1S	2T	3U	4V	5W	6X	7Y	8Z	A1	B2	C3	D4	E5	F6	G7	H8	JA	KB	LC	MD	NE	OF	PG	QH	RJ	SK	TL	UM	VN	WO	XP	+
2R	3S	4T	5U	6V	7W	8X	AY	BZ	C1	D2	E3	F4	G5	H6	J7	K8	LA	MB	NC	OD	PE	QF	RG	SH	TJ	UK	VL	WM	XN	YO	
3Q	4R	5S	6T	7U	8V	AW	BX	CY	DZ	E1	F2	G3	H4	J5	K6	L7	M8	NA	OB	PC	QD	RE	SF	TG	UH	VJ	WK	XL	YM	ZN	
4P	5Q	6R	7S	8T	AU	BV	CW	DX	EY	FZ	G1	H2	J3	K4	L5	M6	N7	O8	PA	QB	RC	SD	TE	UF	VG	WH	XJ	YK	ZL	1M	
5O	6P	7Q	8R	AS	BT	CU	DV	EW	FX	GY	HZ	J1	K2	L3	M4	N5	O6	P7	Q8	RA	SB	TC	UD	VE	WF	XG	YH	ZJ	1K	2L	0
6N	7O	8P	AQ	BR	CS	DT	EU	FV	GW	HX	JY	KZ	L1	M2	N3	O4	P5	Q6	R7	S8	TA	UB	VC	WD	XE	YF	ZG	1H	2J	3K	
7M	8N	AO	BP	CQ	DR	ES	FT	GU	HV	JW	KX	LY	MZ	N1	O2	P3	Q4	R5	S6	T7	U8	VA	WB	XC	YD	ZE	1F	2G	3H	4J	
8L	AM	BN	CO	DP	EQ	FR	GS	HT	JU	KV	LW	MX	NY	OZ	P1	Q2	R3	S4	T5	U6	V7	W8	XA	YB	ZC	1D	2E	3F	4G	5H	
AK	BL	CM	DN	EO	FP	GQ	HR	JS	KT	LU	MV	NW	OX	PY	QZ	R1	S2	T3	U4	V5	W6	X7	Y8	ZA	1B	2C	3D	4E	5F	6G	
BJ	CK	DL	EM	FN	GO	HP	JQ	KR	LS	MT	NU	OV	PW	QX	RY	SZ	T1	U2	V3	W4	X5	Y6	Z7	18	2A	3B	4C	5D	6E	7F	−
CH	DJ	EK	FL	GM	HN	JO	KP	LQ	MR	NS	OT	PU	QV	RW	SX	TY	UZ	V1	W2	X3	Y4	Z5	16	27	38	4A	5B	6C	7D	8E	
DG	EH	FJ	GK	HL	JM	KN	LO	MP	NQ	OR	PS	QT	RU	SV	TW	UX	VY	WZ	X1	Y2	Z3	14	25	36	47	58	6A	7B	8C	AD	
EF	FG	GH	HJ	JK	KL	LM	MN	NO	OP	PQ	QR	RS	ST	TU	UV	VW	WX	XY	YZ	Z1	12	23	34	45	56	67	78	8A	AB	BC	

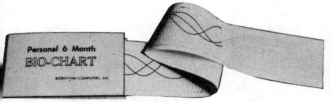
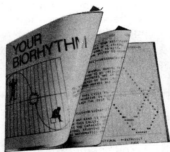

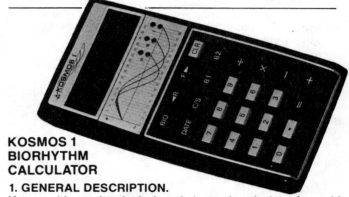

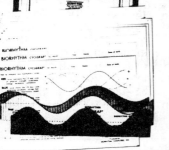
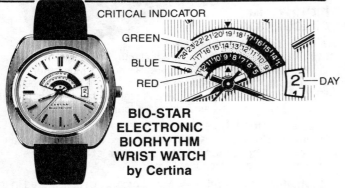